بسم الله الرحمن الرحيم

"The house of al-Arqam is the house of Islam"

Al-Hakim (d. 403 AH) in al-Mustadrak 'Ala al-Sahihayn (6185)

ISBN: 0 9928136 3 5

British Library Cataloguing in Publishing Data
A catalogue record for this book is available from the British Library

Prepared and published by Dar al-Arqam Publishing,
Birmingham, United Kingdom

W. www.daral-arqam.co.uk
E. info@daral-arqam.co.uk
E: daralarqam@hotmail.co.uk

Compiled and translated by Ayman ibn Khalid
Edited by Adnan ibn Fazal Karim

Keep up to date by following us on:

@daralarqampub

@daralarqampub

Printed in Turkey by Mega | export@mega.com.tr

A Commentary on the Depiction of

PROPHET MUHAMMAD

صلى الله عليه وسلم

شرح الشمائل المحمدية

للإمام أبي عيسى محمد بن عيسى الترمذي

(٢٠٩ - ٢٧٩هـ)

Imām

Abū ʿĪsā at-Tirmidhī

(d.279)

DAR AL-ARQAM

"Indeed in the Messenger of Allah you have a good example to follow for him who hopes in [the Meeting with] Allah and the Last Day and remembers Allah much."

[Al-Ahzab: 21]

Contents

IMĀM AL-TIRMIDHI ﷺ

His Name and Birth

He is the *imām*, the *hafīdth*, the great *muhaddith*: Abū Īsa, Muhammad ibn Īsa ibn Sawrah ibn Musa ibn al-Dahhaak al-Sulamī al-Būghī al-Tirmidhī, better known as Imām al-Tirmidhi. There are different views regarding the year in which he was born, but the general consensus is that he was born around 210 AH[1] in the city of Tirmidh.

His Life

Historical works regarding the scholars of hadīth (such as the works of al-Khatīb al-Baghdadī) serve as witnesses that the area of Khurasan was a centre of the study of hadīth during the time of the early generations. From this area arose the *imāms* of hadīth: Muhammad ibn Isma'īl al-Bukhārī, Muslim ibn al-Hajjaj, Abū Dawūd al-Sijistani, Muhammad ibn Mājah, Ahmed ibn Shu'ayb al-Nasa'i and lastly, Abū Īsa al-Tirmidhi. Imām al-Tirmidhi was considered by the scholars

1 As stated by al-Dhahabi in his Siyar A'lam al-Nubala

to be a student of Imām al-Bukhari and he also heard hadīth from Imām Muslim and Abū Dawūd. Though he resided in such a hub of knowledge, he followed the Sunnah of the *muhaddiths* by travelling to the other centres of knowledge such as Iraq and the Hijāz to sit and learn from the scholars. Thus, he travelled to hear from giants such as Abū Musab al-Zuhrī (the son of Ibn Shihab al-Zuhri) from Madīnah, Muhammad ibn Ma'mar from Basrah and Isma'īl al-Fazarī from Kufah.

Imām al-Tirmidhi was considered to be from Imām al-Bukhārī's most exceptional students and he rose to such a high level that he had the privilege of his teacher hearing hadīths from him. Furthermore, it is narrated that Imām al-Bukhārī said to his student, "I have benefitted from you more than you have benefitted from me."[2]

His Works

Imam al-Tirmidhi is most famously known for his vast and highly praised collection of hadīth entitled al-Jami'. Two of the most famous explanations of this are A'ridat-ul-Ahwazi of Abū Bakr ibn al-Arabī and Tuhfat-ul Ahwadhi of Abdul Rahman al-Mubarakfūri (these are amongst the many commentaries that we have referred to for the explanation of the hadīths of the Shama'il). In Ibn al-Arabi's explanation, he states regarding the Jami', "There is no book that matches the rank of Abū Īsa's with respect to the sweetness of its passages, its excellence and its charm." In Abdul Rahman al-Mubarakfūri's explanation, he lists his other works as al-'Ilal al-Kabir, a work on tafsir, al-Tarikh, al-Zuhd and al-Asma wa al-Kuna. Furthermore, he states, **"There is also al-Shama'il al-Muhammadiyyah. It is the best of the books written concerning this subject and full of blessings."**

In al-Bajuri's explanation of Shama'il Muhammadiyyah, he states, "His Jami' is sufficient for you in terms of benefits regarding *fiqh* and hadīth

2 Al-Tadhib

and also regarding the knowledge of the way of the *salaf* and the *khalaf*. Thus, it is sufficient for the *mujtahids* and likewise for the laypeople." In Dhayl Tabaqat al-Hanābilah, it is reported that Abū Isma'īl al-Ansārī said, "In my opinion, the book of al-Tirmidhi is superior in terms of its benefit than the books of al-Bukhārī and Muslim." When he was asked for the reason regarding this, he replied, "Because only those who are well versed in knowledge will benefit from them. As for this book, he has explained the hadīths therein and thus everyone can benefit from it: the *faqīh*, the *muhaddith* and others [i.e. those lesser in knowledge]."

His Personal Qualities and Praise from Scholars for Him

He possessed a great mind, possessing both excellent memory and a high degree of intelligence. His memory is displayed by the following famous narration. Imām al-Dhahabi reports in his Siyar A'lam al-Nubala that al-Tirmidhi said, "Whilst on the route to Makkah I wrote two chapters of hadīth from a shaykh. We met and I requested him to narrate them to me whilst thinking that I had the notes that I previously wrote in my possession. He agreed and began to read whilst I realised that the papers I had were blank. The shaykh realised my papers were devoid of writing and said, 'Have you no shame with me?' I explained to him my circumstances and assured him that I had it all committed to memory. So he asked me to repeat them and I did. However the shaykh was not convinced and he thought that I had reviewed them before our meeting. I asked him to read to me something else and thus he read forty hadīths, then he asked me to repeat them. I did so without error, not even in a single letter."

The praise of the scholars for this great hafidth is vast. What follows are a few examples. In Tabaqāt al-Huffaz, al-Idrisī said, "He was one of the imāms and from the role models in the science of hadīth...

He is mentioned as an example of great memory." In al-Thiqāt, Ibn Hibban said, "He is of those who collected, wrote, took to memory and studied." In Siyar A'lam al-Nubala, it is reported that Hakim said, "I heard 'Umar ibn Alak state, 'Upon al-Bukhāri's passing, he did not leave behind any individual in Khurasan of the same calibre of Abū Īsa in regards to knowledge, memory, piety or ascetism."

His Death

He died in Tirmidh in the year 279 AH on the 13th of Rajab according to al-Dhahabi. It is reported that in the latter part of his life, he lost his sight and became blind. May Allāh have mercy upon him.

COMPILER'S FORWARD

All praise is due to Allāh with Whose grace all good deeds are realised and the *Salāh* and *Salām* of Allāh be upon His Messenger, his family, his companions and all of his loyal followers.

The methodology followed in this book is intended to make the book more appealing to all people and so an in-depth research was made to present to the readers selective gems from a wide array of books and references. The diversity of quotes and texts researched and included therein are intended to enrich the content and allow non-Arabic speakers access to classical books and references that are not yet translated. The commentaries used are taken from the works of early and contemporary scholars from the main four schools of thought (i.e. Hanafi, Shafi'ī, Maliki and Hanbali). This diversity of scholars is hoped to bring people closer and make them more accepting and respectful to the scholars without whom we could not have access to this knowledge. It is also hoped that this work will unite the hearts of people from different backgrounds and it is from Allāh's favours upon us that He united us upon the love of His Prophet ﷺ. To this effect, the selection criteria of commentaries used in this book is based on the added value and benefit that will be brought forth. To make the book more interesting, the quotes were researched based on the subject matter of the hadīth and this required researching tens of classical books and references that covered a wide array of areas such as history, *fiqh*, commentaries, creed, *tazkiyyah* etc. Emphasis was placed upon providing new gems of knowledge (to the English reader) and to present a book with rich content that covers different topics related to *fiqh*, creed, spirituality and hadīth so as to make it more interesting and to suit all tastes.

The references of the hadīths of the Shama'il were taken from the book of al-Shaykh Abdul Razzaq but as some hadīths were not referenced in his book, I researched the references and gave the reference based on the text and not the chain of narrators, and in the case where the exact words were not found in other sources, I would use the reference of a similar hadīth that has the exact same meaning but may have additions or different wording.

Overall, over forty works were used for the commentary. The commentary was based around the books of four main scholars, two of whom are from the contemporary scholars and the other two from the early scholars: (i) Abdul Razzaq ibn Abdul Muhsin al-Badr, (ii) Ibrahim ibn Muhammad al-Bajūrī al-Shafi'ī, (iii) Ibn Hajar al-Haytamī, (iv) al-Mulla Alī ibn Sultan Muhammad al-Qārı. Below is a list of the main books from which commentaries were selected and translated:

1. Sharh Shama'il al-Nabi ﷺ, Abdul Razzaq al-Badr (the book consists of the explanation of this book that the Shaykh gave over forty five lessons in the Masjid of the Prophet ﷺ).
2. Al-Mawahib al-Laduniyyah 'Ala al-Shama'il al-Muhammadiyyah, Ibrahīm ibn Muhammad al-Bajūrī al-Shaf'ī (1198 H.–1277 H.), 2nd Edition (2007), Dar al-Minhaj, Jeddah.
3. Ashraf al-Wasā'il Ila Fahm al-Shama'il, Shihab al-Dīn Ahmad Ibn Hajar al-Haytamī (974 H.), 1st Edition (1998), Dār al-Kutub al-'Ilmiyyah, Beirut.
4. Jam'al-Wasa'il Fi Sharh al-Wasa'il, Ali ibn Sultan Muhammad, Abu al-Hasan, Noor al-Dīn al-Mulla al-Qārī (1014 H.), al-Matb'āh al-Sharafiyyah (1901), Egypt.
5. Fathul Bāri Sharh Sahīh al-Bukhārī, al-Hafidh Ahmad ibn

Hali ibn Hajar, Abu al-Fadl al-'Asqalānī (852 H.), Dār al-Salam, al-Riyadh and Dār al-Fayhaa, Damascus, 3rd Edition (2000).

6. Al-Minhāj Bi Sharh Sahīh Muslim ibn al-Hajjāj, Muhiy al-Dīn ibn Yahya ibn Sharaf al-Nawawī (676 H.), Dār Ibn Hazm, Beirut, 1st Edition (2002).
7. Tuhfatul Ahwadhi bi Sharh Jami' al-Tirmidhi, Abu al 'Ula Muhammad 'Abdul Rahman ibn Abd al-Rahīm al-Mubarakfuri (1353 H.), Dār al-Hadīth, Cairo, 1st Edition (2001).
8. Al-Istidhkār al-Jāmi' Li Madhahib Fuqahā al-Amsār wa 'Ulamā' al-Aqtaar, Yūsuf ibn Abdullāh ibn Mohammed ibn Abdul Barr, Abu Umar al-Namari al-Andalusi al-Qurtubi al-Maliki (463 H.), Dār Qutaybah, Damascus, 1st Edition (1993).
9. Zād al-Ma'ād fi Hady Khayril 'Ibād, Muhammad ibn Abi Bakr ibn Ayyob ibn Sa'd Shams al-dīn, Ibn Qayyim al-Jawziyyah (751 H.), Mu'assasatu al-Risalah, Beirut, 27th Edition (1994).
10. Zahratu al-Khama'il 'Ala al-Shama'il, 'Abdul Rahman ibn Abi Bakr, Jalal al-Deen al-Suyūti (911 H.), Maktabatu al-Quran, Cairo, (1988).
11. Sharh Riyād al-Salihīn, Muhammad ibn Salih ibn Muhammad al-'Uthaymīn (1421 H.), Daar al-Watan, al-Riyadh (1426 H.).
12. Sharh Musnad Abu Hanifah, Ali ibn Sultan Muhammad, Abu al-Hasan, Nūr al-Dīn al-Mulla al-Qārī (1014 H.), Dār al-Kutub al-'Ilmiyyah, Beirut, 1st Edition (1985).
13. Subul al-Salām Sharh Bulūgh al-Maram, Muhammad ibn Ismail ibn Salah al-Amīr al-Kahlani al-San'āni (1182 H.), Dār al-Hadīth, Cairo.
14. Sharh Sahih al-Bukhāri, Abu al-Hasan Ali ibn Khalaf ibn 'Abdil Malik, Ibn Battal, (449 H.), Maktabtu al-Rushd, Al-Riyadh, 2nd Edition (2003).
15. Kifayatu al-Hajah fi Sharh Sunan Ibn Majah, Muhammad ibn 'Abd al-Hādi al-Tatawi, Abu al-Hasan Nūr al-Dīn al-Sindi (1138 H.), Dār al-Jīl, Beirut.

16. Faydul Qadīr Sharh al-Jāmi' al-Saghīr, Zain al-Dīn Muhammad, 'Abdil Ra'ūf ibn Tāj al-'Arifyīn ibn 'Ali ibn Zain al-'Abidīn al-Minnawi (1031 H.), al-Maktabah al-Tijāryyah al-Kubra, Egypt, 1st Edition (1356 H.).
17. Libāb al-Ta'wīl Fi Ma'ani al-Tanzīl, 'Alā al-Dīn Ali ibn Muhammad ibn Ibrahim ibn Umar, Abu al-Hasan, also known as al-Khazin (741 H.), Dār al-Kutub al-'Ilmiyyah, Beirut, 1st Edition (1415 H.).
18. Muntaha al-So'l 'Ala Wasa'il al-Wussūl Ila Shama'il al-Rasūl, Abdullah ibn Sa'īd ibn Muhammad al-Hadrami al-Makki (1410 H.), Dār al-Minhāj, Jeddah, 3rd Edition (2005).
19. Adwā al-Bayān Fi Iydāh al-Quran bil Qurān, Muhammad al-Amīn ibn Muhammad al-Mukhtaar al-Shanqīti (1393 H.), Dār al-Fikr, Beirut (1995).
20. Buhjat al-Mahafil wa Bughyat al-Amāthil Fi Talkhīs al-Mu'jizat wal Siyar wal Shama'il, Yahya ibn Abi Bakr Ibn Muhammad ibn Yahya al'Amri (893 H.), Dār Sādir, Beirut.
21. Latā'if al-Ma'ārif fima lima wasim al-'Aam min al-Wadha'if, Zain al-dīn 'Abdul Rahmān ibn Ahmad ibn Rajab al-Hanbali (795 H.), Dār Ibn Hazm, 1st Edition (2004).
22. Nail al-Awtar, Muhammad ibn Ali ibn Muhammad ibn Abdullah al-Shawkani (1250 H.), Dār al-Hadīth, Egypt, 1st Edition (1993).
23. Ihyā' 'Ulūm al-Dīn, Abu Hamid, Muhammad ibn Muhammad al-Ghazali (505 H.), Dār al-Ma'rifah, Beirut.
24. Madārij al-Salikīn Bayna Manazil Iyyaka Na'bud wa Iyyak Na'sta'īn, Muhammad ibn Abi Bakr ibn Ayyūb ibn Sa'd Shams al-Dīn, Ibn Qayyim al-Jawziyyah (751 H.), Dar al-Kitāb al-Arabi, Beirut, 3rd Edition (1996).
25. 'Uyūn al-Athar Fi Funūn al-Maghazi wal Shama'il wal Siyar, Muhammad ibn Muhammad, Ibn Sayyid al-Nās (734 H.), Dār al-Qalam, Beirut, 2nd Edition (1993).
26. Mukhtasar al-Shama'il al-Muhammadiyyah, Nasiruddin al-Albani, Maktabat al-Marif, Riyadh.

INTRODUCTION OF SHAYKH ABDUL MUHSIN AL-ABBAD

The praise is for Allah. May Allah send salutations, peace, and blessings upon our Prophet Muhammad, upon his family, his Companions and whoever was a supporter of his, held to his sunnah, and was guided by his guidance, until the Day of Reward.

The scholars of hadīth define the Sunnah of the Prophet ﷺ to be all that which is attributed to the Prophet ﷺ in the form of statements, actions, approvals, physical attributes, manners or conduct. This makes the authentic statements of the companions ﷺ regarding his beautiful physical attributes and noble character included in this definition.

These superb character traits and beautiful features are either found scattered in hadīth collections or compiled into dedicated works, the most important of which is "al-Shama'il" by al-Imam al-Tirmidhī, the author of the famous book "al-Jami'", which is known as Sunan al-Tirmidhī. It is indeed a reference of a great importance.

The benefit of learning the physical features of the Prophet ﷺ is that it helps us to distinguish the truthful dream from the false dream in which he appears and the benefit of knowing his character is to follow his example, which Allah has praised: **{There has certainly been for you in the Messenger of Allah an excellent pattern for anyone whose**

hope is in Allah and the Last Day and [who] remembers Allah often.}[3]

3 Qur'ān 33:21

INTRODUCTION OF SHAYKH ABDUL RAZZAQ AL-BADR

In the name of Allah, the most benevolent to mankind, the most Merciful to all believers. All praise is for Allah, Lord of the worlds. Peace and prayers be upon Muhammad, his family, his Companions and all those who follow in their footsteps until the last day.

This book contains a depiction of the physical features and character of the best of mankind and the most beloved and favoured by Allāh the Most High. A depiction of the one who knows his Lord the most and the most capable of mankind at fulfilling the rights of servitude. He was the one chosen to be the link between Allāh and His slaves and chosen to be the messenger who calls towards the good and guidance. Al-Hafith ibn Kathīr commented on the ayah: {**There has certainly been for you in the Messenger of Allah an excellent pattern for anyone whose hope is in Allah and the Last Day and [who] remembers Allah often.**} by saying, "This ayah is a fundamental principle towards following the example of the Messenger of Allāh ﷺ in his statements, actions and conditions."[4]

The following of his example necessitates learning about his guidance in life, character and physical features. It is for this reason, each Muslim

4 Tafsīr Ibn Kathīr (6/391)

ought to give priority to learning about the life of the Prophet ﷺ before learning anything about anyone else.

The benefits of learning the character and physical features of the Prophet ﷺ are many, some of which are:

1. It is from the pillars of *imān* to believe in the Messenger ﷺ and this cannot happen without acquiring the knowledge about him. That being said, the more a person knows about the Prophet ﷺ, the stronger his belief in him becomes.
2. The love of the Prophet ﷺ is an obligation that Allah ﷻ has dictated upon His slaves and He made his love take precedence over one's love for his parents, children and all of mankind including one's own self. The more a person remembers his beloved and knows about his beautiful character, the more a person longs to meet him and feels love for him.
3. Allah ﷻ has set the Prophet ﷺ as the role model that we need to follow. To be able to do this we need to learn about his life and character.
4. The Prophet ﷺ is more worthy of the believers than their own selves. This is because his mercy and efforts to advise and call people to the truth made him more merciful to them than people are merciful to themselves. Also, his favour upon people is incomparable for every good deed that we carry out happens due to his efforts in calling humanity to Islām. Thus, each person should know his great status and this can be acheived through learning about his character and features.
5. Allāh ﷻ has made an oath in the Qur'ān in which He testifies to the perfect character of the Prophet ﷺ. The ayah says: **{And indeed, you are of a great moral character.}**[5] His sense of morality was based on the guidance of the Qur'ān, thus his character was described by Aisha رضي الله عنها as a manifestation of the Qur'ān[6], meaning that he followed all that which is encouraged and made obligatory

5 Qur'ān 68:4

6 Sahīh Muslim (746)

in the Qur'ān and refrained from all that which is admonished and made forbidden in the Qur'ān.

6. Allāh has ordered us in the Qur'ān to pray to Him to confer His Peace and Blessings upon the Prophet ﷺ and the more we are acquainted with his character and life the more we will be encouraged to do so more often. This is why the people who know the Prophet ﷺ more reflect upon matters differently than those who lack this knowledge, whose prayers are nothing but a sound uttered by their tongues.
7. The description of the characteristics of the Prophet ﷺ provides a lifestyle that should be followed by all Muslims desiring to live the best life in this world and the Hereafter. It is a lifestyle that should be taught to the younger generation so that their upbringing can be sound and to keep them away from deviation, instead of letting their generation aspire to the lifestyles of the low-life ones.

For these reasons, there is only one person whose life should be looked into if one desires to find the perfect manners and best conduct, that is the life of the Prophet ﷺ and this is why it is needed to study and learn more about his manners, conduct and lifestyle. Sufyān ibn 'Uyaynah said, "The Messenger of Allah ﷺ is the great balance; whatever complies with his conduct, character and guidance is the truth, otherwise it is falsehood."[7]

This blessed book is from the best and most beneficial books written about the character and depiction of the Prophet ﷺ and its author made it such an excellent work through his structuring of it and the hadiths he included therein. This is the reason why many scholars praise the book and consider it from the best books authored about this topic.

7 Al-Jami' Li Akhlāq al-Rawi wal Sami' (1/9)

CHAPTER ONE

باب ما جاء في خلق رسول الله صلى الله عليه وسلم

THE REPORTS PERTAINING TO THE APPEARANCE OF THE PROPHET ﷺ

Abdul Razzaq al-Badr said,

> With no doubt, Allāh lavished our Prophet ﷺ with a perfect appearance and endowed him with the most beautiful physical attributes and characteristics. Shaykh al-Islām Ibn Taymiyyah said, "He [the Prophet] ﷺ enjoyed the best stature and appearance, indicating his perfection."[1]

Ibn Hajar al-Haytamī said,

> You should know that in order to perfect one's faith, one must believe that there is no human in possession of as good an appearance as the Prophet ﷺ; this is because the outward beauty and handsomeness of the Prophet ﷺ indicates the inward beauty and noble manners he possessed, and no person could ever equal or exceed his status neither in respect to physical appearance nor manners.

1 Taken from al-Jawab al-Sahīh (5/438)

Alī al-Qārī said,

> The Arabic word *bāb* (which translates to chapter in English) means the door through which a person can enter a place and eloquent scholars have understood it to refer to that which leads to one's purpose. In the context [of its use by al-Tirmidhī], it alludes to: the means by which to become acquainted with the hadīths describing the physical appearance of the Prophet ﷺ.

١ : حَدَّثَنَا أَبُو رَجَاءٍ قُتَيْبَةُ بْنُ سَعِيدٍ ، عَنْ مَالِكِ بْنِ أَنَسٍ ، عَنْ رَبِيعَةَ بْنِ أَبِي عَبْدِ الرَّحْمَنِ ، عَنْ أَنَسِ بْنِ مَالِكٍ ، أَنَّهُ سَمِعَهُ ، يَقُولُ : كَانَ رَسُولُ الله صلى الله عليه وسلم ، لَيْسَ بِالطَّوِيلِ الْبَائِنِ ، وَلاَ بِالْقَصِيرِ ، وَلاَ بِالأَبْيَضِ الأَمْهَقِ ، وَلاَ بِالآدَمِ ، وَلاَ بِالْجَعْدِ الْقَطَطِ ، وَلاَ بِالسَّبْطِ ، بَعَثَهُ اللهُ تَعَالَى عَلَى رَأْسِ أَرْبَعِينَ سَنَةً ، فَأَقَامَ بِمَكَّةَ عَشْرَ سِنِينَ ، وَبِالْمَدِينَةِ عَشْرَ سِنِينَ ، وَتَوَفَّاهُ اللهُ تَعَالَى عَلَى رَأْسِ سِتِّينَ سَنَةً ، وَلَيْسَ فِي رَأْسِهِ وَلِحْيَتِهِ عِشْرُونَ شَعَرَةً بَيْضَاءَ[2]

1. Narrated by Rabī'a ibn Abī Abdul Rahman ؓ: "I heard Anas ibn Mālik describing the Prophet ﷺ saying, 'He was neither too tall nor short; neither absolutely white nor brown; his hair was neither very curly nor completely straight. The divine revelation was revealed to him when he was forty years old. He stayed ten years in Makkah, and stayed in Madīnah for ten more years. When he died, he was sixty years old and had [approximately] twenty grey hairs in his head and beard."

Abdul Razzaq al-Badr said,

> "He was neither too tall nor short": The Prophet ﷺ was more apt to be described as tall than short, as it has been explicitly stated in other [authentic] hadīths. This is noted in the choice of words that Anas ibn Mālik ؓ used to describe the height of the Prophet ﷺ i.e.

2 Sahīh al-Bukhārī (5900) and Sahīh Muslim (2347)

he did not use the equivalent antonym of "short" when he negated both attributes; rather, he used the ascription "too tall" to explain that he ﷺ was tall but not to the point where his height exceeded normal or proper limits.

"He stayed ten years in Makkah": This is to specify the length of the period he stayed after receiving the revelation. However, some other hadīths stated that he stayed in Makkah for thirteen years. To reconcile between the two statements, it can be asserted that the mention of ten years refers to the period after the public proclamation of his Message, and the other three years refer to the period he kept this news hidden from others. Another reconciliation to present is that, the ten years refer to the period he stayed in Makkah from the day that Sūrah al-Muddathir was revealed to him wherein he was commanded to warn people, and the other three years refer to the years preceding the aforesaid command. It can even be argued that the narrator counted the age by tens and so he rounded the cardinal number; hence he also omitted the numbers above sixty from the age of the Prophet ﷺ [as Arabs customarily do].

"When he died, he was sixty years old": As it is established in authentic hadīths that the Prophet ﷺ passed away at the age of sixty three, it becomes clear that the narrators chose to count by tens and hence omitted the three years from the earlier part.

Alī al-Qārī said,

> The scholars who explained this hadīth stated that the part, "... When he was forty years old" is structured in the Arabic language to mean he had completed the age of forty.
>
> "And had approximately twenty grey hairs in his head and beard": The wisdom behind the Prophet ﷺ having few grey hairs (though there are many hadīths stating the honour and virtue of grey hair) was so that the affability and love between him and his wives was maintained in a perfect manner [by Allāh], since women are apt to dislike grey hair on men. Further to the point, the statement

of al-Hafith ibn Hajar (see page 1), wherein he mentioned that disliking anything about the Prophet ﷺ is considered a matter of disbelief, cannot be true in all cases because the type of dislike that is naturally implanted in mankind is irrelevant to that which has been dictated.

٢: حَدَّثَنَا حُمَيْدُ بْنُ مَسْعَدَةَ الْبَصْرِيُّ ، قَالَ : حَدَّثَنَا عَبْدُ الْوَهَّابِ الثَّقَفِيُّ ، عَنْ حُمَيْدٍ ، عَنْ أَنَسِ بْنِ مَالِكٍ ، قَالَ : كَانَ رَسُولُ الله صلى الله عليه وسلم رَبْعَةً ، لَيْسَ بِالطَّوِيلِ وَلا بِالْقَصِيرِ ، حَسَنَ الْجِسْمِ ، وَكَانَ شَعَرُهُ لَيْسَ بِجَعْدٍ ، وَلا سَبْطٍ أَسْمَرَ اللَّوْنِ ، إِذَا مَشَى يَتَكَفَّأُ .[3]

2. Anas ibn Mālik ؓ related: "The Prophet ﷺ was of medium height; he was neither [too] tall nor short. He had a good physical build, and his hair was neither curly nor completely straight. He had a tanned complexion, and when he walked, he leaned forward slightly."

Abdul Razzaq al-Badr said,

> It is noted that in the previous hadīth, Anas ibn Mālik ؓ stated that the skin tone of the Prophet ﷺ was not brown. This caused some scholars to believe that this part ("He had a tanned complexion") is not authentic because it was only reported from one person, while the rest of the narrators who reported this from Anas stated that, "He had a rosy complexion."

Alī al-Qārī said,

> The part where it says, "He had a good physical build" refers to his height, skin tone and weight.
>
> The part stating that, "He had a tanned complexion" is intended to negate that he had a skin tone that was absolutely white, though [al-Hafith] al-Iraqī criticised the authenticity of this part. He

3 Sunan al-Tirmidhī (1754)

mentioned that the number of companions who described the skin tone of the Prophet ﷺ was fifteen, and all of them reported that he had a rosy skin tone; furthermore, this description is only reported by one narrator from Anas.

The part where it says, "When he walked, he leaned forward slightly" indicates that he walked with wide steps, because walking with small steps is the way that arrogant people walk.

Ibn Hajar al-Haytamī said,

> Arabs sometimes call the one with a white skin tone that is mixed with some redness a person with a tanned or deep-brown skin colour. This explains the reason why Anas ﷺ stated in this hadīth that the Prophet ﷺ had a tanned complexion. Overall, the hadīths corroborate this understanding regarding the context of the use of the word tanned.
>
> If one argues that, since the skin colour of the Prophet ﷺ is the most noble and honourable of all colours, and so is the skin colour of the dwellers of Paradise, then why is the skin colour of the latter white with some yellowness as stated by the majority of exegetes? I say, the basis of the skin colour of both is the same and the wisdom behind the aforementioned variation is: the red tone mixed with the white is due to the blood and its characteristics, which flows moderately in the veins and it is produced from the worldly nutrition. Whereas the yellow colour that makes the whiteness [of the skin] polished and purified only appears in Paradise as it can only be produced by the nutrition of that world.
>
> From this part, we can understand the statement of some of the Shafi'ī scholars who said it is better for a woman not to wear white or silver clothes, because these can cause a resemblance of men in their clothing, and the reason she is encouraged to change the white coloured garment by dying it with saffron is so that the colour becomes closer to gold as that befits her gender.

٣: حَدَّثَنَا مُحَمَّدُ بْنُ بَشَّارٍ ، قَالَ : حَدَّثَنَا مُحَمَّدُ بْنُ جَعْفَرٍ ، قَالَ : حَدَّثَنَا شُعْبَةُ ، عَنْ أَبِي إِسْحَاقَ ، قَالَ : سَمِعْتُ الْبَرَاءَ بْنَ عَازِبٍ ، يَقُولُ : كَانَ رَسُولُ اللهِ صلى الله عليه وسلم ، رَجُلا مَرْبُوعًا ، بَعِيدَ مَا بَيْنَ الْمَنْكِبَيْنِ ، عَظِيمَ الْجُمَّةِ إِلَى شَحْمَةِ أُذُنَيْهِ الْيُسْرَى ، عَلَيْهِ حُلَّةٌ حَمْرَاءُ ، مَا رَأَيْتُ شَيْئًا قَطُّ أَحْسَنَ مِنْهُ .[4]

3. Al-Barā' ibn 'Āzib ﷺ related: "The Prophet ﷺ was a man of medium build; he had broad shoulders; he had dense hair which reached his earlobes. [I saw him wearing] a *hulla* (red garment) and I never saw anything more beautiful than him."

Abdul Razzaq al-Badr said,

The description given concerning his height is intended to be approximate and not to offer the exact measurement. This is deduced from the fact that other hadīths stated that he ﷺ was closer to tall than short.

The Arabic word *hulla* is used only when the clothing is comprised of two pieces.

To reconcile between the fact that the Prophet ﷺ wore a red garment and his statement wherein he admonished wearing red clothes, it can be said that the order not to wear red clothing refers to clothes comprised completely of red; hence if the garment has other colours such as white or black besides the red, then it does not fall under the category of the forbidden clothing.

The use of the word "anything" rather than "anybody" in the part, "... Anything more beautiful than him" makes the comparison refer to both the animate and inanimate creation.

Alī al-Qārī said,

The use of the word "man" is an addition from one of the narrators and not from the words of the companions. However, as all the

4 Sahīh al-Bukhārī (3551) and Sahīh Muslim (2337)

narrators are trustworthy and creditable we accept this addition, and we understand it to be an adjective that is intended to state that he had all the praised qualities of a man. Alternatively, the use of the word can be understood in the context that it is often used as an introduction to what will come afterwards.

The quality of having broad shoulders is deemed by the Arabs as a sign of one's generosity, profound respect and tolerance.

There are many hadīths about the length of the Prophet's ﷺ hair, some of which indicated that it was up to his ears and some of which indicated that it reached to the middle of his ears. Al-Qadī 'Iyyād explained that the variance of reports regarding this matter is due to the fact that each narrator reported what he saw at a specific time and thus the length of his hair differed.

Al-Nawawī explained that, "*Hulla* refers to clothing that is comprised of two pieces and it often refers to the *izār* (a lower garment wrapped around the waist)." To understand the Prophet's ﷺ wearing of a red garment in light of the knowledge that there are other hadīths wherein he discouraged people from wearing red clothes, we say either the garment he wore had colours other than red in it (but as red was more prominent, it was identified as a red garment), or it could be that the incident reported was before the admonishment he issued (if the garment was purely red), or that wearing these garments [that are completely red] is one of the exclusive characteristics of the Prophet ﷺ that others are not allowed to do.

Ibn Hajar al-Haytamī said,

> There are different hadīths that provide different descriptions of the length of his ﷺ hair and this is because each narrator described what he saw [at that specific time], and because when the Prophet ﷺ would leave his hair uncut, he would leave it until it reached his shoulders and when he shortened it, he would let it reach the level of his earlobes; sometimes to the middle of his ears and sometimes to the level of his ear lobes.

٤ : حَدَّثَنَا مَحْمُودُ بْنُ غَيْلانَ ، قَالَ : حَدَّثَنَا وَكِيعٌ ، قَالَ : حَدَّثَنَا سُفْيَانُ ، عَنْ أَبِي إِسْحَاقَ ، عَنِ الْبَرَاءِ بْنِ عَازِبٍ ، قَالَ : مَا رَأَيْتُ مِنْ ذِي لِمَّةٍ فِي حُلَّةٍ حَمْرَاءَ أَحْسَنَ مِنْ رَسُولِ اللهِ صلى الله عليه وسلم ، لَهُ شَعَرٌ يَضْرِبُ مَنْكِبَيْهِ ، بَعِيدُ مَا بَيْنَ الْمَنْكِبَيْنِ ، لَمْ يَكُنْ بِالْقَصِيرِ ، وَلا بِالطَّوِيلِ .[5]

4. Al-Barā' ibn 'Āzib ؓ related: "I have never seen someone with a *limmah* wearing a red garment more handsome than the Prophet ﷺ. He had long hair that reached his shoulders. The distance between his two shoulders was wide. He was neither tall nor short."

Abdul Razzaq al-Badr said,

> The word "*limmah*" refers to a hairstyle where the length of the hair extends to below the earlobes, whether it reaches the shoulders or not. What follows in this narration comes to state that al-Barā' ؓ considered the Prophet ﷺ to be the most handsome person he ever saw with such a description.

Ibn Hajar al-Haytamī said,

> This hadīth is authentic and it was used by Imām al-Shāfi'ī as evidence that it is permissible to wear red clothing.

٥ : حَدَّثَنَا مُحَمَّدُ بْنُ إِسْمَاعِيلَ ، قَالَ : حَدَّثَنَا أَبُو نُعَيْمٍ ، قَالَ : حَدَّثَنَا الْمَسْعُودِيُّ ، عَنْ عُثْمَانَ بْنِ مُسْلِمِ بْنِ هُرْمُزَ ، عَنْ نَافِعِ بْنِ جُبَيْرِ بْنِ مُطْعِمٍ ، عَنْ عَلِيِّ بْنِ أَبِي طَالِبٍ ، قَالَ : لَمْ يَكُنِ النَّبِيُّ صلى الله عليه وسلم بِالطَّوِيلِ ، وَلا بِالْقَصِيرِ ، شَثْنُ الْكَفَّيْنِ وَالْقَدَمَيْنِ ، ضَخْمُ الرَّأْسِ ، ضَخْمُ الْكَرَادِيسِ ، طَوِيلُ الْمَسْرُبَةِ ، إِذَا مَشَى تَكَفَّأَ تَكَفُّؤًا ، كَأَنَّمَا يَنْحَطُّ مِنْ صَبَبٍ ، لَمْ أَرَ قَبْلَهُ ، وَلا بَعْدَهُ مِثْلَهُ ، صلى الله عليه وسلم.[6]

---

5 Sahīh al-Bukhārī (3549) and Sahīh Muslim (2337)

6 Sunan al-Tirmidhī (3637)

5. Alī ibn Abī Tālib ﷺ narrated: "The Prophet ﷺ was neither extremely tall nor short. He had thickly boned hands and feet and a large head. The joints of his bones were large and he had a line of hair extending from his chest to the navel. When he walked, it appeared as if he was descending from a high place. I have never seen anyone who was comparable to him."

Abdul Razzaq al-Badr said,

> The common attribute that all the narrators who described the Prophet ﷺ mentioned was that he was neither tall nor short.
>
> Having thickly boned fingers does not entail the attribution of rough skin because Anas ﷺ, as shall be mentioned later, stated that the touch of his hand was softer than silk.

Ibn Hajar al-Haytamī said,

> The fact that he had thickly boned fingers and at the same time soft skin (as narrated by Anas ibn Mālik ﷺ in other authentic hadīths) shows that he combined strength with fine-spun skin.

Alī al-Qārī said,

> The last statement of Alī ibn Abī Tālib ﷺ is a statement that is used (in Arabic) to negate the existence of anything that is similar to the described. It is to show that if there is none like him, then evidently there will be no one who is better than him.

٦: حَدَّثَنَا سُفْيَانُ بْنُ وَكِيعٍ ، قَالَ : حَدَّثَنَا أَبِي ، عَنِ الْمَسْعُودِيِّ ، بِهَذَا الإِسْنَادِ ، نَحْوَهُ ، بِمَعْنَاهُ

6. Sufyān ibn Wakī' narrated to us that his father narrated from al-Mas'ūdī through the same chain a similar hadith.

٧: حَدَّثَنَا أَحْمَدُ بْنُ عَبْدَةَ الضَّبِّيُّ الْبَصْرِيُّ ، وَعَلِيُّ بْنُ حُجْرٍ ، وَأَبُو جَعْفَرٍ

مُحَمَّدُ بْنُ الحُسَيْنِ وَهُوَ ابْنُ أَبِي حَلِيمَةَ ، وَالْمَعْنَى وَاحِدٌ ، قَالُوا : حَدَّثَنَا عِيسَى بْنُ يُونُسَ ، عَنْ عُمَرَ بْنِ عَبْدِ الله مَوْلَى غُفْرَةَ ، قَالَ : حَدَّثَنِي إِبْرَاهِيمُ بْنُ مُحَمَّدٍ مِنْ وَلَدِ عَلِيِّ بْنِ أَبِي طَالِبٍ ، قَالَ : كَانَ عَلِيٌّ إِذَا وَصَفَ رَسُولَ الله صلى الله عليه وسلم ، قَالَ : لَمْ يَكُنْ رَسُولُ الله صلى الله عليه وسلم بِالطَّوِيلِ المُمَّغِطِ ، وَلا بِالْقَصِيرِ المُتَرَدِّدِ ، وَكَانَ رَبْعَةً مِنَ الْقَوْمِ ، لَمْ يَكُنْ بِالجَعْدِ الْقَطَطِ ، وَلا بِالسَّبْطِ ، كَانَ جَعْدًا رَجِلا ، وَلَمْ يَكُنْ بِالمُطَهَّمِ ، وَلا بِالمُكَلْثَمِ ، وَكَانَ فِي وَجْهِهِ تَدْوِيرٌ ، أَبْيَضُ مُشْرَبٌ ، أَدْعَجُ الْعَيْنَيْنِ ، أَهْدَبُ الأَشْفَارِ ، جَلِيلُ المُشَاشِ وَالْكَتَدِ ، أَجْرَدُ ، ذُو مَسْرُبَةٍ ، شَثْنُ الْكَفَّيْنِ وَالْقَدَمَيْنِ ، إِذَا مَشَى كَأَنَّمَا يَنْحَطُّ فِي صَبَبٍ ، وَإِذَا الْتَفَتَ الْتَفَتَ مَعًا ، بَيْنَ كَتِفَيْهِ خَاتَمُ النُّبُوَّةِ ، وَهُوَ خَاتَمُ النَّبِيِّينَ ، أَجْوَدُ النَّاسِ صَدْرًا ، وَأَصْدَقُ النَّاسِ لَهْجَةً ، وَأَلْيَنُهُمْ عَرِيكَةً ، وَأَكْرَمُهُمْ عِشْرَةً ، مَنْ رَآهُ بَدِيهَةً هَابَهُ ، وَمَنْ خَالَطَهُ مَعْرِفَةً أَحَبَّهُ ، يَقُولُ نَاعِتُهُ : لَمْ أَرَ قَبْلَهُ ، وَلا بَعْدَهُ مِثْلَهُ صلى الله عليه وسلم[7]

قَالَ أَبُو عِيسَى : سَمِعْتُ أَبَا جَعْفَرٍ مُحَمَّدَ بْنَ الحُسَيْنِ ، يَقُولُ : سَمِعْتُ الأَصْمَعِيَّ يَقُولُ فِي تَفْسِيرِ صِفَةِ النَّبِيِّ صلى الله عليه وسلم

المُمَّغِطُ : الذَّاهِبُ طُولا وَقَالَ : سَمِعْتُ أَعْرَابِيًّا يَقُولُ فِي كَلامِهِ : مَّغَّطَ فِي نَشَّابَتِهِ ، أَيْ مَدَّهَا مَدًّا شَدِيدًا وَالمُتَرَدِّدُ : الدَّاخِلُ بَعْضُهُ فِي بَعْضٍ قِصَرًا

وَأَمَّا الْقَطَطُ : فَالشَّدِيدُ الجُعُودَةِ وَالرَّجِلُ الَّذِي فِي شَعَرِهِ حُجُونَةٌ : أَيْ تَثَنٍّ قَلِيلٌ

وَأَمَّا المُطَهَّمُ فَالْبَادِنُ ، الْكَثِيرُ اللَّحْمِ

وَالمُكَلْثَمُ : المُدَوَّرُ الْوَجْهِ وَالمُشْرَبُ الَّذِي فِي بَيَاضِهِ حُمْرَةٌ

وَالأَدْعَجُ : الشَّدِيدُ سَوَادِ الْعَيْنِ

وَالأَهْدَبُ : الطَّوِيلُ الأَشْفَارِ

7. Ibrahim ibn Muhammad ﷺ (who is from the grandchildren of Alī

---

7 Sunan al-Tirmidhī (3638)

ibn Abī Ṭālib) reported that whenever Alī ﷺ used to describe the Prophet ﷺ, he would say: "The Messenger of Allāh was neither very tall nor very short, but of a medium stature amongst the people. His hair was neither very curly nor completely straight; rather it was in between these two descriptions.

He did not have a fleshy body or a [fully] round face, his face was slightly round. His skin colour was white with some redness. He had extremely black eyes with long eyelashes. He had large joints and broad shoulders. There was no hair [more than normal] on his body and he had a thin line of hair running from the chest to the navel. He had thick hands and feet. When he walked, he lifted his legs with vigour and his steps were firm and strong as if he was descending down a slope. When he wished to look behind, he would turn his whole body, and not just the face. The seal of prophethood was situated between his shoulders. He was the seal of the Prophets, and he had the most generous of hearts and the most truthful tongue. He was the most kind-hearted and tolerant person ever. He was the best to spend time with due to his awe-inspiring character and kind treatment; anyone who came across him unexpectedly would become awestruck; and whoever came in close contact with him would love him. One who describes him can only state, 'I have never seen anyone comparable to him.'"

Abdul Razzaq al-Badr said,

> The part, "He did not have a fleshy body" indicates that he ﷺ was not fat.
>
> The seal of prophethood refers to an area of raised skin between his shoulders.

Ibn Hajar al-Haytamī said,

> The mention of him not turning the neck only is to show that he did not glance secretly or act as the reckless people do whenever they want to look at something.

As Muhammad ﷺ is the last Prophet, when Īsa عليه السلام descends during the end times, he will rule by and abide to the laws of Islām; he will spread justice, pray towards Makkah and take his judgements from the Qur'ān and Sunnah.

The parts that describe his kind-hearted and merciful nature as well as his excellent qualities conform to the event when Jibrīl عليه السلام split his chest and removed the share of the devil from his heart and then washed it with the water of Zamzam.

The part, "... the most truthful tongue" means that he used to utter the letters perfectly, beautifully and eloquently.

Alī al-Qārī said,

> In another version of this hadīth, the part, "He was the most kind-hearted and tolerant person ever" was narrated as, "He is from the most noble tribe" and both versions truly describe him ﷺ.

٨: حَدَّثَنَا سُفْيَانُ بْنُ وَكِيعٍ ، قَالَ : حَدَّثَنَا جُمَيْعُ بْنُ عُمَرَ بْنِ عَبْدِ الرَّحْمَنِ الْعِجْلِيُّ ، إِمْلاءً عَلَيْنَا مِنْ كِتَابِهِ ، قَالَ : أَخْبَرَنِي رَجُلٌ مِنْ بَنِي تَمِيمٍ ، مِنْ وَلَدِ أَبِي هَالَةَ زَوْجِ خَدِيجَةَ ، يُكْنَى أَبَا عَبْدِ اللهِ ، عَنِ ابْنٍ لأَبِي هَالَةَ ، عَنِ الْحَسَنِ بْنِ عَلِيٍّ ، قَالَ : سَأَلْتُ خَالِي هِنْدَ بْنَ أَبِي هَالَةَ ، وَكَانَ وَصَّافًا ، عَنْ حِلْيَةِ رَسُولِ اللهِ صلى الله عليه وسلم ، وَأَنَا أَشْتَهِي أَنْ يَصِفَ لِي مِنْهَا شَيْئًا أَتَعَلَّقُ بِهِ ، فَقَالَ : كَانَ رَسُولُ اللهِ صلى الله عليه وسلم فَخْمًا مُفَخَّمًا ، يَتَلأْلأُ وَجْهُهُ ، تَلأْلُؤَ الْقَمَرِ لَيْلَةَ الْبَدْرِ ، أَطْوَلُ مِنَ الْمَرْبُوعِ ، وَأَقْصَرُ مِنَ الْمُشَذَّبِ ، عَظِيمُ الْهَامَةِ ، رَجِلُ الشَّعْرِ ، إِنِ انْفَرَقَتْ عَقِيقَتُهُ فَرَّقَهَا ، وَإِلا فَلا يُجَاوِزُ شَعَرُهُ شَحْمَةَ أُذُنَيْهِ ، إِذَا هُوَ وَفَّرَهُ ، أَزْهَرُ اللَّوْنِ ، وَاسِعُ الْجَبِينِ ، أَزَجُّ الْحَوَاجِبِ ، سَوَابِغَ فِي غَيْرِ قَرَنٍ ، بَيْنَهُمَا عِرْقٌ ، يُدِرُّهُ الْغَضَبُ ، أَقْنَى الْعِرْنَيْنِ ، لَهُ نُورٌ يَعْلُوهُ ، يَحْسَبُهُ مَنْ لَمْ يَتَأَمَّلْهُ أَشَمَّ ، كَثُّ اللِّحْيَةِ ، سَهْلُ الْخَدَّيْنِ ، ضَلِيعُ الْفَمِ ، مُفْلَجُ الأَسْنَانِ ، دَقِيقُ الْمَسْرُبَةِ ، كَأَنَّ عُنُقَهُ جِيدُ دُمْيَةٍ ، فِي صَفَاءِ الْفِضَّةِ ،

مُعْتَدِلُ الْخَلْقِ ، بَادِنٌ مُتَمَاسِكٌ ، سَوَاءُ الْبَطْنِ وَالصَّدْرِ ، عَرِيضُ الصَّدْرِ ، بَعِيدُ مَا بَيْنَ الْمَنْكِبَيْنِ ، ضَخْمُ الْكَرَادِيسِ ، أَنْوَرُ الْمُتَجَرَّدِ ، مَوْصُولُ مَا بَيْنَ اللَّبَّةِ وَالسُّرَّةِ بِشَعْرٍ يَجْرِي كَالْخَطِّ ، عَارِي الثَّدْيَيْنِ وَالْبَطْنِ مِمَّا سِوَى ذَلِكَ ، أَشْعَرُ الذِّرَاعَيْنِ ، وَالْمَنْكِبَيْنِ ، وَأَعَالِي الصَّدْرِ ، طَوِيلُ الزَّنْدَيْنِ ، رَحْبُ الرَّاحَةِ ، شَثْنُ الْكَفَّيْنِ وَالْقَدَمَيْنِ ، سَائِلُ الأَطْرَافِ أَوْ قَالَ : شَائِلُ الأَطْرَافِ خُمْصَانُ الأَخْمَصَيْنِ ، مَسِيحُ الْقَدَمَيْنِ ، يَنْبُو عَنْهُمَا الْمَاءُ ، إِذَا زَالَ ، زَالَ قَلِعًا ، يَخْطُو تَكَفِّيًا ، وَيَمْشِي هَوْنًا ، ذَرِيعُ الْمِشْيَةِ ، إِذَا مَشَى كَأَنَّمَا يَنْحَطُّ مِنْ صَبَبٍ ، وَإِذَا الْتَفَتَ الْتَفَتَ جَمِيعًا ، خَافِضُ الطَّرْفِ ، نَظَرُهُ إِلَى الأَرْضِ ، أَطْوَلُ مِنْ نَظَرِهِ إِلَى السَّمَاءِ ، جُلُّ نَظَرِهِ الْمُلاحَظَةُ ، يَسُوقُ أَصْحَابَهُ ، وَيَبْدَأُ مَنْ لَقِيَ بِالسَّلامِ [8]

8. Al-Hasan ibn Alī ﷺ reported: "I inquired from my maternal uncle, Hind ibn Abī Hālah about the awe-inspiring characteristics and features of the Prophet ﷺ as he was known for doing so, as I desired to become well acquainted with and memorise his description."

The uncle described the Prophet ﷺ by saying: "His qualities and attributes were the acme of beauty, and his companions and whoever saw him held him in high esteem. His face used to shine like the full moon. He was of a medium height but closer to tall than average and shorter than a lanky person. His head was [moderately] large and his hair was slightly waved. If his hair could [naturally] be parted, he would have it so; otherwise he would make no efforts to part it and his hair would not go beyond his ear lobes. He had a skin tone that was white with a tinge of red and a wide forehead with perfect and complete eyebrows, consisting of hair that reached to the end of the line of his eyes. His eyebrows were separate and did not meet each other in the middle. There was a vein between them that used to expand whenever he became angry. His nose was prominent and was wrapped with a light that shines out. If one did not look at him

---

8 Tahdhīb al-Kamal (1/214)

closely, it would seem as if he had a large nasal bridge. His beard was full and dense and his cheek bones were not high. His mouth was [moderately] wide and he had a space between his teeth.

He had a thin line of hair from the chest to the navel and his neck was as beautiful as the neck of a doll made of ivory. All the parts of his body were of moderate size and fully fleshed. His body was proportionately jointed. His chest and stomach were in line, but his chest was broad and wide. He had a well-built body and the level of his chest and stomach was straight (i.e. he had no extra weight or fat). The space between his shoulders was wide and the bones of his joints were strong and large. His body parts had a brightness that shined whenever he removed his clothing. Between the upper point of the chest and navel he had a thin line of hair while the rest of the area had no hair on it. His forearms were long and his palms were wide. The fingers and toes were moderately thick, and both his hands and legs were moderately long.

The soles of his feet were somewhat high from the ground. His feet were smooth [i.e. had no holes or cracks], such that water would not remain there and flow away quickly. When he walked, he lifted his legs with strength as if he was uprooting a plant; he leaned slightly forward and placed his feet softly on the ground. He walked at a moderate pace and naturally walked with long steps. When he walked it seemed as if he was descending to a lower place. When he wanted to look at something behind him, he would turn his whole body towards it. His gaze would often face down towards the earth; he looked more to the ground than towards the sky, [it was his habit not to stare] and most of his prolonged glances were thoughtful and intended for contemplating. He would let his companions walk in front whilst he himself walked behind, and he always hastened to greet whomsoever he met."

Abdul Razzaq al-Badr said,

The maternal uncle of al-Hasan ibn 'Alī ﷺ was Hind ibn Abī Hālah ﷺ, the son of the mother of believers, Khadījah bint Khuwailid ﷺ

who was raised by the Prophet ﷺ; hence being the stepbrother of Fātimah ﷺ.

The reason why al-Hasan requested to learn the detailed description of the Prophet ﷺ despite the fact that he had the honour to see him in person was because he was very young at that time [when the Prophet ﷺ was alive]. The request of al-Hasan shows that learning the description of the Prophet ﷺ is a knowledge that should be given priority.

Ibn Hajar al-Haytamī said,

"His face used to shine like the full moon": Not only did he possess the most handsome face, but also the best character as reported in the two Sahīh books.

The narrator preferred to use the term "full moon" instead of "the sun" when describing the brightness of the Prophet's ﷺ face. This is because, contrary to the sun, the moon can be looked at without causing the eye any harm.

It is reported in Sahīh Muslim that the Prophet ﷺ used to let his hair hang down while the idolaters used to part their hair, and the People of the Book used to let their hair hang down. He liked to be in harmony with the People of the Book in matters of which he had not received any command. Then later in his life he would part his hair. Though both practices are permissible, parting the hair is preferable since it was the practice that the Prophet ﷺ settled with.

The part of this hadīth that describes the manner in which he would look is intended to mean that he would not glance sneakily when wanting to look at something. "He looked more to the ground than towards the sky," due to his mindfulness of Allāh, his humility and shyness of Him.

Alī al-Qārī said,

The way the Prophet ﷺ walked (i.e. walking with wide steps) is the praised walk for men as walking with short steps is a characteristic of women.

He used to look down to the earth when his glance was not focused on anything because he used to spend the time contemplating and pondering, and it was also his habit due to the humbleness he possessed. Likewise, he used to ask his companions to walk in front of him out of humbleness and also out of his consideration for the weak and wanting to look after them, as they are normally the ones who fall to the back of the group. Furthermore, it was proven in an authentic hadīth that he told his companions, "The angels guard my back, so leave it for them."

The wisdom behind why he used to hasten to greet others (give *salām*) is because this is the nature of the humble and also when one initiates the greeting, his initiation becomes a cause for the one being greeted to reciprocate and attain a reward.

٩ : حَدَّثَنَا أَبُو مُوسَى مُحَمَّدُ بْنُ الْمُثَنَّى ، حَدَّثَنَا مُحَمَّدُ بْنُ جَعْفَرٍ ، حَدَّثَنَا شُعْبَةُ ، عَنْ سِمَاكِ بْنِ حَرْبٍ ، قَالَ : سَمِعْتُ جَابِرَ بْنَ سَمُرَةَ ، يَقُولُ : كَانَ رَسُولُ اللهِ صلى الله عليه وسلم ضَلِيعَ الْفَمِ ، أَشْكَلَ الْعَيْنِ ، مَنْهُوسَ الْعَقِبِ

قَالَ شُعْبَةُ : قُلْتُ لِسِمَاكٍ : مَا ضَلِيعُ الْفَمِ ؟ قَالَ : عَظِيمُ الْفَمِ

قُلْتُ : مَا أَشْكَلُ الْعَيْنِ ؟ قَالَ : طَوِيلُ شَقِّ الْعَيْنِ

قُلْتُ : مَا مَنْهُوسُ الْعَقِبِ ؟

قَالَ : قَلِيلُ لَحْمِ الْعَقِبِ [9]

9. Jābir ibn Samurah رضي الله عنه narrated: "The mouth of the Messenger of Allāh ﷺ was wide and there was some redness in the whites of his eyes, and he had only a small amount of flesh on his heels."[10]

9 Sahīh Muslim (2339)

10 Note: The translation of the part concerning the eyes in this hadīth is based on the explanation of al-Qadī 'Iyyād and the scholars who interpreted the words of this hadīth.

Abdul Razzaq al-Badr said,

> The quality of having white eyes with a hint of redness is a praised physical appearance amongst the Arabs.

Alī al-Qārī said,

> Some scholars interpreted the part "wide mouth" to refer to his teeth but the majority understood this part as referring to the mouth.

١٠ : حَدَّثَنَا هَنَّادُ بْنُ السَّرِيِّ ، قَالَ : حَدَّثَنَا عَبْثَرُ بْنُ الْقَاسِمِ ، عَنْ أَشْعَثَ يَعْنِي ابْنَ سَوَّارٍ ، عَنْ أَبِي إِسْحَاقَ ، عَنْ جَابِرِ بْنِ سَمُرَةَ ، قَالَ : رَأَيْتُ رَسُولَ اللهِ صلى الله عليه وسلم ، فِي لَيْلَةٍ إِضْحِيَانٍ ، وَعَلَيْهِ حُلَّةٌ حَمْرَاءُ ، فَجَعَلْتُ أَنْظُرُ إِلَيْهِ وَإِلَى الْقَمَرِ ، فَلَهُوَ عِنْدِي أَحْسَنُ مِنَ الْقَمَرِ[11]

10. Jābir ibn 'Abdillāh ؓ said: "I saw Allāh's Messenger ﷺ during a night where the moon was full. On that night, he wore a red garment and when I looked at the full moon and compared it with him, by Allāh, he was in my eyes better and more beautiful than the full moon."

Ibn Hajar al-Haytamī said,

> The mention of a "full moon" was intended to show that it was a clear night that was neither dark nor cloudy, having a full moon from its beginning to its end.
>
> The part of the hadīth, "... in my eyes" is to indicate the state he experienced personally and it is not intended to state that it could be otherwise in the eyes of another person.

Abdul Razzaq al-Badr said,

---

11 Sunan al-Tirmidhī (2811)

There are a number of hadīths wherein the face of the Prophet ﷺ was likened to the moon, and this is only to explain his beauty because Allāh, the Most High, lavished him with a beauty that is far beyond the beauty of the moon.

Alī al-Qārī said,

> The part mentioning the red garment indicates that it made his beauty increase, thereby attracting one's eyes and attention.
>
> The part where the narrator mentioned that he found him more beautiful than the moon in his eyes is not intended to state that others may not have considered such, rather the intention was to show his happiness at what he saw as every believing person would see him ﷺ as such.

١١ : حَدَّثَنَا سُفْيَانُ بْنُ وَكِيعٍ ، حَدَّثَنَا حُمَيْدُ بْنُ عَبْدِ الرَّحْمَنِ الرُّؤَاسِيُّ ، عَنْ زُهَيْرٍ ، عَنْ أَبِي إِسْحَاقَ ، قَالَ : سَأَلَ رَجُلٌ الْبَرَاءَ بْنَ عَازِبٍ : أَكَانَ وَجْهُ رَسُولِ اللهِ صلى الله عليه وسلم مِثْلَ السَّيْفِ ؟ قَالَ : لا ، بَلْ مِثْلَ الْقَمَرِ[12]

11. Abū Ishāq related: "A person asked al-Barā' ibn 'Āzib ﷺ, 'Was the face of Allāh's Messenger ﷺ like a sword?' He replied, 'No, it was like the moon.'"

Abdul Razzaq al-Badr said,

> Al-Hafith ibn Hajar commented on this hadīth in Fathul Bārī saying, "It appears as if the questioner intended to ask if his face was long like how a sword is; hence the answer gave the example of the moon to show that his face was more rounded, and it is possible that he intended to ask if his face was as bright and refined as a sword, so the answer was the moon to show that the brightness of his face surpassed that of the sword and so selecting the moon was

12 Sahīh al-Bukhārī (3549) and Sunan al-Tirmidhī (3636)

to combine both qualities."

١٢ : حَدَّثَنَا أَبُو دَاوُدَ الْمَصَاحِفِيُّ سُلَيْمَانُ بْنُ سَلْمٍ ، قَالَ : حَدَّثَنَا النَّضْرُ بْنُ شُمَيْلٍ ، عَنْ صَالِحِ بْنِ أَبِي الأَخْضَرِ ، عَنِ ابْنِ شِهَابٍ ، عَنْ أَبِي سَلَمَةَ ، عَنْ أَبِي هُرَيْرَةَ ، قَالَ : كَانَ رَسُولُ اللهِ صلى الله عليه وسلم أَبْيَضَ كَأَنَّمَا صِيغَ مِنْ فِضَّةٍ ، رَجِلَ الشَّعْرِ[13]

12. Abū Hurairah ﷺ narrated: "The skin tone of the Messenger of Allāh ﷺ was white to a degree that it seemed as if he was moulded from silver, and his hair was slightly curled."

Ibn Hajar al-Haytamī said,

> The expression of "... moulded in silver" refers to the brightness and light shining from his skin. It will come under the chapter of the recitation of the Prophet ﷺ that he said, "Allāh has not sent a Prophet except that he has a beautiful face and a beautiful voice, and your Prophet (i.e. Muhammad) has the most beautiful face and most beautiful voice among them." This indicates that he was more handsome than Prophet Yusuf ﷺ.

١٣ : حَدَّثَنَا قُتَيْبَةُ بْنُ سَعِيدٍ ، قَالَ : أَخْبَرَنِي اللَّيْثُ بْنُ سَعْدٍ ، عَنْ أَبِي الزُّبَيْرِ ، عَنْ جَابِرِ بْنِ عَبْدِ اللهِ ، أَنَّ رَسُولَ اللهِ صلى الله عليه وسلم ، قَالَ : عُرِضَ عَلَيَّ الأَنْبِيَاءُ ، فَإِذَا مُوسَى عَلَيْهِ السَّلامُ ، ضَرْبٌ مِنَ الرِّجَالِ ، كَأَنَّهُ مِنْ رِجَالِ شَنُوءَةَ ، وَرَأَيْتُ عِيسَى بْنَ مَرْيَمَ عَلَيْهِ السَّلامُ ، فَإِذَا أَقْرَبُ مَنْ رَأَيْتُ بِهِ شَبَهًا عُرْوَةُ بْنُ مَسْعُودٍ ، وَرَأَيْتُ إِبْرَاهِيمَ عَلَيْهِ السَّلامُ ، فَإِذَا أَقْرَبُ مَنْ رَأَيْتُ بِهِ شَبَهًا صَاحِبُكُمْ ، يَعْنِي نَفْسَهُ ، وَرَأَيْتُ جِبْرِيلَ عَلَيْهِ السَّلامُ ، فَإِذَا

13 Al-Jamī' al-Saghīr (6471)

أَقْرَبُ مَنْ رَأَيْتُ بِهِ شَبَهًا دِحْيَةُ [14]

13. Jābir ibn 'Abdullāh ﷺ narrated that the Messenger of Allāh ﷺ said: "The Prophets were shown to me. I saw Mūsa ﷺ and his build and height were medium as if he was from the tribe of Shanu'ah. I saw Īsa ﷺ and from among all those whom I have seen, 'Urwah ibn Mas'ūd resembled him the most. I saw Ibrahīm ﷺ and from among all those that I have seen, I resembled him the most. I saw Angel Jibrīl ﷺ and from among all those I have seen, Dihyyah resembled him the most."

Abdul Razzaq al-Badr said,

> It is possible that they were shown to him in a dream or when he ascended to the heavens. The tribe of Shanu'ah is from Yemen and were known for having strong bodies and good physical stature.

Ibn Hajar al-Haytamī said,

> Dihyyah ﷺ was one of the companions and he was considered to be from amongst the most handsome and good looking men. It happened in many cases that Jibrīl ﷺ used to appear in the form of this companion.

Alī al-Qārī said,

> Mirak Shah al-Hanafī stated that this event took place during the night the Prophet ﷺ ascended to the sky as explained in many other authentic hadiths while some other hadīths state that this event happened in different incidents. However, the most correct view, as it appears to be, is that he ﷺ met them in the heavens after he ascended and then when he descended he gathered with them in Bayt al-Maqdis where he led them in prayers.
>
> Perhaps, the reason why the names of only these three prophets

14 Sahīh Muslim (167)

were mentioned is because Ibrahīm ﷺ is the forefather of the Arabs and he is accepted by all faiths, while Mūsa ﷺ and Īsa ﷺ are Prophets of the People of the Book.

١٤ : حَدَّثَنَا سُفْيَانُ بْنُ وَكِيعٍ ، وَمُحَمَّدُ بْنُ بَشَّارٍ ، الْمَعْنَى وَاحِدٌ ، قَالا : أَخْبَرَنَا يَزِيدُ بْنُ هَارُونَ ، عَنْ سَعِيدٍ الْجُرَيْرِيِّ ، قَالَ : سَمِعْتُ أَبَا الطُّفَيْلِ ، يَقُولُ : رَأَيْتُ النَّبِيَّ صلى الله عليه وسلم وَمَا بَقِيَ عَلَى وَجْهِ الأَرْضِ أَحَدٌ رَآهُ غَيْرِي ، قُلْتُ : صِفْهُ لِي ، قَالَ : كَانَ أَبْيَضَ ، مَلِيحًا ، مُقَصَّدًا[15]

14. Sa'īd al-Jarīrī narrated: "I heard Abū al-Tufayl ﷺ say, 'I am the last of the companions who is still alive and saw the Prophet ﷺ.' I asked him to describe him to me and so he said, 'He ﷺ was a handsome man with a white complexion and his body was moderate.'"

Alī al-Qārī said,

> Abū al-Tufayl ﷺ was the last surviving companion of the Prophet ﷺ. He passed away in 110 after Hijrah.

Ibn Hajar al-Haytamī said,

> Abū Tufayl is 'Amir ibn Wathilah al-Laythī and he saw the Prophet ﷺ during the last eight years of his life.

Abdul Razzaq al-Badr said,

> "His body was moderate" means that he was moderate in all physical aspects, whether in terms of height, skin tone, build and hair type etc.

١٥ : حَدَّثَنَا عَبْدُ اللهِ بْنُ عَبْدِ الرَّحْمَنِ ، قَالَ : حَدَّثَنَا إِبْرَاهِيمُ بْنُ الْمُنْذِرِ الْحِزَامِيُّ

15 Sahīh Muslim (2339)

، قَالَ : حَدَّثَنَا عَبْدُ الْعَزِيزِ بْنُ أَبِي ثَابِتٍ الزُّهْرِيُّ ، قَالَ : حَدَّثَنِي إِسْمَاعِيلُ بْنُ إِبْرَاهِيمَ ابْنُ أَخِي مُوسَى بْنِ عُقْبَةَ ، عَنْ مُوسَى بْنِ عُقْبَةَ ، عَنْ كُرَيْبٍ ، عَنِ ابْنِ عَبَّاسٍ ، قَالَ : كَانَ رَسُولُ اللهِ صلى الله عليه وسلم أَفْلَجَ الثَّنِيَّتَيْنِ ، إِذَا تَكَلَّمَ رُئِيَ كَالنُّورِ يَخْرُجُ مِنْ بَيْنِ ثَنَايَاهُ[16]

15. 'Abdullāh ibn 'Abbās ﷺ narrated: "There was a space between the front teeth of the Messenger of Allāh ﷺ. Whenever he talked, light could be seen emitting from his mouth."

Abdul Razzaq al-Badr said,

> There are many hadīths describing the Prophet ﷺ having light emitting from between his teeth and that his face was as bright as the moon and so forth. This has caused some to err as they have understood this literally, as in actual light that shines and enlightens all that surrounds him. In fact, some went to such extremes that they claimed that he did not possess a shadow due to this light. This understanding is obviously fallacious and there are many hadīths that prove it to be untenable, one of which is the report of Aisha ﷺ, which is documented in Sahīh Muslim, wherein she narrated that she woke up in the night and did not find the Prophet ﷺ in bed, so she began to search for him in the dark using her hands until they landed on his feet while he was saying, "*O Allāh! I seek refuge in Your pleasure from Your anger, and in Your forgiveness from Your punishment. I seek refuge with You from You. I cannot count Your praises. You are as You have praised Yourself.*" If the light referred to in these hadīths was an actual light, she would not have needed to search for him in the dark using her hands.

16 Mu'jam al-Tabaranī al-Kabīr (12181)

CHAPTER TWO

باب ما جاء في خاتم النبوة

THE REPORTS PERTAINING TO THE SEAL OF PROPHETHOOD

Abdul Razzaq al-Badr said,

> This is a sub-chapter of the previous one as it is still detailing the physical appearance of the Prophet ﷺ.

Alī al-Qārī said,

> The title of this chapter entails that it will describe the colour, shape and location of the seal.

Ibn Hajar al-Haytamī said,

> The reason it was called a seal was to indicate the authenticity of his prophethood just like how a seal is used to certify the authenticity of documents. It could also be to signify that he is the last prophet as the term "seal" is often used in reference to the end of something.

١٦ : حَدَّثَنَا أَبُو رَجَاءٍ قُتَيْبَةُ بْنُ سَعِيدٍ ، قَالَ : حَدَّثَنَا حَاتِمُ بْنُ إِسْمَاعِيلَ ، عَنِ الْجُعْدِ بْنِ عَبْدِ الرَّحْمَنِ ، قَالَ : سَمِعْتُ السَّائِبَ بْنَ يَزِيدَ ، يَقُولُ : ذَهَبَتْ بِي خَالَتِي إِلَى النَّبِيِّ صلى الله عليه وسلم ، فَقَالَتْ : يَا رَسُولَ اللهِ ، إِنَّ ابْنَ أُخْتِي وَجِعٌ فَمَسَحَ رَأْسِي وَدَعَا لِي بِالْبَرَكَةِ ، وَتَوَضَّأَ ، فَشَرِبْتُ مِنْ وَضُوئِهِ ، وَقُمْتُ خَلْفَ ظَهْرِهِ ، فَنَظَرْتُ إِلَى الْخَاتَمِ بَيْنَ كَتِفَيْهِ ، فَإِذَا هُوَ مِثْلُ زِرِّ الْحَجَلَةِ [17]

16. Al-Sā'ib ibn Yazīd ﷺ narrated: "My maternal aunt took me to the Prophet ﷺ and said to him, 'O Messenger of Allāh, this nephew of mine is ill.' The Prophet ﷺ then wiped his hand over my head and supplicated to Allāh to bless me. Then he ﷺ performed ablution and I drank from the water of his ablution. I saw the seal of prophethood between his shoulders; it was similar to the egg of a partridge."

Abdul Razzaq al-Badr said,

> "This nephew of mine is ill": In other hadīths, it was mentioned that she said to the Prophet ﷺ that her nephew fell down. This made scholars conclude that the injury was to his foot, and this is what al-Hafith ibn Hajar confirmed after he acknowledged the other hadīths.
>
> "Wiped his hand over my head": The Prophet ﷺ rubbed the head instead of the injured area as this is a more kind and sympathetic gesture and through it he could examine the companion's heartbeat and body temperature.
>
> "I drank from the water of his ablution": The use of the remnants of water that the Prophet ﷺ made ablution with for remedy and treatment was practiced by his companions. However, this attribute is exclusive to him and thus no one should seek remedy or blessing through anyone else's spit, sweat or leftovers etc., regardless of their high status and virtue.

17 Sahīh al-Bukhārī (190) and Sahīh Muslim (2345)

"Between his shoulders": Some scholars said that the wisdom of the seal being placed closer to the left side was because that location is closer to the heart.

Alī al-Qārī said,

> Al-Bayhaqī and others reported that the touch of the Prophet ﷺ on the hair of al-Sā'ib ؓ caused his hair to stay black until he died, though grey hairs appeared on his other body parts. The supplication of the Prophet ﷺ was answered and so al-Sā'ib died at the age of ninety six whilst enjoying a very healthy body.

Ibn Hajar al-Haytamī said,

> "This nephew of mine is ill": The boy had pain in his feet and the reason why the Prophet ﷺ wiped his head instead, was either because the boy felt pain in his head as well or because wiping the head is a more noble action than wiping the feet.

١٧ : حَدَّثَنَا سَعِيدُ بْنُ يَعْقُوبَ الطَّالْقَانِيُّ ، قَالَ : حدَّثنا أَيُّوبُ بْنُ جَابِرٍ ، عَنْ سِمَاكِ بْنِ حَرْبٍ ، عَنْ جَابِرِ بْنِ سَمُرَةَ ، قَالَ : رَأَيْتُ الْخَاتَمَ بَيْنَ كَتِفَيْ رَسُولِ اللهِ صلى الله عليه وسلم ، غُدَّةً حَمْرَاءَ ، مِثْلَ بَيْضَةِ الْحَمَامَةِ[18]

17. Jābir ibn Samurah ؓ related: "I saw the seal of the prophethood of Allāh's Messenger ﷺ between his two shoulders. It was red raised flesh that appeared like a pigeon's egg."

Abdul Razzaq al-Badr said,

> "Between his two shoulders": This gives the approximate location only and it is not intended to identify the exact location of the seal. This is because the seal was positioned closer to the left shoulder.
>
> The colour of the seal has been established to be red, just like the

18 Sunan al-Tirmidhī (3643)

colour of the rest of his body.

Alī al-Qārī said,

> "Like a pigeon's egg": This shows the similarity between the size, colour and shape of the pigeon's egg and the seal. Though this comparison entails that the colour of the seal is white, it does not contradict the fact that the skin tone of the Prophet ﷺ was white with some redness. Also, it is possible that the [comparison with something of] white colour was intended to indicate pureness.

Ibn Hajar al-Haytamī said,

> "It was red raised flesh": This indicates that its colour was the same as his skin.

١٨ : حَدَّثَنَا أَبُو مُصْعَبَ الْمُدِينِيُّ ، قَالَ : حَدَّثَنَا يُوسُفُ بْنُ الْمَاجِشُونِ ، عَنْ أَبِيهِ ، عَنْ عَاصِمِ بْنِ عُمَرَ بْنِ قَتَادَةَ ، عَنْ جَدَّتِهِ رُمَيْثَةَ ، قَالَتْ : سَمِعْتُ رَسُولَ اللهِ صلى الله عليه وسلم ، وَلَوْ أَشَاءُ أَنْ أُقَبِّلَ الْخَاتَمَ الَّذِي بَيْنَ كَتِفَيْهِ مِنْ قُرْبِهِ لَفَعَلْتُ ، يَقُولُ لِسَعْدِ بْنِ مُعَاذٍ يَوْمَ مَاتَ : اهْتَزَّ لَهُ عَرْشُ الرَّحْمَنِ[19]

18. Rumaythah ﵂ said: "I heard the Messenger of Allāh ﷺ - and at that time the distance between us was very small, such that if I wanted to, I could have kissed the seal of prophethood – saying after the death of Sā'd ibn Mu'ādh ﵁, 'The Throne of Allāh shook [because of his death].'"

Abdul Razzaq al-Badr said,

> "The distance between us was very small": This is to confirm that she heard him.
>
> "The Throne of Allāh shook [because of his death]": This shows

19 Musnad Ahmad (26793)

the great virtue and status of the companion Sā'd ibn Mu'ādh ﷺ.

Alī al-Qārī said,

> "The death of Sā'd ibn Mu'ādh ﷺ": He was the master of the tribe of the Ansār and he died at the age of thirty seven due to an injury he sustained during the Battle of the Trench.
>
> When the hypocrites joked that his coffin was light, the Prophet ﷺ said that he was carried by seventy thousand angels.

Ibn Hajar al-Haytamī said,

> "The Throne of Allāh shook [because of his death]": It shook literally because it was happy that his soul had ascended above and also to make the angels aware of his virtues and his death. In another interpretation, it was argued that the word "shook" was used metaphorically to mean rejoicing at his arrival.

١٩ : حَدَّثَنَا أَحْمَدُ بْنُ عَبْدَةَ الضَّبِّيُّ ، وَعَلِيُّ بْنُ حُجْرٍ ، وَغَيْرُ وَاحِدٍ ، قَالُوا : حَدَّثَنَا عِيسَى بْنُ يُونُسَ ، عَنْ عُمَرَ بْنِ عَبْدِ اللهِ مَوْلَى غُفْرَةَ ، قَالَ : حَدَّثَنِي إِبْرَاهِيمُ بْنُ مُحَمَّدٍ مِنْ وَلَدِ عَلِيِّ بْنِ أَبِي طَالِبٍ ، قَالَ : كَانَ عَلِيٌّ ، إِذَا وَصَفَ رَسُولَ اللهِ صلى الله عليه وسلم فَذَكَرَ الْحَدِيثَ بِطُولِهِ ، وَقَالَ : بَيْنَ كَتِفَيْهِ خَاتَمُ النُّبُوَّةِ ، وَهُوَ خَاتَمُ النَّبِيِّينَ[20]

19. Ibrahīm ibn Muhammad, the grandson of Alī ibn Abī Tālib said: "Whenever Alī ﷺ used to describe the Prophet ﷺ, he would narrate the complete hadīth and then add, 'The seal of prophethood was between his shoulders, and he was the seal of all Prophets.[21]'"

---

20 See footnote 7

21 It refers to hadīth six in this book wherein 'Alī ibn Abī Tālib ﷺ described the Prophet ﷺ in detail. This hadīth is included here because of the addition related to the seal of prophethood.

٢٠ : حَدَّثَنَا مُحَمَّدُ بْنُ بَشَّارٍ ، قَالَ : حَدَّثَنَا أَبُو عَاصِمٍ ، قَالَ : حَدَّثَنَا عَزْرَةُ بْنُ ثَابِتٍ ، قَالَ : حَدَّثَنِي عِلْبَاءُ بْنُ أَحْمَرَ الْيَشْكُرِيُّ ، قَالَ : حَدَّثَنِي أَبُو زَيْدٍ عَمْرُو بْنُ أَخْطَبَ الأَنْصَارِيُّ ، قَالَ : قَالَ لِي رَسُولُ اللهِ صلى الله عليه وسلم : يَا أَبَا زَيْدٍ ، ادْنُ مِنِّي فَامْسَحْ ظَهْرِي ، فَمَسَحْتُ ظَهْرَهُ ، فَوَقَعَتْ أَصَابِعِي عَلَى الْخَاتَمِ قُلْتُ : وَمَا الْخَاتَمُ ؟ قَالَ : شَعَرَاتٌ مُجْتَمِعَاتٌ[22]

20. Ilyā' ibn Ahmar al-Yashkurī narrated that Abū Zayd, 'Amro ibn Akhtab al-Ansārī ﷺ said: "The Messenger of Allāh ﷺ said to me, 'O Abū Zayd, come closer to me and rub my back.' I began rubbing his back and I felt the seal of prophethood." Ilyā' asked Amro ﷺ, "What is the seal of prophethood?" He replied, "It was a collection of a few hairs."

Ibn Hajar al-Haytamī said,

> "Rub my back": This indicates that it is permissible for one person to touch the body of another person provided that both are from the same gender and the area touched is not from the *'awrah*.

Abdul Razzaq al-Badr said,

> "O Abū Zayd": This shows the kindness and politeness of the Prophet ﷺ when dealing with his companions i.e. he called his companion using his *kunya* and not his actual name.
>
> "It was a collection of a few hairs": However, the seal was not just a collection of hairs. It was a piece of flesh the size of an egg and it was surrounded by a few hairs.
>
> In a different version of this hadīth documented in the Musnad of Imām Ahmad, the Prophet ﷺ wiped his hand over his beard and hair and said, "O Allāh, beautify him and make his beauty last." The supplication was answered and this companion lived over one hundred years, having hardly any grey hairs and skin without

22 Musnad Ahmad (20732)

wrinkles.

We can also benefit from the supplication of the Prophet ﷺ if we look after his Sunnah because he said, "May Allāh enlighten the face of a person who heard my words, understood them and delivered them to others as he heard from me."[23] This is why Sufyān ibn 'Uyayna said, "No one seeks the knowledge of hadīth except that his face is bright."

Alī al-Qārī said,

> 'Amro ibn Zayd al-Ansārī was one of the four companions who memorised the entire Qur'ān at that time.
>
> "Rub my back": he was asked to do so either because the Prophet ﷺ needed to scratch his back, or to check if there was something harmful there, or to receive the honour of touching his noble body.

٢١: حَدَّثَنَا أَبُو عَمَّارٍ الْحُسَيْنُ بْنُ حُرَيْثٍ الْخُزَاعِيُّ ، قَالَ : حَدَّثَنَا عَلِيُّ بْنُ حُسَيْنِ بْنِ وَاقِدٍ ، حَدَّثَنِي أَبِي ، قَالَ : حَدَّثَنِي عَبْدُ اللهِ بْنُ بُرَيْدَةَ ، قَالَ : سَمِعْتُ أَبِي بُرَيْدَةَ ، يَقُولُ : جَاءَ سَلْمَانُ الْفَارِسِيُّ إِلَى رَسُولِ اللهِ صلى الله عليه وسلم ، حِينَ قَدِمَ الْمَدِينَةَ بِمَائِدَةٍ عَلَيْهَا رُطَبٌ ، فَوَضَعَهَا بَيْنَ يَدَيْ رَسُولِ اللهِ صلى الله عليه وسلم ، فَقَالَ : يَا سَلْمَانُ مَا هَذَا ؟ فَقَالَ : صَدَقَةٌ عَلَيْكَ ، وَعَلَى أَصْحَابِكَ ، فَقَالَ : ارْفَعْهَا ، فَإِنَّا لا نَأْكُلُ الصَّدَقَةَ ، قَالَ : فَرَفَعَهَا ، فَجَاءَ الْغَدَ بِمِثْلِهِ ، فَوَضَعَهُ بَيْنَ يَدَيْ رَسُولِ اللهِ صلى الله عليه وسلم ، فَقَالَ : مَا هَذَا يَا سَلْمَانُ ؟ فَقَالَ : هَدِيَّةٌ لَكَ ، فَقَالَ رَسُولُ اللهِ صلى الله عليه وسلم لأَصْحَابِهِ : ابْسُطُوا ثُمَّ نَظَرَ إِلَى الْخَاتَمِ عَلَى ظَهْرِ رَسُولِ اللهِ صلى الله عليه وسلم ، فَآمَنَ بِهِ ، وَكَانَ لِلْيَهُودِ فَاشْتَرَاهُ رَسُولُ اللهِ صلى الله عليه وسلم ، بِكَذَا وَكَذَا دِرْهَمًا عَلَى أَنْ يَغْرِسَ لَهُمْ نَخْلا ، فَيَعْمَلَ سَلْمَانُ فِيهِ ، حَتَّى تُطْعِمَ ، فَغَرَسَ رَسُولُ اللهِ صلى الله عليه وسلم ، النَّخلَ إِلا نَخْلَةً وَاحِدَةً ، غَرَسَهَا

23 Sunan al-Tirmidhī (2658) and Sunan Ibn Mājah (230)

عُمَرُ فَحَمَلَتِ النَّخْلُ مِنْ عَامِهَا ، وَلَمْ تَحْمِلْ نَخْلَةٌ ، فَقَالَ رَسُولُ الله صلى الله عليه وسلم : مَا شَأْنُ هَذِهِ النَّخْلَةِ ؟ فَقَالَ عُمَرُ : يَا رَسُولَ الله ، أَنَا غَرَسْتُهَا ، فَنَزَعَهَا رَسُولُ الله صلى الله عليه وسلم ، فَغَرَسَهَا فَحَمَلَتْ مِنْ عَامِهَا[24]

21. Buraydah ﷺ narrated: "When Salmān al-Fārisī ﷺ came to Madīnah, he visited the Prophet ﷺ and brought a tray on which there were some dates that he placed before the hands of the Prophet ﷺ. The Prophet ﷺ asked, 'What are these?' He replied, 'This is an almsgiving to you and your companions.' Allāh's Messenger ﷺ replied, 'We do not eat from charity; take it away from me.' And so Salmān complied and removed them. On the next day he brought some dates and placed them in front of the Prophet ﷺ who asked him, 'O Salmān, what are these?' To which he replied, 'O Messenger of Allāh, it is a present for you.' The Prophet ﷺ invited his companions to eat from these dates. He then saw the seal of prophethood on the back of Allāh's Messenger ﷺ and embraced Islām.

At that time, he was a slave to a Jew so the Prophet ﷺ made an agreement with his master to grant Salmān his freedom in return of a sum of money and after the planting of [a particular number of] date palms for the Jew that Salmān would tend to until they produced dates. The Messenger of Allāh ﷺ planted all the date palms except one that 'Umar ﷺ planted. On the same year, all the date palms produced dates except one. So the Prophet ﷺ inquired about it and 'Umar replied that he planted that palm tree. The Prophet ﷺ then uprooted it and planted it again. Thereafter the palm tree produced dates in the same year."

Abdul Razzaq al-Badr said,

> The reason why Salmān ﷺ presented the dates to the Prophet ﷺ as a charity on the first occasion and as a gift on the second was because he sought to find the last prophet. He was aware that from

24 Musnad Ahmad (22997)

the signs of this prophet was that he does not eat from charity but he accepts that which is gifted to him. The other sign that he looked for was the seal which he saw on his back.

"All the date palms produced dates except one": The wisdom behind this was so that the miracle of the Prophet ﷺ could be displayed to the people.

Ibn Hajar al-Haytamī said,

> "We do not eat from charity": This includes both the obligatory and voluntary charity as well as all that which is deemed obligatory in religion such as compensation and vows.
>
> "The Prophet ﷺ agreed with his master to free him... In return of": It can be concluded from this that it is recommended to help slaves free themselves.

Alī al-Qārī said,

> "This is an almsgiving to you and your companions": One of the commentators said that charity is something that the superior gives to the inferior, seeking the reward in the Hereafter and it entails that the receiver is pitiable. In contrast, a gift is a means to seek closeness to the recipient and it does not entail any sense of pity towards the recipient.
>
> "We do not eat from charity": The pronoun refers to the prophets as well as his relatives from the tribe of Banī Hashim and al-Muttalib. It does not include the Companions.
>
> "O Salmān, what are these?": The Prophet ﷺ addressed him on the first occasion without mentioning his name but on the second occasion he mentioned his name to show more kindness as he felt he was about to embrace Islām.

٢٢: حَدَّثَنَا مُحَمَّدُ بْنُ بَشَّارٍ ، قَالَ : حَدَّثَنَا بِشْرُ بْنُ الْوَضَّاحِ ، قَالَ : حَدَّثَنَا أَبُو عَقِيلٍ الدَّوْرَقِيُّ ، عَنْ أَبِي نَضْرَةَ الْعَوَقِيِّ ، قَالَ : سَأَلْتُ أَبَا سَعِيدٍ الْخُدْرِيَّ ،

عَنْ خَاتَمِ رَسُولِ الله صلى الله عليه وسلم يَعْنِي خَاتَمَ النُّبُوَّةِ ، فَقَالَ : كَانَ فِي ظَهْرِهِ بَضْعَةٌ نَاشِزَةٌ[25]

22. Abū Nadrah al-'Awaqī related: "I asked Abū Sa'īd al-Khudarī ﷺ about the seal of prophethood of Allāh's Messenger ﷺ. He said, 'It was a raised piece of flesh on his back.'"

Abdul Razzaq al-Badr said,

> "... On his back": As other hadīths show, the seal was located on his back between the two shoulders and it was closer to the left one.

٢٣ : حَدَّثَنَا أَحْمَدُ بْنُ الْمِقْدَامِ أَبُو الأَشْعَثِ الْعِجْلِيُّ الْبَصْرِيُّ ، قَالَ : أَخْبَرَنَا حَمَّادُ بْنُ زَيْدٍ ، عَنْ عَاصِمٍ الأَحْوَلِ ، عَنْ عَبْدِ الله بْنِ سَرْجِسَ ، قَالَ : أَتَيْتُ رَسُولَ الله صلى الله عليه وسلم وَهُوَ فِي نَاسٍ مِنْ أَصْحَابِهِ ، فَدُرْتُ هَكَذَا مِنْ خَلْفِهِ ، فَعَرَفَ الَّذِي أُرِيدُ ، فَأَلْقَى الرِّدَاءَ عَنْ ظَهْرِهِ ، فَرَأَيْتُ مَوْضِعَ الْخَاتَمِ عَلَى كَتِفَيْهِ ، مِثْلَ الْجُمْعِ حَوْلَهَا خِيلانٌ ، كَأَنَّهَا ثَآلِيلُ ، فَرَجَعْتُ حَتَّى اسْتَقْبَلْتُهُ ، فَقُلْتُ : غَفَرَ اللهُ لَكَ يَا رَسُولَ الله ، فَقَالَ : وَلَكَ فَقَالَ الْقَوْمُ : أَسْتَغْفَرَ لَكَ رَسُولُ الله صلى الله عليه وسلم ؟ فَقَالَ : نَعَمْ ، وَلَكُمْ ، ثُمَّ تَلا هَذِهِ الآيَةَ ﴿وَاسْتَغْفِرْ لِذَنْبِكَ وَلِلْمُؤْمِنِينَ وَالْمُؤْمِنَاتِ﴾.[26]

23. 'Abdullāh ibn Sarjas ﷺ narrated: "I came to Allāh's Messenger ﷺ while he was sitting with some of his companions. I went to stand behind him – like this – and so the Prophet ﷺ understood my purpose. So, he dropped the cloak he was wearing on his back and then I saw the place of the seal of prophethood on his shoulders. It was like a clenched fist surrounded by beauty spots. I then walked

---

25 Al-Jamī' al-Saghīr (6484)
26 Sahih Muslim (2346)

and stood in front of him and said, 'O Messenger of Allāh, may Allāh forgive you.' To that he replied, 'May Allāh forgive you too.' The people said to me, 'Allāh's Messenger ﷺ has asked Allāh to forgive you?' I replied, 'Yes, and he asked Him to forgive you too.' Then, he recited, {[O Muhammad] seek forgiveness for yourself and the believing males and females.}"

Ibn Hajar al-Haytamī said,

> "Understood my purpose": He understood that the companion wanted to see the seal.
>
> "O Messenger of Allāh, may Allāh forgive you": He said it to show his gratitude for allowing him to see the seal.

Abdul Razzaq al-Badr said,

> "It was like a clenched fist": All the hadīths describing the size of the seal are similar though each narrator used different examples i.e. some said it was the size of an egg, and some said it was like a piece of flesh, and some said it was like a clenched fist.
>
> "Allāh's Messenger ﷺ has asked Allāh to forgive you": This was a statement they said to express the greatness of the supplication of the Prophet ﷺ. Some people err and misunderstand the statement of Allāh, the Exalted, wherein He said, **{And if, when they wronged themselves, they had come to you, [O Muhammad], and asked forgiveness of Allāh and the Messenger had asked forgiveness for them, they would have found Allāh Accepting of repentance and Merciful.}**[27], thinking that he ﷺ would still ask Allāh to forgive people even after his death. The correct view is that he could ask Allāh to forgive people only during his lifetime as proven in the authentic hadīth in Sahīh al-Bukhārī when Aisha رضي الله عنها said, "O my head!" Allāh's Messenger ﷺ said, "If that (your death) should happen while I am still alive, I would ask Allāh to forgive you and would invoke Allāh for you."

27 Qur'ān: 4:64

The inquiry and surprise of the people who asked whether the Prophet ﷺ asked Allāh to forgive the narrator is another proof because if he could do so after his death they would have not showed such surprise and wishful thinking.

Alī al-Qārī said,

> It is a matter of fact that the Prophet ﷺ was infallible; hence the issue of him seeking Allāh's forgiveness is understood to mean either to forgive him for any thought that crossed his mind unwillingly (as it is the nature of mankind), or to mean that he asked Allāh to maintain his infallibility (though the fact that he was granted it shows his ultimate submission to Allāh), or it can mean that he asked Allāh to forgive his use of lawful matters and his inability to worship Allāh enough to fulfil His ﷻ due rights.

CHAPTER THREE

باب ما جاء في شعر رسول الله صلى الله عليه وسلم
THE REPORTS PERTAINING TO THE HAIR OF THE PROPHET ﷺ

Abdul Razzaq al-Badr said,

> This title is given to show that the subsequent section will include hadīths describing the hair of the Prophet ﷺ; its length, style, and how he used to look after it.

Al-Bajūrī said,

> The Prophet ﷺ never shaved his head except in the year in which the treaty of Hudaybiyah took place, the Umrah al-Qaḍā (i.e. the Umrah he performed in order to make up for the one he missed during the year of Hudaybiyah), the farewell Hajj. And he only cut his hair short once as reported in Sahīh al-Bukhārī and Sahīh Muslim.

٢٤ : حَدَّثَنَا عَلِيُّ بْنُ حُجْرٍ ، قَالَ : أَخْبَرَنَا إِسْمَاعِيلُ بْنُ إِبْرَاهِيمَ ، عَنْ حُمَيْدٍ ، عَنْ أَنَسِ بْنِ مَالِكٍ ، قَالَ : كَانَ شَعَرُ رَسُولِ اللهِ صلى الله عليه وسلم إِلَى نِصْفِ أُذُنَيْهِ[28]

24. Anas ibn Mālik ﷺ narrated: "The hair of Allāh's Messenger ﷺ reached to the mid-portion of his ears."

Abdul Razzaq al-Badr said,

> In other hadīths, the narrators stated that the length of the hair of the Prophet ﷺ reached to his shoulders; hence some scholars explained that this is because the length of his hair differed from one time to another and so each narrator described what he saw.

Al-Suyūtī said,

> Al-Hafith al-Iraqī said, "The hadīths have provided three different descriptions of the hair of the Prophet ﷺ, namely:
> *(1) Wafrah*: It refers to having hair that reaches the earlobe.
> *(2) Lummah*: It refers to having hair that reaches below the earlobe
> *(3) Jumma*: It refers to shoulder length hair.

Alī al-Qārī said,

> There are eights hadīths that describe the length of the hair of the Prophet ﷺ.

٢٥ : حَدَّثَنَا هَنَّادُ بْنُ السَّرِيِّ ، قَالَ : أَخْبَرَنَا عَبْدُ الرَّحْمَنِ بْنُ أَبِي الزِّنَادِ ، عَنْ هِشَامِ بْنِ عُرْوَةَ ، عَنْ أَبِيهِ ، عَنْ عَائِشَةَ ، قَالَتْ : كُنْتُ أَغْتَسِلُ أَنَا وَرَسُولُ اللهِ صَلى الله عليه وسلم مِنْ إِنَاءٍ وَاحِدٍ ، وَكَانَ لَهُ شَعَرٌ فَوْقَ الْجُمَّةِ ، وَدُونَ

28 Sahīh Muslim (2338)

الْوَفْرَةِ[29]

25. Aisha ﵂ narrated: "I used to bathe with the Prophet ﷺ in one utensil, and his hair was below his earlobes but above his shoulders."

Ibn Hajar al-Haytamī said,

> This hadīth is evidence that the water remaining from the bath of women is ritually pure.

٢٦ : حَدَّثَنَا أَحْمَدُ بْنُ مَنِيعٍ ، قَالَ : حَدَّثَنَا أَبُو قَطَنٍ ، قَالَ : حَدَّثَنَا شُعْبَةُ ، عَنْ أَبِي إِسْحَاقَ ، عَنِ الْبَرَاءِ بْنِ عَازِبٍ ، قَالَ : كَانَ رَسُولُ اللهِ صلى الله عليه وسلم مَرْبُوعًا ، بَعِيدَ مَا بَيْنَ الْمَنْكِبَيْنِ ، وَكَانَتْ جُمَّتُهُ تَضْرِبُ شَحْمَةَ أُذُنَيْهِ[30]

26. Al-Barā ibn 'Āzib ﵁ narrated: "The Messenger of Allāh ﷺ was of average height, and the distance between his two shoulders was wide. His hair would fall to his ear lobes."

٢٧ : حَدَّثَنَا مُحَمَّدُ بْنُ بَشَّارٍ ، قَالَ : حَدَّثَنَا وَهْبُ بْنُ جَرِيرِ بْنِ حَازِمٍ ، قَالَ : حَدَّثَنِي أَبِي ، عَنْ قَتَادَةَ ، قَالَ : قُلْتُ لأَنَسٍ : كَيْفَ كَانَ شَعَرُ رَسُولِ اللهِ صلى الله عليه وسلم ؟ قَالَ : لَمْ يَكُنْ بِالْجَعْدِ ، وَلا بِالسَّبْطِ ، كَانَ يَبْلُغُ شَعَرُهُ شَحْمَةَ أُذُنَيْهِ[31]

27. Qatādah narrated: "I asked Anas ibn Mālik ﵁, 'How was the hair of Allāh's Messenger ﷺ?' He replied, 'It was neither very curly nor very straight; it reached his earlobes.'"

29 Sunan al-Tirmidhī (1755)
30 See footnote of hadith 4
31 Sahīh al-Bukhārī (5908) and Sahīh Muslim (2338)

٢٨ : حَدَّثَنَا مُحَمَّدُ بْنُ يَحْيَى بْنِ أَبِي عُمَرَ الْمَكِّيُّ ، قَالَ : حَدَّثَنَا سُفْيَانُ بْنُ عُيَيْنَةَ ، عَنِ ابْنِ أَبِي نَجِيحٍ ، عَنْ مُجَاهِدٍ ، عَنْ أُمِّ هَانِئٍ بِنْتِ أَبِي طَالِبٍ ، قَالَتْ : قَدِمَ رَسُولُ اللهِ صلى الله عليه وسلم مَكَّةَ قَدْمَةً ، وَلَهُ أَرْبَعُ غَدَائِرَ[32]

28. Umm Hanī' bint Abī Tālib ﷺ said: "Allāh's Messenger ﷺ entered Makkah and he had four plaits."

Abdul Razzaq al-Badr said,

> Umm Hanī' is the sister of Alī ibn Abī Tālib ﷺ.

Ibn Hajar al-Haytamī said,

> It appears that she saw him on the day of the conquest of Makkah because he prayed the *Duha* prayer in her house.

Alī al-Qārī said,

> The Prophet ﷺ came to Makkah four times [after the Hijrah]: (i) 'Umrah al-Qadā, (ii) the conquest of Makkah, (iii) 'Umrah al-Ja'ranah, (iv) the farewell Hajj.

٢٩ : حَدَّثَنَا سُوَيْدُ بْنُ نَصْرٍ ، قَالَ : حَدَّثَنَا عَبْدُ اللهِ بْنُ الْمُبَارَكِ ، عَنْ مَعْمَرٍ ، عَنْ ثَابِتٍ الْبُنَانِيِّ ، عَنْ أَنَسٍ : أَنَّ شَعَرَ رَسُولِ اللهِ صلى الله عليه وسلم ، كَانَ إِلَى أَنْصَافِ أُذُنَيْهِ[33]

29. Ma'mar reported that Anas ibn Mālik ﷺ said that: "The hair of Allāh's Messenger ﷺ reached the mid-portion of his ears."

٣٠ : حَدَّثَنَا سُوَيْدُ بْنُ نَصْرٍ حَدَّثَنَا عَبْدُ اللهِ بْنُ الْمُبَارَكِ عَنْ يُونُسَ بْنِ يَزِيدَ

32 Sunan al-Tirmidhī (1781)
33 See footnote of hadīth 27

عَنِ الزُّهْرِيِّ قَالَ : حَدَّثَنَا عُبَيْدُ اللَّهِ بْنُ عَبْدِ اللَّهِ بْنِ عُتْبَةَ عَنِ ابْنِ عَبَّاسٍ أَنَّ رَسُولَ اللَّهِ صلى الله عليه وسلم كَانَ يُسْدِلُ شَعَرَهُ وَكَانَ الْمُشْرِكُونَ يَفْرِقُونَ رُؤُوسَهُمْ وَكَانَ أَهْلُ الْكِتَابِ يُسْدِلُونَ رُؤُوسَهُمْ وَكَانَ يُحِبُّ مُوَافَقَةَ أَهْلِ الْكِتَابِ فِيمَا لَمْ يُؤْمَرْ فِيهِ بِشَيْءٍ ثُمَّ فَرَقَ رَسُولُ اللَّهِ صلى الله عليه وسلم رَأْسَهُ[34]

30. 'Abdullāh ibn 'Abbās ؓ narrated: "The hairstyle of the Messenger of Allāh ﷺ was *sadl* and the polytheists used to part their hair while the hairstyle of the People of the Book was *sadl*. He preferred not to oppose the People of the Book unless he was ordered otherwise."

> The meaning of *sadl* is disputed over among scholars, some of them (such as Al-Bajūrī) stated that it means he let his hair hang down freely around the head, and some (such as al-Nawawī, al-Suyūtī and Alī al-Qārī) were of the view that it means he let his hair fall on his forehead.

Abdul Razzaq al-Badr said,

> Ibn Hajar said that the last practice of the Prophet ﷺ was to part his hair.

Alī al-Qārī said,

> The Prophet ﷺ used to keep a hairstyle similar to that of the People of the Book because he preferred their way over the way of the polytheists, unless he was ordered to oppose them. This is because either they (Christians and Jews) have celestial religions, divine books and prophets, or because they are closer to the truth than the polytheists, since they followed some of the original teachings of their religion during that time (as the known scholar Mirak al-Hanafī explained); hence they deserved better treatment than the

34 Sahīh al-Bukhārī (3588) and Sahīh Muslim (2336)

polytheists.

Al-Bajūrī said,

> "He preferred not to oppose the People of the Book unless he was ordered otherwise": He liked to do so in matters where he was not ordered, regardless whether the divine order entailed an obligation or recommendation. Al-Qurtubī said, "This was only at the beginning when he arrived at Madīnah, during the time he used to pray towards their *qiblah*. The reason behind this was that he wanted to soften their hearts towards Islām but when this approach did not show any benefit and their hearts remained hard, he ordered the Muslims to oppose them in many affairs.

٣١: حَدَّثَنَا مُحَمَّدُ بْنُ بَشَّارٍ ، قَالَ : حَدَّثَنَا عَبْدُ الرَّحْمَنِ بْنُ مَهْدِيٍّ ، عَنْ إِبْرَاهِيمَ بْنِ نَافِعٍ الْمَكِّيِّ ، عَنِ ابْنِ أَبِي نَجِيحٍ ، عَنْ مُجَاهِدٍ ، عَنْ أُمِّ هَانِئٍ ، قَالَتْ : رَأَيْتُ رَسُولَ اللهِ صلى الله عليه وسلم ذَا ضَفَائِرَ أَرْبَعٍ[35]

31. Umm Hanī' bint Abī Tālib رضي الله عنها said: "I saw Allāh's Messenger ﷺ having four plaits."

Abdul Razzaq al-Badr said,

> Shaykh ibn 'Uthaymīn was asked, "Is it from the Sunnah to prolong the hair?" To which he replied, "No, it is not from the Sunnah because the Prophet ﷺ lengthened his hair in a time in which that was the custom of people. This is why he ordered the young boy who shaved part of his head, 'Shave it all or leave it all.' If the hair is supposed to be left to grow long he would have ordered the boy to leave it all only... With that being said, if you live in a place where the custom of the people is to grow their hair long, then do so. Otherwise do not."

---

35 See footnote of hadīth 28

However, it is worthy to mention that one must not imitate women or disbelievers. This is important to mention as we see some youth prolonging their hair and having their hair fashioned in the style of women, to the point they may use the accessories of women to hold their hair, and even worse, their faces are also clean shaved. Likewise some may simulate the disbelievers in their hairstyles or hair dyes, and some of them may argue that prolonging the hair is Sunnah when all the while they do not even commit to praying the obligatory prayers.

Al-Bajūrī said,

> This shows that it is permissible for men to plait their hair and that it is not limited to women, even if it is often the practice of women to plait their hair in this era.

CHAPTER FOUR

باب ما جاء في ترجل رسول اللّه صلى اللّه عليه وسلم

THE REPORTS PERTAINING TO THE HAIR CARE OF THE PROPHET ﷺ

Abdul Razzaq al-Badr said,

> The author dedicated this chapter to listing the hadīths that describe the combing and the hair care of the Prophet ﷺ.
>
> The Prophet ﷺ was moderate and balanced about his hair; neither was he obsessed about his hair or negligent regarding it.

Al-Bajūrī said,

> The hair care is part of the cleanliness and personal hygiene that the legislator encouraged and recommended. The Prophet ﷺ said, "Cleanliness is from *imān*"[36] and, "Whoever has hair should honour it."[37]

---

36 This statement is not from the words of the Prophet ﷺ but the meaning is indicated and supported in other hadiths.

37 Sunan Abu Dawūd (4163)

٣٢: حدثنا إسحاق بن موسى الأنصاري، حدثنا مَعْن بن عيسى، حدثنا مالك بن أنس، عَنْ هِشَام بْنِ عُرْوَةَ، عَنْ أَبِيهِ، عَنْ عَائِشَةَ، قَالَتْ: كُنْتُ أُرَجِّلُ رَأْسَ رَسُولِ اللهِ صَلَى الله عليه وسلم وَأَنَا حَائِضٌ[38]

32. Aisha ﵂ related: "I used to comb the hair of Allāh's Messenger ﷺ even whilst I was in the state of menstruation."

Abdul Razzaq al-Badr said,

> This is evidence that it is permissible for the wife to comb the hair of her husband and touch him while she is menstruating, and that the body of a menstruating woman is not deemed ritually impure.

Ibn Hajar al-Haytamī said,

> This is evidence that it is only the menstrual blood of the woman that is ritually impure while the rest of her body is pure. It also shows that the wife should look after her husband in all cases, and that she can still spend time with her husband during menses as avoiding the wife during her menses is the way of the Jews.

Al-Bajūrī said,

> This hadīth shows that it is recommended to comb the hair, and to comb the beard as well, based on analogy.

٣٣: حَدَّثَنَا يُوسُفُ بْنُ عِيسَى، قَالَ: حَدَّثَنَا وَكِيعٌ، قَالَ: حَدَّثَنَا الرَّبِيعُ بْنُ صَبِيحٍ، عَنْ يَزِيدَ بْنِ أَبَانَ هُوَ الرَّقَاشِيُّ، عَنْ أَنَسِ بْنِ مَالِكٍ، قَالَ: كَانَ رَسُولُ اللَّه صلى الله عليه وسلم يُكْثِرُ دَهْنَ رَأْسِهِ وَتَسْرِيحَ لِحْيَتِهِ، وَيُكْثِرُ الْقِنَاعَ حَتَّى كَأَنَّ ثَوْبَهُ، ثَوْبُ زَيَّاتٍ[39]

---

38 Sahīh al-Bukhārī (295) and Sahīh Muslim (297)
39 Hidayatu al-Ruwāt Ila ahadīth al-masabīh wal Mishkat (4/237)

33. Anas ibn Mālik رضي الله عنه narrated: "The Messenger of Allāh ﷺ used to frequently oil his hair and comb his beard. He would often wear a cloth around his head, which would eventually appear to look like the cloth of an oilman."

Abdul Razzaq al-Badr said,

> "Used to frequently oil his hair": It means that he would often use oil whenever he combed his hair.

Al-Bajūrī said,

> "Would wear a cloth": This is a cloth that is put over the head to protect the turban from the stains of oil.

Alī al-Qārī said,

> "And comb his beard": This indicates that he used to oil his beard when combing it.
>
> "Which would eventually appear to look like the cloth of an oilman": This refers only to the hair-cover. This meaning is the most suitable and it befits the state of the Prophet ﷺ whose clothes were evidently always clean, not to mention the many hadīths wherein he encouraged people to keep their clothes clean. This meaning is also proven from other hadīths that explicitly clarified that it refers to the hair-cover.

Al-Suyūtī said,

> "He would often wear a cloth around his head": He ﷺ also used to cover his head during intercourse often and this was done due to his shyness.

٣٤: حَدَّثَنَا هَنَّادُ بْنُ السَّرِيِّ ، قَالَ : حَدَّثَنَا أَبُو الأَحْوَصِ ، عَنِ الأَشْعَثِ بْنِ أَبِي الشَّعْثَاءِ ، عَنْ أَبِيهِ ، عَنْ مَسْرُوقٍ ، عَنْ عَائِشَةَ ، قَالَتْ : إِنْ كَانَ رَسُولُ

الله صلى الله عليه وسلم لَيُحِبُّ التَّيَمُّنَ فِي طُهُورِهِ إِذَا تَطَهَّرَ ، وَفِي تَرَجُّلِهِ إِذَا
تَرَجَّلَ ، وَفِي انْتِعَالِهِ إِذَا انْتَعَلَ[40]

34. Aisha narrated: "Allāh's Messenger ﷺ used to like to start with the right side when engaging in his ritual purification, combing his hair, and putting on his sandals."

Abdul Razzaq al-Badr said,

> It is recommended to start with the right side in all that which is deemed good such as entering the *masjid*, eating, drinking, shaking the hands, exchanging money or items between people and wearing clothes etc. The opposite should be observed – that is to say – to start with the left side in opposite activities such as entering the toilet, leaving the *masjid*, [taking off shoes and socks] etc.

Al-Bajūrī said,

> "Used to like to start with the right side": Imām al-Bukhārī documented another version that has the addition, "as long as he was able to", which indicates that one should observe this behaviour unless there is something that prevents us from that. The reason why the Prophet ﷺ liked to start with the right side is because the dwellers of Paradise are the people of the right.

Ibn Hajar al-Haytamī said,

> "Engaging in his ritual purification": He liked to start with the right side in ablution when washing the hands and the feet, but did not follow the same manner when washing the cheeks and ears.

Alī al-Qārī said,

> "Engaging in his ritual purification": The purification mentioned

---

40 Sahīh Muslim (268)

in this hadīth includes *wuḍū*, *ghusl* and *tayammum* but it does not include purifying oneself from physical impurity (*istinjah* and *istijmār*).

Al-Nawawī said,

> All scholars are in agreement that starting with the right side in ablution is a Sunnah and whoever opposes it misses its reward but their ablution is valid.

٣٥: حَدَّثَنَا مُحَمَّدُ بْنُ بَشَّارٍ ، قَالَ : حَدَّثَنَا يَحْيَى بْنُ سَعِيدٍ ، عَنْ هِشَامِ بْنِ حَسَّانَ ، عَنِ الْحَسَنِ ، عَنْ عَبْدِ اللهِ بْنِ مُغَفَّلٍ ، قَالَ : نَهَى رَسُولُ اللهِ صلى الله عليه وسلم عَنِ التَّرَجُّلِ ، إِلا غِبًّا[41]

35. 'Abdullāh ibn Mughaffal ؓ narrated: "Allāh's Messenger ﷺ prohibited the combing of hair unless it is done occasionally."

Abdul Razzaq al-Badr said,

> This means that one must not let his haircare occupy all of his time and so one should be neither negligent nor indulgent.

Al-Bajūrī said,

> The reason behind this prohibition was because it gives the impression that one is indulging in luxury and adornment, which is the habit of women.

Abū Bakr ibn al-'Arabī said,

> Taking care of the hair constantly is showing off, neglecting it is foulness and looking after it occasionally is the Sunnah.

41 Sunan al-Tirmidhī (1756)

Ibn Hajar al-Haytamī said,

> This prohibition applies to oiling the hair too.

Alī al-Qārī said,

> 'Abdullāh ibn Mughaffal ؓ was one of the companions who witnessed the Pledge of the Tree.

٣٦: حَدَّثَنَا الْحَسَنُ بْنُ عَرَفَةَ ، قَالَ : حَدَّثَنَا عَبْدُ السَّلام بْنُ حَرْبٍ ، عَنْ يَزِيدَ بْنِ أَبِي خَالِدٍ ، عَنْ أَبِي الْعَلاءِ الأَوْدِيِّ ، عَنْ حُمَيْدِ بْنِ عَبْدِ الرَّحْمَنِ ، عَنْ رَجُلٍ مِنْ أَصْحَابِ النَّبِيِّ صلى الله عليه وسلم : أَنَّ النَّبِيَّ صلى الله عليه وسلم ، كَانَ يَتَرَجَّلُ غِبًّا[42]

36. Humayd ibn Abdul Rahman ؓ narrated from one of the companions that it was the habit of the Prophet ﷺ to comb his hair occasionally.

42 Al-Mughnī 'Ān Hamil al-Asfār Fi Takhrīj Ma Fi al-Ahyā min Akhbar (1/187)

CHAPTER FIVE

باب ما جاء في شيب رسول الله صلى الله عليه وسلم

THE REPORTS PERTAINING TO THE WHITE HAIRS OF THE PROPHET ﷺ

Al-Bajuri said,

> The author dedicated this chapter to listing the hadīths wherein the white hairs of the Prophet ﷺ are mentioned. This chapter was placed after the chapter of the haircare of the Prophet because the latter includes actions (combing, oiling and styling the hair) that we can take as examples to follow.

Abdul Razzaq al-Badr said,

> This chapter will clarify whether the Prophet ﷺ had any white hairs or not on his head or beard, and how many there were.

٣٧: حَدَّثَنَا مُحَمَّدُ بْنُ بَشَّارٍ ، قَالَ : أَخْبَرَنَا أَبُو دَاوُدَ ، قَالَ : أَخْبَرَنَا هَمَّامٌ ، عَنْ قَتَادَةَ ، قَالَ : قُلْتُ لأَنَسِ بْنِ مَالِكٍ : هَلْ خَضَبَ رَسُولُ الله صلى الله عليه وسلم ؟ قَالَ : لَمْ يَبْلُغْ ذَلِكَ ، إِنَّمَا كَانَ شَيْبًا فِي صُدْغَيْهِ وَلَكِنْ أَبُو بَكْرٍ ، خَضَبَ بِالْحِنَّاءِ وَالْكَتَمِ[43]

37. Qatādah ﷺ related: "I asked Anas ibn Mālik ﷺ, 'Did the Messenger of Allāh ﷺ dye his hair?' He replied, 'He did not need to for all he had were a few white hairs on his temples. However, Abū Bakr ﷺ dyed his hair with henna and *katam*.'"

Al-Bajūrī said,

> "Did the Messenger of Allāh ﷺ dye his hair?": Meaning, did he change the colour of the white hairs in his head and beard using the henna or anything else.

Ibn Hajar al-Haytamī said,

> "He did not need to for all he had were a few white hairs on his temples": This indicates that he dyed the few white hairs he had on his temples. The Prophet ﷺ dyed his hair as will be explained in the following chapter.
>
> Abū Bakr dyed his hair using both henna and *katam* at the same time because using *katam* alone would make the hair colour completely black and this is condemned. This is supported by the explicit hadīth found in Sahīh Muslim.

Alī al-Qārī said,

> Henna is a reddish brown dye used especially on hair. *Katam* is a plant that makes the hair black.

43 Sahīh al-Bukhārī (3550) and Sahīh Muslim (2341)

٣٨: حَدَّثَنَا إِسْحَاقُ بْنُ مَنْصُورٍ ، وَيَحْيَى بْنُ مُوسَى ، قَالا : حَدَّثَنا عَبْدُ الرَّزَّاقِ ، عَنْ مَعْمَرٍ ، عَنْ ثَابِتٍ ، عَنْ أَنَسٍ ، قَالَ : مَا عَدَدْتُ فِي رَأْسِ رَسُولِ الله صلى الله عليه وسلم وَلِحْيَتِهِ ، إِلا أَرْبَعَ عَشْرَةَ شَعَرَةً بَيْضَاءَ[44]

38. Anas ibn Mālik ﷺ related: "I did not count more than fourteen white hairs on the head and beard of the Messenger of Allāh ﷺ."

Abdul Razzaq al-Badr said,

> The number of white hairs that Anas ﷺ counted in the hair and beard of the Prophet ﷺ explains why he stated that he did not need to dye his hair (see the previous hadīth).

Ibn Hajar al-Haytamī said,

> "Fourteen white hairs": Anas ﷺ stated in another hadīth that there were seventeen or eighteen white hairs and that could be because he counted them on two different occasions.

Alī al-Qārī said,

> Ibn Hajar said, "In Sahīh al-Bukhārī, 'Abdullāh ibn Busr said that the white hairs of the Prophet did not exceed ten. This could be said in reference to the white hairs he had under his lower lip."

٣٩: حَدَّثَنَا مُحَمَّدُ بْنُ الْمُثَنَّى ، قَالَ : أَخْبَرَنَا أَبُو دَاوُدَ ، قَالَ : حَدَّثَنا شُعْبَةُ ، عَنْ سِمَاكِ بْنِ حَرْبٍ ، قَالَ : سَمِعْتُ جَابِرَ بْنَ سَمُرَةَ ، وَقَدْ سُئِلَ عَنْ شَيْبِ رَسُولِ الله صَلَّى اللهُ عَلَيْهِ وَسَلَّم ، فَقَالَ : كَانَ إِذَا دَهَنَ رَأْسَهُ لَمْ يُرَ مِنْهُ شَيْبٌ ، وَإِذَا لَمْ يَدْهِنْ رُئِيَ مِنْهُ شَيْءٌ[45]

44 Musnad Ahmad (12690)
45 Sahīh Muslim (2344)

39. Jābir ibn Samurah ؓ was asked about the white hair of Allāh's Messenger ﷺ, and so he replied: "Whenever he oiled his hair, it (white hair) did not show. However when he did not oil it, it showed."

Abdul Razzaq al-Badr said,

> This corroborates the statement of Anas ؓ that the Prophet ﷺ only had a few white hairs.

Al-Bajūrī said,

> "Whenever he oiled his hair, it (white hair) did not show": This is because the white hair became mixed with the glittering of the hair after it was oiled.

٤٠ : حَدَّثَنَا مُحَمَّدُ بْنُ عَمْرِو بْنِ الْوَلِيدِ الْكِنْدِيُّ الْكُوفِيُّ ، قَالَ : حَدَّثَنَا يَحْيَى بْنُ آدَمَ ، عَنْ شَرِيكٍ ، عَنْ عُبَيْدِ اللهِ بْنِ عُمَرَ ، عَنْ نَافِعٍ ، عَنْ عَبْدِ اللهِ بْنِ عُمَرَ ، قَالَ : إِنَّمَا كَانَ شَيْبُ رَسُولِ اللهِ صلى الله عليه وسلم نَحْوًا مِنْ عِشْرِينَ شَعَرَةً بَيْضَاءَ[46]

40. 'Abdullāh ibn 'Umar ؓ narrated: "The Messenger of Allāh ﷺ had about twenty white hairs."

Abdul Razzaq al-Badr said,

> This conforms to the reports of Jābir and Anas since Ibn 'Umar gave an approximate number.

Ibn Hajar al-Haytamī said,

> This hadīth does not contradict the previous hadīth of Anas who stated that he had fourteen white hairs. This is because the number fourteen is more than half of twenty and so it can be used to refer

46 Musnad Ahmad (8/27)

to the higher number [i.e. it is to give an approximate number].

٤١ : حَدَّثَنَا أَبُو كُرَيْبٍ مُحَمَّدُ بْنُ الْعَلاءِ ، قَالَ : حَدَّثَنَا مُعَاوِيَةُ بْنُ هِشَامٍ ، عَنْ شَيْبَانَ ، عَنْ أَبِي إِسْحَاقَ ، عَنْ عِكْرِمَةَ ، عَنِ ابْنِ عَبَّاسٍ ، قَالَ : قَالَ أَبُو بَكْرٍ : يَا رَسُولَ اللهِ ، قَدْ شِبْتَ ، قَالَ : شَيَّبَتْنِي هُودٌ ، وَالْوَاقِعَةُ ، وَالْمُرْسَلاتُ ، وَعَمَّ يَتَسَاءَلُونَ ، وَإِذَا الشَّمْسُ كُوِّرَتْ[47]

41. 'Abdullāh ibn 'Abbās ﷺ narrated: "Abū Bakr ﷺ exclaimed, 'O Messenger of Allāh, you have white hairs!' The Messenger of Allāh ﷺ replied, 'Sūrahs Hūd, al-Wāqi`ah, al-Mursalāt, 'Amma Yatasā'alūn (an-Nabā') and Idhā-sh-Shamsu Kuwwirat (at-Takwīr) have turned my hair white."

Ibn Hajar al-Haytamī said,

> The exclamation of Abū Bakr was because he was surprised to see white hairs on the Prophet ﷺ due to the fact that his nature was balanced and his mood was neutral, and white hairs are unlikely to show on one with such characteristics.

Abdul Razzaq al-Badr said,

> The reason why these sūrahs made his hair turn white is because they talk about the terror of the Day of Judgment. This proves that the white hairs he had were not because of experiencing worldly issues but rather due to his concern and thoughtfulness about the Hereafter.

Al-Bajūrī said,

> The reason why the Prophet ﷺ mentioned Sūrah al-Hūd before the other sūrahs is because it includes the order to hold-fast to the

47 Sunan al-Tirmidhī (3297)

straight path that only those whom Allāh has engulfed with the garment of His safety can perfect it.

٤٢ : حَدَّثَنَا سُفْيَانُ بْنُ وَكِيعٍ ، قَالَ : حَدَّثَنَا مُحَمَّدُ بْنُ بِشْرٍ ، عَنْ عَلِيِّ بْنِ صَالِحٍ ، عَنْ أَبِي إِسْحَاقَ ، عَنْ أَبِي جُحَيْفَةَ ، قَالَ : قَالُوا : يَا رَسُولَ اللهِ ، نَرَاكَ قَدْ شِبْتَ ، قَالَ : قَدْ شَيَّبَتْنِي هُودٌ وَأَخَوَاتُهَا[48]

42. Abū Juhaifah ﷺ narrated: "Some people said to the Prophet ﷺ, 'O Messenger of Allāh! Your hair has turned white!' He replied, 'Sūrah Hūd and its sisters have turned my hair white.'"

Al-Bajūrī said,

> "... Its sisters": This refers to all the sūrahs that are similar to Sūrah Hūd – that is to say, all the sūrahs that talk about the terror of the Day of Judgment.

Abdul Razzaq al-Badr said,

> The answer of the Prophet ﷺ was an indirect way of stating that he had white hair because of his concern for the Hereafter. It shows the great effect of the Qur'ān and the immense benefits that can be procured when a person contemplates it and understands its meanings and signs. Whoever ponders upon the Qur'ān in the way it should be, they will be focused on the Hereafter without neglecting the necessary affairs in this worldly life. This is why the Prophet ﷺ said, "O Allāh, do not let this worldly life be our biggest concern,"[49] which entails that it is fine for us to look after our worldly affairs but it should not preoccupy us and distract us from the purpose for which we were created – that is: worshipping Allāh alone and preparing to meet Him on the Last Day.

---

48 Musnad al-Bazzar

49 Sunan al-Tirmidhī (3502)

٤٣ : حَدَّثَنَا عَلِيُّ بْنُ حُجْرٍ ، قَالَ : حَدَّثَنَا شُعَيْبُ بْنُ صَفْوَانَ ، عَنْ عَبْدِ الْمَلِكِ بْنِ عُمَيْرٍ ، عَنْ إِيَادِ بْنِ لَقِيطٍ الْعِجْلِيِّ ، عَنْ أَبِي رِمْثَةَ التَّيْمِيِّ ، تَيْمِ الرَّبَابِ ، قَالَ : أَتَيْتُ النَّبِيَّ صلى الله عليه وسلم ، وَمَعِي ابْنٌ لِي ، قَالَ : فَأُرِيتُهُ ، فَقُلْتُ لَمَّا رَأَيْتُهُ : هَذَا نَبِيُّ اللهِ صلى الله عليه وسلم وَعَلَيْهِ ثَوْبَانِ أَخْضَرَانِ ، وَلَهُ شَعَرٌ قَدْ عَلَاهُ الشَّيْبُ ، وَشَيْبُهُ أَحْمَرُ[50]

43. Abū Rimtha al-Taymī ﷺ related: "I went with my son to see the Prophet ﷺ. When they showed him to me, I said immediately, 'This is the Prophet of Allāh!' He was wearing two pieces of green clothing, and there were some whites in his hair, which were dyed red in colour."

Abdul Razzaq al-Badr said,

> "When they showed him to me": It appears as if this was his first time seeing the Prophet ﷺ as someone pointed him out to him.

Al-Bajūrī said,

> "This is the Prophet of Allāh!": He said it to affirm to the one who led him to see the Prophet ﷺ that he believed that the one whom he was shown was truly the Prophet i.e. it is like saying, "I believe you, O you who showed me the Prophet because I am now confident that he is the Prophet of Allāh after seeing the light of his prophethood and aura of his high-esteem." It is also possible that he said that to his son i.e. "O son, this is the Prophet of Allāh!"

Ibn Hajar al-Haytamī said,

> "Which were red in colour": This conforms to the hadīth of Ibn 'Umar who said that the colour of the edges of his white hair was red; they were dyed.

50 Musnad Ahmad (12/68)

٤٤ : حَدَّثَنَا أَحْمَدُ بْنُ مَنِيعٍ ، قَالَ : حَدَّثَنَا سُرَيْجُ بْنُ النُّعْمَانِ ، قَالَ : حَدَّثَنَا حَمَّادُ بْنُ سَلَمَةَ ، عَنْ سِمَاكِ بْنِ حَرْبٍ ، قَالَ : قِيلَ لِجَابِرِ بْنِ سَمُرَةَ : أَكَانَ فِي رَأْسِ رَسُولِ اللهِ صلى الله عليه وسلم شَيْبٌ ؟ قَالَ : لَمْ يَكُنْ فِي رَأْسِ رَسُولِ اللهِ صلى الله عليه وسلم ، شَيْبٌ إِلا شَعَرَاتٌ فِي مَفْرِقِ رَأْسِهِ ، إِذَا ادَّهَنَ وَارَاهُنَّ الدُّهْنُ[51]

44. Jābir ibn Samurah ﷺ was asked: "Were there any white hairs on the head of Allāh's Messenger ﷺ?" He replied, "He only had a few on the middle parting, but whenever he applied oil to his hair, they did not show."

Abdul Razzaq al-Badr said,

> This description of the companions regarding the white hair of the Prophet ﷺ shows that he used to uncover his head sometimes.

Al-Bajūrī said,

> It is disliked to pluck the white hair according to the majority of scholars based on the hadīth, "Do not pluck out white-hairs, for they are the light of the Muslim."[52]

Alī al-Qārī said,

> As the white hairs did not show when he ﷺ oiled his hair, this indicates that they were few.

51 See hadith 39

52 Musnad Ahmad (11/160)

CHAPTER SIX

باب ما جاء في خضاب رسول الله صلى الله عليه وسلم

THE REPORTS PERTAINING TO THE USAGE OF DYE BY THE PROPHET ﷺ

Abdul Razzaq al-Badr said,

> The author included this chapter in his book to show whether the Prophet ﷺ dyed his hair or not. In summary, the companions differed in opinion about it as mentioned by Ibn al-Qayyim who quoted the statements of many companions such as Anas ibn Mālik ؓ who denied that the Prophet ever dyed his hair and Abū Hurairah ؓ who affirmed that the Prophet dyed his hair. Some other companions said that he used to perfume his hair abundantly, which made his hair appear reddish and that made people think his hair was dyed when it was not.

Al-Bajūrī said,

> Dye refers to colouring the hair with henna or any other dyestuff. According to us – Shāfi'ī scholars, it is the Sunnah to dye the hair with any colour except black and it is forbidden to dye the hair with black.

٤٥ : حَدَّثَنَا أَحْمَدُ بْنُ مَنِيعٍ ، قَالَ : حَدَّثَنَا هُشَيْمٌ ، قَالَ : حَدَّثَنَا عَبْدُ الْمَلِكِ بْنُ عُمَيْرٍ ، عَنْ إِيَادِ بْنِ لَقِيطٍ ، قَالَ : أَخْبَرَنِي أَبُو رِمْثَةَ ، قَالَ : أَتَيْتُ رَسُولَ اللَّهِ صلى الله عليه وسلم مَعَ ابْنٍ لِي ، فَقَالَ : ابْنُكَ هَذَا ؟ فَقُلْتُ : نَعَمْ ، أَشْهَدُ بِهِ ، قَالَ : لاَ يَجْنِي عَلَيْكَ ، وَلاَ تَجْنِي عَلَيْهِ ، قَالَ : وَرَأَيْتُ الشَّيْبَ أَحْمَرَ[53]

قَالَ أَبُو عِيسَى : هَذَا أَحْسَنُ شَيْءٍ رُوِيَ فِي هَذَا الْبَابِ ، وَأَفْسَرُ لأَنَّ الرِّوَايَاتِ الصَّحِيحَةَ أَنَّ النَّبِيَّ صَلَّى اللهُ عَلَيْهِ وَسَلَّمَ لَمْ يَبْلُغِ الشَّيْبَ وَأَبُو رِمْثَةَ اسْمُهُ : رِفَاعَةُ بْنُ يَثْرِبِيٍّ التَّيْمِيُّ

45. Abū Rimthah ﷺ related: "I went with my son to visit the Prophet ﷺ. [When he saw me], he asked, 'Is this your son?' I replied, 'Yes, this is my son. I testify to that.' Then he said, 'You are not held accountable for his crimes, nor is he held accountable for your crimes.'" Abū Rimthah ﷺ then remarked, "I noticed that the white hairs of the Prophet ﷺ had been dyed red."

Al-Tirmidhī commented: "This hadīth is the most correct and explanatory report on the subject of using a dye. This is because the authentic hadīths state that he did not have many white hairs. The name of Abū Rimthah is Rifā'ah ibn Yathrabī al-Taymī"

Abdul Razzaq al-Badr said,

> This hadīth shows that if it is possible for parents to take their children to the gatherings of good such as lectures and visiting scholars etc., then they should do so. This will cause the children to grow up loving the people of knowledge and the circles of knowledge. This should be more emphasised in the current era, as the fruits of deviation and misguidance are everywhere and desires and whims are playing with the Muslim youth. Thus, parents should take their children to the places of knowledge with encouragement and kindness so that the love of these places is instilled into them.

53 Additions of 'Abdullāh ibn Ahmad ibn Hanbal to Musnad Ahmad (7113)

"I noticed that the white hairs of the Prophet ﷺ had been dyed red": This could have been because of dye being applied or due to the effect of the oil that he used to use. The people of knowledge differed on this; some of them such as Umm Salamah ﵂ said it was because of dye, and some said it was because of oil and that he never used dye as affirmed by Anas ibn Mālik ﵁.

Al-Bajūrī said,

"I testify to that": [The Arabic words used for this part] could also mean, "[O Prophet of Allāh] be a witness that he is my son" and so the statement is an affirmation of his answer, "Yes, he is my son." It could also mean, "I testify to that [i.e. I testify and acknowledge that he is my son]" to advise the Prophet ﷺ that he will take the consequences of the actions of his son as this was the norm during the times of *jahiliyyah*.

"This hadīth is the most correct and explanatory report": This statement does not necessitate that the hadīth is authentic because scholars use it even if the hadīth is weak i.e. they intend to mean with that statement that it is the least weak hadīth.

Ibn Hajar al-Haytamī said,

"You are not held accountable for his crime": This response was to show Abū Rimtha that he will not be held accountable or take the burden of his son's sins and mistakes, and that his son will not be held accountable for his father's mistakes and sins. From this, our renowned [Shāfi'ī] scholars concluded that the father and the children of the killer are not liable to contribute in the blood-money.

٤٦ : حَدَّثَنَا سُفْيَانُ بْنُ وَكِيعٍ ، قَالَ : حَدَّثَنَا أَبِي ، عَنْ شَرِيكٍ ، عَنْ عُثْمَانَ بْنِ مَوْهَبٍ ، قَالَ : سُئِلَ أَبُو هُرَيْرَةَ : هَلْ خَضَبَ رَسُولُ اللهِ صلى الله عليه وسلم ؟ قَالَ : نَعَمْ

قَالَ أَبُو عِيسَى : وَرَوَى أَبُو عَوَانَةَ هَذَا الْحَدِيثَ عَنْ عُثْمَانَ بْنِ عَبْدِ اللهِ بْنِ مَوْهَبٍ ، فَقَالَ : عَنْ أُمِّ سَلَمَةَ[54]

46. Abū Hurairah ﷺ was asked: "Did the Messenger of Allāh ﷺ dye his hair?" He replied, "Yes."

Ibn Hajar al-Haytamī said,

> This conforms to the statement of Ibn 'Umar ﷺ which is documented in Sahīh al-Bukhārī and Sahīh Muslim i.e. he narrated that he saw the Prophet ﷺ use a yellow dye. This is our evidence that using a dye colour other than black [i.e. it is not allowed to use black dye] is an act of Sunnah. Other hadīths that are documented by Abū Dawūd also support this.

Al-Nawawī said,

> The view that we adopt is that it is recommended for both men and women to use reddish-brown or yellow dye, and that it is forbidden for them to dye the hair black except in the case where men do this for the purpose of *jihad*.

Al-Bajūrī said,

> This hadīth confirms the other hadīths that the Prophet ﷺ did dye his hair. To reconcile between these hadīths and those hadīths that negate his use of dye, we say that he used to dye his hair at one point, then he stopped doing that most of the time or did it very infrequently; hence each narrator reported what they saw.

٤٧ : حَدَّثَنَا إِبْرَاهِيمُ بْنُ هَارُونَ ، قَالَ : أَنْبَأَنَا النَّضْرُ بْنُ زُرَارَةَ ، عَنْ أَبِي جَنَابٍ ، عَنْ إِيَادِ بْنِ لَقِيطٍ ، عَنِ الْجُهْدَمَةِ ، امْرَأَةِ بِشْرِ ابْنِ الْخَصَاصِيَّةِ ، قَالَتْ

54 Sahīh al-Bukhārī (5896)

: أَنَا رَأَيْتُ رَسُولَ اللهِ صلى الله عليه وسلم يَخْرُجُ مِنْ بَيْتِهِ يَنْفُضُ رَأْسَهُ وَقَدِ اغْتَسَلَ ، وَبِرَأْسِهِ رَدْعٌ مِنْ حِنَّاءٍ أَوْ قَالَ : رَدْعٌ شَكَّ فِي هَذَا الشَّيْخُ[55]

47. Al-Jahdamah ﵂ (the wife of Bashir ibn al-Khasāsiyah ﵁) related: "I saw the Messenger of Allāh ﷺ coming out of his house; after taking a bath, shaking [water from] his hair. I saw on his head the remnants of henna (or saffron)." [The doubt of whether henna or saffron was seen is from Ibrahīm ibn Harūn.]

Abdul Razzaq al-Badr said,

> "I saw on his head the remnants of henna": Some hadīth commentators stated that this part does not necessitate that he dyed his hair. Rather, it is possible that he used the henna for medical purposes or to reduce heat from his head (cool down) or for any other similar purposes.

٤٨ : حَدَّثَنَا عَبْدُ اللهِ بْنُ عَبْدِ الرَّحْمَنِ ، قَالَ : حَدَّثَنَا عَمْرُو بْنُ عَاصِمٍ ، قَالَ : حَدَّثَنَا حَمَّادُ بْنُ سَلَمَةَ ، قَالَ : حَدَّثَنَا حُمَيْدٌ ، عَنْ أَنَسٍ ، قَالَ : رَأَيْتُ شَعَرَ رَسُولِ اللهِ صلى الله عليه وسلم مَخْضُوبًا[56]

48. Anas ibn Mālik ﵁ narrated: "I saw the hair of Allāh's Messenger ﷺ dyed."

Alī al-Qārī said,

> It has been stated in other authentic hadīths that Anas ibn Mālik ﵁ denied that the Prophet ﷺ dyed his hair. With that said, it is possible that he intended to say that he did not use dye most of the

55 Mukhtasar al-Shama'il of al-Albani (39)
56 Translator Note: This hadīth could not be located from other sources with the exact same text but the meaning is correct and supported by many other authentic hadīths.

time, and that he used dye infrequently.

Mirak Shah al-Hanafī said,

> You should know that it is proven in many hadīths documented in the two Sahīh books and other books of hadīth that Anas ﷺ held the view that the Prophet ﷺ did not dye his hair or that he did not possess enough white hairs to warrant the use of dye on them. This hadīth, however, is the only report from him that states otherwise; hence either this hadīth is classified as odd or it refers to when he saw him after his death. This is because it was reported by al-Daraqutnī that Abū Hurairah ﷺ said, "After the death of the Prophet ﷺ, everyone who had some of the hairs of the Prophet ﷺ dyed them in order to preserve them." Hence it is possible that Anas saw his dyed hair in the possession of one of his companions.

Abdul Razzaq al-Badr said,

> The conclusion is that all the authentic hadīths indicate that the Prophet ﷺ had few white hairs, so he had no need to dye them as reported by Anas ibn Mālik ﷺ and others. As for the reddish colour that was noticed in his hair, which was thought to be because of dye, it was most probably due to the use of oil or perfume.

CHAPTER SEVEN

باب ما جاء في كُحل رسول الله صلى الله عليه وسلم

THE REPORTS PERTAINING TO THE KOHL OF THE PROPHET ﷺ

Abdul Razzaq al-Badr said,

> Kohl is a well known stone that is easy to disintegrate and it is used to darken the edges of the eyelids. To produce it [for cosmetic use], it is crushed until it becomes smooth and then it is applied to the eyelids. It comes in two colours, black and red.

Al-Bajūrī said,

> The author listed the chapter of kohl right after the chapter of dye due to the similarity between the two since both are means of adornment.

Ibn Hajar al-Asqalānī said,

> Applying the kohl to the eyelid is a Sunnah according to all Shāfi'ī scholars, based on the hadīths that talk about it.

Abū Bakr ibn al-Arabī said,

There are two benefits of the application of kohl: (i) adornment, which religion did not put a restriction on; thus it is used as needed, (ii) medicine, because it improves the sight and helps eyelashes grow, and it has been religiously prescribed to be done every night so that this benefit can be attained.

٤٩ : حَدَّثَنَا مُحَمَّدُ بْنُ حُمَيْدٍ الرَّازِيُّ ، قَالَ : حَدَّثَنَا أَبُو دَاوُدَ الطَّيَالِسِيُّ ، عَنْ عَبَّادِ بْنِ مَنْصُورٍ ، عَنْ عِكْرِمَةَ ، عَنِ ابْنِ عَبَّاسٍ ، أَنَّ النَّبِيَّ صلى الله عليه وسلم ، قَالَ : اكْتَحِلُوا بِالإِثْمِدِ ، فَإِنَّهُ يَجْلُو الْبَصَرَ ، وَيُنْبِتُ الشَّعْرَ وَزَعَمَ أَنَّ النَّبِيَّ صلى الله عليه وسلم ، كَانَتْ لَهُ مُكْحُلَةٌ يَكْتَحِلُ مِنْهَا كُلَّ لَيْلَةٍ ، ثَلاثَةً فِي هَذِهِ ، وَثَلاثَةً فِي هَذِهِ[57]

49. 'Abdullāh ibn Abbās ﷺ narrated that the Prophet ﷺ said: "Apply the *ithmid* (kohl) on the eye; it strengthens the eyesight, and facilitates the growth of the eyelashes." He also asserted that the Prophet ﷺ had a small container for keeping kohl, from which he applied it on each eyelid three times every night.

Mirak Shah al-Hanafī said,

> "Apply the *ithmid*": It is intended to mean use it frequently.
> "...Every night": Meaning he did it every night before sleeping.

Abdul Razzaq al-Badr said,

> "Facilitates the growth of the eyelashes": Not only do long eyelashes protect the eyes from dust, but they also increase the eyes in beauty.
> "On each eyelid three times": Applying it in an odd number is encouraged because he ﷺ said in another hadīth, "When anyone of

57 Sunan al-Tirmidhī (1757) and Sunan Ibn Mājah (3499)

you applies kohl on their eyes, do it in an odd number."[58] There are two methods that scholars have mentioned based on the different hadīths about this topic: (1) Apply kohl on the right eyelid three times, then apply it on the left eyelid three times. (2) Apply kohl on the right eyelid one time then apply it on the left eyelid one time, then apply it on the right eyelid and then on the left eyelid, and then apply it on the right eyelid. This way, the total number is odd and the right eyelid is preferred over the left eyelid with three things: (i) it was the first to start with, (ii) it was the last to end with, (iii) the kohl is applied on it more than the left eyelid.

Ibn Hajar al-Haytamī said,

> "Three times every night": He preferred three times because it is an odd number, and it is moderate, neither excessive nor little.

٥٠: حَدَّثَنَا عَبْدُ اللهِ بْنُ الصَّبَّاحِ الْهَاشِمِيُّ الْبَصْرِيُّ ، قَالَ : حَدَّثَنَا عُبَيْدُ اللهِ بْنُ مُوسَى ، قَالَ : حَدَّثَنَا إِسْرَائِيلُ ، عَنْ عَبَّادِ بْنِ مَنْصُورٍ (ح) وَحَدَّثَنَا عَلِيُّ بْنُ حُجْرٍ ، قَالَ : حَدَّثَنَا يَزِيدُ بْنُ هَارُونَ ، قَالَ : حَدَّثَنَا عَبَّادُ بْنُ مَنْصُورٍ ، عَنْ عِكْرِمَةَ ، عَنِ ابْنِ عَبَّاسٍ ، قَالَ : كَانَ رَسُولُ اللهِ صلى الله عليه وسلم يَكْتَحِلُ قَبْلَ أَنْ يَنَامَ بِالإِثْمِدِ ، ثَلاثًا فِي كُلِّ عَيْنٍ ، وَقَالَ يَزِيدُ بْنُ هَارُونَ ، فِي حَدِيثِهِ : إِنَّ النَّبِيَّ صلى الله عليه وسلم ، كَانَتْ لَهُ مُكْحُلَةٌ يَكْتَحِلُ مِنْهَا عِنْدَ النَّوْمِ ، ثَلاثًا فِي كُلِّ عَيْنٍ[59]

50. 'Abdullāh ibn Abbās ؓ narrated that the Prophet ﷺ said: "Apply the *ithmid* on the eyelids before sleeping. It clears the eyesight and increases the growth of the eyelashes."

Al-Bajūrī said,

---

58 Musnad Ahmad (8612)
59 Musnad Ibn Abbad (1/471)

"Apply the *ithmid*": Those being addressed regarding this issue are those whose eyes are healthy, because if the eye has a problem then *ithmid* may aggravate it.

Ibn al-Qayyim said,

> Applying the kohl on the eyes maintains their healthiness, improves and clears the eyesight, removes the bad elements and it is an adornment in the case of some types of kohl. It is even more beneficial when the *ithmid* is used before sleeping.

Ibn Hajar al-Asqalānī said,

> The order in this hadīth is understood to mean that it is recommended, as agreed upon by all scholars.

Mirak Shah al-Hanafī said,

> "It clears the eyesight and increases the growth of the eyelashes": Mentioning the worldly benefits of kohl does not negate the fact that it is an act of Sunnah since he ﷺ practiced it and encouraged it. In fact, these worldly benefits are means towards learning the religious acts, such as how to perform purification, assessing the direction of the *qiblah* and other matters that require the use of the eyes. If a person wants to get the reward of following the Sunnah in this matter, they should establish the intention that it is intended for use as a medicine and not just for adornment. This is why Imām Mālik stated that it is disliked for men to apply kohl unless it is for treatment purposes only.

٥١: حَدَّثَنَا أَحْمَدُ بْنُ مَنِيعٍ ، قَالَ : حَدَّثَنَا مُحَمَّدُ بْنُ يَزِيدَ ، عَنْ مُحَمَّدِ بْنِ إِسْحَاقَ ، عَنْ مُحَمَّدِ بْنِ الْمُنْكَدِرِ ، عَنْ جَابِرٍ هُوَ ابْنُ عَبْدِ اللهِ ، قَالَ : قَالَ رَسُولُ اللهِ صلى الله عليه وسلم : عَلَيْكُمْ بِالإِثْمِدِ عِنْدَ النَّوْمِ ، فَإِنَّهُ يَجْلُو

الْبَصَرَ ، وَيُنْبِتُ الشَّعْرَ[60]

51. Jābir ibn 'Abdullāh ؓ narrated: "The Messenger of Allāh ﷺ said, 'The best from among all the kohl used by you is the *ithmid*. It gives strength to the eyesight and increases the growth of the eyelashes.'"

Abdul Razzaq al-Badr said,

> "The best from among all the kohl used by you is the *ithmid*": This indicates that there are many materials that can be used for kohl, the best of which is *ithmid*.

Mirak Shah al-Hanafi said,

> "The best from among all the kohl used by you is the *ithmid*": This indicates that *ithmid* is a special type of kohl. It is said that the meaning is that *ithmid* is the best kohl for protecting the eye when it is healthy as kohl is harmful in the case of ophthalmia (inflamed eyes).

٥٢ : حَدَّثَنَا قُتَيْبَةُ بْنُ سَعِيدٍ ، قَالَ : حَدَّثَنَا بِشْرُ بْنُ الْمُفَضَّلِ ، عَنْ عَبْدِ اللهِ بْنِ عُثْمَانَ بْنِ خُثَيْمٍ ، عَنْ سَعِيدِ بْنِ جُبَيْرٍ ، عَنِ ابْنِ عَبَّاسٍ ، قَالَ : قَالَ رَسُولُ اللهِ صلى الله عليه وسلم : إِنَّ خَيْرَ أَكْحَالِكُمُ الإِثْمِدُ ، يَجْلُو الْبَصَرَ ، وَيُنْبِتُ الشَّعْرَ[61]

52. 'Abdullāh ibn Abbās ؓ reported: "The Messenger of Allāh ﷺ said, 'You should use *ithmid* because it strengthens the eyesight and facilitates the growth of the eyelashes.'"

Mirak Shah al-Hanafi said,

60 Sunan Ibn Mājah (3496)
61 Sunan Abū Dawūd (3878) and Sunan Ibn Mājah (3497)

> The purpose of repeating this hadīth with different chains is to emphasise its content and to strengthen its classification.

Al-Bajūrī said,

> The Prophet ﷺ had a set that included: a mirror that was called "*al-madalla*", a comb made of ivory, a kohl container, a clipper and a *miswāk*.

٥٣: حَدَّثَنَا إِبْرَاهِيمُ بْنُ الْمُسْتَمِرِّ الْبَصْرِيُّ ، قَالَ : حَدَّثَنَا أَبُو عَاصِمٍ ، عَنْ عُثْمَانَ بْنِ عَبْدِ الْمَلِكِ ، عَنْ سَالِمٍ ، عَنِ ابْنِ عُمَرَ ، قَالَ : قَالَ رَسُولُ الله صلى الله عليه وسلم : عَلَيْكُمْ بِالإِثْمِدِ ، فَإِنَّهُ يَجْلُو الْبَصَرَ ، وَيُنْبِتُ الشَّعْرَ[62]

53. 'Abdullāh ibn 'Umar ﷺ reported: "The Messenger of Allāh ﷺ said, 'Apply *ithmid,* for verily it strengthens the eyesight and facilitates the growth of the eyelashes.'"

62 Sunan Ibn Mājah (3495)

CHAPTER EIGHT

باب ما جاء في لباس رسول الله صلى الله عليه وسلم

THE REPORTS PERTAINING TO THE CLOTHING OF THE MESSENGER OF ALLĀH ﷺ

Abdul Razzaq al-Badr said,

> It should be noted that the general rule is that all types of clothing are lawful except that which is forbidden in religion. Al-Bukhārī documented two hadīths establishing this general rule, the first of which is that the Prophet ﷺ said, "Eat, drink, wear clothes and give charity without showing off and being extravagant."[63] The other one is that which Ibn Abbās ﷺ said, "Eat all that you wish and wear all that you like, so long as you are neither showing off nor being extravagant."[64]
>
> The Prophet ﷺ pointed out a number of issues to be avoided in clothing, some of which are:
>
> 1. *Isbāl*: It is letting the garment come below the ankles and according to some scholars it is considered from the major

63 Sahīh al-Bukhārī (51/77)

64 Ibid.

sins.

2. Men wearing clothes made of natural silk.
3. Wearing something that makes the person distinguished from others. It is for this reason that one should wear the clothes that are the norm in the society where they live, provided that such clothes are lawful.
4. Wearing clothes that are known to be worn only by disbelievers and by which a disbeliever is recognised.

Al-Bajūrī said,

> Clothes are subject to five rulings: (i) Clothing that covers the *'awrah* from being shown in the presence of others is obligatory, (ii) It is preferable to wear one's best clothes on Eid and white clothes on Friday, (iii) It is forbidden for men to wear silk clothes, (iv) It is disliked for the rich to wear old clothes constantly and (v) It is lawful to wear anything else.

٥٤: حَدَّثَنَا مُحَمَّدُ بْنُ حُمَيْدٍ الرَّازِيُّ ، قَالَ : حَدَّثَنَا الْفَضْلُ بْنُ مُوسَى ، وَأَبُو تُمَيْلَةَ ، وَزَيْدُ بْنُ حُبَابٍ ، عَنْ عَبْدِ الْمُؤْمِنِ بْنِ خَالِدٍ ، عَنْ عَبْدِ اللهِ بْنِ بُرَيْدَةَ ، عَنْ أُمِّ سَلَمَةَ ، قَالَتْ : كَانَ أَحَبَّ الثِّيَابِ إِلَى رَسُولِ اللهِ صلى الله عليه وسلم الْقَمِيصُ[65]

54. Umm Salamah ﵂ said: "In regards to clothing, the Messenger of Allāh ﷺ liked wearing the *qamīs* the most."

Abdul Razzaq al-Badr said,

> *Qamīs* refers to the well known long robe with sleeves i.e. the *thoub.*

Ibn Hajar al-Haytamī said,

65 Sunan al-Tirmidhī (1762)

> It was his preference as this kind of garment is more concealing than the *izār* (lower wrap) and *ridā'* (upper garment). Al-Hafidh al-Dumyatī narrated a hadīth stating that the *qamīs* of the Prophet ﷺ was made of cotton, short in length and had short sleeves. This hadīth indicates that he preferred the one made of cotton because the one made of wool harms the body, makes one sweat and it has a smell that harms others.

Alī al-Qārī said,

> It was said that the Prophet ﷺ liked wearing the *qamīs* because it is lighter than other types of clothing, it conceals more of the body than other clothes and thus the one who wears it is displaying humility.

٥٥: حَدَّثَنَا عَلِيُّ بْنُ حُجْرٍ ، قَالَ : حَدَّثَنَا الْفَضْلُ بْنُ مُوسَى ، عَنْ عَبْدِ الْمُؤْمِنِ بْنِ خَالِدٍ ، عَنْ عَبْدِ اللهِ بْنِ بُرَيْدَةَ ، عَنْ أُمِّ سَلَمَةَ ، قَالَتْ : كَانَ أَحَبَّ الثِّيَابِ إِلَى رَسُولِ اللهِ صلى الله عليه وسلم الْقَمِيصُ

55. The same report from Umm Salamah ﵂ through a different chain of narrators.

٥٦: حَدَّثَنَا زِيَادُ بْنُ أَيُّوبَ الْبَغْدَادِيُّ ، قَالَ : حَدَّثَنَا أَبُو تُمَيْلَةَ ، عَنْ عَبْدِ الْمُؤْمِنِ بْنِ خَالِدٍ ، عَنْ عَبْدِ اللهِ بْنِ بُرَيْدَةَ ، عَنْ أُمِّهِ ، عَنْ أُمِّ سَلَمَةَ ، قَالَتْ : كَانَ أَحَبَّ الثِّيَابِ إِلَى رَسُولِ اللهِ صلى الله عليه وسلم يَلْبَسُهُ ، الْقَمِيصُ قَالَ : هَكَذَا ، قَالَ زِيَادُ بْنُ أَيُّوبَ ، فِي حَدِيثِهِ : عَنْ عَبْدِ اللهِ بْنِ بُرَيْدَةَ ، عَنْ أُمِّهِ ، عَنْ أُمِّ سَلَمَةَ ، وَهَكَذَا رَوَى غَيْرُ وَاحِدٍ عَنْ أَبِي تُمَيْلَةَ مِثْلَ رِوَايَةِ زِيَادِ بْنِ أَيُّوبَ ، وَأَبُو تُمَيْلَةَ يَزِيدُ فِي هَذَا الْحَدِيثِ : عَنْ أُمِّهِ ، وَهُوَ أَصَحُّ

56. The same report from Umm Salamah ﵂ through a different chain of narrators.

Abdul Razzaq al-Badr said,

> The same hadīth from Umm Salamah رضي الله عنها has been reported three times but the last of them has the chain of narrators that al-Tirmidhī believes to be the most authentic. This is why he mentioned the three different routes for the same text.

٥٧ : حَدَّثَنَا عَبْدُ اللهِ بْنُ مُحَمَّدِ بْنِ الْحَجَّاجِ ، قَالَ : حَدَّثَنَا مُعَاذُ بْنُ هِشَامٍ ، قَالَ : حَدَّثَنِي أَبِي ، عَنْ بُدَيْلٍ يَعْنِي ابْنَ مَيْسَرَةَ الْعُقَيْلِيَّ ، عَنْ شَهْرِ بْنِ حَوْشَبٍ ، عَنْ أَسْمَاءَ بِنْتِ يَزِيدَ ، قَالَتْ : كَانَ كُمُّ قَمِيصِ رَسُولِ اللهِ صلى الله عليه وسلم إِلَى الرُّسْغِ[66]

57. Asmā bint Yazīd رضي الله عنها narrated: "The sleeves of the *qamīs* of the Messenger of Allāh ﷺ would reach his wrists."

Abdul Razzaq al-Badr said,

> This shows that his sleeves did not exceed his wrists.

Al-Bajūrī said,

> The reason behind the sleeves not exceeding the wrists is because if they do exceed them, they hinder the movement of the hands, and if they are too short, they expose the arms to heat and coldness. Therefore, the Prophet ﷺ preferred to be moderate in the length of his sleeves, and moderation is indeed the best of all things.

Al-Jizrī said,

> This hadīth is evidence that the Sunnah is that the sleeves of the *qamīs* do not exceed the wrists. As for other clothes, they (the scholars) said that the Sunnah is that the sleeves should not exceed

66 Sunan al-Tirmidhī (1765) and Sunan Abu Dawūd (4026)

the tips of the fingers.

٥٨: حَدَّثَنَا أَبُو عَمَّارٍ الْحُسَيْنُ بْنُ حُرَيْثٍ ، قَالَ : حَدَّثَنَا أَبُو نُعَيْمٍ ، قَالَ : حَدَّثَنَا زُهَيْرٌ ، عَنْ عُرْوَةَ بْنِ عَبْدِ اللهِ بْنِ قُشَيْرٍ ، عَنْ مُعَاوِيَةَ بْنِ قُرَّةَ ، عَنْ أَبِيهِ ، قَالَ : أَتَيْتُ رَسُولَ اللهِ صلى اللهَ عليه وسلم فِي رَهْطٍ مِنْ مُزَيْنَةَ لِنُبَايِعَهُ ، وَإِنَّ قَمِيصَهُ لَمُطْلَقٌ ، أَوْ قَالَ : زِرُّ قَمِيصِهِ مُطْلَقٌ قَالَ : فَأَدْخَلْتُ يَدِي فِي جَيْبِ قَمِيصِهِ ، فَمَسَسْتُ الْخَاتَمَ[67]

58. Qurrah ibn Iyyas ؓ related: "I came with a group from the tribe of Muzainah to give the pledge to the Messenger of Allāh ﷺ. As I noticed the button of his *qamīs* was open, I inserted my hand into the collar of his *qamīs* and I touched the seal."

Abdul Razzaq al-Badr said,

> The general rule is that one should keep the buttons of the collar fastened unless there is a need to unbutton them. That being said, one should not think that unbuttoning the *qamīs* is a Sunnah because this hadith does not indicate so in any form. This is because the reason why his ﷺ collar was open was not specified and so it could have been for any reason such as attempting to cool down due to excessive heat. In fact, it is most likely that this is not an act of Sunnah. If the Sunnah was to keep the buttons of the collar unbuttoned, there would have been no use for having them.

Al-Bajūrī said,

> The *fiqh* of this hadīth is:
>
> - It is lawful to wear the *qamīs*.
> - It is lawful to have buttons on it.

67 Sunan Abu Dawūd (4082) and Sunan Ibn Mājah (3578)

- It is lawful to unbutton them.
- It is lawful to have a wide collar that is enough for the hand to be inserted into it.
- The Prophet ﷺ allowed others to enter their hands through his collar and touch his skin to seek *barakah*.
- It indicates the humbleness of the Prophet ﷺ.

٥٩ : حَدَّثَنَا عَبْدُ بْنُ حُمَيْدٍ ، قَالَ : حَدَّثَنَا مُحَمَّدُ بْنُ الْفَضْلِ ، قَالَ : حَدَّثنا حَمَّادُ بْنُ سَلَمَةَ ، عَنْ حَبِيبِ بْنِ الشَّهِيدِ ، عَنِ الْحَسَنِ ، عَنْ أَنَسِ بْنِ مَالِكٍ ، أَنَّ النَّبِيَّ صلى الله عليه وسلم خَرَجَ وَهُوَ يَتَّكِئُ عَلَى أُسَامَةَ بْنِ زَيْدٍ عَلَيْهِ ثَوْبٌ قِطْرِيٌّ ، قَدْ تَوَشَّحَ بِهِ ، فَصَلَّى بِهِمْ[68]

وَقَالَ عَبْدُ بْنُ حُمَيْدٍ : قَالَ مُحَمَّدُ بْنُ الْفَضْلِ : سَأَلَنِي يَحْيَى بْنُ مَعِينٍ عَنْ هَذَا الْحَدِيثِ ، أَوَّلَ مَا جَلَسَ إِلَيَّ ، فَقُلْتُ : حَدَّثَنَا حَمَّادُ بْنُ سَلَمَةَ ، فَقَالَ : لَوْ كَانَ مِنْ كِتَابِكَ ، فَقُمْتُ لأُخْرِجَ كِتَابِي فَقَبَضَ عَلَى ثَوْبِي ثُمَّ ، قَالَ : أَمْلِهِ عَلَيَّ فَإِنِّي أَخَافُ أَنْ لا أَلْقَاكَ ، قَالَ : فَأَمْلَيْتُهُ عَلَيْهِ ، ثُمَّ أَخْرَجْتُ كِتَابِي فَقَرَأْتُ عَلَيْهِ

59. Anas ibn Mālik ﷺ reported: "Allāh's Messenger ﷺ came out of his house reclining on Usāmah ibn Zayd ﷺ. He was wearing a *qitrī* wrap and proceeded to lead the prayer."

Abdul Razzaq al-Badr said,

> "He was wearing a *qitrī* wrap": It was placed on his shoulders.

Al-Bajūrī said,

> The *qitrī* wrap is a Yemenī sheet with printed columns, made of cotton and it has some redness in its colour.

68 Musnad Ahmad (13763)

٦٠ : حَدَّثَنَا سُوَيْدُ بْنُ نَصْرٍ ، قَالَ : حَدَّثَنَا عَبْدُ اللهِ بْنُ الْمُبَارَكِ ، عَنْ سَعِيدِ بْنِ إِيَاسٍ الْجُرَيْرِيِّ ، عَنْ أَبِي نَضْرَةَ ، عَنْ أَبِي سَعِيدٍ الْخُدْرِيِّ ، قَالَ : كَانَ رَسُولُ اللهِ صلى الله عليه وسلم ، إِذَا اسْتَجَدَّ ثَوْبًا سَمَّاهُ بِاسْمِهِ عِمَامَةً أَوْ قَمِيصًا أَوْ رِدَاءً ، ثُمَّ يَقُولُ : اللَّهُمَّ لَكَ الْحَمْدُ كَمَا كَسَوْتَنِيهِ ، أَسْأَلُكَ خَيْرَهُ وَخَيْرَ مَا صُنِعَ لَهُ ، وَأَعُوذُ بِكَ مِنْ شَرِّهِ وَشَرِّ مَا صُنِعَ لَهُ[69]

60. Abū Sa'īd al-Khudarī ﷺ narrated: "When the Messenger of Allāh ﷺ would put on a new garment, he would recite the following supplication whilst also identifying the garment (be it a turban, a sheet or a wrap etc.), '*Oh Allāh, all praise is due to You for clothing me with this [garment]. I ask You for the good of it and the good of what it was made for, and I ask Your protection from the evil of it and the evil of what it was made for.*'"

Abdul Razzaq al-Badr said,

> This supplication reminds us that it is Allāh who blessed us with a new garment, and that we did not come to possess it due to our own efforts and power. In other words, it is to direct us to remember the grace of Allāh as was stated in the divine hadīth wherein Allāh says, "O My slaves! All of you are naked except those who I clothe them. Ask me to clothe you and I will clothe you."[70]

Al-Bajūrī said,

> The purpose of mentioning the name of the garment is to show the praise to Allāh for the particular grace that He has bestowed.
>
> The supplication is recited after saying *bismillah* because saying it is an act of Sunnah before wearing the clothes.

Ibn Hajar al-Haytamī said,

---

69 Sunan al-Tirmidhī (1767) and Sunan Abu Dawūd (4020)

70 Sahīh Muslim (2577)

This is to say: "O Allāh you clothed us because of our poverty and need to You and not because You are in need of clothing us; therefore we praise You not because of what You have blessed us with but rather because You deserve it."

٦١ : حَدَّثَنَا هِشَامُ بْنُ يُونُسَ الْكُوفِيُّ ، قَالَ : حَدَّثَنَا الْقَاسِمُ بْنُ مَالِكٍ الْمُزَنِيُّ ، عَنِ الْجُرَيْرِيِّ ، عَنْ أَبِي نَضْرَةَ ، عَنْ أَبِي سَعِيدٍ الْخُدْرِيِّ ، عَنِ النَّبِيِّ صلى الله عليه وسلم ، نَحْوَهُ

61. A similar report was narrated from a different route from Abū Sa'īd al-Khudarī ﷺ.

٦٢ : حَدَّثَنَا مُحَمَّدُ بْنُ بَشَّارٍ ، قَالَ : حَدَّثَنَا مُعَاذُ بْنُ هِشَامٍ ، قَالَ : حَدَّثَنِي أَبِي ، عَنْ قَتَادَةَ ، عَنْ أَنَسِ بْنِ مَالِكٍ ، قَالَ : كَانَ أَحَبَّ الثِّيَابِ إِلَى رَسُولِ اللهِ صلى الله عليه وسلم ، يَلْبَسُهُ الْحِبَرَةُ[71]

62. Anas ibn Mālik ﷺ narrated: "The most beloved garment to the Prophet ﷺ, that he would wear, was the *hibarah*."

Abdul Razzaq al-Badr said,

> A *hibarah* is a kind of cloth made of cotton or linen with patterns to make it more beautiful.

Al-Bajūrī said,

> It seems that he liked this type of clothing due to its softness and nice design. Also, the fabric complimented his body as he possessed very soft skin and due to the softness of the fabric, it suited him perfectly.

71 Sahīh al-Bukhārī (5813) and Sahīh Muslim (2079)

Ibn Hajar al-Haytamī said,

> It has printed patterns on it and although it is disliked to wear a garment with patterns printed on it, the fact that he ﷺ wore it shows that it is permissible to wear them.

٦٣: حَدَّثَنَا مَحْمُودُ بْنُ غَيْلانَ ، قَالَ : حَدَّثَنَا عَبْدُ الرَّزَّاقِ ، قَالَ : حَدَّثَنَا سُفْيَانُ ، عَنْ عَوْنِ بْنِ أَبِي جُحَيْفَةَ ، عَنْ أَبِيهِ ، قَالَ : رَأَيْتُ النَّبِيَّ صلى الله عليه وسلم ، وَعَلَيْهِ حُلَّةٌ حَمْرَاءُ ، كَأَنِّي أَنْظُرُ إِلَى بَرِيقِ سَاقَيْهِ
قَالَ سُفْيَانُ : أُرَاهَا حِبَرَةً [72]

63. Abū Juhayfah ؓ related: "I saw Allāh's Messenger ﷺ wearing a red *hulla*. I can see the radiance of his shins as if they are still before me." Sufyān said, "I think it (his garment) was a *hibarah*."

Abdul Razzaq al-Badr said,

> "I can see the radiance of his shins as if they are still before me": This indicates that the lower wrap of the Prophet ﷺ was to the half point of his shins.

Al-Bajūrī said,

> "I saw Allāh's Messenger ﷺ": This was during the farewell Hajj as stated in the hadīth documented in Sahīh al-Bukhārī.
>
> "I can see the radiance of his shins as if they are still before me": This indicates that it is permissible for the man to look at another man's legs as there is no temptation in it. It indicates that it is recommended to shorten the robe or the *izār* to the mid-point of the shin, though it is permissible to keep its length to the ankles.
>
> "Sufyān said, 'I think it [his garment] was a *hibarah*": As Sufyān

---

72 Sunan al-Tirmidhī (197), Sahīh al-Bukhārī (376) and Sahīh Muslim (503)

(who is the one narrating this hadīth from the companion) holds the view that completely red garments are forbidden, he made the remark that he believes it was a *hibarah* as this would mean it had a pattern with another colour.

Ibn Hajar al-Haytamī said,

> "I can see the radiance of his shins as if they are still before me": While it is recommended for the man to shorten his garment to reach the mid-point of his shin, and it is permissible to make its length reach the ankle, it is recommended for the woman to wear that which covers her and it is allowed to make it long to the point it is dragged on the floor. However, if what she intends with that is showing off then she will be sinful just like if they (men) drag their garments to show off.

٦٤ : حَدَّثَنَا عَلِيُّ بْنُ خَشْرَمٍ ، قَالَ : حَدَّثَنَا عِيسَى بْنُ يُونُسَ ، عَنْ إِسْرَائِيلَ ، عَنْ أَبِي إِسْحَاقَ ، عَنِ الْبَرَاءِ بْنِ عَازِبٍ ، قَالَ : مَا رَأَيْتُ أَحَدًا مِنَ النَّاسِ أَحْسَنَ فِي حُلَّةٍ حَمْرَاءَ ، مِنْ رَسُولِ اللهِ صلى الله عليه وسلم ، إِنْ كَانَتْ جُمَّتُهُ لَتَضْرِبُ قَرِيبًا مِنْ مَنْكِبَيْهِ[73]

64. Al-Barā ibn 'Āzib ﷺ narrated: "I have never seen anybody appear more handsome in red clothing than the Messenger of Allāh ﷺ. At that time, his hair reached his shoulders."

Mirak Shah al-Hanafī said,

> Scholars differed on the permissibility of wearing fully red clothes; some scholars allowed it in all cases, some scholars forbade it in all cases. Some scholars disliked the wearing of clothes which have red prevailing over the other colours, and some scholars said it is disliked in all cases if it is worn for the purpose of adornment and

73 See hadīth 4

to be known, but it is allowed to be worn inside the house and while working. Some scholars said it is not allowed if it is dyed with red after it was woven, and some scholars said only that which is tanned with safflower is forbidden. Some scholars said only that which is dyed red completely is forbidden, and so any garment with additional colours besides red is permissible.

٦٥ : حَدَّثَنَا مُحَمَّدُ بْنُ بَشَّارٍ ، قَالَ : حَدَّثَنَا عَبْدُ الرَّحْمَنِ بْنُ مَهْدِيٍّ ، قَالَ : حَدَّثَنَا عُبَيْدُ اللهِ بْنُ إِيَادٍ ، عَنْ أَبِيهِ ، عَنْ أَبِي رِمْثَةَ ، قَالَ : رَأَيْتُ النَّبِيَّ صلى الله عليه وسلم ، وَعَلَيْهِ بُرْدَانِ أَخْضَرَانِ[74]

65. Abū Rimthah Taymī ؓ said, "I saw the Messenger of Allāh ﷺ and he was dressed in two green coloured *burdahs*."

Abdul Razzaq al-Badr said,

> The colour of the garment was not plain green because a *burdah* always has multiple colours in its pattern design.

٦٦ : حَدَّثَنَا عَبْدُ بْنُ حُمَيْدٍ ، قَالَ : حَدَّثَنَا عَفَّانُ بْنُ مُسْلِمٍ ، قَالَ : حَدَّثَنَا عَبْدُ اللهِ بْنُ حَسَّانَ الْعَنْبَرِيُّ ، عَنْ جَدَّتَيْهِ دُحَيْبَةَ ، وَعُلَيْبَةَ ، عَنْ قَيْلَةَ بِنْتِ مَخْرَمَةَ ، قَالَتْ : رَأَيْتُ النَّبِيَّ صلى الله عليه وسلم وَعَلَيْهِ أَسْمَالُ مُلَيَّتَيْنِ ، كَانَتَا بِزَعْفَرَانٍ ، وَقَدْ نَفَضَتْهُ وَفِي الْحَدِيثِ قِصَّةٌ طَوِيلَةٌ[75]

66. Qaylah bint Makhramah ؓ narrated: "I saw the Messenger of Allāh ﷺ wearing two well worn wraps that had been dyed with saffron yet there was no trace of saffron left upon them."

Al-Bajūrī said,

74 Sunan al-Tirmidhī (2812) and Sunan Abu Dawūd (4065)
75 Sunan al-Tirmidhī (2814)

> The fact that the Prophet ﷺ wore something dyed with saffron does not contradict his order not to wear such garments. This is because his order is related to the case when the colour of saffron is evident and it prevails over other colours.

Alī al-Qārī said,

> It is established that the Prophet ﷺ wore nice clothes but he preferred to wear that which manifested his humility and humbleness before his Lord. The *salaf* followed his way in the type of clothes to wear i.e. wearing clothing that manifests humbleness. This is because they saw people showing off with their fancy garments and adornments; therefore they wanted to remind them of the triviality of what they were proud of. However, later on the heedless started wearing very old clothes as a means to receive worldly pleasures and to make the people like them; thus the Sunnah became to oppose them by wearing nice clothes. It was reported that a man who was wearing old clothes criticized Abū al-Hasan al-Shadhilī for wearing nice garments. To that Abū al-Hasan replied, "The clothes I wear reflect my state praising Allāh, whereas your clothes reflect your state asking people to give you some of their worldly pleasures." In all cases, one must rectify their intention and avoid showing off whilst not refraining from wearing nice clothes due to stinginess, for indeed the beauty lies in the heart but still the body should reflect the beauty of the heart.

٦٧: حَدَّثَنَا قُتَيْبَةُ بْنُ سَعِيدٍ، قَالَ: حَدَّثَنَا بِشْرُ بْنُ الْمُفَضَّلِ، عَنْ عَبْدِ اللهِ بْنِ عُثْمَانَ بْنِ خُثَيْمٍ، عَنْ سَعِيدِ بْنِ جُبَيْرٍ، عَنِ ابْنِ عَبَّاسٍ، قَالَ: قَالَ رَسُولُ اللهِ صلى الله عليه وسلم: عَلَيْكُمْ بِالْبَيَاضِ مِنَ الثِّيَابِ، لِيَلْبَسْهَا أَحْيَاؤُكُمْ، وَكَفِّنُوا فِيهَا مَوْتَاكُمْ، فَإِنَّهَا مِنْ خِيَارِ ثِيَابِكُمْ[76]

76 See hadīth 52

67. 'Abdullāh ibn Abbās ؓ related: "The Prophet ﷺ said, 'Wear garments of white colours. Let the living among you wear them and enshroud the dead therewith, for it is the best of your clothes.'"

Al-Bajūrī said,

> This is to encourage wearing white clothes as it is recommended to wear them when attending the Friday prayer, attending the masjid, events and sittings that the angels witness such as gatherings to recite the Qur'ān or to remember Allāh. As for Eid, it is recommended to wear the best and pricey clothes, even if the colour is not white, because the day is intended to manifest adornment and display Allāh's grace upon us.
>
> The best colours are in the following order: The white, the green and then the yellow colours.

Ibn Hajar al-Haytamī said,

> It is the preferred colour for the shroud because the dead is about to meet the angels. This is why it is recommended, it is also why we are directed to perfume the dead.

Alī al-Qārī said,

> In order for the garment to deserve being called the best of clothes in its absolute form, it has to be (besides being white in colour) pure, neat and not accompanied by pride, showing off etc.

٦٨: حَدَّثَنَا مُحَمَّدُ بْنُ بَشَّارٍ ، قَالَ : حَدَّثَنَا عَبْدُ الرَّحْمَنِ بْنُ مَهْدِيٍّ ، قَالَ : حَدَّثَنَا سُفْيَانُ ، عَنْ حَبِيبِ بْنِ أَبِي ثَابِتٍ ، عَنْ مَيْمُونِ بْنِ أَبِي شَبِيبٍ ، عَنْ سَمُرَةَ بْنِ جُنْدُبٍ ، قَالَ : قَالَ رَسُولُ الله صلى الله عليه وسلم : الْبَسُوا الْبَيَاضَ ، فَإِنَّهَا أَطْهَرُ وَأَطْيَبُ ، وَكَفِّنُوا فِيهَا مَوْتَاكُمْ[77]

77 Sunan al-Tirmidhī (2810)

68. Samurah ibn Jundub ؓ narrated: "The Messenger of Allāh ﷺ said, 'Wear white clothing for it is the purest and most beautiful of your clothing, and also enshroud your dead with it.'"

Abdul Razzaq al-Badr said,

> "It is the purest": It is described as such because dirt or impurity can easily be identified [when wearing a white garment] unlike other colours that may have unseen dirt or impurity. This is why the Prophet ﷺ used to supplicate, "O Allāh, purify me from my sins just like how a white garment is purified from dirt."

Mirak Shah al-Hanafī said,

> "Most beautiful": It is described as such because white clothing indicates the humility of the one wearing it and negates the qualities of pride and showing off.

٦٩: حَدَّثَنَا أَحْمَدُ بْنُ مَنِيعٍ ، حَدَّثَنَا يَحْيَى بْنُ زَكَرِيَّا بْنِ أَبِي زَائِدَةَ ، قَالَ : حَدَّثَنَا أَبِي ، عَنْ مُصْعَبِ بْنِ شَيْبَةَ ، عَنْ صَفِيَّةَ بِنْتِ شَيْبَةَ ، عَنْ عَائِشَةَ ، قَالَتْ : خَرَجَ رَسُولُ اللهِ صلى الله عليه وسلم ذَاتَ غَدَاةٍ ، وَعَلَيْهِ مِرْطٌ مِنْ شَعَرٍ أَسْوَدَ[78]

69. Aisha ؓ narrated: "One day, the Messenger of Allāh ﷺ left the house early in the morning, wearing a long black garment made of hair."

Ibn Hajar al-Haytamī said,

> The way of the Prophet ﷺ was that he did not prefer wearing a particular type of clothing nor did he have an interest in wearing fancy and expensive clothing. This is because showing off with

78 Sahīh Muslim (2082) and Sunan al-Tirmidhī (2813)

fancy clothes is from the qualities of women. However, the quality that is praised in men is to ensure that their clothes are clean, modest and decent; therefore he ﷺ preferred wearing the type of clothing that he needed and encouraged others to wear the other types.

٧٠: حَدَّثَنَا يُوسُفُ بْنُ عِيسَى ، قَالَ : حَدَّثَنَا وَكِيعٌ ، قَالَ : حَدَّثَنَا يُونُسُ بْنُ أَبِي إِسْحَاقَ ، عَنْ أَبِيهِ ، عَنِ الشَّعْبِيِّ ، عَنْ عُرْوَةَ بْنِ الْمُغِيرَةِ بْنِ شُعْبَةَ ، عَنْ أَبِيهِ ، أَنَّ النَّبِيَّ صلى الله عليه وسلم ، لَبِسَ جُبَّةً رُومِيَّةً ، ضَيِّقَةَ الْكُمَّيْنِ[79]

70. Al-Mughīrah ibn Shu'bah ؓ narrated: "The Prophet ﷺ wore a Romanic *jubbah* which had tight sleeves."

Abdul Razzaq al-Badr said,

The *jubbah* is an outer garment that is worn over the *qamīs* (*thawb*).

The hadīths that the author included in this chapter show the variety of clothes that the Prophet ﷺ wore, which indicates that clothing is not a restricted avenue, but rather all garments are lawful except that which is forbidden by evidence.

Al-Bajūrī said,

He wore it whilst travelling and it is reported that this was in the battle of Tabūk.

The fact that the garment was made by the Romans shows that the general rule is that all clothes are pure, even those made by disbelievers.

"Tight sleeves": This means that when he wanted to pull his arms out of the sleeves it was difficult. Some scholars said it is recommended to wear narrow sleeved garments whilst travelling only. The sleeves of the companions were wide.

79 Sahīh Muslim (274)

The beautification of appearance in terms of clothing is praised if it is done to help one in the worship of Allāh such as how the Prophet ﷺ took care of his appearance and clothes when welcoming the delegates and it is dispraised when it is done for worldly benefits or to show off.

CHAPTER NINE

باب ماجاء في عيش رسول الله صلى الله عليه وسلم

THE REPORTS PERTAINING TO THE LIVING CONDITIONS OF THE PROPHET ﷺ

Alī al-Qārī said,

> There is another chapter towards the end of this book that talks about the food and drink of the Prophet ﷺ. However, it seems that this short chapter is intended to highlight the poverty faced by the Prophet and some of his companions while the other long chapter highlights the poverty faced by the Prophet and his family. The other possible explanation is that this short chapter is dedicated to detailing the hardship he experienced at the beginning [of his prophethood] and the long chapter highlights that which he experienced at the end of his life.

Ibn Hajar al-Haytamī said,

> It appears as if this chapter is repeated at the end of the book but this chapter is intended to indicate the poverty of the Prophet ﷺ while the other one is to indicate the type of food and drink he used to consume.

٧١: حَدَّثَنَا قُتَيْبَةُ بْنُ سَعِيدٍ ، حَدَّثَنَا حماد بن زيد عن أيوب عن محمد بن سيرين قال : كُنَّا عِنْدَ أَبِي هُرَيْرَةَ رضي الله عنه وَعَلَيْهِ ثَوْبَانِ مُمَشَّقَانِ مِنْ كَتَّانٍ فَتَمَخَّطَ فِي أحدهما . فَقَالَ أَبُو هُرَيْرَةَ : بَخْ بَخْ يَتَمَخَّطُ أَبُو هُرَيْرَةَ فِي الْكَتَّانِ . لَقَدْ رَأَيْتُنِي وَإِنِّي لَأَخِرُّ فِيمَا بَيْنَ مِنْبَرِ رَسُولِ الله صلى الله عليه وسلم وحُجْرَةِ عَائِشَةَ رضي الله عنها مَغْشِيًّا عَلَيَّ ، فَيَجِيءُ الْجَانِي فَيَضَعُ رِجْلَهُ عَلَى عُنُقِي ، يُرَى أَنَّ بِي جُنُونًا ، وَمَا بِي جُنُونٍ ، وما هو إلا الْجُوعُ[80]

71. Muhammad ibn Sirīn narrated: "We were with Abū Hurayrah ؓ while he was wearing two linen garments dyed with red clay. He cleaned his nose with his garment upon which he said, 'Well done! Well done! Abū Hurairah is cleaning his nose with linen! There came a time when I would fall unconscious between the pulpit of Allāh's Messenger ﷺ and Aisha's dwelling whereupon a passer-by would come and put his foot on my neck, thinking I suffer from epilepsy, while in fact, I suffered nothing but hunger.'"

Al-Bajūrī said,

> "Well done! Well done!": This is often said to express one's pleasure and joy but it could be used in the context of condemnation in the case of this hadīth.

Abdul Razzaq al-Badr said,

> "Abū Hurairah is cleaning his nose with linen": This is an expression of the change he experienced in terms of wealth as he was very poor and then later, he was cleaning his nose with a linen garment.

Alī al-Qārī said,

> "A passer-by would come and put his foot on my neck": The habit of people when seeing a person suffering an epileptic seizure was

---

80 Sahīh al-Bukhārī (7324)

to keep their feet on the neck to hold the person still until the seizure ended.

This hadīth was included in this chapter as it indicates the poverty of the Prophet ﷺ at that time. This is because if he had any food he would have shared it with his companions, particularly due to the fact that he used to look after them and treated them as his guests.

٧٢: حَدَّثَنَا قُتَيْبَةُ حَدَّثَنَا جعفر بن سليمان الضبعي عن مالك بن دِينار قال : مَا شَبِعَ رَسُولِ الله صلى الله عليه وسلم مِنْ خُبْزٍ قَط وَلَحم إلاَّ عَلى ضَفَفَ

قال مالك بن دينار : سألت رجلا من أهل البادية : ما الضفف ؟ فقال : أن يتناول مع الناس[81]

72. Mālik ibn Dinār ﵀ narrated: "The Messenger of Allāh ﷺ never reached the state of being satisfactorily full, neither from bread nor meat, except when he used to eat with people."

Al-Bajūrī said,

> "Except when he used to eat with people": This refers to filling two thirds of his stomach, as in feasts he would stay to show courtesy to the people and to show them that he loves the food. With that said, it is an obvious error on the part of those who claimed that he ﷺ used to reach the state of satiety [or overeat] in feasts. This is because it does not befit his noble status and it would be insulting even if it was said regarding one of us!

Abdul Razzaq al-Badr said,

> Imām Ahmad said, "Four qualities in food will make it perfect: if

81 Sahīh Ibn Hibbān (6359)

> the name of Allāh is mentioned on it in the beginning, Allāh is praised for it at the end, many hands are eating from it, and it is lawful."

Ibn Hajar al-Haytamī said,

> "Neither from bread nor meat": This indicates that he ﷺ never ate bread and meat together except with people. The state of fullness referred to here is interpreted to mean that he would eat until two thirds of his stomach were full or that he would not be full from meat and bread together, or from either of them.

CHAPTER TEN

باب ما جاء في خف رسول الله صلى الله عليه وسلم
THE REPORTS PERTAINING TO THE KHUFF OF THE MESSENGER OF ALLĀH ﷺ

Abdul Razzaq al-Badr said,

> *Khuff* is a well known type of socks. It is made of leather and it covers the entire foot.

٧٣: حَدَّثَنَا هَنَّادُ بْنُ السَّرِيِّ ، قَالَ : حَدَّثَنَا وَكِيعٌ ، عَنْ دَلْهَمِ بْنِ صَالِحٍ ، عَنْ حُجَيْرِ بْنِ عَبْدِ الله ، عَنِ ابْنِ بُرَيْدَةَ ، عَنْ أَبِيهِ ، أَنَّ النَّجَاشِيَّ أَهْدَى لِلنَّبِيِّ صلى الله عليه وسلم ، خُفَّيْنِ ، أَسْوَدَيْنِ ، سَاذَجَيْنِ ، فَلَبِسَهُمَا ثُمَّ تَوَضَّأَ وَمَسَحَ عَلَيْهِمَا[82]

73. Buraydah ﷺ narrated: "Al-Najāshī sent two plain black coloured *khuffs* as a gift to the Messenger of Allāh ﷺ. As soon as he received them, he tried them on, performed ablution and then wiped over them."

Abdul Razzaq al-Badr said,

> "Al-Najāshī" was the title given to the kings of Ethiopia and the name of this particular king was As-Hamah; he embraced Islām and died upon it. When he died, the Prophet ﷺ prayed the absentee funeral prayer on him.

Al-Bajūrī said,

> "As soon as he received them, he tried them on": This indicates that when a person receives a gift from someone, using it immediately shows one's acceptance of the gift and it also indicates the continuous signals of love between the one receiving the gift and the sender of gift. This hadīth also indicates that one should accept gifts even if they come from the People of the Book because at that time al-Najāshī was still a disbeliever, as stated by Abū Bakr ibn al-Arabī.

Ibn Hajar al-Haytamī said,

> "Performed ablution and then wiped over them": This indicates that when an object's purity cannot be ascertained, it is deemed to be pure. It also indicates the permissibility of wiping over the *khuff*.

82 Sunan al-Tirmidhī (2820) and Sunan Abū Dawūd (155)

٧٤: حَدَّثَنَا قُتَيْبَةُ بْنُ سَعِيدٍ ، قَالَ : حَدَّثَنَا يَحْيَى بْنُ زَكَرِيَّا بْنِ أَبِي زَائِدَةَ ، عَنِ الْحَسَنِ بْنِ عَيَّاشٍ ، عَنْ أَبِي إِسْحَاقَ ، عَنِ الشَّعْبِيِّ ، قَالَ : قَالَ الْمُغِيرَةُ بْنُ شُعْبَةَ : أَهْدَى دِحْيَةُ لِلنَّبِيِّ صلى الله عليه وسلم خُفَّيْنِ ، فَلَبِسَهُمَا وَقَالَ إِسْرَائِيلُ : عَنْ جَابِرٍ ، عَنْ عَامِرٍ ، وَجُبَّةً فَلَبِسَهُمَا حَتَّى تَخَرَّقَا لا يَدْرِي النَّبِيُّ صلى الله عليه وسلم ، أَذَكًى هُمَا أَمْ لا[83]

74. Al-Mughīrah ibn Shu'bah ؓ narrated: "Dihiyyah gifted the Prophet ﷺ with a pair of *khuffs* that he wore right away and he kept wearing them until they became torn. The Prophet ﷺ did not know whether the skin of the *khuffs* was from an animal that was slaughtered properly or not."

From another route, it adds, "He was also gifted a robe that he wore until it became torn."

Abdul Razzaq al-Badr said,

> "That he wore right away": This teaches us to hasten in accepting the gift and to use it right away so as to make the one who gave the gift happy and pleased.

Alī al-Qārī said,

> "The Prophet ﷺ did not know whether the skin of the *khuffs* was from an animal that was slaughtered properly or not": [The companion reported this] because either he ﷺ stated it, or the companion determined this because the Prophet ﷺ did not inquire about it.

Al-Bajūrī said,

> "Until they became torn": This indicates that the Prophet ﷺ used to keep wearing the clothes he had until they became worn out, as this is from humility.

83 Sunan al-Tirmidhī (1769)

CHAPTER ELEVEN

باب ماجاء في نعل رسول اللّه صلى اللّه عليه وسلم

THE REPORTS PERTAINING TO THE NA'L (SANDALS) OF THE MESSENGER OF ALLĀH ﷺ

Abdul Razzaq al-Badr said,

> This chapter is dedicated to describing the shoes of the Prophet ﷺ and his guidance in this regard. However, it is noteworthy to mention that it is permissible to wear anything we want, so long as what we wear is not forbidden in the religion. This is because the shoes that people wear in each era and in each culture are different. The general rule regarding clothes is that everything is permissible until there is evidence to prove it is forbidden.

Al-Bajūrī said,

> *Na'l* refers to footwear that keeps the feet away from the floor and when the term is used it does not normally include the *khuff*.
>
> The Prophet ﷺ had three different types of footwear, as Ibn Sa'd narrated in his work Tabaqat al-Kubra:
>
> 1. Footwear that was narrow in the middle.

2. Footwear with a leather piece in the back to support the ankle.
3. Footwear with a long front part, that took the shape of a tongue. It was designed this way to fit his second toe, which was the tallest of his toes.

He ﷺ used to walk barefoot sometimes out of humility, especially when he would go to visit an ill person.

٧٥: حَدَّثَنَا مُحَمَّدُ بْنُ بَشَّارٍ ، قَالَ : حَدَّثَنَا أَبُو دَاوُدَ الطَّيَالِسِيُّ ، قَالَ : حَدَّثَنَا هَمَّامٌ ، عَنْ ، قَالَ : قُلْتُ لأَنَسِ بْنِ مَالِكٍ : كَيْفَ كَانَ نَعْلُ رَسُولِ الله صلى الله عليه وسلم ؟ قَالَ : لَهُمَا قِبَالاَنِ[84]

75. Qatādah narrated: "I asked Anas ibn Mālik ؓ to describe the sandals of Allāh's Messenger ﷺ. He replied, 'Each sandal had two *qibālān*.'"

Ibn Hajar al-Haytamī said,

> *Qibālān* are two ribbons fastened to the sole of the sandal. The joining point of the ribbons separates the middle toe from the next toe (i.e. the fourth toe).

٧٦: حَدَّثَنَا أَبُو كُرَيْبٍ مُحَمَّدُ بْنُ الْعَلاءِ ، قَالَ : حَدَّثَنَا وَكِيعٌ ، عَنْ سُفْيَانَ ، عَنْ خَالِدٍ الْحَذَّاءِ ، عَنْ عَبْدِ الله بْنِ الْحَارِثِ ، عَنِ ابْنِ عَبَّاسٍ ، قَالَ : كَانَ لِنَعْلِ رَسُولِ الله صلى الله عليه وَسَلم قِبَالانِ ، مَثْنِيٌّ شِرَاكُهُمَا[85]

76. 'Abdullāh ibn 'Abbās ؓ related: "The sandal of the Messenger of Allāh ﷺ had two ribbons and two upper straps."

Abdul Muhsin al-Abbad said,

84 Sahīh al-Bukhārī (5857

85 Sunan Ibn Mājah (3614)

The ribbon refers to that which separates the toes, whereas the upper straps are that which secure the sandal to the upper part of the feet.

Abdul Razzaq al-Badr said,

> This means that each sandal had two ribbons and two straps were connected with each ribbon.

٧٧: حَدَّثَنَا أَحْمَدُ بْنُ مَنِيعٍ ، قَالَ : حَدَّثَنَا أَبُو أَحْمَدَ الزُّبَيْرِيُّ ، قَالَ : حَدَّثَنَا عِيسَى بْنُ طَهْمَانَ ، قَالَ : أَخْرَجَ إِلَيْنَا أَنَسُ بْنُ مَالِكٍ نَعْلَيْنِ جَرْدَاوَيْنِ ، لَهُمَا قِبَالانِ

فقَالَ : فَحَدَّثَنِي ثَابِتٌ بَعْدُ عَنْ أَنَسٍ ، أَنَّهُمَا كَانَتَا نَعْلَيِ النَّبِيِّ صلى الله عليه وسلم[86]

77. Īsa ibn Tahmān narrated: "Anas ibn Mālik ﷺ showed us a pair of sandals that had two straps and were hairless. Later on, Thābit told me that these were the sandals of the Prophet ﷺ."

Abdul Razzaq al-Badr said,

> This indicates that Anas kept the sandals of the Prophet ﷺ in his house.

٧٨ : حَدَّثَنَا إِسْحَاقُ بْنُ مُوسَى الأَنْصَارِيُّ ، قَالَ : حَدَّثَنَا مَعْنٌ ، قَالَ : حَدَّثَنَا مَالِكٌ ، قَالَ : حَدَّثَنَا سَعِيدُ بْنُ أَبِي سَعِيدٍ الْمَقْبُرِيُّ ، عَنْ عُبَيْدِ بْنِ جُرَيْجٍ ، أَنَّهُ قَالَ لابْنِ عُمَرَ : رَأَيْتُكَ تَلْبَسُ النِّعَالَ السِّبْتِيَّةَ ، قَالَ : إِنِّي رَأَيْتُ رَسُولَ اللهِ صلى الله عليه وسلم يَلْبَسُ النِّعَالَ الَّتِي لَيْسَ فِيهَا شَعَرٌ ، وَيَتَوَضَّأُ

---

86 Sahīh al-Bukhārī (5858)

فِيهَا ، فَأَنَا أُحِبُّ أَنْ أَلْبَسَهَا[87]

78. Ubayd ibn Jurayj asked Ibn 'Umar ؓ: "Why do you [prefer] wearing the *sibti* type of sandals?" He replied, "I saw the Messenger of Allāh ﷺ wearing sandals that did not have hair on them, performing ablution while he had them on. This is why I like wearing them."

Al-Bajūrī and Abdul Razzaq al-Badr said,

> *Sibti* sandals refer to the sandals made of tanned cow leather and they are called *sibti* because the hair falls off when the leather is dyed.

Alī al-Qārī said,

> The answer of Ibn 'Umar ؓ was to show that he prefers wearing this type of sandal to follow the guidance of the Prophet ﷺ and not because of personal preference.

٧٩: حَدَّثَنَا إِسْحَاقُ بْنُ مَنْصُورٍ ، قَالَ : حَدَّثَنَا عَبْدُ الرَّزَّاقِ ، عَنْ مَعْمَرٍ ، عَنِ ابْنِ أَبِي ذِئْبٍ ، عَنْ صَالِحٍ مَوْلَى التَّوْءَمَةِ ، عَنْ أَبِي هُرَيْرَةَ ، قَالَ : كَانَ لِنَعْلِ رَسُولِ الله صلى الله عليه وسلم قِبَالانِ[88]

79. Abū Hurairah ؓ related: "The sandals of Allāh's Messenger ﷺ had two upper straps."

Al-Bajūrī said,

> Alī ibn Abī Tālib ؓ and Ibn Abbās ؓ encouraged wearing yellow sandals. It is because yellow is from the colours that indicate happiness.

87 Sahīh al-Bukhārī (5851) and Sahīh Muslim (1187)
88 Al-'Ilal al-Kabīr of al-Bukhārī (291)

٨٠ : حَدَّثَنَا أَحْمَدُ بْنُ مَنِيعٍ ، قَالَ : حَدَّثَنَا أَبُو أَحْمَدَ ، قَالَ : حَدَّثَنَا سُفْيَانُ ، عَنِ السُّدِّيِّ ، قَالَ : حَدَّثَنِي مَنْ ، سَمِعَ عَمْرَو بْنَ حُرَيْثٍ ، يَقُولُ : رَأَيْتُ رَسُولَ اللهِ صلى الله عليه وسلم ، يُصَلِّي فِي نَعْلَيْنِ مَخْصُوفَتَيْنِ [89]

80. 'Amr ibn Huraith ؓ narrated: "I saw the Messenger of Allāh ﷺ praying while wearing a pair of sandals that had new soles sewn onto them."

Abdul Razzaq al-Badr said,

> The Prophet ﷺ used to sew the leather sole into his sandals by himself as reported in the hadīth that Imām Ahmad documented in his Musnad[90].

Al-Bajūrī said,

> The Prophet ﷺ had sandals that had one sole and sandals that had more than one sole.

٨١ : حَدَّثَنَا إِسْحَاقُ بْنُ مُوسَى الأَنْصَارِيُّ ، قَالَ : حَدَّثَنَا مَعْنٌ ، قَالَ : حَدَّثَنَا مَالِكٌ ، عَنْ أَبِي الزِّنَادِ ، عَنِ الأَعْرَجِ ، عَنْ أَبِي هُرَيْرَةَ ، أَنَّ رَسُولَ اللهِ صلى الله عليه وسلم ، قَالَ : لا يَمْشِيَنَّ أَحَدُكُمْ فِي نَعْلٍ وَاحِدَةٍ ، لِيُنْعِلْهُمَا جَمِيعًا ، أَوْ لِيُحْفِهِمَا جَمِيعًا [91]

81. Abū Hurairah ؓ narrated that the Prophet ﷺ said: "One should not wear one shoe and walk. Either wear them both or remove them both."

Alī al-Qārī said,

89 Al-Sunan al-Kubra of al-Nasā'ī (9719)
90 Musnad Imam Ahmed, 24749.
91 Sahīh al-Bukhārī (5855) and Sahīh Muslim (2097)

Al-Khattabī said that [it is disliked] because it would be difficult to walk whilst wearing one shoe, not to mention that it does not look good. Others said, it is [disliked] because it would make the person unjust between their own limbs, or because it would make people question their intellect and sensibility. Abū Bakr ibn al-Arabī said, "It is disliked because it makes the person walk the walk of the Shaytan. And it is said that it is disliked because it is immodest." Al-Bayhaqī said, "It is disliked because it makes the person known and famous and we are ordered not to attract the attention of others through our clothing or anything that may make us gain notoriety."

Some scholars applied the same ruling on sleeves i.e. it is disliked to wear a shirt whilst having one arm in a sleeve and the other one bare.

٨٢: حَدَّثَنَا قُتَيْبَةُ ، عَنْ مَالِكِ بْنِ أَنَسٍ ، عَنْ أَبِي الزِّنَادِ نَحْوَهُ

82. Abū Zinād reports the same.

٨٣: حَدَّثَنَا إِسْحَاقُ بْنُ مُوسَى ، قَالَ : حَدَّثَنَا مَعْنٌ ، قَالَ : حَدَّثَنَا مَالِكٌ ، عَنْ أَبِي الزُّبَيْرِ ، عَنْ جَابِرٍ ، أَنَّ النَّبِيَّ صلى الله عليه وسلم نَهَى أَنْ يَأْكُلَ ، يَعْنِي الرَّجُلَ ، بِشِمَالِهِ ، أَوْ يَمْشِيَ فِي نَعْلٍ وَاحِدَةٍ[92]

83. Jābir ibn 'Abdullāh ﷺ narrated: "The Prophet ﷺ prohibited people from eating with the left hand and from wearing one sandal only."

Abdul Razzaq al-Badr said,

> The prohibition of eating with the left hand applies to drinking as well.

92 Sahīh Muslim (2099)

Al-Bajūrī said,

> The ruling on eating with the left hand without a necessity is that it is disliked according to the Shāfi'ī scholars and it is forbidden according to many Hanbalī and Mālikī scholars.

٨٤: حَدَّثَنَا قُتَيْبَةُ ، حوحَدَّثَنَا إِسْحَاقُ بْنُ مُوسَى ، قَالَ : حَدَّثَنَا مَعْنٌ ، قَالَ : حَدَّثَنَا مَالِكٌ ، عَنْ أَبِي الزِّنَادِ ، عَنِ الأَعْرَجِ ، عَنْ أَبِي هُرَيْرَةَ ، أَنَّ النَّبِيَّ صلى الله عليه وسلم ، قَالَ : إِذَا انْتَعَلَ أَحَدُكُمْ فَلْيَبْدَأْ بِالْيَمِينِ ، وَإِذَا نَزَعَ فَلْيَبْدَأْ بِالشِّمَالِ ، فَلْتَكُنِ الْيَمِينُ أَوَّلَهُمَا تُنْعَلُ ، وَآخِرَهُمَا تُنْزَعُ[93]

84. Abū Hurairah ﷺ narrated that the Prophet ﷺ said: "Whenever one amongst you puts on their sandals, he should begin with the right, and when one of you removes them, the left one should be removed first. Let the right side be the first when putting them on and the last when removing them."

Abdul Razzaq al-Badr said,

> This shows the virtue of the right over the left in wearing shoes. It was the guidance of the Prophet ﷺ to start with the right in all that which is honoured and considered a matter of adornment and beauty such as wearing the shoes, clothes, combing the hair etc. Whereas the left side is used to commence anything contrary to that such as removing the shoes, entering the toilet, and leaving the masjid etc.

Al-Bajūrī said,

> The right side is honoured and therefore it comes first in every matter that is intended to be perfect and good, whilst the left side is used in matters that imperfect the status. The right side is

93 Sahīh al-Bukhārī (5856) and Sahīh Muslim (2097)

honoured because it is what Allāh prefers and likes in everything i.e. the dwellers of Paradise stand on the right side of the Throne on the Day of Judgement and receive their books with their right hands, the angel recording the good deeds is on the right side, the scale of good deeds are placed on the right side etc.

٨٥: حَدَّثَنَا أَبُو مُوسَى مُحَمَّدُ بْنُ الْمُثَنَّى ، قَالَ : حَدَّثَنَا مُحَمَّدُ بْنُ جَعْفَرٍ ، قَالَ : حَدَّثَنَا شُعْبَةُ ، قَالَ : حَدَّثَنَا أَشْعَثُ هُوَ ابْنُ أَبِي الشَّعْثَاءِ ، عَنْ أَبِيهِ ، عَنْ مَسْرُوقٍ ، عَنْ عَائِشَةَ ، قَالَتْ : كَانَ رَسُولُ اللهِ صلى الله عليه وسلم يُحِبُّ التَّيَمُّنَ مَا اسْتَطَاعَ فِي تَرَجُّلِهِ ، وَتَنَعُّلِهِ وَطُهُورِهِ[94]

85. Aisha ﷺ narrated: "The Prophet ﷺ liked to begin with the right side as much as possible; he began with his right side when he combed his hair, wore his shoes and washed his limbs when performing ablution."

Abdul Razzaq al-Badr said,

> This emphasises the meaning of the previous hadīth.

٨٦: حَدَّثَنَا مُحَمَّدُ بْنُ مَرْزُوقٍ أَبُو عَبْدِ اللهِ ، قَالَ : حَدَّثَنَا عَبْدُ الرَّحْمَنِ بْنُ قَيْسٍ أَبُو مُعَاوِيَةَ ، قَالَ : حَدَّثَنَا هِشَامٌ ، عَنْ مُحَمَّدٍ ، عَنْ أَبِي هُرَيْرَةَ ، قَالَ : كَانَ لِنَعْلِ رَسُولِ اللهِ صلى الله عليه وسلم قِبَالاَنِ وَأَبِي بَكْرٍ وَعُمَرَ ، وَأَوَّلُ مَنْ عَقَدَ عَقْدًا وَاحِدًا عُثْمَانُ رضي الله عنه.[95]

86. Abū Hurairah ﷺ narrated: "The sandals of the Messenger of Allāh ﷺ had two upper straps, and so did the sandals of Abū Bakr ﷺ and Umar ﷺ. However, 'Uthmān ibn 'Affan ﷺ was the first one to use one strap."

94 See hadīth 34

95 Majma' al-Zawa'id wa Manba' al-Fawa'id (5/141)

Abdul Razzaq al-Badr said,

> This action of 'Uthmān ibn Affan ؓ shows that the Prophet ﷺ had two straps due to his personal preference and not with the intention to draw closer to Allāh. This is because if it was done for this reason, 'Uthmān ؓ would not have left it.

Al-Bajūrī said,

> 'Uthmān ؓ using one strap shows that the two straps were used because that was the custom and not because using one strap is disliked. This illustrates that it is permissible to wear any type of shoes, because wearing sandals at that time was just the custom of people.

Alī al-Qārī said,

> If 'Uthmān ؓ did not use the one strap it would have been assumed that using one strap is disliked. Thus, it shows that not wearing sandals and instead wearing anything else is permissible and not disliked.

CHAPTER TWELVE

باب ما جاء في ذكر خاتم رسول الله صلى الله عليه وسلم

THE REPORTS PERTAINING TO THE RING (SEAL) OF THE PROPHET ﷺ

Abdul Razzaq al-Badr said,

> The Prophet ﷺ used the seal in the latter part of the sixth year of Hijrah when he started writing letters to the kings and leaders in which he called them to the religion of Allāh. This is because when he wanted to write to the Romans, he was advised that they do not read letters without seals on them. For that reason, he made a seal.

٨٧: حَدَّثَنَا قُتَيْبَةُ بْنُ سَعِيدٍ ، وَغَيْرُ وَاحِدٍ ، عَنْ عَبْدِ اللهِ بْنِ وَهْبٍ ، عَنْ يُونُسَ ، عَنِ ابْنِ شِهَابٍ ، عَنْ أَنَسِ بْنِ مَالِكٍ ، قَالَ : كَانَ خَاتَمُ النَّبِيِّ صلى الله عليه وسلم مِنْ وَرِقٍ ، وَكَانَ فَصُّهُ حَبَشِيًّا[96]

87. Anas ibn Mālik ﷺ narrated: "The ring (i.e. seal) of Allāh's Messenger ﷺ was made of silver and its gem stone was Abyssinian."

Abdul Razzaq al-Badr said,

> This indicates that it is permissible for men to wear silver rings.

Al-Bajūrī said,

> The Prophet ﷺ had two seals that the reader of this book needs to distinguish; the seal of prophethood, which is the area of raised skin between his shoulders and the seal of the Prophet, which is the seal he used to stamp his letters.

Ibn Hajar al-Haytamī said,

> It is permissible for men to wear rings; but it is disliked to wear more than two rings as stated by al-Daramī, but the latter view is disputed over.
>
> The gem stone was described as Abyssinian because it was agate, and it was said that its colour was black, or that the one who made it was an Abyssinian.
>
> The preference of the Prophet ﷺ to wear rings made of silver made some of the renowned Shāfi'ī scholars deduce that it is disliked to wear rings made of iron or copper and they relied on many hadīths, one of which is the hadīth wherein the Prophet ﷺ saw a man wearing a ring made of iron and said to him, "Why do you wear the jewellery of the people of Hell?" So the man removed it and then he came wearing a ring made of copper so he said to

96 Sahīh Muslim (2094)

him, "Why do I smell the scent of idols coming from you?!" Upon which the man removed it.[97]

Al-Bayhaqī said, after narrating the hadīths that talk about the gem stone of the Prophet ﷺ wherein some hadīths show that it was made of agate and others show that it was made of silver just like the ring, "These hadīths indicate that he had two rings, one of which the gem stone was agate and another of which the gem stone was silver."

٨٨: حَدَّثَنَا قُتَيْبَةُ حَدَّثَنَا أَبُو عَوَانَةَ ، عَنْ أَبِي بِشْرٍ ، عَنْ نَافِعٍ ، عَنِ ابْنِ عُمَرَ ، أَنَّ النَّبِيَّ صلى الله عليه وسلم اتَّخَذَ خَاتَمًا مِنْ فِضَّةٍ ، فَكَانَ يَخْتِمُ بِهِ وَلا يَلْبَسُهُ[98]

88. 'Abdullāh ibn 'Umar ﷺ narrated: "Allāh's Messenger ﷺ possessed a ring made of silver. He used it to stamp [his letters etc.], and did not wear it."

Abdul Razzaq al-Badr said,

> The last part of this hadīth opposes the many hadīths that state the Prophet ﷺ wore the seal. However, some scholars reconciled this hadīth with the other hadīths by saying that the ring referred to in this hadīth was not made of silver only but rather had other materials that are not permissible to wear such as iron. Imām Ahmad reported that the Prophet ﷺ had a ring made of iron that had some silver on it that he threw away afterwards. Al-Hafith ibn Rajab commented on this hadīth by saying, "Perhaps, this was the ring that he used for stamping and sealing the letters but he never wore it." In any case, if this addition (the last part of the hadīth) is proven to be authentic, then it is understood to refer to a particular case. Some other scholars considered the addition odd and rejected

97 Sunan al-Tirmidhī (1785)
98 Sahīh Ibn Hibbān (5459)

it.

Ibn Hajar al-Haytamī said,

> The last part of this hadīth opposes the other hadīths which indicate that the Prophet ﷺ used to wear the ring on his right hand. However, this contradiction can be reconciled because [it appears] that he had two rings; one that had a gemstone with engraved words to stamp his letters, and this ring he did not wear, and another ring that he wore so that people follow his example. It is also possible that he did not wear it all the time or that he did not wear it at the beginning, and then wore it later to show the people that it is not intended for adornment.

٨٩: حَدَّثَنَا مَحْمُودُ بْنُ غَيْلانَ ، قَالَ : حَدَّثَنَا حَفْصُ بْنُ عُمَرَ بْنِ عُبَيْدٍ هُوَ الطَّنَافِسِيُّ ، قَالَ : حَدَّثَنَا زُهَيْرٌ أَبُو خَيْثَمَةَ ، عَنْ حُمَيْدٍ ، عَنْ أَنَسِ بْنِ مَالِكٍ ، قَالَ : كَانَ خَاتَمُ رَسُولِ اللهِ صلى الله عليه وسلم ، مِنْ فِضَّةٍ ، فَصُّهُ مِنْهُ[99]

89. Anas ibn Mālik ؓ narrated: "The Prophet ﷺ had a ring made of silver and its stone was also of silver."

Alī al-Qārī said,

> The ring that had a gem stone made of silver was the ring that the Prophet ﷺ ordered to be made for him. Al-Daraqutnī reported that Ya'la ibn Umayyah ؓ said, "I myself made for the Prophet ﷺ a ring that no one else helped me with. I engraved on it, 'Muhammad is the Messenger of Allāh.'"

Al-Bajūrī said,

> The meaning of the last part of the hadīth is that the gemstone was part of the ring and not something external added to it.

99 Sahih al-Bukhārī (5870)

٩٠: حَدَّثَنَا إِسْحَاقُ بْنُ مَنْصُورٍ ، قَالَ : حَدَّثَنَا مُعَاذُ بْنُ هِشَامٍ ، قَالَ : حَدَّثَنِي أَبِي ، عَنْ قَتَادَةَ ، عَنْ أَنَسِ بْنِ مَالِكٍ ، قَالَ : لَمَّا أَرَادَ رَسُولُ اللهِ صلى الله عليه وسلم أَنْ يَكْتُبَ إِلَى الْعَجَمِ قِيلَ لَهُ : إِنَّ الْعَجَمَ لا يَقْبَلُونَ إِلاَّ كِتَابًا عَلَيْهِ خَاتَمٌ ، فَاصْطَنَعَ خَاتَمًا ، فَكَأَنِّي أَنْظُرُ إِلَى بَيَاضِهِ فِي كَفِّهِ[100]

90. Anas ibn Mālik ﷺ narrated: "When the Messenger of Allāh ﷺ intended to write letters to the leaders of the non-Arabs [to invite them to Islām], he was advised that they do not accept letters without a seal (stamp) on them. For that reason, he had a ring made for himself. It is as if the brightness of [the ring] which was on his hand is still before my eyes."

Abdul Razzaq al-Badr said,

> This hadīth shows the reason behind the Prophet ﷺ wanting to have a ring (i.e. seal).

Ibn Hajar al-Haytamī said,

> This incident took place after he ﷺ returned from Hudaybiyyah. It is said that the person who advised the Prophet about the seal was a non-Arab or a person from the Quraysh.
>
> The reason they did not accept unstamped letters was because it made them doubt the content or because the stamp indicated that the sender respected them, or that the stamp indicated that access to the contents of the letter was limited to certain people.

Al-Bajuri said,

> This hadīth indicates the permissibility of communication through letters. The first person reported to send a letter was Prophet Sulaymān ﷺ when he sent the hoopoe to deliver his letter to Balqīs, the queen of Saba'. The act of the Prophet ﷺ teaches us to

100 Sahih al-Bukhārī (5875) and Sahīh Muslim (2092)

do what people like and leave that which they dislike.

Alī al-Qārī said,

> The part regarding the brightness of the ring indicates that it was made of silver, and it was said that it refers to the perfection of the ring.

٩١ : حَدَّثَنَا مُحَمَّدُ بْنُ يَحْيَى ، قَالَ : حَدَّثَنَا مُحَمَّدُ بْنُ عَبْدِ اللهِ الأَنْصَارِيُّ ، قَالَ : حَدَّثَنِي أَبِي ، عَنْ ثُمَامَةَ ، عَنْ أَنَسِ بْنِ مَالِكٍ ، قَالَ : كَانَ نَقْشُ خَاتَمِ رَسُولِ اللهِ صلى الله عليه وسلم : مُحَمَّدٌ سَطْرٌ ، وَرَسُولٌ سَطْرٌ ، وَاللهُ سَطْرٌ[101]

91. Anas ibn Mālik ﷺ narrated: "The inscription engraved on the ring of Allāh's Messenger ﷺ was 'Muhammad' on one line, 'Messenger' on the next, and 'Allāh' on the last."

Abdul Razzaq al-Badr said,

> This shows that the inscription engraved on the ring consisted of three words, each written on a separate line.

Al-Bajūrī said,

> The word "Muhammad" was written on the first line at the top and the other words were written below. This is supported by another narration reported by al-Isma'īlī that explicitly stated the order of the lines, and it is also the apparent meaning of the narration reported by al-Bukhārī.

٩٢ : حَدَّثَنَا نَصْرُ بْنُ عَلِيٍّ الْجَهْضَمِيُّ أَبُو عَمْرٍو ، قَالَ : حَدَّثَنَا نُوحُ بْنُ قَيْسٍ ، عَنْ خَالِدِ بْنِ قَيْسٍ ، عَنْ قَتَادَةَ ، عَنْ أَنَسِ بْنِ مَالِكٍ ، أَنَّ النَّبِيَّ صلى الله عليه

101 Sahīh al-Bukhārī (3106)

وسلم كَتَبَ إِلَى كِسْرَى وَقَيْصَرَ وَالنَّجَاشِيِّ ، فَقِيلَ لَهُ : إِنَّهُمْ لا يَقْبَلُونَ كِتَابًا ، إلا بِخَاتَم ، فَصَاغَ رَسُولُ الله صلى الله عليه وسلم ، خَاتمًا حَلْقَتُهُ فِضَّةٌ ، وَنُقِشَ فِيهِ : مُحَمَّدٌ رَسُولُ اللهِ[102]

92. Anas ibn Mālik ؓ related: "Allāh's Messenger ﷺ [intended to] write letters to Kisra [of the Persians), Caesar (of the Romans) and al-Najāshī (of the Abyssinians). The Prophet ﷺ was advised that they do not accept letters without a stamp. For this reason, he ﷺ had a ring made of silver, and had 'Muhammad is the Messenger of Allāh' engraved upon it."

Al-Bajūrī said,

> Kisra was the title given to the kings of Persia. Caesar was the title given to the kings of the Romans. Al-Najāshī was the title given to the kings of Abyssinia. Pharaoh was the title given to the kings of the region of Copt in Egypt. Al-'Azīz was the title given to the kings of Egypt. Tubba' was the title given to the kings of the tribe of Himyar. Khaqan was the title given to the kings of the Turks.

٩٣ : حَدَّثَنَا إِسْحَاقُ بْنُ مَنْصُورٍ ، قَالَ : حَدَّثَنَا سَعِيدُ بْنُ عَامِرٍ ، وَالْحَجَّاجُ بْنُ مِنْهَالٍ ، عَنْ هَمَّام ، عَنِ ابْنِ جُرَيْجٍ ، عَنِ الزُّهْرِيِّ ، عَنْ أَنَسِ بْنِ مَالِكٍ ، أَنَّ النَّبِيَّ صلى الله عليه وسلم كَانَ إِذَا دَخَلَ الْخَلاءَ نَزَعَ خَاتَمَهُ[103]

93. Anas ibn Mālik ؓ related: "Whenever the Messenger of Allāh ﷺ entered the place where he relieved himself, he would remove his ring."

Alī al-Qārī said,

> He ﷺ used to remove his ring before entering the place where he

102 See hadīth 90
103 Sunan al-Tirmidhī (1746)

relieved himself because the ring had the name of Allāh engraved on it.

Before gold was made forbidden for men to wear, the Prophet ﷺ had a ring made of gold and so the people began to wear golden rings in imitation of him. When he became aware of this, he removed it and said that he would not wear a golden ring again and so the people followed suit. Then he wore a ring made of silver as an adornment, so people followed him in that. However, he saw that this may lead to arrogance and pride so he removed it and so did the people. Later on, he needed to wear a ring for the purpose of stamping letters so he wore it but he said to the people, "I have made myself a ring and engraved on it some words; so do not engrave on your rings [the same words I have used]."

Ibn Hajar al-Haytamī said,

> It is disliked to keep the Name of Allāh in ones possession whilst being in the place where people relieve themselves, and it was said that this is forbidden. The same ruling applies to anything that is glorified in religion such as the Qur'ān, the name of a prophet or an angel. As for names that people use that are also the names of prophets [or angels etc.] such as Muhammad, then the ruling is based on the intention of the person. If the intention is that it is a normal person's name then it is permissible but if it is intended to refer to one who is glorified in the religion, then it is disliked.

٩٤: حَدَّثَنَا إِسْحَاقُ بْنُ مَنْصُورٍ ، قَالَ : حَدَّثنا عَبْدُ الله بْنُ نُمَيْرٍ ، قالَ : حَدَّثَنَا عُبَيْدُ الله بْنُ عُمَرَ ، عَنْ نَافِعٍ ، عَنِ ابْنِ عُمَرَ ، قالَ : اتَّخَذَ رَسُولُ الله صلى الله عليه وَسلم ، خَاتمًا مِنْ وَرِقٍ ، فَكَانَ فِي يَدِهِ ثُمَّ كَانَ فِي يَدِ أَبِي بَكْرٍ ، وَيَدِ عُمَرَ ، ثُمَّ كَانَ فِي يَدِ عُثْمانَ ، حَتَّى وَقَعَ فِي بِئْرِ أَرِيسٍ ، نَقْشُهُ : مُحَمَّدٌ رَسُولُ الله[104]

104 Sahīh al-Bukhārī (5873) and Sahīh Muslim (2091)

94. 'Abdullāh ibn 'Umar ؓ narrated: "The Messenger of Allāh ﷺ had a ring made of silver that he wore on his hand. Then, [after the death of the Prophet], Abū Bakr ؓ wore it on his hand, and then [after the death of Abū Bakr] 'Umar ibn al-Khattab ؓ kept it and wore it on his hand. Then [after the death of 'Umar], 'Uthmān ibn 'Affan ؓ kept it and wore it until it fell into the well of Arīs. The inscription on the ring was 'Muhammad is the Messenger of Allāh.'"

Abdul Razzaq al-Badr said,

> The well of Arīs is a well in a garden located near the Masjid al-Qubā'. The ring fell when 'Uthmān ؓ was moving the ring on his finger while standing at the edge of the well. He spent three days, along with his companions, searching for it but they could not find it. Thus, the claim that the ring was found is a baseless claim and to prove something is from the belongings of the Prophet ﷺ requires authentic evidence.

Al-Bajūrī said,

> This hadīth shows that it is permissible to use a seal that has the name of someone else engraved on it after their death.

Ibn Hajar al-Haytamī said,

> The seal of the Prophet ﷺ was not from his heritance because it was treated like his weapons that were allocated as a charity for the Muslims that the ruler would utilise in the way that serves their best interest. This is why Abū Bakr, Umar and Uthmān used it as it was from the tools that the Caliphate needed.
>
> None of our fellow Shāfi'ī scholars discussed the weight of the ring, but some later scholars such as al-Adhra'ī stated that it is forbidden for it to exceed one *mithqal* (a unit of mass equal to 4.25 grams) whilst other scholars said it is permissible such as al-Hafidh al-'Iraqī who said that it is [not forbidden but rather] disliked for the ring to weigh one *mithqal*. However, the appropriate,

permissible weight depends on the norms of the people in their culture as the *mithqal* was the norm of the people at that time.

CHAPTER THIRTEEN

باب ماجاء في تختم رسول الله صلى الله عليه وسلم

THE REPORTS STATING THAT THE PROPHET ﷺ WORE THE RING ON HIS RIGHT HAND

Abdul Razzaq al-Badr said,

> The title used for this chapter is intended to show that it is the Sunnah to wear the ring on the right hand. This is the view adopted by the author as he considered the hadīth wherein it states that he ﷺ wore the ring on the left hand to be weak. However, Ibn al-Qayyim said, "There are hadīths indicating that he wore his ring on the right hand and other hadīths stating that he wore it on the left hand, and the chains of all these hadīths are authentic."
>
> Al-Nawawī said, "The scholars are in agreement that it is permissible to wear the ring on the right hand or the left hand as neither is disliked. However, they differed on what is better. Many of the *salaf* used to wear the ring on the right hand and many of them used to wear the ring on the left hand. Imām Mālik preferred wearing the ring on the left hand and he disliked wearing it on the right hand. In our madhab (Shāfi'ī) there are two views, but the most correct is that wearing the ring on the right hand is better

because it is a form of adornment and the right hand is more deserving of being honoured and beautified."

٩٥: حَدَّثَنَا مُحَمَّدُ بْنُ سَهْلِ بْنِ عَسْكَرٍ الْبَغْدَادِيُّ، وَعَبْدُ اللهِ بْنُ عَبْدِ الرَّحْمَنِ، قَالا: أَخْبَرَنَا يَحْيَى بْنُ حَسَّانَ، قَالَ: حَدَّثَنَا سُلَيْمَانُ بْنُ بِلَالٍ، عَنْ شَرِيكِ بْنِ عَبْدِ اللهِ بْنِ أَبِي نَمِرٍ، عَنْ إِبْرَاهِيمَ بْنِ عَبْدِ اللهِ بْنِ حُنَيْنٍ، عَنْ أَبِيهِ، عَنْ عَلِيِّ بْنِ أَبِي طَالِبٍ: أَنَّ النَّبِيَّ صلى الله عليه وسلم كَانَ يَلْبَسُ خَاتَمَهُ فِي يَمِينِهِ[105]

95. Alī ibn Abī Tālib ؓ narrated: "The Messenger of Allāh ﷺ wore his ring on the right hand."

Al-Bajūrī said,

> The author (al-Tirmidhī) quoted al-Bukhārī who said, "The hadīths stating that he ﷺ wore the ring on his left hand are the most authentic hadīths."
>
> The hadīths can be reconciled i.e. he ﷺ had two rings, one he wore on his left hand and [on other occasions] he wore his other ring on his right hand, which goes in line with the hadīths that stated he had a ring with a gemstone made of silver and another from Abyssinia.

Ibn Hajar al-Haytamī said,

> Imām Ahmad disliked wearing a ring on the index finger or the middle finger.

Alī al-Qārī said,

> Ibn Hajar al-Asqalānī said, "If the ring is worn as an adornment then wearing it on the right hand is better but if it is worn to use

105 Sunan Abū Dawūd (4226)

for stamping letters, then wearing it on the left hand is better."

٩٦: حَدَّثَنَا مُحَمَّدُ بْنُ يَحْيَى ، قَالَ : حَدَّثَنَا أَحْمَدُ بْنُ صَالِحٍ ، قَالَ : حَدَّثَنَا عَبْدُ اللهِ بْنُ وَهْبٍ ، عَنْ سُلَيْمَانَ بْنِ بِلالٍ ، عَنْ شَرِيكِ بْنِ عَبْدِ اللهِ بْنِ أَبِي نَمِرٍ ، نَحْوَهُ

96. Sharīk ibn 'Abdullāh ibn Abū Namir reports the same.

٩٧: حدثنا أحمد بن منيع أحدثنا يزيد بن هارون أعن حماد بن سلمة أ قَالَ رأيت ابن أبي رافع يتختم في يَمِينِهِ وقَالَ عَبْدِ اللهِ بن جعفر : كان رَسُولُ اللهِ صلى الله عليه وسلم يتختم فِي يَمِينِهِ[106]

97. Hammād ibn Salamah narrated that he saw Abdur Rahmān ibn Abī Rāfi' wearing a ring on his right hand. He inquired regarding the reason behind this and he replied: "I had seen 'Abdullāh ibn Ja'far ﷺ wearing a ring on his right hand, and he said that he had seen the Prophet ﷺ wear a ring on his right hand."

٩٨: حَدَّثَنَا يَحْيَى بْنُ مُوسَى ، قَالَ : حَدَّثَنَا عَبْدُ اللهِ بْنُ نُمَيْرٍ ، قَالَ : حَدَّثَنَا إِبْرَاهِيمُ بْنُ الْفَضْلِ ، عَنْ عَبْدِ اللهِ بْنِ مُحَمَّدِ بْنِ عَقِيلَ ، عَنْ عَبْدِ اللهِ بْنِ جَعْفَرٍ ، أَنَّ النَّبِيَّ صلى الله عليه وسلم كَانَ يَتَخَتَّمُ فِي يَمِينِهِ[107]

98. 'Abdullāh ibn Ja'far ﷺ narrates: "The Messenger of Allāh wore a ring on his right hand."

٩٩ : حَدَّثَنَا أَبُو الْخَطَّابِ زِيَادُ بْنُ يَحْيَى ، قَالَ : حَدَّثَنَا عَبْدُ اللهِ بْنُ مَيْمُونٍ ، عَنْ جَعْفَرِ بْنِ مُحَمَّدٍ ، عَنْ أَبِيهِ ، عَنْ جَابِرِ بْنِ عَبْدِ اللهِ : أَنَّ النَّبِيَّ صلى الله

106 Sunan al-Tirmidhī (1744)
107 Musnad Ahmad (3/195)

عليه وسلم كَانَ يَتَخَتَّمُ فِي يَمِينِهِ[108]

99. Jābir ibn 'Abdullāh ؓ narrated: "The Prophet ﷺ wore the ring on the right hand."

Al-Bajūrī said,

> These hadīths did not show what finger he ﷺ used to wear the ring on but the hadīths in the two Sahīh books show that he wore his ring on the pinkie. With that said, the Sunnah is to wear the ring on the pinkie only. The wisdom behind this is that the pinkie is far from the actions of the hand and [due to it being the farthest finger from the thumb] it does not hinder the work of the hand unlike if it was worn on the index finger.

١٠٠ : حَدَّثَنَا مُحَمَّدُ بْنُ حُمَيْدٍ الرَّازِيُّ ، قَالَ : حَدَّثَنَا جَرِيرٌ ، عَنْ مُحَمَّدِ بْنِ إِسْحَاقَ ، عَنِ الصَّلتِ بْنِ عَبْدِ الله ، قَالَ : كَانَ ابْنُ عَبَّاسٍ ، يَتَخَتَّمُ فِي يَمِينِهِ ، وَلا إِخَالُهُ إِلا قَالَ : كَانَ رَسُولُ اللهِ صلى الله عليه وسلم يَتَخَتَّمُ فِي يَمِينِهِ[109]

100. Salt ibn 'Abdullāh narrated: "Ibn Abbās ؓ wore a ring on the right hand, and as far as I can recall he used to say that the Prophet ﷺ wore it on the right hand."

١٠١ : حَدَّثَنَا مُحَمَّدُ بْنُ أَبِي عُمَرَ ، قَالَ : حَدَّثَنَا سُفْيان ، عَنْ أَيُّوبَ بْنِ مُوسَى ، عَنْ نَافِعٍ ، عَنِ ابْنِ عُمَرَ : أَنَّ النَّبِيَّ صلى الله عليه وسلم اتَّخَذَ خَاتَمًا مِنْ فِضَّةٍ ، وَجَعَلَ فَصَّهُ مِمَّا يَلِي كَفَّهُ ، وَنَقَشَ فِيهِ مُحَمَّدٌ رَسُولُ الله ، وَنَهَى أَنْ يَنْقُشَ أَحَدٌ عَلَيْهِ وَهُوَ الَّذِي سَقَطَ مِنْ مُعَيْقِيبٍ فِي بِئْرِ أَرِيسٍ[110]

---

108 Al-'Ilal al-Kabīr of al-Bukhārī (287) who said this report [from Jābir through this chain] is not authentic.
109 Sunan al-Tirmidhī (1742) and Sunan Abū Dawūd (4229)
110 Sahīh Muslim (2091)

101. 'Abdullāh ibn 'Umar ﷺ related: "The Prophet ﷺ had a ring made of silver which had its gemstone facing his palm. He [ordered] the words, 'Muhammad is the Messenger of Allāh' to be engraved on it and prohibited people from putting the same inscription on their rings. This is the same ring that fell from the hands of Mu'ayqib ﷺ into the well of Arīs."

Abdul Razzaq al-Badr said,

> The Prophet ﷺ positioned its gemstone facing towards his palm so that it would not show, which indicates that the ring was for the purpose of stamping letters and not for adornment.
>
> This hadīth can be reconciled with the other hadīth where it stated that the ring fell from the hand of 'Uthmān ﷺ: It is possible that 'Uthmān gave Mu'ayqib ﷺ the ring to use and then when he wanted to give it back to 'Uthmān, it fell from his hand. This is why both were referred to as the one from whom the ring fell down.

Alī al-Qārī said,

> Al-Nawawī said that the reason for keeping the gemstone of the ring towards the palm was because that would protect the inscription and because keeping it away from the eye would prevent showing off and pride.

Al-Bajūrī said,

> The Prophet ﷺ prohibited people from making this inscription on their rings to avert confusion and corruption. However, al-Zain al-'Iraqī stated that this prohibition was only applicable during his life ﷺ.

١٠٢ : حَدَّثَنَا قتيبة بن سعيد أ حَدَّثَنَا حاتم بن إسماعيل أ عن جَعْفَرِ بن محمد

عن أبيه قَالَ : كان الحسن والحسين يتختمان في يسارهما[111]

102. Muhammad al-Baqir related: "Al-Hasan and al-Hussain ؓ wore their rings on their left hands."

Ibn Hajar al-Haytamī said,

> They wore their rings on the left hand to follow the example of the Prophet ﷺ who wore it on the left hand often. The reason the author included this hadīth though it opposes the title of the chapter is because he wanted to explain that such hadīths do not negate that wearing it on the right hand is better.

Abdul Razzaq al-Badr said,

> This shows that it is permissible to wear it on the left hand or the right hand.

١٠٣ : حَدَّثَنَا عَبْدُ اللهِ بْنُ عَبْدِ الرَّحْمَنِ ، قَالَ : حَدَّثَنَا مُحَمَّدُ بْنُ عِيسَى وَهُوَ ابْنُ الطَّبَّاعِ ، قَالَ : حَدَّثَنَا عَبَّادُ بْنُ الْعَوَّامِ ، عَنْ سَعِيدِ بْنِ أَبِي عَرُوبَةَ ، عَنْ قَتَادَةَ ، عَنْ أَنَسِ بْنِ مَالِكٍ : أَنَّهُ صلى الله عَليه وسلم كَانَ يَتَخَتَّمُ فِي يَمِينِهِ[112]

103. Anas ibn Mālik ؓ related: "The Prophet ﷺ wore a ring on his right hand."

١٠٤ : حَدَّثَنَا مُحَمَّدُ بْنُ عُبَيْدِ اللهِ الْمُحَارِبِيُّ ، قَالَ : حَدَّثَنَا عَبْدُ الْعَزِيزِ بْنُ أَبِي حَازِمٍ ، عَنْ مُوسَى بْنِ عُقْبَةَ ، عَنْ نَافِعٍ ، عَنِ ابْنِ عُمَرَ ، قَالَ : اتَّخَذَ رَسُولُ اللهِ صَلى الله عليه وسلم خَاتَمًا مِنْ ذَهَبٍ ، فَكَانَ يَلْبَسُهُ فِي يَمِينِهِ ، فَاتَّخَذَ النَّاسُ خَوَاتِيمَ مِنْ ذَهَبٍ فَطَرَحَهُ صلى الله عليه وسلم ، وَقَالَ : لا أَلْبَسُهُ

111 Sunan al-Tirmidhī (1743)
112 Sunan al-Nasā'ī (5204)

أَبدًا فَطَرَحَ النَّاسُ خَوَاتِيمَهُمْ[113]

104. 'Abdullāh ibn 'Umar ؓ related: "The Prophet ﷺ possessed a ring made of gold which he wore on his right hand. To follow the example of the Prophet ﷺ, the companions also had gold rings made for themselves. Upon seeing this, the Prophet ﷺ removed the gold ring and said, 'I will never wear it again.' Accordingly, the people removed their gold rings too."

Alī al-Qārī said,

> This hadīth refers to the period where gold was not yet made prohibited for men. The Prophet ﷺ removed the ring after it was revealed to him that gold was not allowed for men.

Al-Nawawī said,

> The scholars are in agreement that the Sunnah for men is to wear the ring on their pinkie fingers whilst women can wear the ring on the finger of their choosing.

Al-Bajūrī said,

> He ﷺ removed it because he saw that people showed off with their gold rings and it coincided that the revelation came down to make gold forbidden for men.

113 Sahīh al-Bukhārī (5865) and Sahīh Muslim (2091)

CHAPTER FOURTEEN

باب ماجاء في صفة سَيْفِ رَسُولِ اللّٰهِ صلى اللّٰه عليه وسلم

THE REPORTS PERTAINING TO THE DESCRIPTION OF THE SWORD OF ALLĀH'S MESSENGER ﷺ

Abdul Razzaq al-Badr said,

> This chapter and some subsequent chapters are dedicated to describing the weapons of the Prophet ﷺ that he used in battles and wars. There is a benefit that can be derived from the ordering of the chapters in that the author placed the chapter of the sword after the chapter of the ring. This ordering was deliberate and was to indicate that calling to Allāh using words comes before fighting with the sword. This is because the ring was used to stamp letters that were sent to disbelievers inviting them to Islām and so al-Tirmidhī placed it before the sword to show that preaching and advising people takes priority over calling them to Islām with the sword.

Al-Bajūrī said,

> The Prophet ﷺ had many swords; the first sword he ever had was

called "al-Ma'thūr" which he inherited from his father. The other swords he had were called: al-Qadīb, al-Qula'i, al-Battār, al-Hatif, al-Mikhdham, al-Rasūb, al-Samsām, al-Lahīf and Dhul-Fiqār.

Ibn Hajar al-Haytamī said,

> The reason why the author started with the sword as the first weapon is because it was the most frequently used and most effective during battles.

١٠٥ : حَدَّثَنَا مُحَمَّدُ بْنُ بَشَّارٍ ، قَالَ : حَدَّثَنَا وَهْبُ بْنُ جَرِيرٍ ، قَالَ : حَدَّثَنَا أَبِي ، عَنْ قَتَادَةَ ، عَنْ أَنَسٍ ، قَالَ : كَانَتْ قَبِيعَةُ سَيْفِ رَسُولِ الله صلى الله عليه وسلم مِنْ فِضَّةٍ[114]

105. Anas ibn Mālik ﷺ narrated: "The handle of the sword of the Messenger of Allāh ﷺ was made of silver."

Alī al-Qārī said,

> This hadīth proves that it is permissible to adorn the sword and any other weapon with silver. As for adorning them with gold, this is forbidden.

Al-Bajūrī said,

> The sword referred to in this hadīth is the sword Dhul-Fiqār, which is the sword that the Prophet ﷺ always carried and had when he conquered Makkah.

١٠٦ : حَدَّثَنَا مُحَمَّدُ بْنُ بَشَّارٍ ، قَالَ : حَدَّثَنَا مُعَاذُ بْنُ هِشَامٍ ، قَالَ : حَدَّثَنِي أَبِي ، عَنْ قَتَادَةَ ، عَنْ سَعِيدِ بْنِ أَبِي الْحَسَنِ ، قَالَ : كَانَتْ قَبِيعَةُ سَيْفِ رَسُولِ

114 Sunan al-Tirmidhī (1691) and Sunan Abū Dawūd (2583)

اللهِ صلى الله عليه وسلم مِنْ فِضَّةٍ[115]

106. Sa'īd ibn Abil Hasan related: "The handle of the sword of the Prophet ﷺ was made of silver."

١٠٧: حَدَّثَنَا أَبُو جَعْفَرٍ مُحَمَّدُ بْنُ صُدْرَانَ الْبَصْرِيُّ، قَالَ: حَدَّثَنَا طَالِبُ بْنُ حُجَيْرٍ، عَنْ هُودٍ وَهُوَ ابْنُ عَبْدِ اللهِ بْنِ سَعْدٍ، عَنْ جَدِّهِ، قَالَ: دَخَلَ رَسُولُ اللهِ صلى الله عليه وسلم مَكَّةَ يَوْمَ الْفَتْحِ وَعَلَى سَيْفِهِ ذَهَبٌ، وَفِضَّةٌ، قَالَ طَالِبٌ: فَسَأَلْتُهُ عَنِ الْفِضَّةِ، فَقَالَ: كَانَتْ قَبِيعَةُ السَّيْفِ فِضَّةً[116]

107. The grandfather of Hūd ibn 'Abdullāh ibn Sa'd narrated: "When the Prophet ﷺ entered Makkah on the day it was conquered, his sword was adorned with gold and silver. Tālib (who is one of the narrators of this hadīth) asked Hūd, 'On which part of the sword was the silver?' He replied, 'The handle was made of silver.'"

Al-Bajūrī said,

> This hadīth is weak insofar as al-Qattan ruled it as a *munkar* hadīth. Hence, it cannot be used as evidence to allow adorning the weapons with gold.

Ibn Hajar al-Haytamī said,

> This *hadīth* does not contradict the ruling of prohibition regarding adorning weapons with gold because it is weak. It is incorrect to claim that the incident mentioned in this hadīth was before gold was made forbidden because this ruling occurred before the conquest of Makkah, as has been reported.

---

115 Sunan Abū Dawūd (2584)
116 Sunan Abū Dawūd (1690)

١٠٨ : حَدَّثَنَا محمد بن شجاع البغدادى حَدَّثَنَا أبو عبيدة الحداد عن عثمان بن سعد عن ابن سيرين قال : صنعت سيفي على سيف سمرة بن جندب وزعم سمرة أنه صنع سَيْفِه على سيف رَسُولِ اللهِ صلى الله عليه وسلم : وكان حنيفيا[117]

108. Ibn Sirīn narrated: "I based [the design of] my sword upon the sword of Samurah ibn Jundub ﷺ because he said that he had his sword made like the sword of the Prophet ﷺ. The sword was the type used by the tribe of Banī Hanīfah."

Abdul Razzaq al-Badr said,

> The last part could be from the words of Ibn Sirīn or Samurah and the sword was described as such because the tribe of Banī Hanīfah was known for making exceptional swords or because the one who made the sword was from the tribe of Banī Hanīfah.

١٠٩ : حدثنا عقبة بن مكرم البصري قال : حدثنا محمد بن بكر عن عثمان بن سعد بهذا الإسناد نحوه .

109. 'Uthmān ibn Sa'd reports the same.

117 Sunan al-Tirmidhī (1683)

CHAPTER FIFTEEN

باب ماجاء في صفة درع رَسُولِ اللّٰه صلى اللّٰه عليه وسلم

THE REPORTS PERTAINING TO THE DESCRIPTION OF THE ARMOUR OF THE MESSENGER ﷺ

Ibn al-Qayyim said,

> The Prophet ﷺ had seven suits of armour, the names of which are: Dhat al-Fudūl, which is the armour that he pawned for a year with a Jewish man for thirty *sā'* (a cubic measure) of barley and it was made of iron, Dhat al-Wishāh, Dhat al-Hawāshi, al-Su'diyyah, Fiddah, al-Batrā' and al-Khirnaq.

Al-Bajūrī said,

> This chapter is dedicated to describing the way the Prophet ﷺ used to wear his armour, rather than describing the suits of armour.

١١٠ : حَدَّثَنَا أَبُو سَعِيدٍ عَبْدُ اللهِ بْنُ سَعِيدٍ الأَشَجُّ ، قَالَ : حَدَّثَنَا يُونُسُ بْنُ بُكَيْرٍ ، عَنْ مُحَمَّدِ بْنِ إِسْحَاقَ ، عَنْ يَحْيَى بْنِ عَبَّادِ بْنِ عَبْدِ اللهِ بْنِ الزُّبَيْرِ ، عَنْ أَبِيهِ ، عَنْ جَدِّهِ عَبْدِ اللهِ بْنِ الزُّبَيْرِ ، عَنِ الزُّبَيْرِ بْنِ الْعَوَّامِ ، قَالَ : كَانَ عَلَى النَّبِيِّ صلى الله عليه وَسلم يَوْمَ أُحُدٍ دِرْعَانِ ، فَنَهَضَ إِلَى الصَّخْرَةِ فَلَمْ يَسْتَطِعْ ، فَأَقْعَدَ طَلْحَةَ تَحْتَهُ ، وَصَعِدَ النَّبِيُّ صلى الله عليه وسلم حَتَّى اسْتَوَى عَلَى الصَّخْرَةِ ، قَالَ : سَمِعْتُ النَّبِيَّ صلى الله عليه وسلم ، يَقُولُ : أَوْجَبَ طَلْحَةُ[118]

110. Al-Zubair ibn Al-'Awwām ﷻ related: "The Messenger of Allāh ﷺ wore two suits of armour during the Battle of Uhud. He tried to climb a rock but he could not do so. Thus, he requested Talhah ﷻ to sit and, with his aid, climbed the rock until he rose on it." Al-Zubair ﷻ said, "I heard the Prophet ﷺ then say, 'Talhah has necessitated Paradise for himself.'"

Abdul Razzaq al-Badr said,

> The two suits of armour that he ﷺ wore on that day were Dhat al-Fudūl and Fiddah. The scholars concluded that the reality of reliance on Allāh lies in the heart and that a person is required to take the means [of protecting oneself] whilst the heart is fully dependent on the Causer and not the causes.

Al-Bajūrī said,

> The Prophet ﷺ wanted to climb the rock so that his army could see that he was still alive and gather around him[119].

Ibn Hajar al-Haytamī said,

---

118 Sunan al-Tirmidhī (1692)

119 [Translator's Note] This was due to a rumour spreading during the battle that he had been martyred, causing confusion amongst the Muslim army.

> He ﷺ could not climb the rock because of the two suits of armour weighing him down. This (their thickness and weight) indicates how well made they were as it serves the ultimate purpose of wearing a suit of armour i.e. protection. This part [of the hadīth] provides a description of the suit of armour. However, some said that he could not climb the rock because of the wound he received on his noble head which resulted in losing a lot of blood.

Alī al-Qārī said,

> Talhah ؓ deserved Paradise because he sacrificed his life for the sake of the Prophet ﷺ as he kept protecting his body from arrows with his hand until his hand became paralysed and the rest of his body was wounded.

١١١ : حَدَّثَنَا مُحَمَّدُ بْنُ أَبِي عُمَرَ ، قَالَ : حَدَّثَنَا سُفْيَانُ بْنُ عُيَيْنَةَ ، عَنْ يَزِيدَ بْنِ خُصَيْفَةَ ، عَنِ السَّائِبِ بْنِ يَزِيدَ ، أَنَّ رَسُولَ اللهِ صلى الله عليه وسلم ، كَانَ عَلَيْهِ يَوْمَ أُحُدٍ دِرْعَانِ ، قَدْ ظَاهَرَ بَيْنَهُمَا[120]

111. Al-Sāib ibn Yazīd ؓ narrated: "In the Battle of Uhud the Messenger of Allāh ﷺ wore two suits of armour. He wore them one over the other."

Abdul Razzaq al-Badr said,

> Al-Sāib ibn Yazīd was the last companion who died in al-Madīnah; he died on 91 H.

Al-Bajūrī said,

> His wearing of two suits of armour indicates that reliance on Allāh should be accompanied by taking the means of protection.

---

120 Sunan Ibn Majah (2806)

CHAPTER SIXTEEN

باب ما جاء في صفة مغفر رسول الله صلى الله عليه وسلم

THE REPORTS PERTAINING TO THE DESCRIPTION OF THE MAIL COIF OF ALLĀH'S MESSENGER ﷺ

Al-Bajūrī said,

> The mail coif is a flexible type of armour made of interlinked metal rings that is made to fit the size of the head and worn underneath the turban. It is considered to be from his weapons because a weapon refers to that which is used to fight and that which is used for protection.

١١٢ : حَدَّثَنَا قُتَيْبَةُ بْنُ سَعِيدٍ ، قَالَ : حَدَّثَنَا مَالِكُ بْنُ أَنَسٍ ، عَنِ ابْنِ شِهَابٍ ، عَنْ أَنَسِ بْنِ مَالِكٍ : أَنَّ النَّبِيَّ صلى الله عليه وسلم دَخَلَ مَكَّةَ وَعَلَيْهِ مِغْفَرٌ ، فَقِيلَ لَهُ : هَذَا ابْنُ خَطَلٍ مُتَعَلِّقٌ بِأَسْتَارِ الْكَعْبَةِ ، فَقَالَ : اقْتُلُوهُ[121]

112. Anas ibn Mālik ﷺ reported: "The Prophet ﷺ was wearing a mail coif when he entered Makkah. Someone came to him and said, 'O Messenger of Allāh, Ibn Khatal is holding the cover (black cloth) of the Ka'bah.' The Prophet ﷺ replied, 'Kill him.'"

Abdul Razzaq al-Badr said,

> Ibn Khatal was one of those who the Prophet ﷺ ordered to kill wherever and whenever he was found. This was because he embraced Islām and had a Muslim servant but afterwards apostated, killed the servant and started to defame the Prophet with foul language in his poetry and employed two female singers to sing his foul poetry against the Prophet and his companions.

Al-Bajūrī said,

> Ibn Khatal was holding the cover of the Ka'bah because it was the habit of the Arabs before Islām to give refuge to anyone who did this, regardless of their crimes.

Ibn Hajar al-Haytamī said,

> It is reported in Sahīh Muslim that the Prophet ﷺ said, "It is unlawful for anyone to carry a weapon in Makkah."[122] This appears contradictory to the incident narrated in this hadīth. However, there is no contradiction because it is proven authentic that Allāh made it lawful for the Prophet ﷺ to fight for one hour of a day in

121 Sahīh al-Bukhārī (3044) and Sahīh Muslim (1357)
122 Sahih Muslim (1356)

Makkah[123]

Alī al-Qārī said,

> There are four persons that the Prophet ﷺ ordered to be killed whenever and wherever they were found: al-Huwairith ibn Nuqayd, Hilal ibn Khatal, Maqīs ibn Subabah and 'Abdullāh ibn Abī Sarh. The companion who killed Ibn Khatal is reported to be Sa'īd ibn Huraith but it was reported in a more authentic hadīth that the one who killed him was Abū Barzah al-Aslamī.

١١٣: حَدَّثَنَا عِيسَى بْنُ أَحْمَدَ ، قَالَ : حَدَّثَنَا عَبْدُ اللهِ بْنُ وَهْبٍ ، قَالَ : حَدَّثَنِي مَالِكُ بْنُ أَنَسٍ ، عَنِ ابْنِ شِهَابٍ ، عَنْ أَنَسِ بْنِ مَالِكٍ ، أَنَّ رَسُولَ اللهِ صلى الله عليه وسلم ، دَخَلَ مَكَّةَ عَامَ الْفَتْحِ ، وَعَلَى رَأْسِهِ الْمِغْفَرُ ، قَالَ : فَلَمَّا نَزَعَهُ جَاءَهُ رَجُلٌ ، فَقَالَ لَهُ : ابْنُ خَطَلٍ مُتَعَلِّقٌ بِأَسْتَارِ الْكَعْبَةِ ، فَقَالَ : اقْتُلُوهُ ، قَالَ ابْنُ شِهَابٍ : وَبَلَغَنِي أَنَّ رَسُولَ اللهِ صلى الله عليه وسلم ، لَمْ يَكُنْ يَوْمَئِذٍ مُحْرِمًا[124]

113. Anas ibn Mālik ﷺ narrated: "The Prophet ﷺ wore a mail coif on his head when he entered Makkah as a conqueror. After he removed it, a person came and said, 'O Messenger of Allāh, Ibn Khatal is clinging to the cover of the Ka'bah.' The Prophet ﷺ replied, 'Kill him.'"

---

123 Al-Hafith Ibn Hajar said in Fathul Barī commenting on this hadith (no. 1737) "Al-Mawardi said, 'From the exclusive qualities of Makkah is that it is not allowed to fight its inhabitants. If they transgress and rebel against the Muslims, if their evil can be stopped without fighting then it is not allowed to fight them, and if fighting is the only solution then the majority said it is allowed because fighting the rebellious is from the rights of Allāh and cannot be overlooked whilst others said that they should be pressured until they become obedient again.'"

124 Muwatta Mālik (1271) – See hadīth 112

Ibn Shihāb (the one narrating from Anas) said, "I have been informed that the Prophet ﷺ was not in the state of *ihram* on that day."

Abdul Razzaq al-Badr said,

> The statement of Ibn Shihāb al-Zuhrī indicates that if a person is entering Makkah without intending to enter the state of *ihram*, then he is not required to wear the clothes of *ihram* as this is only required for the one who wants to perform 'Umrah or Hajj.

CHAPTER SEVENTEEN

باب ما جاء في عمامة رسول الله صلى الله عليه وسلم

THE REPORTS PERTAINING TO THE HEADDRESS OF THE MESSENGER OF ALLĀH ﷺ

Ibn Hajar al-Haytamī said,

> The Prophet ﷺ had a turban called "al-Sahāb" that he used to wear underneath a head cap.

Ibn al-Qayyim said,

> The size of the turban of the Prophet ﷺ was neither too large so as to make it a burden on the head nor too small so that it could not protect the head from heat and cold. Rather, it was moderate in size and indeed the best of things are those that are moderate and balanced.

Al-Bajūrī said,

> The headdress refers to the clothing of the head and it includes the turban, the head cap, and the mail coif etc. However, in this

chapter it excludes the mail coif as it has been addressed in the previous one.

١١٤ : حَدَّثَنَا مُحَمَّدُ بْنُ بَشَّارٍ ، قَالَ : حَدَّثَنَا عَبْدُ الرَّحْمَنِ بْنُ مَهْدِيٍّ ، عَنْ حَمَّادِ بْنِ سَلَمَةَ (ح) حَدَّثَنَا مَحْمُودُ بْنُ غَيْلانَ ، قَالَ : حَدَّثَنَا وَكِيعٌ ، عَنْ حَمَّادِ بْنِ سَلَمَةَ ، عَنْ أَبِي الزُّبَيْرِ ، عَنْ جَابِرٍ ، قَالَ : دَخَلَ النَّبِيُّ صلى الله عليه وسلم ، مَكَّةَ يَوْمَ الْفَتْحِ ، وَعَلَيْهِ عِمَامَةٌ سَوْدَاءُ[125]

114. Jābir ibn 'Abdullāh ﷺ narrated: "When Makkah was conquered, the Messenger of Allāh ﷺ entered the city wearing a black turban."

Abdul Razzaq al-Badr said,

> It was mentioned in the preceding chapter that he ﷺ was wearing a mail coif on his head whereas this hadīth mentions that he was wearing a black turban. There is no contradiction between the two hadīths as it is possible that he wore the mail coif underneath the turban or that he removed the mail coif and then wore the black turban to deliver his speech.

Al-Bajūrī said,

> The reason why he ﷺ preferred the black turban over the white colour (though the latter is a praised colour) on that day was because the black colour indicates that Islām has prevailed and that Islām does not change, similar to how the colour black does not change to another colour.

١١٥ : حَدَّثَنَا ابْنُ أَبِي عُمَرَ ، قَالَ : حَدَّثَنَا سُفْيَانُ ، عَنْ مُسَاوِرٍ الْوَرَّاقِ ، عَنْ جَعْفَرِ بْنِ عَمْرِو بْنِ حُرَيْثٍ ، عَنْ أَبِيهِ ، قَالَ : رَأَيْتُ النَّبِيَّ صلى الله عليه

125 Sahīh Muslim (1358)

وسلم يَخْطُبُ عَلَى الْمِنْبَرِ ، وَعَلَيْهِ عِمَامَةٌ سَوْدَاءُ[126]

115. Amr ibn Huraith ؓ narrated: "I once saw a black turban upon the head of the Messenger of Allāh ﷺ."

١١٦ : حَدَّثَنَا مَحْمُودُ بْنُ غَيْلَانَ ، وَيُوسُفُ بْنُ عِيسَى ، قَالا : حَدَّثَنَا وَكِيعٌ ، عَنْ مُسَاوِرٍ الْوَرَّاقِ ، عَنْ جَعْفَرِ بْنِ عَمْرِو بْنِ حُرَيْثٍ ، عَنْ أَبِيهِ ، أَنَّ النَّبِيَّ صلى الله عليه وسلم ، خَطَبَ النَّاسَ ، وَعَلَيْهِ عِمَامَةٌ سَوْدَاءُ[127]

116. Amr ibn Huraith ؓ narrated: "I had seen the Messenger of Allāh ﷺ address the people from the pulpit whilst wearing a black turban."

Alī al-Qārī said,

> This hadīth proves that he ﷺ wore a black turban more than once because there was no pulpit when he gave his speech in Makkah as he gave it while standing in front of the gate of the Ka'bah. The author of al-Masabīh included this hadīth under the chapter of "Friday Khutbah".

Al-Nawawī said,

> It is permissible to wear black clothing when delivering the Khutbah on Friday but wearing white clothing is better.

١١٧ : حَدَّثَنَا هَارُونُ بْنُ إِسْحَاقَ الْهَمْدَانِيُّ ، قَالَ : حَدَّثَنَا يَحْيَى بْنُ مُحَمَّدٍ الْمَدَنِيُّ ، عَنْ عَبْدِ الْعَزِيزِ بْنِ مُحَمَّدٍ ، عَنْ عُبَيْدِ اللهِ بْنِ عُمَرَ ، عَنْ نَافِعٍ ، عَنِ ابْنِ عُمَرَ ، قَالَ : كَانَ النَّبِيُّ صلى الله عليه وسلم ، إِذَا اعْتَمَّ ، سَدَلَ عِمَامَتَهُ

---

126 Sahīh Muslim (1359)
127 Ibid.

بَيْنَ كَتِفَيْهِ .
قَالَ نَافِعٌ : وَكَانَ ابْنُ عُمَرَ ، يَفْعَلُ ذَلِكَ .
قَالَ عُبَيْدُ اللهِ : وَرَأَيْتُ الْقَاسِمَ بْنَ مُحَمَّدٍ ، وَسَالِمًا يَفْعَلانِ ذَلِكَ[128]

117. 'Abdullāh ibn 'Umar ﵁ reported: "Whenever Allāh's Messenger ﷺ wrapped his turban around his head, he made its loose end in the form of a tail that he hung down between his shoulders."

Nafi says, "I saw 'Abdullāh ibn Umar ﵁ do it in the same manner."

Ubaidullah, the student of Nafi, said, "In my time, al-Qasim ibn Muhammad and Salim did the same."

Abdul Razzaq al-Badr said,

> He ﷺ used to keep the loose end of the turban hanging down between his shoulders, behind his back.

Al-Bajūrī said,

> It can be concluded from this hadīth that wrapping the turban while leaving its loose end hanging down is recommended, and to have it hang down on the back between the shoulders is the best. However, if the tail was left to hang down on the front as Sufis and some people of knowledge do, it is debatable whether it is better to keep it hanging down from the left side or the right side. This is because there is a weak hadīth specifying that it should hang to the right side and the Sufis preferred the left side because it is the side where the heart is located (leaving it to hang on the left side is to remind them to keep the heart empty of everything but Allāh).

Ibn Hajar al-Haytamī said,

> He ﷺ made the tail of the turban of Abdul Rahman ibn 'Awf ﵁ to fall in front of him.

128 Sunan al-Tirmidhī (1736)

Abū 'Abdullāh ibn al-Hāj said,

> It is a surprise that some late scholars considered leaving the tail hanging down to the front an innovation while there are explicit authentic hadīths citing that the early *salaf* did this.

١١٨ : حَدَّثَنَا يُوسُفُ بْنُ عِيسَى ، قَالَ : حَدَّثَنَا وَكِيعٌ ، قَالَ : حَدَّثَنَا أَبُو سُلَيْمَانَ وَهُوَ عَبْدُ الرَّحْمَنِ بْنُ الْغَسِيلِ ، عَنْ عِكْرِمَةَ ، عَنِ ابْنِ عَبَّاسٍ : أَنَّ النَّبِيَّ صلى الله عليه وسلم خَطَبَ النَّاسَ ، وَعَلَيْهِ عِصَابَةٌ دَسْمَاءُ[129]

118. 'Abdullāh ibn Abbās reported: "The Prophet ﷺ was once delivering a sermon whilst wearing an oily headdress."

Abdul Razzaq al-Badr said,

> There are no authentic hadīths from the Prophet ﷺ regarding the virtue of wearing a turban. The only authentic hadīths mention him wearing turbans. Thus, a person should not oblige people to wear a particular dress. This is because a person should wear the normal clothes that are known in their society so long as the clothes are not unlawful to wear. A person should not wear that which makes him stand out because the Prophet ﷺ forbade people from wearing what would make an individual known or famous amongst people.

Ibn Hajar al-Haytamī said,

> This sermon was delivered whilst he was afflicted with the sickness of which he died.

Alī al-Qārī said,

> Al-Haytamī in his commentary concerning the reason why the Prophet ﷺ preferred to keep the tail of his turban hang down

---

129 Sahīh al-Bukhārī (927)

behind his back, between his shoulders condemned and defamed Ibn al-Qayyim and Ibn Taymiyyah and accused them of advocating anthropomorphism! However, whoever reads the explanation of Manazil al-Sa'irīn will come to know that they (Ibn Taymiyyah and Ibn al-Qayyim) are from the esteemed major scholars of Ahlu al-Sunnah wal-Jama'ah and from the pious ones of this nation. Shaykh al-Islām, 'Abdullāh al-Ansārī al-Hanbalī explains the great status and merits of Ibn Taymiyyah and that he is innocent from the accusations made by his enemies that he was an advocate of anthropomorphism but it is the habit of the enemies of the people of hadīth and Sunnah to falsely accuse... These accusations are the heritage that those deviated people received from the enemies of the Messenger of Allāh ﷺ who called the Prophet and his companions apostates and claimed that they invented a new religion!

CHAPTER EIGHTEEN

باب ما جاء في صفة إزار رسول الله صلى الله عليه وسلم

THE REPORTS PERTAINING TO THE IZĀR OF THE MESSENGER OF ALLĀH ﷺ

Abdul Razzaq al-Badr said,

> The *izār* refers to the voluminous garment that is wrapped around the lower part of the body.

Al-Bajūrī said,

> The title also refers to the *ridā'*, which is the garment that covers the upper part of the body. This is similar to the use of the ayah: **{And has made for you garments which protect you from the heat}**[130] which actually refers to the cold too.

130 Qur'ān: 16:81

١١٩ : حَدَّثَنَا أَحْمَدُ بْنُ مَنِيعٍ ، قَالَ : حَدَّثَنَا إِسْمَاعِيلُ بْنُ إِبْرَاهِيمَ ، قَالَ : حَدَّثَنَا أَيُّوبُ ، عَنْ حُمَيْدِ بْنِ هِلالٍ ، عَنْ أَبِي بُرْدَةَ ، قَالَ : أَخْرَجَتْ إِلَيْنَا عَائِشَةُ ، كِسَاءً مُلَبَّدًا ، وَإِزَارًا غَلِيظًا ، فَقَالَتْ : قُبِضَ رُوحُ رَسُولِ اللهِ صلى الله عليه وسلم ، فِي هَذَيْنِ[131]

119. Abū Mūsa al-Ash'arī narrated: "Aisha showed us a patched garment that is worn to cover the upper part, and a coarse *izār*. She then said, 'The Messenger of Allāh ﷺ passed away whilst wearing these two garments.'"

Abdul Razzaq al-Badr said,

> The meaning of this hadīth is that he ﷺ passed away while he had these garments to wear.

Al-Bajūrī said,

> The reason Aisha kept the two garments of the Prophet ﷺ was to seek blessing from his clothes. She also kept his jubbah (loose outer robe) and after she passed away, her sister Asmā' took it and kept it.

Ibn Hajar al-Haytamī said,

> The Prophet ﷺ wore these rough clothes despite the fact he conquered many lands, subdued his enemies and had all the treasures before his hand. This is because he never cared about worldly pleasures and favoured the pleasures found in the Hereafter, and because he ﷺ wanted his nation to follow the example of his lifestyle, especially when they are old.

١٢٠ : حَدَّثَنَا مَحْمُودُ بْنُ غَيْلانَ ، قَالَ : حَدَّثَنَا أَبُو دَاوُدَ ، عَنْ شُعْبَةَ ، عَنِ

131 Sahīh al-Bukhārī (3108) and Sahīh Muslim (2080)

الأَشْعَثِ بْنِ سُلَيْمٍ ، قَالَ : سَمِعْتُ عَمَّتِي ، تُحَدِّثُ عَنْ عَمِّهَا ، قَالَ : بَيْنَا أَنَا أَمْشِي بِالْمَدِينَةِ ، إِذَا إِنْسَانٌ خَلْفِي يَقُولُ : ارْفَعْ إِزَارَكَ ، فَإِنَّهُ أَتْقَى وَأَبْقَى فَإِذَا هُوَ رَسُولُ اللهِ صلى الله عليه وسلم ، فَقُلْتُ : يَا رَسُولَ اللهِ إِنَّمَا هِيَ بُرْدَةٌ مَلْحَاءُ ، قَالَ : أَمَا لَكَ فِيَّ أُسْوَةٌ ؟ فَنَظَرْتُ فَإِذَا إِزَارُهُ إِلَى نِصْفِ سَاقَيْهِ[132]

120. Ubayd bin Khālid ؓ narrated: "I was once walking in Madīnah and I then heard a person from behind me say, 'Lift your *izār* higher for that shows more piety and makes it last longer.' When I turned to see who this was, I saw that it was the Messenger of Allāh ﷺ. I said, 'O Messenger of Allāh! This is a black garment with white patterns!' He replied, 'Are you not taking me as your example?' I looked at him and I saw that his *izār* reached until the halfway point of his shins."

Alī al-Qārī said,

> Lifting the garment up [above the ankles] negates the arrogance and showing off that a long garment [hanging below the ankles] entails, and so one follows the order of Allāh ﷻ. This is why the Prophet ﷺ said it shows more piety.

Abdul Razzaq al-Badr said,

> The reason why the companion ؓ stated the description of the wrap was to say that this kind of clothing cannot be used to show off or make one arrogant even if it reached below the ankle due to its simplicity.

Al-Bajūrī said,

> The guidance of the Prophet ﷺ in respect to lifting the garment above the ankle applies to all types of clothes. This ruling is only applicable to men because it is recommended for women to let one inch of her clothes drag on the floor.

---

132 Musnad Ahmad (23086)

Ibn Hajar al-Haytamī said,

> This hadīth shows us that a person should look after their clothes so that they do not become worn out as that will make one waste his money.

١٢١ : حَدَّثَنَا سُوَيْدُ بْنُ نَصْرٍ ، قَالَ : حَدَّثَنَا عَبْدُ اللهِ بْنُ الْمُبَارَكِ ، عَنْ مُوسَى بْنِ عُبَيْدَةَ ، عَنْ إِيَاسِ بْنِ سَلَمَةَ بْنِ الأَكْوَعِ ، عَنْ أَبِيهِ ، قَالَ : كَانَ عُثْمَانُ بْنُ عَفَّانَ ، يَأْتَزِرُ إِلَى أَنْصَافِ سَاقَيْهِ ، وَقَالَ : هَكَذَا كَانَتْ إِزْرَةُ صَاحِبِي ، يَعْنِي النَّبِيَّ صلى الله عليه وسلم[133]

121. Salamah ibn al-Akwa' ﷺ narrated: "The *izār* of 'Uthmān ibn 'Affān ﷺ would fall to the middle of his shins. 'Uthmān said, 'This is how my companion, the Messenger of Allāh ﷺ wore his *izār*.'"

١٢٢ : حَدَّثَنَا قُتَيْبَةُ بْنُ سَعِيدٍ ، قَالَ : حَدَّثَنَا أَبُو الأَحْوَصِ ، عَنْ أَبِي إِسْحَاقَ ، عَنْ مُسْلِمِ بْنِ نَذِيرٍ ، عَنْ حُذَيْفَةَ بْنِ الْيَمَانِ ، قَالَ : أَخَذَ رَسُولُ اللهِ صلى الله عليه وسلم ، بِعَضَلَةِ سَاقِي أَوْ سَاقِهِ ، فَقَالَ : هَذَا مَوْضِعُ الإِزَارِ ، فَإِنْ أَبَيْتَ فَأَسْفَلَ ، فَإِنْ أَبَيْتَ فَلا حَقَّ لِلإِزَارِ فِي الْكَعْبَيْنِ[134]

122. Hudhaifah ibn al-Yamān ﷺ reported: "The Messenger of Allāh ﷺ caught the shin of my leg (the narrator doubted whether he heard it was his leg or the companion's leg) and said, 'This is where the *izār* should reach, and if not, then slightly lower, and if not, then it has no right to reach the ankles.'"

Al-Bajūrī said,

> The last part of the hadīth illustrates that one should be very

133 Musannaf ibn Abī Shaybah (24240)
134 Sunan Ibn Mājah (3572)

cautious in ensuring that the *izār* does not even reach the ankle.

Ibn Hajar al-Haytamī said,

> The ruling on the length of clothes after considering all the hadīths is that the Sunnah is to keep it to the halfway-point of the shin, and that it is lawful to let it reach to the ankle, and that it is disliked to let it reach below the ankle if no showing off is intended, otherwise it would be forbidden.

CHAPTER NINETEEN

باب ما جاء في مشية رسول الله صلى الله عليه وسلم

THE REPORTS PERTAINING TO THE WALKING OF ALLĀH'S MESSENGER ﷺ

Abdul Razzaq al-Badr said,

> The walking of the Prophet ﷺ was in compliance with the guidance of the ayah: **{And be moderate in your pace...}**[135]

135 Qur'ān: 31:19

١٢٣ : حَدَّثَنَا قُتَيْبَةُ بْنُ سَعِيدٍ ، قَالَ : حَدَّثَنَا ابْنُ لَهِيعَةَ ، عَنْ أَبِي يُونُسَ ، عَنْ أَبِي هُرَيْرَةَ ، قَالَ : وَلا رَأَيْتُ شَيْئًا أَحْسَنَ مِنْ رَسُولِ الله صلى الله عليه وسلم كَأَنَّ الشَّمْسَ تَجْرِي فِي وَجْهِهِ ، وَمَا رَأَيْتُ أَحَدًا أَسْرَعَ فِي مِشْيَتِهِ مِنْ رَسُولِ الله صلى الله عليه وسلم كَأَنَّمَا الأَرْضُ تُطْوَى لَهُ إِنَّا لَنُجْهِدُ أَنْفُسَنَا وَإِنَّهُ لَغَيْرُ مُكْتَرِثٍ[136]

123. Abū Hurairah ؓ narrated: "I have not seen anything more handsome than the Messenger of Allāh ﷺ. It was as if the brightness of the sun shone from his face. I have not seen anyone walk faster than him. It was as if the earth would fold up for him; we found it difficult to keep up the pace when we walked with him, yet he walked at his normal pace."

Abdul Razzaq al-Badr said,

> Abū Hurairah ؓ intentionally used the word "anything" to include everything, meaning that his beauty excelled the beauty of everything that a person can see such as the sun, nature, the moon, and anything that is described as beautiful.
>
> The fast pace indicates that he possessed strong stamina.

Al-Bajūrī said,

> The reason that Abū Hurairah ؓ referred to the face only to explain the beauty of the Prophet ﷺ is because the face is the focal point of a person's beauty and often the body conforms to the status of the face.

Ibn Hajar al-Haytamī said,

> Despite his fast pace, he walked in a manner that maintained his respect and status; hence his pace was moderate [for him].

---

136 Sunan al-Tirmidhī (3648)

١٢٤ : حَدَّثَنَا عَلِيُّ بْنُ حُجْرٍ ، وَغَيْرُ وَاحِدٍ ، قَالُوا : حَدَّثَنَا عِيسَى بْنُ يُونُسَ ، عَنْ عُمَرَ بْنِ عَبْدِ اللهِ مَوْلَى غُفْرَةَ ، قَالَ : أَخْبَرَنِي إِبْرَاهِيمُ بْنُ مُحَمَّدٍ مِنْ وَلَدِ عَلِيِّ بْنِ أَبِي طَالِبٍ ، قَالَ : كَانَ عَلِيٌّ إِذَا وَصَفَ النَّبِيَّ صلى الله عليه وسلم ، قَالَ : كَانَ إِذَا مَشَى تَقَلَّعَ كَأَنَّمَا يَنْحَطُّ مِنْ صَبَبٍ[137]

124. Alī ibn Abī Tālib ﵁ used to describe the Messenger of Allāh ﷺ, saying: "When he walked, he lifted his legs with vigour; it seemed as if he was descending from a higher place."

Al-Bajūrī said,

> He ﷺ lifted his legs with vigour and did not lift them in an arrogant manner or slowly as that is the way women walk.

١٢٥ : حَدَّثَنَا سُفْيَانُ بْنُ وَكِيعٍ ، قَالَ : حَدَّثَنَا أَبِي ، عَنِ الْمَسْعُودِيِّ ، عَنْ عُثْمَانَ بْنِ مُسْلِمِ بْنِ هُرْمُزَ ، عَنْ نَافِعِ بْنِ جُبَيْرِ بْنِ مُطْعِمٍ ، عَنْ عَلِيِّ بْنِ أَبِي طَالِبٍ ، قَالَ : كَانَ النَّبِيُّ صلى الله عليه وسلم إِذَا مَشَى ، تَكَفَّأَ تَكَفُّؤًا ، كَأَنَّمَا يَنْحَطُّ مِنْ صَبَبٍ[138]

125. Alī ibn Abī Tālib ﵁ narrated: "When the Messenger of Allāh ﷺ walked, he bent forward slightly as if he was descending from a high place."

Alī al-Qārī said,

> This is to show that he did not drag his feet on the ground or walk in an arrogant manner.

137 See hadīth 7
138 See hadīth 5 and 6

CHAPTER TWENTY

باب ما جاء في تقنع رسول الله صلى الله عليه وسلم

THE REPORTS PERTAINING TO THE HEAD-COVER OF THE MESSENGER OF ALLĀH ﷺ

Abdul Razzaq al-Badr said,

> The head-cover referred to here is a cloth that is put over the head to protect the turban from the stains of oil.

Al-Bajūrī said,

> The head-cover (Arabic: *qinā'*) refers, in its broader meaning, to the sheet that a person places upon the turban and which partially covers the face. However in the context of this chapter, it refers to the cloth worn underneath the turban to protect it from the stains of oil or the heat.

١٢٦ : حَدَّثَنَا يُوسُفُ بْنُ عِيسَى ، قَالَ : حَدَّثَنَا وَكِيعٌ ، قَالَ : حَدَّثَنَا الرَّبِيعُ بْنُ صَبِيحٍ ، عَنْ يَزِيدَ بْنِ أَبَانَ ، عَنْ أَنَسِ بْنِ مَالِكٍ ، قَالَ : كَانَ رَسُولُ اللهِ صلى الله عليه وسلم يُكْثِرُ الْقِنَاعَ ، كَأَنَّ ثَوْبَهُ ثَوْبُ زَيَّاتٍ[139]

126. Anas ibn Mālik ﷺ narrated: "Allāh's Messenger ﷺ often wore a cloth on his head. This cloth, because of its greasiness, looked as if it had been oiled."

Al-Bajūrī said,

> The benefits of covering the turban with a sheet so that it covers most of the face are many, some of them are: it is a sign of one's shyness and fear of Allāh because it is the habit of the fearful to hide and cover themselves, it helps the heart to be more attentive to Allāh and not distracted by the surroundings, it gives the person [the opportunity] to have a minor solitude, as some Sufis have said.

139 See hadīth 33

CHAPTER TWENTY ONE

باب ما جاء في جلسته صلى الله عليه وسلم

THE REPORTS PERTAINING TO THE SITTING OF THE MESSENGER ﷺ

Abdul Razzaq al-Badr said,

> This chapter is dedicated to describing the manner in which the Prophet ﷺ used to sit.

١٢٧ : حَدَّثَنَا عَبْدُ بْنُ حُمَيْدٍ ، قَالَ : حَدَّثَنَا عَفَّانُ بْنُ مُسْلِمٍ ، قَالَ : حَدَّثَنَا عَبْدُ اللهِ بْنُ حَسَّانَ ، عَنْ ، جَدَّتَيْهِ ، عَنْ قَيْلَةَ بِنْتِ مَخْرَمَةَ ، أَنَّهَا رَأَتْ رَسُولَ اللهِ صلى الله عليه وسلم فِي الْمَسْجِدِ ، وَهُوَ قَاعِدٌ الْقُرْفُصَاءَ ، قَالَتْ : فَلَمَّا رَأَيْتُ رَسُولَ اللهِ صلى الله عليه وسلم ، الْمُتَخَشِّعَ فِي الْجِلْسَةِ ، أُرْعِدْتُ مِنَ الْفَرَقِ [140]

127. Qaylah bint Makhramah ﵂ reported: "I saw the Messenger ﷺ in the masjid sitting in a *qurfusā'* posture. Whilst watching him [and observing his personality] I became overwhelmed due to his overwhelming tranquillity, and this caused me to shiver."

Abdul Razzaq al-Badr said,

> This hadīth is part of a longer one wherein Qaylah narrates the story of how she embraced Islām.

Al-Bajūrī said,

> The *qurfusā'* (also pronounced as *qarfasā'* and *qirfisā'*) is to sit on the ground with the thighs pressing against the stomach and the arms enfolding the legs. This position is also known as *al-ihtibā'*.

Ibn Hajar al-Haytamī said,

> He ﷺ was sitting in a humble state, gazing at the floor whilst his body parts were calm and tranquil due to his excessive fear of Allāh, the Most High.

Alī al-Qārī said,

> The sitting posture of the Prophet ﷺ manifested his true slavery to Allāh, the Most High as he said in a hadīth, "I sit like how a

140 Sunan Abū Dawūd (4847)

slave sits and I eat just like how a slave eats."[141] He did not sit in the manner of the arrogant and the proud. Qaylah was affected in the way she mentioned due to his overwhelming prestige and awe-inspiring personality that caused people to respect him highly and glorify him.

١٢٨ : حَدَّثَنَا سَعِيدُ بْنُ عَبْدِ الرَّحْمَنِ الْمَخْزُومِيُّ ، وَغَيْرُ وَاحِدٍ ، قَالُوا : حَدَّثَنَا سُفْيَانُ ، عَنِ الزُّهْرِيِّ ، عَنْ عَبَّادِ بْنِ تَمِيمٍ ، عَنْ عَمِّهِ ، أَنَّهُ رَأَى النَّبِيَّ صلى الله عليه وسلم مُسْتَلْقِيًا فِي الْمَسْجِدِ وَاضِعًا إِحْدَى رِجْلَيْهِ عَلَى الأُخْرَى[142]

128. 'Abdullāh ibn Zayd ﷺ reported: "I saw the Messenger of Allāh ﷺ lying on his back in the masjid with one leg placed upon the other."

Abdul Razzaq al-Badr said,

> This kind of posture is not common when a person is sitting with a group of people. Rather, a person adopts this posture when resting, when alone or whilst sitting in the company of a few people.

Al-Bajūrī said,

> This hadīth indicates that lying down is considered a form of sitting.

Ibn Hajar al-Haytamī said,

> It is reported in Sahīh Muslim that the Prophet ﷺ admonished this kind of posture. The reconciliation between his admonishment of sitting in such a position and his action [in the hadīth] is that his action shows that it is permissible to sit in that position when one knows that his *'awrah* will not become uncovered.

141 Al-Mughni 'Ān Hamil al-Asfār Fi Takhrīj Ma Fi al-Ahyā min Akhbar (2/454)

142 Sahīh al-Bukhārī (6287) and Sahīh Muslim (2100)

Alī al-Qārī said,

> Al-Khattabī said: "This indicates that the hadīth wherein the Prophet ﷺ admonished this form of sitting is either abrogated or that it is admonished only when the *'awrah* will show. This is because the *izār* could be tight and so placing the leg on the other would make most of the leg show. It was also said that this incident happened before he ﷺ admonished this posture or that the admonishment does not apply to the case where one does it because of being tired or to rest, or that his action was to show that it is permissible. It is also said that resting one leg upon the other is done in two ways: (i) the two legs stretched out while one is on the other and this posture does not expose the *'awrah*, (ii) one leg is lifted and bent whilst the other leg is on it, and so the hadīth in this chapter refers to the first type while the admonishment [in Sahīh Muslim] refers to the second type.

١٢٩ : حَدَّثَنَا سَلَمَةُ بْنُ شَبِيبٍ ، قَالَ : حَدَّثَنَا عَبْدُ اللهِ بْنُ إِبْرَاهِيمَ الْمَدَنِيُّ ، قَالَ : حَدَّثَنَا إِسْحَاقُ بْنُ مُحَمَّدٍ الأَنْصَارِيُّ ، عَنْ رُبَيْحِ بْنِ عَبْدِ الرَّحْمَنِ بْنِ أَبِي سَعِيدٍ ، عَنْ أَبِيهِ ، عَنْ جَدِّهِ أَبِي سَعِيدٍ الْخُدْرِيِّ ، قَالَ : كَانَ رَسُولُ اللهِ صلى الله عليه وسلم إِذَا جَلَسَ فِي الْمَسْجِدِ ، احْتَبَى بِيَدَيْهِ[143]

129. Abū Sa'īd al-Khudarī ﷺ narrated: "When Allāh's Messenger ﷺ sat in the masjid, he did *ihtibā'* with his hands."

Al-Bajūrī said,

> The exception to this posture is that which he ﷺ used to do after the prayer of *Fajr* as he used to sit with his legs-crossed as reported by Abū Dawūd with an authentic chain of narrators.
>
> *Ihtibā'* is the common posture of the Bedouins and it is to sit on the ground and to have the thighs pressing against the stomach by

143 Al-Sunan Al-Kubra of al-Bayhaqī (3/236)

wrapping them with a turban and its likes [such as the arms] to give support to the back. The Bedouins used to do it as they had no walls to lean their backs upon.

CHAPTER TWENTY TWO

باب ما جاء في تكأة رسول الله صلى الله عليه وسلم

THE REPORTS PERTAINING TO THE MESSENGER OF ALLĀH'S ﷺ RECLINING UPON PILLOWS

Abdul Razzaq al-Badr said,

> This chapter is dedicated to describing that which the Prophet ﷺ used to rest on for support.

١٣٠ : حَدَّثَنَا عَبَّاسُ بْنُ مُحَمَّدٍ الدُّورِيُّ الْبَغْدَادِيُّ ، قَالَ : حَدَّثَنَا إِسْحَاقُ بْنُ مَنْصُورٍ ، عَنْ إِسْرَائِيلَ ، عَنْ سِمَاكِ بْنِ حَرْبٍ ، عَنْ جَابِرِ بْنِ سَمُرَةَ ، قَالَ : رَأَيْتُ رَسُولَ اللهِ صلى الله عليه وسلم ، مُتَّكِئًا عَلَى وِسَادَةٍ عَلَى يَسَارِهِ[144]

130. Jābir ibn Samurah ؓ narrated: "I saw the Messenger of Allāh ﷺ reclining upon a pillow which was on his left side."

Ibn Hajar al-Haytamī said,

> This hadīth describes the event and is not intended to restrict the side on which a person should lean on because it is allowed to lean towards both sides.

١٣١ : حَدَّثَنَا حُمَيْدُ بْنُ مَسْعَدَةَ ، قَالَ : حَدَّثَنَا بِشْرُ بْنُ الْمُفَضَّلِ ، قَالَ : حَدَّثَنَا الْجُرَيْرِيُّ ، عَنْ عَبْدِ الرَّحْمَنِ بْنِ أَبِي بَكْرَةَ ، عَنْ أَبِيهِ ، قَالَ : قَالَ رَسُولُ اللهِ صلى الله عليه وسلم : أَلا أُحَدِّثُكُمْ بِأَكْبَرِ الْكَبَائِرِ ؟ قَالُوا : بَلَى يَا رَسُولَ اللهِ قَالَ : الإِشْرَاكُ بِاللهِ ، وَعُقُوقُ الْوَالِدَيْنِ قَالَ : وَجَلَسَ رَسُولُ اللهِ صلى الله عليه وسلم ، وَكَانَ مُتَّكِئًا ، قَالَ : وَشَهَادَةُ الزُّورِ ، أَوْ قَوْلُ الزُّورِ ، قَالَ : فَمَا زَالَ رَسُولُ اللهِ صلى الله عليه وسلم ، يَقُولُهَا حَتَّى قُلْنَا : لَيْتَهُ سَكَتَ[145]

131. Abū Bakrah ؓ related: "The Messenger of Allāh ﷺ said, 'Shall I not inform you of the most severe of the major sins?' The Messenger of Allāh ﷺ asked this question thrice. We said, 'Yes, O Messenger of Allāh! [Please inform us.]' He said, 'Ascribing partners to Allāh, and being undutiful to your parents.' [Then] the Messenger of Allāh ﷺ sat up from his reclining position and said, 'And I warn you against giving forged statements and false testimony.' The Messenger of Allāh ﷺ kept on repeating that warning until we wished he would stop."

---

144 Sunan al-Tirmidhī (2770) and Sunan Abū Dawūd (4143)
145 Sahīh al-Bukhārī (2654) and Sahīh Muslim (87)

Abdul Razzaq al-Badr said,

> The style of the introductory statement was often used by the Prophet ﷺ as it attracts the attention of the audience and it is a good educational method.

Ibn Hajar al-Haytamī said,

> Ibn Abbās ﷺ considered all that which Allāh has admonished and made forbidden to be major sins as he did not believe that there is a minor sin given the fact that the one being disobeyed is Allāh ﷻ. However, the most correct view is that sins are of two types, major and minor. The major sins are those that have been warned against in the Qur'ān and Sunnah.

Al-Bajūrī said,

> The greatest of the major sins is disbelief but ascribing partners to Allāh is mentioned in this hadīth as it is the most common type of disbelief that people do. The second major sin is being undutiful to the parents and this includes all that which harms them in action or words. The mention of parents here also refers to the grandparents.
>
> This hadīth shows that it is permissible for a person to remember Allāh and teach others whilst reclining upon a pillow and that this act does not imperfect one's mannerisms. It also shows that the preacher should repeat the message until the audience becomes moved by the enthusiasm that they see.

١٣٢ : حَدَّثَنَا قُتَيْبَةُ بْنُ سَعِيدٍ ، قَالَ : حَدَّثَنَا شَرِيكٌ ، عَنْ عَلِيِّ بْنِ الأَقْمَرِ ، عَنْ أَبِي جُحَيْفَةَ ، قَالَ : قَالَ رَسُولُ اللهِ صلى الله عليه وسلم : أَمَّا أَنَا ، فَلاَ آكُلُ مُتَّكِئًا[146]

146 Sahīh al-Bukhārī (5389)

132. Abū Juhayfah ﷺ reported: "The Messenger of Allāh ﷺ said, 'As for me, I do not eat whilst reclining.'"

Alī al-Qārī said,

> The statement of the Prophet ﷺ was intended to condemn the practice of non-Muslims and leaders of the non-Arabs at that time as they used to eat while leaning to one side to show their greatness, pride and arrogance. This statement hints that neither the Prophet ﷺ nor his followers would lean when they ate as Allāh ﷻ said: **{Say, "This is my way; I invite to Allāh with insight, I and those who follow me."}**[147]

Mirak Shah al-Hanafī said,

> Scholars explained that reclining is of four types: to lean on one side, to rest on one of the hands for support, sitting cross-legged on a pillow, resting the back against a pillow. Adopting any of these positions whilst eating is disliked as doing so indicates arrogance. The Sunnah is to eat while sitting down, leaning forward towards the food.

Al-Bayhaqī said,

> If a person is sick and cannot eat unless they are reclining, then it is permissible to eat in such a position.

Al-Bajūrī said,

> It is fine for a person to lean and eat nuts, based on the practice of Alī ibn Abī Tālib ﷺ and al-Ghazalī said, "Arabs may do that but eating while sitting down is better and it is not disliked to eat while standing. As for eating whilst sitting with crossed-legs, it is not the best position to eat in."

---

147 Qur'ān: 12:108

١٣٣ : حَدَّثَنَا مُحَمَّدُ بْنُ بَشَّارٍ ، قَالَ : حَدَّثَنَا عَبْدُ الرَّحْمَنِ بْنُ مَهْدِيٍّ ، قَالَ : حَدَّثَنَا سُفْيَانُ ، عَنْ عَلِيِّ بْنِ الأَقْمَرِ ، قَالَ : سَمِعْتُ أَبَا جُحَيْفَةَ ، يَقُولُ : قَالَ رَسُولُ الله صلى الله عليه وسلم : لا آكُلُ مُتَّكِئًا[148]

133. Abū Juhayfah ﷺ reported the same.

١٣٤ : حَدَّثَنَا يُوسُفُ بْنُ عِيسَى ، قَالَ : حَدَّثَنَا وَكِيعٌ ، قَالَ : حَدَّثَنَا إِسْرَائِيلُ ، عَنْ سِمَاكِ بْنِ حَرْبٍ ، عَنْ جَابِرِ بْنِ سَمُرَةَ ، قَالَ : رَأَيْتُ النَّبِيَّ صلى الله عليه وسلم مُتَّكِئًا عَلَى وِسَادَةٍ ،

قَالَ أَبُو عِيسَى : لَمْ يَذْكُرْ وَكِيعٌ عَلَى يَسَارِهِ ، وَهَكَذَا رَوَى غَيْرُ وَاحِدٍ عَنْ إِسْرَائِيلَ ، نَحْوَ رِوَايَةِ وَكِيعٍ ، وَلا نَعْلَمُ أَحَدًا رَوَى فِيهِ عَلَى يَسَارِهِ ، إِلا مَا رَوَاهُ إِسْحَاقُ بْنُ مَنْصُورٍ ، عَنْ إِسْرَائِيلَ[149]

134. Jābir ibn Samurah ﷺ narrated: "I saw the Messenger of Allāh reclining upon a pillow."

---

148 See hadīth 132

149 See hadīth 130

CHAPTER TWENTY THREE

باب ما جاء في اتكاء رسول الله صلى الله عليه وسلم

THE REPORTS PERTAINING TO THE MESSENGER OF ALLĀH ﷺ LEANING UPON PEOPLE

Abdul Razzaq al-Badr said,

> This chapter describes the manner in which the Prophet ﷺ leaned whilst standing whereas the previous chapter described how he did so whilst sitting.

١٣٥ : حَدَّثَنَا عَبْدُ اللهِ بْنُ عَبْدِ الرَّحْمَنِ ، قَالَ : حَدَّثَنَا عَمْرُو بْنُ عَاصِمٍ ، قَالَ : حَدَّثَنَا حَمَّادُ بْنُ سَلَمَةَ ، عَنْ حُمَيْدٍ ، عَنْ أَنَسٍ : أَنَّ النَّبِيَّ صلى الله عليه وسلم كَانَ شَاكِيًا ، فَخَرَجَ يَتَوَكَّأُ عَلَى أُسَامَةَ بْنِ زَيْدٍ وَعَلَيْهِ ثَوْبٌ قِطْرِيٌّ ، قَدْ تَوَشَّحَ بِهِ فَصَلَّى بِهِمْ[150]

135. Anas ibn Mālik ﷺ reported that he saw the Messenger of Allāh ﷺ, while he was sick, coming out of his room leaning upon Usāmah ibn Zayd ﷺ for support. He headed to the prayer leading the Muslims whilst wearing a Yemenī shawl that he put on his shoulders.

١٣٦ : حَدَّثَنَا عَبْدُ اللهِ بْنُ عَبْدِ الرَّحْمَنِ ، قَالَ : حَدَّثَنَا مُحَمَّدُ بْنُ الْمُبَارَكِ ، قَالَ : حَدَّثَنَا عَطَاءُ بْنُ مُسْلِمٍ الْخَفَّافُ الْحَلَبِيُّ ، قَالَ : حَدَّثَنَا جَعْفَرُ بْنُ بُرْقَانَ ، عَنْ عَطَاءِ بْنِ أَبِي رَبَاحٍ ، عَنِ الْفَضْلِ بْنِ عَبَّاسٍ ، قَالَ : دَخَلْتُ عَلَى رَسُولِ اللهِ صلى الله عليه وسلم ، فِي مَرَضِهِ الَّذِي تُوُفِّيَ فِيهِ ، وَعَلَى رَأْسِهِ عِصَابَةٌ صَفْرَاءُ ، فَسَلَّمْتُ عَلَيْهِ ، فَقَالَ : يَا فَضْلُ قُلْتُ : لَبَّيْكَ يَا رَسُولَ الله ، قَالَ : اشْدُدْ بِهَذِهِ الْعِصَابَةِ رَأْسِي قَالَ : فَفَعَلْتُ ، ثُمَّ قَعَدَ فَوَضَعَ كَفَّهُ عَلَى مَنْكِبِي ، ثُمَّ قَامَ فَدَخَلَ فِي الْمَسْجِدِ
وَفِي الْحَدِيثِ قِصَّةٌ[151]

136. Al-Fadl ibn al-'Abbās ﷺ narrated: "I came to Allāh's Messenger ﷺ during the time of his last illness before he passed away and I saw that a yellow band had been tied around his head. I greeted him and after replying, he requested that I fasten the band tightly around his head. I did so and then he sat. He placed his hands upon my shoulders, stood and then he entered the masjid."

Al-Bajūrī said,

150 See hadīth 59
151 Mukhtasar al-Shama'il of Al-Albani (107)

> This hadīth is the evidence used as the basis for wearing yellow turbans and the evidence for wearing black turbans is the hadīth that states that he ﷺ entered Makkah whilst wearing a black turban. However, the white turban is the best as we have explained before.

Ibn Hajar al-Haytamī said,

> The request of the Prophet ﷺ to fasten the band around his head was to relieve his headache. This shows that seeking treatment and medicine does not contradict full reliance on Allāh; rather it shows one's humility and need for Allāh.

CHAPTER TWENTY FOUR

باب ما جاء في أكل رسول الله صلى الله عليه وسلم

THE REPORTS PERTAINING TO THE MANNER OF EATING OF THE MESSENGER OF ALLĀH ﷺ

١٣٧ : حَدَّثَنَا مُحَمَّدُ بْنُ بَشَّارٍ ، قَالَ : حَدَّثَنَا عَبْدُ الرَّحْمَنِ بْنُ مَهْدِيٍّ ، عَنْ سُفْيَانَ ، عَنْ سَعْدِ بْنِ إِبْرَاهِيمَ ، عَنِ ابْنٍ لِكَعْبِ بْنِ مَالِكٍ ، عَنْ أَبِيهِ ، أَنَّ النَّبِيَّ صلى الله عليه وسلم كَانَ يَلْعَقُ أَصَابِعَهُ ثَلاثًا

قَالَ أَبُو عِيسَى : وَرَوَى غَيْرُ مُحَمَّدِ بْنِ بَشَّارٍ هَذَا الْحَدِيثَ ، قَالَ : يَلْعَقُ أَصَابِعَهُ الثَّلاثَ[152]

137. Ka'b ibn Mālik ؓ narrated: "The Messenger of Allāh ﷺ used to lick his fingers thrice after eating."

Abū 'Īsa [al-Tirmidhī] said: "The narration transmitted from the other narrators of this hadīth, which Muhammad ibn Bashar narrated, is that he ﷺ used to lick his three fingers."

Abdul Razzaq al-Badr said,

> The hadīth wherein it says that he ﷺ licked his fingers three times is an odd narration. The preserved narration is that he licked his three fingers.

Al-Bajūrī said,

> The wisdom of licking the fingers is explained in another hadīth wherein he said, "When one of you finishes eating, he should lick his fingers. You do not know in which [part] of your food is the *barakah* (blessing)."[153]

Ibn Hajar al-Haytamī said,

> The reconciliation between this hadīth and the other one where it says that he licked his three fingers (rather than each finger thrice) is that he licked each of the three fingers thrice. The three fingers he used for eating were the thumb, index and middle fingers. The

152 Sahīh Muslim (2032)
153 Sunan al-Tirmidhī (1801)

middle finger should be licked first after finishing the meal because it is the longest and so it will have more food stuck to it, then the index finger should be licked, followed by the thumb. It is the Sunnah to lick the fingers before washing them or wiping them.

Al-Qadī 'Iyyād said,

> The wisdom of licking the fingers is so that a person does not belittle the food and appreciates it even if it is little.

Alī al-Qārī said,

> It is disliked to lick the fingers while eating because the fingers will then touch the food whilst having some traces of saliva upon them.

١٣٨ : حَدَّثَنَا الْحُسَنُ بْنُ عَلِيٍّ الْخَلَالُ ، قَالَ : حَدَّثَنَا عَفَّانُ ، قَالَ : حَدَّثَنَا حَمَّادُ بْنُ سَلَمَةَ ، عَنْ ثَابِتٍ ، عَنْ أَنَسٍ ، قَالَ : كَانَ النَّبِيُّ صلى الله عليه وسلم إِذَا أَكَلَ طَعَامًا لَعِقَ أَصَابِعَهُ الثَّلَاثَ[154]

138. Anas ibn Mālik ﷺ narrated: "The Messenger of Allāh ﷺ used to lick his three fingers after he finished eating."

١٣٩ : حَدَّثَنَا الْحُسَيْنُ بْنُ عَلِيِّ بْنِ يَزِيدَ الصُّدَائِيُّ الْبَغْدَادِيُّ ، قَالَ : حَدَّثَنَا يَعْقُوبُ بْنُ إِسْحَاقَ يَعْنِي الْحَضْرَمِيَّ ، قَالَ : حَدَّثَنَا شُعْبَةُ ، عَنْ سُفْيَانَ الثَّوْرِيِّ ، عَنْ عَلِيِّ بْنِ الأَقْمَرِ ، عَنْ أَبِي جُحَيْفَةَ ، قَالَ : قَالَ النَّبِيُّ صلى الله عليه وسلم : أَمَّا أَنَا فَلا آكُلُ مُتَّكِئًا[155]

139. Abū Juhaifah ﷺ narrated: "The Messenger of Allāh ﷺ said, 'As for me, I do not eat whilst I am reclining [upon something].'"

154 Sahīh Muslim (2034)
155 See hadīth 130

١٤٠ : حَدَّثَنَا مُحَمَّدُ بْنُ بَشَّارٍ ، قَالَ : حَدَّثَنَا عَبْدُ الرَّحْمَنِ بْنُ مَهْدِيٍّ ، قَالَ : حَدَّثَنَا سُفْيَانُ ، عَنْ عَلِيِّ بْنِ الأَقْمَرِ نَحْوَهُ

140. Alī ibn al-Aqmar reports the same.

١٤١ : حَدَّثَنَا هَارُونُ بْنُ إِسْحَاقَ الْهَمْدَانِيُّ ، قَالَ : حَدَّثَنَا عَبْدَةُ بْنُ سُلَيْمَانَ ، عَنْ هِشَامِ بْنِ عُرْوَةَ ، عَنِ ابْنٍ لِكَعْبِ بْنِ مَالِكٍ ، عَنْ أَبِيهِ ، قَالَ : كَانَ رَسُولُ اللهِ صلى الله عليه وسلم يَأْكُلُ بِأَصَابِعِهِ الثَّلاثِ وَيَلْعَقُهُنَّ[156]

141. Ka'b ibn Mālik ؓ narrated: "The Messenger of Allāh ﷺ used to eat with his three fingers and lick them after finishing the meal."

Abdul Razzaq al-Badr said,

> There are two etiquettes to learn from this hadīth, they are: (i) eating with three fingers and licking them after finishing eating. However, some scholars have said that eating with three fingers is not for soupy types of food i.e. it is for finger foods that can be collected in the three fingers, and (ii) licking the fingers after finishing the meal.

١٤٢ : حَدَّثَنَا أَحْمَدُ بْنُ مَنِيعٍ ، قَالَ : حَدَّثَنَا الْفَضْلُ بْنُ دُكَيْنٍ ، قَالَ : حَدَّثَنَا مُصْعَبُ بْنُ سُلَيْمٍ ، قَالَ : سَمِعْتُ أَنَسَ بْنَ مَالِكٍ ، يَقُولُ : أُتِيَ رَسُولُ اللهِ صلى الله عليه وسلم بِتَمْرٍ فَرَأَيْتُهُ يَأْكُلُ وَهُوَ مُقْعٍ مِنَ الْجُوعِ[157]

142. Anas ibn Mālik ؓ said: "Dates were presented to the Messenger of Allāh ﷺ. Due to hunger, I saw him kneeling with his feet upright, resting on his heels whilst eating the dates."

---

156 Musannaf Ibn Abi Shaybah (23869)
157 Sahīh Muslim (2044)

Ibn al-Uthaymīn said,

> The Prophet ﷺ ate like that so that he would not become too comfortable and eat too much. This is because, usually when a person sits in this manner, he does not feel too comfortable and this causes him to become unable to eat excessively. If he is not comfortable he will never eat to excess, but if he is comfortable he will.

Abdul Razzaq al-Badr said,

> This hadīth is fully narrated in the Musnad of Imām Ahmad and its wording is: "Dates were presented to the Prophet ﷺ so he divided it equally to be distributed amongst the [needy] people and I was the one who was sent to give it away. After he finished, I saw him eating whilst sitting in a kneeling position and this made me realise that he was hungry."[158]
>
> This hadīth shows he gave priority to other persons who had a similar condition (i.e. hunger) despite the fact that he was hungry himself.

Ibn Hajar al-Asqalānī said,

> The Sunnah when sitting to eat is to kneel down with the top of the feet resting upon the floor, or to sit with the right knee up, resting on the left foot.

158 Musnad Ahmad (13101)

CHAPTER TWENTY FIVE

باب ما جاء في صفة خبز رسول الله صلى الله عليه وسلم

THE REPORTS PERTAINING TO THE DESCRIPTION OF THE BREAD OF ALLĀH'S MESSENGER ﷺ

١٤٣ : حدثني مُحَمَّدُ بْنُ الْمُثَنَّى ، وَمُحَمَّدُ بْنُ بَشَّارٍ ، قَالا : حَدَّثَنَا مُحَمَّدُ بْنُ جَعْفَرٍ ، قَالَ : حَدَّثَنَا شُعْبَةُ ، عَنْ أَبِي إِسْحَاقَ ، قَالَ : سَمِعْتُ عَبْدَ الرَّحْمَنِ بْنَ يَزِيدَ ، يُحَدِّثُ عَنِ الأَسْوَدِ بْنِ يَزِيدَ ، عَنْ عَائِشَةَ ، أَنَّهَا قَالَتْ : مَا شَبِعَ آلُ مُحَمَّدٍ صلى الله عليه وسلم مِنْ خُبْزِ الشَّعِيرِ يَوْمَيْنِ مُتَتَابِعَيْنِ حَتَّى قُبِضَ رَسُولُ اللهِ صلى الله عليه وسلم[159]

143. Aisha ﵂ related: "The family of Muhammad ﷺ never ate a full stomach of barley bread for two consecutive days until the day he passed away."

Abdul Razzaq al-Badr said,

> This hadīth shows that the Prophet ﷺ used to eat little and that this worldly life held no weight upon his heart. He is the best of mankind but still he used to sleep hungry. This shows that the worldly life is trivial in the sight of Allāh. If it had any value, He would have endowed the best of His creation with all of its adornments and pleasures.

Al-Bajūrī said,

> It is possible that the word 'family' mentioned in this hadīth is just an unnecessary addition i.e. if it is removed the meaning will still be the same. That is to say that the statement does not include the family of the Prophet ﷺ and the following hadīth confirms this meaning. It is also possible that the wording is an integral part of the hadīth and in this case the word 'family' refers to those under the responsibility of the Prophet ﷺ, and not the family in its broader sense.

١٤٤ : حَدَّثَنَا عَبَّاسُ بْنُ مُحَمَّدٍ الدُّورِيُّ ، قَالَ : حَدَّثَنَا يَحْيَى بْنُ أَبِي بُكَيْرٍ ،

---

159 See hadith 149

قَالَ : حَدَّثَنَا حَرِيزُ بْنُ عُثْمَانَ ، عَنْ سُلَيْمِ بْنِ عَامِرٍ ، قَالَ : سَمِعْتُ أَبَا أُمَامَةَ الْبَاهِلِيَّ ، يَقُولُ : مَا كَانَ يَفْضُلُ عَنْ أَهْلِ بَيْتِ رَسُولِ اللهِ صلى الله عليه وسلم خُبْزُ الشَّعِيرِ[160]

144. Abū Umāmah al-Bāhilī ﷺ narrated: "The family of the Messenger of Allāh ﷺ never had any barley bread left over."

Alī al-Qārī said,

> This indicates that they were never full from food.

١٤٥ : حَدَّثَنَا عَبْدُ اللهِ بْنُ مُعَاوِيَةَ الْجُمَحِيُّ ، قَالَ : حَدَّثَنَا ثَابِتُ بْنُ يَزِيدَ ، عَنْ هِلَالِ بْنِ خَبَّابٍ ، عَنْ عِكْرِمَةَ ، عَنِ ابْنِ عَبَّاسٍ ، قَالَ : كَانَ رَسُولُ اللهِ صلى الله عليه وسلم ، يَبِيتُ اللَّيَالِيَ الْمُتَتَابِعَةَ طَاوِيًا هُوَ وَأَهْلُهُ ، لا يَجِدُونَ عَشَاءً وَكَانَ أَكْثَرُ خُبْزِهِمْ ، خُبْزَ الشَّعِيرِ[161]

145. 'Abdullāh ibn Abbās ﷺ related: "The Messenger ﷺ and his family spent many consecutive nights hungry as there would be no supper. Often, their bread was made of barley."

Al-Bajūrī said,

> This hadīth shows the noble character, dignity and self-esteem of the Prophet ﷺ as he took precautions so that none of his companions would know that he and his family slept hungry for several nights. This is evident as it is certain that if they were aware about it they would have raced each other to give him priority over themselves and their families. This indicates the virtue of the poor and directs people not to ask for food even when one is hungry.

160 Sunan al-Tirmidhī (2359)

161 Sunan al-Tirmidhī (2359)

١٤٦ : حَدَّثَنَا عَبْدُ اللهِ بْنُ عَبْدِ الرَّحْمَنِ ، قَالَ : حَدَّثَنَا عُبَيْدُ اللهِ بْنُ عَبْدِ الْمَجِيدِ الْحَنَفِيُّ ، حَدَّثَنَا عَبْدُ الرَّحْمَنِ بْنُ عَبْدِ اللهِ بْنِ دِينَارٍ ، قَالَ : حَدَّثَنَا أَبُو حَازِمٍ ، عَنْ سَهْلِ بْنِ سَعْدٍ ، أَنَّهُ قِيلَ لَهُ : أَكَلَ رَسُولُ اللهِ صلى الله عليه وسلم النَّقِيَّ ؟ يَعْنِي الْحُوَّارَى فَقَالَ سَهْلٌ : مَا رَأَى رَسُولُ اللهِ صلى الله عليه وسلم النَّقِيَّ حَتَّى لَقِيَ اللهَ عَزَّ وَجَلَّ تَعَالَى ، فَقِيلَ لَهُ : هَلْ كَانَتْ لَكُمْ مَنَاخِلُ عَلَى عَهْدِ رَسُولِ اللهِ صلى الله عليه وسلم ؟

قَالَ : مَا كَانَتْ لَنَا مَنَاخِلُ قِيلَ : كَيْفَ كُنْتُمْ تَصْنَعُونَ بِالشَّعِيرِ ؟

قَالَ : كُنَّا نَنْفُخُهُ فَيَطِيرُ مِنْهُ مَا طَارَ ، ثُمَّ نَعْجِنُهُ[162]

146. Someone asked Sahl ibn Sa'd ﷺ: "Did the Messenger of Allāh ﷺ ever eat bread made of white bran-free flour?" He replied, "The Messenger ﷺ never ate it in his lifetime." The questioner then asked, "Did you people use sieved flour in the time of the Messenger ﷺ?" He replied, "We did not have sieves." The questioner then asked, "How did you sieve the barley?" He replied, "We used to blow out the particles and then knead that which remained."

Abdul Razzaq al-Badr said,

> The reason why the questioner asked about barley is because it has grains that if they remain in the dough, the bread would be difficult to chew.

Ibn Hajar al-Haytamī said,

> This hadīth shows that the Prophet ﷺ was not fussy about food and so he ate the barley bread just like everyone else. It is only the fools and idle people who are fussy about food.

١٤٧ : حَدَّثَنَا مُحَمَّدُ بْنُ بَشَّارٍ ، قَالَ : حَدَّثَنَا مُعَاذُ بْنُ هِشَامٍ ، قَالَ : حَدَّثَنِي

162 Sahīh al-Bukhārī (5413)

أَبِي ، عَنْ يُونُسَ ، عَنْ قَتَادَةَ ، عَنْ أَنَسِ بْنِ مَالِكٍ ، قَالَ : مَا أَكَلَ نَبِيُّ اللهِ عَلَى خِوَانٍ ، وَلا فِي سُكُرُّجَةٍ ، وَلا خُبِزَ لَهُ مُرَقَّقٌ قَالَ : فَقُلْتُ لِقَتَادَةَ : فَعَلامَ كَانُوا يَأْكُلُونَ ؟ قَالَ : عَلَى هَذِهِ السُّفَرِ[163]

قَالَ مُحَمَّدُ بْنُ بَشَّارٍ : يُونُسُ هَذَا الَّذِي رَوَى عَنْ قَتَادَةَ هُوَ يُونُسُ الإِسْكَافُ

147. Anas ibn Mālik ﷺ reported: "The Messenger ﷺ never ate food from a table, nor from a *sukurrujah* (i.e. a small plate), nor was thin soft bread ever made for him."

Yūnus asked Qatādah (who narrated this hadīth from Anas): "Then upon what did they eat their food?" He replied: "Upon these floor-sheets."

Abdul Razzaq al-Badr said,

> This shows the moderation of the Prophet ﷺ even in food as he ate neither from a table nor on the floor without placing a sheet underneath. This is because eating on the table was considered as a luxury whilst eating on the floor without placing anything underneath would expose the food to dirt. Thus, eating on the floor while having a sheet underneath is a humble way of eating that protects the food from dirt.

Al-Bajūrī said,

> Eating on dining tables was the practice followed amongst the non-Arabs so that their heads would not nod down while eating. However, it is allowed to eat from the table if there is no pride or arrogance involved.

Ibn Hajar al-Haytamī said,

> The *sukurrujah* is a small plate that is used for side dishes and appetisers.

163 Sahīh al-Bukhārī (5415)

١٤٨ : حَدَّثَنَا أَحْمَدُ بْنُ مَنِيع ، قَالَ : حَدَّثَنَا عَبَّادُ بْنُ عَبَّادٍ الْمُهَلَّبِيُّ ، عَنْ مُجَالِدٍ ، عَنِ الشَّعْبِيِّ ، عَنْ مَسْرُوقٍ ، قَالَ : دَخَلْتُ عَلَى عَائِشَةَ ، فَدَعَتْ لِي بطَعَام وَقَالَتْ : مَا أَشْبَعُ مِنْ طَعَام فَأَشَاءُ أَنْ أَبْكِيَ إِلا بَكِيتُ قَالَ : قُلْتُ لِمَ ؟ قَالَتْ : أَذْكُرُ الْحَالَ الَّتِي فَارَقَ عَلَيْهَا رَسُولُ الله صلى الله عليه وسلم الدُّنْيَا ، وَاللَّهَ مَا شَبعَ مِنْ خُبْزٍ وَلَحمٍ مَرَّتَيْنِ فِي يَوْمٍ[164]

148. Masrūq narrated: "I visited Aisha ﵂ and she ordered food for me and then said, 'I never eat to my full except that I wish to cry, then I begin to cry.' I asked, 'Why is that?' She replied, 'I remember the state of the Messenger of Allāh ﷺ upon which he left us for the next world. I swear by Allāh that he never filled his stomach twice in one day with meat or bread.'"

Abdul Razzaq al-Badr said,

> Masrūq was born during the lifetime of the Prophet ﷺ but never saw him as he was living in the city of Kufa in Iraq. The name Masrūq means "stolen" and he was given this name because he was kidnapped when he was a child and then later on his family managed to find him.

Ibn Hajar al-Haytamī said,

> The reason Aisha ﵂ used to cry every time she ate to her full was because she missed the hard life that she had experienced with the Prophet ﷺ. This is because that lifestyle was the highest level of virtuousness since it was the lifestyle that the Prophet chose for himself ﷺ and his family.

Al-Bajūrī said,

> He ﷺ never had a full stomach from either meat and bread twice in

164 Sunan al-Tirmidhī (2356)

one day i.e. enjoying much of the lawful matters is disliked whereas enjoying less of it is recommended, and humbleness is required.

١٤٩ : حَدَّثَنَا مَحْمُودُ بْنُ غَيْلاَنَ ، قَالَ : حَدَّثَنَا أَبُو دَاوُدَ ، قَالَ : حَدَّثنا شُعْبَةُ ، عَنْ أَبِي إِسْحَاقَ ، قَالَ : سَمِعْتُ عَبْدَ الرَّحْمَنِ بْنَ يَزِيدَ يُحَدِّثُ ، عَنِ الأَسْوَدِ بْنِ يَزِيدَ ، عَنْ عَائِشَةَ ، قَالَتْ : مَا شَبِعَ رَسُولُ الله صلى الله عليه وسلم مِنْ خُبْزِ الشَّعِيرِ يَوْمَيْنِ مُتَتَابِعَيْنِ حَتَّى قُبِضَ[165]

149. Aisha ﵂ narrated: "The Messenger of Allāh ﷺ never filled his stomach with barley bread for two consecutive days until he passed away."

Alī al-Qārī said,

> He ﷺ never filled his stomach with bread made of barley, let alone bread made of wheat. This was because he acted upon the decision he made when he was given the choice to either be a prophet who is a king in this world or just a slave of Allāh, and so he chose, "I prefer to be a Prophet who is a [true] slave of Allāh; I starve on one day so I bear it with patience and I eat well on another day so I praise Him."[166]

Al-Bajūrī said,

> He did not eat to his full twice in one day because he avoided that and preferred the state of hunger.

١٥٠ : حَدَّثَنَا عَبْدُ الله بْنُ عَبْدِ الرَّحْمَنِ ، قَالَ : حَدَّثَنَا عَبْدُ الله بْنُ عَمْرٍو أَبُو مَعْمَرٍ ، حَدَّثَنَا عَبْدُ الْوَارِثِ ، عَنْ سَعِيدِ بْنِ أَبِي عَرُوبَةَ ، عَنْ قَتَادَةَ ، عَنْ أَنَسٍ

165 Sahīh al-Bukhārī (5416) and Sahīh Muslim (2970)
166 Musnad Ahmad (12/143)

، قَالَ : مَا أَكَلَ رَسُولُ الله صلى الله عليه وسلم عَلَى خِوَانٍ ، وَلا أَكَلَ خُبْزًا مُرَقَّقًا حَتَّى مَاتَ[167]

150. Anas ibn Mālik ﷺ narrated: "Until the end of his life; the Messenger of Allāh ﷺ never ate on a table and never ate thin soft bread."

167 Sahīh al-Bukhārī (6450)

CHAPTER TWENTY SIX

ما جاء في إدام رسول الله صلى الله عليه وسلم

THE REPORTS PERTAINING TO THE IDĀM OF THE PROPHET ﷺ

Al-Bajūrī said,

> The *idām* refers to all that which is eaten with bread, be it liquid or solid, and so it includes even meat. The fact that meat is considered a type of *idām* is based on the linguistic meaning of the word but it is not considered an *idām* based on the norms of people.

Ibn Hajar al-Haytamī said,

> This is because the habit of people is to eat the *idām* to facilitate the eating of other food [i.e. it is used to eat the bread].

١٥١ : حَدَّثَنَا مُحَمَّدُ بْنُ سَهْلِ بْنِ عَسْكَرٍ ، وَعَبْدُ اللهِ بْنُ عَبْدِ الرَّحْمَنِ ، قَالا : حَدَّثَنَا يَحْيَى بْنُ حَسَّانَ ، قَالَ : حَدَّثَنَا سُلَيْمَانُ بْنُ بِلالٍ ، عَنْ هِشَامِ بْنِ عُرْوَةَ ، عَنْ أَبِيهِ ، عَنْ عَائِشَةَ ، أَنَّ رَسُولَ اللهِ صلى الله عليه وسلم ، قَالَ : نِعْمَ الإِدَامُ الْخَلُّ ، قَالَ عَبْدُ اللهِ بْنُ عَبْدِ الرَّحْمَنِ ، فِي حَدِيثِهِ : نِعْمَ الإِدَامُ أَوِ الأُدْمُ الْخَلُّ[168]

151. Aisha ﵂ narrated: "The Messenger of Allāh ﷺ said, 'What an excellent *idām* vinegar is.'"

Ibn al-Qayyim said,

> This hadīth is intended to praise vinegar, given the circumstances of the event, and so it does not intend to prefer it over all other types of *idām*, as some ignorant people think. The context behind this statement is that he ﷺ went home and took a piece of bread. He then asked his family if there was an *idām* to eat with the bread and so they replied that they have nothing but vinegar. Upon that he praised the *idām*.

Al-Bajūrī said,

> The Prophet ﷺ praised vinegar to complement and bring comfort to the heart of the one presenting it to him. Otherwise if the available *idām* was milk or meat or honey, they would have been praised instead.

١٥٢ : حَدَّثَنَا قُتَيْبَةُ ، قَالَ : حَدَّثَنَا أَبُو الأَحْوَصِ ، عَنْ سِمَاكِ بْنِ حَرْبٍ ، قَالَ : سَمِعْتُ النُّعْمَانَ بْنَ بَشِيرٍ ، يَقُولُ : أَلَسْتُمْ فِي طَعَامٍ وَشَرَابٍ مَا شِئْتُمْ ؟ لَقَدْ رَأَيْتُ نَبِيَّكُمْ صلى الله عليه وسلم ، وَمَا يَجِدُ مِنَ الدَّقَلِ مَا يَمْلأُ بَطْنَهُ[169]

168 Sahīh Muslim (2051)
169 Sahīh Muslim (2977)

152. Al-Nu'mān ibn Bashīr ؓ said: "You are in enough luxury to eat and drink all that you wish! By Allāh, I have seen your Prophet ﷺ not having the worst type of dates to fill his stomach."

Abdul Razzaq al-Badr said,

> The purpose of al-Nu'mān's statement was to remind the remaining companions and the generation that did not have the pleasure and honour to see the Prophet ﷺ of the blessings and favours of Allāh upon them.

Al-Bajūrī said,

> The purpose of al-Nu'mān was to admonish those whom he addressed and advise them to suffice with the little that is enough and to follow the example of the Prophet ﷺ in this regard. The reason he said "your Prophet" was to emphasise the meaning of the advice that followed and to encourage them.

١٥٣ : حَدَّثَنَا عَبْدَةُ بْنُ عَبْدِ اللهِ الْخُزَاعِيُّ ، قَالَ : حَدَّثَنَا مُعَاوِيَةُ بْنُ هِشَامٍ ، عَنْ سُفْيَانَ ، عَنْ مُحَارِبِ بْنِ دِثَارٍ ، عَنْ جَابِرِ بْنِ عَبْدِ اللهِ ، قَالَ : قَالَ رَسُولُ اللهِ صلى الله عليه وسلم : نِعْمَ الإِدَامُ الأُدْمُ : الْخَلُّ [170]

153. Jābir ibn 'Abdullāh ؓ related: "The Messenger of Allāh ﷺ said, 'What a wonderful *idām* vinegar is.'"

١٥٤ : حَدَّثَنَا هَنَّادٌ ، حَدَّثَنَا وَكِيعٌ ، عَنْ سُفْيَانَ ، عَنْ أَيُّوبَ ، عَنْ أَبِي قِلَابَةَ ، عَنْ زَهْدَمٍ الْجَرْمِيِّ ، قَالَ : كُنَّا عِنْدَ أَبِي مُوسَى الأَشْعَرِيِّ ، فَأُتِيَ بِلَحْمِ دَجَاجٍ فَتَنَحَّى رَجُلٌ مِنَ الْقَوْمِ ، فَقَالَ : مَا لَكَ ؟ فَقَالَ : إِنِّي رَأَيْتُهَا تَأْكُلُ شَيْئًا فَحَلَفْتُ أَنْ لا آكُلَهَا

170 Sunan al-Tirmidhī (1839)

قَالَ : ادْنُ ، فَإِنِّي رَأَيْتُ رَسُولَ الله صلى الله عليه وسلم ، يَأْكُلُ لَحْمَ دَجَاجٍ [171]

154. Zahdam al-Jarmī narrated that: "We were in the presence of Abū Mūsa al-Ash'arī ﷺ when chicken was served to us. A person from among those present distanced himself from the gathering. Abū Mūsa ﷺ asked him the reason [for doing so]. He replied, 'I have seen the chicken eat something unclean so I swore that I would not eat it.' Abū Mūsa ﷺ said, 'Come, for I have seen the Messenger of Allāh ﷺ eat the meat of the chicken.'"

Al-Bajūrī said,

> The direction of Abū Mūsa ﷺ given to the man was to indicate that it is better for him that he offers expiation for his oath and eats from the chicken to follow the example of the Prophet ﷺ based on the hadīth, "None of you shall believe until his desire conforms to that which I brought."[172] It also indicates that the host serving the food should try to make the person break any similar oath if the reason for leaving a particular food is for a matter that is not disliked in religion (except in the case where the man made a conditional divorce).

Ibn Hajar al-Haytamī said,

> If the chicken was of the type that lives on dirt and garbage then one should not break his oath because it is forbidden to eat. However, it seems that the chicken was not from that type and it happened that it ate something dirty on that day.

Abdul Razzaq al-Badr said,

> The man did not specify the type of dirt that he saw the chicken eating so that he would not make the people feel disgust towards

171 Sahīh al-Bukhārī (5517) and Sahīh Muslim (1649)
172 Al-Arba'ūn al-Nawawiyyah (41)

the food. This is because it suffices for a person who dislikes a type of food just to state that he does not feel like eating it, thus following the guidance of the Prophet ﷺ in this kind of situation.

١٥٥ : حَدَّثَنَا الْفَضْلُ بْنُ سَهْلٍ الأَعْرَجُ الْبَغْدَادِيُّ ، قَالَ : حَدَّثَنَا إِبْرَاهِيمُ بْنُ عَبْدِ الرَّحْمَنِ بْنِ مَهْدِيٍّ ، عَنْ إِبْرَاهِيمَ بْنِ عُمَرَ بْنِ سَفِينَةَ ، عَنْ أَبِيهِ ، عَنْ جَدِّهِ ، قَالَ : أَكَلْتُ مَعَ رَسُولِ اللهِ صلى الله عليه وسلم لَحْمَ حُبَارَى[173]

155. Safina ﷺ narrated: "I ate bustard meat with the Messenger of Allāh ﷺ."

Safina is a nick name given to him. It means a ship because he carried a lot of luggage when travelling. He was one of the slaves that the Prophet ﷺ freed and his name is disputed over but some stated that his actual name is Mihrān.

١٥٦ : حَدَّثَنَا عَلِيُّ بْنُ حُجْرٍ ، قَالَ : حَدَّثَنَا إِسْمَاعِيلُ بْنُ إِبْرَاهِيمَ ، عَنْ أَيُّوبَ ، عَنِ الْقَاسِمِ التَّمِيمِيِّ ، عَنْ زَهْدَمٍ الْجَرْمِيِّ ، قَالَ : كُنَّا عِنْدَ أَبِي مُوسَى الأَشْعَرِيِّ ، قَالَ : فَقَدَّمَ طَعَامَهُ وَقَدَّمَ فِي طَعَامِهِ لَحْمَ دَجَاجٍ وَفِي الْقَوْمِ رَجُلٌ مِنْ بَنِي تَيْمِ اللهِ أَحْمَرُ كَأَنَّهُ مَوْلًى ، قَالَ : فَلَمْ يَدْنُ فَقَالَ لَهُ أَبُو مُوسَى : ادْنُ ، فَإِنِّي قَدْ رَأَيْتُ رَسُولَ اللهِ صلى الله عليه وسلم أَكَلَ مِنْهُ ، فَقَالَ : إِنِّي رَأَيْتُهُ يَأْكُلُ شَيْئًا ، فَقَذِرْتُهُ فَحَلَفْتُ أَنْ لا أَطْعَمَهُ أَبَدًا[174]

156. Zahdam al-Jarmī narrated: "We were present in a gathering with Abū Mūsa al-Ash'arī ﷺ and in the food that was served there was poultry. Among those present was a man from the tribe of Banī Taymullah who was reddish in complexion and seemed to be a freed slave. He moved back and sat to one side, staying away from the

173 Sunan Abū Dawūd (3797)
174 See hadīth 154.

food. Abū Mūsa asked him to come near [and eat from the food] and related to him that he saw the Messenger ﷺ also eat chicken. He excused himself saying, 'I had seen it eating something unclean. For this reason I swore an oath that I would not eat it.'"[175]

١٥٧ : حَدَّثَنَا مَحْمُودُ بْنُ غَيْلانَ ، قَالَ : حَدَّثَنَا أَبُو أَحْمَدَ الزُّبَيْرِيُّ ، وَأَبُو نُعَيْم ، قَالا : حَدَّثَنَا سُفْيَانُ ، عَنْ عَبْدِ اللهِ بْنِ عِيسَى ، عَنْ رَجُلٍ مِنْ أَهْلِ الشَّام ، يُقَالُ : لَهُ عَطَاءٌ ، عَنْ أَبِي أَسِيدٍ ، قَالَ : قَالَ رَسُولُ اللهِ صلى الله عليه وسلم : كُلُوا الزَّيْتَ ، وَادَّهِنُوا بِهِ ، فَإِنَّهُ مِنْ شَجَرَةٍ مُبَارَكَةٍ[176]

157. Abū Asīd ﷺ narrated: "The Messenger of Allāh ﷺ said, 'Use olive oil as a food and for rubbing [on the body], for it is from a blessed tree.'"

Abdul Razzaq al-Badr said,

> The direction to eat olive oil relates to eating it with bread (i.e. using it as an *idām*).

Al-Bajūrī said,

> The direction to rub the body with olive oil should be moderate. Ibn al-Qayyim said, "Using oil in hot lands such as the region of Hejaz is good for heath but it is harmful if it is used in cold lands."

Alī al-Qārī said,

> The olive tree is blessed because it grows in the blessed land (i.e. the region of al-Shām) and that makes its olives blessed. It was reported that the Prophet ﷺ encouraged using it as a medicine to treat haemorrhoids, and in another hadīth that olive oil cures

175 Previously explained in hadith 154.
176 Sunan al-Tirmidhī (1852)

seventy diseases.

١٥٨ : حَدَّثَنَا يَحْيَى بْنُ مُوسَى ، قَالَ : حَدَّثَنَا عَبْدُ الرَّزَّاقِ ، قَالَ : حَدَّثَنَا مَعْمَرٌ ، عَنْ زَيْدِ بْنِ أَسْلَمَ ، عَنْ أَبِيهِ ، عَنْ عُمَرَ بْنِ الْخَطَّابِ ، قَالَ : قَالَ رَسُولُ اللهِ صلى الله عليه وسلم : كُلُوا الزَّيْتَ وَادَّهِنُوا بِهِ ، فَإِنَّهُ مِنْ شَجَرَةٍ مُبَارَكَةٍ[177]

قَالَ أَبُو عِيسَى : وكَانَ عَبْدُ الرَّزَّاقِ يَضْطَرِبُ فِي هَذَا الْحَدِيثِ ، فَرُبَّمَا أَسْنَدَهُ ، وَرُبَّمَا أَرْسَلَهُ

158. 'Umar ibn al-Khattab ﷺ narrated: "The Messenger of Allāh ﷺ said, 'Use olive oil as a food and for rubbing [on the body], for it is from a blessed tree.'"[178]

١٥٩ : حَدَّثَنَا السِّنْجِيُّ وَهُوَ أَبُو دَاوُدَ سُلَيْمَانُ بْنُ مَعْبَدٍ السِّنْجِيُّ ، قَالَ : حَدَّثَنَا عَبْدُ الرَّزَّاقِ ، عَنْ مَعْمَرٍ ، عَنْ زَيْدِ بْنِ أَسْلَمَ ، عَنْ أَبِيهِ ، عَنِ النَّبِيِّ صلى الله عليه وسلم نَحْوَهُ ، وَلَمْ يَذْكُرْ فِيهِ عَنْ عُمَرَ[179]

159. Zayd ibn Aslam reports the same from his father.

١٦٠ : حَدَّثَنَا مُحَمَّدُ بْنُ بَشَّارٍ ، قَالَ : حَدَّثَنَا مُحَمَّدُ بْنُ جَعْفَرٍ ، وَعَبْدُ الرَّحْمَنِ بْنُ مَهْدِيٍّ ، قَالا : حَدَّثَنَا شُعْبَةُ ، عَنْ قَتَادَةَ ، عَنْ أَنَسِ بْنِ مَالِكٍ ، قَالَ : كَانَ النَّبِيُّ صلى الله عليه وسلم يُعْجِبُهُ الدُّبَّاءُ فَأُتِيَ بِطَعَامٍ ، أَوْ دُعِيَ لَهُ فَجَعَلْتُ أَتَتَبَّعُهُ ، فَأَضَعُهُ بَيْنَ يَدَيْهِ لِمَا أَعْلَمُ أَنَّهُ يُحِبُّهُ[180]

177 Sunan al-Tirmidhī (1851) and Sunan Ibn Mājah (3319)
178 See hadīth 157.
179 Musannad Abdul Razzaq (19568)
180 Musnad Ahmad (12811)

160. Anas ibn Mālik ﷺ narrated: "The Prophet ﷺ loved eating gourd. Once food was presented to him (or he attended an invitation) where gourd was served. As I knew that he loved it; I sought its pieces in the platter and then placed them in front of him so that he could eat them."

Al-Bajūrī said,

> The reason the Prophet ﷺ liked eating gourd is because it sharpens the mind, cures headaches, extinguishes thirst, it is good for the one who has a fever and is suitable for one who feels cold.

Ibn Hajar al-Haytamī said,

> The Prophet ﷺ liked gourd because he knew that this vine possesses hidden benefits since Allāh caused it to grow over Prophet Yūnus ﷺ. Yūnus subsisted and lived under the shade of this vine [during his rehabilitation].
>
> One of the benefits concluded from this hadīth is that it is allowed for a person to reach for the food that is not in front of him if the food consists of different types.

١٦١ : حَدَّثَنَا قُتَيْبَةُ بْنُ سَعِيدٍ ، قَالَ : حَدَّثَنَا حَفْصُ بْنُ غِيَاثٍ ، عَنْ إِسْمَاعِيلَ بْنُ أَبِي خَالِدٍ ، عَنْ حَكِيمِ بْنِ جَابِرٍ ، عَنْ أَبِيهِ ، قَالَ : دَخَلْتُ عَلَى النَّبِيِّ صلى الله عليه وسلم ، فَرَأَيْتُ عِنْدَهُ دُبَّاءً يُقَطَّعُ ، فَقُلْتُ : مَا هَذَا ؟ قَالَ : نُكَثِّرُ بِهِ طَعَامَنَا[181]

161. Jābir ibn Tariq ﷺ narrated: "I visited the Prophet ﷺ and I observed that a gourd was being sliced. I inquired, 'What is the reason for cutting it into pieces?' He replied, 'We use it to increase the quantity of our food.'"

181 Sunan Ibn Mājah (3304)

Abdul Razzaq al-Badr said,

> This hadīth shows that gourd is from the *idām*.

Al-Bajūrī said,

> The slicing of the gourd into pieces indicates that one should take care of the cooking as this does not contradict asceticism or reliance on Allāh, as one can live moderately in a manner that leads to contentment.

١٦٢ : حَدَّثَنَا قُتَيْبَةُ بْنُ سَعِيدٍ ، عَنْ مَالِكِ بْنِ أَنَسٍ ، عَنْ إِسْحَاقَ بْنِ عَبْدِ اللهِ بْنِ أَبِي طَلْحَةَ ، أَنَّهُ سَمِعَ أَنَسَ بْنَ مَالِكٍ ، يَقُولُ : إِنَّ خَيَّاطًا دَعَا رَسُولَ اللهِ صلى الله عليه وسلم ، لِطَعَامٍ صَنَعَهُ ، قَالَ أَنَسٌ : فَذَهَبْتُ مَعَ رَسُولِ اللهِ صَلَى الله عليه وسلم ، إِلَى ذَلِكَ الطَّعَامِ ، فَقَرَّبَ إِلَى رَسُولِ الله صلى الله عليه وسلم خُبْزًا مِنْ شَعِيرٍ ، وَمَرَقًا فِيهِ دُبَّاءٌ وَقَدِيدٌ ، قَالَ أَنَسٌ : فَرَأَيْتُ النَّبِيَّ صلى الله عليه وسلم يَتَتَبَّعُ الدُّبَّاءَ حَوَالَيِ الْقَصْعَةِ فَلَمْ أَزَلْ أُحِبُّ الدُّبَّاءَ مِنْ يَوْمِئِذٍ[182]

162. Anas ibn Mālik ؓ narrated: "A tailor once invited the Messenger of Allāh ﷺ to a feast he had prepared. I went with Allāh's Messenger ﷺ and attended the gathering. The host presented the Messenger ﷺ with some bread made of barley and a broth with pieces of meat and gourd in it. I saw the Messenger ﷺ look for pieces of gourd from all sides of the bowl. Thenceforth, I began loving gourd."

Abdul Razzaq al-Badr said,

> From the etiquettes of good hospitality is to place the food near the guest.

182 Sahīh al-Bukhārī (5379) and Sahīh Muslim (2041)

Al-Bajūrī said,

> Anas ibn Mālik ؓ attended the invitation with the Prophet ﷺ because he was his servant or because he was asked to.
>
> The fact that the Prophet ﷺ ate from all sides of the plate does not contradict his command that a person should eat only from in front of him. This is because the command was given so that other diners would not be harmed [by the person reaching], and no one would ever be harmed if the hand of the Prophet ﷺ reached in front of them because people seek blessing with that.

Ibn Hajar al-Haytamī said,

> The *fiqh* of this hadīth is as follows:
>
> 1. It is recommended to accept the invitation of others even if the food made is little or the social status of the host is less than that of the invitee.
> 2. It is recommended to like gourd because the Prophet ﷺ liked it and the same applies to all that which he ﷺ liked.
> 3. It is recommended to eat with the servant. The Prophet ﷺ allowing his servant to accompany him and join him is an example of his humble character and kind treatment to the young companions.

١٦٣ : حَدَّثَنَا أَحْمَدُ بْنُ إِبْرَاهِيمَ الدَّوْرَقِيُّ ، وَسَلَمَةُ بْنُ شَبِيبٍ ، وَمَحْمُودُ بْنُ غَيْلَانَ ، قَالُوا : حَدَّثَنَا أَبُو أُسَامَةَ ، عَنْ هِشَامِ بْنِ عُرْوَةَ ، عَنْ أَبِيهِ ، عَنْ عَائِشَةَ ، قَالَتْ : كَانَ النَّبِيُّ صلى الله عليه وسلم يُحِبُّ الْحَلْوَاءَ وَالْعَسَلَ[183]

163. Aisha ؓ narrated: "The Prophet ﷺ loved *halwā* and honey."

Ibn Hajar al-Haytamī said,

183 Sahīh al-Bukhārī (5431) and Sahīh Muslim (1473)

Halwā refers to all that which is sweet, and it can be used to refer to fruits. Al-Khattabī said that it refers to the manmade sweets. Al-Tha'alibī said that the *halwā* that the Prophet ﷺ liked was the mixture of dates that is knead with milk.

Al-Khattabī said, "He ﷺ did not like *halwā* in the sense that he used to crave for it but rather he would like to eat more of it when it was presented to him and that is how it was known that he liked it."

١٦٤ : حَدَّثَنَا الْحَسَنُ بْنُ مُحَمَّدٍ الزَّعْفَرَانِيُّ ، قَالَ : حَدَّثَنَا الْحَجَّاجُ بْنُ مُحَمَّدٍ ، قَالَ : قَالَ ابْنُ جُرَيْجٍ : أَخْبَرَنِي مُحَمَّدُ بْنُ يُوسُفَ ، أَنَّ عَطَاءَ بْنَ يَسَارٍ أَخْبَرَهُ ، أَنَّ أُمَّ سَلَمَةَ أَخْبَرَتْهُ ، أَنَّهَا قَرَّبَتْ إِلَى رَسُولِ الله صلى الله عليه وسلم ، جَنْبًا مَشْوِيًّا ، فَأَكَلَ مِنْهُ ، ثُمَّ قَامَ إِلَى الصَّلاةِ ، وَمَا تَوَضَّأَ[184]

164. Umm Salamah رضي الله عنها related: "I presented a roasted side portion of sheep to the Messenger of Allāh ﷺ. He ate from it and then prayed without performing ablution."

Abdul Razzaq al-Badr said,

> The last practice of the Prophet ﷺ was not to perform ablution after eating meat cooked on fire except for the meat of camels, according to the most correct view of scholars.

Al-Bajūrī said,

> Mentioning the roasted meat after *halwā* and honey indicates that these are the best types of food. However, Ibn al-Qayyim mentioned that one should not eat meat all the time as that can cause illness.

184 Sunan al-Tirmidhī (1829)

١٦٥ : حَدَّثَنَا قُتَيْبَةُ ، قَالَ : حَدَّثَنَا ابْنُ لَهِيعَةَ ، عَنْ سُلَيْمَانَ بْنِ زِيَادٍ ، عَنْ عَبْدِ اللهِ بْنِ الْحَارِثِ ، قَالَ : أَكَلْنَا مَعَ رَسُولِ اللهِ صلى الله عليه وسلم شِوَاءً فِي الْمَسْجِدِ[185]

165. 'Abdullāh ibn al-Hārith ﷺ narrated: "We ate roasted meat with the Messenger of Allāh ﷺ whilst in the masjid."

Al-Bajūrī said,

> The Sunan of Ibn Majah includes the following addition to the hadīth, "Then, he got up and prayed and we prayed with him. We did not do anything after finishing the meal more than wiping our hands with stones." It is possible that this incident took place during their *'itikāf* though it is permissible to eat in the masjid if one can assure that the food will not cause mess.

١٦٦ : حَدَّثَنَا مَحْمُودُ بْنُ غَيْلَانَ ، قَالَ : حَدَّثَنَا وَكِيعٌ ، قَالَ : حَدَّثَنَا مِسْعَرٌ ، عَنْ أَبِي صَخْرَةَ جَامِعِ بْنِ شَدَّادٍ ، عَنِ الْمُغِيرَةِ بْنِ عَبْدِ اللهِ ، عَنِ الْمُغِيرَةِ بْنِ شُعْبَةَ ، قَالَ : ضِفْتُ مَعَ رَسُولِ اللهِ صلى الله عليه وسلم ذَاتَ لَيْلَةٍ ، فَأُتِيَ بِجَنْبٍ مَشْوِيٍّ ، ثُمَّ أَخَذَ الشَّفْرَةَ فَجَعَلَ يَحُزُّ ، فَحَزَّ لِي بِهَا مِنْهُ ، قَالَ : فَجَاءَ بِلَالٌ يُؤْذِنُهُ بِالصَّلَاةِ فَأَلْقَى الشَّفْرَةَ ، فَقَالَ : مَا لَهُ تَرِبَتْ يَدَاهُ ؟ ، قَالَ : وَكَانَ شَارِبُهُ قَدْ وَفَى ، فَقَالَ لَهُ : أَقُصُّهُ لَكَ عَلَى سِوَاكٍ أَوْ قُصُّهُ عَلَى سِوَاكٍ[186]

166. Al-Mughīrah ibn Shu'bah ﷺ narrated: "One night, I and the Messenger of Allāh ﷺ were the guests of an individual. The host served us a roasted side portion of sheep and then he ﷺ took a big knife and started cutting pieces from it and he cut some for me to eat. During this period, Bilal ﷺ came and began the call to prayer, and so the Prophet ﷺ put down the knife and said, 'May both his hands

185 Sunan Ibn Mājah (3311)
186 Sunan Abu Dawud (188)

be in dust. What made him call out for the prayer at this moment?'"

Al-Mughīrah said that his moustache had grown long and so the Messenger of Allāh ﷺ said to him, "Come let me put a *siwāk* on it and then trim the hair that goes below its level."

Ibn Hajar al-Haytamī said,

> The Messenger of Allāh ﷺ cutting the meat for al-Mughīrah shows his modesty and it was an action done to show kindness to al-Mughīrah who had recently embraced Islām at that time.
>
> The Messenger of Allāh ﷺ blamed Bilal for calling him to the prayer in the presence of food when there was still time remaining for the time of the prayer.[187]

Alī al-Qārī said,

> The statement of the Messenger of Allāh ﷺ to Bilal could be interpreted either in the sense of blame or praise. To assume it is intended to mean the latter, then it was said to praise Bilal for notifying him of the prayer. If it is the former then, it was said because delaying the prayer of *'Ishā* is better than praying it at the beginning of its time.

Ibn Hajar al-Asqalānī said,

> The scholars differed on whether it is better to trim the moustache or to shave it. Some scholars held the view that shaving the moustache is better based on a hadīth but the majority stated that trimming it is better.

١٦٧ : حَدَّثَنَا وَاصِلُ بْنُ عَبْدِ الأَعْلَى ، قَالَ : حَدَّثَنَا مُحَمَّدُ بْنُ فُضَيْلٍ ، عَنْ أَبِي حَيَّانَ التَّيْمِيِّ ، عَنْ أَبِي زُرْعَةَ ، عَنْ أَبِي هُرَيْرَةَ ، قَالَ : أُتِيَ النَّبِيُّ صلى الله عليه

---

187 The Prophet ﷺ said: When the supper is brought and the prayer begins, one should first take food" [Sahīh Muslim]

وسلم بِلَحْمٍ ، فَرُفِعَ إِلَيْهِ الذِّرَاعُ ، وَكَانَتْ تُعْجِبُهُ ، فَنَهَسَ مِنْهَا[188]

167. Abū Hurairah ؓ narrated: "Someone sent the Messenger of Allāh ﷺ some meat. From it the forearm was presented to him as he loved this portion of the meat, and so he ate a morsel of it with his front teeth."

Al-Qadī 'Iyyād said,

> He ﷺ liked the meat of the forearm because it is delicious, quick to be cooked, easy to chew and swallow, and it is far from the parts of the animal that are exposed to dirt and harm.

١٦٨ : حَدَّثَنَا مُحَمَّدُ بْنُ بَشَّارٍ ، قَالَ : حَدَّثَنَا أَبُو دَاوُدَ ، عَنْ زُهَيْرٍ يَعْنِي ابْنَ مُحَمَّدٍ ، عَنِ أَبِي إِسْحَاقَ ، عَنْ سَعْدِ بْنِ عِيَاضٍ ، عَنِ ابْنِ مَسْعُودٍ ، قَالَ : كَانَ النَّبِيُّ صلى الله عليه وسلم يُعْجِبُهُ الذِّرَاعُ ، قَالَ : وَسُمَّ فِي الذِّرَاعِ ، وَكَانَ يَرَى أَنَّ الْيَهُودَ سَمُّوهُ[189]

168. 'Abdullāh ibn Mas'ūd ؓ narrated: "The Messenger of Allāh ﷺ loved the meat of the forearm." He also narrated that: "He ﷺ was given poison in the forearm portion of the meat and it was believed that the Jews poisoned him."

Al-Bajūrī said,

> In another hadīth, it mentions that he loved the shoulder. He ﷺ also liked the meat of the neck because it is similar to the meat of the forearm in that it is far from the places of harm.
>
> Ibn 'Umar ؓ narrated that he ﷺ disliked eating seven things from the sheep: (i) the gall bladder, (ii) the bladder, (iii) the testicles, (iv) the penis, (v) the vagina, (vi) the blood, (vii) and the gland.

188 Sahīh al-Bukhārī (4712) and Sahīh Muslim (194)
189 Sunan Abu Dawud (3780)

Alī al-Qārī said,

> The lethal poisoned meat did not harm the Prophet ﷺ when he ate it but it used to affect him every year until he ﷺ died because of it. This was in order to double his reward. It was narrated that he ﷺ only ate one bite of it and then Jibrīl ﷺ informed him about the poison upon which he ﷺ informed his companions to refrain from eating it. However, some of them passed away. In another hadīth, it was the poisoned forearm that informed the Prophet ﷺ about it. The Jewish woman who did this was questioned about her motives and she answered that she believed if he ﷺ was a Prophet then the poison would not harm him and for that he ﷺ forgave her and the woman embraced Islām after she saw the outcome of her test. However, later on she was executed because her poison led to the death of one of the other companions who ate from the meat. The wisdom behind Jibrīl and the forearm (according to the other narration) not informing him ﷺ until after he ate from the meat was to manifest the truthfulness of his status as a Prophet, to be a reason for the Jewish woman to embrace Islām, and to be an evidence against anyone who insists after that on disbelief.

١٦٩ : حَدَّثَنَا مُحَمَّدُ بْنُ بَشَّارٍ ، قَالَ : حَدَّثَنَا مُسْلِمُ بْنُ إِبْرَاهِيمَ ، قَالَ : حَدَّثَنَا أَبَانُ بْنُ يَزِيدَ ، عَنْ قَتَادَةَ ، عَنْ شَهْرِ بْنِ حَوْشَبٍ ، عَنْ أَبِي عُبَيْدَةَ ، قَالَ : طَبَخْتُ لِلنَّبِيِّ صلى الله عليه وسلم ، قِدْرًا ، وَقَدْ كَانَ يُعْجِبُهُ الذِّرَاعُ ، فَنَاوَلْتُهُ الذِّرَاعَ ، ثُمَّ قَالَ : نَاوِلْنِي الذِّرَاعَ ، فَنَاوَلْتُهُ ، ثُمَّ قَالَ : نَاوِلْنِي الذِّرَاعَ ، فَقُلْتُ : يَا رَسُولَ اللهِ ، وَكَمْ لِلشَّاةِ مِنْ ذِرَاعٍ ، فَقَالَ : وَالَّذِي نَفْسِي بِيَدِهِ لَوْ سَكَتَّ لَنَاوَلْتَنِي الذِّرَاعَ مَا دَعَوْتُ[190]

169. Abū 'Ubaydah ﷺ narrated: "I once prepared food for the Messenger of Allāh ﷺ. Because he loved the forearm portion of

190 Al-Bidaya wal Nihayah (6/127)

the meat, I served him that portion. He then ordered another one, I served the second one. He then ordered one again. I replied, 'O Messenger of Allāh! The goat has only two forearms!' To that he said, 'I swear by the One in whose Hand is my soul, if you kept quiet, you could have served me every time I requested one from you.'"

Abdul Razzaq al-Badr said,

> This is a hadīth that shows one of the miracles of the Messenger of Allāh ﷺ and signs of his truthfulness.

Ibn Hajar al-Haytamī said,

> The reason why the inquisitive statement of the companion resulted in not witnessing this miracle is because witnessing such a miracle is an honour by itself and only a person whose submission is perfect and free of any personal desire or opinion deserves to witness it.

١٧٠ : حَدَّثَنَا الْحَسَنُ بْنُ مُحَمَّدٍ الزَّعْفَرَانِيُّ ، قَالَ : حَدَّثَنَا يَحْيَى بْنُ عَبَّادٍ ، عَنْ فُلَيْحِ بْنِ سُلَيْمَانَ ، قَالَ : حَدَّثَنِي رَجُلٌ ، مِنْ بَنِي عَبَّادٍ يُقَالُ لَهُ : عَبْدُ الْوَهَّابِ بْنُ يَحْيَى بْنُ عَبَّادٍ ، عَنْ عَبْدِ اللهِ بْنِ الزُّبَيْرِ ، عَنْ عَائِشَةَ ، قَالَتْ : مَا كَانَتِ الذِّرَاعُ أَحَبَّ اللَّحْمِ إِلَى رَسُولِ اللهِ صلى الله عليه وسلم ، وَلَكِنَّهُ كَانَ لا يَجِدُ اللَّحْمَ إِلا غِبًّا ، وَكَانَ يَعْجَلُ إِلَيْهَا ، لأَنَّهَا أَعْجَلُهَا نُضْجًا[191]

170. Aisha ﵂ narrated: "The Messenger of Allāh ﷺ did not like the forearm portion of meat the best (i.e. due to its taste). Rather, as meat was only available occasionally, and as this portion of the meat cooked quickly, he liked it."

Alī al-Qārī said,

191 Sunan al-Tirmidhī (1838)

> This is supported by the statement of Aisha ﵂ that it would pass a whole month without them having anything to cook and that they would live on dates and water unless they received some meat. This hadīth also shows that he ﷺ liked other portions of meat such as the meat of the back (the meat that is along the backbone of the animal), as stated in the next hadīth.

Ibn Hajar al-Haytamī said,

> The statement of Aisha ﵂ negating that he ﷺ liked the meat of the forearm as a personal preference seems to be given to indicate that the noble status of the Prophet ﷺ transcended any inclination to the worldly pleasures. Thus she explained that he liked it because it cooks fast and that saved him time so he could return quickly to his commitments and look after the affairs of Muslims. However, to love the meat of the forearm as a personal preference does not contravene his perfection because imperfection is to work hard to attain a worldly pleasure or feeling sorry for missing it.

١٧١ : حَدَّثَنَا مَحْمُودُ بْنُ غَيْلانَ ، قَالَ : حَدَّثَنَا أَبُو أَحْمَدَ ، قَالَ : حَدَّثَنَا مِسْعَرٌ ، قَالَ : سَمِعْتُ شَيْخًا ، مِنْ فَهْمٍ ، قَالَ : سَمِعْتُ عَبْدَ اللهِ بْنَ جَعْفَرٍ ، يَقُولُ : سَمِعْتُ رَسُولَ اللهِ صلى الله عليه وسلم ، يَقُولُ : إِنَّ أَطْيَبَ اللَّحْمِ لَحْمُ الظَّهْرِ [192]

171. 'Abdullāh ibn Ja'far ﵁ narrated: "I heard the Prophet ﷺ saying, 'The best meat is the meat of the back (the meat that is along the backbone of the animal).'"

Abdul Razzaq al-Badr said,

> This praise shows that the Prophet ﷺ ate the meat of the back as well.

192 Sunan Ibn Mājah (3308)

١٧٢ : حَدَّثَنَا سُفْيَانُ بْنُ وَكِيعٍ ، قَالَ : حَدَّثَنَا زَيْدُ بْنُ الْحُبَابِ ، عَنْ عَبْدِ اللهِ بْنِ الْمُؤَمَّلِ ، عَنِ ابْنِ أَبِي مُلَيْكَةَ ، عَنْ عَائِشَةَ : أَنَّ النَّبِيَّ صلى الله عليه وسلم ، قَالَ : نِعْمَ الإِدَامُ الْخَلُّ[193]

172. Aisha ﵂ narrated that the Prophet ﷺ said: "Vinegar is an excellent *idām*."[194]

١٧٣ : حَدَّثَنَا أَبُو كُرَيْبٍ مُحَمَّدُ بْنُ الْعَلاءِ ، قَالَ : حَدَّثَنَا أَبُو بَكْرِ بْنُ عَيَّاشٍ ، عَنْ ثَابِتٍ أَبِي حَمْزَةَ الثُّمَالِيِّ ، عَنِ الشَّعْبِيِّ ، عَنْ أُمِّ هَانِئٍ ، قَالَتْ : دَخَلَ عَلَيَّ النَّبِيُّ صلى الله عليه وسلم ، فَقَالَ : أَعِنْدَكِ شَيْءٌ ؟ فَقُلْتُ : لا ، إِلا خُبْزٌ يَابِسٌ ، وَخَلٌّ فَقَالَ : هَاتِي ، مَا أَقْفَرَ بَيْتٌ مِنْ أُدْمٍ فِيهِ الخل[195]

173. Umm Hanī' ﵂ related: "The Messenger of Allāh ﷺ came to my house and asked if there was something to eat. I replied, 'Nothing besides dry bread and vinegar.' The Messenger of Allāh ﷺ said, 'Bring it. The house that has vinegar in it is not a house that has bread without an *idām*.'"

Abdul Razzaq al-Badr said,

> This incident happened on the day that Makkah was conquered.

Alī al-Qārī said,

> It was said that the statement of Umm Hanī began with a negative word to indicate that there was no food in the house even though there was some. This was because she glorified the status of the Prophet ﷺ and thought that dry bread and vinegar were not suitable foods to be served to a person with such a high, noble

193 Sunan Abu Dawūd (3820)
194 Previously explained in hadith 151.
195 Sunan al-Tirmidhī (1841)

status.

The meaning of the statement of the Prophet ﷺ is that a house that has vinegar will not be in need of another *idām*.

Ibn Hajar al-Haytamī said,

> The *fiqh* of this hadīth is:
>
> 1. Encouraging not belittling bread and vinegar as a food.
> 2. It is permissible to ask someone for food if the relationship is strong enough that the questioner will not feel embarrassment when asking.

١٧٤ : حَدَّثَنَا مُحَمَّدُ بْنُ الْمُثَنَّى ، قَالَ : حَدَّثَنَا مُحَمَّدُ بْنُ جَعْفَرٍ ، قَالَ : حَدَّثَنَا شُعْبَةُ ، عَنْ عَمْرِو بْنِ مُرَّةَ ، عَنْ مُرَّةَ الْهَمْدَانِيِّ ، عَنْ أَبِي مُوسَى الأَشْعَرِيِّ ، عَنِ النَّبِيِّ صلى الله عليه وسلم ، قَالَ : فَضْلُ عَائِشَةَ عَلَى النِّسَاءِ كَفَضْلِ الثَّرِيدِ عَلَى سَائِرِ الطَّعَامِ[196]

174. Abū Mūsa al-Ash'arī ﷺ narrated: "The Messenger of Allāh ﷺ said, 'The excellence of Aisha ﷺ over other women is like the excellence of *tharīd* over other foods.'"

Al-Bajūrī said,

> This description of Aisha ﷺ is a merit she earned due to her good character, eloquence in speech, sensibility and wisdom, and her constant efforts to please her husband. This hadīth is intended to mean that she was the best of his wives because the best of women are in the following order: Maryam bint 'Imrān, Fātimah al-Zahrā' (daughter of the Prophet ﷺ), Khadījah bint Khuwailid (the first wife of the Prophet ﷺ) and then comes Aisha. This is the view of many of the *salaf* and many of the latter scholars.

196 Sahīh al-Bukhārī (5418) and Sahīh Muslim (2431)

Ibn Hajar al-Haytamī said,

> *Tharīd* is a dish made of pieces of bread in meat broth. This dish does not always include pieces of meat.

١٧٥ : حَدَّثَنَا عَلِيُّ بْنُ حُجْرٍ ، قَالَ : حَدَّثَنَا إِسْمَاعِيلُ بْنُ جَعْفَرٍ ، قَالَ : حَدَّثَنَا عَبْدُ اللهِ بْنُ عَبْدِ الرَّحْمَنِ بْنِ مَعْمَرٍ الأَنْصَارِيُّ أَبُو طُوَالَةَ ، أَنَّهُ سَمِعَ أَنَسَ بْنَ مَالِكٍ ، يَقُولُ : قَالَ رَسُولُ اللهِ صلى الله عليه وسلم : فَضْلُ عَائِشَةَ عَلَى النِّسَاءِ كَفَضْلِ الثَّرِيدِ عَلَى سَائِرِ الطَّعَامِ[197]

175. Anas ibn Mālik ﷺ narrated: "The Messenger of Allāh ﷺ said, 'The excellence of Aisha ﷺ over other women is like the excellence of *tharīd* over other foods.'"

١٧٦ : حَدَّثَنَا قُتَيْبَةُ بْنُ سَعِيدٍ ، قَالَ : حَدَّثَنَا عَبْدُ الْعَزِيزِ بْنُ مُحَمَّدٍ ، عَنْ سُهَيْلِ بْنِ أَبِي صَالِحٍ ، عَنْ أَبِيهِ ، عَنْ أَبِي هُرَيْرَةَ ، أَنَّهُ رَأَى رَسُولَ اللهِ صلى الله عليه وسلم ، تَوَضَّأَ مِنْ أَكْلِ ثَوْرِ أَقِطٍ ، ثُمَّ رَآهُ أَكَلَ مِنْ كَتِفِ شَاةٍ ، ثُمَّ صَلَّى ، وَلَمْ يَتَوَضَّأْ[198]

176. Abū Hurairah ﷺ narrated: "He once saw the Messenger of Allāh ﷺ performing ablution after he ate a piece of hard dry yoghurt (made from ewe or goat's milk), and he saw him on another occasion eating from the shoulder of a lamb, and then he prayed without performing ablution."

Abdul Razzaq al-Badr said,

> The word ablution (Arabic: *wudū*) is used in this hadīth twice but each mention entails a different meaning; the lingual meaning and

197 Sahīh al-Bukhārī (5428) and Sahīh Muslim (2446)
198 Musnad Ahmad (9050)

the religious meaning. The word was used in reference to eating dry yoghurt to mean that he ﷺ washed his hands after he ate it, and the word was used in the second instance to refer to the actual ablution. Thus, the meaning of the hadīth is that he ﷺ washed his hands after eating the first meal, and he did not perform ablution after eating from the sheep because it does not invalidate one's ablution.

١٧٧ : حَدَّثَنَا ابْنُ أَبِي عُمَرَ ، قَالَ : حَدَّثنا سُفْيَانُ بْنُ عُيَيْنَةَ ، عَنْ وَائِلِ بْنِ دَاوُدَ ، عَنِ ابْنِهِ ، وَهُوَ بَكْرُ بْنُ وَائِلٍ ، عَنِ الزُّهْرِيِّ ، عَنْ أَنَسِ بْنِ مَالِكٍ ، قَالَ : أَوْلَمَ رَسُولُ الله صلى الله عليه وسلم عَلَى صَفِيَّةَ بِتَمْرٍ وَسَوِيقٍ[199]

177. Anas ibn Mālik ﷺ reported: "The Messenger of Allāh ﷺ had his wedding feast in celebration of his marriage with Safiyyah ﷺ with dates and *sawīq*."

Abdul Razzaq al-Badr said,

The mother of the believers Safiyyah was the daughter of Huyay ibn Akhtab and she was from the captives (slaves) but the Prophet ﷺ freed her and married her, making her freedom her wedding gift (Arabic: *mahr*). The *sawīq* is a meal made of wheat or barley. However, in Sahīh Bukhārī it states that the feast was a meal made of dates, *ghee* and dried milk or wheat.

Al-Bajūrī said,

The father of Safiyyah was the famous master of the Jewish tribe Banī al-Nadīr and his daughter was one of the female captives on the day of Khaybar. Before she was captured and entered Islām, she saw a dream that the moon fell upon her lap. When she told her father about the dream he hit her hard on the face, leaving a

199 Sunan Abū Dawūd (3744) and Sunan Ibn Mājah (1909)

mark on it and he said to her, "You will keep looking high until you become the woman of the kind of the Arabs."

١٧٨ : حَدَّثَنَا الحُسَيْنُ بْنُ مُحَمَّدٍ الْبَصْرِيُّ ، قَالَ : حَدَّثَنَا الْفُضَيْلُ بْنُ سُلَيْمَانَ ، قَالَ : حَدَّثَنِي فَائِدٌ ، مَوْلَى عُبَيْدِ اللهِ بْنِ عَلِيِّ بْنِ أَبِي رَافِعٍ مَوْلَى رَسُولِ اللهِ صلى الله عليه وسلم ، قَالَ : حَدَّثَنِي عُبَيْدُ اللهِ بْنُ عَلِيٍّ ، عَنْ جَدَّتِهِ سَلْمَى ، أَنَّ الحَسَنَ بْنَ عَلِيٍّ ، وَابْنَ عَبَّاسٍ ، وَابْنَ جَعْفَرٍ أَتَوْهَا فَقَالُوا لَهَا : اصْنَعِي لَنَا طَعَامًا مِمَّا كَانَ يُعْجِبُ رَسُولَ اللهِ صلى الله عليه وسلم ، وَيُحْسِنُ أَكْلَهُ فَقَالَتْ : يَا بُنَيَّ لا تَشْتَهِيهِ الْيَوْمَ ، قَالَ : بَلَى اصْنَعِيهِ لَنَا قَالَ : فَقَامَتْ فَأَخَذَتْ مِنْ شَعِيرٍ فَطَحَنَتْهُ ، ثُمَّ جَعَلَتْهُ فِي قِدْرٍ ، وَصَبَّتْ عَلَيْهِ شَيْئًا مِنْ زَيْتٍ ، وَدَقَّتِ الْفُلْفُلَ ، وَالتَّوَابِلَ ، فَقَرَّبَتْهُ إِلَيْهِمْ ، فَقَالَتْ : هَذَا مِمَّا كَانَ يُعْجِبُ رَسُولَ اللهِ صلى الله عليه وسلم ، وَيُحْسِنُ أَكْلَهُ[200]

178. Salma ﵂, the grandmother of 'Ubaidullāh ibn Alī narrated that Al-Hasan ibn Alī, Ibn 'Abbās and Ibn Ja'far ﵃ visited her and asked her to make them a food that the Messenger of Allāh ﷺ liked and ate with pleasure. However, she replied, "O my children, you will not like it now." They replied, "We will surely like it." She stood up and gathered some barley, crushed it and put it in a pot, poured a little olive oil over it, then crushed some pepper and spices and added that to the pot and served it whilst saying, "This is from the food that the Messenger of Allāh ﷺ liked and ate with pleasure."

Al-Bajūrī said,

> The grandmother of 'Ubaidullāh ibn Alī was the one who helped deliver Ibrahīm, the son of the Prophet ﷺ. She was the servant of the Prophet ﷺ and the one who cooked for him. This is why she was approached and asked about the food he ﷺ used to like.

200 Al-Targhīb wal Tarhīb (4/173)

Alī al-Qārī said,

> Her stating that they would not like the food was meant to indicate that it would not meet their personal preferences in terms of what constitutes a good food. This was due to this food being eaten during difficult times whereas the food they (the companions who visited her) were now accustomed to was far more diverse as life had become more comfortable. Their answering that they will like it meant that they will surely like it since the Prophet ﷺ liked it and they were seeking the blessings of following the example of the Prophet ﷺ.

١٧٩ : حَدَّثَنَا مَحْمُودُ بْنُ غَيْلانَ ، قَالَ : حَدَّثَنَا أَبُو أَحْمَدَ ، قَالَ : حَدَّثَنَا سُفْيَانُ ، عَنِ الأَسْوَدِ بْنِ قَيْسٍ ، عَنْ نُبَيْحٍ الْعَنَزِيِّ ، عَنْ جَابِرِ بْنِ عَبْدِ اللهِ ، قَالَ : أَتَانَا النَّبِيُّ صلى الله عليه وسلم ، فِي مَنْزِلِنَا ، فَذَبَحْنَا لَهُ شَاةً ، فَقَالَ : كَأَنَّهُمْ عَلِمُوا أَنَّا نُحِبُّ اللَّحْمَ وَفِي الْحَدِيثِ قِصَّةٌ[201]

179. Jābir ibn 'Abdullāh ؓ narrated: "The Messenger of Allāh ﷺ came to our house and we slaughtered a sheep in his honour. He ﷺ said, 'It is as if they knew we like meat.'"

Imām al-Tirmidhī said: "There is a story behind the visit of the Prophet ﷺ."

Al-Bajūrī said,

> The statement of the Messenger of Allāh ﷺ was intended to compliment the hosts and make them happy, not to show his admiration for meat. This hadīth teaches us that the host should serve that which the guest likes, if he knows about it, and that the guest should mention to his host the food he likes (unless he knows that it would burden the host).

201 Al-Ajwibah al-Murdiyyah (1/177)

Abdul Razzaq al-Badr said,

> The reason behind the visit of the Prophet ﷺ to the house of Jābir ﷺ is explained in the hadīth documented in the Musnad of Imām Ahmad wherein it states that Jābir asked the Prophet ﷺ to help him pay the debts of his father, so he ﷺ said that he would pay a visit to his house. Then Jābir went home and told his wife not to talk to or ask the Prophet ﷺ for anything. So, when he ﷺ visited them, he slaughtered for him a sheep and so he ﷺ said, "It is as if they knew we like meat." But, when he ﷺ went out, Jābir's wife asked the Prophet ﷺ to pray on her and her husband so the Prophet ﷺ said, "O Allāh, may your *Salah* be upon them." This made Jābir chastise his wife for disobeying him but she said, "Did you want him ﷺ to enter our house and leave without supplicating for us!"[202]

١٨٠ : حَدَّثَنَا ابْنُ أَبِي عُمَرَ ، قَالَ : حَدَّثَنَا سُفْيَانُ ، قَالَ : حَدَّثَنَا عَبْدُ اللهِ بْنُ مُحَمَّدِ بْنِ عَقِيلٍ ، أَنَّهُ سمعَ جَابِرًا (ح) قَالَ سُفْيَانُ : وَحَدَّثَنَا مُحَمَّدُ بْنُ الْمُنْكَدِرِ ، عَنْ جَابِرٍ ، قَالَ : خَرَجَ رَسُولُ اللهِ صلى الله عليه وسلم ، وَأَنَا مَعَهُ فَدَخَلَ عَلَى امْرَأَةٍ مِنَ الأَنْصَارِ ، فَذَبَحَتْ لَهُ شَاةً ، فَأَكَلَ مِنْهَا ، وَأَتَتْهُ بِقِنَاعٍ مِنْ رُطَبٍ ، فَأَكَلَ مِنْهُ ، ثُمَّ تَوَضَّأَ لِلظُّهْرِ ، وَصَلَّى ، صلى الله عليه وسلم ، ثُمَّ انْصَرَفَ ، فَأَتَتْهُ بِعُلالَةٍ مِنْ عُلالَةِ الشَّاةِ ، فَأَكَلَ ثُمَّ صَلَّى الْعَصْرَ ، وَلَمْ يَتَوَضَّأْ[203]

180. Jābir ﷺ narrated: "The Messenger of Allāh ﷺ went out to the house of a woman from among the Ansār and I accompanied him. The hostess slaughtered a sheep for the Messenger of Allāh ﷺ and so he ate from it. She then served him fresh dates upon a tray made of palm leaves. The Messenger of Allāh ﷺ ate some from it, then performed ablution and prayed *Dhuhr*. After returning from the

---

202 Musnad Ahmad (14245)
203 Sunan al-Tirmidhī (80)

prayer, she served him some of the remaining meat. The Messenger of Allāh ﷺ ate from it and then prayed '*Asr* without performing ablution."

Abdul Razzaq al-Badr said,

> The statement of Jābir when he said, "I accompanied him" demonstrates the high level of politeness and good etiquette of the companions when talking about the Prophet ﷺ as their choice of words always implied that they were following the Prophet ﷺ.

Al-Bajūrī said,

> This hadīth shows us that the Prophet ﷺ ate meat twice in one day and this does not contradict the statement of Aisha ﷺ wherein she mentioned that he ﷺ never had a full stomach from meat. This is because eating meat twice on the same say does not necessitate that he had a full stomach.

Ibn Hajar al-Haytamī said,

> This hadīth teaches us that it is allowed to eat twice even if the food from the first time has not yet fully digested if one knows that he will not overeat, or if the food served first was little.

١٨١ : حَدَّثَنَا الْعَبَّاسُ بْنُ مُحَمَّدٍ الدُّورِيُّ ، قَالَ : حَدَّثَنَا يُونُسُ بْنُ مُحَمَّدٍ ، قَالَ : حَدَّثَنَا فُلَيْحُ بْنُ سُلَيْمَانَ ، عَنْ عُثْمَانَ بْنِ عَبْدِ الرَّحْمَنِ ، عَنْ يَعْقُوبَ بْنِ أَبِي يَعْقُوبَ ، عَنْ أُمِّ الْمُنْذِرِ ، قَالَتْ : دَخَلَ عَلَيَّ رَسُولُ اللهِ صلى الله عليه وسلم ، وَمَعَهُ عَلِيٌّ ، وَلَنَا دَوَالٍ مُعَلَّقَةٌ ، قَالَتْ : فَجَعَلَ رَسُولُ اللهِ صلى الله عليه وسلم يَأْكُلُ وَعَلِيٌّ مَعَهُ يَأْكُلُ ، فَقَالَ رَسُولُ اللهِ صلى الله عليه وسلم ، لِعَلِيٍّ : مَهْ يَا عَلِيُّ ، فَإِنَّكَ نَاقِةٌ ، قَالَتْ : فَجَلَسَ عَلِيٌّ ، وَالنَّبِيُّ صلى الله عليه وسلم يَأْكُلُ ، قَالَتْ : فَجَعَلْتُ لَهُمْ سِلْقًا وَشَعِيرًا ، فَقَالَ النَّبِيُّ صلى الله عليه

وسلم لِعَلِيٍّ : مِنْ هَذَا فَأَصِبْ فَإِنَّ هَذَا أَوْفَقُ لَكَ[204]

181. Umm al-Mundhir ﵂ narrated: "The Messenger of Allāh ﷺ visited me and Alī ﵁ was with him. We had some dates hanging and the Messenger of Allāh ﷺ began eating from them and so did Alī ﵁. The Messenger of Allāh ﷺ stopped him saying, 'You have not fully recovered from your illness and should not eat this.' Alī ﵁ stopped and the Messenger of Allāh ﷺ continued eating. Then I prepared for them some barley and *silq* (similar to the arugula plant). The Messenger of Allāh ﷺ said to Alī ﵁, 'Eat of this, for it is more suitable for you.'"

Abdul Razzaq al-Badr said,

> It is said that Umm al-Mundhir was one of the maternal aunts of the Prophet ﷺ.

Al-Bajūrī said,

> The directions of the Prophet ﷺ show that it is prescribed to seek medication and that this does not contradict reliance on Allāh.

١٨٢ : حَدَّثَنَا مَحْمُودُ بْنُ غَيْلانَ ، قَالَ : حَدَّثَنَا بِشْرُ بْنُ السَّرِيِّ ، عَنْ سُفْيَانَ ، عَنْ طَلْحَةَ بْنِ يَحْيَى ، عَنْ عَائِشَةَ بِنْتِ طَلْحَةَ ، عَنْ عَائِشَةَ ، أُمِّ الْمُؤْمِنِينَ ، قَالَتْ : كَانَ النَّبِيُّ صلى الله عليه وسلم يَأْتِينِي فَيَقُولُ : أَعِنْدَكِ غَدَاءٌ ؟ فَأَقُولُ : لا قَالَتْ : فَيَقُولُ : إِنِّي صَائِمٌ قَالَتْ : فَأَتَانِي يَوْمًا ، فَقُلْتُ : يَا رَسُولَ اللهِ ، إِنَّهُ أُهْدِيَتْ لَنَا هَدِيَّةٌ ، قَالَ : وَمَا هِيَ ؟ قُلْتُ : حَيْسٌ ، قَالَ : أَمَا إِنِّي أَصْبَحْتُ صَائِمًا ، قَالَتْ : ثُمَّ أَكَلَ[205]

182. Aisha, the mother of the believers ﵂, narrated: "The Messenger

204 Sunan Al-Tirmidhī (2037)
205 Sahīh Muslim (1154)

of Allāh ﷺ used to come to me and ask if there was any food available for lunch. When I would say no, he would reply, 'In that case, I make the intention to fast.' On one occasion he came and enquired, I replied, 'We have received a gift.' He asked, 'What is it?' I replied, '*Hays* (dates mixed with ghee and dry yoghurt or ghee and wheat).' He said, 'I woke up with the intention of fasting.' He then ate some from it."

Abdul Razzaq al-Badr said,

> It is not a condition of voluntary fasting to establish the intention to fast before the time of *Fajr*. Thus, if a person wakes up and did not eat or drink, he can make the intention to fast at any point until the time before *Dhuhr*.

Al-Bajūrī said,

> The wives of the Prophet ﷺ are called the mothers of the believers because they are unlawful for the Muslims to marry. It is said so because it is obligatory to look after them and respect them [as mothers].
>
> The statement of the Prophet ﷺ wherein he disclosed his intention to fast shows that it is fine to show others your voluntary good deeds if the purpose is to educate them.

Ibn Hajar al-Haytamī said,

> The act of the Prophet ﷺ where he ate whilst he was fasting indicates that it is allowed for a person to break his voluntary fast and this view is supported by a number of other hadīths.

١٨٣ : حَدَّثَنَا عَبْدُ اللهِ بْنُ عَبْدِ الرَّحْمَنِ ، قَالَ : حَدَّثَنَا عُمَرُ بْنُ حَفْصِ بْنِ غِيَاثٍ ، قَالَ : حَدَّثَنَا أَبِي ، عَنْ مُحَمَّدِ بْنِ أَبِي يَحْيَى الأَسْلَمِيِّ ، عَنْ يَزِيدَ بْنِ أَبِي أُمَيَّةَ الأَعْوَرِ ، عَنْ يُوسُفَ بْنِ عَبْدِ اللهِ بْنِ سَلامٍ ، قَالَ : رَأَيْتُ النَّبِيَّ صلى

الله عليه وسلم أَخَذَ كِسْرَةً مِنْ خُبْزِ الشَّعِيرِ فَوَضَعَ عَلَيْهَا تَمْرَةً وَقَالَ : هَذِهِ إِدَامُ هَذِهِ ، وأكل[206]

183. Yūsuf ibn 'Abdullāh ibn Salām ؓ narrated: "I once saw the Messenger of Allāh ﷺ taking a piece of bread made of barley and putting a date on it. He then said, 'This [date] is the *idām* for this [bread].' He then ate it."

Alī al-Qārī said,

> This hadīth teaches us to utilise the resources available to have good nutrition, for the bread made of barley is cold and dry whilst the date is warm and moist. It also teaches that one should be self-content with whatever one has.

١٨٤ : حَدَّثَنَا عَبْدُ اللهِ بْنُ عَبْدِ الرَّحْمَنِ ، قَالَ : حَدَّثَنَا سَعِيدُ بْنُ سُلَيْمَانَ ، عَنْ عَبَّادِ بْنِ الْعَوَّامِ ، عَنْ حُمَيْدٍ ، عَنْ أَنَسٍ : أَنَّ رَسُولَ اللهِ صلى الله عليه وسلم كَانَ يُعْجِبُهُ الثُّفْلُ ، قَالَ عَبْدُ اللهِ : يَعْنِي مَا بَقِيَ مِنَ الطَّعَامِ[207]

184. Anas ibn Mālik ؓ narrated: "The Messenger of Allāh ﷺ liked to eat the remains of food."

Abdul Razzaq al-Badr said,

The remains of food refers to the food that remains in the bottom of the pot as it is the most cooked and tastiest of the food cooked in the pot.

206 Sunan Abū Dawūd (3260)
207 Musnad Ahmad (13300)

CHAPTER TWENTY SEVEN

باب ما جاء في صفة وضوء رسول الله صلى الله عليه وسلم عند الطعام

THE REPORTS PERTAINING TO THE *WUDŪ* OF THE MESSENGER OF ALLĀH ﷺ AT THE TIME OF EATING

Al-Bajūrī said,

> The word "*wuḍū*" used in the title of this chapter is used in its linguistic and religious sense. The former means to wash and cleanse the hands and the latter means to perform ablution.
>
> This chapter is dedicated to explaining that ablution is neither obligatory nor recommended at the time of eating and that washing the hands is recommended.

١٨٥ : حَدَّثَنَا أَحْمَدُ بْنُ مَنِيعٍ ، قَالَ : حَدَّثَنَا إِسْمَاعِيلُ بْنُ إِبْرَاهِيمَ ، عَنْ أَيُّوبَ ، عَنِ ابْنِ أَبِي مُلَيْكَةَ ، عَنِ ابْنِ عَبَّاسٍ ، أَنَّ رَسُولَ اللهِ صلى الله عليه وسلم خَرَجَ مِنَ الْخَلاءِ ، فَقُرِّبَ إِلَيْهِ الطَّعَامُ ، فَقَالُوا : أَلا نَأْتِيكَ بِوَضُوءٍ ؟ قَالَ : إِنَّمَا أُمِرْتُ بِالْوُضُوءِ ، إِذَا قُمْتُ إِلَى الصَّلاةِ[208]

185. 'Abdullāh ibn Abbās ؓ narrated: "Once after the Messenger of Allāh ﷺ finished relieving himself from the call of nature, food was served to him. He was asked if the water for ablution should be brought. He replied, 'I have only been commanded to perform ablution when I want to pray.'"

Abdul Razzaq al-Badr said,

> The statement of the Messenger of Allāh ﷺ was to explain to the companions that ablution is not required when a person wants to eat; rather only when one wants to pray.

Al-Bajūrī said,

> The command that the Messenger of Allāh ﷺ referred to was the ayah: **{O you who have believed, when you rise to [perform] prayer, wash your faces and your forearms to the elbows and wipe over your heads and wash your feet to the ankles.}**[209]
>
> Al-Walī al-Irāqī said, "This hadīth is a proof that the Messenger of Allāh ﷺ liked to perform ablution before each prayer, whether he was in a state of purity or not, except on the day Makkah was conquered as he prayed the five daily prayers with one ablution. This made 'Umar ibn al-Khattab ؓ exclaim saying, 'I saw you today doing something you never did before.' The Prophet ﷺ replied, 'O Umar! I did that intentionally.'"[210]

---

208 Sunan Abu Dawūd (3760) and Sunan al-Tirmidhī (1847)
209 Qur'ān: 5:6
210 Sahīh al-Nasai' (133)

١٨٦ : حَدَّثَنَا سَعِيدُ بْنُ عَبْدِ الرَّحْمَنِ الْمَخْزُومِيُّ ، قَالَ : حَدَّثنَا سُفْيَانُ بْنُ عُيَيْنَةَ ، عَنْ عَمْرِو بْنِ دِينَارٍ ، عَنْ سَعِيدِ بْنِ الْحُوَيْرِثِ ، عَنِ ابْنِ عَبَّاسٍ ، قَالَ : خَرَجَ رَسُولُ الله صلى الله عليه وسلم مِنَ الْغَائِطِ فَأُتِيَ بِطَعَامٍ ، فَقِيلَ لَهُ : أَلا تَتَوَضَّأُ ؟ فَقَالَ : أَأُصَلِّي ، فَأَتَوَضَّأُ[211]

186. 'Abdullāh ibn Abbās ؓ narrated: "Once after the Messenger of Allāh ﷺ finished relieving himself from the call of nature, food was served to him. He was asked if he was going to perform ablution. He replied, 'Am I going to offer a prayer so that I need to perform ablution?'"

١٨٧ : حَدَّثَنَا يَحْيَى بْنُ مُوسَى ، قَالَ : حَدَّثَنَا عَبْدُ الله بْنُ نُمَيْرٍ ، قَالَ : حَدَّثنَا قَيْسُ بْنُ الرَّبِيعِ (ح) وَحَدَّثَنَا قُتَيْبَةُ ، قَالَ : حَدَّثنَا عَبْدُ الْكَرِيمِ الْجُرْجَانِيُّ ، عَنْ قَيْسِ بْنِ الرَّبِيعِ ، عَنْ أَبِي هَاشِمٍ ، عَنْ زَاذَانَ ، عَنْ سَلْمَانَ ، قَالَ : قَرَأْتُ فِي التَّوْرَاةِ ، أَنَّ بَرَكَةَ الطَّعَامِ الْوُضُوءُ بَعْدَهُ ، فَذَكَرْتُ ذَلِكَ لِلنَّبِيِّ صلى الله عليه وسلم ، وَأَخْبَرْتُهُ بِمَا قَرَأْتُ فِي التَّوْرَاةِ ، فَقَالَ رَسُولُ الله صلى الله عليه وسلم : بَرَكَةُ الطَّعَامِ الْوُضُوءُ قَبْلَهُ ، وَالْوُضُوءُ بَعْدَهُ[212]

187. Salmān al-Fārisī ؓ narrated: "I have read in the Torah that to attain the blessings from food one should wash the hands after eating. I mentioned this to the Messenger of Allāh ﷺ and so he said, 'The blessing in food is attained when washing the hands before and after eating.'"

Al-Bajūrī said,

> It is recommended to allow the children to wash their hands first before old people as the hands of children are more likely to be

211 Sahīh Muslim (374)
212 Sunan Abu Dawūd (3761) and Sunan al-Tirmidhi (1846)

dirty compared to the hands of old people and water may run out if the old people take the lead. This is recommended before eating and the opposite is the case after eating, meaning the old people should be given priority to wash their hands over the youngsters to show respect to their age. As for the host, he takes the priority to wash his hands first before everyone but should be the last to wash his hands. It is recommended to dry the washed hands after eating but not before eating. This is because if the towel has some dirt on it and hands were dried using it before eating, then the dirt may transfer to the hands, and also because wet hands will prevent the ghee (butter) from sticking to the hands.

Al-Qurtubī said,

> If the one who reads it (the Qur'ān) will have a tenfold reward or more for each letter, according to what we mentioned in the introduction to this book, then turning away from it and towards other scriptures is misguidance and loss, and this is a poor trade off and waste of time.

Ibn Hajar al-Asqalānī said,

> It is important to note that in the case of those who are not well-versed in knowledge and are lacking in faith, it is not permissible for them to read any of those books.

CHAPTER TWENTY EIGHT

باب ما جاء في قول رسول الله صلى الله عليه وسلم قبل الطعام وعند الفراغ منه

THE REPORTS PERTAINING TO WHAT THE MESSENGER OF ALLĀH ﷺ SAID BEFORE AND AFTER EATING

Al-Bajūrī said,

> This chapter includes all that which the Messenger of Allah ﷺ used to say before and after eating and drinking.

١٨٨ : حَدَّثَنَا قُتَيْبَةُ بْنُ سَعِيدٍ ، قَالَ : حَدَّثَنَا ابْنُ لَهِيعَةَ ، عَنْ يَزِيدَ بْنِ أَبِي حَبِيبٍ ، عَنْ رَاشِدِ بْنِ جَنْدَلٍ الْيَافِعِيِّ ، عَنْ حَبِيبِ بْنِ أَوْسٍ ، عَنْ أَبِي أَيُّوبَ الأَنْصَارِيِّ ، قَالَ : كُنَّا عِنْدَ النَّبِيِّ صلى الله عليه وسلم ، يَوْمًا ، فَقَرَّبَ طَعَامًا ، فَلَمْ أَرَ طَعَامًا كَانَ أَعْظَمَ بَرَكَةً مِنْهُ ، أَوَّلَ مَا أَكَلْنَا ، وَلا أَقَلَّ بَرَكَةً فِي آخِرِهِ ، قُلْنَا : يَا رَسُولَ اللهِ ، كَيْفَ هَذَا ؟ قَالَ : إِنَّا ذَكَرْنَا اسْمَ اللهِ حِينَ أَكَلْنَا ، ثُمَّ قَعَدَ مَنْ أَكَلَ وَلَمْ يُسَمِّ اللهَ تَعَالَى فَأَكَلَ مَعَهُ الشَّيْطَانُ[213]

188. Abū Ayyūb al-Ansārī ؓ narrated: "We were once sitting with the Messenger of Allāh ﷺ. Food was presented to him and I have never seen any food that had such a large amount of blessings at the beginning and less blessings left in the food at the end. We therefore asked, 'O Messenger of Allāh ﷺ! How did this happen?' He replied, 'In the beginning we all mentioned the name of Allāh before we began eating. Then someone in the end joined us, and did not recite '*Bismillah*' and so Satan ate with him.'"

Abdul Razzaq al-Badr said,

> The statement of Abū Ayyūb ؓ at the beginning demonstrates the perfect manners of the companions when talking about the Prophet ﷺ as they used statements that indicated that they were his followers.

Al-Bajūrī said,

> The answer of the Messenger of Allāh ﷺ proves that saying '*Bismillah*' is enough to fulfil the Sunnah of mentioning the name of Allāh before eating, which is the reason why the food had so much blessing in it. However, al-Ghazalī and al-Nawawī said that adding '*al-Rahman al-Rahīm*' to '*Bismillah*' is better and closer to perfection. This is recommended to say even if the woman is menstruating or in postpartum, or when the person is in a state of

213 Musnad Ahmad (23522)

major impurity due to intercourse. However, it is stipulated that they (those in a state of major impurity) do not intend to say this with the intention to recite from the Qur'ān.

Ibn Hajar al-Haytamī said,

> It is recommended to say *'Bismillah'* before commencing anything that is important and virtuous except in the case of remembrance of Allāh and supplications (i.e. it is not prescribed for us to say *Bismillah* before we invoke Allah or before reciting any *dhikr*).

١٨٩ : حَدَّثَنَا يَحْيَى بْنُ مُوسَى ، قَالَ : حَدَّثَنَا أَبُو دَاوُدَ ، قَالَ : حَدَّثَنَا هِشَامٌ الدَّسْتُوائِيُّ ، عَنْ بُدَيْلٍ الْعُقَيْلِيِّ ، عَنْ عَبْدِ اللهِ بْنِ عُبَيْدِ بْنِ عُمَيْرٍ ، عَنْ أُمِّ كُلْثُومٍ ، عَنْ عَائِشَةَ ، قَالَتْ : قَالَ رَسُولُ اللهِ صلى الله عليه وسلم : إِذَا أَكَلَ أَحَدُكُمْ ، فَنَسِيَ أَنْ يَذْكُرَ اللهَ تَعَالَى عَلَى طَعَامِهِ ، فَلْيَقُلْ : بِسْمِ اللهِ أَوَّلَهُ وَآخِرَهُ[214]

189. Aisha ﵂ narrated: "The Messenger of Allāh ﷺ said, 'When a person eats and has forgotten to recite '*Bismillah*' [before starting to eat], then one should recite, *'Bismillahi awwalahu wa aa-khirahu'* ('*Bismillah* at the beginning and at the end')."

Abdul Razzaq al-Badr said,

> This is a direction to those who may forget to mention the name of Allāh before eating and then remember it before they finish eating. In such a case, the person should say, *"Bismillahi awwalahu wa aa-khirahu"* in order to attain the blessings of the food, by the will of Allāh.

Al-Bajūrī said,

214 See Sahīh al-Jami' (1323)

The statement "*Bismillah* at the beginning and at the end" includes all that comes in the middle and it is possible that it refers to the first half and second half of the time spent eating. In other words, it means "*Bismillah* throughout the time spent eating."

١٩٠ : حَدَّثَنَا عَبْدُ اللهِ بْنُ الصَّبَّاحِ الْهَاشِمِيُّ الْبَصْرِيُّ ، قَالَ : حَدَّثَنَا عَبْدُ الأَعْلَى ، عَنْ مَعْمَرٍ ، عَنْ هِشَامِ بْنِ عُرْوَةَ ، عَنْ أَبِيهِ ، عَنْ عُمَرَ بْنِ أَبِي سَلَمَةَ ، أَنَّهُ دَخَلَ عَلَى رَسُولِ اللهِ صلى الله عليه وسلم ، وَعِنْدَهُ طَعَامٌ ، فَقَالَ : ادْنُ يَا بُنَيَّ ، فَسَمِّ اللهَ تَعَالَى ، وَكُلْ بِيَمِينِكَ ، وَكُلْ مِمَّا يَلِيكَ[215]

190. Umar ibn Abī Salamah ؓ narrated: "I entered upon the Messenger of Allāh ﷺ whilst some food had been served to him. He ﷺ said, 'O my son! Come near, say *Bismillah*, and eat with your right hand from that which is in front of you.'"

Abdul Razzaq al-Badr said,

> This hadīth teaches us that it is allowed to call those other than one's own children "son" and it includes three etiquettes pertaining to food:
>
> 1. To say *Bismillah* before eating.
> 2. To eat with the right hand.
> 3. To eat from the portion in front of you.

Al-Bajūrī said,

> The ruling on eating with the right hand is that it is recommended but other scholars stated that it is obligatory due to the existence of the hadīth wherein the Prophet ﷺ admonished the person who ate with his left hand.

---

215 Sunan Ibn Mājah (3265) and Sunan al-Tirmidhī (1857)

Ibn Hajar al-Haytamī said,

> This hadīth teaches us the following:
>
> 1. It is recommended for the elders to be kind with the youth, especially when food is served so as to break the ice since there can be elements of shyness on such occasions.
> 2. It is recommended to say *Bismillah* audibly so others can hear it.
> 3. It is obligatory on the person to eat from the portion in front of themselves except in the case of fruits.
> 4. It is recommended for a person to teach others who eat about any of the etiquettes of food if a person does not act upon them.

١٩١ : حَدَّثَنَا مَحْمُودُ بْنُ غَيْلانَ ، قَالَ : حَدَّثَنَا أَبُو أَحْمَدَ الزُّبَيْرِيُّ ، قَالَ : حَدَّثَنَا سُفْيَانُ الثَّوْرِيُّ ، عَنْ أَبِي هَاشِمٍ ، عَنْ إِسْمَاعِيلَ بْنِ رِيَاحٍ ، عَنْ أَبِيهِ رِيَاحِ بْنِ عَبِيدَةَ ، عَنْ أَبِي سَعِيدٍ الْخُدْرِيِّ ، قَالَ : كَانَ رَسُولُ اللَّهِ صلى الله عليه وسلم إِذَا فَرَغَ مِنْ طَعَامِهِ ، قَالَ : الْحَمْدُ لِلَّهِ الَّذِي أَطْعَمَنَا وَسَقَانَا وَجَعَلَنَا مُسْلِمِينَ[216]

191. Abū Sa'īd al-Khudarī ؓ narrated: "After the Messenger of Allāh ﷺ finished eating he recited, '*All praise is due only to Allāh, who has fed us, granted us something to drink and has made us Muslims*.'"

Abdul Razzaq al-Badr said,

> There are different statements that the Prophet ﷺ used to say to praise Allāh and it is prescribed for a person to recite these various phrases of praise at different times so that on a certain occasion one is said and at another time something else and so forth. The

---

216 Sunan Abu Dawūd (3850) and Sunan al-Tirmidhī (3457)

minimum one can say is "*Alhamdulillah*" but it is better to say that which is reported from the Prophet ﷺ.

Al-Bajūrī said,

> Praising Allāh for the food after finishing the meal is to show gratefulness and appreciation to Allāh who has blessed us with that. The reason why he mentioned food before the drink is because drinks complement the food, not the other way around. The reason behind praising Allāh for making us Muslims is to combine praising Him for that which we receive in this world and that which we will receive in the Hereafter. It also indicates that one who praises Allāh for a worldly matter should praise Him for the blessings of Islām because through Islām we learnt to praise Him.

١٩٢ : حَدَّثَنَا مُحَمَّدُ بْنُ بَشَّارٍ ، قَالَ : حَدَّثَنَا يَحْيَى بْنُ سَعِيدٍ ، قَالَ : حَدَّثَنَا ثَوْرُ بْنُ يَزِيدَ ، عَنْ خَالِدُ بْنُ مَعْدَانَ ، عَنْ أَبِي أُمَامَةَ ، قَالَ : كَانَ رَسُولُ اللهِ صلى الله عليه وسلم إِذَا رُفِعَتِ الْمَائِدَةُ مِنْ بَيْنِ يَدَيْهِ ، يَقُولُ : الْحَمْدُ للهِ حَمْدًا كَثِيرًا طَيِّبًا مُبَارَكًا فِيهِ ، غَيْرَ مُودَعٍ ، وَلا مُسْتَغْنًى عَنْهُ رَبَّنَا[217]

192. Abū Umāmah ؓ narrated: "The Messenger of Allāh ﷺ used to say after the food was removed, '*All praise is due to Allāh alone; praise which is abundant, good and blessed that is neither insufficient, nor abandoned, nor ignored from our Lord.*'"

Alī al-Qārī said,

> The Sunnah is not to say "*Alhamdulillah*" after finishing the meal whist other people are still eating as that may make them stop eating.

217 Sahīh al-Bukhārī (5458)

The meaning of "praise which is abundant, good and blessed" is a praise that is endless just like how His blessings and favours upon us are endless, with sincerity and no element of showing off, and a praise that is ceaseless and blessed.

The Prophet ﷺ used to supplicate for the person at whose house he ate before leaving. The Sunnah is not to leave the food even if one is full until the other people in the group finish too. This is so that they do not feel embarrassed and leave the food whilst they still wish to eat.

١٩٣: حَدَّثَنَا أَبُو بَكْرٍ مُحَمَّدُ بْنُ أَبَانَ ، قَالَ : حَدَّثَنَا وَكِيعٌ ، عَنْ هِشَامٍ الدَّسْتُوائِيِّ ، عَنْ بُدَيْلِ بْنِ مَيْسَرَةَ الْعُقَيْلِيِّ ، عَنْ عَبْدِ اللهِ بْنِ عُبَيْدِ بْنِ عُمَيْرٍ ، عَنْ أُمِّ كُلْثُومٍ ، عَنْ عَائِشَةَ ، قَالَتْ : كَانَ النَّبِيُّ صلى الله عليه وسلم يَأْكُلُ الطَّعَامَ فِي سِتَّةٍ مِنْ أَصْحَابِهِ ، فَجَاءَ أَعْرَابِيٌّ ، فَأَكَلَهُ بِلُقْمَتَيْنِ ، فَقَالَ رَسُولُ اللهِ صلى الله عليه وسلم : لَوْ سَمَّى لَكَفَاكُمْ[218]

193. Aisha ﵂ related: "While six of the companions were eating with the Messenger of Allāh ﷺ, a nomad came and ate all the food in two bites. The Messenger of Allah ﷺ said, 'If he had said '*Bismillah*' it would have been sufficient for all of you.'"

Abdul Razzaq al-Badr said,

> This shows that leaving the *Bismillah* removes the blessings of the food.

١٩٤: حَدَّثَنَا هَنَّادٌ ، وَمَحْمُودُ بْنُ غَيْلانَ ، قَالا : حَدَّثَنَا أَبُو أُسَامَةَ ، عَنْ زَكَرِيَّا بْنِ أَبِي زَائِدَةَ ، عَنْ سَعِيدِ بْنِ أَبِي بُرْدَةَ ، عَنْ أَنَسِ بْنِ مَالِكٍ ، قَالَ : قَالَ رَسُولُ اللهِ صلى الله عليه وسلم : إِنَّ اللهَ لَيَرْضَى عَنِ الْعَبْدِ أَنْ يَأْكُلَ الأَكْلَةَ ،

218 Sunan al-Tirmidhī (1858)

أَوْ يَشْرَبَ الشَّرْبَةَ فَيَحْمَدَهُ عَلَيْهَا[219]

194. Anas ibn Mālik ؓ related: "The Messenger of Allāh ﷺ said, 'Allāh is pleased with His slave who praises Him after eating a morsel of food or taking a sip of a beverage.'"

Abdul Razzaq al-Badr said,

> The author kept this hadīth until the end of the chapter because it includes the reward of praising Allāh for one's food and drink – that is winning the pleasure of Allāh.

219 Sahīh Muslim (2734)

CHAPTER TWENTY NINE

باب ما جاء في قدح رسول الله صلى الله عليه وسلم

THE REPORTS PERTAINING TO THE CUP OF THE MESSENGER OF ALLĀH ﷺ

Abdul Razzaq al-Badr said,

> The cup refers to all that which is used to drink from.

١٩٥ : حَدَّثَنَا الحُسَيْنُ بْنُ الأَسْوَدِ الْبَغْدَادِيُّ ، قَالَ : حَدَّثَنَا عَمْرُو بْنُ مُحَمَّدٍ ، قَالَ : حَدَّثَنَا عِيسَى بْنُ طَهْمَانَ ، عَنْ ثَابِتٍ ، قَالَ : أَخْرَجَ إِلَيْنَا أَنَسُ بْنُ مَالِكٍ ، قَدَحَ خَشَبٍ ، غَلِيظًا ، مُضَبَّبًا بِحَدِيدٍ ، فَقَالَ : يَا ثَابِتُ ، هَذَا قَدَحُ رَسُولِ اللهِ صلى الله عليه وسلم[220]

195. Thābit narrated: "Anas ﷺ presented to us a thick wooden cup, which was lined with metal, and said, 'O Thābit, this is the cup of the Messenger of Allāh ﷺ.'"

Mirak Shah al-Hanafī said,

> It is proven in the authentic hadīth that the cup of the Prophet ﷺ that Anas ibn Mālik ﷺ possessed was a good cup with a length shorter than its width, and that this cup had a crack in it so the Prophet ﷺ fixed it with a silver chain.

١٩٦ : حَدَّثَنَا عَبْدُ اللهِ بْنُ عَبْدِ الرَّحْمَنِ ، قَالَ : أَنْبَأَنَا عَمْرُو بْنُ عَاصِمٍ ، قَالَ : أَنْبَأَنَا حَمَّادُ بْنُ سَلَمَةَ ، قَالَ : أَنْبَأَنَا حُمَيْدٌ ، وَثَابِتٌ ، عَنْ أَنَسٍ ، قَالَ : لَقَدْ سَقَيْتُ رَسُولَ اللهِ صلى الله عليه وسلم ، بِهَذَا الْقَدَحِ الشَّرَابَ كُلَّهُ ، الْمَاءَ ، وَالنَّبِيذَ ، وَالْعَسَلَ ، وَاللَّبَنَ[221]

196. Anas ibn Mālik ﷺ narrated: "I presented the Messenger of Allāh ﷺ with drinks in this cup from all those things which are drunk; water, *nabīdh*, honey and milk."

Abdul Razzaq al-Badr said,

> The *nabīdh* is water that has had dates or grapes put in it and left overnight. By morning the water becomes sweetened with the taste of dates or grapes.

---

220 Sharh al-Sunnah of al-Baghawī (2935)
221 Sahīh Muslim (2008)

CHAPTER THIRTY

باب ما جاء في صفة فاكهة رسول الله صلى الله عليه وسلم

THE REPORTS PERTAINING TO THE FRUITS EATEN BY THE MESSENGER OF ALLĀH ﷺ

١٩٧ : حَدَّثَنَا إِسْمَاعِيلُ بْنُ مُوسَى الْفَزَارِيُّ ، قَالَ : حَدَّثَنَا إِبْرَاهِيمُ بْنُ سَعْدٍ ، عَنْ أَبِيهِ ، عَنْ عَبْدِ اللهِ ، قَالَ : كَانَ النَّبِيُّ صلى الله عليه وسلم ، يَأْكُلُ الْقِثَّاءَ بِالرُّطَبِ[222]

197. 'Abdullāh ibn Ja'far ﷺ narrated: "The Messenger of Allāh ﷺ ate *qithā'* with ripe dates (*rutab*)."

Abdul Razzaq al-Badr said,

> *Qithā'* is a type of cucumber that is larger than the normal cucumber.

Al-Bajūrī said,

> He ﷺ combined between dates and cucumber to attain the benefits and avert the harms of each. This is because the hotness of dates neutralises the coolness of cucumber i.e. dates neutralise the negative effects of cucumber and the latter neutralises the negative effects of dates.

Ibn Hajar al-Haytamī said,

> You should know that the Messenger of Allāh ﷺ used to eat from the fruits grown in his town and never refrained from it. This is a means of maintaining one's health.
>
> This hadīth teaches us that it is allowed to combine between two types of *idām* and the hadīth does not state that both are chewed at once. Rather, it means that both are eaten one after another so they are both in the digestive tract.

١٩٨ : حَدَّثَنَا عَبْدَةُ بْنُ عَبْدِ اللهِ الْخُزَاعِيُّ الْبَصْرِيُّ ، قَالَ : حَدَّثَنَا مُعَاوِيَةُ بْنُ هِشَامٍ ، عَنْ سُفْيَانَ ، عَنْ هِشَامِ بْنِ عُرْوَةَ ، عَنْ أَبِيهِ ، عَنْ عَائِشَةَ : أَنَّ النَّبِيَّ

222 Sahīh al-Bukhārī (5440) and Sahīh Muslim (2043)

صلى الله عليه وسلم ، كَانَ يَأْكُلُ الْبِطِّيخَ بِالرُّطَبِ[223]

198. Aisha ﵂ narrated: "The Messenger of Allāh ﷺ ate watermelon with ripe dates (*rutab*)."

Abdul Razzaq al-Badr said,

> All the hadīths about the virtue of watermelon are fabricated or very weak except this hadīth.

Al-Bajūrī said,

> The combination of fruits that he ﷺ used to eat shows that he followed the logic of medicine i.e. he ate that which would neutralise the bad effects of the other food.

١٩٩ : حَدَّثَنَا إِبْرَاهِيمُ بْنُ يَعْقُوبَ ، قَالَ : حَدَّثنَا وَهْبُ بْنُ جَرِير ، قَالَ : حَدَّثَنَا أَبِي ، قَالَ : سَمِعْتُ حُمَيْدًا ، أَوْ قَالَ : حَدَّثَنِي حُمَيْدٌ ، قَالَ وَهْبٌ : وَكَانَ صَدِيقًا لَهُ ، عَنْ أَنَسِ بْنِ مَالِكٍ ، قَالَ : رَأَيْتُ رَسُولَ الله صلى الله عليه وسلم ، يَجْمَعُ بَيْنَ الْخِرْبِزِ وَالرُّطَبِ[224]

199. Anas ibn Mālik ﵁ reported: "I saw the Messenger of Allāh ﷺ eating muskmelon together with ripe dates (*rutab*)."

٢٠٠ : حَدَّثَنَا مُحَمَّدُ بْنُ يَحْيَى ، قَالَ : حَدَّثَنَا مُحَمَّدُ بْنُ عَبْدِ الْعَزِيزِ الرَّمْلِيُّ ، قَالَ : حَدَّثَنَا عَبْدُ الله بْنُ يَزِيدَ بْنِ الصَّلْتِ ، عَنْ مُحَمَّدِ بْنِ إِسْحَاقَ ، عَنْ يَزِيدَ بْنِ رُومَانَ ، عَنْ عُرْوَةَ ، عَنْ عَائِشَةَ : أَنَّ النَّبِيَّ صلى الله عليه وسلم أَكَلَ الْبِطِّيخَ بِالرُّطَبِ[225]

---

223 Sunan Abū Dawūd (3836) and Sunan al-Tirmidhī (1843)
224 Musnad Ahmad (12460)
225 See hadīth 195

200. Aisha ﵂ narrated: "The Messenger of Allāh ﷺ ate watermelon with ripe dates (*rutab*)."

٢٠١ : حَدَّثَنَا قُتَيْبَةُ بْنُ سَعِيدٍ ، عَنْ مَالِكِ بْنِ أَنَسٍ (ح) وَحَدَّثَنَا إِسْحَاقُ بْنُ مُوسَى ، قَالَ : حَدَّثَنَا مَعْنٌ ، قَالَ : حَدَّثَنَا مَالِكٌ ، عَنْ سُهَيْلِ بْنِ أَبِي صَالِحٍ ، عَنْ أَبِيهِ ، عَنْ أَبِي هُرَيْرَةَ ، قَالَ : كَانَ النَّاسُ إِذَا رَأَوْا أَوَّلَ الثَّمَرِ جَاءُوا بِهِ إِلَى رَسُولِ اللهِ صلى الله عليه وسلم ، فَإِذَا أَخَذَهُ رَسُولُ اللهِ صلى الله عليه وسلم ، قَالَ : اللَّهُمَّ بَارِكْ لَنَا فِي ثِمَارِنَا ، وَبَارِكْ لَنَا فِي مَدِينَتِنَا ، وَبَارِكْ لَنَا فِي صَاعِنَا وَفِي مُدِّنَا ، اللَّهُمَّ إِنَّ إِبْرَاهِيمَ عَبْدُكَ وَخَلِيلُكَ وَنَبِيُّكَ ، وَإِنِّي عَبْدُكَ وَنَبِيُّكَ ، وَإِنَّهُ دَعَاكَ لِمَكَّةَ ، وَإِنِّي أَدْعُوكَ لِلْمَدِينَةِ ، بِمِثْلِ مَا دَعَاكَ بِهِ لِمَكَّةَ وَمِثْلِهِ مَعَهُ ، قَالَ : ثُمَّ يَدْعُو أَصْغَرَ وَلِيدٍ يَرَاهُ ، فَيُعْطِيهِ ذَلِكَ الثَّمَرَ[226]

201. Abū Hurairah ﵁ narrated: "People used to pick their new fruit, and then present it to the Messenger of Allāh ﷺ. He ﷺ then would take it and supplicate, '*O Allāh! Bless us in our fruits. Bless our city. Bless us in our sā', and bless us in our mudd* (these are two units of measurement used to measure dates). *O Allāh! Ibrahīm ﵇ is Your slave, close friend, and Prophet, and I am Your slave and Prophet. And, he supplicated to You for Makkah and I supplicate to You for Madīnah for the like of what He prayed to You for Makkah.*' Then, he would call the youngest child he could see and give him that fruit."

Abdul Razzaq al-Badr said,

> This hadīth shows an allowed type of intercession - that is intercession through one's state as a slave of Allāh and humility before Him.
>
> It was his perfect manners, kindness and mercy that made him give the fruit to the youngest child present because children long the most for fruits.

226 Sahīh Muslim (2038)

Al-Bajūrī said,

> The Prophet ﷺ is also the *khalīl* of Allāh (i.e. close friend of Allāh) but he did not mention it either out of reverence for Ibrahīm ﵇ or because he was granted a higher level of love and closeness to Allāh.
>
> The fact that the Prophet ﷺ did not eat the fruit brought to him and instead gave it to children demonstrates that noble people with pure souls and high manners do not long to eat something until after everyone else can have it.
>
> The scholars are in agreement that Makkah and Madīnah are the best places on earth, and the three *imāms* hold the view that Makkah is better than Madīnah whereas Imām Mālik stated otherwise. However, the dispute is not over the noble area where he ﷺ is buried for it is indeed better than the heavens and the earth.

Ibn Hajar al-Haytamī said,

> The people brought the fruits to the Prophet ﷺ because they favoured him over themselves and to seek his blessings.

٢٠٢ : حَدَّثَنَا مُحَمَّدُ بْنُ حُمَيْدٍ الرَّازِيُّ ، قَالَ : حَدَّثَنَا إِبْرَاهِيمُ بْنُ الْمُخْتَارِ ، عَنْ مُحَمَّدِ بْنِ إِسْحَاقَ ، عَنْ أَبِي عُبَيْدَةَ بْنِ مُحَمَّدِ بْنِ عَمَّارِ بْنِ يَاسِرٍ ، عَنِ الرُّبَيِّعِ بِنْتِ مُعَوِّذِ بْنِ عَفْرَاءَ ، قَالَتْ : بَعَثَنِي مُعَاذُ بْنُ عَفْرَاءَ بِقِنَاعٍ مِنْ رُطَبٍ وَعَلَيْهِ أَجْرٌ مِنْ قِثَّاءٍ زُغْبٍ وَكَانَ النَّبِيُّ صلى الله عليه وسلم يُحِبُّ الْقِثَّاءَ ، فَأَتَيْتُهُ بِهِ وَعِنْدَهُ حِلْيَةٌ قَدْ قَدِمَتْ عَلَيْهِ مِنَ الْبَحْرَيْنِ ، فَمَلأَ يَدَهُ مِنْهَا فَأَعْطَانِيهِ[227]

202. Al-Rubayyi' bint Mu'awwidh ibn 'Afrā ﵄ narrated: "Mu'ādh ibn Afrā sent me with a plate of ripe dates (*rutab*), which had small cucumbers upon it, to the Messenger of Allāh ﷺ. He ﷺ liked

227 Sharh al-Sunnah of al-Baghawī (2897)

cucumbers. I took the plate to him and when I entered on him, I saw jewellery that was sent to him from Bahrain. He took hold of a handful from it and gave it to me."

Abdul Razzaq al-Badr said,

> He ﷺ gave her from the jewellery because it was suitable for women.

Al-Bajūrī said,

> Mu'ādh ibn 'Afrā was the uncle of al-Rubayyi' and he and his brother were the ones who killed Abū Jahl in the battle of Badr.
>
> The jewellery refers to money and pieces of jewellery.

٢٠٣: حَدَّثَنَا عَلِيُّ بْنُ حُجْرٍ ، قَالَ : حَدَّثَنَا شَرِيكٌ ، عَنْ عَبْدِ اللهِ بْنِ مُحَمَّدِ بْنِ عَقِيلٍ ، عَنِ الرُّبَيِّعِ بِنْتِ مُعَوِّذِ بْنِ عَفْرَاءَ ، قَالَتْ : أَتيتُ النَّبِيَّ صلى الله عليه وسلم ، بِقِنَاعٍ مِنْ رُطَبٍ ، وَأَجْرٍ زُغْبٍ ، فَأَعْطَانِي مِلْءَ كَفِّهِ حُلِيًّا أَوْ قَالَتْ : ذَهَبًا [228]

203. Al-Rubayyi' bint Mu'awwidh ibn 'Afrā ﵁ narrated: "I took a plate of ripe dates (*rutab*) and small cucumbers to the Messenger of Allāh ﷺ. He gifted me with a handful of jewellery, or a handful of gold."

228 Musnad Ahmad (27020)

CHAPTER THIRTY ONE

باب ما جاء في صفة شراب رسول الله صلى الله عليه وسلم

THE REPORTS PERTAINING TO THE DRINKS OF THE MESSENGER OF ALLĀH ﷺ

Abdul Razzaq al-Badr said,

> This chapter is dedicated to describing that which the Prophet ﷺ used to drink and the following chapter will describe the manner in which he used to drink.

٢٠٤: حَدَّثَنَا ابْنُ أَبِي عُمَرَ ، قَالَ : حَدَّثَنَا سُفْيَانُ ، عَنْ مَعْمَرٍ ، عَنِ الزُّهْرِيِّ ، عَنْ عُرْوَةَ ، عَنْ عَائِشَةَ ، قَالَتْ : كَانَ أَحَبَّ الشَّرَابِ إِلَى رَسُولِ الله صلى الله عليه وسلم ، الْحُلْوُ الْبَارِدُ[229]

204. Aisha ﵂ narrated: "The drink most liked by the Messenger of Allāh ﷺ was that which was sweet and cold."

Ibn Hajar al-Haytamī said,

> The drink being referred to in this hadīth is water as he ﷺ liked to drink water cold and sweetened. It was referred to as "sweet" because he ﷺ used to like having honey, dates or raisins mixed with the cold water.

Al-Bajūrī said,

> Liking the drink to be sweet and cold does not contradict asceticism as it is intended to witness and observe more of the graces of Allāh and accordingly to show sincere gratitude.

Ibn Battal said,

> Drinking sweetened water does not contravene asceticism and it is not included in the admonished types of luxury, contrary to scenting the water, not to mention that there is no benefit or virtue in salty water. Allāh made a likeness of the disbeliever with salty water and of the believer with sweet water: **{And not alike are the two bodies of water. One is fresh and sweet, palatable for drinking, and one is salty and bitter.}**[230]

Alī al-Qārī said,

> It was said that the sweet water mentioned in this hadīth refers

229 Sunan al-Tirmidhī (1895)
230 Qur'ān: 35:12

to the water mixed with honey because the Prophet ﷺ did not use sugar at all, not to mention that honey is a cure in itself.

٢٠٥: حَدَّثَنَا أَحْمَدُ بْنُ مَنِيعٍ ، قَالَ : حَدَّثَنَا إِسْمَاعِيلُ بْنُ إِبْرَاهِيمَ ، قَالَ : حَدَّثَنَا عَلِيُّ بْنُ زَيْدٍ ، عَنْ عُمَرَ هُوَ ابْنُ أَبِي حَرْمَلَةَ ، عَنِ ابْنِ عَبَّاسٍ ، قَالَ : دَخَلْتُ مَعَ رَسُولِ اللهِ صلى الله عليه وسلم ، أَنَا ، وَخَالِدُ بْنُ الْوَلِيدِ عَلَى مَيْمُونَةَ ، فَجَاءَتْنَا بِإِنَاءٍ مِنْ لَبَنٍ ، فَشَرِبَ رَسُولُ اللهِ صلى الله عليه وسلم ، وَأَنَا عَلَى يَمِينِهِ ، وَخَالِدٌ عَلَى شِمَالِهِ ، فَقَالَ لِي : الشَّرْبَةُ لَكَ ، فَإِنْ شِئْتَ آثَرْتَ بِهَا خَالِدًا ، فَقُلْتُ : مَا كُنْتُ لأُوثِرَ عَلَى سُؤْرِكَ أَحَدًا ، ثُمَّ قَالَ رَسُولُ اللهِ صلى الله عليه وسلم : مَنْ أَطْعَمَهُ اللهُ طَعَامًا ، فَلْيَقُلِ : اللَّهُمَّ بَارِكْ لَنَا فِيهِ ، وَأَطْعِمْنَا خَيْرًا مِنْهُ ، وَمَنْ سَقَاهُ اللهُ عَزَّ وَجَلَّ لَبَنًا ، فَلْيَقُلِ : اللَّهُمَّ بَارِكْ لَنَا فِيهِ ، وَزِدْنَا مِنْهُ ثُمَّ قَالَ : قَالَ رَسُولُ اللهِ صلى الله عليه وسلم : لَيْسَ شَيْءٌ يُجْزِئُ مَكَانَ الطَّعَامِ وَالشَّرَابِ ، غَيْرُ اللَّبَنِ[231]

205. 'Abdullāh ibn Abbās ؓ narrated: "Khālid ibn al-Walīd and I both accompanied the Messenger of Allāh ﷺ to the house of Maymūnah ؓ. There, she presented us with milk in a vessel and the Messenger of Allāh ﷺ drank from it. I was upon his right and Khālid to his left. The Messenger of Allāh ﷺ said to me, 'You possess the right of drinking but if you wish you could give your right to Khālid.' I replied that I would not give up his leftovers to anyone else. After that the Messenger of Allāh ﷺ said, 'Whenever Allāh feeds someone anything, the following supplication should be recited, '*O Allāh grant us blessings in it, and feed us something better than it*,' and whenever Allāh gives someone milk to drink one should read, '*O Allāh grant us blessing in it and increase it for us*.' Then, the Messenger of Allāh ﷺ added, 'There is nothing that serves the place of both food and drink except for milk.'"

231 Sunan Abū Dawūd (3730) and Sunan al-Tirmidhī (2455)

Al-Tirmidhī said: "Maymūnah bint al-Hārith ﵂ is the wife of the Messenger of Allāh ﷺ and the maternal aunt of Ibn Abbās and Khālid ibn al-Walīd."

Abdul Razzaq al-Badr said,

> This hadīth shows that the one to the right of the person has more right to be served first than the one on the left. It also shows that it is permissible for the one on the right to give his right to the person on the left.

Al-Bajūrī said,

> The Sunnah of giving preference to the one on the right applies to food, drink, clothing etc. The Prophet ﷺ explained that Ibn Abbās had the right to drink first because he was on the right side but as Khālid was older than Ibn Abbās and a leader in his tribe as well as being a new Muslim at that time, he informed Ibn Abbās that he could give Khālid this right to show Khālid that he was not being disrespected or overlooked.

Ibn Hajar al-Haytamī said,

> The response of Ibn Abbās began with the excuse of not wanting to give that right to anyone so that it would not give the impression that he was refusing to comply.

CHAPTER THIRTY TWO

باب ما جاء في شرب رسول الله صلى الله عليه وسلم

THE REPORTS PERTAINING TO THE MANNER IN WHICH THE MESSENGER OF ALLĀH ﷺ DRANK

٢٠٦: حَدَّثَنَا أَحْمَدُ بْنُ مَنِيعٍ ، قَالَ : حَدَّثَنَا هُشَيْمٌ ، قَالَ : حَدَّثَنَا عَاصِمٌ الأَحْوَلُ ، وَمُغِيرَةُ ، عَنِ الشَّعْبِيِّ ، عَنِ ابْنِ عَبَّاسٍ : أَنَّ النَّبِيَّ صلى الله عليه وسلم ، شَرِبَ مِنْ زَمْزَمَ ، وَهُوَ قَائِمٌ[232]

206. 'Abdullāh ibn Abbās ﷺ narrated: "The Prophet ﷺ drank Zamzam water whilst standing."

Ibn al-Qayyim said,

> The guidance of the Prophet ﷺ in drinking was to drink whilst sitting down and it is proven authentic that he forbade people to drink while they are standing but at the same time it is proven authentic that he drank while he was standing. Some scholars reconciled between the two, stating that the latter abrogated the former, and other scholars stated that the order not to drink while standing was to show that it is not the best thing to do, and some scholars said that there is no need for reconciliation at all as he drank while he was standing because the situation required that. This was because, as he ﷺ arrived to the well of Zamzam, people were drinking and he was handed a bottle of Zamzam water.

Ibn Hajar al-Haytamī said,

> The reason he ﷺ drank while he was standing was to show that this is permissible as he ordered people [at an earlier point] to only drink while they are sitting down.

٢٠٧: حَدَّثَنَا قُتَيْبَةُ بْنُ سَعِيدٍ ، قَالَ : حَدَّثَنَا مُحَمَّدُ بْنُ جَعْفَرٍ ، عَنْ حُسَيْنٍ الْمُعَلِّمِ ، عَنْ عَمْرِو بْنِ شُعَيْبٍ ، عَنْ أَبِيهِ ، عَنْ جَدِّهِ ، قَالَ : رَأَيْتُ رَسُولَ اللهِ صلى الله عليه وسلم ، يَشْرَبُ قَائِمًا ، وَقَاعِدًا[233]

---

232 Sahīh al-Bukhārī (5617) and Sahīh Muslim (2027)

233 Sunan Abu Dawūd (653) and Sunan al-Tirmidhī (1883)

207. 'Abdullāh ibn Amr ؓ related: "I saw the Messenger of Allāh ﷺ drink while he was sitting and also whilst stood."

Ibn Hajar al-Haytamī said,

> This indicates that he ﷺ drank while he was sitting many times and he drank while he was standing one time to display its permissibility. The known practice of him ﷺ was to drink while he was sitting.

٢٠٨: حَدَّثَنَا عَلِيُّ بْنُ حُجْرٍ، قَالَ: حَدَّثَنَا ابْنُ الْمُبَارَكِ، عَنْ عَاصِمٍ الأَحْوَلِ، عَنِ الشَّعْبِيِّ، عَنِ ابْنِ عَبَّاسٍ، قَالَ: سَقَيْتُ النَّبِيَّ صلى الله عليه وسلم، مِنْ زَمْزَمَ، فَشَرِبَ، وَهُوَ قَائِمٌ[234]

208. 'Abdullāh ibn Abbās ؓ narrated: "I gave the Prophet ﷺ Zamzam water to drink, so he drank it while he was standing."

٢٠٩: حَدَّثَنَا أَبُو كُرَيْبٍ مُحَمَّدُ بْنُ الْعَلاءِ، وَمُحَمَّدُ بْنُ طَرِيفٍ الْكُوفِيُّ، قَالا: حَدَّثَنَا ابْنُ الْفُضَيْلِ، عَنِ الأَعْمَشِ، عَنْ عَبْدِ الْمَلِكِ بْنِ مَيْسَرَةَ، عَنِ النَّزَّالِ بْنِ سَبْرَةَ، قَالَ: أَتَى عَلِيٌّ، بِكُوزٍ مِنْ مَاءٍ، وَهُوَ فِي الرَّحْبَةِ، فَأَخَذَ مِنْهُ كَفًّا، فَغَسَلَ يَدَيْهِ، وَمَضْمَضَ، وَاسْتَنْشَقَ، وَمَسَحَ وَجْهَهُ وَذِرَاعَيْهِ وَرَأْسَهُ، ثُمَّ شَرِبَ وَهُوَ قَائِمٌ، ثُمَّ قَالَ: هَذَا وُضُوءُ مَنْ لَمْ يُحْدِثْ، هَكَذَا رَأَيْتُ رَسُولَ اللهِ صلى الله عليه وسلم فَعَلَ[235]

209. Al-Nazzāl ibn Sabrah ؓ related: "Water in a clay pot was brought to Alī ibn Abī Tālib ؓ whilst he was in the courtyard of the masjid. He took a handful from this water and used it to wash his hands. Then he rinsed his mouth, sniffed the water to clean his nose

---

234 See hadith 206

235 Sahīh al-Bukhārī (5615)

and washed his face, forearms and head. Thereafter, he stood and drank from it. He then said, 'This is the ablution of a person who is already in a state of purity. I have observed the Messenger of Allāh ﷺ perform it so.'"

Ibn Hajar al-Haytamī said,

> This hadīth describes how to renew the ablution without being in a state of impurity. This ablution is intended for cleansing and not to remove the state of ritual impurity.

Abdul Razzaq al-Badr said,

> The relevant part in this hadīth is that he ﷺ drank the water whilst he was standing.

Alī al-Qārī said,

> In another version it added, "And he washed his feet."

٢١٠ : حَدَّثَنَا قُتَيْبَةُ بْنُ سَعِيدٍ ، وَيُوسُفُ بْنُ حَمَّادٍ ، قَالا : حَدَّثَنَا عَبْدُ الْوَارِثِ بْنُ سَعِيدٍ ، عَنْ أَبِي عِصَامٍ ، عَنْ أَنَسِ بْنِ مَالِكٍ ، أَنَّ النَّبِيَّ صلى الله عليه وسلم : كَانَ يَتَنَفَّسُ فِي الإِنَاءِ ثَلاثًا إِذَا شَرِبَ ، وَيَقُولُ : هُوَ أَمْرَأُ ، وَأَرْوَى[236]

210. Anas ibn Mālik ؓ narrated: "The Messenger of Allāh ﷺ drank water from the vessel in three breaths (i.e. in three sips) and used to say, 'It is more pleasing and thirst quenching in this manner.'"

Alī al-Qārī said,

> The practice that is admonished is to breathe in the bottle or vessel and then drink because this changes the nature of the water in addition to the benefits mentioned in this hadīth. It is also

236 Sahīh Muslim (2028)

admonished to drink the contents of the vessel all at once because the Prophet ﷺ stated it is the way Shaytān drinks, not to mention that this could cause the person to choke and block the throat.

٢١١ : حَدَّثَنَا عَلِيُّ بْنُ خَشْرَمٍ ، قَالَ : حَدَّثَنَا عِيسَى بْنُ يُونُسَ ، عَنْ رِشْدِينَ بْنِ كُرَيْبٍ ، عَنْ أَبِيهِ ، عَنِ ابْنِ عَبَّاسٍ : أَنَّ النَّبِيَّ صلى الله عليه وسلم كَانَ إِذَا شَرِبَ ، تَنَفَّسَ مَرَّتَيْنِ[237]

211. 'Abdullāh ibn Abbās ؓ narrated: "The Prophet ﷺ drank water in two breaths."

Abdul Razzaq al-Badr said,

> This hadīth is not an explicit evidence that he ﷺ drank water in two breaths because it is possible that the narrator did not count the last breath, which is bound to happen by default, and only described the two pauses that happened while drinking.

٢١٢ : حَدَّثَنَا ابْنُ أَبِي عُمَرَ ، قَالَ : حَدَّثَنَا سُفْيَانُ ، عَنْ يَزِيدَ بْنِ يَزِيدَ بْنِ جَابِرٍ ، عَنْ عَبْدِ الرَّحْمَنِ بْنِ أَبِي عَمْرَةَ ، عَنْ جَدَّتِهِ كَبْشَةَ ، قَالَتْ : دَخَلَ عَلَيَّ النَّبِيُّ صلى الله عليه وسلم فَشَرِبَ مِنْ قِرْبَةٍ مُعَلَّقَةٍ قَائِمًا ، فَقُمْتُ إِلَى فِيهَا فَقَطَعْتُهُ[238]

212. Kabshah bint Thābit ؓ narrated: "The Prophet ﷺ once visited me at home and he drank while he was standing from a leather water bag that was suspended. Then, I got up and cut out the mouth [part] of the bag."

Abdul Razzaq al-Badr said,

---

237 Sunan Ibn Mājah (3417) and Sunan al-Tirmidhī (1886)
238 Sunan Ibn Mājah (3423) and Sunan al-Tirmidhī (1892)

Kabshah bint Thābit is the sister of Hassan ibn Thābit, the poet of the Prophet ﷺ.

Ibn Hajar al-Haytamī said,

> Him ﷺ drinking while standing shows that his order not to drink while standing was to refer to it as disliked and not forbidden.
> She cut out the mouth part of the bag after he ﷺ drank from it in order to preserve the place where the Prophet ﷺ placed his mouth upon and to keep it for seeking its blessings.

٢١٣: حَدَّثَنَا مُحَمَّدُ بْنُ بَشَّارٍ ، قَالَ : حَدَّثَنَا عَبْدُ الرَّحْمَنِ بْنُ مَهْدِيٍّ ، قَالَ : حَدَّثَنَا عُزْرَةُ بْنُ ثَابِتٍ الأَنْصَارِيُّ ، عَنْ ثُمَامَةَ بْنِ عَبْدِ اللهِ ، قَالَ : كَانَ أَنَسُ بْنُ مَالِكٍ ، يَتَنَفَّسُ فِي الإِنَاءِ ثَلاثًا ، وَزَعَمَ أَنَسٌ ، أَنَّ النَّبِيَّ صلى الله عليه وسلم ، كَانَ يَتَنَفَّسُ فِي الإِنَاءِ ثَلاثًا[239]

213. Thumāmah ibn 'Abdullāh ﷺ narrated: "Anas ibn Mālik ﷺ used to drink water in three breaths, and he stated that the Prophet ﷺ drank water in the same manner."

Abdul Razzaq al-Badr said,

> This shows how keen the companions ﷺ were to follow the Sunnah and adhere to the manners and etiquettes of the Prophet ﷺ.

٢١٤: حَدَّثَنَا عَبْدُ اللهِ بْنُ عَبْدِ الرَّحْمَنِ ، قَالَ : حَدَّثَنَا أَبُو عَاصِمٍ ، عَنِ ابْنِ جُرَيْجٍ ، عَنْ عَبْدِ الْكَرِيمِ ، عَنِ الْبَرَاءِ بْنِ زَيْدٍ ابْنِ ابْنَةِ أَنَسِ بْنِ مَالِكٍ ، عَنْ أَنَسِ بْنِ مَالِكٍ ، أَنَّ النَّبِيَّ صلى الله عليه وسلم ، دَخَلَ عَلَى أُمِّ سُلَيْمٍ ، وَقِرْبَةٌ مُعَلَّقَةٌ ، فَشَرِبَ مِنْ فَمِ الْقِرْبَةِ وَهُوَ قَائِمٌ ، فَقَامَتْ أُمُّ سُلَيْمٍ إِلَى رَأْسِ الْقِرْبَةِ

239 Sahīh al-Bukhārī (5631) and Sahīh Muslim (2028)

فَقَطَعَتْهَا[240]

214. Anas ibn Mālik ﷺ narrated: "The Prophet ﷺ once visited Umm Salīm ﷺ at her home and he drank while he was standing, from a leather water bag that was suspended. Then, she got up and cut out the mouth [part] of the bag."

٢١٥: حَدَّثَنَا أَحْمَدُ بْنُ نَصْرٍ النَّيْسَابُورِيُّ ، قَالَ : حَدَّثَنَا إِسْحَاقُ بْنُ مُحَمَّدٍ الْفَرْوِي ، قَالَ : حَدَّثَتْنَا عَبِيدَةُ بِنْتُ نَائِلٍ ، عَنْ عَائِشَةَ بِنْتِ سَعْدِ بْنِ أَبِي وَقَّاصٍ ، عَنْ أَبِيهَا ، أَنَّ النَّبِيَّ صلى الله عليه وسلم ، كَانَ يَشْرَبُ قَائِمًا.[241]
قَالَ أَبُو عِيسَى : وَقَالَ بَعْضُهُمْ : عُبَيْدَةُ بِنْتُ نَابِلٍ

215. Sa'd ibn Abī Waqqās ﷺ narrated: "The Prophet ﷺ used to drink whilst standing."

Al-Bajūrī said,

> Sa'd ibn Abī Waqqās ﷺ was one of the ten people who were given the glad tidings of Paradise, the first person in Islām who shot an arrow in a battle and he witnessed all the battles [of his time], so he was called the Knight of Islām.
>
> As it was explained, the common practice of the Prophet ﷺ was to drink while he was sitting and on some rare occasions he drank while standing.

240 Musnad Ahmad (12188)
241 Mukhtasar al-Shama'il of al-Albani (184)

CHAPTER THIRTY THREE

باب ما جاء في تعطررسول الله صلى الله عليه وسلم

THE REPORTS PERTAINING TO THE PERFUME OF THE MESSENGER OF ALLĀH ﷺ

Abdul Razzaq al-Badr said,

> This chapter is dedicated to describing the guidance of the Prophet ﷺ in respect to perfume.

Ibn al-Qayyim said,

> The Prophet ﷺ liked applying perfume and he always wore it. His scent was the best and the scent of his perspiration was even better than that of perfume.

Al-Bajūrī said,

> It is more emphasised for men to wear perfume on Fridays, days of Eid, when entering the state of *ihram*, when intending to pray in congregation, when attending gatherings, reciting the Qur'ān, learning and teaching knowledge, remembrance of Allāh. It is also

recommended for the husband and wife to perfume themselves before being intimate.

٢١٦: حَدَّثَنَا مُحَمَّدُ بْنُ رَافِعٍ ، وَاحِدٍ ، قَالُوا : حَدَّثَنَا أَبُو أَحْمَدَ الزُّبَيْرِيُّ ، قَالَ : حَدَّثَنَا شَيْبَانُ ، عَنْ عَبْدِ اللهِ بْنِ الْمُخْتَارِ ، عَنْ مُوسَى بْنِ أَنَسِ بْنِ مَالِكٍ ، عَنْ أَبِيهِ ، قَالَ : كَانَ لِرَسُولِ اللهِ صلى الله عليه وسلم سُكَّةٌ يَتَطَيَّبُ مِنْهَا[242]

216. Anas ibn Mālik ﷺ narrated: "The Messenger of Allāh ﷺ had a container that he would apply perfume from."

Al-Bajūrī said,

> *Sukkah* refers here to the perfume bottle based on the context of the hadīth though one of its meanings is a perfume that is made of a mixture of elements.

٢١٧: حَدَّثَنَا مُحَمَّدُ بْنُ بَشَّارٍ ، قَالَ : حَدَّثَنَا عَبْدُ الرَّحْمَنِ بْنُ مَهْدِيٍّ ، قَالَ : حَدَّثَنَا عَزْرَةُ بْنُ ثَابِتٍ ، عَنْ ثُمَامَةَ بْنِ عَبْدِ اللهِ ، قَالَ : كَانَ أَنَسُ بْنُ مَالِكٍ ، لا يَرُدُّ الطِّيبَ ، وَقَالَ أَنَسٌ : إِنَّ النَّبِيَّ صلى الله عليه وسلم كَانَ لا يَرُدُّ الطِّيبَ[243]

217. Thumāmah ibn 'Abdullāh ﷺ narrated: "Anas ibn Mālik ﷺ never refused accepting perfume whenever it was offered and he narrated that, 'The Messenger of Allāh ﷺ never refused perfume whenever it was offered to him.'"

Abdul Razzaq al-Badr said,

> Anas ibn Mālik ﷺ never rejected perfume to follow the example of the Messenger of Allāh ﷺ.

Ibn Hajar al-Asqalānī said,

> The reason why he ﷺ never rejected an offering of perfume was

242 Sunan Abū Dawūd (4162)
243 Sahīh al-Bukhārī (5929)

because it is light in weight and has a good smell.

Abū Bakr ibn al-'Arabī said,

> The reason why he ﷺ never rejected an offering of perfume was because he liked it and needed it more than anyone else as he was always receiving revelation from his Lord.

٢١٨: حَدَّثَنَا قُتَيْبَةُ بْنُ سَعِيدٍ ، قَالَ : حَدَّثَنَا ابْنُ أَبِي فُدَيْكٍ ، عَنْ عَبْدِ اللهِ بْنِ مُسْلِمِ بْنِ جُنْدُبٍ ، عَنْ أَبِيهِ ، عَنِ ابْنِ عُمَرَ ، قَالَ : قَالَ رَسُولُ اللهِ صلى الله عليه وسلم : ثَلاثٌ لا تُرَدُّ : الْوَسَائِدُ ، وَالدُّهْنُ ، وَاللَّبَنُ[244]

218. 'Abdullāh ibn 'Umar ؓ narrated: "The Messenger of Allāh ﷺ said, 'Three things should not be refused: cushions (pillows), incense and milk.'"

Al-Bajūrī said,

> This hadīth can be understood in two ways: that these gifts are not refused to avoid the gift giver feeling hurt by the rejection and this is the apparent meaning, or that the guest should not refuse any of these three things when the host offers them.
>
> This applies to all that which people do not consider a favour conferred upon others i.e. it applies to all items and gifts that do not cause the recipient to feel like he will owe a favour to the individual who gifted him.

Al-Suyūtī said,

> The Sunnah is to accept and not to refuse seven things when they are offered: sweets, milk, incense, cushions, provision given to a person in need, perfume and basil.

244 Sunan al-Tirmidhī (2790)

٢١٩ : حَدَّثَنَا مَحْمُودُ بْنُ غَيْلانَ ، قَالَ : حَدَّثَنَا أَبُو دَاوُدَ الْحَفَرِيُّ ، عَنْ سُفْيَانَ ، عَنِ الْجُرَيْرِيِّ ، عَنْ أَبِي نَضْرَةَ ، عَنْ رَجُلٍ ، عَنْ أَبِي هُرَيْرَةَ ، قَالَ : قَالَ رَسُولُ اللهِ صلى الله عليه وسلم : طِيبُ الرِّجَالِ مَا ظَهَرَ رِيحُهُ ، وَخَفِيَ لَوْنُهُ ، وَطِيبُ النِّسَاءِ مَا ظَهَرَ لَوْنُهُ وَخَفِيَ رِيحُهُ[245]

219. Abū Hurairah ﷺ narrated: "The Messenger of Allāh ﷺ said: 'The perfume of men is that which possesses a fragrance that spreads yet is colourless, and the perfume of women is that which has a colour yet its fragrance does not spread.'"

Alī al-Qārī said,

> Qatādah said that scholars understood the perfume prescribed for women in this hadīth as that which she wears when she wants to go outside her house, and she can wear any type of perfume she wants when she is with her husband. It was reported that Abū Musah ﷺ narrated that the Prophet ﷺ said, "The eye is liable to commit adultery; and the woman who wears perfume and then passes by people, she is considered an adulteress."[246]

Al-Bajūrī said,

> The perfume of men is of types such as musk, rosewater and camphor and the perfume of women is of types such as sandalwood.

٢٢٠ : حَدَّثَنَا عَلِيُّ بْنُ حُجْرٍ ، قَالَ : أَنْبَأَنَا إِسْمَاعِيلُ بْنُ إِبْرَاهِيمَ ، عَنِ الْجُرَيْرِيِّ ، عَنْ أَبِي نَضْرَةَ ، عَنِ الطُّفَاوِيِّ ، عَنْ أَبِي هُرَيْرَةَ ، عَنِ النَّبِيِّ صلى الله عليه وسلم ، مِثْلَهُ بِمَعْنَاهُ[247]

245 Sunan Abū Dawūd (2174) and Sunan al-Tirmidhī (2787)
246 Reported by al-Tirmidhī
247 See hadīth 219

220. Abū Hurairah ؓ narrated a similar report.

٢٢١ : حَدَّثَنَا مُحَمَّدُ بْنُ خَلِيفَةَ ، وَعَمْرُو بْنُ عَلِيٍّ ، قَالا : حَدَّثَنَا يَزِيدُ بْنُ زُرَيْعٍ ، قَالَ : حَدَّثَنَا حَجَّاجٌ الصَّوَّافُ ، عَنْ حَنَانٍ ، عَنْ أَبِي عُثْمَانَ النَّهْدِيِّ ، قَالَ : قَالَ رَسُولُ اللهِ صلى الله عليه وسلم : إِذَا أُعْطِيَ أَحَدُكُمُ الرَّيْحَانَ فَلا يَرُدَّهُ ، فَإِنَّهُ خَرَجَ مِنَ الْجَنَّةِ[248]

221. Abū Uthmān al-Nahdī narrated: "The Messenger of Allāh ﷺ said, 'If one is given fragrance of basil, he should not refuse it, because it originated from Paradise.'"

Al-Qadī 'Iyyād said,

> I find it possible to interpret the use of basil here in this context to refer to all types of perfume.

Al-Nawawī said,

> This hadīth shows that it is disliked to refuse fragrance of basil unless there is a reason to reject it (i.e. a person cannot handle its smell etc.).

Alī al-Qārī said,

> The original seed of basil is from Paradise. Allāh has created the good scents in this worldly life to remind His creation of the scents of the Hereafter. This is to make them want to enter Paradise and thus increase in good deeds.

٢٢٢ : حَدَّثَنَا عمر بن إسماعيل بن مجالد بن سعيد الهمذاني حدثني أبي عن بيان عن قيس بن أبي حازم عن جرير بن عبد الله قَالَ :عرضت بين

248 Sunan al-Tirmidhī (2791)

يدى عمر بن الخطاب، فألقى جرير رداءه، ومشى في إزار، فقال له : خذ رداءك، فقال للقوم : ما رأيت رجلاً أحسن صورة من جرير، إلا ما بلغنا من صورة يوسف عليه السلام.[249]

222. Jarīr ibn 'Abdullāh ﷺ related that he was presented to 'Umar ibn al-Khattāb ﷺ and then he threw off his top cloak and walked in his izār only. 'Umar told him to take his top and put it back on and then addressed the people saying, "I have not seen anyone more handsome than Jarīr except what has been reported to us about Yūsuf ﷺ."

Al-Bajūrī said,

> The reason Jarīr ﷺ was presented to 'Umar ﷺ and was asked to take his top off was so 'Umar ﷺ could check if he was physically fit to join the army.

Ibn Hajar al-Haytamī said,

> Jarīr was known for his inability to remain on the back of the horse until the Prophet ﷺ hit him on his chest and asked Allāh to rid him of this fault. This incident happened forty nights before the death of the Prophet ﷺ. He took off his upper garment to show his strength and skills.

Abdul Razzaq al-Badr said,

> The reason why this hadīth was included in this chapter though it does not mention anything regarding perfume was to hint that being good looking necessitates smelling good as well.
>
> It is known that there is no one more handsome than the Prophet ﷺ and the statement of 'Umar ﷺ was said in respect to the physical build of Jarīr ﷺ, since he made that statement after Jarīr took off his top cloak.

---

249 Musnad al-Farūq of Ibn Kathīr (2/682)

CHAPTER THIRTY FOUR

باب كيف كان كلام رسول اللّه صلى اللّه عليه وسلم

THE REPORTS PERTAINING TO THE SPEECH OF THE MESSENGER OF ALLĀH ﷺ

Abdul Razzaq al-Badr said,

> This chapter is dedicated to describing how the Prophet ﷺ used to talk.

٢٢٣: حَدَّثَنَا حُمَيْدُ بْنُ مَسْعَدَةَ الْبَصْرِيُّ ، قَالَ : حَدَّثَنَا حُمَيْدُ بْنُ الأَسْوَدِ ، عَنْ أُسَامَةَ بْنِ زَيْدٍ ، عَنِ الزُّهْرِيِّ ، عَنْ عُرْوَةَ ، عَنْ عَائِشَةَ ، قَالَتْ : مَا كَانَ رَسُولُ اللهِ صلى الله عليه وسلم يَسْرُدُ سَرْدَكُمْ هَذَا ، وَلَكِنَّهُ كَانَ يَتَكَلَّمُ بِكَلامٍ بَيِّنٍ فَصْلٍ ، يَحْفَظُهُ مَنْ جَلَسَ إِلَيْهِ[250]

223. Aisha ﵂ related: "The speech of the Messenger of Allāh ﷺ was not fast paced as that of yours. He spoke clearly, enunciating each word slowly so that anyone sitting with him would remember what he said."

Abdul Razzaq al-Badr said,

> This shows that due to his eloquence and concise use of words, anyone sitting with him would easily remember all that he ﷺ said.

Al-Bajūrī said,

> Enunciating each word slowly ensures the clearness of the sentence and it leaves no room for doubts. It also helps the listener memorise that which he has heard.

٢٢٤: حَدَّثَنَا مُحَمَّدُ بْنُ يَحْيَى ، قَالَ : حَدَّثَنَا أَبُو قُتَيْبَةَ سَلْمُ بْنُ قُتَيْبَةَ ، عَنْ عَبْدِ اللهِ بْنِ الْمُثَنَّى ، عَنْ ثُمَامَةَ ، عَنْ أَنَسِ بْنِ مَالِكٍ ، قَالَ : كَانَ رَسُولُ اللهِ صلى الله عليه وسلم ، يُعِيدُ الْكَلِمَةَ ثَلاثًا لِتُعْقَلَ عَنْهُ[251]

224. Anas ibn Mālik ﵁ related: "The Messenger of Allāh ﷺ used to repeat a word thrice, in order that they (his listeners) could understand what was said correctly."

Ibn Hajar al-Haytamī said,

---

250 Sunan al-Tirmidhī (3639)

251 Sahih al-Bukhārī (6244)

The Messenger of Allāh ﷺ used to repeat the word or the sentence for a variety of reasons: to ensure he had the attention of the people, to ensure the audience understood the meaning or when the audience was increasing around him, to ensure everybody heard what he said. This exhibits the perfection of his compassion and mercy for his nation.

Based on this hadīth, it is recommended for the teacher to talk slowly and repeat his words to ensure the audience understands him.

٢٢٥ : حَدَّثَنَا سُفْيَانُ بْنُ وَكِيعٍ ، قَالَ : حَدَّثَنَا جُمَيْعُ بْنُ عُمَرَ بْنِ عَبْدِ الرَّحْمَنِ الْعِجْلِيُّ ، قَالَ : حدَّثني رَجُلٌ مِنْ بَنِي تَمِيمٍ مِنْ وَلَدِ أَبِي هَالَةَ زَوْجِ خَدِيجَةَ يُكْنَى أَبَا عَبْدِ الله ، عَنِ ابْنٍ لأَبِي هَالَةَ ، عَنِ الْحَسَنِ بْنِ عَلِيٍّ ، قَالَ : سَأَلْتُ خَالِي هِنْدُ بْنُ أَبِي هَالَةَ ، وَكَانَ وَصَّافًا ، فَقُلْتُ : صِفْ لِي مَنْطِقَ رَسُولِ الله صلى الله عليه وسلم ، قَالَ : كَانَ رَسُولُ الله صلى الله عليه وسلم مُتَوَاصِلَ الأَحْزَانِ ، دَائِمَ الْفِكْرَةِ ، لَيْسَتْ لَهُ رَاحَةٌ ، طَوِيلُ السَّكْتِ ، لا يَتَكَلَّمُ فِي غَيْرِ حَاجَةٍ ، يَفْتَتِحُ الْكَلامَ ، وَيَخْتِمُهُ بِاسْمِ الله تَعَالَى ، وَيَتَكَلَّمُ بِجَوَامِعِ الْكَلِمِ ، كَلامُهُ فَصْلٌ ، لا فُضُولَ ، وَلا تَقْصِيرَ ، لَيْسَ بِالْجَافِي ، وَلا الْمُهِينِ ، يُعَظِّمُ النِّعْمَةَ وَإِنْ دَقَّتْ لا يَذُمُّ مِنْهَا شَيْئًا ، غَيْرَ أَنَّهُ لَمْ يَكُنْ يَذُمُّ ذَوَّاقًا وَلا يَمْدَحُهُ ، وَلا تُغْضِبُهُ الدُّنْيَا ، وَلا مَا كَانَ لَهَا ، فَإِذَا تُعُدِّيَ الْحَقُّ ، لَمْ يَقُمْ لِغَضَبِهِ شَيْءٌ ، حَتَّى يَنْتَصِرَ لَهُ ، وَلا يَغْضَبُ لِنَفْسِهِ ، وَلا يَنْتَصِرُ لَهَا ، إِذَا أَشَارَ بِكَفِّهِ كُلِّهَا ، وَإِذَا تَعَجَّبَ قَلَبَهَا ، وَإِذَا تَحَدَّثَ اتَّصَلَ بِهَا ، وَضَرَبَ بِرَاحَتِهِ الْيُمْنَى بَطْنَ إِبْهَامِهِ الْيُسْرَى ، وَإِذَا غَضِبَ أَعْرَضَ وَأَشَاحَ ، وَإِذَا فَرِحَ غَضَّ طَرْفَهُ ، جُلُّ ضَحِكِهِ التَّبَسُّمُ ، يَفْتَرُّ عَنْ مِثْلِ حَبِّ الْغَمَامِ[252]

225. Al-Hasan ibn Alī ؓ narrated: "I asked my maternal uncle Hind ibn Abī Hālah, who was known as one who would describe the

---

252 See hadīth 8

features of the Prophet ﷺ, to describe to me the manner in which the Messenger of Allāh ﷺ spoke. He replied, 'The Messenger of Allāh ﷺ was in a continual state of worry, constantly thoughtful and his mind was never at rest.

He would remain silent for long periods and he would not speak without need. He used to begin and end his speech with the name of Allāh, and his speech was concise yet comprehensive. He kept pauses between each sentence and word he uttered. There was no exaggeration in his speech, nor was there deficiency. He was not rude or unkind, nor did he disgrace anyone. He always glorified and appreciated the blessings of Allāh, and he never criticised food or drink even when it might be very minute. He did not criticise food, nor over-praise it. He was never angered for anything worldly. However if someone transgressed the limits in religious matters, he would not calm down until he avenged it. He neither became angry for a personal matter nor avenged for himself.

If he wanted to make a gesture or point at something, he would do so with his full hand. Whenever he was surprised by something, he turned his hands upside down, and when he spoke he moved his hands. He would hit the palm of his right hand with the inside part of his left thumb. When he became angry with someone, he would direct his attention away from that person. When he was happy he would gaze down. The laugh of his was mostly a smile and at that moment his front teeth glittered like shining hailstones piercing the clouds.'"

Abdul Razzaq al-Badr said,

> This hadīth is not authentic and it has some parts that are questionable. This is also the view of Ibn al-Qayyim.

Al-Bajūrī said,

> The state of worry refers to his constant fear of Allāh and this is a common trait of all Prophets. However, in public he used to

maintain a smile on his face for the people, to soften their hearts.

He glorified and appreciated the blessings of Allāh, those which are hidden, those which are apparent and those which are related to this world and the Hereafter. He did that by praising Allāh with his tongue and using these blessings in obeying Him.

Ibn Taymiyyah said,

> The state of worry mentioned is intended to mean that he was always alert and attentive to what he received and this involves the heart and the eyes whilst silence and thoughtfulness involve the tongue and the heart. It is factual that he was never worried or concerned about a worldly matter.

Ibn Hajar al-Haytamī said,

> He ﷺ never rested because he was always busy in good deeds. He started and ended his speeches with the name of Allāh, meaning he started with the *Bismillah* and ended them with *Alhamdulillah* or *Astaghfirullah*. This was with the intention of making his speeches engulfed with the blessings of His Name.

Alī al-Qārī said,

> He ﷺ never became angry for a worldly matter, following the divine order: {**And do not extend your eyes toward that by which We have given enjoyment to [some] categories of them, [its being but] the splendour of worldly life by which We test them. And the provision of your Lord is better and more enduring.**}[253]
>
> He neither became angry for a personal matter nor avenged for himself as he always encountered insult with forbearance, and harm with forgiveness, following the divine order: {**Enjoin what is good, and turn away from the ignorant.**}[254]

253 Qur'ān: 20:131
254 Qur'ān: 7:199

He pointed out using his full hand because pointing out with some fingers is from the acts of the arrogant.

CHAPTER THIRTY FIVE

باب ما جاء في ضحك رسول الله صلى الله عليه وسلم
THE REPORTS PERTAINING TO THE LAUGHTER OF THE MESSENGER OF ALLĀH ﷺ

Abdul Razzaq al-Badr said,

> The guidance of the Prophet ﷺ in respect to laughing was to be moderate just as he was moderate in all of his affairs. On most occasions, his laugh was just a smile and if he laughed audibly, he would not laugh boisterously.

٢٢٦: حَدَّثَنَا أَحْمَدُ بْنُ مَنِيعٍ ، قَالَ : حَدَّثَنَا عَبَّادُ بْنُ الْعَوَّامِ ، قَالَ : أَخْبَرَنَا الْحَجَّاجُ وَهُوَ ابْنُ أَرْطَاةَ ، عَنْ سِمَاكِ بْنِ حَرْبٍ ، عَنْ جَابِرِ بْنِ سَمُرَةَ ، قَالَ : كَانَ فِي سَاقَيْ رَسُولِ الله صلى الله عليه وسلم ، حُمُوشَةٌ ، وَكَانَ لا يَضْحَكُ إِلا تَبَسُّمًا ، فَكُنْتُ إِذَا نَظَرْتُ إِلَيْهِ ، قُلْتُ : أَكْحَلُ الْعَيْنَيْنِ ، وَلَيْسَ بِأَكْحَلَ[255]

226. Jābir ibn Samurah ﷺ narrated: "The legs of the Messenger of Allāh ﷺ were slightly thin. His laugh was only that of a smile. Every time I looked at him, I would think that kohl had been applied to his eyes even though it hadn't."

Abdul Razzaq al-Badr said,

> The slight thinness in his legs befitted the structure of his body and so it is a characteristic that people praise.

Al-Bajūrī said,

> The statement that 'his laugh was only that of a smile' does not mean that he never laughed but rather it is to state that most of the time he used to smile. This is because it was reported that the Messenger of Allāh ﷺ laughed until his molars showed. Some scholars offered a nice explanation to highlight the difference between the reasons that made him laugh and the reasons that made him smile. This explanation is that the Messenger of Allāh ﷺ smiled in matters related to this worldly life and laughed in matters related to the Hereafter.

Ibn Hajar al-Haytamī said,

> The eyelashes of the Messenger of Allāh ﷺ were dark enough to give the impression that he had applied kohl.

255 Sunan al-Tirmidhi (3645)

٢٢٧: حَدَّثَنَا قُتَيْبَةُ بْنُ سَعِيدٍ ، قَالَ : أَخْبَرَنَا ابْنُ لَهِيعَةَ ، عَنْ عُبَيْدِ اللهِ بْنِ الْمُغِيرَةِ ، عَنْ عَبْدِ اللهِ بْنِ الْحَارِثِ بْنِ جَزْءٍ ، أَنَّهُ قَالَ : مَا رَأَيْتُ أَحَدًا أَكْثَرَ تَبَسُّمًا مِنْ رَسُولِ اللهِ صلى الله عليه وسلم .[256]

227. 'Abdullāh ibn al-Hārith ؓ narrated: "I never saw a person who smiled more than the Messenger of Allāh ﷺ."

Al-Bajūrī said,

> This is a characteristic that indicates his perfection as he used to smile in the face of people despite the feelings of concern regarding the Hereafter that he concealed in his heart.

٢٢٨: حَدَّثَنَا أَحْمَدُ بْنُ خَالِدٍ الْخَلاَّلُ ، قَالَ : حَدَّثَنَا يَحْيَى بْنُ إِسْحَاقَ السَّيْلَحَانِيُّ ، قَالَ : حَدَّثَنَا لَيْثُ بْنُ سَعْدٍ ، عَنْ يَزِيدَ بْنِ أَبِي حَبِيبٍ ، عَنْ عَبْدِ اللهِ بْنِ الْحَارِثِ ، قَالَ : مَا كَانَ ضَحِكُ رَسُولِ اللهِ صلى الله عليه وسلم إِلا تَبَسُّمًا[257]

228. 'Abdullāh ibn al-Hārith narrated: "The laughter of the Messenger of Allāh ﷺ was naught but a smile."

٢٢٩: حَدَّثَنَا أَبُو عَمَّارٍ الْحُسَيْنُ بْنُ حُرَيْثٍ ، قَالَ : حَدَّثَنَا وَكِيعٌ ، قَالَ : حَدَّثَنَا الأَعْمَشُ ، عَنِ الْمَعْرُورِ بْنِ سُوَيْدٍ ، عَنْ أَبِي ذَرٍّ ، قَالَ : قَالَ رَسُولُ اللهِ صلى الله عليه وسلم : إِنِّي لأَعْلَمُ أَوَّلَ رَجُلٍ يَدْخُلُ الْجَنَّةَ ، وَآخِرَ رَجُلٍ يَخْرُجُ مِنَ النَّارِ ، يُؤْتَى بِالرَّجُلِ يَوْمَ الْقِيَامَةِ ، فَيُقَالُ : اعْرِضُوا عَلَيْهِ صِغَارَ ذُنُوبِهِ وَيُخَبَّأُ عَنْهُ كِبَارُهَا ، فَيُقَالُ لَهُ : عَمِلْتَ يَوْمَ كَذَا وَكَذَا ، كَذَا ، وَهُوَ مُقِرٌّ ، لا يُنْكِرُ ، وَهُوَ مُشْفِقٌ مِنْ كِبَارِهَا ، فَيُقَالُ : أَعْطُوهُ مَكَانَ كُلِّ سَيِّئَةٍ عَمِلَهَا

---

256 Sunan al-Tirmidhī (3641)

257 Sunan al-Tirmidhī (3642)

حَسَنَةً ، فَيَقُولُ : إِنَّ لِي ذُنُوبًا مَا أَرَاهَا هَاهُنَا ... قَالَ أَبُو ذَرٍّ : فَلَقَدْ رَأَيْتُ رَسُولَ الله صلى الله عَلَيه وسلم ، ضَحِكَ حَتَّى بَدَتْ نَوَاجِذُهُ[258]

229. Abū Dhar ؓ narrated: "The Messenger of Allāh ﷺ said, 'I know the person who will enter Paradise first and also the last person to be taken out of the Hellfire. On the Day of Judgment, a person will be brought forward and then it shall be commanded that all the minor sins of that person be put forward to him and the major sins be concealed. Then, it will be said to him, 'On such a day you did this and on such a day you did this.' He will attest to this without protest whilst being filled with anxiety due to the pending disclosure of his major sins. Then, it shall be commanded that for every sin of that person he be given a good deed. Upon hearing this, the person says, 'I still have many sins left to account for, that I do not find here.'"

Abū Dhar ؓ related: "By Allāh, I saw the Messenger ﷺ laughing [because of the response of the person] until his molar teeth began to show."

Abdul Razzaq al-Badr said,

> The first person who will enter Paradise is the Messenger of Allāh ﷺ and the last person who is taken out from the Hellfire will be the last person to enter Paradise, leaving behind in the Hellfire all those who will remain there forever. The ones who will remain there forever are the disbelievers because the sinners amongst the believers will eventually leave Hell.

Al-Bajūrī said,

> The story of the person in the hadīth is separate from the statement wherein he ﷺ mentioned the first and last person to enter Paradise.
>
> The reason that he was given a good deed for every misdeed is because Allāh, the Most High, said: **{Except for those who repent, believe and do righteous work. For them Allāh will**

258 Sahīh Muslim (190)

replace their evil deeds with good. And ever is Allāh Forgiving and Merciful.}[259]

The reason the Prophet ﷺ laughed was because he was astonished [at what this man will be granted]. The man was anxious at first because he feared his major sins being exposed but after he saw that his minor sins turned into good deeds, he started looking forward to seeing his major sins too. Abū Dhar swore that he saw the Prophet ﷺ laughing so no one doubts his statement since he ﷺ was known for smiling and not laughing.

Ibn Hajar al-Haytamī said,

> The response of the man was because he was overwhelmed with the great Mercy that Allāh bestowed upon him so he wanted to find more sins hoping that they will be replaced with good deeds too.

٢٣٠: حَدَّثَنَا أَحْمَدُ بْنُ مَنِيعٍ ، قَالَ : حَدَّثَنَا مُعَاوِيَةُ بْنُ عَمْرٍو ، قَالَ : حَدَّثَنَا زَائِدَةُ ، عَنْ بَيَانٍ ، عَنْ قَيْسِ بْنِ أَبِي حَازِمٍ ، عَنْ جَرِيرِ بْنِ عَبْدِ اللهِ ، قَالَ : مَا حَجَبَنِي رَسُولُ اللهِ صلى الله عليه وسلم مُنْذُ أَسْلَمْتُ ، وَلا رَآنِي إِلا ضَحِكَ.[260]

230. Jarīr ibn ʿAbdullāh ؓ narrated: "From the day I accepted Islām, the Messenger of Allāh ﷺ never prevented me from entering upon him and every time he saw me, he would laugh."

Al-Bajūrī said,

> Jarīr ibn ʿAbdullāh ؓ embraced Islām forty days before the death of the Messenger of Allāh ﷺ.

259 Qur'ān: 25:70
260 Sahih al-Bukhārī (3035) and Sahīh Muslim (2475)

Ibn Hajar al-Haytamī said,

> Jarīr ibn 'Abdullāh's ﷺ statement was to say that the Messenger of Allāh ﷺ never prevented him from entering upon him when he was with his close companions. This shows the special status of Jarīr.

٢٣١ : حَدَّثَنَا أَحْمَدُ بْنُ مَنِيعٍ ، قَالَ : حَدَّثَنَا مُعَاوِيَةُ بْنُ عَمْرٍو ، قَالَ : حَدَّثَنَا زَائِدَةُ ، عَنْ إِسْمَاعِيلَ بْنِ أَبِي خَالِدٍ ، عَنْ قَيْسٍ ، عَنْ جَرِيرٍ ، قَالَ : مَا حَجَبَنِي رَسُولُ اللهِ صلى الله عليه وسلم ، وَلا رَآنِي مُنْذُ أَسْلَمْتُ إِلا تَبَسَّمَ[261]

231. Jarīr ibn 'Abdullāh ﷺ narrated: "From the day I accepted Islām, the Messenger of Allāh ﷺ never prevented me from entering upon him and every time he saw me, he would smile."

Ibn Hajar al-Haytamī said,

> This hadīth explains that the meaning intended with 'laughing' mentioned in the previous hadīth referred to smiling i.e. he ﷺ used to smile whenever he saw Jarīr ﷺ.

٢٣٢ : حَدَّثَنَا هَنَّادُ بْنُ السَّرِيِّ ، قَالَ : حَدَّثَنَا أَبُو مُعَاوِيَةَ ، عَنِ الأَعْمَشِ ، عَنْ إِبْرَاهِيمَ ، عَنْ عَبِيدَةَ السَّلْمَانِيِّ ، عَنْ عَبْدِ اللهِ بْنِ مَسْعُودٍ ، قَالَ : قَالَ رَسُولُ اللهِ صلى الله عليه وسلم : إِنِّي لأَعْرِفُ آخِرَ أَهْلِ النَّارِ خُرُوجًا ، رَجُلٌ يَخْرُجُ مِنْهَا زَحْفًا ، فَيُقَالُ لَهُ : انْطَلِقْ فَادْخُلِ الْجَنَّةَ ، قَالَ : فَيَذْهَبُ لِيَدْخُلَ الْجَنَّةَ ، فَيَجِدُ النَّاسَ قَدْ أَخَذُوا الْمَنَازِلَ ، فَيَرْجِعُ فَيَقُولُ : يَا رَبِّ ، قَدْ أَخَذَ النَّاسُ الْمَنَازِلَ ، فَيُقَالُ لَهُ : أَتَذْكُرُ الزَّمَانَ الَّذِي كُنْتَ فِيهِ ، فَيَقُولُ : نَعَمْ ، قَالَ : فَيُقَالُ لَهُ : تَمَنَّ ، قَالَ : فَيَتَمَنَّى ، فَيُقَالُ لَهُ : فَإِنَّ لَكَ الَّذِي تَمَنَّيْتَ

261 Sunan al-Tirmidhī (3821)

وَعَشَرَةَ أَضْعَافِ الدُّنْيَا ، قَالَ : فَيَقُولُ : تَسْخَرُ بِي وَأَنْتَ الْمَلِكُ قَالَ : فَلَقَدْ رَأَيْتُ رَسُولَ اللهِ صلى الله عليه وسلم ، ضَحِكَ ، حَتَّى بَدَتْ نَوَاجِذُهُ [262]

232. 'Abdullāh ibn Mas'ūd ﷺ narrated: "The Messenger of Allāh ﷺ said, 'I know the last of the people of Hell to be brought forth, and the last of the people of Paradise to enter therein. It will be a man who will emerge crawling from Hell, and Allāh, may He be blessed and exalted, will say to him, 'Go and enter Paradise.' He will come to it and it will appear to him to be full. He will go back and say, 'O Lord, I found it full.' Allāh, may He be blessed and exalted, will say to him, 'Do you remember your time before [on Earth]?' The man answers, 'Yes, I do.' Allāh, may He be blessed and exalted, will say to him, 'Make a wish,' and so the man makes a wish and then Allāh, the Most High, says to him, 'You will have that which you wished and ten times as much.' He will say, 'Are You mocking me – or laughing at me – yet You are the Sovereign?'"

'Abdullāh ibn Mas'ūd said: "And I saw the Messenger of Allāh ﷺ laugh so that his molars appeared."

Ibn Hajar al-Haytamī said,

> The statement of the man, "Are You mocking me – or laughing at me – when You are the King and Sovereign," was said due to the overwhelming surprise felt by the man. This made him unaware of his words in a similar manner to the incident reported in the hadīth of the man who lost all of his provisions and his camel and then awaited death as he was in the middle of desert. When he saw that his camel had returned, he said out of overwhelming surprise, "O Lord, you are my slave and I am your Lord!"[263]

Al-Bajūrī said,

262 Sahīh al-Bukhārī (6571) and Sahīh Muslim (186)
263 Sahīh Muslim (2747)

The reason the man returned after he reached Paradise was because his thought process was according to the rules of this worldly life, his understanding caused him to believe that Paradise only accommodates a specific number of people and so it was full.

Allāh, the Most High, asked the man to make a wish in order to show him that the rules of the worldly life do not apply to Paradise, and thus he could wish for what he likes.

٢٣٣: حَدَّثَنَا قُتَيْبَةُ بْنُ سَعِيدٍ، قَالَ: حَدَّثَنَا أَبُو الأَحْوَصِ، عَنْ أَبِي إِسْحَاق، عَنْ عَلِيِّ بْنِ رَبِيعَةَ، قَالَ: شَهِدْتُ عَلِيًّا، أُتِيَ بِدَابَّةٍ لِيَرْكَبَهَا فَلَمَّا وَضَعَ رِجْلَهُ فِي الرِّكَابِ، قَالَ: بِسْمِ اللهِ، فَلَمَّا اسْتَوَى عَلَى ظَهْرِهَا، قَالَ: الْحَمْدُ للهِ، ثُمَّ قَالَ: سُبْحَانَ الَّذِي سَخَّرَ لَنَا هَذَا وَمَا كُنَّا لَهُ مُقْرِنِينَ وَإِنَّا إِلَى رَبِّنَا لَمُنْقَلِبُونَ، ثُمَّ قَالَ: الْحَمْدُ للهِ ثَلاثًا، وَاللهُ أَكْبَرُ ثَلاثًا، سُبْحَانَكَ إِنِّي ظَلَمْتُ نَفْسِي، فَاغْفِرْ لِي فَإِنَّهُ لا يَغْفِرُ الذُّنُوبَ إِلا أَنْتَ، ثُمَّ ضَحِكَ فَقُلْتُ: مِنْ أَيِّ شَيْءٍ ضَحِكْتَ يَا أَمِيرَ الْمُؤْمِنِينَ؟ قَالَ: رَأَيْتُ رَسُولَ اللهِ صلى الله عليه وسلم صَنَعَ كَمَا صَنَعْتُ ثُمَّ ضَحِكَ، فَقُلْتُ: مِنْ أَيِّ شَيْءٍ ضَحِكْتَ يَا رَسُولَ اللهِ؟ قَالَ: إِنَّ رَبَّكَ لَيَعْجَبُ مِنْ عَبْدِهِ، إِذَا قَالَ: رَبِّ اغْفِرْ لِي ذُنُوبِي، إِنَّهُ لاَ يَغْفِرُ الذُّنُوبَ غَيْرُكَ.[264]

233. Alī ibn Rabī'a ﵁ narrated: "I was present when an animal (i.e. a horse or a donkey) was brought to Alī ibn Abī Tālib ﵁. When he put his feet on the stirrup, he recited '*Bismillah*' and after he had mounted he said '*Alhamdulillah*' and supplicated: '*Subhān Allāh, He who has subjected this to us, and we could not have [otherwise] subdued it. And indeed we, to our Lord, will [surely] return. Alhamdulillah, Alhamdulillah, Alhamdulillah, Allāhu Akbar, Allāhu Akbar, Allāhu Akbar. Subhānak, I have wronged myself so forgive me as no one can forgive me save You.*' Then, he laughed and I asked him, 'O Chief of Believers! What is the reason for laughing?' He replied, 'The

264 Sunan al-Tirmidhī (3446)

Messenger of Allāh ﷺ also supplicated in this manner and thereafter laughed (smiled). I inquired from him the reason for laughing. The Messenger of Allāh ﷺ said, 'Allāh, the Most High, becomes pleased when His servants say, 'My Lord, forgive my sins. No one can forgive sins save You.'"

Al-Bajūrī said,

> *Bismillah* is recited to mean, "By the blessings of the name of Allāh I mount." The basis for saying *bismillah* when mounting is from the statement of Nūh ﷺ when he mounted the ship as reported in the Qur'ān.
>
> The reason for saying after mounting, "*and indeed we, to our Lord, will surely return,*" is because a person may fall off and die and so the statement is to remind the person that he will return to Allāh. It is for this reason that it is recommended for a person who takes a means that could lead to death (translator's note: such as driving cars, taking trains, flying on airplanes etc.) to repent and turn to Allāh during the trip.

Alī al-Qārī said,

> The praise is said to praise Allāh, the Most High, for the blessing of having a means of transport.
>
> The statement, 'Exalted be He' is to reflect on how the strong horse and camel is tamed to serve the humans who have weak bodies when compared to these animals.
>
> Repeating the praise three times is to show one's gratitude for the blessing and repeating *Allāhu Akbar* is to glorify the perfection of Allāh manifested in His creation.

Abdul Razzaq al-Badr said,

> "*I have wronged myself so forgive me,*" is said to acknowledge one's shortcomings as opposed to the blessings that one has been granted. Thus, with all these blessings it befits that one asks for

Allāh's forgiveness.

٢٣٤: حَدَّثَنَا مُحَمَّدُ بْنُ بَشَّارٍ ، قَالَ : حَدَّثَنَا مُحَمَّدُ بْنُ عَبْدِ اللهِ الأَنْصَارِيُّ ، قَالَ : حَدَّثَنَا عَبْدُ اللهِ بْنُ عَوْنٍ ، عَنْ مُحَمَّدِ بْنِ مُحَمَّدِ بْنِ الأَسْوَدِ ، عَنْ عَامِرِ بْنِ سَعْدٍ ، قَالَ : قَالَ سَعْدٌ : لَقَدْ رَأَيْتُ النَّبِيَّ صلى الله عليه وسلم ، ضَحِكَ يَوْمَ الْخَنْدَقِ حَتَّى بَدَتْ نَوَاجِذُهُ قَالَ : قُلْتُ : كَيْفَ كَانَ ؟ قَالَ : كَانَ رَجُلٌ مَعَهُ تُرْسٌ ، وَكَانَ سَعْدٌ رَامِيًا ، وَكَانَ يَقُولُ كَذَا وَكَذَا بِالتُّرْسِ يُغَطِّي جَبْهَتَهُ ، فَنَزَعَ لَهُ سَعْدٌ بِسَهْمٍ ، فَلَمَّا رَفَعَ رَأْسَهُ رَمَاهُ فَلَمْ يُخْطِئْ هَذِهِ مِنْهُ يَعْنِي جَبْهَتَهُ وَانْقَلَبَ الرَّجُلُ ، وَشَالَ بِرِجْلِهِ : فَضَحِكَ النَّبِيُّ صلى الله عليه وسلم حَتَّى بَدَتْ نَوَاجِذُهُ قَالَ : قُلْتُ : مِنْ أَيِّ شَيْءٍ ضَحِكَ ؟ قَالَ : مِنْ فِعْلِهِ بِالرَّجُلِ[265]

234. 'Āmir ibn al-Aswad narrated from Sa'd ibn Abī Waqqās ﷺ that: "[Sa'd said] 'The Messenger of Allāh ﷺ laughed on the day of the Battle of the Trench until his teeth showed.' I asked Sa'd, 'What caused him to laugh?' He replied, 'A disbeliever had a shield, and Sa'd was an archer. He was swaying the shield from side to side to protect his forehead, whilst making derogatory remarks. Sa'd took an arrow and kept it ready in the bow. When the disbeliever exposed his head, he quickly aimed at his forehead and did not miss the target. The enemy immediately fell down with his legs rising into the air. On that the Messenger of Allāh ﷺ laughed until his molar teeth were displayed.' I asked, 'Why did the Messenger of Allāh ﷺ laugh?' He replied, 'Because of what Sa'd did to the man.'"

Abdul Razzaq al-Badr said,

> The Messenger of Allāh ﷺ laughed because he was happy that an enemy of Allāh was killed and not because of how the man fell down. This was because that disbeliever caused a lot of harm.

---

265 Musnad Ahmad (1620)

CHAPTER THIRTY SIX

باب ما جاء في صفة مزاح رسول الله صلى الله عليه وسلم

THE REPORTS PERTAINING TO THE SENSE OF HUMOUR OF THE MESSENGER OF ALLĀH ﷺ

Abdul Razzaq al-Badr said,

> The jokes of the Prophet ﷺ were always truthful and intended to bring forth affability. He joked with his companions only according to the need. For this reason, one should be moderate in his sense of humour and refrain from insulting and mocking others.

Al-Nawawi said,

> The forbidden type of joking is that which is immoderate and highly frequent for this hardens the heart and makes laughing a habit of the person, distracting the individual from the remembrance of Allāh and the religious obligations. Not to mention that excessive joking can often lead to hurting the feelings of others, thereby inducing hatred and compromising one's dignity and respect before the people. If the joke is free of all these defects, then it is the lawful joking that the Prophet ﷺ did.

٢٣٥ : حَدَّثَنَا مَحْمُودُ بْنُ غَيْلانَ ، قَالَ : حَدَّثَنَا أَبُو أُسَامَةَ ، عَنْ شَرِيكٍ ، عَنْ عَاصِمٍ الأَحْوَلِ ، عَنْ أَنَسِ بْنِ مَالِكٍ ، قَالَ : إِنَّ النَّبِيَّ صلى الله عليه وسلم ، قَالَ لَهُ : يَا ذَا الأُذُنَيْنِ.[266]
قَالَ مَحْمُودٌ : قَالَ أَبُو أُسَامَةَ : يَعْنِي يُمَازِحُهُ

235. Anas ibn Mālik ﷺ narrated: "The Messenger of Allāh ﷺ once called me, 'O two eared one!'"

Abdul Razzaq al-Badr said,

> The statement of the Messenger of Allāh ﷺ to Anas ﷺ was to joke with him and it shows his humbleness as he joked with his servant.

Al-Bajūrī said,

> The statement of the Messenger of Allāh ﷺ was said to praise Anas for being an attentive listener who understands the words he hears accurately. The humorous aspect of the statement is that it gives the impression that the person possesses no sense except for that which emanates from the ears.

٢٣٦ : حَدَّثَنَا هَنَّادُ بْنُ السَّرِيِّ ، قَالَ : حَدَّثَنَا وَكِيعٌ ، عَنْ شُعْبَةَ ، عَنْ أَبِي التَّيَّاحِ ، عَنْ أَنَسِ بْنِ مَالِكٍ ، قَالَ : إِنْ كَانَ رَسُولُ الله صلى الله عليه وسلم ، لَيُخَالِطُنَا حَتَّى يَقُولَ لأَخٍ لِي صَغِيرٍ : يَا أَبَا عُمَيْرٍ ، مَا فَعَلَ النُّغَيْرُ ؟ .[267]
قَالَ أَبُو عِيسَى : وَفِقْهُ هَذَا الْحَدِيثِ أَنَّ النَّبِيَّ صلى الله عليه وسلم ، كَانَ يُمَازِحُ وَفِيهِ أَنَّهُ كَنَّى غُلامًا صَغِيرًا ، فَقَالَ لَهُ : يَا أَبَا عُمَيْرٍ .
وَفِيهِ أَنَّهُ لا بَأْسَ أَنْ يُعْطَى الصَّبِيُّ الطَّيْرَ ، لِيَلْعَبَ بِهِ وَإِنَّمَا ، قَالَ لَهُ النَّبِيُّ صلى الله عليه وسلم : يَا أَبَا عُمَيْرٍ ، مَا فَعَلَ النُّغَيْرُ ؟ لأَنَّهُ كَانَ لَهُ نُغَيْرٌ يَلْعَبُ بِهِ

266 Sunan Abū Dawūd (5002) and Sunan al-Tirmidhī (1992)
267 Sahīh al-Bukhārī (6129) and Sahīh Muslim (2150)

فَمَاتَ ، فَحَزِنَ الْغُلَامُ عَلَيْهِ فَمَازَحَهُ النَّبِيُّ صلى الله عليه وسلم : يَا أَبَا عُمَيْرٍ ، مَا فَعَلَ النُّغَيْرُ ؟

236. Anas ibn Mālik ﷺ narrated: "The Messenger of Allāh ﷺ used to mix with us (i.e. me and my family) to the extent that he said to my younger brother, 'Abū Umayr, what happened to the Nughayr?'"

Al-Tirmidhī said: "This hadīth shows that the Prophet ﷺ used to joke with others and that it is allowed to give young children birds to play with."

Ibn Hajar al-Haytamī said,

> Al-Nughayr is a type of bird and the Prophet ﷺ used a *kunya* to call the young child to bring joy to his heart as he knew that his bird had died.
>
> Al-Baghawī said, "This hadīth shows that it is allowed to rhyme if it is natural and intended."
>
> The *fiqh* of this hadīth is:
>
> 1. It is allowed to have birds in a cage to enjoy their colour or play with so long as they are fed and looked after.
> 2. It is allowed to call children with a *kunya* (i.e. the father of so and so).
> 3. It is allowed to joke so long as the joke does not involve sins.
> 4. It shows the kind manners and compassion of the Prophet ﷺ.
> 5. It is from the recommended good manners to look after the vulnerable ones and bring happiness to their hearts.

٢٣٧ : حَدَّثَنَا عَبَّاسُ بْنُ مُحَمَّدٍ الدُّورِيُّ ، قَالَ : حَدَّثَنَا عَلِيُّ بْنُ الْحَسَنِ بْنِ شَقِيقٍ ، قَالَ : أَنبأَنَا عَبْدُ اللهِ بْنُ الْمُبَارَكِ ، عَنْ أُسَامَةَ بْنِ زَيْدٍ ، عَنْ سَعِيدٍ الْمَقْبُرِيِّ ، عَنْ أَبِي هُرَيْرَةَ ، قَالَ : قَالُوا : يَا رَسُولَ اللهِ ، إِنَّكَ تُدَاعِبُنَا ، قَالَ :

إِنِّي لا أَقُولُ إِلا حَقًّا [268]

237. Abū Hurairah narrated: "The companions said, 'O Messenger of Allāh ﷺ! Verily, you joke with us!' He said, 'Yes, except I do not say but the truth.'"

Abdul Razzaq al-Badr said,

> The Prophet ﷺ joked but his jokes did not include anything unlawful as all of his statements were truthful.

٢٣٨: حَدَّثَنَا قُتَيْبَةُ بْنُ سَعِيدٍ ، قَالَ : حَدَّثَنَا خَالِدُ بْنُ عَبْدِ الله ، عَنْ حُمَيْدٍ ، عَنْ أَنَسِ بْنِ مَالِكٍ ، أَنَّ رَجُلا اسْتَحْمَلَ رَسُولَ الله صلى الله عليه وسلم ، فَقَالَ : إِنِّي حَامِلُكَ عَلَى وَلَدِ نَاقَةٍ ، فَقَالَ : يَا رَسُولَ الله ، مَا أَصْنَعُ بِوَلَدِ النَّاقَةِ ؟ فَقَالَ صلى الله عليه وسلم : وَهَلْ تَلِدُ الإِبِلَ إِلا النُّوقُ ؟ . [269]

238. Anas ibn Mālik narrated: "A man requested from the Messenger of Allāh ﷺ a means of transport. The Messenger of Allāh ﷺ said, 'I will give you the baby of a camel to ride.' The man said, 'O Messenger of Allāh! What shall I do with the baby camel?' He replied, '[Do you not know that] every camel is the baby of a camel?'"

Al-Bajūrī said,

> The response of the Prophet ﷺ to the reaction of the man teaches us that one should contemplate the words he hears and not rush to respond and reject a statement or offering until after it is understood well.

٢٣٩: حَدَّثَنَا إِسْحَاقُ بْنُ مَنْصُورٍ ، قَالَ : حَدَّثَنَا عَبْدُ الرَّزَّاقِ ، قَالَ : حَدَّثَنَا

268 Sunan al-Tirmidhī (1990)
269 Sunan Abū Dawūd (4998) and Sunan al-Tirmidhī (1991)

مَعْمَرٌ ، عَنْ ثَابِتٍ ، عَنْ أَنَسِ بْنِ مَالِكٍ ، أَنَّ رَجُلا مِنْ أَهْلِ الْبَادِيَةِ كَانَ اسْمُهُ زَاهِرًا ، وَكَانَ يُهْدِي إِلَى النَّبِيِّ صلى الله عليه وسلم ، هَدِيَّةً مِنَ الْبَادِيَةِ ، فَيُجَهِّزُهُ النَّبِيُّ صلى الله عليه وسلم ، إِذَا أَرَادَ أَنْ يَخْرُجَ ، فَقَالَ النَّبِيُّ صلى الله عليه وسلم : إِنَّ زَاهِرًا بَادِيَتُنَا وَنَحْنُ حَاضِرُوهُ وَكَانَ صلى الله عليه وسلم يُحِبُّهُ وَكَانَ رَجُلا دَمِيمًا ، فَأَتَاهُ النَّبِيُّ صلى الله عليه وسلم ، يَوْمًا وَهُوَ يَبِيعُ مَتَاعَهُ وَاحْتَضَنَهُ مِنْ خَلْفِهِ وَهُوَ لا يُبْصِرُهُ ، فَقَالَ : مَنْ هَذَا ؟ أَرْسِلْنِي فَالْتَفَتَ فَعَرَفَ النَّبِيُّ صلى الله عليه وسلم فَجَعَلَ لا يَأْلُو مَا أَلْصَقَ ظَهْرَهُ بِصَدْرِ النَّبِيِّ صلى الله عليه وسلم حِينَ عَرَفَهُ ، فَجَعَلَ النَّبِيُّ صلى الله عليه وسلم ، يَقُولُ : مَنْ يَشْتَرِي هَذَا الْعَبْدَ ، فَقَالَ : يَا رَسُولَ اللهِ ، إِذًا وَاللهِ تَجِدُنِي كَاسِدًا ، فَقَالَ النَّبِيُّ صلى الله عليه وسلم : لَكِنْ عِنْدَ اللهِ لَسْتَ بِكَاسِدٍ أَوْ قَالَ : أَنتَ عِنْدَ اللهِ غَالٍ .[270]

239. Anas ibn Mālik ؓ narrated: "There was a resident of the desert whose name was Zāhir, whenever he visited the Messenger of Allāh ﷺ he brought with him a present to give to the Messenger of Allāh ﷺ and when he intended to leave Madīnah, the Messenger of Allāh ﷺ used to present him with provisions of the city. Once the Messenger of Allāh ﷺ said, 'Zāhir is our desert, and we are his city.' The Messenger of Allāh ﷺ had a strong bond with him though he had an unpleasant appearance. One day, the Messenger of Allāh ﷺ approached him while he was selling his merchandise in the market and caught him in between the arms from the back in such a manner that he could not be seen. Zāhir ؓ said, 'Who is this? Let me go.' But when he turned and saw with the corner of his eye that it was the Messenger of Allāh ﷺ, he straightened his back and began pressing it to the chest of the Messenger of Allāh ﷺ. The Prophet ﷺ then said, 'Who will purchase this slave?' Zāhir ؓ replied, 'O Messenger of Allāh, if you shall sell me, you will be selling something defective.' The Messenger of Allāh ﷺ replied, 'No, you are not defective in the

270 Musnad Ahmad (12669)

sight of Allāh, but very valuable.'"

Abdul Razzaq al-Badr said,

> Zāhir ؓ used to gift the Messenger of Allāh ﷺ from the items that the Bedouins used to make such as dry milk, ghee etc. In return, the Messenger of Allāh ﷺ used to reciprocate with a better gift when Zāhir wanted to leave Madīnah.
>
> The statement of the Prophet ﷺ that, "Zāhir is our desert and we are his city" was to show that both sets of people complete each other as the people in the desert need the ones in the city and the people in the city need the ones living in the desert.
>
> This hadīth shows that joking is not limited to words but can also include action as can be seen from the act of the Messenger of Allāh ﷺ when he held Zāhir from the back.
>
> The reason Anas ؓ mentioned Zāhir's appearance was to clarify the reason why Zāhir described himself as defective merchandise that no one would want to buy.
>
> The statement of the Prophet ﷺ to Zāhir shows the virtue of this companion and at the same time goes in line with the other hadīth, "Allāh does not look at your image and wealth, rather He looks at your deeds and hearts."[271] The virtue of a person depends on his piety and not his physical appearance.

٢٤٠: حَدَّثَنَا عَبْدُ بْنُ حُمَيْدٍ ، قَالَ : حَدَّثَنَا مُصْعَبُ بْنُ الْمِقْدَامِ ، قَالَ : حَدَّثَنَا الْمُبَارِكُ بْنُ فَضَالَةَ ، عَنِ الْحَسَنِ ، قَالَ : أَتَتْ عَجُوزٌ إِلَى النَّبِيِّ صلى الله عليه وسلم ، فَقَالَتْ : يَا رَسُولَ اللهِ ، ادْعُ اللهَ أَنْ يُدْخِلَنِي الْجَنَّةَ ، فَقَالَ : يَا أُمَّ فُلَانٍ ، إِنَّ الْجَنَّةَ لا تَدْخُلُهَا عَجُوزٌ ، قَالَ : فَوَلَّتْ تَبْكِي ، فَقَالَ : أَخْبِرُوهَا أَنَّهَا لا تَدْخُلُهَا وَهِيَ عَجُوزٌ إِنَّ اللهَ تَعَالَى ، يَقُولُ : إِنَّا أَنْشَأْنَاهُنَّ إِنْشَاءً ، فَجَعَلْنَاهُنَّ أَبْكَارًا ، عُرُبًا أَتْرَابًا[272]

271 Sahīh Muslim (4657)
272 Ma'alim al-Tanzīl (1203)

240. Al-Hasan al-Basrī narrated: "An old woman came to the Messenger of Allāh ﷺ and said, 'O Messenger of Allāh! Ask Allāh to grant me entrance into Paradise.' The Messenger of Allāh ﷺ replied, 'O mother of so and so! No old women will enter Paradise.' The woman started crying and began to leave. The Messenger of Allāh ﷺ said, 'Say to the woman that she will not enter Paradise in a state of old age. Allāh ﷻ says: {Lo! We have created them a [new] creation and made them virgins, lovers, equal in age.}[273]'"

Al-Bajūrī said,

> The statement of the Prophet ﷺ was intended to teach the woman in a humorous manner that old women will be created new and their age when they enter Paradise will be thirty three as stated in the hadīth reported by Mu'ādh ibn Jabal ﷺ and documented in the Musnad of Imām Ahmad.

273 Qur'ān: 35-37

CHAPTER THIRTY SEVEN

باب ما جاء في صفة كلام رسول اللّه صلى اللّه عليه وسلم في الشعر

THE REPORTS PERTAINING TO THE LINES OF POETRY SAID BY THE MESSENGER OF ALLĀH ﷺ

Abdul Razzaq al-Badr said,

> Poetry takes the same ruling as any other speech: that which is good is allowed and can be recited, but that which is otherwise, it is not allowed to recite it or listen to it. The Prophet ﷺ said that some poetry contains wisdom. This shows that not all poetry is good; hence you find poetry that encourages sins, innovation and superstition, and some that encourages guidance and promotes the truth.

٢٤١: حَدَّثَنَا عَلِيُّ بْنُ حُجْرٍ ، قَالَ : حَدَّثَنَا شَرِيكٌ ، عَنِ الْمِقْدَامِ بْنِ شُرَيْحٍ ، عَنْ أَبِيهِ ، عَنْ عَائِشَةَ ، قَالَتْ : قِيلَ لَهَا : هَلْ كَانَ النَّبِيُّ صلى الله عليه وسلم ، يَتَمَثَّلُ بِشَيْءٍ مِنَ الشِّعْرِ ؟ قَالَتْ : كَانَ يَتَمَثَّلُ بِشِعْرِ ابْنِ رَوَاحَةَ ، وَيَتَمَثَّلُ بِقَوْلِهِ : يَأْتِيكَ بِالأَخْبَارِ مَنْ لَمْ تُزَوِّدِ[274]

241. Aisha ﵂ was asked: "Did the Prophet ﷺ quote from poetry that which he used as a proverb?" She replied: "He recited a line of poetry of 'Abdullāh ibn Rawāhah but without following its structure and rhyme. He recited this couplet of his, 'News is brought to you by a person whom you have not compensated.'"

Ibn Hajar al-Haytamī said,

> It was narrated that the most disliked of speech to him ﷺ was poetry but he would quote some proverbs taken from poetry on occasion. Such as when he recited a line of poetry of the brother of Qais ibn Turfah whilst changing the order of the words i.e. he did not follow the order of words in the line so he said, "News is brought to you by a person whom you have not compensated." Abū Bakr ﵁ said, "O Messenger of Allāh! The couplet is not as you have recited!" The Messenger of Allah ﷺ replied, "I am not a poet." Meaning that he only intended to mention the message of the words and not to recite the poem.
>
> 'Abdullāh ibn Rawāhah ﵁ was one of the poets who defended the Prophet ﷺ but the most active influential poets who defended him were Ka'b ibn Mālik and Hassan ibn Thābit ﵄.

٢٤٢: حَدَّثَنَا مُحَمَّدُ بْنُ بَشَّارٍ ، قَالَ : حَدَّثَنَا عَبْدُ الرَّحْمَنِ بْنُ مَهْدِيٍّ ، قَالَ : حَدَّثَنَا سُفْيَانُ الثَّوْرِيُّ ، عَنْ عَبْدِ الْمَلِكِ بْنِ عُمَيْرٍ ، قَالَ : حَدَّثَنَا أَبُو سَلَمَةَ ، عَنْ أَبِي هُرَيْرَةَ ، قَالَ : قَالَ رَسُولُ اللهِ صلى الله عليه وسلم : إِنَّ أَصْدَقَ

---

274 Sunan al-Tirmidhī (2848)

كَلِمَةٍ قَالَهَا الشَّاعِرُ ، كَلِمَةُ لَبِيدٍ : أَلا كُلُّ شَيْءٍ مَا خَلا اللَّهَ بَاطِلُ ، وَكَادَ أُمَيَّةُ بْنُ أَبِي الصَّلْتِ أَنْ يُسْلِمَ [275]

242. Abū Hurairah ؓ narrated: "The Messenger of Allāh ﷺ said, 'The most truthful statement said by a poet is that of Labīd, 'Indeed, be aware, everything besides Allāh is false.' Umayyah ibn Abī al-Salt was close to accepting Islām.'"

Al-Bajūrī said,

> Labīd ibn Rabiash al-'Amirī was one of the renowned poets, he embraced Islām and did not recite any poetry from that point on as he said, "The Qur'ān suffices me."
>
> The meaning of the line is that everything else besides Allāh is doomed to perish.

Alī al-Qārī said,

> The reason he ﷺ described these words as being the most truthful statement a poet has ever said was because the statement conforms to the ayah: **{Everything will be destroyed except His Face}**[276] and this is the core of monotheism.
>
> Umayyah ibn Abī al-Salt was a poet whose poems conformed to the tenets of Islām and he believed in the Resurrection and was a worshipper but he did not embrace Islām, though he died after the emergence of Islām.

٢٤٣ : حَدَّثَنَا مُحَمَّدُ بْنُ الْمُثَنَّى ، قَالَ : حَدَّثَنَا مُحَمَّدُ بْنُ جَعْفَرٍ ، قَالَ : حَدَّثَنَا شُعْبَةُ ، عَنِ الأَسْوَدِ بْنِ قَيْسٍ ، عَنْ جُنْدُبِ بْنِ سُفْيَانَ الْبَجَلِيِّ ، قَالَ : أَصَابَ حَجَرٌ أُصْبُعَ رَسُولِ اللَّهِ صلى الله عليه وسلم فَدَمِيَتْ ، فَقَالَ : هَلْ أَنْتِ إِلا

---

275 Sahīh al-Bukhārī (6147) and Sahīh Muslim (3841)
276 Qur'ān: 28:88

أُصْبُعٌ دَمِيتِ وَفِي سَبِيلِ اللهِ مَا لَقِيتِ [277]

243. Jundub ibn Sufyān ؓ narrated: "Once a rock fell upon the toe of the Messenger of Allāh ﷺ and caused it to bleed. Thereupon, he recited this couplet, 'You are but a toe that has bled. This is not fruitless, for reward has been obtained in the path of Allāh.'"

Abdul Razzaq al-Badr said,

> The bleeding was caused by the toe of the Messenger of Allāh ﷺ hitting a stone while he was walking. This hadīth is evidence that the Muslim is rewarded for every difficulty and test he goes through if he shows patience and seeks the reward of Allāh.

٢٤٤: حَدَّثَنَا ابْنُ أَبِي عُمَرَ ، قَالَ : حَدَّثَنَا سُفْيَانُ بْنُ عُيَيْنَةَ ، عَنِ الأَسْوَدِ بْنِ قَيْسٍ ، عَنْ جُنْدُبِ بْنِ عَبْدِ اللهِ الْبَجَلِيِّ ، نَحْوَهُ . [278]

244. The same is reported through another route.

٢٤٥: حَدَّثَنَا مُحَمَّدُ بْنُ بَشَّارٍ ، قَالَ : حَدَّثَنَا يَحْيَى بْنُ سَعِيدٍ ، قَالَ : حَدَّثَنَا سُفْيَانُ الثَّوْرِيُّ ، قَالَ : أَنْبَأَنَا أَبُو إِسْحَاقَ ، عَنِ الْبَرَاءِ بْنِ عَازِبٍ ، قَالَ : قَالَ لَهُ رَجُلٌ : أَفَرَرْتُمْ عَنْ رَسُولِ اللهِ صلى الله عليه وسلم يَا أَبَا عُمَارَةَ ؟ فَقَالَ : لا وَاللهِ مَا وَلَّى رَسُولُ اللهِ صلى الله عليه وسلم ، وَلَكِنْ وَلَّى سَرَعَانُ النَّاسِ ، تَلَقَّتْهُمْ هَوَازِنُ بِالنَّبْلِ ، وَرَسُولُ اللهِ صلى الله عليه وسلم ، عَلَى بَغْلَتِهِ ، وَأَبُو سُفْيَانَ بْنُ الْحَارِثِ بْنِ عَبْدِ الْمُطَّلِبِ آخِذٌ بِلِجَامِهَا ، وَرَسُولُ اللهِ يَقُولُ : أَنَا النَّبِيُّ لا كَذِبْ أَنَا ابْنُ عَبْدِ الْمُطَّلِبْ [279]

---

277 Sahīh al-Bukhārī (2802) and Sahīh Muslim (1796)
278 See hadīth 243
279 Sahīh al-Bukhārī (2824) and Sahīh Muslim (1776)

245. A man asked al-Barā ibn Āzib ؓ: "O Abū 'Umārah! Did you all flee the battle?" He replied, "No, not all of us. The Messenger of Allāh ﷺ did not turn away but [some] people in the army were hasty [to collect the spoils of war] and so the people of the tribe of Hawāzin began to shower arrows [on their heads]. The Messenger of Allāh ﷺ was upon a mule and Abū Sufyān ibn Al-Hārith ibn Abdul Muttalib ؓ was leading it by its reins. The Messenger of Allāh ﷺ was reciting the following couplet, 'Verily, I am the Prophet, and it is no lie. I am from the children [grandsons] of Abdul Muttalib.'"

Al-Bajūrī said,

> The answer of al-Barā that not everyone fled the battle on that day required him to state that he ﷺ did not turn away to show that the major companions remained with him too. However, al-Barā did not use the term "flee" when talking about the Prophet ﷺ to avoid attributing him with such an ugly defective characteristic. This is because it is forbidden to describe him with such a trait and it would nullify one's Islām to call him as such if he intends to degrade him, and if no degrading is intended then the person deserves severe punishment according al-Shāfi'ī and deserves the death penalty according to Imām Mālik. This is because the term "turn away" can be used to show that the person is changing his tactics whereas the term "flee" necessitates cowardice and fear.

Ibn Hajar al-Haytamī said,

> The hasty ones refer to those in whose hearts Islām was not established deeply such as the new Muslims, those who embraced Islām after the conquest of Makkah and those like them.
>
> The battle referred to here is the battle of Hunayn, which happened after the conquest of Makkah when the tribes of Hawāzin and Thaqīf agreed to unite to fight the Muslims. In light of this, the Prophet ﷺ led a force of ten thousand persons from Madīnah and two thousand from those who embraced Islām after

Makkah was conquered (who are the ones who the Prophet ﷺ freed on that day) and eighty disbelievers, including Safwan ibn Umayyah as he ﷺ borrowed one hundred shields from him to use in the battle.

This battle was amongst the toughest that the Prophet ﷺ participated in because after some of the army fled, the Prophet ﷺ asked al-Abbās to call the Ansār and those who gave the pledge under the tree, and his voice was heard from the distance of eight miles, upon which the army returned to the battle swiftly. Then, after they engaged in the fight and it became extremely heated, the Prophet ﷺ picked up some pebbles from the ground and threw them in the air and said, "May their faces be deformed!" Subsequently, the pebbles entered the eyes of the disbelievers and the Muhajirūn and Ansār engaged in the battle fiercely, causing the disbelievers to flee the battle and be defeated.

Angels fought alongside the Muslims in the battle of Badr and the battle of Hunayn only, where in the latter they wore red turbans.

The reason why the Prophet ﷺ was riding his white mule although he had horses and riding a mule in the battle is not suitable for engagement, was to show the Muslims that victory was guaranteed from Allāh so that their hearts would be filled with tranquillity and they would return to the battle. This action of the Prophet ﷺ shows his great courage and bravery.

The meaning of the couplet is that he is truthfully the Prophet ﷺ and thus he will not run away and will not be defeated, and it is no lie because a Prophet does not lie and so he was certain of victory.

٢٤٦: حَدَّثَنَا إِسْحَاقُ بْنُ مَنْصُورٍ ، قَالَ : حَدَّثَنَا عَبْدُ الرَّزَّاقِ ، قَالَ : حَدَّثَنَا جَعْفَرُ بْنُ سُلَيْمَانَ ، قَالَ : حَدَّثَنَا ثَابِتٌ ، عَنْ أَنَسٍ : أَنَّ النَّبِيَّ صلى الله عليه وسلم دَخَلَ مَكَّةَ فِي عُمْرَةِ الْقَضَاءِ ، وَابْنُ رَوَاحَةَ يَمْشِي بَيْنَ يَدَيْهِ ، وَهُوَ يَقُولُ : خَلُّوا بَنِي الْكُفَّارِ عَنْ سَبِيلِهِ الْيَوْمَ نَضْرِبُكُمْ عَلَى تَنْزِيلِهِ ضَرْبًا يُزِيلُ

الْهَامَ عَنْ مَقِيلِهِ وَيُذْهِلُ الْخَلِيلَ عَنْ خَلِيلِهِ فَقَالَ لَهُ عُمَرُ : يَا ابْنَ رَوَاحَةَ ، بَيْنَ يَدِي رَسُولِ الله صلى الله عليه وسلم ، وَفِي حَرَمِ الله تَقُولُ الشِّعْرَ ، فَقَالَ صلى الله عليه وَسلم : خَلِّ عَنْهُ يَا عُمَرُ ، فَلَهِيَ أَسْرَعُ فِيهِمْ ، مِنْ نَضْحِ النَّبْلِ [280]

246. Anas ibn Mālik ﷺ narrated: "The Messenger of Allāh ﷺ entered Makkah for Umratul Qadā while 'Abdullāh ibn Rawāhah ﷺ was walking ahead of him reciting these couplets:

O non-believers clear his path and leave today,
For today we shall strike you upon his arrival,
Such a strike that we will separate the head from its body,
And will cause a friend to forget his friend.

'Umar ﷺ said, 'O Ibn Rawāhah! How do you recite poetry in the presence of the Messenger of Allāh ﷺ and in the Sacred House of Allāh?' The Messenger of Allāh ﷺ said, 'O 'Umar, leave him! These couplets have more impact than showering arrows onto them.'"

Abdul Razzaq al-Badr said,

> The statement of the Messenger of Allāh ﷺ shows that poetry scares the enemy and troubles them, strengthening the believers to avert the harm of the disbelievers and protect the religion of Allāh.

'Alī al-Qārī said,

> Umratul Qadā refers to the Umrah that the Messenger of Allāh ﷺ wanted to make up as he could not perform it due to the truce signed between the Muslims and disbelievers on the day of Hudaybiyyah that made the Muslims agree not to perform Umrah on that day. This is evidence that if a person intended to perform Umrah or Hajj and after entering the state *ihrām* could not continue it, he should make it up.

280 Sunan al-Tirmidhī (2847)

The couplets were said after the day of Hudaybiyyah to celebrate this victory of the Muslims and to threaten the disbelievers of what will happen to them should they breach the truce.

The reason behind the statement of 'Umar was because he thought poetry was condemned in all cases as he read it in the Qur'ān and heard it from the Messenger of Allāh ﷺ. The response of the Messenger of Allāh ﷺ was to show that not all poetry is condemned and admonished.

٢٤٧: حَدَّثَنَا عَلِيُّ بْنُ حُجْرٍ ، قَالَ : حَدَّثَنَا شَرِيكٌ ، عَنْ سِمَاكِ بْنِ حَرْبٍ ، عَنْ جَابِرِ بْنِ سَمُرَةَ ، قَالَ : جَالَسْتُ النَّبِيَّ صلى الله عليه وسلم ، أَكْثَرَ مِنْ مِائَةِ مَرَّةٍ ، وَكَانَ أَصْحَابُهُ يَتَنَاشَدُونَ الشِّعْرَ ، وَيَتَذَاكَرُونَ أَشْيَاءَ مِنْ أَمْرِ الْجَاهِلِيَّةِ ، وَهُوَ سَاكِتٌ وَرُبَّمَا تَبَسَّمَ مَعَهُمْ [281]

247. Jābir ibn Samurah ﷺ narrated: "I sat with the Prophet ﷺ more than a hundred times. His companions ﷺ would recite poetry and relate certain stories from the days of Jāhiliyyah. The Prophet ﷺ listened to them silently and at times he smiled with them."

Abdul Razzaq al-Badr said,

> The reason he ﷺ mentioned the number of times was to assure the listener that the statement he was about to narrate was true.

Al-Bajūrī said,

> This hadīth teaches us that it is allowed to recite poetry and listen to it even if it includes mentioning the days before Islām and events, on the condition that it has nothing that is considered as disliked or unlawful in religion.

281 Sunan al-Tirmidhī (2850)

٢٤٨ : حَدَّثَنَا عَلِيُّ بْنُ حُجْرٍ ، قَالَ : حَدَّثَنَا شَرِيكٌ ، عَنْ عَبْدِ الْمَلِكِ بْنِ عُمَيْرٍ ، عَنْ أَبِي سَلَمَةَ ، عَنْ أَبِي هُرَيْرَةَ ، عَنِ النَّبِيِّ صلى الله عليه وسلم ، قَالَ : أَشْعَرُ كَلِمَةٍ تَكَلَّمَتْ بِهَا الْعَرَبُ كَلِمَةُ لَبِيدٍ : أَلا كُلُّ شَيْءٍ مَا خَلا اللَّهَ بَاطِلٌ[282]

248. Abū Hurairah ﷺ narrated: "The Messenger of Allāh ﷺ said: 'The best couplet that the Arabs ever recited is that of Labīd, 'Indeed, be aware, everything besides Allāh is false.''"

٢٤٩ : حَدَّثَنَا أَحْمَدُ بْنُ مَنِيعٍ ، قَالَ : حَدَّثَنَا مَرْوَانُ بْنُ مُعَاوِيَةَ ، عَنْ عَبْدِ اللهِ بْنِ عَبْدِ الرَّحْمَنِ الطَّائِفِيِّ ، عَنْ عَمْرِو بْنِ الشَّرِيدِ ، عَنْ أَبِيهِ ، قَالَ : كُنْتُ رِدْفَ النَّبِيِّ صلى الله عليه وسلم ، فَأَنْشَدْتُهُ مِائَةَ قَافِيَةٍ مِنْ قَوْلِ أُمَيَّةَ بْنِ أَبِي الصَّلْتِ الثَّقَفِيِّ ، كُلَّمَا أَنْشَدْتُهُ بَيْتًا ، قَالَ لِيَ النَّبِيُّ صلى الله عليه وسلم : هِيهْ حَتَّى أَنْشَدْتُهُ مِائَةً يَعْنِي بَيْتًا ، فَقَالَ النَّبِيُّ صلى الله عليه وسلم : إِنْ كَادَ لَيُسْلِمُ[283]

249. Amr ibn Sharīd reported that his father ﷺ said: "I once rode behind the Prophet ﷺ. I recited for him one hundred couplets of Umayyah ibn Salt's poetry. After reciting each couplet, he asked me to continue until I recited a hundred couplets. In the end, he said, 'He (Umayyah) came close to accepting Islām.'"

Ibn Hajar al-Haytamī said,

> The liking that the Prophet ﷺ took to the poetry of Umayyah and his request to hear more of it is evidence that poetry is recommended if it includes affirmation of Allāh's Oneness and fine gems and wisdoms.

---

282 See hadīth 242

283 Sahīh Muslim (2255)

Al-Bajūrī said,

> It is said that Umayyah is the famous poet Umayyah ibn Abī al-Salt al-Thaqafī who Allāh ﷻ revealed an ayah regarding: {**And recite to them, [O Muhammad], the news of him to whom we gave [knowledge of] Our signs, but he detached himself from them; so Satan pursued him, and he became of the deviators.**}[284] He read the Torah and the Bible before the emergence of Islām, and knew that a prophet would appear. However, he desired for himself to be that prophet and that was the reason why he rejected the Prophet ﷺ and caused him to envy him and disbelieve.
>
> The statement of the Prophet ﷺ was said after he heard the content of the poem as it included words indicating monotheism and good wisdom.

٢٥٠: حَدَّثَنَا إِسْمَاعِيلُ بْنُ مُوسَى الْفَزَارِيُّ ، وَعَلِيُّ بْنُ حُجْرٍ ، وَالْمَعْنَى وَاحِدٌ ، قَالا : حَدَّثَنَا عَبْدُ الرَّحْمَنِ بْنُ أَبِي الزِّنَادِ ، عَنْ هِشَامِ بْنِ عُرْوَةَ ، عَنْ أَبِيهِ ، عَنْ عَائِشَةَ ، قَالَتْ : كَانَ رَسُولُ الله صلى الله عليه وسلم يَضَعُ لِحَسَّانَ بْنِ ثَابِتٍ مِنْبَرًا فِي الْمَسْجِدِ يَقُومُ عَلَيْهِ قَائِمًا يُفَاخِرُ عَنْ رَسُولِ الله صلى الله عليه وسلم أَوْ قَالَ : يُنَافِحُ عَنْ رَسُولِ الله صلى الله عليه وسلم وَيَقُولُ صلى الله عليه وسلم : إِنَّ اللهَ يُؤَيِّدُ حَسَّانَ بِرُوحِ الْقُدُسِ ، مَا يُنَافِحُ أَوْ يُفَاخِرُ عَنْ رَسُولِ الله صلى الله عليه وسلم[285]

250. Aisha ؓ narrated: "The Messenger of Allāh ﷺ would place something high in the Masjid for Hassan ibn Thābit ؓ, so that he could stand upon it and recite poetry praising the Messenger of Allāh ﷺ (or it was said: defending the Messenger of Allāh ﷺ). He ﷺ would say, 'Verily, Allāh aids Hassan with the Rūh al-Quds as long as he defends or praises the Messenger of Allāh ﷺ.'"

---

284 Qur'ān: 7:175

285 Sunan Abū Dawūd (5015) and Sunan al-Tirmidhī (2846)

Al-Bajūrī said,

> Rūh al-Quds (the Holy Spirit) refers to Jibrīl ﵇ and he was referred to as the "spirit" because the spirit (soul) brings life to the heart and because he is the one who delivers the revelations that provide eternal life to the Prophets.
>
> He (Hassan) defended the Prophet ﷺ in response to the false accusations and abuse of the disbelievers.

٢٥١: حَدَّثَنَا إِسْمَاعِيلُ بْنُ مُوسَى ، وَعَلِيُّ بْنُ حُجْرٍ ، قَالا : حَدَّثَنَا ابْنُ أَبِي الزِّنَادِ ، عَنْ أَبِيهِ ، عَنْ عُرْوَةَ ، عَنْ عَائِشَةَ ، عَنِ النَّبِيِّ صلى الله عليه وسلم ، مِثْلَهُ

251. Aisha ﵁ reported a similar hadīth through a different route.

CHAPTER THIRTY EIGHT

باب ما جاء في كلام رسول الله صلى الله عليه وسلم في السمر

THE REPORTS PERTAINING TO THE CONVERSATIONS OF THE MESSENGER OF ALLĀH ﷺ AT NIGHT

٢٥٢: حَدَّثَنَا الْحَسَنُ بْنُ صَبَّاحِ الْبَزَّارُ ، قَالَ : حَدَّثَنَا أَبُو النَّضْرِ ، قَالَ : حَدَّثَنَا أَبُو عَقِيلٍ الثَّقَفِيُّ عَبْدُ اللَّهِ بْنُ عَقِيلٍ ، عَنْ مُجَالِدٍ ، عَنِ الشَّعْبِيِّ ، عَنْ مَسْرُوقٍ ، عَنْ عَائِشَةَ ، قَالَتْ : حَدَّثَ رَسُولُ الله صلى الله عليه وسلم ، ذَاتَ لَيْلَةٍ نِسَاءَهُ حَدِيثًا ، فَقَالَتِ امْرَأَةٌ مِنْهُنَّ : كَأَنَّ الْحَدِيثَ حَدِيثُ خُرَافَةَ ، فَقَالَ : أَتَدْرُونَ مَا خُرَافَةُ ؟ إِنَّ خُرَافَةَ كَانَ رَجُلا مِنْ عُذْرَةَ ، أَسَرَتْهُ الْجِنُّ فِي الْجَاهِلِيَّةِ ، فَمَكَثَ فِيهِمْ دَهْرًا ، ثُمَّ رَدُّوهُ إِلَى الإِنْسِ ، فَكَانَ يُحَدِّثُ النَّاسَ بِمَا رَأَى فِيهِمْ مِنَ الأَعَاجِيبِ ، فَقَالَ النَّاسُ : حَدِيثُ خُرَافَةَ[286]

252. Aisha ﵂ reported: "One night, the Messenger of Allāh ﷺ related an [astonishing] story to his wives. One of his wives commented, 'This story is as astonishing as the stories of Khurāfah.' The Messenger of Allāh ﷺ said, 'Do you know the original story of Khurāfah? He was a man from the tribe of 'Udhrah, whom the Jinn kidnapped. They kept him for a long time, and then they returned him to the people. He began to relate the wonders and strange things that he saw during his stay with them. Thenceforth, the people began to call every story that was incredible or too much for the mind to handle, a story of Khurāfah.'"

Abdul Razzaq al-Badr said,

> Khurāfah is the name of a man who was kidnapped by the Jinn during the pre-Islamic era and after some time they brought him back to the people. He used to relate strange stories about matters that people had never heard of or saw in their lifetimes, which made them feel astonished. From that time, it became a proverb to describe any unbelievable story as being a story of Khurāfah.

Al-Bajūrī said,

> The purpose of the Prophet ﷺ entertaining his wives at night was

286 Musnad Ahmad (25244)

to make them happy and show them kindness. As for the hadīths concerning disallowing talking after praying *Ishā*, they refer to the talk that has no benefit in it.

٢٥٣: حَدَّثَنَا عَلِيُّ بْنُ حُجْرٍ ، قَالَ : حَدَّثَنَا عِيسَى بْنُ يُونُسَ ، عَنْ هِشَامِ بْنِ عُرْوَةَ ، عَنْ أَخِيهِ عَبْدِ اللهِ بْنِ عُرْوَةَ ، عَنْ عُرْوَةَ ، عَنْ عَائِشَةَ ، قَالَتْ : جَلَسَتْ إِحْدَى عَشْرَةَ امْرَأَةً فَتَعَاهَدْنَ وَتَعَاقَدْنَ أَنْ لا يَكْتُمْنَ مِنْ أَخْبَارِ أَزْوَاجِهِنَّ شَيْئًا : فَقَالَتِ الأُولَى : زَوْجِي لَحْمُ جَمَلٍ غَثٍّ عَلَى رَأْسِ جَبَلٍ وَعْرٍ ، لا سَهْلٌ فَيُرْتَقَى ، وَلا سَمِينٌ فَيُنْتَقَلُ قَالَتِ الثَّانِيَةُ : زَوْجِي لا أُبِثُّ خَبَرَهُ ، إِنِّي أَخَافُ أَنْ لا أَذَرَهُ ، إِنْ أَذْكُرْهُ أَذْكُرْ عُجَرَهُ ، وَبُجَرَهُ قَالَتِ الثَّالِثَةُ : زَوْجِي الْعَشَنَّقُ ، إِنْ أَنْطِقْ أُطَلَّقْ ، وَإِنْ أَسْكُتْ أُعَلَّقْ قَالَتِ الرَّابِعَةُ : زَوْجِي كَلَيْلِ تِهَامَةَ ، لا حَرٌّ ، وَلا قُرٌّ ، وَلا مَخَافَةَ ، وَلا سَآمَةَ قَالَتِ الْخَامِسَةُ : زَوْجِي إِنْ دَخَلَ فَهِدَ ، وَإِنْ خَرَجَ أَسِدَ ، وَلا يَسْأَلُ عَمَّا عَهِدَ قَالَتِ السَّادِسَةُ : زَوْجِي إِنْ أَكَلَ لَفَّ ، وَإِنْ شَرِبَ اشْتَفَّ ، وَإِنِ اضْطَجَعَ الْتَفَّ ، وَلا يُولِجُ الْكَفَّ ، لِيَعْلَمَ الْبَثَّ قَالَتِ السَّابِعَةُ : زَوْجِي عَيَايَاءُ ، أَوْ غَيَايَاءُ طَبَاقَاءُ ، كُلُّ دَاءٍ لَهُ دَاءٌ ، شَجَّكِ ، أَوْ فَلَّكِ ، أَوْ جَمَعَ كُلا لَكِ قَالَتِ الثَّامِنَةُ : زَوْجِي الْمَسُّ ، مَسُّ أَرْنَبٍ وَالرِّيحُ ، رِيحُ زَرْنَبٍ قَالَتِ التَّاسِعَةُ : زَوْجِي رَفِيعُ الْعِمَادِ ، طَوِيلُ النِّجَادِ عَظِيمُ الرَّمَادِ ، قَرِيبُ الْبَيْتِ مِنَ النَّادِ قَالَتِ الْعَاشِرَةُ : زَوْجِي مَالِكٌ ، وَمَا مَالِكٌ مَالِكٌ خَيْرٌ مِنْ ذَلِكِ ، لَهُ إِبِلٌ كَثِيرَاتُ الْمَبَارِكِ ، قَلِيلاتُ الْمَسَارِحِ ، إِذَا سَمِعْنَ صَوْتَ الْمِزْهَرِ ، أَيْقَنَّ أَنَّهُنَّ هَوَالِكُ قَالَتِ الْحَادِيَةَ عَشْرَةَ : زَوْجِي أَبُو زَرْعٍ وَمَا أَبُو زَرْعٍ ؟ أَنَاسَ مِنْ حُلِيٍّ أُذُنَيَّ ، وَمَلأَ مِنْ شَحْمٍ عَضُدَيَّ ، وَبَجَّحَنِي ، فَبَجِحَتْ إِلَيَّ نَفْسِي ، وَجَدَنِي فِي أَهْلِ غُنَيْمَةٍ بِشَقٍّ فَجَعَلَنِي فِي أَهْلِ صَهِيلٍ ، وَأَطِيطٍ وَدَائِسٍ وَمُنَقٍّ ، فَعِنْدَهُ أَقُولُ ، فَلا أُقَبَّحُ ، وَأَرْقُدُ ، فَأَتَصَبَّحُ ، وَأَشْرَبُ ، فَأَتَقَمَّحُ ، أُمُّ أَبِي زَرْعٍ فَمَا أُمُّ أَبِي زَرْعٍ ، عُكُومُهَا رَدَاحٌ ، وَبَيْتُهَا فَسَاحٌ ، ابْنُ أَبِي زَرْعٍ ، فَمَا ابْنُ أَبِي زَرْعٍ ، مَضْجَعُهُ كَمَسَلِّ شَطْبَةٍ ،

وَتُشْبِعُهُ ذِرَاعُ الْجُفْرَةِ ، بِنْتُ أَبِي زَرْعٍ ، فَمَا بِنْتُ أَبِي زَرْعٍ ، طَوْعُ أَبِيهَا وَطَوْعُ أُمِّهَا ، مِلْءُ كِسَائِهَا ، وَغَيْظُ جَارَتِهَا ، جَارِيَةُ أَبِي زَرْعٍ ، فَمَا جَارِيَةُ أَبِي زَرْعٍ ، لا تَبُثُّ حَدِيثَنَا تَبْثِيثًا ، وَلا تُنَقِّثُ مِيرَتَنَا تَنْقِيثًا ، وَلا تَمْلأُ بَيْتَنَا تَعْشِيشًا ، قَالَتْ : خَرَجَ أَبُو زَرْعٍ ، وَالأَوْطَابُ تُمْخَضُ ، فَلَقِيَ امْرَأَةً مَعَهَا وَلَدَانِ لَهَا ، كَالْفَهْدَيْنِ ، يَلْعَبَانِ مِنْ تَحْتِ خَصْرِهَا بِرُمَّانَتَيْنِ ، فَطَلَّقَنِي وَنَكَحَهَا ، فَنَكَحْتُ بَعْدَهُ رَجُلا سَرِيًّا ، رَكِبَ شَرِيًّا ، وَأَخَذَ خَطِّيًّا ، وَأَرَاحَ عَلَيَّ نَعَمًا ثَرِيًّا ، وَأَعْطَانِي مِنْ كُلِّ رَائِحَةٍ زَوْجًا ، وَقَالَ : كُلِي أُمَّ زَرْعٍ ، وَمِيرِي أَهْلَكِ ، فَلَوْ جَمَعْتُ كُلَّ شَيْءٍ أَعْطَانِيهِ ، مَا بَلَغَ أَصْغَرَ آنِيَةِ أَبِي زَرْعٍ قَالَتْ عَائِشَةُ : فَقَالَ لِي رَسُولُ اللهِ صلى الله عليه وسلم : كُنْتُ لَكِ كَأَبِي زَرْعٍ لأُمِّ زَرْعٍ[287]

253. 'Aisha ﵂ reported:

[One day] there sat together eleven women making an explicit promise amongst themselves that they would conceal nothing about their spouses.

The first one said, "My husband is like the meat of a lean, weak camel which is kept on the top of a mountain which is neither easy to climb, nor is the meat fat, so that one might put up with the trouble of fetching it."

The second one said, "I shall not relate my husband's news, for I fear that I may not be able to finish his story, for if I describe him, I will mention all of his defects and bad traits."

The third one said, "My husband is a tall man [who is useless due to being thick-headed and ill-mannered]; if I describe him [and he hears of that] he will divorce me, and if I keep quiet, he will neither divorce me nor treat me as a wife."

The fourth one said, "My husband is a moderate person like the night of Tihāma which is neither hot nor cold. I am neither afraid of him, nor am I discontented with him."

The fifth one said, "My husband, when entering [the house] is a

---

287 Sahīh al-Bukhārī (5189) and Sahīh Muslim (2448)

leopard, and when he is outside he is a lion. He does not ask about the state of his home."

The sixth one said, "If my husband eats. he eats too much [leaving the dishes empty], and if he drinks he leaves nothing, and if he sleeps he sleeps alone [away from me] covered in garments and he does not stretch his hands to avoid touching my body as he may see my grief."

The seventh one said, "My husband is an impotent wrong-doer, weak and foolish. All the defects are present in him. He may injure your head, your body or may do both."

The eighth one said, "My husband is soft to the touch like a rabbit and smells like a *zarnab* (a kind of good smelling grass)."

The ninth one said, "My husband is a tall generous man wearing a long strap for carrying his sword. His ashes are abundant and his house is near to the people who can easily consult him."

The tenth one said, "My husband is Mālik, and what is Mālik? Mālik is greater than whatever I say about him. He is beyond and above all praises which can come to my mind. Most of his camels are kept at home [ready to be slaughtered for the guests] and only a few are taken to the pastures. When the camels hear the sound of the lute (or the tambourine) they realise that they are going to be slaughtered for the guests."

The eleventh one said, "My husband is Abū Zar and what is Abū Zar (i.e. what should I say about him)? He has given me many ornaments and my ears are heavily loaded with them and my arms have become fat (i.e. I have become fat). And he has pleased me, and I have become so happy that I feel proud of myself. He found me with my family who were mere owners of sheep and living in poverty, and brought me to a respected family having horses, camels, threshing and purifying grain. Whatever I say, he does not rebuke or insult me. When I sleep, I sleep till late in the morning, and when I drink water (or milk), I drink to my fill. The mother of Abū Zar, what could one say in praise of the mother of Abū Zar? Her saddle bags were always full of provision and her house was spacious. As for the son of Abū Zar, what could one say about the son of Abū Zar? His

bed is as narrow as an unsheathed sword and an arm of a lamb [of four months] satisfies his hunger. As for the daughter of Abū Zar, she is obedient to her father and to her mother. She has a fat, well-built body and that arouses the jealousy of her husband's other wife. As for the slave girl of Abū Zar, what could one say about the slave girl of Abū Zar? She does not disclose our secrets but keeps them, and does not waste our provisions and does not leave the rubbish scattered everywhere in our house."

The eleventh woman added, "One day it so happened that Abū Zar went out at the time when the milk was being milked from the animals, and he saw a woman who had two sons like two leopards playing with her two breasts. [On seeing her] he divorced me and married her. Thereafter I married a noble man who used to ride a fast tireless horse and keep a spear in his hand. He gave me many things, and also a pair of every kind of livestock and said, 'Eat (of this), O Umm Zar, and give provision to your relatives.'" She added, "Yet, all those things which my second husband gave me could not fill the smallest utensil of Abū Zar's."

Aisha then said: "Allāh's Messenger ﷺ said to me, 'I am to you as Abū Zar was to his wife Umm Zar.'"

Abdul Razzaq al-Badr said,

> The author listed this hadīth to show how the Prophet ﷺ used to interact with his wives in a manner that brought joy to their hearts and how he used to give pleasant remarks and comments.
>
> This is a famous hadīth that some scholars dedicated books to due to the many gems and benefits it possesses. From the scholars who covered this hadīth in one book is al-Qadī 'Iyyād in his book "*Bughyatu al-Ra'id lima Tadamanahu Hadīth Umm Zar' minal Fawaid*" and from the scholars who explained this hadīth in depth is al-Hafidh ibn Hajar in his book "*Fathul Bari*".

CHAPTER THIRTY NINE

باب في صفة نوم رسول الله صلى الله عليه وسلم في السمر

THE REPORTS PERTAINING TO THE SLEEPING OF THE MESSENGER OF ALLĀH ﷺ

Abdul Razzaq al-Badr said,

> Sleeping is one of the great signs of Allāh ﷻ that indicates Allāh's Oneness, Perfect Power and Arrangement of this Universe. It is a mercy from Allāh ﷻ to His slaves and one of His favours. Allāh ﷻ said: **{And of His signs are your sleep by night and day and your seeking of His bounty. Indeed in that are signs for a people who listen.}**[288] **{And out of His mercy He made for you the night and the day that you may rest therein and [by day] seek from His bounty and [that] perhaps you will be grateful.}**[289]

Ibn Hajar al-Haytamī said,

> Know that he ﷺ used to sleep at the beginning of the night, wake

288 Qur'ān: 30:23
289 Qur'ān: 28:73

up in the second half of the night and then cleanse his teeth with a *siwāk*, perform ablution and pray until a sixth of the night remained. Then, he would sleep or talk with his wives until *Fajr*. He ﷺ would sleep with a light stomach and on his right side, remembering Allāh until he fell into the state of sleep.

٢٥٤: حَدَّثَنَا مُحَمَّدُ بْنُ الْمُثَنَّى ، قَالَ : حَدَّثَنَا عَبْدُ الرَّحْمَنِ بْنُ مَهْدِيٍّ ، قَالَ : حَدَّثَنَا إِسْرَائِيلُ ، عَنْ أَبِي إِسْحَاقَ ، عَنْ عَبْدِ اللهِ بْنِ يَزِيدَ ، عَنِ الْبَرَاءِ بْنِ عَازِبٍ ، أَنَّ النَّبِيَّ صلى الله عليه وسلم ، كَانَ إِذَا أَخَذَ مَضْجَعَهُ وَضَعَ كَفَّهُ الْيُمْنَى تَحْتَ خَدِّهِ الأَيْمَنِ ، وَقَالَ : رَبِّ قِنِي عَذَابَكَ يَوْمَ تَبْعَثُ عِبَادَكَ [290]

254. Al-Barā' ibn al-'Āzib رضي الله عنه narrated: "When the Prophet ﷺ used to lie down on his bed, he would put his right hand under his right cheek, and recite, '*O Allāh, save me from Your Punishment on the Day of Judgment*.'"

Abdul Razzaq al-Badr said,

> This hadīth provides us with three etiquettes related to sleep:
>
> 1. Lie down on the right side.
> 2. Put the right hand under the right cheek.
> 3. Supplicate: "*O Allāh, save me from Your Punishment on the Day of Resurrection.*"

Al-Bajūrī said,

> The Prophet ﷺ recited this supplication, despite his high rank and infallibility, to show humility before Allāh and to give Him His due right as the Lord of mankind. He ﷺ recited such so that his nation would follow his example. [Reciting this du'a] ensures

290 Musnad Ahmad (18672)

that the words of remembrance of Allāh are the last words uttered before sleeping. Furthermore, the words of this specific du'a are said to seek protection from one's shortcomings that necessitate punishment as it is possible that the individual may never wake up from his sleep. The mention of the Day of Resurrection indicates that death is the twin of sleep and waking up is similar to the state of resurrection. This is why he ﷺ used to say after waking up, "*All praise be to Allāh Who restored life into us after He took our souls, and to Him we shall be resurrected,*" as shall be mentioned later in the book.

٢٥٥: حَدَّثَنَا مُحَمَّدُ بْنُ الْمُثَنَّى ، قَالَ : حَدَّثَنَا عَبْدُ الرَّحْمَنِ ، قَالَ : حَدَّثَنَا إِسْرَائِيلُ ، عَنْ أَبِي إِسْحَاقَ ، عَنْ أَبِي عُبَيْدَةَ ، عَنْ عَبْدِ اللهِ ، مِثْلَهُ وَقَالَ : يَوْمَ تَجْمَعُ عِبَادَكَ[291]

255. 'Abdullāh ibn Mas'ūd ؓ narrated the same but with the end of the supplication as: "*On the Day where You will gather your slaves.*"

٢٥٦: حَدَّثَنَا مَحْمُودُ بْنُ غَيْلانَ ، قَالَ : حَدَّثَنَا عَبْدُ الرَّزَّاقِ ، قَالَ : حَدَّثَنَا سُفْيَانُ ، عَنْ عَبْدِ الْمَلِكِ بْنِ عُمَيْرٍ ، عَنْ رِبْعِيِّ بْنِ حِرَاشٍ ، عَنْ حُذَيْفَةَ ، قَالَ : كَانَ النَّبِيُّ صلى الله عليه وسلم إِذَا أَوَى إِلَى فِرَاشِهِ ، قَالَ : اللَّهُمَّ بِاسْمِكَ أَمُوتُ وَأَحْيَا ، وَإِذَا اسْتَيْقَظَ ، قَالَ : الْحَمْدُ للهِ الَّذِي أَحْيَانَا بَعْدَمَا أَمَاتَنَا وَإِلَيْهِ النُّشُورُ[292]

256. Hudhaifah ؓ narrated: "When the Prophet ﷺ used to lie down on his bed, he would say, '*O Allāh! On [the remembrance of] Your Name, I die and I live.*' Then upon waking he would say, '*All praise be to Allāh Who restored life into us after He took our souls, and to Him we shall be resurrected.*'"

291 Musnad Ahmad (3664)
292 Sahīh al-Bukhārī (6312)

Ibn Hajar al-Haytamī said,

> "*I die and I live*": The reason sleeping is resembled to death is because a person loses control over all their senses just like it is the case in death. Also, a life can be described as such when it is spent in good deeds and obedience; otherwise the disobedient spends his life as a dead person.
>
> Praising Allāh for life is because this is from the most important blessings as it distinguishes the human from the non-human and whereby one comes to learn about Allāh and His worship.
>
> The last part of the supplication recited after waking up is to remind us that just as we awake to life at the cessation of sleep, there will be resurrection after death and then people will be judged.
>
> The wisdom behind reciting these supplications is so the last deed of the day consists of the remembrance of Allāh and the first deed a statement of monotheism and *taqwa*. This reminds the person that it is important to be conscious of Allāh and His Grandeur throughout the day and not to utter anything unless it is good.

٢٥٧ : حَدَّثَنَا قُتَيْبَةُ بْنُ سَعِيدٍ ، قَالَ : حَدَّثَنَا الْمُفَضَّلُ بْنُ فَضَالَةَ ، عَنْ عُقَيْلٍ ، أُرَاهُ عَنِ الزُّهْرِيِّ ، عَنْ عُرْوَةَ ، عَنْ عَائِشَةَ ، قَالَتْ : كَانَ رَسُولُ الله صلى الله عليه وسلم ، إِذَا أَوَى إِلَى فِرَاشِهِ كُلَّ لَيْلَةٍ جَمَعَ كَفَّيْهِ فَنَفَثَ فِيهِمَا ، وَقَرَأَ فِيهِمَا : قُلْ هُوَ اللهُ أَحَدٌ وَ قُلْ أَعُوذُ بِرَبِّ الْفَلَقِ وَ قُلْ أَعُوذُ بِرَبِّ النَّاسِ ، ثُمَّ مَسَحَ بِهِمَا مَا اسْتَطَاعَ مِنْ جَسَدِهِ ، يَبْدَأُ بِهِمَا رَأْسَهُ وَوَجْهَهُ وَمَا أَقْبَلَ مِنْ جَسَدِهِ ، يَصْنَعُ ذَلِكَ ثَلاثَ مَرَّاتٍ [293]

257. Aisha ﵂ narrated: "Every night before the Messenger of Allāh ﷺ slept upon his bed he would join his hands, lightly blow into them

293 Sahīh al-Bukhārī (5017)

and recite the last three sūrahs of the Qur'ān (i.e. Sūrah al-Ikhlās, Sūrah al-Falaq, and Sūrah al-Nās). He would then wipe his hands over whatever parts of his body he could. He began with the head and face, and then the front part of his body. He did so thrice."

Abdul Razzaq al-Badr said,

> The regular practice of this indicates the keenness of the Prophet ﷺ to do so, to the extent that he ordered Aisha ﵂ to do so on his behalf during his sickness whereof he died.
>
> The Prophet ﷺ passed his hands over wherever he could reach to attain the blessings of the ayāt as this protects the person from the devil and other harmful things.
>
> It is important that a person understands and contemplates the meanings of these ayāt by reading the tafsīr of Ibn Kathīr or the tafsīr of al-Sa'di, for example. This is because the person who recites them while understanding their meaning is not like the one who recites them without this knowledge.

٢٥٨: حَدَّثَنَا مُحَمَّدُ بْنُ بَشَّارٍ ، قَالَ : حَدَّثنا عَبْدُ الرَّحْمَنِ بْنُ مَهْدِيٍّ ، قَالَ : حَدَّثَنَا سُفْيَانُ ، عَنْ سَلَمَةَ بْنِ كُهَيلٍ ، عَنْ كُرَيْب ، عَنِ ابْنِ عَبَّاسٍ : أَنَّ رَسُولَ الله صلى الله عليه وسلم ، نَامَ حَتَّى نَفَخَ ، وَكَانَ إِذَا نَامَ نَفَخَ ، فَأَتَاهُ بِلالٌ فَآذَنَهُ بِالصَّلاةِ ، فَقَامَ وَصَلَّى وَلَمْ يَتَوَضَّأْ وَفِي الْحَدِيثِ قِصَّةٌ[294]

258. 'Abdullāh ibn Abbās ﵄ narrated: "Once the Messenger of Allāh ﷺ slept and began to blow. It was the nature of the Messenger of Allāh ﷺ that he blew when he slept. Bilal ﵁ came and gave the call for the prayer. The Messenger of Allāh ﷺ awakened and offered the prayer without performing the ablution." This hadith has a detailed story behind it.

Al-Bajūrī said,

294 Sahīh al-Bukhārī (138)

Blowing is a sign of deep sleep and knowing that it was the nature of the Messenger of Allāh ﷺ, we know that blowing while sleeping is not something that is dispraised.

The Messenger of Allāh ﷺ did not perform ablution though he entered a state of deep sleep. This is an exclusive quality of his due to his heart always remaining awake (i.e. conscious) as he stated in the hadith, "We Prophets, the eyes close in sleep whilst the hearts remain awake."[295]

The detailed story of this hadīth will be mentioned in the chapter detailing his worship.

٢٥٩: حَدَّثَنَا إِسْحَاقُ بْنُ مَنْصُورٍ، قَالَ: حَدَّثَنَا عَفَّانُ، قَالَ: حَدَّثَنَا حَمَّادُ بْنُ سَلَمَةَ، عَنْ ثَابِتٍ، عَنْ أَنَسِ بْنِ مَالِكٍ، أَنَّ رَسُولَ الله صلى الله عليه وسلم، كَانَ إِذَا أَوَى إِلَى فِرَاشِهِ، قَالَ: الْحَمْدُ لله الَّذِي أَطْعَمَنَا وَسَقَانَا وَكَفَانَا وَآوَانَا، فَكَمْ مِمَّنْ لا كَافِيَ لَهُ وَلا مُؤْوِيَ[296]

259. Anas ibn Mālik ؓ narrated: "When the Messenger of Allāh ﷺ would lie down on his bed, he would say, '*All praise is for Allāh, Who fed us and gave us drink, and Who is sufficient for us, and has sheltered us, for how many have none to suffice them or shelter them!*'"

Alī al-Qārī said,

> The Prophet ﷺ praised Allāh for providing food and drink before he slept because without these, one's life cannot be sustained, and because sleeping occurs after one eats and drinks (i.e. it is difficult to sleep when one is hungry and thus easier to sleep when one has eaten and drunk).
>
> Al-Mudhhir describes Allāh's sufficiency as meaning that He averts the harm of people and facilitates for one shelter. So all

295 Musnad Ahmad (24171)
296 Sahīh Muslim (2715)

praise be to Allāh for making us from amongst the protected for there are many people who Allāh does not protect against the harm of evil people and they are left to fend for themselves against the evil, and thus the vile people overcome them. Likewise, there are many people bereft of shelter and so He left them to be harmed by the elements.

Al-Nawawī said,

> The meaning of the last part of the supplication means that many people have no one to have mercy on them, to be compassionate with them and many have no shelter to stay in.

٢٦٠: حَدَّثَنَا الْحُسَيْنُ بْنُ مُحَمَّدٍ الْجُرَيْرِيُّ ، قَالَ : حَدَّثَنَا سُلَيْمَانُ بْنُ حَرْبٍ ، قَالَ : حَدَّثَنَا حَمَّادُ بْنُ سَلَمَةَ ، عَنْ حُمَيْدٍ ، عَنْ بَكْرِ بْنِ عَبْدِ اللهِ الْمُزَنِيِّ ، عَنْ عَبْدِ اللهِ بْنِ رَبَاحٍ ، عَنْ أَبِي قَتَادَةَ : أَنَّ النَّبِيَّ صلى الله عليه وسلم، كَانَ إِذَا عَرَّسَ بِلَيْلٍ اضْطَجَعَ عَلَى شِقِّهِ الأَيْمَنِ ، وَإِذَا عَرَّسَ قُبَيْلَ الصُّبْحِ نَصَبَ ذِرَاعَهُ ، وَوَضَعَ رَأْسَهُ عَلَى كَفِّهِ[297]

260. Abū Qatādah ﷺ narrated: "When the Prophet ﷺ was journeying and stopped for rest and there was enough time in the night, he slept on his right side. However, if he stopped close to the time of the morning, he would lift his right arm, put his head upon it and sleep."

Abdul Razzaq al-Badr said,

> This shows the concern he had for performing the prayer of *Fajr* as sleeping in that position would make it difficult for the person to enter the state of deep sleep.

297 Sahih Muslim (2715)

CHAPTER FORTY

باب ما جاء في عبادة النبي صلى اللّٰه عليه وسلم

THE REPORTS PERTAINING TO THE WORSHIP OFFERED BY THE PROPHET ﷺ

Abdul Razzaq al-Badr said,

> Though the title of the chapter is general, the hadīths included in this chapter relate to the night prayer.

٢٦١ : حَدَّثَنَا قُتَيْبَةُ بْنُ سَعِيدٍ ، وَبِشْرُ بْنُ مُعَاذٍ ، قَالا : حَدَّثَنَا أَبُو عَوَانَةَ ، عَنْ زِيَادِ بْنِ عِلاقَةَ ، عَنِ الْمُغِيرَةِ بْنِ شُعْبَةَ ، قَالَ : صَلَّى رَسُولُ الله صلى الله عليه وسلم ، حَتَّى انْتَفَخَتْ قَدَمَاهُ ، فَقِيلَ لَهُ : أَتَتَكَلَّفُ هَذَا ، وَقَدْ غَفَرَ اللهُ لَكَ مَا تَقَدَّمَ مِنْ ذَنْبِكَ وَمَا تَأَخَّرَ ؟ قَالَ : أَفَلا أَكُونُ عَبْدًا شَكُورًا [298]

261. Al-Mughīrah ibn Shu'bah ﷺ narrated: "The Messenger of Allāh ﷺ performed prayers of such length that his feet would become swollen. It was said to him, 'You exert yourself to such a degree yet Allāh has forgiven your past and future sins?' The Messenger of Allāh ﷺ said, 'Should I not be a grateful servant?'"

Ibn Hajar al-Asqalānī said,

> This response of the Messenger of Allāh ﷺ could be expanded in other words as: "Praying at night is to show appreciation and thankfulness for Allāh's forgiveness; hence how could it be possible for me to stop this!"
>
> If a person fears becoming bored due to excessive worship, then he should not force himself to do it. If otherwise, one should push himself to worship as much as possible.

Ibn 'Allan al Shafi'ī said,

> The companion thought that the reason the Messenger of Allāh ﷺ underwent such difficulties in worship was because he feared the punishment of his sins or hoped for the reward [of the prayers]. But the Messenger of Allāh ﷺ clarified that the reason was nobler and higher: to show appreciation, gratitude and acknowledgement of one's servitude.

Alī al-Qārī said,

> The Messenger of Allāh ﷺ is infallible and the sins referred to

298 Sahīh al-Bukhārī (1130) and Sahīh Muslim (2819)

in this hadīth are not understood at face value because the good deeds of the pious are viewed as sins for the ones in higher ranks (meaning: the inability of a person to praise, worship, thank Allāh and give Him His due right is looked upon as a shortcoming that equals sins for those who are at a higher state).

٢٦٢: حَدَّثَنَا أَبُو عَمَّارٍ الْحُسَيْنُ بْنُ حُرَيْثٍ ، قَالَ : حَدَّثَنَا الْفَضْلُ بْنُ مُوسَى ، عَنْ مُحَمَّدِ بْنِ عَمْرٍو ، عَنْ أَبِي سَلَمَةَ ، عَنْ أَبِي هُرَيْرَةَ ، قَالَ : كَانَ رَسُولُ اللهِ صلى الله عليه وسلم ، يُصَلِّي حَتَّى تَرِمَ قَدَمَاهُ ، قَالَ : فَقِيلَ لَهُ : أَتَفْعَلُ هَذَا وَقَدْ جَاءَكَ أَنَّ اللهَ تَعَالَى قَدْ غَفَرَ لَكَ مَا تَقَدَّمَ مِنْ ذَنْبِكَ وَمَا تَأَخَّرَ ؟ قَالَ : أَفَلا أَكُونُ عَبْدًا شَكُورًا [299]

262. Abū Hurairah ؓ narrated: "The Messenger of Allāh ﷺ used to pray at night until his feet became swollen. It was said to him, 'You do this although Allāh has forgiven your past and future sins?' The Messenger of Allāh ﷺ replied, 'Should I not be a grateful servant?'"

٢٦٣: حَدَّثَنَا عِيسَى بْنُ عُثْمَانَ بْنِ عِيسَى بْنِ عَبْدِ الرَّحْمَنِ الرَّمْلِيُّ ، قَالَ : حَدَّثَنَا عَمِّي يَحْيَى بْنُ عِيسَى الرَّمْلِيُّ ، عَنِ الأَعْمَشِ ، عَنْ أَبِي صَالِحٍ ، عَنْ أَبِي هُرَيْرَةَ ، قَالَ : كَانَ رَسُولُ اللهِ صلى الله عليه وسلم يَقُومُ يُصَلِّي حَتَّى تَنْتَفِخَ قَدَمَاهُ فَيُقَالُ لَهُ : يَا رَسُولَ اللهِ ، تَفْعَلُ هَذَا وَقَدْ غَفَرَ اللهُ لَكَ مَا تَقَدَّمَ مِنْ ذَنْبِكَ وَمَا تَأَخَّرَ ؟ ، قَالَ : أَفَلا أَكُونُ عَبْدًا شَكُورًا [300]

263. Abū Hurairah ؓ narrated: "The Messenger of Allāh ﷺ performed such lengthy prayers that his feet became swollen. It was said to him, 'You do this although Allāh has forgiven your past and future sins?' The Messenger of Allāh ﷺ said, 'Should I not be a

299 See hadīth 261
300 See hadīth 261

grateful servant?'"

٢٦٤: حَدَّثَنَا مُحَمَّدُ بْنُ بَشَّارٍ ، قَالَ : حَدَّثَنَا مُحَمَّدُ بْنُ جَعْفَرٍ ، قَالَ : حَدَّثَنَا شُعْبَةُ ، عَنْ أَبِي إِسْحَاقَ ، عَنِ الأَسْوَدِ بْنِ يَزِيدَ ، قَالَ : سَأَلْتُ عَائِشَةَ ، عَنْ صَلاةِ رَسُولِ اللهِ صلى الله عليه وسلم بِاللَّيْلِ ؟ فَقَالَتْ : كَانَ يَنَامُ أَوَّلَ اللَّيْلِ ثُمَّ يَقُومُ ، فَإِذَا كَانَ مِنَ السَّحَرِ أَوْتَرَ ، ثُمَّ أَتَى فِرَاشَهُ ، فَإِذَا كَانَ لَهُ حَاجَةٌ أَلَمَّ بِأَهْلِهِ ، فَإِذَا سَمِعَ الأَذَانَ وَثَبَ ، فَإِنْ كَانَ جُنُبًا أَفَاضَ عَلَيْهِ مِنَ الْمَاءِ ، وَإِلا تَوَضَّأَ وَخَرَجَ إِلَى الصَّلاةِ [301]

264. Al-Aswad ibn Yazīd enquired from Aisha ؓ regarding the prayer of the Messenger of Allāh ﷺ at night. She replied: "The Messenger of Allāh ﷺ used to sleep for the first half portion of the night (after praying *Ishā*). He would then wake up and pray at night but when the time of the last sixth of the night entered, he would pray the *witr* and then go to his bed. If he had a desire, he would approach his wife. And, when he would hear the call for prayer, he would get up actively. If he was in a state of major ritual impurity, he performed *ghusl*. If not, he performed ablution and then went to pray."

Abdul Razzaq al-Badr said,

> The beginning of the night starts from sunset but the time intended in this hadīth refers to after the prayer of *Ishā* because the Prophet ﷺ disliked sleeping before *Ishā* and disliked talking after it, so he would sleep right after praying *Ishā*.
>
> He ﷺ used to wake up after the middle of the night as explained in the authentic hadīth found in Sahīh al-Bukharī (1131) and Sahīh Muslim (1159).

Al-Bajūrī said,

301 Sahih al-Bukhārī (1146) and Sahīh Muslim (739)

The intention of the question regarding his prayer at night was to ask about the time that he used to pray the night prayers and *witr*.

It is possible that he ﷺ performed ablution because his ablution was nullified for a reason other than sleeping or that he renewed his ablution. This hadīth teaches us to care for the acts of worship, not to be lazy in sleep and to perform the worship whilst being active and energetic.

٢٦٥: حَدَّثَنَا قُتَيْبَةُ بْنُ سَعِيدٍ، عَنْ مَالِكِ بْنِ أَنَسٍ (ح) وَحَدَّثَنَا إِسْحَاقُ بْنُ مُوسَى الأَنْصَارِيُّ، قَالَ: حَدَّثَنَا مَعْنٌ، عَنْ مَالِكٍ، عَنْ مَخْرَمَةَ بْنِ سُلَيْمَانَ، عَنْ كُرَيْبٍ، عَنِ ابْنِ عَبَّاسٍ، أَنَّهُ أَخْبَرَهُ، أَنَّهُ بَاتَ عِنْدَ مَيْمُونَةَ وَهِيَ خَالَتُهُ، قَالَ: فَاضْطَجَعْتُ فِي عَرْضِ الْوِسَادَةِ، وَاضْطَجَعَ رَسُولُ الله صلى الله عليه وسلم فِي طُولِهَا، فَنَامَ رَسُولُ الله صلى الله عليه وسلم، حَتَّى إِذَا انْتَصَفَ اللَّيْلُ أَوْ قَبْلَهُ بِقَلِيلٍ أَوْ بَعْدَهُ بِقَلِيلٍ، فَاسْتَيْقَظَ رَسُولُ الله صلى الله عليه وسلم، فَجَعَلَ يَمْسَحُ النَّوْمَ عَنْ وَجْهِهِ، ثُمَّ قَرَأَ الْعَشْرَ الآيَاتِ الْخَوَاتِيمَ مِنْ سُورَةِ آلِ عِمْرَانَ، ثُمَّ قَامَ إِلَى شَنٍّ مُعَلَّقٍ فَتَوَضَّأَ مِنْهَا، فَأَحْسَنَ الْوُضُوءَ، ثُمَّ قَامَ يُصَلِّي، قَالَ عَبْدُ الله بْنُ عَبَّاسٍ: فَقُمْتُ إِلَى جَنْبِهِ فَوَضَعَ رَسُولُ الله صلى الله عليه وسلم، يَدَهُ الْيُمْنَى عَلَى رَأْسِي ثُمَّ أَخَذَ بِأُذُنِي الْيُمْنَى، فَفَتَلَهَا فَصَلَّى رَكْعَتَيْنِ، ثُمَّ رَكْعَتَيْنِ، ثُمَّ رَكْعَتَيْنِ، ثُمَّ رَكْعَتَيْنِ، ثُمَّ رَكْعَتَيْنِ، ثُمَّ رَكْعَتَيْنِ، قَالَ مَعْنٌ: سِتَّ مَرَّاتٍ ثُمَّ أَوْتَرَ، ثُمَّ اضْطَجَعَ حَتَّى جَاءَهُ الْمُؤَذِّنُ، فَقَامَ فَصَلَّى رَكْعَتَيْنِ خَفِيفَتَيْنِ، ثُمَّ خَرَجَ فَصَلَّى الصُّبْحَ[302]

265. 'Abdullāh ibn Abbās ﷺ reported that he once slept at the house of his maternal aunt Maymūnah ﷺ. He said: "I slept on the width of the cushion and the Messenger of Allāh ﷺ slept on the length of the cushion and he slept until the middle of the night, or a little before or after that. He ﷺ then awoke, began wiping off the signs of sleep

302 See hadīth 258

from his face and then recited the last ten ayāt of Sūrah al-'Imrān.

He then stood and used the water he found in a leather bag that was hanging to perform his ablution. He performed his ablution thoroughly and commenced the prayer."

'Abdullāh ibn Abbās ؓ added: "I stood next to him [on his left]. The Messenger of Allāh ﷺ put his right hand on my head, took hold of my ear and twisted it. He performed two units, then two units, then two units, then two units, then two units, then two units. [Ma'n (a narrator of this hadīth from Ibn 'Abbās) says the Messenger of Allāh ﷺ prayed two units six times (a total of twelve units)].

The Messenger of Allāh ﷺ then performed the *witr* and lied down [for a short period] until the *mu'adhin* came to inform him of the *Fajr* prayer. He then prayed two short units and headed for the masjid."

Al-Bajūrī said,

> The reason Ibn Abbās ؓ slept at the house of his maternal aunt was because his father, al-Abbās (the uncle of the Prophet) wanted to know the worship of the Prophet ﷺ at night so he could follow his guidance.
>
> The Prophet ﷺ normally slept upon a bed besides one of his wives and this was his habit. However, whenever he wanted to perform worship he would leave his wives and focus on his worship. This way he fulfilled the rights of his wives and did justice to the rights of his Lord.

Ibn Hajar al-Haytamī said,

> It can be extracted from this hadīth that it is recommended to recite the last ten *ayāt* of Sūrah al-Imrān after waking up and that it is allowed to recite the Qur'ān in a state of minor ritual impurity.
>
> He ﷺ twisted the ear of Ibn Abbās ؓ either to notify him that he was not following the Sunnah when he stood on his left side, to keep him alert so that he could memorise the Sunnah or to remove his sleepiness.

The habit of the Prophet ﷺ was to pray the *witr* at the end of the night but sometimes he prayed it at the mid-point and sometimes at the beginning. The variation most likely occurred due to the necessities of different situations, as it is possible that he prayed the *witr* at the beginning of the night due to sickness and at the middle of the night because he was travelling.

The *fiqh* of this hadīth is:

1. It is recommended for a congregation made of two that the person following the i*mām* stands to his right side, and to move to the right side if he was standing on the left side. If he does not move to the correct side, it is recommended for the imām to move him to his right side.

2. It is recommended for the *imām* to physically instruct the person praying behind him to the Sunnah if he notices him not following it. This shows that a small amount of physical action in the prayer does not nullify the prayer, and it can be the Sunnah in some cases as exemplified in this hadīth.

3. The congregation is valid with a young boy and he takes the same ruling as adults in congregation.

4. It is valid to pray a voluntary prayer in congregation.

5. It is recommended to pray the *witr* and voluntary prayers, two units by two units.

6. It is recommended for the *muadhin* to notify the *imām* in person to come to the prayer.

7. It is recommended to make the Sunnah of *Fajr* short.

٢٦٦: حَدَّثَنَا أَبُو كُرَيْبٍ مُحَمَّدُ بْنُ الْعَلاءِ ، قَالَ : حَدَّثَنَا وَكِيعٌ ، عَنْ شُعْبَةَ ، عَنْ أَبِي جَمْرَةَ ، عَنِ ابْنِ عَبَّاسٍ ، قَالَ : كَانَ النَّبِيُّ صلى الله عليه وسلم يُصَلِّي

مِنَ اللَّيْلِ ثَلاثَ عَشْرَةَ رَكْعَةً[303]

266. 'Abdullah ibn Abbās ﵄ narrated: "The Prophet ﷺ used to pray during the night thirteen units."

Abdul Razzaq al-Badr said,

> There are other hadīths stating that he ﷺ prayed eleven units and nine units. However, scholars understood these hadīths in the context that each refers to a different situation and incident.

Al-Bajūrī said,

> The thirteen units mentioned consist of two units as the Sunnah of *Ishā* or the Sunnah of ablution and eleven units as *witr*.

٢٦٧ : حَدَّثَنَا قُتَيْبَةُ بْنُ سَعِيدٍ ، قَالَ : حَدَّثَنَا أَبُو عَوَانَةَ ، عَنْ قَتَادَةَ ، عَنْ زُرَارَةَ بْنِ أَوْفَى ، عَنْ سَعْدِ بْنِ هِشَامٍ ، عَنْ عَائِشَةَ : أَنَّ النَّبِيَّ صلى الله عليه وسلم كَانَ إِذَا لَمْ يُصَلِّ بِاللَّيْلِ ، مَنَعَهُ مِنْ ذَلِكَ النَّوْمُ ، أَوْ غَلَبَتْهُ عَيْنَاهُ ، صَلَّى مِنَ النَّهَارِ ثِنْتَيْ عَشْرَةَ رَكْعَةً[304]

267. Aisha ﵂ reported: "Whenever the Prophet ﷺ could not pray the night prayers due to sleep or excessive fatigue; he would pray twelve units during the daytime."

Abdul Razzaq al-Badr said,

> This shows that the Prophet ﷺ did not pray *witr* during the daytime. It teaches us that if a person misses his regular night prayers, it is prescribed for him to make them up during the day.

Al-Bajūrī said,

303 Sahih al-Bukhārī (1138) and Sahīh Muslim (764)
304 Sahīh Muslim (746)

The night prayers mentioned in the hadith refer to the *tahajjud* and *witr*.

The reason the Prophet ﷺ did not pray at night, based on the wording of the hadīth, shows that the narrator was uncertain as he mentioned two possibilities, each of which gives a different meaning i.e. if the reason was that he slept, that means he made the choice to sleep though he could stay awake, but if the reason was that he was too fatigued, it means that he was in a state where he could not stay awake.

٢٦٨: حَدَّثَنَا مُحَمَّدُ بْنُ الْعَلاءِ ، قَالَ : حَدَّثَنَا أَبُو أُسَامَةَ ، عَنْ هِشَامٍ يَعْنِي ابْنَ حَسَّانَ ، عَنْ مُحَمَّدِ بْنِ سِيرِينَ ، عَنْ أَبِي هُرَيْرَةَ ، عَنِ النَّبِيِّ صَلَّى الله عليه وسلم ، قَالَ : إِذَا قَامَ أَحَدُكُمْ مِنَ اللَّيْلِ فَلْيَفْتَتِحْ صَلاتَهُ بِرَكْعَتَيْنِ خَفِيفَتَيْنِ[305]

268. Abū Hurairah رضي الله عنه narrated: "The Prophet ﷺ said: 'When one awakes at night, let him begin [his night prayers] with two short units of prayer.'"

Al-Bajūrī said,

> These two units are recommended to be an introductory to the *witr* so that one can pray the *witr* actively while being fully awake. This is similar to how it is recommended to precede the obligatory prayer with the Sunnah prayer.

٢٦٩: حَدَّثَنَا قُتَيْبَةُ بْنُ سَعِيدٍ ، عَنْ مَالِكِ بْنِ أَنَسٍ (ح) وَحَدَّثَنَا إِسْحَاقُ بْنُ مُوسَى ، قَالَ : حَدَّثَنَا مَعْنٌ ، قَالَ : حَدَّثَنَا مَالِكٌ ، عَنْ عَبْدِ الله بْنِ أَبِي بَكْرٍ ، عَنْ أَبِيهِ ، أَنَّ عَبْدَ الله بْنَ قَيْسِ بْنِ مَخْرَمَةَ أَخْبَرَهُ ، عَنْ زَيْدِ بْنِ خَالِدٍ الْجُهَنِيِّ

---

305 Sahīh Muslim (768)

، أَنَّهُ قَالَ : لأَرْمُقَنَّ صَلاةَ النَّبِيِّ صلى الله عليه وسلم ، فَتَوَسَّدْتُ عَتَبَتَهُ ، أَوْ فُسْطَاطَهُ فَصَلَّى رَسُولُ الله صلى الله عليه وسلم ، رَكْعَتَيْنِ خَفِيفَتَيْنِ ، ثُمَّ صَلَّى رَكْعَتَيْنِ طَوِيلَتَيْنِ ، طَوِيلَتَيْنِ ، طَوِيلَتَيْنِ ، ثُمَّ صَلَّى رَكْعَتَيْنِ وَهُمَا دُونَ اللَّتَيْنِ قَبْلَهُمَا ، ثُمَّ صَلَّى رَكْعَتَيْنِ وَهُمَا دُونَ اللَّتَيْنِ قَبْلَهُمَا ، ثُمَّ صَلَّى رَكْعَتَيْنِ وَهُمَا دُونَ اللَّتَيْنِ قَبْلَهُمَا ، ثُمَّ صَلَّى رَكْعَتَيْنِ وَهُمَا دُونَ اللَّتَيْنِ قَبْلَهُمَا ، ثُمَّ أَوْتَرَ فَذَلِكَ ثَلاثَ عَشْرَةَ رَكْعَةً [306]

269. Zayd ibn Khālid ﷺ narrated: "I decided that I would closely observe how the Prophet ﷺ performed his prayers. Thus, I lied down on the threshold [of his house or his tent]. The Messenger of Allāh ﷺ first prayed two short units, and then he prayed two long units, two long units, two long units. He then prayed two units shorter than the previous ones, and then prayed two more units shorter than the ones before. And again, he prayed two more units shorter than the previous ones. He again prayed two units shorter than the previous ones. He then prayed the *witr*. They amounted to thirteen units of prayer in total."

Al-Bajūrī said,

> The person who narrated from Zayd doubted whether it was the threshold of his house or his tent, and it is most likely the latter because the Prophet ﷺ would be with his wives in his house and so it is inappropriate to say that Zayd stood there watching him inside in such circumstances. However, during his travels, he ﷺ would be in his tent and not with his wives so Zayd could remain on the threshold of his tent and watch.
>
> The reason Zayd repeated thrice that the first two units were long was to show how lengthy they were, as if they were equivalent in length to six long units. The reason he ﷺ made the first two units very long was because a person is more active and possesses

306 Sahīh Muslim (765)

more energy at the beginning of the prayer as opposed to the end. This is why it is recommended to make the first unit of the prayer longer than the second one in obligatory prayers.

The thirteen units mentioned include the introductory two units and the remaining eleven units are *witr* prayer.

٢٧٠: حَدَّثَنَا إِسْحَاقُ بْنُ مُوسَى، قَالَ: حَدَّثَنَا مَعْنٌ، قَالَ: حَدَّثَنَا مَالِكٌ، عَنْ سَعِيدِ بْنِ أَبِي سَعِيدٍ الْمَقْبُرِيِّ، عَنْ أَبِي سَلَمَةَ بْنِ عَبْدِ الرَّحْمَنِ، أَنَّهُ أَخْبَرَهُ أَنَّهُ سَأَلَ عَائِشَةَ، كَيْفَ كَانَتْ صَلاةُ رَسُولِ الله صلى الله عليه وسلم فِي رَمَضَانَ؟ فَقَالَتْ: مَا كَانَ رَسُولُ الله صلى الله عليه وسلم لِيَزِيدَ فِي رَمَضَانَ وَلا فِي غَيْرِهِ عَلَى إِحْدَى عَشْرَةَ رَكْعَةً، يُصَلِّي أَرْبَعًا، لا تَسْأَلْ عَنْ حُسْنِهِنَّ، وَطُولِهِنَّ، ثُمَّ يُصَلِّي أَرْبَعًا لا تَسْأَلْ عَنْ حُسْنِهِنَّ وَطُولِهِنَّ، ثُمَّ يُصَلِّي ثَلاثًا، قَالَتْ عَائِشَةُ: قُلْتُ: يَا رَسُولَ الله، أَتَنَامُ قَبْلَ أَنْ تُوتِرَ؟ فَقَالَ: يَا عَائِشَةُ، إِنَّ عَيْنَيَّ تَنَامَانِ، وَلا يَنَامُ قَلْبِي[307]

270. Abū Salamah asked Aisha ﵂ to describe for him the prayer of the Messenger of Allāh ﷺ so she said: "The Messenger of Allāh ﷺ did not pray more than eleven units, whether he prayed in the month of Ramadan or outside of it. He used to pray four units and it is too difficult to describe their length and earnestness. Then, in the same manner he prayed four more units. After that he prayed three units of prayer." Aisha ﵂ said, "I asked him, 'O Messenger of Allāh. How come you sleep before praying the *witr*?' He replied, 'O Aisha, my eyes sleep but my heart does not.'"

Abdul Razzaq al-Badr said,

> This hadīth does not contradict the other hadīths by stating that he ﷺ prayed eleven units of prayer. This is because Aisha ﵂ did not count the two introductory units that he ﷺ prayed at the beginning

307 Sahīh al-Bukhārī (1147) and Sahīh Muslim (738)

as can be noted when she detailed how the units were divided four by four.

Al-Bajūrī said,

> Each set of four units were prayed two by two and not as the apparent meaning of the statement of Aisha ﵂. This way, the hadīth conforms to the previous hadīth narrated by Zayd. The reason the four units were mentioned as a whole is because the two sets of two units were similar in length and performance.
>
> This hadīth shows that prolonging the standing in prayer is better than praying a higher quantity of short units. The hadīth about the closeness to our Lord in prostration[308] teaches us that supplications are more likely to be answered therein. The last three units were not described in the same manner as the preceding ones to show that they were short.
>
> The reason Aisha ﵂ asked the question [regarding sleeping before *witr*] is because it was known that he ﷺ ordered some of his companions such as Abū Hurairah ﵁ not to sleep before praying *witr* due to fearing that they may oversleep and miss it. The answer of the Prophet ﷺ came to show that the possibility to miss the *Fajr* is inapplicable in his case as his heart is awake. Thus, it is recommended for the one who is certain that he will wake up before *Fajr* to postpone the *witr* and pray it after waking up, if otherwise he should pray it before.

٢٧١ : حَدَّثَنَا إِسْحَاقُ بْنُ مُوسَى ، قَالَ : حَدَّثَنَا مَعْنٌ ، قَالَ : حَدَّثَنَا مَالِكٌ ، عَنِ ابْنِ شِهَابٍ ، عَنْ عُرْوَةَ ، عَنْ عَائِشَةَ : أَنَّ رَسُولَ الله صلى الله عليه وسلم ، كَانَ يُصَلِّي مِنَ اللَّيْلِ إِحْدَى عَشْرَةَ رَكْعَةً ، يُوتِرُ مِنْهَا بِوَاحِدَةٍ ، فَإِذَا

308 "The closest a servant comes to his Lord is in *Sujūd*; therefore make excessive du'a, for it is most likely to be answered." Collected in Sahīh Muslim.

فَرَغَ مِنْهَا ، اضْطَجَعَ عَلَى شِقِّهِ الأَيْمَنِ[309]

271. Aisha ﵂ narrated: "The Messenger of Allāh ﷺ used to pray eleven units at night, one of which was a unit of *witr*. After he finished, he would lie down on his right side."

Abdul Razzaq al-Badr said,

> Some scholars extracted a gem from this hadīth: The number of units that he ﷺ prayed at night was exactly the same as the units performed for the daytime obligatory prayers, which are D*huhr*, *Asr* and *Maghrib*.

Ibn Hajar al-Haytamī said,

> This is an explicit statement to show that the least number of units for *witr* is one, and that a prayer of one unit is valid.

٢٧٢ : حَدَّثَنَا ابْنُ أَبِي عُمَرَ ، قَالَ : حَدَّثَنَا مَعْنٌ ، عَنْ مَالِكٍ ، عَنِ ابْنِ شِهَابٍ ، نَحْوَهُ (ح) وَحَدَّثَنَا قُتَيْبَةُ ، عَنْ مَالِكٍ ، عَنِ ابْنِ شِهَابٍ ، نَحْوَهُ

272. Ibn Shihāb reported the same through two different routes.

٢٧٣ : حَدَّثَنَا هَنَّادٌ ، قَالَ : حَدَّثَنَا أَبُو الأَحْوَصِ ، عَنِ الأَعْمَشِ ، عَنِ إِبْرَاهِيمَ ، عَنِ الأَسْوَدِ ، عَنْ عَائِشَةَ ، قَالَتْ : كَانَ رَسُولُ اللهِ صلى الله عليه وسلم ، يُصَلِّي مِنَ اللَّيْلِ تِسْعَ رَكَعَاتٍ[310]

273. Aisha ﵂ narrated: "The Messenger of Allāh ﷺ used to pray nine units during the night."

309 Sahīh al-Bukhārī (994) and Sahīh Muslim (736)
310 Sunan Ibn Mājah (1360) and Sunan al-Tirmidhī (443)

٢٧٤: حَدَّثَنَا مَحْمُودُ بْنُ غَيْلَانَ ، قَالَ : حَدَّثَنَا يَحْيَى بْنُ آدَمَ ، قَالَ : حَدَّثَنَا سُفْيَانُ الثَّوْرِيُّ ، عَنِ الأَعْمَشِ ، نَحْوَهُ

274. Al-A'mash reported the same through a different route.

٢٧٥: حَدَّثَنَا مُحَمَّدُ بْنُ الْمُثَنَّى ، قَالَ : حَدَّثَنَا مُحَمَّدُ بْنُ جَعْفَرٍ ، قَالَ : حَدَّثَنَا شُعْبَةُ ، عَنْ عَمْرِو بْنِ مُرَّةَ ، عَنْ أَبِي حَمْزَةَ ، رَجُلٍ مِنَ الأَنْصَارِ ، عَنْ رَجُلٍ مِنْ بَنِي عَبْسٍ ، عَنْ حُذَيْفَةَ بْنِ الْيَمَانِ ، أَنَّهُ صَلَّى مَعَ النَّبِيِّ صلى الله عليه وسلم مِنَ اللَّيْلِ ، قَالَ : فَلَمَّا دَخَلَ فِي الصَّلَاةِ ، قَالَ : اللهُ أَكْبَرُ ذُو الْمَلَكُوتِ وَالْجَبَرُوتِ ، وَالْكِبْرِيَاءِ وَالْعَظَمَةِ ، قَالَ : ثُمَّ قَرَأَ الْبَقَرَةَ ، ثُمَّ رَكَعَ رُكُوعَهُ نَحْوًا مِنْ قِيَامِهِ ، وَكَانَ يَقُولُ : سُبْحَانَ رَبِّيَ الْعَظِيمِ ، سُبْحَانَ رَبِّيَ الْعَظِيمِ ثُمَّ رَفَعَ رَأْسَهُ ، فَكَانَ قِيَامُهُ نَحْوًا مِنْ رُكُوعِهِ ، وَكَانَ يَقُولُ : لِرَبِّيَ الْحَمْدُ ، لِرَبِّيَ الْحَمْدُ ثُمَّ سَجَدَ ، فَكَانَ سُجُودُهُ نَحْوًا مِنْ قِيَامِهِ ، وَكَانَ يَقُولُ : سُبْحَانَ رَبِّيَ الأَعْلَى ، سُبْحَانَ رَبِّيَ الأَعْلَى ثُمَّ رَفَعَ رَأْسَهُ ، فَكَانَ مَا بَيْنَ السَّجْدَتَيْنِ نَحْوًا مِنَ السُّجُودِ ، وَكَانَ يَقُولُ : رَبِّ اغْفِرْ لِي ، رَبِّ اغْفِرْ لِي حَتَّى قَرَأَ الْبَقَرَةَ ، وَآلَ عِمْرَانَ ، وَالنِّسَاءَ ، وَالْمَائِدَةَ ، أَوِ الأَنْعَامَ ، شُعْبَةُ الَّذِي شَكَّ فِي الْمَائِدَةِ ، وَالأَنْعَامِ [٣١١]

275. Hudhaifah ibn al-Yamān ؓ narrated: "I prayed with the Prophet ﷺ wherein he commenced the prayer with the following statement, '*Allāhu Akbar dhul Malakūtī wal Jabarūtī wal Kibryā wal 'Adhamah*.' Then he recited Sūrah al-Baqarah (after al-Fātihah) and proceeded to bow. The length of the bowing was as long as the standing posture, during which he said repeatedly, '*Subhana rabbiy al-Adhim*.' Then, he raised his torso and the length of his standing was like that of his bowing, during which he said repeatedly, '*Li-Rabbi al-Hamd*.' Then, he prostrated and the length of his prostration was similar

311 Sunan Abū Dawūd (874)

to his standing, during which he said repeatedly, '*Subhan Rabbi al-'Ala*.' Then he raised himself from prostration. The length of the sitting posture was similar to the prostration, during which he said, '*Rabbi Ighfir Lī*.' He prayed each unit in the same manner and in that prayer he recited al-Baqarah, al-Imrān, al-Nisā' and [al-Maidah or al-An'ām]."

Al-Bajūrī said,

> Regarding the meaning of the opening statement: *Dhul Malakūt* means the One with Dominion and Pride. *Dhul Jabarūtī* means the Subduer and Surmounter. *Dhul Kibriyā* means the One who transcends all defects and shortcomings while everything submits to Him. *Dhul 'Adhama* means the One Who nothing can encompass. It is said that *Kibryā* refers to the perfection of His essence while *'Adhamah* refers to the beauty of His Attributes.
>
> The narrator who heard this from Hudhaifah doubted whether it was Sūrah al-Ma'ida or al-An'ām that was recited in the fourth unit.

٢٧٦: حَدَّثَنَا أَبُو بَكْرٍ مُحَمَّدُ بْنُ نَافِعٍ الْبَصْرِيُّ ، قَالَ : حَدَّثَنَا عَبْدُ الصَّمَدِ بْنُ عَبْدِ الْوَارِثِ ، عَنْ إِسْمَاعِيلَ بْنِ مُسْلِمٍ الْعَبْدِيِّ ، عَنْ أَبِي الْمُتَوَكِّلِ ، عَنْ عَائِشَةَ ، قَالَتْ : قَامَ رَسُولُ اللهِ صلى الله عليه وسلم بِآيَةٍ مِنَ الْقُرْآنِ لَيْلَةً[312]

276. Aisha ﵂ narrated: "The Messenger of Allāh ﷺ stood in a [complete] night's prayer reciting one ayah of the Qur'ān."

Abdul Razzaq al-Badr said,

> The ayah mentioned is: **{If You should punish them - indeed they are Your servants; but if You forgive them - indeed it is You**

312 Sunan al-Tirmidhī (448)

who is the Exalted in Might, the Wise.}[313] As stated in the hadīth collected in the Musnad of Imam Ahmad.

Ibn al-Qayyim said,

> If people knew the benefits of contemplating the Qur'ān they would busy themselves with it and leave everything else. A person should recite the Qur'ān with contemplation and if he comes across an ayah that touches his heart, repeat it one hundred times or even the whole night to attain its benefit. The recitation of an ayah with contemplation and understanding is better than reciting the whole Qur'ān without understanding and contemplating it. It is certainly more beneficial to the heart and increases one's *imān* in it. Furthermore, it lets the person taste the sweetness of the Qur'ān. This was the habit of the *salaf* who used to repeat one ayah until the time of *Fajr*.

٢٧٧: حَدَّثَنَا مَحْمُودُ بْنُ غَيْلانَ ، قَالَ : حَدَّثَنَا سُلَيْمَانُ بْنُ حَرْبٍ ، قَالَ : حَدَّثَنَا شُعْبَةُ ، عَنِ الأَعْمَشِ ، عَنْ أَبِي وَائِلٍ ، عَنْ عَبْدِ اللهِ بْنِ مَسْعُودٍ ، قَالَ : صَلَّيْتُ لَيْلَةً مَعَ رَسُولِ اللهِ صلى الله عليه وسلم فَلَمْ يَزَلْ قَائِمًا حَتَّى هَمَمْتُ بِأَمْرِ سُوءٍ قِيلَ لَهُ : وَمَا هَمَمْتَ بِهِ ؟ قَالَ : هَمَمْتُ أَنْ أَقْعُدَ وَأَدَعَ النَّبِيَّ صلى الله عليه وسلم[314]

277. 'Abdullāh ibn Mas'ūd ؓ narrated: "Once at night I prayed in congregation with the Messenger of Allāh ﷺ wherein he stood for such a long time that I intended to do a bad deed." Someone asked: "What deed did you intend to do?" He replied: "I was about to sit down and leave the Prophet ﷺ standing alone."

Abdul Razzaq al-Badr said,

313 Qur'ān: 5:118

314 Sahīh al-Bukhārī (1135) and Sahīh Muslim (773)

This is intended to show how long the night prayer of the Prophet ﷺ was.

٢٧٨: حَدَّثَنَا سُفْيَانُ بْنُ وَكِيعٍ ، قَالَ : حَدَّثَنَا جَرِيرٌ ، عَنِ الأَعْمَشِ ، نَحْوَهُ

278. A similar report is narrated through a different route from al-A'mash

٢٧٩: حَدَّثَنَا إِسْحَاقُ بْنُ مُوسَى الأَنْصَارِيُّ ، قَالَ : حَدَّثَنَا مَعْنٌ ، قَالَ : حَدَّثَنَا مَالِكٌ ، عَنْ أَبِي النَّضْرِ ، عَنْ أَبِي سَلَمَةَ ، عَنْ عَائِشَةَ : أَنَّ النَّبِيَّ صلى الله عليه وسلم كَانَ يُصَلِّي جَالِسًا ، فَيَقْرَأُ وَهُوَ جَالِسٌ ، فَإِذَا بَقِيَ مِنْ قِرَاءَتِهِ قَدْرُ مَا يَكُونُ ثَلاثِينَ أَوْ أَرْبَعِينَ آيَةً ، قَامَ فَقَرَأَ وَهُوَ قَائِمٌ ، ثُمَّ رَكَعَ وَسَجَدَ ، ثُمَّ صَنَعَ فِي الرَّكْعَةِ الثَّانِيَةِ مِثْلَ ذَلِكَ[315]

279. Aisha ﵂ narrated: "The Prophet ﷺ prayed in a sitting posture until about thirty or forty ayāt were remaining. At this point he stood up and completed them standing. He then bowed and prostrated. He would subsequently do the same in the second unit."

Al-Bajūrī said,

> This was the case when he ﷺ became old in age as Aisha explicitly stated in the hadīth documented in Sahīh al-Bukharī and Sahīh Muslim.
>
> It shows that it is allowed to pray while sitting in voluntary prayers.

٢٨٠: حَدَّثَنَا أَحْمَدُ بْنُ مَنِيعٍ ، قَالَ : حَدَّثَنَا هُشَيْمٌ ، قَالَ : حَدَّثَنَا خَالِدٌ الْحَذَّاءُ ، عَنْ عَبْدِ اللهِ بْنِ شَقِيقٍ ، قَالَ : سَأَلْتُ عَائِشَةَ ، عَنْ صَلاةِ رَسُولِ اللهِ صلى

315 Sahīh al-Bukhārī (1119) and Sahīh Muslim (731)

الله عليه وسلم ، عَنْ تَطَوُّعِهِ ، فَقَالَتْ : كَانَ يُصَلِّي لَيْلا طَوِيلا قَائِمًا ، وَلَيْلا طَوِيلا قَاعِدًا ، فَإِذَا قَرَأَ وَهُوَ قَائِمٌ رَكَعَ وَسَجَدَ وَهُوَ قَائِمٌ ، وَإِذَا قَرَأَ وَهُوَ جَالِسٌ رَكَعَ وَسَجَدَ وَهُوَ جَالِسٌ [316]

280. 'Abdullāh ibn Shaqīq asked Aisha ﷺ about the prayer of the Messenger of Allāh ﷺ. She said: "He used to pray lengthy periods of the night whilst standing and lengthy periods of the night whilst sitting. If he prayed standing, he would bow and prostrate whilst standing, and if he prayed whilst sitting, he would bow and prostrate from the sitting posture."

Abdul Razzaq al-Badr said,

> The reward for praying while sitting down is half of praying while standing. However, this does not apply to the Prophet ﷺ as he himself stated in the hadīth documented in Sahīh Muslim:
>
> 'Abdullāh ibn 'Amr ﷺ reported: "It was narrated to me that the Messenger of Allāh ﷺ had said, 'The prayer observed by a person sitting is half of the prayer.' I came to him ﷺ and found him praying in a sitting position. I placed my hand on his head. He said, 'O 'Abdullāh ibn 'Amr, what is the matter with you?' I replied, 'Messenger of Allāh, it has been narrated to me that you said, 'The prayer of a man in a sitting position is half of the prayer,' and you are observing the prayer sitting.' He ﷺ said, 'Yes, it is so, but I am not like anyone amongst you.'"[317]

٢٨١ : حَدَّثَنَا إِسْحَاقُ بْنُ مُوسَى الأَنْصَارِيُّ ، قَالَ : حَدَّثَنَا مَعْنٌ ، قَالَ : حَدَّثَنَا مَالِكٌ ، عَنِ ابْنِ شِهَابٍ ، عَنِ السَّائِبِ بْنِ يَزِيدَ ، عَنِ الْمُطَّلِبِ بْنِ أَبِي وَدَاعَةَ ، عَنْ حَفْصَةَ ، زَوْجِ النَّبِيِّ صلى الله عليه وسلم ، قَالَتْ : كَانَ رَسُولُ

316 Sahīh Muslim (730)
317 Sahīh Muslim (735)

اللهِ يُصَلِّي فِي سُبْحَتِهِ قَاعِدًا ، وَيَقْرَأُ بِالسُّورَةِ وَيُرَتِّلُهَا ، حَتَّى تَكُونَ أَطْوَلَ مِنْ أَطْوَلَ مِنْهَا[318]

281. The wife of the Prophet ﷺ Hafsah ﵂ narrated: "The Messenger of Allāh ﷺ prayed voluntary prayers whilst sitting. He would recite with slow, distinct and clear intonation, such that the sūrah became longer than a sūrah that was actually lengthier."

Abdul Razzaq al-Badr said,

> He prayed most of the time whilst sitting towards the end of his life as he was sick and could not stand for long durations as he used to.
>
> The manner in which he ﷺ recited was to recite slowly, contemplating the ayāt. If there was an ayah about punishment, he would take refuge in Allāh from it, and if an ayah contained *tasbih* , he would glorify Allāh, and if an ayah contained a mercy, he would ask Allāh for His mercy. This is why the sūrah appeared longer than other lengthier ones.

٢٨٢ : حَدَّثَنَا الْحَسَنُ بْنُ مُحَمَّدٍ الزَّعْفَرَانِيُّ ، قَالَ : حَدَّثَنَا الْحَجَّاجُ بْنُ مُحَمَّدٍ ، عَنِ ابْنِ جُرَيْجٍ ، قَالَ : أَخْبَرَنِي عُثْمَانُ بْنُ أَبِي سُلَيْمَانَ ، أَنَّ أَبَا سَلَمَةَ بْنَ عَبْدِ الرَّحْمَنِ أَخْبَرَهُ ، أَنَّ عَائِشَةَ أَخْبَرَتْهُ ، أَنَّ النَّبِيَّ صلى الله عليه وسلم ، لَمْ يَمُتْ ، حَتَّى كَانَ أَكْثَرُ صَلاتِهِ وَهُوَ جَالِسٌ[319]

282. Aisha ﵂ reported: "The Prophet ﷺ, towards the end of his life, would perform most of his prayers whilst sitting."

Abdul Razzaq al-Badr said,

> This was close to the time of his death and due to the toll inflicted

318 Sahīh Muslim (733)
319 Musannaf Abdul Razzaq (3959)

by age and his illness.

Ibn Hajar al-Haytamī said,

> This refers to the optional prayers.

٢٨٣: حَدَّثَنَا أَحْمَدُ بْنُ مَنِيعٍ ، قَالَ : حَدَّثَنَا إِسْمَاعِيلُ بْنُ إِبْرَاهِيمَ ، قَالَ : حَدَّثَنَا أَيُّوبَ ، عَنْ نَافِعٍ ، عَنِ ابْنِ عُمَرَ ، قَالَ : صَلَّيْتُ مَعَ النَّبِيِّ صلى الله عليه وسلم ، رَكْعَتَيْنِ قَبْلَ الظُّهْرِ ، وَرَكْعَتَيْنِ بَعْدَهَا ، وَرَكْعَتَيْنِ بَعْدَ الْمَغْرِبِ فِي بَيْتِهِ ، وَرَكْعَتَيْنِ بَعْدَ الْعِشَاءِ فِي بَيْتِهِ[320]

283. 'Abdullāh ibn 'Umar ﷺ narrated: "I prayed with the Prophet ﷺ two units before and after *Dhuhr*, two units after *Maghrib* in his house, and [also] two units after *Ishā* in his house."

Abdul Razzaq al-Badr said,

> This hadīth talks about the regular Sunnah units associated with the obligatory prayers while the previous hadīth was regarding optional prayers.

٢٨٤: حَدَّثَنَا أَحْمَدُ بْنُ مَنِيعٍ ، قَالَ : حَدَّثَنَا إِسْمَاعِيلُ بْنُ إِبْرَاهِيمَ ، قَالَ : حَدَّثَنَا أَيُّوبُ ، عَنْ نَافِعٍ ، عَنِ ابْنِ عُمَرَ ، قَالَ : حَدَّثَتْنِي حَفْصَةُ : أَنَّ رَسُولَ الله صلى الله عليه وسلم ، كَانَ يُصَلِّي رَكْعَتَيْنِ حِينَ يَطْلُعُ الْفَجْرُ وَيُنَادِي الْمُنَادِي ، قَالَ أَيُّوبُ : وَأُرَاهُ ، قَالَ : خَفِيفَتَيْنِ[321]

284. 'Abdullāh ibn 'Umar ﷺ narrated: "Hafsah related to me that the Messenger of Allāh ﷺ used to pray two units upon the commencement of *Fajr*, when the call to prayer was made." Ayyūb

---

320 Sahīh al-Bukhārī (937) and Sahīh Muslim (729)
321 Part of hadīth 283

(one of the narrators) said: "I think he said: 'Short units.'"

Abdul Razzaq al-Badr said,

> This hadīth talks about the supererogatory prayers of the Prophet ﷺ that he prayed before *Fajr* and with these two units, the total number of the units is ten. Ibn 'Umar ؓ saw him pray eight units and then his sister Hafsah ؓ, the wife of the Prophet, informed him of the other two units. The Sunnah is to recite in the first unit of the Sunnah of *Fajr* "al-Kafirūn" and the second unit "al-Ikhlās".

Al-Bajūrī said,

> The two short units referred to here are the Sunnah of *Fajr*.

٢٨٥: حَدَّثَنَا قُتَيْبَةُ بْنُ سَعِيدٍ ، قَالَ : حَدَّثَنَا مَرْوَانُ بْنُ مُعَاوِيَةَ الْفَزَارِيُّ ، عَنْ جَعْفَرِ بْنِ بُرْقَانَ ، عَنْ مَيْمُونِ بْنِ مِهْرَانَ ، عَنِ ابْنِ عُمَرَ ، قَالَ : حَفِظْتُ مِنْ رَسُولِ اللهِ صلى الله عليه وسلم ، ثَمَانِيَ رَكَعَاتٍ : رَكْعَتَيْنِ قَبْلَ الظُّهْرِ ، وَرَكْعَتَيْنِ بَعْدَهَا ، وَرَكْعَتَيْنِ بَعْدَ الْمَغْرِبِ ، وَرَكْعَتَيْنِ بَعْدَ الْعِشَاءِ ، قَالَ ابْنُ عُمَرَ : وَحَدَّثَتْنِي حَفْصَةُ بِرَكْعَتَيِ الْغَدَاةِ ، وَلَمْ أَكُنْ أَرَاهُمَا مِنَ النَّبِيِّ صلى الله عليه وسلم[322]

285. 'Abdullāh ibn 'Umar ؓ narrated: "I memorised from the Messenger of Allāh ﷺ eight units of prayer; two before *Dhuhr* and two after it; two units after *Maghrib* and two after *Ishā*. Hafsah related to me about the two units before *Fajr*, which I did not observe from the Prophet ﷺ."

Ibn Hajar al-Haytamī said,

> This shows that he ﷺ prayed the regular Sunnah of the obligatory

---

322 See hadīth 283

prayers in the masjid; therefore Ibn 'Umar saw them. Unlike the Sunnah of *Fajr* which he always prayed at home.

٢٨٦: حَدَّثَنَا أَبُو سَلَمَةَ يَحْيَى بْنُ خَلَفٍ ، قَالَ : حَدَّثَنَا بِشْرُ بْنُ الْمُفَضَّلِ ، عَنْ خَالِدٍ الْحَذَّاءِ ، عَنْ عَبْدِ اللهِ بْنِ شَقِيقٍ ، قَالَ : سَأَلْتُ عَائِشَةَ ، عَنْ صَلاَةِ النَّبِيِّ صلى الله عليه وسلم ، قَالَتْ : كَانَ يُصَلِّي قَبْلَ الظُّهْرِ رَكْعَتَيْنِ وَبَعْدَهَا رَكْعَتَيْنِ ، وَبَعْدَ الْمَغْرِبِ رَكْعَتَيْنِ ، وَبَعْدَ الْعِشَاءِ رَكْعَتَيْنِ ، وَقَبْلَ الْفَجْرِ ثِنْتَيْنِ[323]

286. 'Abdullāh ibn Shaqīq asked Aisha ﵂ about the optional prayers of the Prophet ﷺ. She replied: "He used to pray two units before and two after *Dhuhr*, two units after *Maghrib*, two units after *'Ishā* and two before *Fajr*."

٢٨٧: حَدَّثَنَا مُحَمَّدُ بْنُ الْمُثَنَّى ، قَالَ : حَدَّثَنَا مُحَمَّدُ بْنُ جَعْفَرٍ ، قَالَ : حَدَّثَنَا شُعْبَةُ ، عَنْ أَبِي إِسْحَاقَ ، قَالَ : سَمِعْتُ عَاصِمَ بْنَ ضَمْرَةَ ، يَقُولُ : سَأَلْنَا عَلِيًّا ، عَنْ صَلاَةِ رَسُولِ اللهِ صلى الله عليه وسلم مِنَ النَّهَارِ ، فَقَالَ : إِنَّكُمْ لا تُطِيقُونَ ذَلِكَ ، قَالَ : فَقُلْنَا : مَنْ أَطَاقَ ذَلِكَ مِنَّا صَلَّى ، فَقَالَ : كَانَ إِذَا كَانَتِ الشَّمْسُ مِنْ هَهُنَا كَهَيْئَتِهَا مِنْ هَهُنَا عِنْدَ الْعَصْرِ صَلَّى رَكْعَتَيْنِ ، وَإِذَا كَانَتِ الشَّمْسُ مِنْ هَهُنَا ، كَهَيْئَتِهَا مِنْ هَهُنَا عِنْدَ الظُّهْرِ صَلَّى أَرْبَعًا ، وَيُصَلِّي قَبْلَ الظُّهْرِ أَرْبَعًا ، وَبَعْدَهَا رَكْعَتَيْنِ ، وَقَبْلَ الْعَصْرِ أَرْبَعًا ، يَفْصِلُ بَيْنَ كُلِّ رَكْعَتَيْنِ بِالتَّسْلِيمِ عَلَى الْمَلائِكَةِ الْمُقَرَّبِينَ وَالنَّبِيِّينَ ، وَمَنْ تَبِعَهُمْ مِنَ الْمُؤْمِنِينَ وَالْمُسْلِمِينَ[324]

287. 'Āsim ibn Damrah narrated: "We asked Alī ibn Abī Tālib ﵁ about the optional prayers that the Messenger of Allāh ﷺ performed

323 See hadīth 280
324 Sunan al-Tirmidhī (599)

during the daytime. Alī replied, 'You do not have the capability to perform them.' We replied, 'Whoever from amongst us that possesses the capability will do so.' Alī said, 'In the morning when the sun rises to the height, the same as it is at the time for *'Asr*. At that time he performed two units. When the sun rises in the east to a similar height as it is in the west at the time of *Dhuhr*, he performed four units. He performed four units before *Dhuhr* and two after. Four units were performed before *'Asr*. In between the two units [of a four unit prayer] he would sit and send salutations to the close angels, Prophets, and those who followed them from the devoted believers and Muslims.'"

Abdul Razzaq al-Badr said,

> The inquiry of 'Āsim shows the keen interest of the *salaf* towards learning the guidance of the Prophet ﷺ and following it.
>
> The first set of two units mentioned in the hadīth refers to the *Duha* prayer.
>
> The first set of four units mentioned in the hadīth refers to, as explained by some commentators, the prayer of *awwabyeen* which is offered when the pebbles become overheated (i.e. when the temperature is high).
>
> The second set of four units mentioned in the hadīth refers to the regular Sunnah preceding the prayer of *Dhuhr*, which confirms the previous hadīths.
>
> The two units performed after *Dhuhr* and four units before *Asr* are not the regular Sunnah associated with these two prayers. These two prayers have a great reward mentioned in other hadīths.
>
> The statement he ﷺ said could be the *taslīm* with which he concluded the prayer or the *tashahud* wherein salutations are sent to all pious slaves of Allāh, which includes angels and the Prophets. However, the former is more likely to be the case and more obvious in the context of this hadīth and other hadīths.

CHAPTER FORTY ONE

باب صلاة الضحى

THE DUHA PRAYER (FORENOON PRAYER)

Al-San'āni said,

> Ibn al-Qayyim compiled all the views of the scholars regarding the ruling on praying the *Duha* prayer, and they totalled to six different views, as follows:
>
> 1. It is a recommended Sunnah.
> 2. It is not prescribed unless there is a reason for it.
> 3. It is not recommended.
> 4. It is recommended to pray it but not on a regular basis.
> 5. It is preferable to pray it at home.
> 6. It is an innovation.
>
> The most correct view of these is that it is a recommended Sunnah as stated by Ibn Daqīq al-'Eid.

٢٨٨: حَدَّثَنَا مَحْمُودُ بْنُ غَيْلانَ ، قَالَ : حَدَّثَنَا أَبُو دَاوُدَ الطَّيَالِسِيُّ ، قَالَ : حَدَّثَنَا شُعْبَةُ ، عَنْ يَزِيدَ الرِّشْكِ ، قَالَ : سَمِعْتُ مُعَاذَةَ ، قَالَتْ : قُلْتُ لِعَائِشَةَ : أَكَانَ النَّبِيُّ صلى الله عليه وسلم يُصَلِّي الضُّحَى ؟ قَالَتْ : نَعَمْ ، أَرْبَعَ رَكَعَاتٍ ، وَيَزِيدُ مَا شَاءَ اللهُ عَزَّ وَجَلَّ[325]

288. Mu'ādhah narrated: "I asked Aisha ﵂, 'Did the Prophet ﷺ pray the *Duha* prayer?' She replied, 'Yes, he prayed four units, and would also increase upon that [number] whatever Allāh willed.'"

Ibn Battal said,

> Masrūq said: "We used to recite Qur'ān [after *Fajr*] in the masjid and would remain in the masjid after Ibn Mas'ūd ﵁ would leave, and then [later we would] perform the *Duha* prayer. The news reached Ibn Mas'ūd and so he said to us, 'Why do you dictate upon people that which Allāh did not oblige them to do. If you want to pray it, then do so at home.'"
>
> The *salaf* preferred praying the *Duha* prayer in secret and not to pray it in public.

Al-Sindī said,

> The affirmative answer of Aisha ﵂ indicates that he ﷺ prayed it sometimes. This is because she related in other hadīths that he did not pray it; thus to reconcile between these hadīths, it appears she meant that he did not pray it all the time or that she did not see him pray it but was then informed by someone at a later point that he did pray it.

Hafith al-'Iraqī said,

> Al-Nawawī and al-Bayhaqī said that scholars understood the hadīths indicating that the Prophet ﷺ did not pray it to mean

325 Sahīh Muslim (719)

that he did not pray it regularly as he feared that it may become obligatory. This is evident in the statement of Aisha ﵂ wherein she said, "The Messenger of Allāh ﷺ would not do an act of worship he liked to perform just out of fear that the people would follow suit and accordingly, it would become obligatory."

Al-Minnawī said,

> This hadīth was used as evidence by some scholars that the number of its units is open.

٢٨٩ : حَدَّثَنَا مُحَمَّدُ بْنُ الْمُثَنَّى ، قَالَ : حَدَّثَنِي حَكِيمُ بْنُ مُعَاوِيَةَ الزِّيَادِيُّ ، قَالَ : حَدَّثَنَا زِيَادُ بْنُ عُبَيْدِ اللهِ بْنِ الرَّبِيعِ الزِّيَادِيُّ ، عَنْ حُمَيْدٍ الطَّوِيلِ ، عَنْ أَنَسِ بْنِ مَالِكٍ : أَنَّ النَّبِيَّ صلى الله عليه وسلم ، كَانَ يُصَلِّي الضُّحَى سِتَّ رَكَعَاتٍ [326]

289. Anas ibn Mālik ﵁ narrated: "The Prophet ﷺ used to pray six units as the *Duha* prayer."

Al-Minnawī said,

> The *Duha* prayer is an established Sunnah. The Shafi'ī scholars stated that the minimum number of its units is two, the best is eight units and the maximum is twelve (based on the hadīths narrating the number of units of this prayer).

٢٩٠ : حَدَّثَنَا مُحَمَّدُ بْنُ الْمُثَنَّى ، قَالَ : حَدَّثَنَا مُحَمَّدُ بْنُ جَعْفَرٍ ، قَالَ : حَدَّثَنَا شُعْبَةُ ، عَنْ عَمْرِو بْنِ مُرَّةَ ، عَنْ عَبْدِ الرَّحْمَنِ بْنِ أَبِي لَيْلَى ، قَالَ : مَا أَخْبَرَنِي أَحَدٌ ، أَنَّهُ رَأَى النَّبِيَّ صلى الله عليه وسلم يُصَلِّي الضُّحَى إِلا أُمُّ هَانِئٍ ، فَإِنَّهَا حَدَّثَتْ أَنَّ رَسُولَ اللهِ صلى الله عليه وسلم ، دَخَلَ بَيْتَهَا يَوْمَ فَتْحِ مَكَّةَ

326 Al-Mu'jam al-Awsat (1276)

فَاغْتَسَلَ فَسَبَّحَ ثَمَانِيَ رَكَعَاتٍ مَا رَأَيْتُهُ صلى الله عليه وسلم ، صَلَّى صَلاَةً قَطُّ أَخَفَّ مِنْهَا ، غَيْرَ أَنَّهُ كَانَ يُتِمُّ الرُّكُوعَ وَالسُّجُودَ[327]

290. 'Abdul Rahman ibn Abī Laylah narrated: "None had informed me that they had observed the Prophet ﷺ pray the *Duha* prayer besides Umm Hānī' ؓ for she related, 'The Messenger of Allāh ﷺ came to my house on the day Makkah was conquered, and there he performed *ghusl* and then prayed eight units that I did not observe him perform any prayer shorter than, but he still bowed and prostrated his normal length.'"

Alau'ddin al-Baghdadī said,

> Ibn Abbās ؓ said: "I did not know *Duha* prayer was mentioned in the ayah: **{Indeed, We subjected the mountains [to praise] with him, exalting [Allāh] in the [late] afternoon and [after] sunrise.}**[328] until I heard Umm Hānī' tell me that the Messenger of Allāh visited her and asked for water to perform ablution and then prayed the *Duha* prayer. After he finished, he said to her, 'O Umm Hānī'! This is the *Duha* prayer.'"[329]

Ibn Hajar al-Asqalānī said,

> Though this hadīth indicates that it is prescribed to shorten the *Duha* prayer, this is something debatable due to the possibility that he ﷺ shortened it due to the multitude of tasks he was burdened with when Makkah was conquered, particularly as it is proven that he ﷺ prayed lengthy *Duha* prayers at other times. However, al-Qadī 'Iyyād reported from some scholars that the prayer mentioned in this hadīth is the prayer of conquest which Khālid ibn al-Walīd ؓ prayed in some of his conquests.

327 Sahih al-Bukhārī (1103) and Sahīh Muslim (336)
328 Qur'ān: 38:18
329 Al-Mu'jam al-Awsat (4/296)

Al-Tirmidhī narrated from Imām Ahmad that the most authentic hadīth about the *Duha* prayer is the hadīth of Umm Hānī', and it is as he stated. This is the reason Al-Nawawī said that the best number of units to pray are eight, while the maximum is twelve (though many other scholars did not place a restriction on the maximum number of units).

٢٩١: حدثنا ابن أبي عمر أحدثنا وكيع ، حدثنا كهمس بن الحسن ، عن عبد الله بن شقيق قال : قلت لعائشة : أكان النبي صلى الله عليه وسلم يصلي الضحى ؟

قالت :لا إلا يجيء من مغيبه[330]

291. 'Abdullāh ibn Shaqīq related: "I asked Aisha ﵂, 'Did the Prophet ﷺ pray the *Duha* prayer?' She replied, 'No. He did not perform it except when he would return from a journey.'"

Ibn Hajar al-Asqalānī said,

> He ﷺ prayed it after his return from travelling because he admonished arriving home from a journey at night and so he would arrive early in the morning and the first thing he would do was to go to the masjid and pray during the forenoon time.

Al-Suyūtī said,

> This clarifies the other hadīth of Aisha ﵂ wherein she negated that the Prophet ﷺ prayed the *Duha* prayer as she meant that he did not pray it regularly.

٢٩٢: حَدَّثَنَا زِيَادُ بْنُ أَيُّوبَ الْبَغْدَادِيُّ ، قَالَ : حَدَّثَنَا مُحَمَّدُ بْنُ رَبِيعَةَ ، عَنْ فُضَيْلِ بْنِ مَرْزُوقٍ ، عَنْ عَطِيَّةَ ، عَنْ أَبِي سَعِيدٍ الْخُدْرِيِّ ، قَالَ : كَانَ النَّبِيُّ

330 Sahīh Muslim (336)

صلى الله عليه وسلم ، يُصَلِّي الضُّحَى حَتَّى نَقُولَ : لا يَدَعُهَا ، وَيَدَعُهَا حَتَّى نَقُولَ : لا يُصَلِّيهَا[331]

292. Abu Sa'īd al-Khudarī ﷺ narrated: "The Prophet ﷺ used to pray the *Duha* prayer with such regularity that we thought he would not leave it. And, he would not pray it [for such a lengthy period of time], that we thought he would not pray it again."

Ibn Hajar al-Asqalānī said,

> 'Ikrimah related that Ibn Abbās ﷺ used to pray it for ten days and then leave it for ten days. Sufyān al-Thawrī related that Mansūr said, "They (the *salaf*) disliked praying the *Duha* prayer on a regular basis just like they observe the obligatory prayer." Sa'īd ibn Jubair said, "I do not pray it [sometimes], though I like praying it as I fear I might start obliging myself to pray it."

Zain al-Dīn al-Iraqī said,

> The reason he ﷺ did not pray it on a regular basis was because he feared it becoming obligatory upon his nation. However, as he ﷺ passed away and the religion is now complete and perfect, one should try to pray it as much as possible.

٢٩٣ : حَدَّثَنَا أَحْمَدُ بْنُ مَنِيعٍ ، عَنْ هُشَيْمٍ ، قَالَ : حَدَّثَنَا عُبَيْدَةُ ، عَنِ إِبْرَاهِيمَ ، عَنْ سَهْمِ بْنِ مِنْجَابٍ ، عَنْ قَرْثَعٍ الضَّبِّيِّ ، أَوْ عَنْ قَزَعَةَ ، عَنْ قَرْثَعٍ ، عَنْ أَبِي أَيُّوبَ الأَنْصَارِيِّ ، أَنَّ النَّبِيَّ صلى الله عليه وسلم ، كَانَ يُدْمِنُ أَرْبَعَ رَكَعَاتٍ عِنْدَ زَوَالِ الشَّمْسِ ، فَقُلْتُ : يَا رَسُولَ الله ، إِنَّكَ تُدْمِنُ هَذِهِ الأَرْبَعَ رَكَعَاتٍ عِنْدَ زَوَالِ الشَّمْسِ ، فَقَالَ : إِنَّ أَبْوَابَ السَّمَاءِ تُفْتَحُ عِنْدَ زَوَالِ الشَّمْسِ فَلا تُرْتَجُ حَتَّى تُصَلَّى الظُّهْرُ ، فَأُحِبُّ أَنْ يَصْعَدَ لِي فِي تِلْكَ السَّاعَةِ خَيْرٌ ، قُلْتُ :

331 Sunan al-Tirmidhī (477)

أَفِي كُلِّهِنَّ قِرَاءَةٌ ؟ قَالَ : نَعَمْ قُلْتُ : هَلْ فِيهِنَّ تَسْلِيمٌ فَاصِلٌ ؟ قَالَ : لا [332]

293. Abu Ayyūb al-Ansārī ﷺ narrated: "The Prophet ﷺ always prayed four units when the sun passed the zenith. I said, 'O Messenger of Allāh! You constantly pray these four units when the sun passes the zenith!' The Messenger ﷺ replied, 'The doors of the heavens open from the time the sun passes the zenith until the *Dhuhr* prayer is performed; hence I like that a good deed of mine reaches the heavens at that time.' I asked, 'Is there a recital in every unit?' He replied, 'Yes.' I enquired, 'Is there a taslīm in between?' He replied, 'No.'"

Abdul Rahman al-Mubarakfūrī said,

> These four units are known as the Sunnah of *Zawāl* which is different to the four units of Sunnah preceding the *Dhuhr* prayer and they are linked to the time of the sun passing the zenith. The wisdom for praying it at that time is because the time of midday mirrors the time of midnight; the doors of the heavens are open at midday and Allāh ﷻ descends after midnight; thus both times are times of mercy.
>
> Ibn al-Qayyim said that the Prophet ﷺ prayed these four units after the sun passed the zenith.

Abdullah ibn Sa'īd al-Hadramī al-Makkī said,

> The inquiry about whether these units included any Qur'ān recitation refers to anything in addition to the Fātihah. This is because a prayer is not accepted without reciting the Fātihah even if it is an optional prayer, and this is something well known.
>
> The inquiry about the taslīm was to find out whether the four units are prayed with one taslīm or prayed two units by two. This hadīth was used as evidence by the scholars who hold the view that the optional prayers of the daytime should consist of four units with one taslīm. However, other scholars understood the statement of

332 Musnad Ahmad (23532)

the Prophet ﷺ to mean that the taslīm is not obligatory. Meaning one is not obligated to pray them two units by two and so it does not contradict that the best manner of praying the optional prayers is two by two.

٢٩٤ : حدثنا أَحْمَدُ بْنُ مَنِيعٍ ، قَالَ : حَدَّثَنَا أَبُو مُعَاوِيَةَ ، قَالَ : حَدَّثَنَا عُبَيْدَةُ ، عَنْ إِبْرَاهِيمَ ، عَنْ سَهْمِ بْنِ مِنْجَابٍ ، عَنْ قَزَعَةَ ، عَنْ قَرْثَعٍ ، عَنْ أَبِي أَيُّوبَ الأَنْصَارِيِّ ، عَنِ النَّبِيِّ صلى الله عليه وسلم ، نَحْوَهُ

294. Abu Ayyūb al-Ansārī ؓ narrated from the Prophet ﷺ a similar narration through a different route.

٢٩٥ : حَدَّثَنَا مُحَمَّدُ بْنُ الْمُثَنَّى ، قَالَ : حَدَّثَنَا أَبُو دَاوُدَ ، قَالَ : حَدَّثَنَا مُحَمَّدُ بْنُ مُسْلِمِ بْنِ أَبِي الْوَضَّاحِ ، عَنْ عَبْدِ الْكَرِيمِ الْجَزَرِيِّ ، عَنْ مُجَاهِدٍ ، عَنْ عَبْدِ اللهِ بْنِ السَّائِبِ ، أَنَّ رَسُولَ اللهِ صلى الله عليه وسلم كَانَ يُصَلِّي أَرْبَعًا بَعْدَ أَنْ تَزُولَ الشَّمْسُ قَبْلَ الظُّهْرِ وَقَالَ : إِنَّهَا سَاعَةٌ تُفْتَحُ فِيهَا أَبْوَابُ السَّمَاءِ ، فَأُحِبُّ أَنْ يَصْعَدَ لِي فِيهَا عَمَلٌ صَالِحٌ [333]

295. 'Abdullāh ibn al-Sāi'b ؓ narrated: "The Messenger of Allāh ﷺ used to pray four units between the time of the sun passing the zenith and the prayer of *Dhuhr*, and he ﷺ said, 'The doors of the heavens open at this moment; therefore I like that a good deed of mine ascends at this moment.'"

٢٩٦ : حَدَّثَنَا أَبُو سَلَمَةَ يَحْيَى بْنُ خَلَفٍ ، قَالَ : حَدَّثَنَا عُمَرُ بْنُ عَلِيٍّ الْمُقَدَّمِيُّ ، عَنْ مِسْعَرِ بْنِ كِدَامٍ ، عَنْ أَبِي إِسْحَاقَ ، عَنْ عَاصِمِ بْنِ ضَمْرَةَ ، عَنْ عَلِيٍّ ، أَنَّهُ كَانَ يُصَلِّي قَبْلَ الظُّهْرِ أَرْبَعًا ، وَذَكَرَ أَنَّ رَسُولَ اللهِ صلى الله عليه وسلم

333 Sunan al-Tirmidhī (478)

كَانَ يُصَلِّيهَا عِنْدَ الزَّوَالِ وَيَمُدُّ فِيهَا[334]

296. Alī ibn Abī Tālib ﷺ used to pray four units before the prayer of *Dhuhr* and he mentioned that the Messenger of Allāh ﷺ used to pray these four units when the sun passed the zenith and he would make the units long in duration.

Ibn Hajar al-Haytamī said,

> This shows that it is recommended to prolong the *Duha* prayer.

334 Al-Targhīb fī Fada'il al-A'māl (82)

CHAPTER FORTY TWO

باب صلاة التطوع في البيت

PRAYING SUPEREROGATORY PRAYERS AT HOME

Abdul Razzaq al-Badr said,

> It is more rewarding to pray supererogatory prayers at home than in the masjid even if the masjid is one of the three wherein the reward is doubled. Praying at home brings life to it and whenever a home is devoid of prayer then it is devoid of life. From the benefits of praying supererogatory prayers at home is that it encourages the children to pray, expels devils from the home and brings tranquillity and peace therein.

٢٩٧: حَدَّثَنَا عَبَّاسٌ الْعَنْبَرِيُّ ، قَالَ : حَدَّثَنَا عَبْدُ الرَّحْمَنِ بْنُ مَهْدِيٍّ ، عَنْ مُعَاوِيَةَ بْنِ صَالِحٍ ، عَنِ الْعَلَاءِ بْنِ الْحَارِثِ ، عَنْ حَرَامِ بْنِ مُعَاوِيَةَ ، عَنْ عَمِّهِ عَبْدِ اللهِ بْنِ سَعْدٍ ، قَالَ : سَأَلْتُ رَسُولَ اللهِ صلى الله عليه وسلم عَنِ الصَّلاةِ فِي بَيْتِي وَالصَّلاةِ فِي الْمَسْجِدِ ، قَالَ : قَدْ تَرَى مَا أَقْرَبَ بَيْتِي مِنَ الْمَسْجِدِ ، فَلأَنْ أُصَلِّيَ فِي بَيْتِي أَحَبُّ إِلَيَّ مِنْ أَنْ أُصَلِّيَ فِي الْمَسْجِدِ ، إِلا أَنْ تَكُونَ صَلاةً مَكْتُوبَةً [335]

297. 'Abdullāh ibn Sa'd ﷺ related: "I asked the Messenger of Allāh ﷺ which is more meritorious, praying at home or praying at the masjid?" He replied, "You can see that my house is very close to the masjid yet besides the five obligatory prayers, I prefer to pray in my house rather than in the masjid."

Muhammad al-Amīn al-Shanqītī said,

> The scholars differed on whether it is better to pray the supererogatory prayers at home or at the masjid of the Prophet ﷺ because each group understood the overall texts differently. The views of the scholars are as follows:
>
> Imam Abū Hanifah said that praying supererogatory prayers at home is better and there would be no difference in reward if they were prayed at the masjid of the Prophet ﷺ.
>
> Imam al-Shafi'ī had two views reported from him as noted in Sharh Sahīh Muslim of al-Nawawī and al-Majmū' of the same author.
>
> Mālikī scholars hold the view that praying supererogatory prayers at the masjid of the Prophet ﷺ is better than praying them at home.
>
> It should be noted that the reward for women praying at home is greater than them praying at the masjid, be it supererogatory prayers or obligatory prayers.

---

335 Sunan Abū Dawūd (311) and Sunan Ibn Mājah (651)

Al-Nabhānī said,

> The reason he ﷺ preferred to offer supererogatory prayers at home was so the blessings of prayer encompass the home and the household members, through this angels enter the house and devils leave it.

CHAPTER FORTY THREE

باب ماجاء في صوم رسول الله صلى الله عليه وسلم

THE REPORTS PERTAINING TO THE FASTING OF THE MESSENGER OF ALLĀH ﷺ

Abdul Razzaq al-Badr said,

This chapter is dedicated to clarifying the recommended and obligatory fasting of the Prophet ﷺ – that which he repeated every week such as the fast of Mondays and Thursdays, and that which he repeated every month such as the three days of each month, and that which he repeated every year such as the month of Ramadān and the day of 'Ashūrā.

The lingual meaning of the Arabic word '*sawm*' is abstaining and refraining. In its religious context it means refraining from food, drink and sexual activities during the day from the time of *Fajr* until sunset.

Fasting is of two types, the first of which is to refrain from food, drink and sexual activities and this must be observed during each day of the month of Ramadān, from *Fajr* until sunset. The other type of fasting is to refrain from sins and this must be observed all of the time. It is for this reason that each bodily limb must fast, the ears must refrain from listening to the forbidden, the tongue must refrain from uttering the forbidden and so forth.

٢٩٨: حَدَّثَنَا قُتَيْبَةُ بْنُ سَعِيدٍ ، قَالَ : حَدَّثَنَا حَمَّادُ بْنُ زَيْدٍ ، عَنْ أَيُّوبَ ، عَنْ عَبْدِ اللهِ بْنِ شَقِيقٍ ، قَالَ : سَأَلْتُ عَائِشَةَ ، عَنْ صِيَامِ رَسُولِ اللهِ صلى الله عليه وسلم ، قَالَتْ : كَانَ يَصُومُ حَتَّى نَقُولَ قَدْ صَامَ ، وَيُفْطِرُ حَتَّى نَقُولَ قَدْ أَفْطَرَ قَالَتْ : وَمَا صَامَ رَسُولُ اللهِ صلى الله عليه وسلم ، شَهْرًا كَامِلا مُنْذُ قَدِمَ الْمَدِينَةَ إِلا رَمَضَانَ [336]

298. 'Abdullāh ibn Shaqīq ﵁ narrated: "I inquired from Aisha ﵂ regarding the supererogatory fasting of the Messenger of Allāh ﷺ. She replied, 'At times he would fast continuous days to the point that we thought he would not cease fasting. And at times he would not fast, until we began thinking he would continue to not fast. The Messenger of Allāh ﷺ did not fast a whole month from the time he entered Madinah, except the month of Ramadan.'"

Al-Nawawī said,

> This hadith shows that it is recommended for a person to fast a day or more from each month, and that optional fasting does not have a specific time as it can be offered anytime during the year except the month of Ramadan, Eid days and the days of Tashrīq.

Ibn Hajar al-Haytamī said,

> The reason it was mentioned that this was his practice from the day he entered Madinah is because most of the rulings were revealed after immigration.
>
> This is a proof that optional fasting during the month of Ramadān is invalid.

---

336 Sahīh Muslim (1156)

٢٩٩ : حَدَّثَنَا عَلِيُّ بْنُ حُجْرٍ ، قَالَ : حَدَّثَنَا إِسْمَاعِيلُ بْنُ جَعْفَرٍ ، عَنْ حُمَيْدٍ ، عَنْ أَنَسِ بْنِ مَالِكٍ ، أَنَّهُ سُئِلَ عَنْ صَوْمِ النَّبِيِّ صلى الله عليه وسلم ، فَقَالَ : كَانَ يَصُومُ مِنَ الشَّهْرِ حَتَّى نَرَى أَنْ لا يُرِيدَ أَنْ يُفْطِرَ مِنْهُ ، وَيُفْطِرُ مِنْهُ حَتَّى نَرَى أَنْ لا يُرِيدَ أَنْ يَصُومَ مِنْهُ شَيْئًا وَكُنْتَ لا تَشَاءُ أَنْ تَرَاهُ مِنَ اللَّيْلِ مُصَلِّيًا إِلا رَأَيْتَهُ مُصَلِّيًا ، وَلا نَائِمًا إِلا رَأَيْتَهُ نَائِمًا [337]

299. Anas ibn Mālik ﷺ was asked about the fasting of the Prophet ﷺ. He replied: "It was his habit that in some months he fasted for so many days, that it was thought he would continue fasting the whole month. In other months, he did not fast to the point that it was thought he would not fast any day from the month. If anyone wanted to observe him praying at night, it was possible, and if one wanted to observe him sleeping at night, this too was possible."

Yahya ibn Yahya al-Amirī said,

> You should know that fasting is from the best acts of worship and it is an act of striving. Its virtue has been reported in many hadīths, the loftiest of which is the hadīth mentioned in Sahīh al-Bukharī and Sahīh Muslim wherein Allāh ﷻ said on the tongue of the Prophet ﷺ, "Every deed of the son of Adam is for him except fasting; it is for Me and I shall reward him for it."[338]

Abdul Rahman al-Mubarakfūri said,

> Al-Hafith ibn Hajar said that the meaning of this hadīth is that he ﷺ did not follow a particular pattern in his worship. An example of this is that he used to pray night prayers at the beginning of the night, some other times in the middle of the night and some other times at the end of the night. Likewise, he used to fast the beginning of the month, and some other times in the middle of

337 Sahīh al-Bukhārī (1141)
338 Sahīh al-Bukhārī (1780) and Sahīh Muslim (1949)

the month and some other times at the end of the month. Thus, if a person wanted to observe his worship, he would certainly be able to see him either fasting or praying.

٣٠٠: حَدَّثَنَا مَحْمُودُ بْنُ غَيْلانَ ، قَالَ : حَدَّثَنَا أَبُو دَاوُدَ ، قَالَ : حَدَّثَنَا شُعْبَةُ ، عَنْ أَبِي بِشْرٍ ، قَالَ : سَمِعْتُ سَعِيدَ بْنَ جُبَيْرٍ ، عَنِ ابْنِ عَبَّاسٍ ، قَالَ : كَانَ النَّبِيُّ صلى الله عليه وسلم يَصُومُ حَتَّى نَقُولَ مَا يُرِيدُ أَنْ يُفْطِرَ مِنْهُ ، وَيُفْطِرُ حَتَّى نَقُولَ مَا يُرِيدُ أَنْ يَصُومَ مِنْهُ ، وَمَا صَامَ شَهْرًا كَامِلا مُنْذُ قَدِمَ الْمَدِينَةَ إِلا رَمَضَانَ[339]

300. 'Abdullāh ibn Abbās ؓ narrated: "The Prophet ﷺ at times would fast continuously to such an extent that we began to think that he would not discontinue fasting. And, at times he would not fast to such an extent that we began thinking he would not restart fasting. The Messenger of Allāh ﷺ did not fast a whole month from the time he entered Madinah, except the month of Ramadan."

٣٠١: حَدَّثَنَا مُحَمَّدُ بْنُ بَشَّارٍ ، قَالَ : حَدَّثَنَا عَبْدُ الرَّحْمَنِ بْنُ مَهْدِيٍّ ، عَنْ سُفْيَانَ ، عَنْ مَنْصُورٍ ، عَنْ سَالِمِ بْنِ أَبِي الْجَعْدِ ، عَنْ أَبِي سَلَمَةَ ، عَنْ أُمِّ سَلَمَةَ ، قَالَتْ : مَا رَأَيْتُ النَّبِيَّ صلى الله عليه وسلم يَصُومُ شَهْرَيْنِ مُتَتَابِعَيْنِ إِلا شَعْبَانَ وَرَمَضَانَ[340] قَالَ أَبُو عِيسَى : هَذَا إِسْنَادٌ صَحِيحٌ وَهَكَذَا ، قَالَ : عَنْ أَبِي سَلَمَةَ ، عَنْ أُمِّ سَلَمَةَ وَرَوَى هَذَا الْحَدِيثَ غَيْرُ وَاحِدٍ ، عَنْ أَبِي سَلَمَةَ ، عَنْ عَائِشَةَ ، عَنِ النَّبِيِّ صلى الله عليه وسلم ، وَيُحْتَمَلُ أَنْ يَكُونَ أَبُو سَلَمَةَ بْنُ عَبْدِ الرَّحْمَنِ قَدْ رَوَى الْحَدِيثَ عَنْ عَائِشَةَ ، وَأُمِّ سَلَمَةَ جَمِيعًا ، عَنِ النَّبِيِّ صلى الله عليه وسلم

339 Sahīh al-Bukhārī (1971) and Sahīh Muslim (1157)
340 Sunan Abū Dawūd (2336) and Sunan Ibn Mājah (1648)

301. Umm Salamah ﵂ narrated: "I did not see the Prophet ﷺ fast two consecutive months except the months of Sha'bān and Ramadān."

Ibn Abdul Barr said,

> 'Abdullāh ibn al-Mubarak said, "In the Arabic language saying 'fasted the whole month' can refer to someone who fasted most of the month."

Ibn Rajab said,

> The Prophet ﷺ used to fast during the month of Sha'bān more than any other months. The most correct view is that he ﷺ fasted most of the month as evidenced in many other explicit hadīths. Ibn Abbās ﵁ used to forbid people from fasting a whole month (except the month of Ramadān). The month of Sha'bān is the most virtuous month after the month of Ramadān due to the fact that it is the closest month to the month of Ramadan. Thus when one offers optional fasting in Sha'ban and then follows it with obligatory fasting in Ramadan, it is like the regular Sunnah prayers preceding and following the obligatory prayers.

٣٠٢: حَدَّثَنَا هَنَّادٌ ، قَالَ : حَدَّثَنَا عَبْدَةُ ، عَنْ مُحَمَّدِ بْنِ عَمْرٍو ، قَالَ : حَدَّثَنَا أَبُو سَلَمَةَ ، عَنْ عَائِشَةَ ، قَالَتْ : لَمْ أَرَ رَسُولَ اللهِ صلى الله عليه وسلم ، يَصُومُ فِي شَهْرٍ أَكْثَرَ مِنْ صِيَامِهِ لِلَّهِ فِي شَعْبَانَ ، كَانَ يَصُومُ شَعْبَانَ إِلا قَلِيلا ، بَلْ كَانَ يَصُومُهُ كُلَّهُ [341]

302. Aisha ﵂ narrated: "I did not see the Messenger of Allāh ﷺ fast in a month [excluding Ramadān] more than he did in Sha'bān. He fasted the month except for a few days; rather he fasted the full month."

341 Sahih al-Bukhārī (1969) and Sahīh Muslim (1156)

Ibn al-Qayyim said,

> The statement of Aisha ﵂ indicates that he nearly fasted the whole month of Sha'bān and the days he left out were insignificant in number. Al-Nawawī said that the Prophet ﷺ did not fast a whole month except Ramadān so people would not make this act of his obligatory.

Al-Shawkānī said,

> The first part of the statement of Aisha ﵂ seems to contradict her last statement and scholars reconciled the meanings of the two statements by concluding that she meant that he nearly fasted the whole month. However, al-Taybī dismissed such reconciliation based on the meanings of the word "*kul*" (English: whole) mentioned in the hadith, and so he stated that she meant that he fasted the whole month of Sha'bān but not every year so that people would not think that it is obligatory to fast it.

٣٠٣: حَدَّثَنَا الْقَاسِمُ بْنُ دِينَارٍ الْكُوفِيُّ ، قَالَ : حَدَّثَنَا عُبَيْدُ اللهِ بْنُ مُوسَى ، وَطَلْقُ بْنُ غَنَّامٍ ، عَنْ شَيْبَانَ ، عَنْ عَاصِمٍ ، عَنْ زِرِّ بْنِ حُبَيْشٍ ، عَنْ عَبْدِ اللهِ ، قَالَ : كَانَ رَسُولُ اللهِ صلى الله عليه وسلم ، يَصُومُ مِنْ غُرَّةِ كُلِّ شَهْرٍ ثَلاثَةَ أَيَّامٍ ، وَقَلَّمَا كَانَ يُفْطِرُ يَوْمَ الْجُمُعَةِ [342]

303. 'Abdullah ibn Mas'ūd ﵁ narrated: "The Messenger of Allāh ﷺ fasted for three days at the beginning of every month, and rarely would he miss fasting on Fridays."

Ibn Hajar al-Asqalanī said,

> Reconciling all the hadīths related to fasting on Friday, it is disliked to single out Friday for fasting and the wisdom behind that is

342 Sunan Abū Dawūd (2450) and Sunan Ibn Mājah (1725)

because Friday is a day of celebration and such days are not fasted. However, the counterargument is that the Prophet ﷺ allowed its fasting if Thursday or Saturday is fasted with it, and Ibn al-Qayyim and other scholars responded saying that fasting another day with it negates the intention of fasting Friday in particular.

Al-Shawkānī said,

This hadīth entails that he ﷺ fasted Friday along with Thursday or Saturday.

٣٠٤: حَدَّثَنَا أَبُو حَفْصٍ عَمْرُو بْنُ عَلِيٍّ ، قَالَ : حَدَّثَنَا عَبْدُ اللهِ بْنُ دَاوُدَ ، عَنْ ثَوْرِ بْنِ يَزِيدَ ، عَنْ خَالِدِ بْنِ مَعْدَانَ ، عَنْ رَبِيعَةَ الْجُرَشِيِّ ، عَنْ عَائِشَةَ ، قَالَتْ : كَانَ النَّبِيُّ صلى الله عليه وسلم يَتَحَرَّى صَوْمَ الاثْنَيْنِ وَالْخَمِيسِ[343]

304. Aisha رضي الله عنها narrated: "The Prophet ﷺ was keen to fast on Mondays and Thursdays."

Muhammad Alī al-Shafi'ī said,

He ﷺ used to fast these two days due to their great virtue.

Abdul Rahman al-Mubarakfūrī said,

This shows that he ﷺ had great keenness towards the fasting of these two days.

٣٠٥: حَدَّثَنَا مُحَمَّدُ بْنُ يَحْيَى ، قَالَ : حَدَّثَنَا أَبُو عَاصِمٍ ، عَنْ مُحَمَّدِ بْنِ رِفَاعَةَ ، عَنْ سُهَيْلِ بْنِ أَبِي صَالِحٍ ، عَنْ أَبِيهِ ، عَنْ أَبِي هُرَيْرَةَ ، أَنَّ النَّبِيَّ صلى الله عليه وسلم ، قَالَ : تُعْرَضُ الأَعْمَالُ يَوْمَ الاثْنَيْنِ وَالْخَمِيسِ ، فَأُحِبُّ أَنْ

343 Sunan Ibn Mājah (1649) and Sunan al-Tirmidhī (745)

يُعْرَضَ عَمَلِي وَأَنَا صَائِمٌ [344]

305. Abū Hurairah ﷺ narrated: "The Prophet ﷺ said, 'Deeds are presented before Allāh ﷻ on Mondays and Thursdays; therefore I like for my good deeds to be presented whilst I am fasting.'"

Ibn al-Uthaymīn said,

> The virtue of the day of Monday is established in other hadīths wherein he ﷺ mentioned that it was the day on which he was born, the day he was sent to people and also the day on which he received the first revelation. Fasting the day of Thursday is a Sunnah but it is less virtuous than the day of Monday. However, the most virtuous kind of fasting is the fasting of Prophet Dawūd ﷺ which is to fast alternate days.

٣٠٦: حَدَّثَنَا مَحْمُودُ بْنُ غَيْلانَ ، قَالَ : حَدَّثَنَا أَبُو أَحْمَدَ ، وَمُعَاوِيَةُ بْنُ هِشَامِ ، قَالا : حَدَّثَنَا سُفْيَانُ ، عَنْ مَنْصُورٍ ، عَنْ خَيْثَمَةَ ، عَنْ عَائِشَةَ ، قَالَتْ : كَانَ النَّبِيُّ صلى الله عليه وسلم يَصُومُ مِنَ الشَّهْرِ السَّبْتَ وَالأَحَدَ وَالاثْنَيْنَ ، وَمِنَ الشَّهْرِ الآخَرِ الثُّلاثَاءَ وَالأَرْبَعَاءَ وَالْخَمِيسَ [345]

306. Aisha ﷺ narrated: "The Prophet ﷺ used to fast in one month Saturdays, Sundays and Mondays, and in the following month he would fast on Tuesdays, Wednesdays and Thursdays."

Ibn Hajar al-Asqalānī said,

> The purpose of dividing his fasting was so that he could be able to fast most of the days of the week.

Al-San'anī said,

---

344 Sunan al-Tirmidhī (747)
345 Sunan al-Tirmidhī (746)

The reason behind him ﷺ fasting Saturdays and Sundays is explained in another hadīth wherein he mentioned that he fasted them because they are the Eid days of the disbelievers. Subsequently, he wanted to oppose them by fasting these days since on their days of Eid the disbelievers would be indulging in feasts, drinks and merriment.

Ibn al-Qayyim said,

> It is disliked to single out Saturday for fasting and this hadīth can be reconciled with other hadīths as the ruling of "disliked" is removed when another day is fasted with it (i.e. Friday or Sunday). The reason it is disliked to single out Saturday is so that the day venerated by the Jews as a day of rest is not glorified [by the Muslims].

٣٠٧: حَدَّثَنَا أَبُو مُصْعَبٍ الْمَدِينِيُّ ، عَنْ مَالِكِ بْنِ أَنَسٍ ، عَنْ أَبِي النَّضْرِ ، عَنْ أَبِي سَلَمَةَ بْنِ عَبْدِ الرَّحْمَنِ ، عَنْ عَائِشَةَ ، قَالَتْ : مَا كَانَ رَسُولُ اللهِ صلى الله عليه وسلم يَصُومُ فِي شَهْرٍ أَكْثَرَ مِنْ صِيَامِهِ فِي شَعْبَانَ[346]

307. Aisha ﵂ narrated: "The Messenger of Allāh ﷺ did not fast in any month more than he did in the month of Sha'bān."

٣٠٨: حَدَّثَنَا مَحْمُودُ بْنُ غَيْلانَ ، قَالَ : حَدَّثَنَا أَبُو دَاوُدَ ، قَالَ : حَدَّثَنَا شُعْبَةُ ، عَنْ يَزِيدَ الرِّشْكِ ، قَالَ : سَمِعْتُ مُعَاذَةَ ، قَالَتْ : قُلْتُ لِعَائِشَةَ : أَكَانَ رَسُولُ اللهِ صلى الله عليه وسلم ، يَصُومُ ثَلاثَةَ أَيَّامٍ مِنْ كُلِّ شَهْرٍ ؟ قَالَتْ : نَعَمْ قُلْتُ : مِنْ أَيِّهِ كَانَ يَصُومُ ؟ قَالَتْ : كَانَ لا يُبَالِي مِنْ أَيِّهِ صَامَ[347]

308. Mu'ādhah narrated: "I asked 'Aisha ﵂ whether the Messenger

346 See hadīth 302
347 Sahih Muslim (1160)

of Allāh ﷺ used to fast three days of each month and she ؓ confirmed that. Thus, I asked her, 'On which days of the month did he fast?' She replied, 'He did not specify any particular days.'"

Ibn Rajab said,

> This hadīth shows that he ﷺ did not have any specific days selected to fast the three days from each month.

٣٠٩: حَدَّثَنَا هَارُونُ بْنُ إِسْحَاقَ الْهَمْدَانِيُّ ، قَالَ : حَدَّثَنَا عَبْدَةُ بْنُ سُلَيْمَانَ ، عَنْ هِشَامِ بْنِ عُرْوَةَ ، عَنْ أَبِيهِ ، عَنْ عَائِشَةَ ، قَالَتْ : كَانَ عَاشُورَاءُ يَوْمًا تَصُومُهُ قُرَيْشٌ فِي الْجَاهِلِيَّةِ ، وَكَانَ رَسُولُ اللهِ صلى الله عليه وسلم يَصُومُهُ ، فَلَمَّا قَدِمَ الْمَدِينَةَ صَامَهُ وَأَمَرَ بِصِيَامِهِ ، فَلَمَّا افْتُرِضَ رَمَضَانُ كَانَ رَمَضَانُ هُوَ الْفَرِيضَةُ وَتُرِكَ عَاشُورَاءُ ، فَمَنْ شَاءَ صَامَهُ وَمَنْ شَاءَ تَرَكَهُ [348]

309. Aisha ؓ narrated: "The day of 'Ashūra was a day that the Quraysh used to fast before Islām and the Messenger of Allāh ﷺ observed this fast too. When he came to Madīnah he observed its fast and commanded others to fast it too. However, when the command to fast the month of Ramadān was revealed, it became the obligatory fasting and the fast of 'Ashūra was left; whoever wished, observed its fast and whoever did not, left it."

Abdul Rahman al-Mubarakfūrī said,

> This shows that the fast of 'Ashūra[349] was made obligatory but

348 Sahih al-Bukhari (1592) and Sahih Muslim (1125)

349 Ibn Abbās narrated that the Prophet ﷺ came to Madīnah and saw the Jews fasting on the day of 'Ashūra. He said, "What is this?" They said, "This is a good day, this is the day when Allāh saved the Children of Israel from their enemy and Mūsa fasted on this day." He ﷺ said, "We are closer to Mūsa than you." So he fasted on this day and told the people to fast. (Sahīh al-Bukhārī (1865))

the ruling was abrogated when it was revealed that the fast of Ramadan is obligatory.

'Abdullāh al-Hadramī al-Makkī said,

> Al-Qadī 'Iyyād said it is possible that he ﷺ fasted the day of 'Ashūra to incline the hearts of the Jews to Islām just as he did when he prayed toward their *qiblah* (Jerusalem). However, when Makkah was conquered and Islām spread, he preferred to oppose them and so he said that he will fast another day with the day of 'Ashūra.
>
> According to some scholars the best manner of fasting the day of 'Ashūra is by fasting it with the day that precedes it and the day that follows it. Then, to fast 'Ashūra and the day before it, and the last in rank is to fast the day alone.

٣١٠: حَدَّثَنَا مُحَمَّدُ بْنُ بَشَّارٍ ، قَالَ : حَدَّثَنَا عَبْدُ الرَّحْمَنِ بْنُ مَهْدِيٍّ ، قَالَ : حَدَّثَنَا سُفْيَانُ ، عَنْ مَنْصُورٍ ، عَنِ إِبْرَاهِيمَ ، عَنْ عَلْقَمَةَ ، قَالَ : سَأَلْتُ عَائِشَةَ ، أَكَانَ رَسُولُ اللهِ صلى الله عليه وسلم ، يَخُصُّ مِنَ الأَيَّامِ شَيْئًا ؟ قَالَتْ : كَانَ عَمَلُهُ دِيمَةً ، وَأَيُّكُمْ يُطِيقُ مَا كَانَ رَسُولُ اللهِ صلى الله عليه وسلم ، يُطِيقُ[350]

310. 'Alqamah narrated: "I asked Aisha ﵂, 'Did the Messenger of Allāh ﷺ set aside particular days for worship?' She replied, 'The worship of the Prophet ﷺ was of a continuous nature, and who amongst you would have the strength that the Messenger of Allāh ﷺ possessed?'"

Ibn Battāl said,

> This means that he did not specify an act of worship to a particular day but it was narrated that his optional fasting was increased

350 Sahīh al-Bukhārī (1987) and Sahīh Muslim (783)

during the month of Sha'bān and that he encouraged fasting Mondays and Thursdays. We understand this by stating that he ﷺ fasted according to his energy level and so it happened that the fasting often coincided with the days he preferred.

Ibn Rajab said,

> The Prophet ﷺ admonished discontinuing good deeds when they have become routine for the individual as noted in the hadīth wherein he addressed 'Abdullāh ibn 'Umar ﷺ, "Do not be like so and so, he used to offer night prayers and then he stopped."[351]

Ibn Hajar al-Asqalānī said,

> The virtue of continuing to do a good deed after it becomes habitual is so the individual does not become a person who breaks contact with his beloved. A person like that deserves admonishment. A similar case is the one who memorises from the Qur'ān and forgets it; there are many hadīths admonishing this. In this hadīth lies an encouragement for people to spare no efforts in worship, striving to reach their maximum individual capacity, provided that the exertion does not reach to the degree that will cause the person to leave the worship due to reasons such as boredom.

Al-Ghazālī said,

> It was narrated that if Allāh accustoms a person to an act of worship but later on he stops it out of boredom, Allāh will despise him. This is why it is reported that the Prophet ﷺ continuously prayed the two units after *'Asr* to make up the two units he missed after the prayer of *Dhuhr* due to his visitors.[352] However, he prayed

351 Sahīh al-Bukhārī (1090)

352 Kuraib, the freed slave of Ibn Abbās stated: "Ibn Abbās, Abdur-Rahman ibn Azhar and Al-Miswar bin Makhrama sent me to Aisha saying, "Pay her our greetings and ask her about our offering of the two rakat after *Asr* Prayer,

them in his house and not outside so that the people would not imitate him in this matter.

٣١١: حَدَّثَنَا هَارُونُ بْنُ إِسْحَاقَ ، قَالَ : حَدَّثَنَا عَبْدَةُ ، عَنْ هِشَامِ بْنِ عُرْوَةَ ، عَنْ أَبِيهِ ، عَنْ عَائِشَةَ ، قَالَتْ : دَخَلَ عَلَيَّ رَسُولُ اللهِ صلى الله عليه وسلم وَعِنْدِي امْرَأَةٌ ، فَقَالَ : مَنْ هَذِهِ ؟ قُلْتُ : فُلانَةُ لا تَنَامُ اللَّيْلَ ، فَقَالَ رَسُولُ اللهِ صلى الله عليه وسلم : عَلَيْكُمْ مِنَ الأَعْمَالِ مَا تُطِيقُونَ ، فَوَاللهِ لا يَمَلُّ اللهُ حَتَّى تَمَلُّوا ، وَكَانَ أَحَبَّ ذَلِكَ إِلَى رَسُولِ اللهِ صلى الله عليه وسلم الَّذِي

---

and tell her that we have been informed that you offer these two rak'at while we have heard that the Prophet ﷺ had forbidden their offering." Ibn Abbas said, "I and 'Umar used to beat the people for their offering of them." I entered upon her and delivered their message to her. She said, "Ask Umm Salamah." So, I informed them [of Aisha's answer] and they sent me to Umm Salamah for the same purpose as they sent me to Aisha. Umm Salamah replied, "I heard the Prophet ﷺ forbidding the offering of these two rak'at. Once the Prophet ﷺ offered the *Asr* prayer, and then came to me. And at that time an Ansāri women from the tribe of Banū Haram was with me. Then [the Prophet ﷺ] offered those two rak'at, and I sent my [lady] servant to him, saying, "Stand beside him and say [to him]: "Umm Salamah says, "O Allāh's Apostle! Didn't I hear you forbidding the offering of these two rak'at [after the *Asr* prayer] yet I see you offering them?" And if he beckons to you with his hand, then wait behind." So the lady slave did that and the Prophet ﷺ beckoned to her with his hand, and she stayed behind. When the Prophet ﷺ finished his prayer, he said, "O the daughter of Abu Umaiya (i.e. Umm Salamah), you were asking me about these two rak'at after the *Asr* prayer. In fact, some people from the tribe of Abdul Qais came to me to embrace Islām and busied me so much that I did not offer the two rak'at that are offered after the *Dhuhr* compulsory prayer, and these two rak'at [you have seen me offering] make up for those." (Sahīh al-Bukhari)

Abū Salamah narrated that he asked Aisha about the two prostrations (i.e. rak'ahs) that the Messenger of Allah ﷺ used to pray after *Asr*. She said, "He used to pray them before *Asr*, but if he got distracted or forgot them, he would pray them after *Asr*, and if he performed a prayer he would be consistent in it." (Sahīh Muslim)

يَدُومُ عَلَيْهِ صَاحِبُهُ[353]

311. Aisha ﷺ narrated: "The Messenger of Allāh ﷺ once came home while a woman was present at that time. He inquired, 'Who is this woman?' I told him the name of the woman and then said, 'She does not sleep at night.' The Messenger ﷺ said, 'One should offer deeds that befit one's capacity. By Allāh! Allāh will not get bored until you get bored [from the act of worship].'" [Aisha added], "The most beloved of deeds to the Messenger ﷺ were those that were performed with consistency."

Ibn Abdul Barr said,

> The scholars understand the part, "Allāh will not get bored until you get bored" to mean that Allāh will continue to reward the individual until he becomes bored of offering the good deed. Boredom in worship arises when one overburdens himself with that which he cannot bear.

Ibn al-Qayyim said,

> Extremism in worship is of two types. The first type is that which negates the nature of the act of worship. Subsequently, the act is no longer considered to be an act of obedience. Examples of such cases are: a person who adds one unit to an obligatory prayer, fasts everyday or [during the days of *tashrīq*] instead of throwing pebbles, one throws big rocks. The second type is that which causes the person to cease his habitual acts of worship such as praying all night without sleeping, fasting every day except the forbidden days and overburdening oneself with anything similar.

Ibn Rajab said,

> Performing a good deed that the body can bear throughout its

353 Sahīh al-Bukhārī (43) and Sahīh Muslim (785)

anointed time, during one's weakness and strength will uphold the right path, and whoever performs a deed he cannot bear during weakness and sickness may end up discontinuing it.

٣١٢: حَدَّثَنَا أَبُو هِشَامٍ مُحَمَّدُ بْنُ يَزِيدَ الرِّفَاعِيُّ ، قَالَ : حَدَّثَنَا ابْنُ فُضَيْلٍ ، عَنِ الأَعْمَشِ ، عَنْ أَبِي صَالِحٍ ، قَالَ : سَأَلْتُ عَائِشَةَ ، وَأُمَّ سَلَمَةَ ، أَيُّ الْعَمَلِ كَانَ أَحَبَّ إِلَى رَسُولِ اللهِ صلى الله عليه وسلم ؟ قَالَتَا : مَا دِيمَ عَلَيْهِ ، وَإِنْ قَلَّ[354]

312. Abu Sālih narrated: "I enquired from Aisha and Umm Salamah ﵄ about the act that was the most beloved to the Messenger of Allāh ﷺ. Both answered, 'That deed which was practiced continuously, regardless of its size.'"

٣١٣: حَدَّثَنَا مُحَمَّدُ بْنُ إِسْمَاعِيلَ ، قَالَ : حَدَّثَنَا عَبْدُ اللهِ بْنُ صَالِحٍ ، قَالَ : حَدَّثَنِي مُعَاوِيَةُ بْنُ صَالِحٍ ، عَنْ عَمْرِو بْنِ قَيْسٍ ، أَنَّهُ سَمِعَ عَاصِمَ بْنَ حُمَيْدٍ ، قَالَ : سَمِعْتُ عَوْفَ بْنَ مَالِكٍ ، يَقُولُ : كُنْتُ مَعَ رَسُولِ اللهِ صلى الله عليه وسلم ، لَيْلَةً فَاسْتَاكَ ، ثُمَّ تَوَضَّأَ ، ثُمَّ قَامَ يُصَلِّي ، فَقُمْتُ مَعَهُ فَبَدَأَ فَاسْتَفْتَحَ الْبَقَرَةَ ، فَلا يَمُرُّ بِآيَةِ رَحْمَةٍ ، إِلا وَقَفَ فَسَأَلَ ، وَلا يَمُرُّ بِآيَةِ عَذَابٍ ، إِلا وَقَفَ فَتَعَوَّذَ ، ثُمَّ رَكَعَ فَمَكَثَ رَاكِعًا بِقَدْرِ قِيَامِهِ ، وَيَقُولُ فِي رُكُوعِهِ : سُبْحَانَ ذِي الْجَبَرُوتِ وَالْمَلَكُوتِ ، وَالْكِبْرِيَاءِ وَالْعَظَمَةِ ، ثُمَّ سَجَدَ بِقَدْرِ رُكُوعِهِ ، وَيَقُولُ فِي سُجُودِهِ : سُبْحَانَ ذِي الْجَبَرُوتِ وَالْمَلَكُوتِ ، وَالْكِبْرِيَاءِ وَالْعَظَمَةِ ثُمَّ قَرَأَ آلَ عِمْرَانَ ثُمَّ سُورَةً ، يَفْعَلُ مِثْلَ ذَلِكَ فِي كل ركعة[355]

313. 'Awf ibn Mālik ﵁ related: "I spent a night with the Messenger of Allāh ﷺ. He brushed his teeth with the *siwāk*, performed ablution

354 Sunan al-Tirmidhī (2856)
355 Sunan Abū Dawūd (873)

and then stood up to commence the prayer, and so I joined him in the prayer. He began reciting Sūrah al-Baqarah [after al-Fātihah] and whenever he came across an ayah about Allāh's mercy, he paused and beseeched Allāh for His Mercy. Likewise, when he came across an ayah regarding His punishment, he paused and sought refuge in Allāh from His punishment. Then, he bowed and remained bowing for as long as he had spent in the standing posture. He recited whilst bowing, '*Subhāna dhil Malakūti wal Jabarūti wal Kibriyā wal 'Adhamah' Dhul Malakūt.*' Then he prostrated for a similar length to the bowing and recited the same in the prostration. Then, he recited [in the second unit] Sūrah al-Imrān and repeated the same in each unit."

Al-Bajūrī said,

> *Dhul Malakūt* means the One with Dominion and Pride. *Dhul Jabarūti* means the Subduer and Surmounter. *Dhul Kibriyā* means the One who transcends all defects and shortcomings whilst everything submits to Him. *Dhul 'Adhama* means the One Whom nothing can encompass. It is said that *Kibryā* refers to the perfection of His essence while *'Adhamah* refers to the beauty of His Attributes.

Ibn Sayyid al-Nās said,

> This is one of the hadīths that provide a vivid insight into his fear of his Lord ﷻ and his worship.

CHAPTER FORTY FOUR

باب ماجاء في قراءة رسول الله صلى الله عليه وسلم

THE REPORTS PERTAINING TO THE QUR'ĀNIC RECITATION OF THE MESSENGER ﷺ

Ibn al-Qayyim said,

> The Prophet ﷺ used to recite the Qur'ān whilst standing, sitting and lying down. He recited it with ablution and without ablution. The only thing that prevented him from reciting it was the state of major impurity.

٣١٤: حَدَّثَنَا قُتَيْبَةُ بْنُ سَعِيدٍ ، قَالَ : حَدَّثَنَا اللَّيْثُ ، عَنِ ابْنِ أَبِي مُلَيْكَةَ ، عَنْ يَعْلَى بْنِ مَمْلَكٍ ، أَنَّهُ سَأَلَ أُمَّ سَلَمَةَ ، عَنْ قِرَاءَةِ رَسُولِ اللَّهِ صلى الله عليه وسلم ، فَإِذَا هِيَ تَنْعَتُ قِرَاءَةً مُفَسَّرَةً حَرْفًا حَرْفًا [356]

314. Ya'lā ibn Mamlak narrated that he asked Umm Salamah ﵂ about the way the Messenger of Allāh ﷺ recited the Qur'ān, and she described his recitation as clear, thoughtful and slow, letter by letter.

Al-Ghazalī said,

> The recommended way to recite the Qur'ān is to recite it slowly and clearly (Arabic: *tartīl*). It was narrated that Ibn Abbās ﵁ said, "I prefer to recite Sūrah al-Baqarah and al-Imrān slowly and contemplate them than reciting the whole Qur'ān hastily."

٣١٥: حَدَّثَنَا مُحَمَّدُ بْنُ بَشَّارٍ ، قَالَ : حَدَّثَنَا وَهْبُ بْنُ جَرِيرِ بْنِ حَازِمٍ ، قَالَ : حَدَّثَنَا أَبِي ، عَنْ قَتَادَةَ ، قَالَ : قُلْتُ لأَنَسِ بْنِ مَالِكٍ : كَيْفَ كَانَتْ قِرَاءَةُ رَسُولِ اللَّهِ صلى الله عليه وسلم ؟ فَقَالَ : مَدًّا [357]

315. Qatādah narrated: "I asked Anas ibn Mālik ﵁, 'How was the recital of the Messenger of Allāh ﷺ?' He replied, 'He prolonged the recitation of Qur'ān.'"

Al-Taybī said,

> The letters that are prolonged in the recitation of the Qur'ān are three letters, namely (أ – و – ي) and the length of the prolonged letter depends on the letter that follows and whether it is paused or not.

---

356 Sunan Abū Dawūd (1466) and Sunan al-Tirmidhī (2923)
357 Sahīh al-Bukhārī (5045)

٣١٦: حَدَّثَنَا عَلِيُّ بْنُ حُجْرٍ، قَالَ: حَدَّثَنَا يَحْيَى بْنُ سَعِيدٍ الأُمَوِيُّ، عَنِ ابْنِ جُرَيْجٍ، عَنِ ابْنِ أَبِي مُلَيْكَةَ، عَنْ أُمِّ سَلَمَةَ، قَالَتْ: كَانَ النَّبِيُّ صلى الله عليه وسلم، يَقْطَعُ قِرَاءَتَهُ، يَقُولُ: الْحَمْدُ للهِ رَبِّ الْعَالَمِينَ ثُمَّ يَقِفُ، ثُمَّ يَقُولُ: الرَّحْمَنِ الرَّحِيمِ ثُمَّ يَقِفُ، وَكَانَ يَقْرَأُ مَلِكِ يَوْمِ الدِّينِ[358]

316. Umm Salamah ﵂ narrated: "The Prophet ﷺ recited every ayah separately; he recited '*Alhamdulillāhī Rabbil 'Ālamīn*' and paused, then recited '*Ar-Rahmānir Rahīm*' and paused. Then he would pause after reciting '*Mālikī Yawmiddīn*.'"

Al-Sakhawī said,

> This is evidence that he ﷺ used to recite Sūrah al-Fātihah audibly.

Ibn Battal said,

> He ﷺ used to recite in this way to fulfil the command of Allāh to recite the Qur'ān slowly and thoughtfully. Thus, he ﷺ recited in such a manner to teach his nation the way to recite the Qur'ān and how to contemplate it.

Ibn al-Qayyim said,

> The method of recitation mentioned in this hadīth is the most recommended way. It is better to pause after each ayah even if the following ayah depends on the ayah that precedes it.

٣١٧: حَدَّثَنَا قُتَيْبَةُ، قَالَ: حَدَّثَنَا اللَّيْثُ، عَنْ مُعَاوِيَةَ بْنِ صَالِحٍ، عَنْ عَبْدِ اللهِ بْنِ أَبِي قَيْسٍ، قَالَ: سَأَلْتُ عَائِشَةَ، عَنْ قِرَاءَةِ النَّبِيِّ صلى الله عليه وسلم أَكَانَ يُسِرُّ بِالْقِرَاءَةِ أَمْ يَجْهَرُ؟ قَالَتْ: كُلُّ ذَلِكَ قَدْ كَانَ يَفْعَلُ قَدْ كَانَ رُبَّمَا

358 Sunan al-Tirmidhī (2927)

أَسَرَّ وَرُبَّمَا جَهَرَ فَقُلْتُ : الْحَمْدُ للهِ ، الَّذِي جَعَلَ فِي الأَمْرِ سَعَةً [359]

317. 'Abdullāh ibn Abī Qays ﷺ reported: "I inquired from Aisha ﷺ about the recital of the Prophet ﷺ: whether he recited quietly or audibly. She replied, 'He recited in both ways; he recited quietly and audibly.' I said, 'Praise be to Allāh, who has accorded ease in this matter.'"

Al-Nabhānī said,

> Ibn Abbās ﷺ said, "When the Prophet ﷺ recited the Qur'ān in his house, those in the same house would be able to hear his recital but he would not let it reach [to the ears of those] outside his house."

٣١٨: حَدَّثَنَا مَحْمُودُ بْنُ غَيْلانَ ، قَالَ : حَدَّثَنَا وَكِيعٌ ، قَالَ : حَدَّثَنَا مِسْعَرٌ ، عَنْ أَبِي الْعَلاءِ الْعَبْدِيِّ ، عَنْ يَحْيَى بْنِ جَعْدَةَ ، عَنْ أُمِّ هَانِئٍ ، قَالَتْ : كُنْتُ أَسْمَعُ قِرَاءَةَ النَّبِيِّ صلى الله عليه وسلم ، بِاللَّيْلِ وَأَنَا عَلَى عَرِيشِي [360]

318. Umm Hānī' ﷺ narrated: "I heard the Prophet ﷺ reciting the Qur'ān at night, whilst I was upon my bed."

Al-Qasim ibn Salam said,

> Umm Hanī intended to mean that she heard his recitation during the night.

'Abdullāh ibn Sa'īd al-Hadramī said,

> This hadīth refers to an instance when the Prophet ﷺ was in Makkah and he was offering his night prayers next to the Ka'bah. This happened before the time of Hijrah.

---

359 Sunan Abū Dawūd (226)
360 Sunan Ibn Mājah (1349)

٣١٩: حَدَّثَنَا مَحْمُودُ بْنُ غَيْلانَ ، قَالَ : حَدَّثَنَا أَبُو دَاوُدَ ، قَالَ : حَدَّثَنَا شُعْبَةُ ، عَنْ مُعَاوِيَةَ بْنِ قُرَّةَ ، قَالَ : سَمِعْتُ عَبْدَ اللهِ بْنَ مُغَفَّلٍ ، يَقُولُ : رَأَيْتُ النَّبِيَّ صلى الله عليه وسلم ، عَلَى نَاقَتِهِ يَوْمَ الْفَتْحِ ، وَهُوَ يَقْرَأُ : إِنَّا فَتَحْنَا لَكَ فَتْحًا مُبِينًا لِيَغْفِرَ لَكَ اللهُ مَا تَقَدَّمَ مِنْ ذَنْبِكَ وَمَا تَأَخَّرَ ، قَالَ : فَقَرَأَ وَرَجَّعَ ، قَالَ : وَقَالَ مُعَاوِيَةُ بْنُ قُرَّةَ : لَوْلا أَنْ يَجْتَمِعَ النَّاسُ عَلَيَّ لأَخَذْتُ لَكُمْ فِي ذَلِكَ الصَّوْتِ أَوْ قَالَ : اللَّحْنِ [361]

319. 'Abdullāh ibn Mughaffal ؓ narrated: "I saw the Prophet ﷺ riding his camel on the day of the conquest of Makkah and he was reciting, {Indeed, We have given you, [O Muhammad], a clear conquest, that Allāh may forgive for you what preceded of your sin and what will follow.}[362] He ﷺ recited it and did *tarjī*'[363]."

Mu'awiya ibn Qurrah ؓ (a narrator of this hadīth) said, "If I did not fear that people would gather around me, I would have recited it for you in the same tone."

'Abdullāh ibn Sa'īd al-Hadramī said,

> This indicates that reciting audibly is better than reciting inaudibly in some places especially when it is to glorify Allāh and awake the heedless. The conquest referred to is either the conquest of Makkah, as reported from Anas ibn Mālik, or Khaybar, as reported from Mujāhid, or the Hudaybiyyah Truce as reported from the majority because it was the basis of all the conquests that followed.

361 Sahīh al-Bukhārī (4281) and Sahīh Muslim (794)

362 Qur'ān: 48:1-2

363 Translator Note: The scholars differed on the actual meaning of "*tarjī*", some said it refers to the coming and going of sound in the larynx, or technically speaking, rolling of the sound in it, and some said it means beautifying the voice, and some said it happens unwillingly due to joy, and some said it happened when he ﷺ was riding his camel so it happened unwillingly due to the movement of the camel, and some said it means repeating the words in a lower tone.

He ﷺ recited the entire Sūrah of al-Fath as stated in the hadīth mentioned by al-Bukharī. *Tarjī'* means the coming and going of sound and it often happens due to joy as it happened to the Prophet ﷺ on that day.

٣٢٠: حَدَّثَنَا قُتَيْبَةُ بْنُ سَعِيدٍ ، قَالَ : حَدَّثَنَا نُوحُ بْنُ قَيْسٍ الْحُدَّانِيُّ ، عَنْ حُسَامِ بْنِ مِصَكٍّ ، عَنْ قَتَادَةَ ، قَالَ : مَا بَعَثَ اللهُ نَبِيًّا إِلا حَسَنَ الْوَجْهِ ، حَسَنَ الصَّوْتِ ، وَكَانَ نَبِيُّكُمْ صلى الله عليه وسلم حَسَنَ الْوَجْهِ ، حَسَنَ الصَّوْتِ ، وَكَانَ لا يُرَجِّعُ[364]

320. Qatādah ﷺ said: "Allāh blessed every Prophet that He had sent with a beautiful face and beautiful voice. Your Prophet ﷺ had a beautiful face and a beautiful voice, and did not recite with *tarjī'*."

Ibn al-Athīr said,

> This refers to his recital when he was not riding since the instance of the *tarjī'* happened while he was riding.

Muhammad ibn Yūsuf al-Shāmī said,

> Ibn al-Munīr, al-Zarkashī and others commented on the statement of the Prophet ﷺ wherein he mentioned that Prophet Yūsuf ﷺ was given half of the beauty, saying, "Some people think that the other half of beauty, based on this hadīth, is divided among the rest of people while, in fact, it means that Prophet Yūsuf was given half of the beauty given to Prophet Muhammad ﷺ.

٣٢١: حَدَّثَنَا عَبْدُ اللهِ بْنُ عَبْدِ الرَّحْمَنِ ، قَالَ : حَدَّثَنَا يَحْيَى بْنُ حَسَّانَ ، قَالَ : حَدَّثَنَا عَبْدُ الرَّحْمَنِ بْنُ أَبِي الزِّنَادِ ، عَنْ عَمْرِو بْنِ أَبِي عَمْرٍو ، عَنْ عِكْرِمَةَ

---

364 Tabaqat Ibn Sa'd (879)

، عَنِ ابْنِ عَبَّاسٍ ، قَالَ : كَانَتْ قِرَاءَةُ النَّبِيِّ صلى الله عليه وسلم ، رُبَّمَا يَسْمَعُهَا مَنْ فِي الْحُجْرَةِ وَهُوَ فِي الْبَيْتِ[365]

321. 'Abdullāh ibn 'Abbās ؓ narrated: "The recitation of the Prophet ﷺ was audible enough that it might have been possible that if he recited in the house, those in the courtyard would be able to hear it."

Abdul Razzaq al-Badr said,

> This explains the previous hadīths regarding the audibleness of his recitation, which is to state that if he recited audibly in the night then it would be loud enough to be heard by those who were near to him, meaning he did not recite very loudly.

365 Sunan Abu Dawūd (1327)

CHAPTER FORTY FIVE

باب ماجاء في بكاء رسول الله صلى الله عليه وسلم

THE REPORTS PERTAINING TO THE CRYING OF THE MESSENGER OF ALLĀH ﷺ

Ibn al-Qayyim said.

> The nature of his crying was similar to that of his laughing; he neither laughed out loud nor did he laugh boisterously. Likewise when he cried, he neither wailed nor was his breath taken away due to it. Rather, his eyes would shed tears and a sound would emit from his chest; he cried out of his mercy for the deceased and sometimes he cried out of his concern and mercy for his nation. Sometimes he would cry due to his fear of Allāh, and sometimes when he heard the Qur'ān, due to his love of Allāh. Thus embodying the required combination of love and fear of Allāh.

٣٢٢: حَدَّثَنَا سُوَيْدُ بْنُ نَصْرٍ ، قَالَ : حَدَّثَنَا عَبْدُ اللهِ بْنُ الْمُبَارِكِ ، عَنْ حَمَّادِ بْنِ سَلَمَةَ ، عَنْ ثَابِتٍ ، عَنْ مُطَرِّفٍ وَهُوَ ابْنُ عَبْدِ اللهِ بْنِ الشِّخِّيرِ ، عَنْ أَبِيهِ ، قَالَ : أَتَيْتُ رَسُولَ اللهِ صلى الله عليه وسلم وَهُوَ يُصَلِّي ، وَلِجَوْفِهِ أَزِيزٌ كَأَزِيزِ الْمِرْجَلِ مِنَ الْبُكَاءِ[366]

322. 'Abdullāh ibn Shikhīr ؓ narrated: "I entered upon the Messenger of Allāh ﷺ whilst he was praying. Due to his crying, such sound emitted from his chest like that of a boiling kettle."

Abdul-Karīm al-Khudair said,

> This description given by the narrator is to show the high level of humility and piety of the Prophet ﷺ from the effect of the Qur'ān. However, it is unfortunate that many people enter the prayer and end it without being affected by the Qur'ān they recite. The description given in this hadīth is what happens to those who follow the Prophet's example which results from the fear of Allāh that one feels whilst standing before Him in the prayer.
>
> You find some people who are touched by the recitation of some individuals but never feel anything when the same ayāt are recited by someone else. This could be due to the beauty of the voice but one ought to be blamed if he only becomes touched by particular voices and does not get touched if the Qur'ān is recited beautifully by other people. This is because a person should feel touched and effected by the words of the Qur'ān, per se, and so the beauty of the voice should serve to help the person to increase this feeling and not be that which makes the person cry.
>
> Sometimes, there are individuals who we hear cry aloud in the prayer. If this happens because the person is overwhelmed and cannot control himself, then the person is not blamed. It is noticed that the effect on some people is short i.e. they cry when they come across an ayah and after the ayah ends, they return to their normal

366 Sunan Abū Dawūd (904)

status. It should be noted that the real crying that affects the heart is that which does not end quickly. It was reported that many of the righteous predecessors would fall sick in the next morning because of their crying in the night while praying. Thus, the heart which cannot maintain this effect is indicative of the effect being weak upon it. I saw during the last Ramadān someone who was weeping out loud in the prayer and after the prayer ended he entered into a verbal altercation with other people over some issue. This shows that the heart is still taken away by this worldly life and the sins are not yet cleansed.

٣٢٣: حَدَّثَنَا مَحْمُودُ بْنُ غَيْلانَ ، قَالَ : حَدَّثَنَا مُعَاوِيَةُ بْنُ هِشَامٍ ، قَالَ : حَدَّثَنَا سُفْيَانُ ، عَنِ الأَعْمَشِ ، عَنْ إِبْرَاهِيمَ ، عَنْ عُبَيْدَةَ ، عَنْ عَبْدِ اللهِ بْنِ مَسْعُودٍ ، قَالَ : قَالَ لِي رَسُولُ اللهِ صلى الله عليه وسلم : اقْرَأْ عَلَيَّ فَقُلْتُ : يَا رَسُولَ اللهِ ، أَقَرَأُ عَلَيْكَ وَعَلَيْكَ أُنْزِلَ ، قَالَ : إِنِّي أُحِبُّ أَنْ أَسْمَعَهُ مِنْ غَيْرِي ، فَقَرَأْتُ سُورَةَ النِّسَاءِ ، حَتَّى بَلَغْتُ وَجِئْنَا بِكَ عَلَى هَؤُلاءِ شَهِيدًا ، قَالَ : فَرَأَيْتُ عَيْنَيْ رَسُولِ اللهِ تَهمِلانِ[367]

323. 'Abdullāh ibn Mas'ūd ﵁ related: "The Messenger of Allāh ﷺ once asked me to recite the Qur'ān to him. I said, 'O Messenger of Allāh! How could I recite it to you when it has been revealed to you?' He ﷺ said, 'I love to hear it from other people.' Thereupon I began reciting Sūrah al-Nisā and when I reached this ayah, {But how [will it be with them] when We bring of every people a witness, and We bring thee [O Muhammad] a witness against these?}[368] I saw tears begin to flow from the eyes of the Messenger of Allāh ﷺ."

Al-Qastalanī said,

This effect is what a person would have when listening to the

367 Sahīh al-Bukhārī (4582) and Sahīh Muslim (800)
368 Qur'ān: 4:41

Qur'ān with his heart and not just his ears. Allāh ﷻ said: **{And when they hear what has been revealed to the Messenger, you see their eyes overflowing with tears because of what they have recognized of the truth.}**[369]

Alī al-Qārī said,

> Ibn Battal said: "It is possible that he ﷺ requested to hear the Qur'ān from Ibn Mas'ūd ؓ to show that listening to the Qur'ān is Sunnah (even if the person has memorised it) or to contemplate it and reflect upon it because the listener is more focused and more able to contemplate than the reciter who is busy reciting."

Abū Hafs al-Sūhrawardī said,

> This is indeed the truthful manner for listening to the Qur'ān. It is a truthfulness that no two believers would ever dispute over its truthfulness, and evidence testifying to the guidance of the person who is listening in such a lofty manner. The ignited flame of this thoughtful listening overcomes the coldness of certainty, causing the eyes to be flushed with tears. The combination of the element of certainty with the element of attentive and thoughtful listening brings forth different emotions; sometimes it produces grief, which is an enkindled emotion, and some other times it brings forth the flames of yearning, which is an enkindled emotion, and sometimes it sets the fire of regret, which is also an enkindled emotion. If listening to the Qur'ān manages to call forth these emotions from a heart that is filled with the coolness of certainty, the eyes will have no power but to release the tears therein because water is a result of the engagement between heat and cold. When the heat of listening emerges into the layers of the heart, its effect reflects on the bodily limbs through goose bumps; Allāh ﷻ said: **{Allāh has sent down the best statement: a consistent Book wherein is reiteration. The skins shiver there from of those who fear their**

369 Qur'ān: 5:83

Lord.}[370] And when its effect escalates, it reaches into the brain causing the eyes to drop its tears, and when its effect crosses the borders and reaches into the soul, the waves can no longer be constrained within and so crying and disturbance manifest upon the body. Each person, depending on his level, experiences these conditions.

٣٢٤: حَدَّثَنَا قُتَيْبَةُ ، قَالَ : حَدَّثَنَا جَرِيرٌ ، عَنْ عَطَاءِ بْنِ السَّائِبِ ، عَنْ أَبِيهِ ، عَنْ عَبْدِ اللهِ بْنِ عَمْرٍو ، قَالَ : انْكسفَتِ الشَّمْسُ يَوْمًا عَلَى عَهْدِ رَسُولِ اللهِ صلى الله عليه وسلم ، فَقَامَ رَسُولُ اللهِ صلى الله عليه وسلم يُصَلِّي ، حَتَّى لَمْ يَكَدْ يَرْكَعُ ثُمَّ رَكَعَ ، فَلَمْ يَكَدْ يَرْفَعُ رَأْسَهُ ، ثُمَّ رَفَعَ رَأْسَهُ ، فَلَمْ يَكَدْ أَنْ يَسْجُدَ ، ثُمَّ سَجَدَ فَلَمْ يَكَدْ أَنْ يَرْفَعَ رَأْسَهُ ، ثُمَّ رَفَعَ رَأْسَهُ ، فَلَمْ يَكَدْ أَنْ يَسْجُدَ ، ثُمَّ سَجَدَ فَلَمْ يَكَدْ أَنْ يَرْفَعَ رَأْسَهُ ، فَجَعَلَ يَنْفُخُ وَيَبْكِي ، وَيَقُولُ : رَبِّ أَلَمْ تَعِدْنِي أَنْ لا تُعَذِّبَهُمْ وَأَنَا فِيهِمْ ؟ رَبِّ أَلَمْ تَعِدْنِي أَنْ لا تُعَذِّبَهُمْ وَهُمْ يَسْتَغْفِرُونَ ؟ وَنَحْنُ نَسْتَغْفِرُكَ فَلَمَّا صَلَّى رَكْعَتَيْنِ انْجَلَتِ الشَّمْسُ ، فَقَامَ فَحَمِدَ اللهَ تَعَالَى ، وَأَثْنَى عَلَيْهِ ، ثُمَّ قَالَ : إِنَّ الشَّمْسَ وَالْقَمَرَ آيَتَانِ مِنْ آيَاتِ اللهِ لا يَنْكَسِفَانِ لِمَوْتِ أَحَدٍ وَلا لِحَيَاتِهِ ، فَإِذَا انْكَسَفَا ، فَافْزَعُوا إِلَى ذِكْرِ اللهِ تَعَالَى[371]

324. 'Abdullāh ibn 'Amr ؓ narrated: "In the time of the Messenger of Allāh ﷺ there once occurred a solar eclipse. Subsequently, the Messenger of Allāh ﷺ began to pray and he stood for such a period that it seemed that he did not intend to bow. He then remained bowing to such an extent that it seemed that he did not intend to rise. Then in the same manner after standing up from bowing, he stood for such a long period that it seemed that he did not intend to prostrate. He remained in the position of prostration for such a

370 Qur'ān: 29:23

371 Musnad Ahmad (6483)

long period that it seemed that he did not intend to raise his head. In this manner he did the same after lifting his head and sitting between the two prostrations. He did the same [as he did in the first prostration] in the second one. After he arose from the prostration he began breathing heavily and crying whilst pleading, 'O Allāh! You have promised me that you will not punish them so long as I am among them. O Allāh! You have promised me that you will not punish them while they seek forgiveness. O Allāh! We beseech you for your forgiveness.'

When he ﷺ completed the prayer, the sun had already cleared. Thereupon, he ﷺ delivered a sermon wherein he praised and exalted Allāh ﷻ then he said, 'Indeed, the sun and moon are from the signs of Allāh that do not eclipse because of the death or birth of anyone. Whenever eclipses happen, hasten to resort to the remembrance of Allāh.'"

Abdul Karīm al-Khudair said,

> The Prophet ﷺ refuted the claim of the disbelievers before Islam that eclipses occur because of the death of persons who possess great status. This great sign is taken lightly today because the people perceive it as a mere natural phenomenon whose time of occurrence can be expected based on calculation. In other words, people have started to look at it through the lens of science to the extent that they will buy sunglasses and travel to other countries just to watch an eclipse while they should fear Allāh and rush to perform prayers in light of the guidance of the Prophet ﷺ in this regard.

Muhib al-Dīn al-Tabarī said,

> It coincided on this day that the son of the Prophet ﷺ died. The sun would often eclipse, according to their observations, on the twenty eighth or twenty ninth of the month. Thus, when they saw it had eclipsed on the tenth they said it must have eclipsed due to

the death of the son of the Prophet ﷺ.

Abū al-Hasan al-Nadwī said,

> Had this emotional sad event (i.e. the death of the son of the Prophet ﷺ) happened to any other leader, ruler or preacher, the least they would have done is to remain silent so as not to negate the speculations of people about the relation between the event and the occurrence of the eclipse. This is because the occurrence would serve their cause and movements and would allow them to enforce a layer of glorification that would make people trust them more. However, in this great event, the position of the Prophet ﷺ stands out, drawing the line between Prophets and all other leaders due to his refusal to take advantage of any event to attract more praise and glorification. This is why Allāh ﷻ prescribed to pray upon the occurrence of this event so as to prevent any opportunity for this deviated notion to grow in the hearts of people and strengthen the bond between the people and Allāh ﷻ.

٣٢٥: حَدَّثَنَا مَحْمُودُ بْنُ غَيْلانَ ، قَالَ : حَدَّثَنَا أَبُو أَحْمَدَ ، قَالَ : حَدَّثَنَا سُفْيَانُ ، عَنْ عَطَاءِ بْنِ السَّائِبِ ، عَنْ عِكْرِمَةَ ، عَنِ ابْنِ عَبَّاسٍ ، قَالَ : أَخَذَ رَسُولُ اللهِ صلى الله عليه وسلم ابْنَةً لَهُ تَقْضِي فَاحْتَضَنَهَا فَوَضَعَهَا بَيْنَ يَدَيْهِ ، فَمَاتَتْ وَهِيَ بَيْنَ يَدَيْهِ وَصَاحَتْ أُمُّ أَيْمَنَ ، فَقَالَ يَعْنِي صلى الله عليه وسلم : أَتَبْكِينَ عِنْدَ رَسُولِ اللهِ ؟ فَقَالَتْ : أَلَسْتُ أَرَاكَ تَبْكِي ؟ قَالَ : إِنِّي لَسْتُ أَبْكِي ، إِنَّمَا هِيَ رَحْمَةٌ ، إِنَّ الْمُؤْمِنَ بِكُلِّ خَيْرٍ عَلَى كُلِّ حَالٍ ، إِنَّ نَفْسَهُ تُنْزَعُ مِنْ بَيْنِ جَنْبَيْهِ ، وَهُوَ يَحْمَدُ اللهَ تعالى[372]

325. 'Abdullāh ibn Abbās ؓ related: "One of the daughters of the Messenger of Allāh ﷺ was on her death bed. He picked her up and placed her before him. Thus she passed away whilst in front of him.

---

372 Musnad Ahmad (2412)

Umm Ayman began wailing aloud at her passing. The Messenger of Allāh ﷺ said, 'Are you crying in the presence of the Messenger of Allāh!?' She said, 'Do I not see you cry?' He replied, 'The tears you see are not from crying, but rather they are a mercy from Allāh. A believer is in a good state at all times, his soul is taken out whilst still praising Allāh ﷻ.'"

'Abdullāh ibn Sa'īd al-Hadramī said,

> It is prohibited to wail loudly but as she saw him shedding tears she thought what she did was permissible. This is why when he ﷺ admonished her act, she replied, "I saw you crying." Meaning, "I followed your guidance and I thought it is allowed to wail along with shedding the tears." The response of the Prophet ﷺ was to teach her that he was not crying due to an inability to be patient or due to panic but rather his tears fell due to the mercy that Allāh had planted in his heart. This hadīth does not contradict the hadīth wherein Aisha رضي الله عنها mentioned that, "The Prophet ﷺ never cried over a dead person; the most he would do was to hold his own beard." This is because she meant that he never cried due to grieving over the deceased but his tears were due to his mercy for his nation.

٣٢٦: حَدَّثَنَا مُحَمَّدُ بْنُ بَشَّارٍ ، قَالَ : حَدَّثَنَا عَبْدُ الرَّحْمَنِ بْنُ مَهْدِيٍّ ، قَالَ : حَدَّثَنَا سُفْيَانُ ، عَنْ عَاصِمِ بْنِ عُبَيْدِ اللهِ ، عَنِ الْقَاسِمِ بْنِ مُحَمَّدٍ ، عَنْ عَائِشَةَ ، أَنَّ رَسُولَ اللهِ صلى الله عليه وسلم ، قَبَّلَ عُثْمَانَ بْنَ مَظْعُونٍ وَهُوَ مَيِّتٌ وَهُوَ يَبْكِي أَوْ قَالَ : عَيْنَاهُ تَهْرَاقَانِ[373]

326. Aisha رضي الله عنها narrated: "The Messenger of Allāh ﷺ kissed [the forehead] of 'Uthmān ibn Madh'ūn رضي الله عنه [after his death] and his eyes were shedding tears whilst he was doing so."

Abdul Muhsin al-Abbad said,

---

373 Sunan Abū Dawūd (3163) and Sunan Ibn Mājah (1456)

This shows that kissing the dead is permissible and there are other hadīths that indicate this permissibility.

Ibn al-Qayyim said,

> From the guidance of the Prophet ﷺ is to cover the face and body of the deceased and to close the eyes of the person. Sometimes he would kiss the deceased just as he did with 'Uthmān ibn Madh'ūn.

٣٢٧: حَدَّثَنَا إِسْحَاقُ بْنُ مَنْصُورٍ ، قَالَ : أَخْبَرَنَا أَبُو عَامِرٍ ، قَالَ : حَدَّثَنَا فُلَيْحٌ وَهُوَ ابْنُ سُلَيْمَانَ ، عَنْ هِلَالِ بْنِ عَلِيٍّ ، عَنْ أَنَسِ بْنِ مَالِكٍ ، قَالَ : شَهِدْنَا ابْنَةً لِرَسُولِ اللهِ صلى الله عليه وسلم ، وَرَسُولُ اللهِ جَالِسٌ عَلَى الْقَبْرِ ، فَرَأَيْتُ عَيْنَيْهِ تَدمَعَانِ ، فَقَالَ : أَفِيكُمْ رَجُلٌ لَمْ يُقَارِفِ اللَّيْلَةَ ؟ ، قَالَ أَبُو طَلْحَةَ : أَنَا ، قَالَ : انْزِلْ فَنَزَلَ فِي قَبْرِهَا [374]

327. Anas ibn Mālik ؓ reported: "We witnessed with the Messenger of Allāh ﷺ the burial of one of his daughters. He was sitting next to the grave whilst the tears flowed from his eyes. The Messenger of Allāh ﷺ said, 'Is there any person here who did not have sexual relations today.' Abū Talhah ؓ replied, 'I did not.' The Prophet ﷺ told him to enter the grave and so he entered her grave and buried her."

Abdul Muhsin al-Abbad said,

> This hadīth indicates that a person who has sexual relations on the same day should not enter the grave to bury the deceased.

Al-Qastalanī said,

> The reason Abū Talhah ؓ was given precedence over 'Uthmān ؓ (the husband of Umm Kulthūm ؓ) was because 'Uthmān had

374 Sahīh al-Bukhārī (1285)

sexual intercourse with one of his women that night and so the Prophet ﷺ did not want him to enter the grave of his wife. This was because he ﷺ did not like that he left his wife on her death bed to fulfil his desires. It is possible that the sickness of his wife was long and 'Uthmān needed to fulfil his desire that night and did not think she may die on the same night.

CHAPTER FORTY SIX

باب ماجاء في فراش رسول اللّه صلى اللّه عليه وسلم

THE REPORTS PERTAINING TO THE BED OF THE MESSENGER OF ALLĀH ﷺ

Abdul Razzaq al-Badr said,

> The Prophet ﷺ slept only to provide his body with rest and thus he would not oversleep, sufficing with the amount of sleep that provided this. It is for this reason that he did not sleep upon luxurious mattresses or beds. This is because he had great things to achieve in his lifetime, for he is the Messenger of Allāh and the role model for mankind.

٣٢٨: حَدَّثَنَا عَلِيُّ بْنُ حُجْرٍ ، قَالَ : حَدَّثَنَا عَلِيُّ بْنُ مُسْهِرٍ ، عَنْ هِشَامِ بْنِ عُرْوَةَ ، عَنْ أَبِيهِ ، عَنْ عَائِشَةَ ، قَالَ : إِنَّمَا كَانَ فِرَاشُ رَسُولِ اللهِ صلى الله عليه وسلم ، الَّذِي يَنَامُ عَلَيْهِ مِنْ أَدَمٍ ، حَشْوُهُ لِيفٌ [375]

328. Aisha ﵂ narrated: "The bed on which the Messenger of Allāh ﷺ slept upon was made of leather stuffed with the fibre of palm trees."

Al-Qadī 'Iyyād said,

> This indicates the permissibility of pillows, sleeping pads and to have sleeping pads that are made of leather and stuffed.

Ibn al-Jawzī said,

> Aisha ﵂ narrated, "A woman from the Ansār visited me and saw that the pad on which the Prophet ﷺ used to lie on was a folded robe so she left and returned with a pad filled with wool. The Messenger of Allāh ﷺ came afterwards and saw it so he asked about it. I mentioned to him what happened so he told me to return it three times but as he saw that I liked it and wanted to keep it he said, 'O Aisha, return it for by Allāh if I wanted, Allāh would have given me mountains of gold and silver.'"[376]

٣٢٩: حَدَّثَنَا أَبُو الْخَطَّابِ زِيَادُ بْنُ يَحْيَى الْبَصْرِيُّ ، قَالَ : حَدَّثَنَا عَبْدُ اللهِ بْنُ مَيْمُونٍ ، قَالَ : حَدَّثَنَا جَعْفَرُ بْنُ مُحَمَّدٍ ، عَنْ أَبِيهِ ، قَالَ : سُئِلَتْ عَائِشَةُ ، : - وَسُئِلَتْ حَفْصَةُ ، مَا كَانَ فِرَاشُ رَسُولِ اللهِ صلى الله عليه وسلم فِي بَيْتِكِ ؟ قَالَتْ : مِسْحًا نَثْنِيهِ ثَنِيَّتَيْنِ فَيَنَامُ عَلَيْهِ ، فَلَمَّا كَانَ ذَاتَ لَيْلَةٍ ، قُلْتُ : لَوْ ثَنَيْتَهُ أَرْبَعَ ثَنْيَاتٍ ، لَكَانَ أَوْطَأَ لَهُ ، فَثَنَيْنَاهُ لَهُ بِأَرْبَعِ ثَنْيَاتٍ ، فَلَمَّا أَصْبَحَ ، قَالَ : مَا فَرَشْتُمْ لِيَ اللَّيْلَةَ قَالَتْ : قُلْنَا : هُوَ فِرَاشُكَ ، إِلا أَنَّا ثَنَيْنَاهُ بِأَرْبَعِ ثَنْيَاتٍ ،

375 Sahīh al-Bukhārī (6456) and Sahīh Muslim (2082)
376 Al-Mu'jam al-Awsat [6195)

قُلْنَا : هُوَ أَوْطَأُ لَكَ ، قَالَ : رُدُّوهُ لِحَالَتِهِ الأُولَى ، فَإِنَّهُ مَنَعَتْنِي وَطَاءَتُهُ صَلاتِيَ اللَّيْلَةَ [377]

329. Muhammad al-Baqir narrated that someone asked Aisha ﵂ [... to the end of the previous hadith] and then asked Hafsah ﵂: "How was the bed of the Messenger of Allāh ﷺ in your house?" She replied: "It was a rough canvas made of wool folded into two, which was spread for him to sleep on. On one night we thought if we folded it into four and spread it, it would become more comfortable and so we folded it and spread it that way. In the morning, he asked, 'What did you spread out for me last night?' We replied, 'It was your bed but we folded it into four so that it may become softer.' He ﷺ said, 'Leave it in its original state. Its softness prevented me from praying the night prayers.'"

'Abdullāh ibn Sa'īd al-Hadramī said,

> The Prophet ﷺ thought that his sleeping pad was changed as he noticed it felt softer and he asked his wife to fold it into two layers (the manner in which he was accustomed to) because a softer bed can cause one to fall into deep sleep.

377 Akhlāq al-Nabi (454)

CHAPTER FORTY SEVEN

باب ماجاء في تواضع رسول الله صلى الله عليه وسلم

THE REPORTS PERTAINING TO THE HUMILITY OF THE MESSENGER OF ALLĀH ﷺ

Abdul Razzaq al-Badr said,

> Humility is to show kindness in treatment and interaction, and also to refrain from false pride and arrogance. The humility of the Prophet ﷺ manifested in his mannerisms, character and dealings with people as will be explained in this chapter.

٣٣٠: حَدَّثَنَا أَحْمَدُ بْنُ مَنِيعٍ ، وَسَعِيدُ بْنُ عَبْدِ الرَّحْمَنِ الْمَخْزُومِيُّ ، وَغَيْرُ وَاحِدٍ ، قَالُوا : حَدَّثَنَا سُفْيَانُ بْنُ عُيَيْنَةَ ، عَنِ الزُّهْرِيِّ ، عَنْ عُبَيْدِ اللهِ ، عَنِ ابْنِ عَبَّاسٍ ، عَنْ عُمَرَ بْنِ الْخَطَّابِ ، قَالَ : قَالَ رَسُولُ اللهِ صلى الله عليه وسلم : لاَ تُطْرُونِي كَمَا أَطْرَتِ النَّصَارَى ابْنَ مَرْيَمَ ، إِنَّمَا أَنَا عَبْدٌ ، فَقُولُوا : عَبْدُ اللهِ وَرَسُولُهُ[378]

330. 'Umar ibn al-Khattab ﷺ narrated: "The Messenger of Allāh ﷺ said, 'Do not over praise me as the Christians over praised Īsa ibn Maryam ﷺ for I am just a slave of Allāh, so call me the slave of Allāh and His Messenger.'"

Ibn Shamah said,

> Apart from the fact that the Mawlid is an innovation, it often includes other wrongdoings such as mixing between men and women, songs, musical instruments, liquor and drugs. However, what is even worse is the major shirk committed when they go to extremes towards the Messenger of Allāh ﷺ or any awliyā' by seeking his or their help and believing he knows the future and such similar acts of disbelief that people do when they celebrate the birthday of the Prophet ﷺ. They do such acts even though they have been ordered not to go to extremes in praise for him ﷺ as reported in the hadīth.
>
> The irony is that many people are enthusiastic, energetic and keen to attend these innovated celebrations whilst you will find them too slack and lazy to attend that which Allāh has dictated for them to attend such as the congregational and Friday prayers and still they do not find their slackness as a serious issue. Evidently, this is due to their weak *imān*, poor insight of their hearts and the many sins that cover their hearts. We ask Allāh to protect us from all of that, for us and all Muslims.

378 Sahīh al-Bukhārī (2462) and Sahīh Muslim (1691)

Ibn Hajar al-Asqalānī said,

> The admonished over praise that is mentioned in this hadīth refers to that which is false praise. This is similar to how the Christians praise Jesus ﷺ with false praise when they claim that he is the son of God.

٣٣١: حَدَّثَنَا عَلِيُّ بْنُ حُجْرٍ ، قَالَ : حَدَّثَنَا سُوَيْدُ بْنُ عَبْدِ الْعَزِيزِ ، عَنْ حُمَيْدٍ ، عَنْ أَنَسِ بْنِ مَالِكٍ ، أَنَّ امْرَأَةً جَاءَتْ إِلَى النَّبِيِّ صلى الله عليه وسلم ، فَقَالَتْ لَهُ : إِنَّ لِي إِلَيْكَ حَاجَةً ، فَقَالَ : اجْلِسِي فِي أَيِّ طَرِيقِ الْمَدِينَةِ شِئْتِ ، أَجْلِسْ إِلَيْكِ[379]

331. Anas ibn Mālik ﷺ reported: "A woman came to the Prophet ﷺ and said, 'I wish to speak to you in private.' He replied, 'Choose any street of Madīnah and I will come there and listen to you.'"

Al-Nawawī said,

> This hadīth shows the closeness of the Prophet ﷺ to his people and his desire to help people have their rights fulfilled and guide those who need guidance, so that people can see his actions and follow his example. This hadīth does not condone sitting with women in privacy as [the Prophet ﷺ made it a point to meet her in public]. They met on the road and though people were passing by, no one could hear her question as she wanted to ask it in private.

٣٣٢: حَدَّثَنَا عَلِيُّ بْنُ حُجْرٍ ، قَالَ : حَدَّثَنَا عَلِيُّ بْنُ مُسْهِرٍ ، عَنْ مُسْلِمٍ الأَعْوَرِ ، عَنْ أَنَسِ بْنِ مَالِكٍ ، قَالَ : كَانَ رَسُولُ اللهِ صلى الله عليه وسلم يَعُودُ الْمَرِيضَ ، وَيَشْهَدُ الْجَنَائِزَ ، وَيَرْكَبُ الْحِمَارَ ، وَيُجِيبُ دَعْوَةَ الْعَبْدِ ، وَكَانَ يَوْمَ

379 Sunan Abū Dawūd (4818)

بَنِي قُرَيْظَةَ عَلَى حِمَارٍ مَخْطُومٍ بِحَبْلٍ مِنْ لِيفٍ ، وَعَلَيْهِ إِكَافٌ مِنْ لِيفٍ[380]

332. Anas ibn Mālik ﷺ related: "The Messenger of Allāh ﷺ would visit the sick, attend funerals, ride donkeys and accept the invitations of slaves. On the day of the battle of Banu Quraydhah, he rode upon a donkey, the reigns of which were made of date palm leaves, and the saddle was also made of date palm leaves."

'Abdullāh ibn Sa'īd said,

> Some people preferred solitude and that made them lose the immense reward of these good deeds despite the fact that their solitude brought forth great benefit to them.
>
> The guidance of the Prophet ﷺ when visiting the sick is to sit near his head and then inquire about the condition of the person's health.
>
> He used to attend the *janazah* and witness the burial of the deceased. The way of the Prophet ﷺ when walking in funerals was that his sadness would manifest upon him, he would speak little and he would be engaged in contemplation of the event.

٣٣٣: حَدَّثَنَا وَاصِلُ بْنُ عَبْدِ الأَعْلَى الْكُوفِيُّ ، قَالَ : حَدَّثَنَا مُحَمَّدُ بْنُ فُضَيْلٍ ، عَنِ الأَعْمَشِ ، عَنْ أَنَسِ بْنِ مَالِكٍ ، قَالَ : كَانَ النَّبِيُّ صلى الله عليه وسلم ، يُدْعَى إِلَى خُبْزِ الشَّعِيرِ ، وَالإِهَالَةِ السَّنِخَةِ ، فَيُجِيبُ وَلَقَدْ كَانَ لَهُ دِرْعٌ عِنْدَ يَهُودِيٍّ ، فَمَا وَجَدَ مَا يَفُكُّهَا حَتَّى مَاتَ[381]

333. Anas ibn Mālik ﷺ narrated: "The Messenger of Allāh ﷺ accepted and attended invitations to places where bread made of barley and days old stale fat was served. The armour he possessed had been pawned to a Jew. [He passed away] without possessing a sufficient amount to release it."'

380 Sunan Ibn Mājah (2296) and Sunan al-Tirmidhī (1017)
381 Musnad Ahmad (11993)

'Abdullāh ibn Sa'īd said,

> This shows that it is allowed to eat old food so long as it does not cause harm. The story of the armour is that he ﷺ pawned it for thirty *sā'* of barley as stated in Sahīh al-Bukharī, and the name of the armour was "Dhāt al-Fudūl" as stated by Ibn al-Qayyim. The reason he ﷺ went to the Jewish man instead of his companions was to show that dealing with Jews and pawnbrokers is permissible and because the companions would not agree to take money from him ﷺ or accept it as a pawn type agreement. The armour was released by Abū Bakr [after the Prophet's ﷺ death] and handed to Alī ibn Abī Tālib ؓ. The hadīth also shows the rigorous self-discipline employed by the Prophet ﷺ.

٣٣٤: حَدَّثَنَا مَحْمُودُ بْنُ غَيْلانَ ، قَالَ : حَدَّثَنَا أَبُو دَاوُدَ الْحُفَرِيُّ ، عَنْ سُفْيَانَ ، عَنِ الرَّبِيعِ بْنِ صَبِيحٍ ، عَنْ يَزِيدَ بْنِ أَبَانَ ، عَنْ أَنَسِ بْنِ مَالِكٍ ، قَالَ : حَجَّ رَسُولُ اللهِ صلى الله عليه وسلم ، عَلَى رَحْلٍ رَثٍّ ، وَعَلَيْهِ قَطِيفَةٌ ، لا تُسَاوِي أَرْبَعَةَ دَرَاهِمَ ، فَقَالَ : اللَّهُمَّ اجْعَلْهُ حَجًّا ، لا رِيَاءَ فِيهِ ، وَلا سُمْعَةَ[382]

334. Anas ibn Mālik ؓ narrated: "The Messenger of Allāh ﷺ performed Hajj upon an old and worn saddle. On it was a piece of cloth, the value of which did not equate to four Dirhams. He ﷺ supplicated, 'O Allāh! Make this Hajj one that has no element of showing off or seeking fame.'"

Al-Zarqanī said,

> Despite the infallibility of the Prophet ﷺ and the impossibility that he would do an act for fame or showing off, he asked Allāh to make his Hajj free from these two traits due to his great humility and his consideration of himself as just a normal person. This is because ostentation and seeking fame can easily creep upon

382 Sunan Ibn Mājah (2890)

someone mounting a fancy ride and wearing fancy garments.

'Abdullāh ibn Sa'īd said,

> Given that Hajj entails detachment from all worldly pleasures, it befitted the most that he ﷺ manifested the highest level of humility in this event.

٣٣٥: حَدَّثَنَا عَبْدُ اللهِ بْنُ عَبْدِ الرَّحْمَنِ ، قَالَ : حَدَّثَنَا عَفَّانُ ، قَالَ : حَدَّثَنَا حَمَّادُ بْنُ سَلَمَةَ ، عَنْ حُمَيْدٍ ، عَنْ أَنَسِ بْنِ مَالِكٍ ، قَالَ : لَمْ يَكُنْ شَخْصٌ أَحَبَّ إِلَيْهِمْ مِنْ رَسُولِ اللهِ صلى الله عليه وسلم ، قَالَ : وَكَانُوا إِذَا رَأَوْهُ لَمْ يَقُومُوا ، لِمَا يَعْلَمُونَ مِنْ كَرَاهَتِهِ لِذَلِكَ[383]

335. Anas ibn Mālik ؓ narrated: "There was no individual more beloved to the companions than the Messenger of Allāh ﷺ. When they saw him they would not stand up as they knew that he disliked it."

Ibn Hajar al-Asqalānī said,

> Al-Nawawī said that the reason he ﷺ disliked them standing up for him is he feared that this would lead to them over glorifying him just as he stated, "Do not over praise me." However, he did not dislike that they stand up for each other because he stood up for some of his companions and they stood up for other people in his presence and he did not object to this. The other reason is that the level of love and bond between him and his companions was perfect to the extent that standing up would not have manifested more love or honouring.

٣٣٦: حَدَّثَنَا سُفْيَانُ بْنُ وَكِيعٍ ، قَالَ : حَدَّثَنَا جُمَيْعُ بْنُ عُمَرَ بْنِ عَبْدِ الرَّحْمَنِ

---

383 Sunan al-Tirmidhi (2754)

الْعِجْلِيُّ ، قَالَ : أَنْبَأَنَا رَجُلٌ مِنْ بَنِي تَمِيمٍ مِنْ وَلَدِ أَبِي هَالَةَ زَوْجِ خَدِيجَةَ ، يُكْنَى أَبَا عَبْدِ الله ، عَنِ ابْنٍ لأَبِي هَالَةَ ، عَنِ الْحَسَنِ بْنِ عَلِيٍّ ، قَالَ : سَأَلْتُ خَالِي هِنْدَ بْنَ أَبِي هَالَةَ ، وَكَانَ وَصَّافًا عَنْ حِلْيَةِ رَسُولِ الله صلى الله عليه وسلم ، وَأَنَا أَشْتَهِي أَنْ يَصِفَ لِي مِنْهَا شَيْئًا ، فَقَالَ : كَانَ رَسُولُ الله صلى الله عليه وسلم فَخْمًا مُفَخَّمًا، يَتَلَأْلأُ وَجْهُهُ تَلأْلُؤَ الْقَمَرِ لَيْلَةَ الْبَدْرِ، فَذَكَرَ الْحُدِيثَ بِطُولِهِ ، قالَ الْحَسَنُ: فَكَتَّمْتُهَا الْحُسَيْنَ زَمَانًا، ثُمَّ حَدَّثْتُهُ فَوَجَدْتُهُ قَدْ سَبَقَنِي إِلَيْهِ. فَسَأَلَهُ عَمَّا سَأَلْتُهُ عَنْهُ وَوَجَدْتُهُ قَدْ سَأَلَ أَبَاهُ عَنْ مَدْخَلِهِ وَمَخْرَجِهِ وَشَكْلِهِ فَلَمْ يَدَعْ مِنْهُ شَيْئًا. قَالَ الْحُسَيْنُ: فَسَأَلْتُ أَبِي، عَنْ دُخُولِ رَسُولِ اللهِ صَلَّى اللهُ عَلَيْهِ وَسَلَّمَ فَقَالَ: كَانَ إِذَا أَوَى إِلَى مَنْزِلِهِ جَزَّأَ دُخُولَهُ ثَلَاثَةَ أَجْزَاءٍ، جُزْءًا للهِ، وَجُزْءًا لِأَهْلِهِ، وَجُزْءًا لِنَفْسِهِ، ثُمَّ جَزَّأَ جُزْأَهُ بَيْنَهُ وَبَيْنَ النَّاسِ، فَيَرُدُّ ذَلِكَ بِالْخَاصَّةِ عَلَى الْعَامَّةِ، وَلَا يَدَّخِرُ عَنْهُمْ شَيْئًا، وَكَانَ مِنْ سِيرَتِهِ فِي جُزْءِ الْأُمَّةِ إِيثَارُ أَهْلِ الْفَضْلِ بِإِذْنِهِ وَقَسْمِهِ عَلَى قَدْرِ فَضْلِهِمْ فِي الدِّينِ، فَمِنْهُمْ ذُو الْحَاجَةِ، وَمِنْهُمْ ذُو الْحَاجَتَيْنِ، وَمِنْهُمْ ذُو الْحَوَائِجِ، فَيَتَشَاغَلُ بِهِمْ وَيَشْغَلُهُمْ فِيمَا يُصْلِحُهُمْ وَالْأُمَّةَ مِنْ مُسَاءَلَتِهِمْ عَنْهُ وَإِخْبَارِهِمْ بِالَّذِي يَنْبَغِي لَهُمْ وَيَقُولُ: «لِيُبَلِّغِ الشَّاهِدُ مِنْكُمُ الْغَائِبَ، وَأَبْلِغُونِي حَاجَةَ مَنْ لَا يَسْتَطِيعُ إِبْلَاغَهَا، فَإِنَّهُ مَنْ أَبْلَغَ سُلْطَانًا حَاجَةَ مَنْ لَا يَسْتَطِيعُ إِبْلَاغَهَا ثَبَّتَ اللهُ قَدَمَيْهِ يَوْمَ الْقِيَامَةِ» ، لَا يُذْكَرُ عِنْدَهُ إِلَا ذَلِكَ، وَلَا يُقْبَلُ مِنْ أَحَدٍ غَيْرِهِ، يَدْخُلُونَ رُوَّادًا وَلَا يَفْتَرِقُونَ إِلَا عَنْ ذَوَاقٍ، وَيَخْرُجُونَ أَدِلَّةً يَعْنِي عَلَى الْخَيْرِ.

قَالَ الحسين : فَسَأَلْتُهُ عَنْ مَخْرَجِهِ كَيْفَ يَصْنَعُ فِيهِ ؟ قَالَ : كَانَ رَسُولُ الله صلى الله عليه وسلم يَخْزِنُ لِسَانَهُ إلا فِيمَا يَعْنِيهِ ، وَيُؤَلِّفُهُمْ وَلا يُنَفِّرُهُمْ ، وَيُكْرِمُ كَرِيمَ كُلِّ قَوْمٍ وَيُوَلِّيهِ عَلَيْهِمْ ، وَيُحَذِّرُ النَّاسَ وَيَحْتَرِسُ مِنْهُمْ مِنْ غَيْرِ أَنْ يَطْوِيَ عَنْ أَحَدٍ مِنْهُمْ بِشْرَهُ وَخُلُقَهُ ، وَيَتَفَقَّدُ أَصْحَابَهُ ، وَيَسْأَلُ النَّاسَ عَمَّا فِي النَّاسِ ، وَيُحَسِّنُ الْحُسَنَ وَيُقَوِّيهِ ، وَيُقَبِّحُ الْقَبِيحَ وَيُوَهِّيهِ ، مُعْتَدِلُ الأَمْرِ غَيْرُ مُخْتَلِفٍ ، لا يَغْفُلُ مَخَافَةَ أَنْ يَغْفُلُوا أَوْ يَمِيلُوا ، لِكُلِّ حَالٍ عِنْدَهُ عَتَادٌ ،

لا يُقَصِّرُ عَنِ الْحَقِّ وَلا يُجَاوِزُهُ الَّذِينَ يَلُونَهُ مِنَ النَّاسِ خِيَارُهُمْ ، أَفْضَلُهُمْ عِنْدَهُ أَعَمُّهُمْ نَصِيحَةً ، وَأَعْظَمُهُمْ عِنْدَهُ مَنْزِلَةً أَحْسَنُهُمْ مُوَاسَاةً وَمُؤَازَرَةً قَالَ : فَسَأَلْتُهُ عَنْ مَجْلِسِهِ ، فَقَالَ : كَانَ رَسُولُ الله صلى الله عليه وسلم لا يَقُومُ وَلا يَجْلِسُ ، إلا عَلَى ذِكْرٍ ، وَإِذَا انْتَهَى إِلَى قَوْمٍ ، جَلَسَ حَيْثُ يَنْتَهِي بِهِ الْمَجْلِسُ ، وَيَأْمُرُ بِذَلِكَ ، يُعْطِي كُلَّ جُلَسَائِهِ بِنَصِيبِهِ ، لا يَحْسَبُ جَلِيسُهُ أَنَّ أَحَدًا أَكْرَمُ عَلَيْهِ مِنْهُ ، مَنْ جَالَسَهُ أَوْ فَاوَضَهُ فِي حَاجَةٍ ، صَابَرَهُ حَتَّى يَكُونَ هُوَ الْمُنْصَرِفُ عَنْهُ ، وَمَنْ سَأَلَهُ حَاجَةً لَمْ يَرُدَّهُ إلا بِهَا ، أَوْ بِمَيْسُورٍ مِنَ الْقَوْلِ ، قَدْ وَسِعَ النَّاسَ بَسْطُهُ وَخُلُقُهُ ، فَصَارَ لَهُمْ أَبًا وَصَارُوا عِنْدَهُ فِي الْحَقِّ سَوَاءً ، مَجْلِسُهُ مَجْلِسُ عِلْمٍ وَحِلْمٍ وَحَيَاءٍ وَأَمَانَةٍ وَصَبْرٍ ، لا تُرْفَعُ فِيهِ الأَصْوَاتُ ، وَلا تُؤْبَنُ فِيهِ الْحُرَمُ ، وَلا تُثَنَّى فَلَتَاتُهُ ، مُتَعَادِلِينَ ، بَلْ كَانُوا يَتَفَاضَلُونَ فِيهِ بِالتَّقْوَى ، مُتَوَاضِعِينَ يُوَقِّرُونَ فِيهِ الْكَبِيرَ ، وَيَرْحَمُونَ فِيهِ الصَّغِيرَ ، وَيُؤْثِرُونَ ذَا الْحَاجَةِ ، وَيَحْفَظُونَ الْغَرِيبَ [384]

336. Al-Hasan ibn 'Alī ﷺ reported: "I asked my maternal uncle, Hind ibn Abī Hālah ﷺ, who was known for his skill of describing, about the awe-inspiring characteristics and features of the Prophet ﷺ, whilst hoping he could describe to me some of his features to be well acquainted with his description. My maternal uncle described the Prophet ﷺ by saying, 'His qualities and attributes were the acme of beauty, and his companions and whoever saw him held him in high esteem. His face used to shine like the full moon… [To the end of the hadith].'

I withheld this information from al-Hussain ﷺ but when I shared it with him I realised that he had inquired about it before me and I found out that he had asked our father about the interaction of the Prophet ﷺ both outside and within his house and his features, leaving nothing to inquire about."

Al-Hussain ibn Alī ibn Abī Tālib ﷺ narrated: "I asked my father

384 See hadīth 8

about what the Prophet ﷺ did when he was at home. He said: "He ﷺ distributed his time into three portions; one portion for Allāh, another portion for his family and a portion for himself. Then, he distributed his personal portion in two, one for himself and one for the people; in such a manner that he communicated knowledge to the masses through his close companions when they visited him and he did not conceal anything from them. During the portion he dedicated for people, he gave preference to the people of greater piety and status to enter upon him and he distributed this time according to their level of piety. From among those who visited him, some had one need, some had two needs, and some had many needs. He ﷺ sacrificed the time to fulfil all their requirements and busied them in things that would rectify them and the entire nation. When they inquired on matters related to religion, he replied to them in a manner that benefited them and he used to say, 'Those that are present, should convey to those that are absent regarding these beneficial matters.' He also used to say, 'Those people who for some reason cannot bring forth their needs, you should inform me about them. This is because the person who conveys to a ruler the need of another, who is unable to do so himself, Allāh ﷻ will keep that person firm on the Day of Judgment.' No issues besides those of importance and benefit were presented to him in his gatherings and he did not accept listening except to that which was beneficial and lawful. The companions came to his assemblies for their religious and lawful needs and they did not depart without enjoying the taste of his knowledge, and they left with guidance for the people.'

I then asked him about his interaction with people outside his house. He replied, 'The Messenger of Allāh ﷺ controlled his tongue, only speaking regarding that which concerned him. He brought unity amongst the people and did not alienate them. He honoured the esteemed ones of every group and made them the leaders of their groups. He warned the people and was cautious when dealing with people to preserve his status among them but he never lacked courtesy towards others.

He inquired about his companions if one of them was absent and he made himself aware about the affairs and conditions of people. He praised good deeds and encouraged them and admonished the misdeeds and discouraged them. He was moderate and consistent in all matters. He did not neglect guiding the people out of fear that they become either heedless or inclined to the worldly pleasures. He was prepared for every scenario, and he established the rights of others in all matters, and did not exceed the limits in this.

Those who were close to him were the best of people, the best of whom in his eyes were the ones who wished everybody well, and the ones with the highest status in his eyes were the ones with the most compassion, who aided the creation the most.'

I then asked my father regarding the gatherings of the Messenger ﷺ. He replied, 'The Messenger of Allāh ﷺ began and ended all of his sittings with the remembrance of Allāh. When he came to a gathering, he sat where there was space available, and instructed the people to do the same. He gave every attendee his due respect and rights to a degree that led every individual present to think that he ﷺ was honouring him the most. When an individual came to sit with him or came regarding some issue, he ﷺ would remain seated until that person began to rise. Whenever he was asked for something, he would fulfil that request, and did not refuse it; [if he did not possess that which was required] he would advise the person with soft and kind words. His affection and good manners were for all and not restricted to certain people. He was like a father to them and he was just and fair with each one of them.

His gatherings were the gatherings of knowledge, humility, patience and trustworthiness. In his gatherings, voices were not raised and vile and unlawful topics were refrained from. If anyone committed a fault, it was not publicised. All were regarded as equals amongst themselves and superiority was according to the piety possessed. Therein the old were respected, the young were loved, the needy were given preference, and strangers and travellers were cared for and his gems were observed attentively and memorised.'"

'Abdullāh ibn Sa'īd said,

> The Prophet ﷺ did not talk unless there was a need, be it related to religion or worldly affairs, following the guidance of the ayah: **{And they who turn away from idle speech}**[385] and he would repeat his speech twice or thrice to ensure the listeners understood and memorised his statements.
>
> He ﷺ used to bring the hearts of people together and removed all disputes and animosity from their hearts so that they became like one person and he did not do anything that could cause dispute due to his overwhelming compassion and forgiveness.
>
> He ﷺ inquired about the affairs of people to see if there were cases of injustice to be removed, rights to be restored or oppressed people to help. This manner should be followed by the rulers, scholars and pious people and anyone who has followers as they should follow up the news of their followers to avoid neglecting them.
>
> He ﷺ drew close to the best of his people because they would benefit the most from his knowledge and learn it. The teacher should make his best students stay close to him because this will ensure that those who will be entrusted with knowledge are those whose piety is trusted.

Abdul Razzaq al-Badr said,

> Al-Hasan did not inform al-Hussain about his inquiry about the description of the Prophet ﷺ but later on he found out that al-Hussain had already enquired about it. So he asked him regarding what he had acquired since al-Hussain had collected more information than him.
>
> The Prophet ﷺ was cautious in his interactions due to the fact that people are of different natures; there are the rude, the aggressive, the kind and the well-mannered etc. Thus, he dealt with each individual in a suitable and appropriate manner to keep

385 Qur'ān 23:3

everyone close to him.

This hadīth proves that the virtue of the companions differs from one to another. The best of them was Abū Bakr, then 'Umar, then Uthmān, then Alī, and then the ten companions who were given the glad tidings of Paradise.

Fatherhood is of two types, religious and biological. The former is established for the Prophet ﷺ, meaning he is the father of all believers and the latter is negated, as stated in the Qur'ān: **{Muhammad is not the father of [any] one of your men, but [he is] the Messenger of Allah and last of the prophets. And ever is Allah, of all things, Knowing.}**[386]

٣٣٧: حَدَّثَنَا مُحَمَّدُ بْنُ عَبْدِ اللهِ بْنِ بَزِيعٍ ، قَالَ : حَدَّثَنَا بِشْرُ بْنُ الْمُفَضَّلِ ، قَالَ : حَدَّثَنَا سَعِيدٌ ، عَنْ قَتَادَةَ ، عَنْ أَنَسِ بْنِ مَالِكٍ ، قَالَ : قَالَ رَسُولُ اللَّهِ صلى الله عليه وسلم : لَوْ أُهْدِيَ إِلَيَّ كُرَاعٌ لَقَبِلْتُ ، وَلَوْ دُعِيتُ عَلَيْهِ لأَجَبْتُ[387]

337. Anas ibn Mālik ﷺ reported: "The Messenger of Allāh ﷺ said, 'Even if the foot of a goat was gifted to me, I would accept it, and if I was invited to eat from it, I would surely accept that invitation.'"

Ibn Battal said,

> Al-Muhallab said, "This hadīth shows that one should show humility, refrain from arrogance and bring the hearts together by accepting the invitation even if it is for something minute and by accepting gifts. This is because these acts confirm the bond between people and invitations for food cannot be given unless this bond of affability pre-exists between people. It is for these reasons that the Messenger ﷺ encouraged accepting the gift (even if it is little) and answering the invitation of people.

---

386 Qur'ān 33:40

387 Sunan al-Tirmidhī (1338)

٣٣٨: حَدَّثَنَا مُحَمَّدُ بْنُ بَشَّارٍ ، قَالَ : حَدَّثَنَا عَبْدُ الرَّحْمَنِ ، قَالَ : حَدَّثَنَا سُفْيَانُ ، عَنْ مُحَمَّدِ بْنِ الْمُنْكَدِرِ ، عَنْ جَابِرٍ ، قَالَ : جَاءَنِي رَسُولُ اللهِ صلى الله عليه وسلم لَيْسَ بِرَاكِبِ بَغْلٍ وَلا بِرْذَوْنٍ [388]

338. Jabir ﷺ narrated: "The Messenger of Allāh ﷺ came to visit me [while I was sick] and he did not come on the back of a mule or on a Turkish horse."

Ibn Battal said,

> This hadīth teaches us that visiting the sick whether on a ride or by foot is a rewarding deed when the intention is sincerely for the sake of Allāh alone, even if the effort required to reach the sick is minimal.

Badr al-Din al-'Aynī said,

> This hadīth shows the virtue of walking over riding when visiting the sick as it shows more humility.

٣٣٩: حَدَّثَنَا عَبْدُ اللهِ بْنُ عَبْدِ الرَّحْمَنِ ، قَالَ : حَدَّثَنَا أَبُو نُعَيْمٍ ، قَالَ : أَنْبَأَنَا يَحْيَى بْنُ أَبِي الْهَيْثَمِ الْعَطَّارُ ، قَالَ : سَمِعْتُ يُوسُفَ بْنَ عَبْدِ اللهِ بْنِ سَلامٍ ، قَالَ : سَمَّانِي رَسُولُ اللهِ صلى الله عليه وسلم يُوسُفَ ، وَأَقْعَدَنِي فِي حِجْرِهِ ، وَمَسَحَ عَلَى رَأْسِي [389]

339. Yūsuf ibn 'Abdullāh ibn Salām ﷺ reported: "The Messenger of Allāh ﷺ named me Yūsuf and he put me on his lap and then wiped his hand over my head."

Ibn Hajar al-Haytamī said,

---

388 Sahīh al-Bukhārī (194) and Sahīh Muslim (1616)
389 Musnad Ahmad (16404)

It is recommended for a person of high esteem, whose example is followed to name the children of his companions and to choose for them good names. This hadīth also shows that the names of the Prophets are good names.

٣٤٠: حَدَّثَنَا إِسْحَاقُ بْنُ مَنْصُورٍ ، قَالَ : حَدَّثَنَا أَبُو دَاوُدَ الطَّيَالِسِيُّ ، قَالَ : حَدَّثَنَا الرَّبِيعُ وَهُوَ ابْنُ صَبِيحٍ ، قَالَ : حَدَّثَنَا يَزِيدُ الرَّقَاشِيُّ ، عَنْ أَنَسِ بْنِ مَالِكٍ ، أَنَّ رَسُولَ الله صلى الله عليه وسلم ، حَجَّ عَلَى رَحْلٍ رَثٍّ وَقَطِيفَةٍ ، كُنَّا نَرَى ثَمَنَهَا أَرْبَعَةَ دَرَاهِمَ ، فَلَمَّا اسْتَوَتْ بِهِ رَاحِلَتُهُ ، قَالَ : لَبَّيْكَ بِحَجَّةٍ لا سُمْعَةَ فِيهَا وَلا رِيَاءَ [390]

340. Anas ibn Mālik ﷺ narrated: "The Messenger of Allāh ﷺ performed Hajj upon an old and worn saddle. Upon it was a piece of cloth, the value of which was less than four *dirhams*. He ﷺ supplicated, 'O Allāh! Make this Hajj one that has no element of showing off or seeking fame.'"

٣٤١: حَدَّثَنَا عَبْدُ الرَّزَّاقِ ، قَالَ : حَدَّثَنَا مَعْمَرٌ ، عَنْ ثَابِتٍ الْبُنَانِيِّ ، وَعَاصِمٍ الأَحْوَلِ ، عَنْ أَنَسِ بْنِ مَالِكٍ ، أَنَّ رَجُلا خَيَّاطًا دَعَا رَسُولَ الله صلى الله عليه وسلم ، فَقَرَّبَ مِنْهُ ثَرِيدًا عَلَيْهِ دُبَّاءُ ، قَالَ : فَكَانَ رَسُولُ الله صلى الله عليه وسلم ، يَأْخُذُ الدُّبَّاءَ ، وَكَانَ يُحِبُّ الدُّبَّاءَ [391].
قَالَ ثَابِتٌ : فَسَمِعْتُ أَنَسًا ، يَقُولُ : فَمَا صُنِعَ لِي طَعَامٌ ، أَقْدَرُ عَلَى أَنْ يُصْنَعَ فِيهِ دُبَّاءُ ، إِلا صُنِعَ

341. Anas ibn Mālik ﷺ reported: "A tailor once invited the Messenger of Allāh ﷺ to his home. *Tharīd* was served, in which gourd was added, and he ﷺ began eating it as he liked the gourd."

390 See hadīth 334
391 Sahīh Muslim (2041)

Anas ؓ added, "After that, whenever food was prepared for me, if gourd could be added to it, it was added."

Ibn Hajar al-Haytamī said,

> *Tharīd* is a dish made of pieces of bread in meat broth. This dish may or may not include pieces of meat. This hadīth shows that it is recommended to like all that which the Prophet ﷺ liked.

٣٤٢: حَدَّثَنَا عَبْدُ اللهِ بْنُ صَالِحٍ ، قَالَ : حَدَّثَنَا مُعَاوِيَةُ بْنُ صَالِحٍ ، عَنْ يَحْيَى بْنِ سَعِيدٍ ، عَنْ عَمْرَةَ ، قَالَتْ : قِيلَ لِعَائِشَةَ : مَاذَا كَانَ يَعْمَلُ رَسُولُ اللهِ صلى الله عليه وسلم فِي بَيْتِهِ ؟ قَالَتْ : كَانَ بَشَرًا مِنَ الْبَشَرِ ، يَفْلِي ثَوْبَهُ ، وَيَحْلُبُ شَاتَهُ ، وَيَخْدُمُ نَفْسَهُ[392]

342. 'Amrah ؓ reported that someone asked Aisha ؓ: "What was the normal routine of the Messenger of Allāh ﷺ at home?" She replied: "He was a man from amongst men. He himself removed anything that was attached to his clothing, milked his goats, and did all of his work himself."

Abū Bakr ibn al-Arabī said,

> The best work that a person can do individually without the help of others is the acts of worship so that they are all sincerely for Allāh alone. This includes doing everything that leads to these acts of worship as that will amplify the reward.

Al-Taybī said,

> The reason Aisha ؓ mentioned first that he ﷺ was a man is because disbelievers believed that it does not befit the status of Prophets to do what normal people do. Their belief was mentioned

392 Al-Adab al-Mufrad (541)

in the Qur'ān wherein Allāh ﷻ said: **{And they say, "What is this messenger that eats food and walks in the markets?"}**[393] And so she wanted to show that he ﷺ was simply a man from the sons of Ādam whom Allāh honoured with Prophethood and the Message. Thus, he was like all other humans and humble in all of his affairs.

393 Qur'ān 25:7

CHAPTER FORTY EIGHT

باب ماجاء في خلق رسول الله صلى الله عليه وسلم

THE REPORTS PERTAINING TO THE CHARACTER OF THE MESSENGER OF ALLĀH ﷺ

Abdul Razzaq al-Badr said,

> The character consists of inward etiquettes such as shyness, patience and generosity, and outward etiquettes such as cheerful countenance, good treatment, and honesty in speech.
>
> The character of the Prophet ﷺ is the most perfect of all characters for his character resembled the Qur'an.

٣٤٣: حَدَّثَنَا عَبَّاسُ بْنُ مُحَمَّدٍ الدُّورِيُّ ، قَالَ : حَدَّثَنَا عَبْدُ اللهِ بْنُ يَزِيدَ الْمُقْرِئُ ، قَالَ : حَدَّثَنَا لَيْثُ بْنُ سَعْدٍ ، قَالَ : حَدَّثَنِي أَبُو عُثْمَانَ الْوَلِيدُ بْنُ أَبِي الْوَلِيدِ ، عَنْ سُلَيْمَانَ بْنِ خَارِجَةَ ، عَنْ خَارِجَةَ بْنِ زَيْدِ بْنِ ثَابِتٍ ، قَالَ : دَخَلَ نَفَرٌ عَلَى زَيْدِ بْنِ ثَابِتٍ ، فَقَالُوا لَهُ : حَدِّثْنَا أَحَادِيثَ رَسُولِ اللهِ صلى الله عليه وسلم ، قَالَ : مَاذَا أُحَدِّثُكُمْ ؟ كُنْتُ جَارَهُ فَكَانَ إِذَا نَزَلَ عَلَيْهِ الْوَحْيُ بَعَثَ إِلَيَّ فَكَتَبْتُهُ لَهُ ، فَكُنَّا إِذَا ذَكَرْنَا الدُّنْيَا ذَكَرَهَا مَعَنَا ، وَإِذَا ذَكَرْنَا الآخِرَةَ ذَكَرَهَا مَعَنَا ، وَإِذَا ذَكَرْنَا الطَّعَامَ ذَكَرَهُ مَعَنَا ، فَكُلُّ هَذَا أُحَدِّثُكُمْ عَنْ رَسُولِ اللهِ صلى الله عليه وسلم[394]

343. Khārijah ibn Zayd ibn Thābit related: "A group of people came to Zayd ibn Thābit ﷺ and requested him to tell them about the Messenger of Allāh ﷺ. He replied, 'What should I tell you? I was his neighbour and he used to send for me every time something was revealed to him, so that I could transcribe it for him. If we entered into discussion regarding worldly affairs, he would join us in doing so. If we entered into discussion regarding the Hereafter, he would join us in doing so. If we entered into discussion regarding food, he also did so. All of this that I have stated regarding him is factual.'"

Alī al-Qārī said,

> Zayd ibn Thābit was one of the scribes of the Qur'ān who transcribed it directly from the mouth of the Prophet ﷺ. He was the most knowledgeable companion in the science of inheritance and one of the most esteemed Qur'ān reciters.
>
> He ﷺ mentioned that he was the neighbour of the Prophet ﷺ to show his closeness to him in terms of location and companionship and to indicate that he was more familiar with him than other companions.
>
> The Prophet ﷺ joined their conversations because this life is

394 Al-Sunan al-Kubrah (12345)

the farmland of deeds where people plant their seeds to reap the harvest in the Hereafter. Thus, he would join them in order to help them survive this life and to reach the Hereafter safe. This is why he joined their conversations regarding the Hereafter, to inspire them towards the attainment of good deeds. The mentioning of food indicates that he ﷺ showed them its benefits and etiquettes.

In summary he ﷺ used to join them in conversation so that they would not become bored and share with them through the means of conversation, religious rulings and exhortations.

٣٤٤: حَدَّثَنَا إِسْحَاقُ بْنُ مُوسَى ، قَالَ : حَدَّثَنَا يُونُسُ بْنُ بُكَيْرٍ ، عَنْ مُحَمَّدِ بْنِ إِسْحَاقَ ، عَنْ زِيَادِ بْنِ أَبِي زِيَادٍ ، عَنْ مُحَمَّدِ بْنِ كَعْبٍ الْقُرَظِيِّ ، عَنْ عَمْرِو بْنِ الْعَاصِ ، قَالَ : كَانَ رَسُولُ الله صلى الله عليه وسلم ، يُقْبِلُ بِوَجْهِهِ وَحَدِيثِهِ عَلَى أَشَرِّ الْقَوْمِ ، يَتَأَلَّفُهُمْ بِذَلِكَ فَكَانَ يُقْبِلُ بِوَجْهِهِ وَحَدِيثِهِ عَلَيَّ ، حَتَّى ظَنَنْتُ أَنِّي خَيْرُ الْقَوْمِ ، فَقُلْتُ : يَا رَسُولَ الله ، أَنَا خَيْرٌ أَوْ أَبُو بَكْرٍ ؟ فَقَالَ : أَبُو بَكْرٍ ، فَقُلْتُ : يَا رَسُولَ الله ، أَنَا خَيْرٌ أَوْ عُمَرُ ؟ فَقَالَ : عُمَرُ ، فَقُلْتُ : يَا رَسُولَ الله ، أَنَا خَيْرٌ أَوْ عُثْمَانُ ؟ فَقَالَ : عُثْمَانُ ، فَلَمَّا سَأَلْتُ رَسُولَ الله صلى الله عليه وسلم ، فَصَدَقَنِي فَلَوَدِدْتُ أَنِّي لَمْ أَكُنْ سَأَلْتُهُ[395]

344. 'Amr ibn al-'Ās ؓ reported: "The Messenger of Allāh ﷺ embraced and spoke to vile people with a cheerful countenance to soften their hearts. He used to embrace me and speak to me in a manner that made me feel that I was the best amongst the people. I asked, 'O Messenger of Allāh! Who is better, me or Abū Bakr ؓ?' He replied, 'Abū Bakr.' I then asked, 'Am I better, or is 'Umar ؓ?' He replied, "Umar.' I asked, 'Am I better or is 'Uthmān ؓ?' He replied, "Uthman.' After I asked him these questions and he told me the truth, I wished I had not asked him such."

395 Tahdhīb al-Kamāl (939)

'Abdullāh ibn Sa'īd said,

> The Prophet ﷺ used to embrace people with a cheerful countenance to either make them more inclined towards Islām, to aid them in remaining steadfast in religion or to avoid their evil. It is allowed to avoid the evil of bad people by showing them a cheerful countenance but it is not allowed to praise the evil people as this constitutes lying.
>
> The extra attention he ﷺ gave them does not contradict the fact that he gave equal attention to all of his companions. This is because that (i.e. giving them equal attention) was the case in normal circumstances when there was no necessity or need to show more attention. From the benefits of meeting vile people with cheerful countenance is that it prevents arrogance and pride.
>
> The reason why the Prophet ﷺ showed more attention to 'Amr ibn al-'Ās ؓ is because he was new to Islām and from the leaders of his tribe.
>
> The reason he ؓ regretted enquiring such is because he thought the attention and good treatment he received was due to his status in the religion but then he realised it was to soften his heart. It is for this reason a person should not ask about a matter before verifying it, in order to avoid embarrassment.
>
> The kind of mannerisms mentioned in this hadīth reflects the ayah: **{So by mercy from Allāh, [O Muhammad], you were lenient with them. And if you had been rude [in speech] and harsh in heart, they would have disbanded from about you. So pardon them and ask forgiveness for them and consult them in the matter.}**[396]

٣٤٥: حَدَّثَنَا قُتَيْبَةُ بْنُ سَعِيدٍ ، قَالَ : حَدَّثَنَا جَعْفَرُ بْنُ سُلَيْمَانَ الضُّبَعِيُّ ، عَنْ ثَابِتٍ ، عَنْ أَنَسِ بْنِ مَالِكٍ ، قَالَ : خَدَمْتُ رَسُولَ اللهِ صلى الله عليه وسلم

396 Qur'ān 3:159

عَشْرَ سِنِينَ ، فَمَا قَالَ لِي أُفٍّ قَطُّ ، وَمَا قَالَ لِشَيْءٍ صَنَعْتُهُ ، لِمَ صَنَعْتَهُ ، وَلا لِشَيْءٍ تَرَكْتُهُ ، لِمَ تَرَكْتَهُ ؟ وَكَانَ رَسُولُ اللهِ صلى الله عليه وسلم ، مِنْ أَحْسَنِ النَّاسِ خُلُقًا ، وَلا مَسَسْتُ خَزًّا وَلا حَرِيرًا ، وَلا شَيْئًا كَانَ أَلْيَنَ مِنْ كَفِّ رَسُولِ اللهِ صلى الله عليه وسلم ، وَلا شَمَمْتُ مِسْكًا قَطُّ ، وَلا عِطْرًا كَانَ أَطْيَبَ مِنْ عَرَقِ رسول الله صلى الله عليه وسلم[397]

345. Anas ibn Mālik ؓ related: "I served the Messenger of Allāh ﷺ for ten years. He never once said *uff* to me and he never asked me the reason behind anything I did, nor did he ever ask me the reason behind anything that I left. The Messenger of Allāh ﷺ was the most beautiful of people in character. I have never felt any fabric, pure silk or anything else softer than his palm. Nor did I smell any musk or any other fragrance, with a sweeter scent than the perspiration of the Messenger of Allāh ﷺ."

Ibn Hajar al-Asqalānī said,

> The act of refraining from asking others regarding things that have been done or not done shows that one should avoid blaming others for things that have already occurred. It shows that one should safeguard his tongue from admonishing and rebuking others [for actions that have no religious implications] and that one should soften the heart of the servant by not admonishing him if it is regarding something personal (i.e. worldly) but issues related to religion must be addressed.
>
> The softness of his hands and pleasant scent of his body indicates the perfect character and features of the Prophet ﷺ for the pleasant scent he possessed was due to his interactions with angels.

٣٤٦: حَدَّثَنَا قُتَيْبَةُ بْنُ سَعِيدٍ ، وَأَحْمَدُ بْنُ عَبْدَةَ هُوَ الضَّبِّيُّ ، وَالْمَعْنَى وَاحِدٌ

397 Sahīh al-Bukhārī (6041) and Sahīh Muslim (2330)

، قَالا : حَدَّثَنَا حَمَّادُ بْنُ زَيْدٍ ، عَنْ سَلْمٍ الْعَلَوِيِّ ، عَنْ أَنَسِ بْنِ مَالِكٍ ، عَنْ رَسُولِ اللهِ صلى الله عليه وسلم ، أَنَّهُ كَانَ عِنْدَهُ رَجُلٌ بِهِ أَثَرُ صُفْرَةٍ ، قَالَ : وَكَانَ رَسُولُ اللهِ صلى الله عليه وسلم ، لا يَكَادُ يُوَاجِهُ أَحَدًا بِشَيْءٍ يَكْرَهُهُ ، فَلَمَّا قَامَ ، قَالَ لِلْقَوْمِ : لَوْ قُلْتُمْ لَهُ يَدَعُ هَذِهِ الصُّفْرَةَ [398]

346. Anas ibn Mālik ﷺ reported: "A man wearing a yellow coloured garment sat with the Messenger of Allāh ﷺ and the habit of the Messenger of Allāh ﷺ was that he would often avoid bluntly expressing things that other people would dislike. After the man left, he said to those who were present, 'It would have been better if you told him not to wear yellow clothing.'"

Ibn Hajar al-Haytamī said,

> The Prophet ﷺ tended to avoid saying or doing something to an individual if that was something that the person would dislike. The reason he ﷺ did not ask the individual to remove it directly, though wearing yellow clothes is not allowed, is because it was not yet made forbidden otherwise he ﷺ would have not postponed giving the advice. This is supported by another hadīth wherein the Prophet ﷺ saw 'Amr ibn al-'Ās ﷺ wearing yellow garments and ordered him to remove them right away. If someone asks why the Prophet ﷺ ordered 'Amr bluntly but delegated this task to the other companions in the case of the man mentioned in this hadīth, the answer is: 'Amr was wearing something that was deemed unlawful while at the time of the other incident it was not yet made forbidden. And, if we assume that wearing yellow clothing is not forbidden, then the answer is: it could be that the man was a new Muslim, and he ﷺ feared that such a blunt direct order would lead to an undesired outcome whilst in the case of 'Amr, he would be very happy to hasten to obey the Messenger ﷺ.
>
> The argument of some who said that he ﷺ disliked the colour

398 Sunan Abū Dawūd (4182)

yellow because it is a distinguishing sign of the Jews is incorrect. This is because this colour was made as the sign that distinguishes them from Muslims only recently as it happened in some countries like Egypt. Ibn Abī Hajlah mentioned that the Christians wore blue turbans, the Jews wore yellow turbans and al-Samirah wore red turbans in 701 H. The reason they wore such distinctive colours is because it happened that one day a man from Morocco was sitting at the door of a castle and a Christian man came wearing a white turban. Thereupon, the Moroccan man got up and stood in respect thinking he was a Muslim. However after he realised that he was a Christian, he went to the Sultan, Al-Nasir Muhammad ibn Qalawūn and requested the change of the dress code of the non-Muslims living in the lands of Islām so that they could be distinguished from the Muslims and he accepted his request.

٣٤٧: حَدَّثَنَا مُحَمَّدُ بْنُ بَشَّارٍ ، قَالَ : حَدَّثَنَا مُحَمَّدُ بْنُ جَعْفَرٍ ، قَالَ : حَدَّثَنَا شُعْبَةُ ، عَنْ أَبِي إِسْحَاقَ ، عَنْ أَبِي عَبْدِ اللهِ الْجَدَلِيِّ وَاسْمُهُ عَبْدُ بْنُ عَبْدٍ ، عَنْ عَائِشَةَ ، أَنَّهَا قَالَتْ : لَمْ يَكُنْ رَسُولُ اللهِ صَلى الله عليه وسلم ، فَاحِشًا ، وَلا مُتَفَحِّشًا وَلا صَخَّابًا فِي الأَسْوَاقِ ، وَلاَ يَجْزِئُ بِالسَّيِّئَةِ السَّيِّئَةَ ، وَلَكِنْ يَعْفُو وَيَصْفَحُ[399]

347. Aisha ﵂ narrated: "The Messenger of Allāh ﷺ was never indecent or offensive. Nor did he shout in the market. He did not respond to a bad deed with a bad deed. Rather, he forgave and pardoned it."

Bakr Abū Zayd said,

The Prophet ﷺ was selective in his words and he was always keen to use the most respectful and kindest words which were far from the words used by rude and vulgar people. He disliked

399 Sunan al-Tirmidhī (2016)

giving respectful titles to those who did not deserve them and also using insulting words against those who should be honoured. For example, he ﷺ prevented people from addressing the hypocrite with the title "master" and from calling Abū Jahl with the *kunya* Abul Hakam, or a slave person from calling his master 'my lord' and a master calling his slave "my slave". Rather, he directed the master to say "my boy" or "my girl" and the slave to say to their masters "my master" etc.

٣٤٨: حَدَّثَنَا هَارُونُ بْنُ إِسْحَاقَ الْهَمْدَانِيُّ ، قَالَ : حَدَّثَنَا عَبْدَةُ ، عَنْ هِشَامِ بْنِ عُرْوَةَ ، عَنْ أَبِيهِ ، عَنْ عَائِشَةَ ، قَالَتْ : مَا ضَرَبَ رَسُولُ اللهِ صلى الله عليه وسلم ، بِيَدِهِ شَيْئًا قَطُّ ، إِلا أَنْ يُجَاهِدَ فِي سَبِيلِ اللهِ ، وَلا ضَرَبَ خَادِمًا وَلا امْرَأَةً[400]

348. Aisha ﵂ narrated: "The Messenger of Allāh ﷺ never hit anything or anyone with his hands, unless he was fighting in the Path of Allāh, and he did not hit a servant or a woman."

Ibn Abdul Barr said,

> This hadīth indicates that it is recommended for rulers and scholars not to avenge themselves. By doing so, they follow the example of the Prophet ﷺ by forgiving those who were unjust to them.

٣٤٩: حَدَّثَنَا أَحْمَدُ بْنُ عَبْدَةَ الضَّبِّيُّ ، قَالَ : حَدَّثَنَا فُضَيْلُ بْنُ عِيَاضٍ ، عَنْ مَنْصُورٍ ، عَنِ الزُّهْرِيِّ ، عَنْ عُرْوَةَ ، عَنْ عَائِشَةَ ، قَالَتْ : مَا رَأَيْتُ رَسُولَ اللهِ صلى الله عليه وسلم مُنْتَصِرًا مِنْ مَظْلَمَةٍ ظُلِمَهَا قَطُّ ، مَا لَمْ يُنْتَهَكْ مِنْ مَحَارِمِ اللهِ تَعَالَى شَيْءٌ ، فَإِذَا انْتُهِكَ مِنْ مَحَارِمِ اللهِ شَيْءٌ كَانَ مِنْ أَشَدِّهِمْ فِي

400 Sahīh Muslim (2328)

ذَلِكَ غَضَبًا ، وَمَا خُيِّرَ بَيْنَ أَمْرَيْنِ ، إِلا اخْتَارَ أَيْسَرَهُمَا ، مَا لَمْ يَكُنْ مَأْثَمًا[401]

349. Aisha ؓ narrated: "I have never seen the Messenger of Allāh ﷺ avenge the injustice he was subjected to unless there was a case where the laws of Allāh were transgressed or broken. If the laws of Allāh were transgressed, there was no one angrier than him. If the situation arose where he was given a choice between two things, he always chose the one that was easier, unless it was sinful."

Ibn Abdul Barr said,

> There are three benefits concluded from this hadīth:
>
> 1. It is recommended for rulers and scholars not to avenge themselves, thereby following the example of the Prophet ﷺ and to forgive those who show injustice towards them. The scholars agreed that the judge cannot judge in a case in which he is involved.
> 2. It is allowed to take concessions.
> 3. The Messenger ﷺ never avenged in personal matters related to worldly affairs. As for the cases where he was abused verbally, then it is mandatory to avenge because this is from the rights of Allāh and it is an act of disbelief. If a person apostates then he cannot be left without a punishment.

٣٥٠: حَدَّثَنَا ابْنُ أَبِي عُمَرَ ، قَالَ : حَدَّثَنَا سُفْيَانُ ، عَنْ مُحَمَّدِ بْنِ الْمُنْكَدِرِ ، عَنْ عُرْوَةَ ، عَنْ عَائِشَةَ ، قَالَتِ : اسْتَأْذَنَ رَجُلٌ عَلَى رَسُولِ اللهِ صلى الله عليه وسلم ، وَأَنَا عِنْدَهُ ، فَقَالَ : بِئْسَ ابْنُ الْعَشِيرَةِ أَوْ أَخُو الْعَشِيرَةِ ، ثُمَّ أَذِنَ لَهُ ، فَأَلانَ لَهُ الْقَوْلَ ، فَلَمَّا خَرَجَ ، قُلْتُ : يَا رَسُولَ اللهِ ، قُلْتَ مَا قُلْتَ ثُمَّ أَلَنْتَ لَهُ الْقَوْلَ ؟ فَقَالَ : يَا عَائِشَةُ ، إِنَّ مِنْ شَرِّ النَّاسِ مَنْ تَرَكَهُ النَّاسُ أَوْ وَدَعَهُ

401 Sahīh al-Bukhārī (3560) and Sahīh Muslim (2327)

النَّاسُ اتِّقَاءَ فُحْشِهِ[402]

350. Aisha ﷺ narrated: "A man sought permission from the Messenger of Allāh ﷺ to enter his presence whilst I was with him. He ﷺ said, 'What a wretched person is he amongst his community,' and then he gave him permission to enter. After the person entered, he spoke in a kind manner to him. When the man left I said, 'O Messenger of Allāh! You said what you said before he entered and then you spoke so kindly to him!' The Messenger ﷺ said, 'O Aisha! Indeed, from the vilest are those who people avoid to avert their wickedness.'"

Al-Khattabī said,

> The fact that the Prophet ﷺ mentioned the bad trait of this man in his absence does not make it an act of backbiting. This is because this kind of statement is intended to warn people from the person and admonish others from following his ways. It is possible that the wickedness of the man was done in public and in religion mentioning the wrongdoing of a person who does it in public is not considered backbiting.

Ibn Battal said,

> Whoever Allāh has guided to take the path of sensibility to accustom his tongue to saying good words follows the example of the Prophets. They are indeed the best role models that all should follow. This hadīth shows that it is not considered backbiting when mentioning the public sins of a *fāsiq* (a person who does sins in public). It also indicates that kindness should be employed towards the *fāsiq* if there is a benefit hoped from him. The person mentioned in this hadīth is 'Uyaynah ibn Badr al-Fazarī who was the leader of his people and he was known as, "The idiot who people obey." The Prophet ﷺ hoped with his kind treatment towards him that

402 Sahīh al-Bukhārī (6032) and Sahīh Muslim (2591)

he would embrace Islām and subsequently his people would follow suit in doing so.

٣٥١: حَدَّثَنَا سُفْيَانُ بْنُ وَكِيعٍ ، قَالَ : حَدَّثَنَا جُمَيْعُ بْنُ عُمَرَ بْنِ عَبْدِ الرَّحْمَنِ الْعِجْلِيُّ ، قَالَ : أَنْبَأَنَا رَجُلٌ مِنْ بَنِي تَمِيمٍ مِنْ وَلَدِ أَبِي هَالَةَ زَوْجِ خَدِيجَةَ ، وَيُكْنَى أَبَا عَبْدِ اللهِ ، عَنِ ابْنٍ لأَبِي هَالَةَ ، عَنِ الْحَسَنِ بْنِ عَلِيٍّ ، قَالَ : قَالَ الْحُسَيْنُ : سَأَلْتُ أَبِي عَنْ سِيرَةِ النَّبِيِّ صلى الله عليه وسلم ، فِي جُلَسَائِهِ ، فَقَالَ : كَانَ رَسُولُ اللهِ صلى الله عليه وسلم ، دَائِمَ الْبِشْرِ ، سَهْلَ الْخُلُقِ ، لَيِّنَ الْجَانِبِ ، لَيْسَ بِفَظٍّ وَلا غَلِيظٍ ، وَلا صَخَّابٍ وَلا فَحَّاشٍ ، وَلا عَيَّابٍ وَلا مُشَاحٍ ، يَتَغَافَلُ عَمَّا لا يَشْتَهِي ، وَلا يُؤْيِسُ مِنْهُ رَاجِيهِ وَلَا يُخَيَّبُ فِيهِ ، قَدْ تَرَكَ نَفْسَهُ مِنْ ثَلاثٍ : الْمِرَاءِ ، وَالإِكْثَارِ ، وَمَا لا يَعْنِيهِ ، وَتَرَكَ النَّاسَ مِنْ ثَلاثٍ : كَانَ لا يَذُمُّ أَحَدًا ، وَلا يَعِيبُهُ ، وَلا يَطْلُبُ عَوْرَتَهُ ، وَلا يَتَكَلَّمُ إِلا فِيمَا رَجَا ثَوَابَهُ ، وَإِذَا تَكَلَّمَ أَطْرَقَ جُلَسَاؤُهُ ، كَأَنَّمَا عَلَى رُؤُوسِهِمُ الطَّيْرُ ، فَإِذَا سَكَتَ تَكَلَّمُوا لا يَتَنَازَعُونَ عِنْدَهُ الْحَدِيثَ ، وَمَنْ تَكَلَّمَ عِنْدَهُ أَنْصَتُوا لَهُ حَتَّى يَفْرُغَ ، حَدِيثُهُمْ عِنْدَهُ حَدِيثُ أَوَّلِهِمْ ، يَضْحَكُ مِمَّا يَضْحَكُونَ مِنْهُ ، وَيَتَعَجَّبُ مِمَّا يَتَعَجَّبُونَ مِنْهُ ، وَيَصْبِرُ لِلْغَرِيبِ عَلَى الْجَفْوَةِ فِي مَنْطِقِهِ وَمَسْأَلَتِهِ ، حَتَّى إِنْ كَانَ أَصْحَابُهُ ، وَيَقُولُ : إِذَا رَأَيْتُمْ طَالِبَ حَاجَةٍ يَطْلُبُهَا فَأَرْفِدُوهُ ، وَلا يَقْبَلُ الثَّنَاءَ إِلا مِنْ مُكَافِئٍ وَلا يَقْطَعُ عَلَى أَحَدٍ حَدِيثَهُ حَتَّى يَجُوزَ فَيَقْطَعَهُ بِنَهْيٍ أَوْ قِيَامٍ[403]

351. Al-Hasan ibn Alī ؓ narrated that al-Hussain ibn Alī ؓ said: "I inquired from my father regarding the conduct of the Prophet ﷺ with his company. He replied, 'The Messenger of Allāh ﷺ maintained a cheerful countenance and he was easy mannered. He was soft-natured; neither rude nor harsh, and neither stone-hearted nor loud or offensive in his speech. He did not mention the faults

403 See hadīth 8

of anything and he was not narrow-minded or argumentative. If he heard or saw something he disliked he would turn his attention away as if he did not notice it. He did not make people fall into despair or feel disheartened, and he did not respond negatively to the requests that he disliked. He refrained from three traits related to himself: stubbornness in arguments (in some versions: pretension), excessiveness (in some versions: pride), and that which did not concern him. He refrained from three traits related to people: he did not disgrace or insult anyone, nor look for the hidden faults of others; he only spoke that from which reward was hoped.

When he spoke, those present bowed their heads in such a manner, as if birds were perched upon them. When he was silent, the others would begin speaking. They would not dispute in his presence regarding anything and whenever a person spoke to him the others would keep quiet and listen until he would finish. They would speak in order (i.e. the first person to arrive would be the first person to speak and so forth). When those around him laughed due to some reason, he would laugh as well and he would show surprise at the things that surprised the people. He exercised patience at the crude and indecent questions of the traveller and his companions would bring travellers to his assemblies. He used to say to his companions, 'When you see a person in need, always help that person.' If someone praised him, he would detest it unless it came from someone, who in the process of giving thanks praised him. He did not interrupt someone speaking. However, if one exceeded the limits he would stop him or would get up and leave."

'Abdullāh ibn Sa'īd said,

> The cheerful countenance of the Prophet ﷺ does not negate the sad state of his heart due to his concern about the Hereafter and his nation.
>
> He ﷺ never uttered a word or did something that hurt others without any lawful right. He was merciful and soft-hearted with the believers. He never dispraised a food or anything lawful and

this does not contradict that he dispraised the forbidden and admonished it.

If someone asked him for something that he disliked, he would not make the person hopeful to achieve it nor resigned to give up on it. Rather, he would remain silent.

This hadīth manifests the perfect character of the Prophet ﷺ.

٣٥٢: حَدَّثَنَا مُحَمَّدُ بْنُ بَشَّارٍ ، قَالَ : حَدَّثَنَا عَبْدُ الرَّحْمَنِ بْنُ مَهْدِيٍّ ، قَالَ : حَدَّثَنَا سُفْيَانُ ، عَنْ مُحَمَّدِ بْنِ الْمُنْكَدِرِ ، قَالَ : سَمِعْتُ جَابِرَ بْنَ عَبْدِ اللهِ ، يَقُولُ : مَا سُئِلَ رَسُولُ اللهِ صلى الله عليه وسلم ، شَيْئًا قَطُّ فَقَالَ : لا[404]

352. Jābir ibn 'Abdullāh ؓ narrated: "The Messenger of Allāh ﷺ was never asked of something to which he said 'No.'"

Al-Nawawī said,

> This shows the excessive generosity of the Prophet ﷺ for he was never asked for anything from this worldly life except that he agreed to give it away.

Ibn al-Uthaymīn said,

> This hadīth along with other hadīths encourages us to spend for the sake of Allāh for Allāh has provided people with money to test them. Allāh ﷻ said: **{Your wealth and your children are but a trial and Allāh has with Him a great reward.}**[405] Thus, some people spend it to fulfil their unlawful desires and pleasures which keep them distant from Allāh whilst some other people spend it in the path of Allāh seeking His reward. As for those who spend it in matters that are neither prescribed in religion nor forbidden, then they have just wasted their wealth.

---

404 Sahīh al-Bukhārī (6034) and Sahīh Muslim (2311)

405 Qur'ān 64:15

٣٥٣: حَدَّثَنَا عَبْدُ اللهِ بْنُ عِمْرَانَ أَبُو الْقَاسِمِ الْقُرَشِيُّ الْمَكِّيُّ ، قَالَ : حَدَّثَنَا إِبْرَاهِيمُ بْنُ سَعْدٍ ، عَنِ ابْنِ شِهَابٍ ، عَنْ عُبَيْدِ اللهِ ، عَنِ ابْنِ عَبَّاسٍ ، قَالَ : كَانَ رَسُولُ اللهِ صلى الله عليه وسلم ، أَجْوَدَ النَّاسِ بِالْخَيْرِ ، وَكَانَ أَجْوَدَ مَا يَكُونُ فِي شَهْرِ رَمَضَانَ ، حَتَّى يَنْسَلِخَ ، فَيَأْتِيهِ جِبْرِيلُ ، فَيَعْرِضُ عَلَيْهِ الْقُرْآنَ ، فَإِذَا لَقِيَهُ جِبْرِيلُ كَانَ رَسُولُ اللهِ صلى الله عليه وسلم ، أَجْوَدَ بِالْخَيْرِ مِنَ الرِّيحِ الْمُرْسَلَةِ [406]

353. 'Abdullāh ibn Abbās ﷺ narrated: "The Messenger of Allāh ﷺ was the most generous amongst the people in performing good deeds. He would increase in generosity during the month of Ramadān until the month's end. In this month Jibrīl ﷺ used to visit him and recite the Qur'ān to him. Every time Jibrīl met him, the generosity of the Messenger of Allāh ﷺ was more than that of a wind that brings forth heavy rains."

Ibn Battal said,

> Al-Muhallab said, "This hadīth shows the benefits and blessings of being in the company of pious and righteous people as this reminds the person to do good deeds and increase his share from good deeds. This is why the Prophet ﷺ ordered us to sit with the learned ones and spend time in the gatherings of Allāh's remembrance and gave the example of the righteous friend as the perfume seller. It also shows the blessings attained through good deeds and that a good deed leads to another i.e. the blessing of fasting, meeting Jibrīl and reciting the Qur'ān increased the generosity of the Prophet ﷺ.

٣٥٤: حَدَّثَنَا قُتَيْبَةُ بْنُ سَعِيدٍ ، قَالَ : أَخْبَرَنَا جَعْفَرُ بْنُ سُلَيْمَانَ ، عَنْ ثَابِتٍ ، عَنْ أَنَسِ بْنِ مَالِكٍ ، قَالَ : كَانَ النَّبِيُّ صلى الله عليه وسلم ، لا يَدَّخِرُ شَيْئًا

406 Sahih al-Bukhari (1902) and Sahih Muslim (2308)

لِغَدٍ[407]

354. Anas ibn Mālik ؓ narrated: "The Prophet ﷺ would not store anything for the following day."

Al-Qastalanī said,

> It is permissible to store the food for one's wife and children and this does not negate reliance on Allāh because the Prophet ﷺ did it and he is the master of those who rely on Allāh ﷻ. This is because taking the means (whilst the reliance on Allāh is established in the heart) does not contradict one's reliance. The fact that he ﷺ stored for his family their sustenance for one year does not contradict that he did not store anything for the next day because this was either before he ﷺ had access to sustenance or it means that he did not store anything for himself.

٣٥٥: حَدَّثَنَا هَارُونُ بْنُ مُوسَى بْنِ أَبِي عَلْقَمَةَ الْمَدِينِيُّ ، قَالَ : حَدَّثَنِي أَبِي ، عَنْ هِشَامِ بْنِ سَعْدٍ ، عَنْ زَيْدِ بْنِ أَسْلَمَ ، عَنْ أَبِيهِ ، عَنْ عُمَرَ بْنِ الْخَطَّابِ ، أَنَّ رَجُلاً جَاءَ إِلَى النَّبِيِّ صلى الله عليه وسلم ، فَسَأَلَهُ أَنْ يُعْطِيَهُ ، فَقَالَ النَّبِيُّ صلى الله عليه وسلم : مَا عِنْدِي شَيْءٌ ، وَلَكِنِ ابْتَعْ عَلَيَّ ، فَإِذَا جَاءَنِي شَيْءٌ قَضَيْتُهُ فَقَالَ عُمَرُ : يَا رَسُولَ اللهِ ، قَدْ أَعْطَيْتَهُ فَمَا كَلَّفَكَ اللهُ مَا لا تَقْدِرُ عَلَيْهِ ، فَكَرِهَ النَّبِيُّ صلى الله عليه وسلم قَوْلَ عُمَرَ ، فَقَالَ رَجُلٌ مِنَ الأَنْصَارِ : يَا رَسُولَ اللهِ ، أَنْفِقْ وَلا تَخَفْ مِنْ ذِي الْعَرْشِ إِقْلالا ، فَتَبَسَّمَ رَسُولُ اللهِ صلى الله عليه وَسلم وَعُرِفَ فِي وَجْهِهِ الْبِشْرَ لِقَوْلِ الأَنْصَارِيِّ ، ثُمَّ قَالَ : بِهَذَا أُمِرْتُ[408]

355. 'Umar ibn al-Khattab ؓ narrated: "A man came to the Prophet

---

407 Sunan al-Tirmidhī (2362)
408 Al-Ahadīth al-Mukhtarah (78)

ﷺ asking for something. The Prophet ﷺ replied, 'I do not have anything at present but go and purchase something on my name and I will pay for it when I have sufficient money.' 'Umar ؓ said, 'O Messenger of Allāh! You have already given him that which you had and Allāh ﷻ did not make you responsible for that which is beyond your means.' The Messenger ﷺ disliked this statement of 'Umar ؓ. A man from the Ansār said, 'O Messenger of Allāh! Spend whatever you wish, and do not fear any diminution from the Lord of the Throne.' The Messenger ﷺ smiled and the happiness could be seen on his face due to the statement of the man. He ﷺ then said, 'With this I have been ordered.'"

Abdullah ibn Sa'īd said,

> The statement of 'Umar either meant that he ﷺ gave to that person before, therefore there was no need to promise him more since he ﷺ did not have anything at that time or that he ﷺ answered the man in a kind manner when he explained that he did not have anything to give away. The reason why the Prophet ﷺ disliked the statement of 'Umar is that it made the man feel disappointed and that the promise made was not considered a burden given that he ﷺ used to be lavished with the blessings of Allāh.

٣٥٦: حَدَّثَنَا عَلِيُّ بْنُ حُجْرٍ ، قَالَ : أَخْبَرَنَا شَرِيكٌ ، عَنْ عَبْدِ اللهِ بْنِ مُحَمَّدِ بْنِ عَقِيلٍ ، عَنِ الرُّبَيِّعِ بِنْتِ مُعَوِّذِ بْنِ عَفْرَاءَ ، قَالَتْ : أَتَيْتُ النَّبِيَّ صلى الله عليه وسلم ، بِقِنَاعٍ مِنْ رُطَبٍ وَأَجْرٍ زُغْبٍ ، فَأَعْطَانِي مِلْءَ كَفِّهِ حُلِيًّا وَذَهَبًا[409]

356. Al-Rubayyi' bint Mu'awwidh ibn 'Afrā ؓ narrated: "I took a plate of ripe dates (*rutab*) and small cucumbers to the Messenger of Allāh ﷺ. He gave me a handful of jewellery, or a handful of gold."

409 See hadīth 203

٣٥٧: حَدَّثَنَا عَلِيُّ بْنُ خَشْرَمٍ ، وَغَيْرُ وَاحِدٍ ، قَالُوا : حَدَّثَنَا عِيسَى بْنُ يُونُسَ ، عَنْ هِشَامِ بْنِ عُرْوَةَ ، عَنْ أَبِيهِ ، عَنْ عَائِشَةَ : أَنَّ النَّبِيَّ صلى الله عليه وسلم ، كَانَ يَقْبَلُ الْهَدِيَّةَ ، وَيُثِيبُ عَلَيْهَا[410]

357. Aisha ﵂ narrated: "The Messenger of Allāh ﷺ accepted gifts and would reciprocate in return."

Al-Khattabī said,

> Accepting gifts is a form of generosity and from the kind manners that bring hearts together and it was reported that he ﷺ ordered people to exchange gifts as that will bring forth love between people. The acceptance of gifts was one of the signs of his prophethood mentioned in previous scriptures wherein he was described as a person who accepts gifts and does not take charity. The Prophet ﷺ used to reward those who gave him gifts so that no one could have the upper hand over him or hold favours over him. Allāh ﷻ said: **{O my people, I do not ask you for it any reward. My reward is only from the one who created me. Then will you not reason?}**[411] And if he ﷺ accepted gifts without rewarding those who presented the gifts, it would have been as if he was receiving rewards for his mission. It is for this reason, giving gifts to rulers is considered a form of bribery because it was not allowed for the Messenger ﷺ to accept gifts without reciprocating or to take without giving, and he is the leader and master of all humanity.

410 Sahīh al-Bukhārī (2585)
411 Qur'ān 11:51

CHAPTER FORTY NINE

باب ماجاء في حياء رسول الله صلى الله عليه وسلم

THE REPORTS PERTAINING TO THE MODESTY AND SHYNESS OF THE MESSENGER OF ALLĀH ﷺ

Abdul Razzaq al-Badr said,

> The quality of *haya'* is an attribute that brings forth nothing but good and it is one of the parts of *imān*. It induces the person to do the good in all of his affairs, be it related to worship, etiquettes or social life. It also keeps the person away from the ugly sins, wrongdoings and ill-manners.

٣٥٨: حَدَّثَنَا مَحْمُودُ بْنُ غَيْلانَ ، قَالَ : حَدَّثَنَا أَبُو دَاوُدَ ، قَالَ : حَدَّثَنَا شُعْبَةُ ، عَنْ قَتَادَةَ ، قَالَ : سَمِعْتُ عَبْدَ اللهِ بْنَ أَبِي عُتْبَةَ ، يُحَدِّثُ عَنْ أَبِي سَعِيدٍ الْخُدْرِيِّ ، قَالَ : كَانَ النَّبِيُّ صلى الله عليه وسلم أَشَدَّ حَيَاءً مِنَ الْعَذْرَاءِ فِي خِدْرِهَا ، وَكَانَ إِذَا كَرِهَ شَيْئًا عَرَفْنَاهُ فِي وَجْهِهِ[412]

358. Abū Sa'īd al-Khudarī ﷺ narrated: "The Prophet ﷺ was the most modest, more so than a virgin in her private quarters. If he did not like something, we could notice that on his face."

Ibn Hajar al-Asqalānī said,

> Al-Qadī 'Iyyād said, "Shyness and modesty were made part of *imān* though it is a human instinct. For a characteristic to fall in line with the guidelines of religion [rather than being a mere human instinct], one would need to establish the intention, endeavour and possess the knowledge to do so. As for stating that shyness brings about nothing but goodness, it is found problematic because someone may argue that sometimes shyness prevents one from facing and stopping a wrongdoer or not fulfilling rights and obligations. The answer to this is that there are two types of shyness; one that conforms to religion and that does not lead to the aforementioned weakness whilst the other type is given the same name (i.e. shyness) because it shares the trait of preventing one from low and ugly acts.
>
> Abū al-'Abbās al-Qurtubī said that cultivated shyness is the type of shyness that Allāh has made part of *imān* and the characteristic that people ought to acquire. However, the instinctual type of shyness could support the attained shyness and it could integrate with the attained shyness until the prescribed shyness becomes an innate nature and the Prophet ﷺ enjoyed both types; his instinctual shyness made him more modest than a virgin girl in her private quarters and his attained shyness elevated him to the

412 Sahīh al-Bukhārī (3562) and Sahīh Muslim (2320)

highest status.

٣٥٩: حَدَّثَنَا مَحْمُودُ بْنُ غَيْلانَ ، قَالَ : حَدَّثَنَا وَكِيعٌ ، قَالَ : حَدَّثَنَا سُفْيَانُ ، عَنْ مَنْصُورٍ ، عَنْ مُوسَى بْنِ عَبْدِ اللهِ بْنِ يَزِيدَ الْخَطْمِيِّ ، عَنْ مَوْلًى لِعَائِشَةَ ، قَالَ : قَالَتْ عَائِشَةُ : مَا نَظَرْتُ إِلَى فَرْجِ رَسُولِ اللهِ صلى الله عليه وسلم أَوْ قَالَتْ : مَا رَأَيْتُ فَرْجَ رَسُولِ اللهِ صلى الله عليه وسلم قَطُّ[413]

359. Aisha ﵂ reported: "I never looked towards the private parts of the Messenger of Allāh ﷺ, [or she said] that I never saw the private parts of the Messenger of Allāh ﷺ."

Ibn Hajar al-Haytamī said,

> This hadīth manifests the perfect level of shyness possessed by the Prophet ﷺ because he did not do anything that would allow her to look at his private parts. This is because a woman would not dare to see the private parts of her husband unless he would allow it and give his consent.

413 Sunan Ibn Mājah (662)

CHAPTER FIFTY

باب ماجاء في حجامة رسول الله صلى الله عليه وسلم

THE REPORTS PERTAINING TO THE CUPPING OF THE MESSENGER OF ALLĀH ﷺ

Abdul Razzaq al-Badr said,

> Cupping is a medical treatment that the Prophet ﷺ had administered upon himself many times and he paid the cupper for it. He also encouraged it and stated that it is a cure. Ibn Abbas narrated that the Prophet ﷺ said "Healing is in three things: in the incision of the cupper, in drinking honey, and in cauterizing with fire, but I forbid my Ummah (nation) from cauterization (branding with fire)."[414]

414 Sahīh al-Bukhārī (3436)

٣٦٠: حَدَّثَنَا عَلِيُّ بْنُ حُجْرٍ ، قَالَ : حَدَّثَنَا إِسْمَاعِيلُ بْنُ جَعْفَرٍ ، عَنْ حُمَيْدٍ ، قَالَ : سُئِلَ أَنَسُ بْنُ مَالِكٍ عَنْ كَسْبِ الْحُجَّامِ ، فَقَالَ : احْتَجَمَ رَسُولُ الله صلى الله عليه وسلم ، حَجَمَهُ أَبُو طَيْبَةَ ، فَأَمَرَ لَهُ بِصَاعَيْنِ مِنْ طَعَامٍ ، وَكَلَّمَ أَهْلَهُ فَوَضَعُوا عَنْهُ مِنْ خَرَاجِهِ ، وَقَالَ : إِنَّ أَفْضَلَ مَا تَدَاوَيْتُمْ بِهِ الْحِجَامَةُ ، أَوْ إِنَّ مِنْ أَمْثَلِ دَوَائِكُمُ الْحِجَامَةَ[415]

360. Anas ibn Mālik ﷺ was asked about the ruling on the income of the cupper. He said: "The Messenger of Allāh ﷺ had the treatment of cupping administered upon him by Abū Taybah ﷺ. In return, he ﷺ gave Abū Taybah two *sā'* of food, and interceded on his behalf with his masters that the stipulated labour tax imposed upon him be reduced. He also said, 'Indeed the best of treatments is cupping.'"

Abdul Rahman al-Mubarakfūrī said,

> This hadīth shows that it is allowed to charge fees for medical treatment and it is recommended to intercede for people so that the person receiving the request reduces some of their rights and becomes easy with others in this regard. It shows that it is permissible for the master to let his slave work independently in return of a fixed payment with the rest of the earnings going to the slave.
>
> The scholars differed on the ruling of the income of the cupper, the majority stated that it is lawful as stated by al-Hafith ibn Hajar.

٣٦١: حَدَّثَنَا عَمْرُو بْنُ عَلِيٍّ ، قَالَ : حَدَّثَنَا أَبُو دَاوُدَ ، قَالَ : حَدَّثَنَا وَرْقَاءُ بْنُ عُمَرَ ، عَنْ عَبْدِ الأَعْلَى ، عَنْ أَبِي جَمِيلَةَ ، عَنْ عَلِيٍّ : أَنَّ النَّبِيَّ صلى الله عليه وسلم ، احْتَجَمَ وَأَمَرَنِي فَأَعْطَيْتُ الْحُجَّامَ أَجْرَهُ[416]

415 Sahīh al-Bukhārī (2102) and Sahīh Muslim (1577)
416 Sunan Ibn Mājah (2163)

361. Alī ibn Abī Tālib ؓ narrated: "The Prophet ﷺ had the treatment of cupping administered upon him and ordered me to pay the cupper his fees, so I did."

Alī al-Qārī said,

> Ibn al-Jawzī mentioned that the Prophet ﷺ disliked the income of cuppers because cupping is from the things that Muslims ought to offer for free when it is required by fellow Muslims.

٣٦٢: حَدَّثَنَا هَارُونُ بْنُ إِسْحَاقَ الْهَمْدَانِيُّ ، قَالَ : حَدَّثَنَا عَبْدَةُ ، عَنْ سُفْيَانَ الثَّوْرِيِّ ، عَنْ جَابِرٍ ، عَنِ الشَّعْبِيِّ ، عَنِ ابْنِ عَبَّاسٍ ، قَالَ : إِنَّ النَّبِيَّ صلى الله عليه وسلم احْتَجَمَ فِي الأَخْدَعَيْنِ ، وَبَيْنَ الْكَتِفَيْنِ ، وَأَعْطَى الْحَجَّامَ أَجْرَهُ ، وَلَوْ كَانَ حَرَامًا لَمْ يُعْطِهِ[417]

362. 'Abdullāh ibn Abbās ؓ narrated: "The Prophet ﷺ had the treatment of cupping administered on both sides of his neck and the top area between his shoulders, and paid the cupper his fees. Had it been forbidden to charge fees for cupping, he would have not paid it."

Alī al-Qārī said,

> It is proven in many hadīths that he had cupping administered on different parts of his body depending on the treatment needed on each occasion. The majority of scholars relied on this hadīth amongst others to state that the income of cuppers is lawful.

٣٦٣: حَدَّثَنَا هَارُونُ بْنُ إِسْحَاقَ ، قَالَ : حَدَّثَنَا عَبْدَةُ ، عَنِ ابْنِ أَبِي لَيْلَى ، عَنْ نَافِعٍ ، عَنِ ابْنِ عُمَرَ ، أَنَّ النَّبِيَّ صلى الله عليه وسلم ، دَعَا حَجَّامًا

---

417 See Sahīh al-Bukhārī (2103) and Sahīh Muslim (1202)

فَحَجَمَهُ وَسَأَلَهُ : كَمْ خَرَاجُكَ ؟ فَقَالَ : ثَلاثَةُ آصُعٍ ، فَوَضَعَ عَنْهُ صَاعًا وَأَعْطَاهُ أَجْرَهُ[418]

363. 'Abdullāh ibn 'Umar ﷺ narrated: "The Prophet ﷺ requested a cupper to treat him. After he finished, he ﷺ inquired from him regarding the amount of labour tax he paid his master. The cupper replied, 'Three *sā*.' So he ﷺ had it reduced to two *sā*', and gave him his remuneration."

Ibn Hajar al-Haytamī said,

> The name of the cupper mentioned in this hadīth is said to be Abū Taybah as mentioned in the previous hadīth.

٣٦٤: حَدَّثَنَا عَبْدُ الْقُدُّوسِ بْنُ مُحَمَّدٍ الْعَطَّارُ الْبَصْرِيُّ ، قَالَ : حَدَّثَنَا عَمْرُو بْنُ عَاصِمٍ ، قَالَ : حَدَّثَنَا هَمَّامٌ ، وَجَرِيرُ بْنُ حَازِمٍ ، قَالَ : حَدَّثَنَا قَتَادَةُ ، عَنْ أَنَسِ بْنِ مَالِكٍ ، قَالَ : كَانَ رَسُولُ اللهِ صلى الله عليه وسلم يَحْتَجِمُ فِي الأَخْدَعَيْنِ وَالْكَاهِلِ ، وَكَانَ يَحْتَجِمُ لِسَبْعَ عَشْرَةَ ، وَتِسْعَ عَشْرَةَ ، وَإِحْدَى وَعِشْرِينَ[419]

364. Anas ibn Mālik ﷺ narrated: "The Messenger of Allāh ﷺ used to have the treatment of cupping administered upon both sides of his neck and between the two shoulders. He used to take this treatment on the seventeenth, nineteenth or the twenty first of the lunar month."

Ibn Muflih said,

> The reason why the Prophet ﷺ cupped the top area between the shoulders is because this is the closest area to the heart which can

418 See al-Mu'jam al-Kabīr (12427)
419 Sunan Abū Dawūd (3860) and Sunan Ibn Mājah (3483)

be cupped.

Ibn al-Qayyim said,

> The administration of cupping on both sides of the neck can treat sicknesses related to the head and its parts such as the face, teeth, ears, eyes, nose and throat if the sickness is due to excessive or corrupted blood.

'Abdullāh ibn Sa'īd said,

> The companions ﷺ used to follow his example in choosing the time for cupping as they liked doing it on the odd nights of the month. This is due to the virtue of odd numbers as Allāh loves odd numbers. The best day to have cupping administered is on a Monday if it coincides with the seventeenth, nineteenth or twenty first of the month.

٣٦٥: حَدَّثَنَا إِسْحَاقُ بْنُ مَنْصُورٍ ، قَالَ : أَنْبَأَنَا عَبْدُ الرَّزَّاقِ ، عَنْ مَعْمَرٍ ، عَنْ قَتَادَةَ ، عَنْ أَنَسِ بْنِ مَالِكٍ : أَنَّ رَسُولَ اللهِ صلى الله عليه وسلم احْتَجَمَ وَهُوَ مُحْرِمٌ بِمَلَلٍ عَلَى ظَهْرِ الْقَدَمِ[420]

365. Anas bin Mālik ﷺ narrated: "The Messenger of Allāh ﷺ had cupping administered upon the top of his foot at a place called Malal whilst he was in the state of *ihrām*."

Ibn Hajar al-Haytamī said,

> Malal is a place between Makkah and Madīnah. It is about seventeen miles away from Madīnah.
>
> It is allowed to administer cupping whilst a person is still in the state of *ihrām* if the treatment does not include removing hair; otherwise it is considered to be forbidden unless there is a

420 Sunan Abū Dawūd (1837)

necessity and in such a case the person is required to slaughter a sacrifice as expiation.

CHAPTER FIFTY ONE

باب ماجاء في أسماء رسول الله صلى الله عليه وسلم

THE REPORTS PERTAINING TO THE NAMES OF THE MESSENGER OF ALLĀH ﷺ

Abdul Razzaq al-Badr said,

> The names of the Prophet ﷺ are more than just names as they reflect his character and nature.

٣٦٦: عن سَعِيدُ بْنُ عَبْدِ الرَّحْمَنِ الْمَخْزُومِيُّ ، وَغَيْرُ وَاحِدٍ ، قَالُوا : حَدَّثَنَا سُفْيَانُ ، عَنِ الزُّهْرِيِّ ، عَنْ مُحَمَّدِ بْنِ جُبَيْرِ بْنِ مُطْعِمٍ ، عَنْ أَبِيهِ ، قَالَ : قَالَ رَسُولُ اللهِ صلى الله عليه وسلم : إِنَّ لِي أَسْمَاءً ، أَنَا مُحَمَّدٌ ، وَأَنَا أَحْمَدُ ، وَأَنَا الْمَاحِي الَّذِي يَمْحُو اللَّهُ بِيَ الْكُفْرَ ، وَأَنَا الْحَاشِرُ الَّذِي يُحْشَرُ النَّاسُ عَلَى قَدَمِي ، وَأَنَا الْعَاقِبُ الَّذِي لَيْسَ بَعْدَهُ نَبِيٌّ[421]

366. Jubair ibn Mut'im ﷺ narrated: "The Messenger of Allāh ﷺ said, 'I have many names. I am Muhammad, I am Ahmad. I am al-Māhi [the obliterator] with whom Allāh obliterates disbelief. I am al-Hāshir [the gatherer] as the people will be gathered after I am gathered [on the Day of Resurrection], and I am al-'Āqib [i.e. the one who succeeds the other Prophets in bringing about good], after whom there will come no prophet."

Ibn Hajar al-Asqalānī said,

> The Prophet ﷺ will be the first one to be resurrected as stated in the authentic hadīth. His other agreed upon names that are mentioned in the Qur'ān are: al-Shāhid (the witness), al-Mubashir (giver of glad tidings), al-Nadhīr al-Mubīn (the evident warner), al-Dā'ī ila Allāh (caller to Allāh), al-Sirāj al-Munīr (enlightening luminary), al-Mudhakir (the reminder), al-Rahmah (the mercy), al-Ni'mah (the grace), al-Hādi (the guide), al-Amīn (the trustworthy), al-Muzzamil (enwrapped in his raiment), and al-Muddathir (the one shrouded in his mantle).

٣٦٧: حَدَّثَنَا مُحَمَّدُ بْنُ طَرِيفٍ الْكُوفِيُّ ، قَالَ : حَدَّثَنَا أَبُو بَكْرِ بْنُ عَيَّاشٍ ، عَنْ عَاصِمٍ ، عَنْ أَبِي وَائِلٍ ، عَنْ حُذَيْفَةَ ، قَالَ : لَقِيتُ النَّبِيَّ صلى الله عليه وسلم ، فِي بَعْضِ طُرُقِ الْمَدِينَةِ ، فَقَالَ : أَنَا مُحَمَّدٌ ، وَأَنَا أَحْمَدُ ، وَأَنَا نَبِيُّ الرَّحْمَةِ

421 Sahīh al-Bukhārī (3532) and Sahīh Muslim (2354)

، وَنَبِيُّ التَّوْبَةِ ، وَأَنَا المُقَفَّى ، وَأَنَا الحَاشِرُ ، وَنَبِيُّ المَلاحِمِ[422]

367. Hudhaifah ﷺ narrated: "I once met the Messenger of Allāh ﷺ in one of the roads of Madīnah. He said, 'I am Muhammad, and I am Ahmad, and I am the Prophet of Mercy, the Prophet of Repentance, I am Muqaffā (the last Prophet), I am al-Hāshir (the first one to be gathered), and the Prophet of the battlefield.'"

Ibn al-Jawzī said,

> Ibn Qutaybah said, "From the signs and evidence regarding the coming of the Prophet Muhammad ﷺ is that his name (i.e. Ahmad or Muhammad) was prophesised in the previous scriptures and yet no one was given it before him. This was so that Allāh could protect this name and avert any doubts and false claims should someone be named with it. Thus, when his time came and the People of the Book spread the news that he was about to come out, his name was given."

Al-Taybī said,

> He is the Prophet of the battlefield because of his keenness for *jihad* and the great courage he possessed on the battlefield.

٣٦٨: حَدَّثَنَا إِسْحَاقُ بْنُ مَنْصُورٍ ، قَالَ : حَدَّثَنَا النَّضْرُ بْنُ شُمَيْلٍ ، قَالَ : أَنْبَأَنَا حَمَّادُ بْنُ سَلَمَةَ ، عَنْ عَاصِمٍ ، عَنْ زِرٍّ ، عَنْ حُذَيْفَةَ ، عَنِ النَّبِيِّ صلى الله عليه وسلم ، نَحْوَهُ بِمَعْنَاهُ ، هَكَذَا ، قَالَ حَمَّادُ بْنُ سَلَمَةَ ، عَنْ عَاصِمٍ ، عَنْ زِرٍّ ، عَنْ حُذَيْفَةَ

368. The same is reported from Hudhaifah ﷺ through another route.

422 Musnad Ahmad (23445)

CHAPTER FIFTY TWO

باب ماجاء في عيش رسول الله صلى الله عليه وسلم

THE REPORTS PERTAINING TO THE MANNER OF LIVING OF THE MESSENGER OF ALLĀH ﷺ

Abdul Razzaq al-Badr said,

> The subject of this chapter has already been addressed in chapter nine under which two hadīths were listed, and it is addressed here again to emphasise his ﷺ concern regarding the Hereafter and his disinterest regarding the worldly pleasures.

٣٦٩: حَدَّثَنَا قُتَيْبَةُ بْنُ سَعِيدٍ ، قَالَ : حَدَّثَنَا أَبُو الأَحْوَصِ ، عَنْ سِمَاكِ بْنِ حَرْبٍ ، قَالَ : سَمِعْتُ النُّعْمَانَ بْنَ بَشِيرٍ ، يَقُولُ : أَلَسْتُمْ فِي طَعَامٍ وَشَرَابٍ مَا شِئْتُمْ ؟ لَقَدْ رَأَيْتُ نَبِيَّكُمْ صلى الله عليه وسلم ، وَمَا يَجِدُ مِنَ الدَّقَلِ ، مَا يَمْلأُ بَطْنَهُ[423]

369. Al-Nu'mān ibn Bashīr ؓ said: "You are in enough luxury to eat and drink all that you wish! By Allāh, I have seen your Prophet ﷺ not having the worst type of dates to fill his stomach."

٣٧٠: حَدَّثَنَا هَارُونُ بْنُ إِسْحَاقَ ، قَالَ : حَدَّثَنَا عَبْدَةُ ، عَنْ هِشَامِ بْنِ عُرْوَةَ ، عَنْ أَبِيهِ ، عَنْ عَائِشَةَ ، قَالَتْ : إِنْ كُنَّا آلَ مُحَمَّدٍ نَمكُثُ شَهْرًا مَا نَسْتَوْقِدُ بِنَارٍ ، إِنْ هُوَ إِلا التَّمْرُ وَالْمَاءُ [424]

370. Aisha ؓ narrated: "We, the family of Muhammad ﷺ would pass a whole month without kindling a fire in our homes. [During this time] we would sustain ourselves on dates and water."

Abū Bakr ibn al-Arabī said,

> Al-Tirmidhī reported from al Zubair ibn al-'Awwām ؓ that when the ayah: **{Then you will surely be asked that Day about the delight [you indulged in, in this world]!}**[425] was revealed, he asked, "O Messenger of Allāh! What delight will we be asked about when all that we have is just dates and water?" The Prophet ﷺ replied, "Indeed, it will happen."[426]

Ibn Battal said,

---

423 See hadīth 152
424 Sahīh al-Bukhārī (6458) and Sahīh Muslim (2971)
425 Qur'ān 102:8
426 Sunan al-Tirmidhī (3356)

This shows the rigorous self-denial and self-restraint of the Prophet ﷺ and his favouring of the Hereafter over the worldly pleasures. This is because when he was given the choice between receiving the pleasures of this worldly life and the pleasures of the Hereafter, he chose the latter, and when he was given the choice either to be a Prophet and a slave to Allāh or a Prophet who is a king, he chose the former. It is also an evidence for those who favour poverty over possessing riches.

٣٧١: حَدَّثَنَا عَبْدُ اللهِ بْنُ أَبِي زِيَادٍ ، قَالَ : حَدَّثَنَا سَيَّارٌ ، قَالَ : حَدَّثَنَا سَهْلُ بْنُ أَسْلَمَ ، عَنْ يَزِيدَ بْنِ أَبِي مَنْصُورٍ ، عَنْ أَنَسٍ ، عَنْ أَبِي طَلْحَةَ ، قَالَ : شَكَوْنَا إِلَى رَسُولِ اللهِ صلى الله عليه وسلم ، الْجُوعَ وَرَفَعْنَا عَنْ بُطُونِنَا عَنْ حَجَرٍ ، فَرَفَعَ رَسُولُ اللهِ صلى الله عليه وسلم ، عَنْ بَطْنِهِ عَنْ حَجَرَيْنِ[427] قَالَ أَبُو عِيسَى : هَذَا حَدِيثٌ غَرِيبٌ مِنْ حَدِيثِ أَبِي طَلْحَةَ لا نَعْرِفُهُ إِلا مِنْ هَذَا الْوَجْهِ ، وَمَعْنَى قَوْلِهِ : وَرَفَعْنَا عَنْ بُطُونِنَا عَنْ حَجَرٍ حَجَرٍ ، كَانَ أَحَدُهُمْ يَشُدُّ فِي بَطْنِهِ الْحَجَرَ مِنَ الْجُهْدِ وَالضَّعْفِ الَّذِي بِهِ مِنَ الْجُوعِ

371. Abu Talhah ﷺ narrated: "We complained to the Messenger of Allāh ﷺ regarding the hunger we suffered, and showed him the stones fastened on our stomachs. Thereupon, he ﷺ raised his garment and revealed two stones that he had fastened onto his stomach."

Al-Tirmidhī said: "They fastened stones on their stomachs due to the severe exhaustion and hunger they suffered from."

Alī al-Qārī said,

> It was said that the benefit of fastening a stone onto the stomach is that it averts intestinal emphysema, gives support to the back and thus allows easy movement. Al-Hafith ibn Hajar mentioned that this was the habit of Arabs or the people of Madīnah.

427 Sunan al-Tirmidhī (2371)

٣٧٢: حَدَّثَنَا مُحَمَّدُ بْنُ إِسْمَاعِيلَ ، قَالَ : حَدَّثَنَا آدَمُ بْنُ أَبِي إِيَاسٍ ، قَالَ : حَدَّثَنَا شَيْبَانُ أَبُو مُعَاوِيَةَ ، قَالَ : حَدَّثَنَا عَبْدُ الْمَلِكِ بْنُ عُمَيْرٍ ، عَنْ أَبِي سَلَمَةَ بْنِ عَبْدِ الرَّحْمَنِ ، عَنْ أَبِي هُرَيْرَةَ ، قَالَ : خَرَجَ رَسُولُ اللهِ صلى الله عليه وسلم ، فِي سَاعَةٍ لا يَخْرُجُ فِيهَا ، وَلا يَلْقَاهُ فِيهَا أَحَدٌ ، فَأَتَاهُ أَبُو بَكْرٍ ، فَقَالَ : مَا جَاءَ بِكَ يَا أَبَا بَكْرٍ ؟ ، قَالَ : خَرَجْتُ أَلْقَى رَسُولَ اللهِ صلى الله عليه وسلم وَأَنْظُرُ فِي وَجْهِهِ ، وَالتَّسْلِيمَ عَلَيْهِ ، فَلَمْ يَلْبَثْ أَنْ جَاءَ عُمَرُ ، فَقَالَ : مَا جَاءَ بِكَ يَا عُمَرُ ؟ ، قَالَ : الْجُوعُ يَا رَسُولَ اللهِ ، قَالَ صلى الله عليه وسلم : وَأَنَا قَدْ وَجَدْتُ بَعْضَ ذَلِكَ ، فَانْطَلَقُوا إِلَى مَنْزِلِ أَبِي الْهَيْثَمِ بْنِ التَّيِّهَانِ الأَنْصَارِيِّ ، وَكَانَ رَجُلا كَثِيرَ النَّخْلِ وَالشَّاءِ ، وَلَمْ يَكُنْ لَهُ خَدَمٌ ، فَلَمْ يَجِدُوهُ ، فَقَالُوا لامْرَأَتِهِ : أَيْنَ صَاحِبُكِ ؟ فَقَالَتِ : انْطَلَقَ يَسْتَعْذِبُ لَنَا الْمَاءَ ، فَلَمْ يَلْبَثُوا أَنْ جَاءَ أَبُو الْهَيْثَمِ بِقِرْبَةٍ يَزْعَبُهَا ، فَوَضَعَهَا ثُمَّ جَاءَ يَلْتَزِمُ النَّبِيَّ صلى الله عليه وسلم وَيُفَدِّيهِ بِأَبِيهِ وَأُمِّهِ ، ثُمَّ انْطَلَقَ بِهِمْ إِلَى حَدِيقَتِهِ فَبَسَطَ لَهُمْ بِسَاطًا ، ثُمَّ انْطَلَقَ إِلَى نَخْلَةٍ فَجَاءَ بِقِنْوٍ فَوَضَعَهُ ، فَقَالَ النَّبِيُّ صلى الله عليه وسلم : أَفَلا تَنَقَّيْتَ لَنَا مِنْ رُطَبِهِ ؟ فَقَالَ : يَا رَسُولَ اللهِ ، إِنِّي أَرَدْتُ أَنْ تَخْتَارُوا ، أَوْ تَخَيَّرُوا مِنْ رُطَبِهِ وَبُسْرِهِ ، فَأَكَلُوا وَشَرِبُوا مِنْ ذَلِكَ الْمَاءِ فَقَالَ صلى الله عليه وسلم : هَذَا وَالَّذِي نَفْسِي بِيَدِهِ مِنَ النَّعِيمِ الَّذِي تُسْأَلُونَ عَنْهُ يَوْمَ الْقِيَامَةِ ظِلٌّ بَارِدٌ ، وَرُطَبٌ طَيِّبٌ ، وَمَاءٌ بَارِدٌ فَانْطَلَقَ أَبُو الْهَيْثَمِ لِيَصْنَعَ لَهُمْ طَعَامًا فَقَالَ النَّبِيُّ صلى الله عليه وسلم : لا تَذْبَحَنَّ ذَاتَ دَرٍّ ، فَذَبَحَ لَهُمْ عَنَاقًا أَوْ جَدْيًا ، فَأَتَاهُمْ بِهَا فَأَكَلُوا ، فَقَالَ صلى الله عليه وسلم : هَلْ لَكَ خَادِمٌ ؟ ، قَالَ : لا ، قَالَ : فَإِذَا أَتَانَا ، سَبْيٌ ، فَأْتِنَا فَأُتِيَ النَّبِيُّ صلى الله عليه وسلم بِرَأْسَيْنِ لَيْسَ مَعَهُمَا ثَالِثٌ ، فَأَتَاهُ أَبُو الْهَيْثَمِ ، فَقَالَ النَّبِيُّ صلى الله عليه وسلم : اخْتَرْ مِنْهُمَا فَقَالَ : يَا رَسُولَ اللهِ ، اخْتَرْ لِي فَقَالَ النَّبِيُّ صلى الله عليه وسلم : إِنَّ الْمُسْتَشَارَ مُؤْتَمَنٌ ، خُذْ هَذَا ، فَإِنِّي رَأَيْتُهُ يُصَلِّي ، وَاسْتَوْصِ بِهِ مَعْرُوفًا فَانْطَلَقَ أَبُو الْهَيْثَمِ إِلَى امْرَأَتِهِ ، فَأَخْبَرَهَا بِقَوْلِ رَسُولِ اللهِ صلى الله عليه وسلم ، فَقَالَتِ امْرَأَتُهُ

: مَا أَنْتَ بِبَالِغٍ حَقَّ مَا ، قَالَ فِيهِ النَّبِيُّ صلى الله عليه وسلم إلا بِأَنْ تَعْتِقَهُ ، قَالَ : فَهُوَ عَتِيقٌ ، فَقَالَ صلى الله عليه وسلم : إِنَّ اللهَ لَمْ يَبْعَثْ نَبِيًّا وَلا خَلِيفَةً إلا وَلَهُ بِطَانَتَانِ : بِطَانَةٌ تَأْمُرُهُ بِالْمَعْرُوفِ وَتَنْهَاهُ عَنِ الْمُنْكَرِ ، وَبِطَانَةٌ لا تَأْلُوهُ خَبَالا ، وَمَنْ يُوقَ بِطَانَةَ السُّوءِ فَقَدْ وُقِيَ[428]

372. Abu Hurairah ﷺ narrated: "Once, the Messenger of Allāh ﷺ exited his house at such a time that he would not normally leave his home, a time at which people would not meet him. Abū Bakr ﷺ came to him and so he ﷺ asked, 'O Abū Bakr! Why have you come out?' Abū Bakr ﷺ replied, 'I came out to meet the Messenger of Allāh, to look at his face and greet him.'

Soon after, 'Umar ﷺ came and so he ﷺ said, 'O Umar! Why have you come out?' 'Umar ﷺ replied, 'O Messenger of Allāh, due to hunger!' The Messenger of Allāh ﷺ said, 'I too am slightly hungry.' They then proceeded to the house of Abū al-Haytham al-Tayhān al-Ansārī ﷺ. He owned many date palms, trees and sheep, but he did not have any servants. However, after arriving, they did not find him present. They asked his wife, 'Where is your husband?' She replied, 'He has gone to bring us fresh water.' It was not long until he arrived whilst carrying a water bag with difficulty. He placed it to the ground, embraced the Prophet ﷺ and said, 'May my father and mother be sacrificed for you.'

He then invited them to his garden where he spread out for them a mat to sit upon and then went to a palm tree and brought a large cluster of dates, placing it before his guests. The Messenger of Allāh ﷺ said, 'Why did you not just pick for us the ripe ones [rather than bringing forth a whole cluster?]' The host replied, 'O Messenger of Allāh! I wanted that you could eat what pleases you from it.' They ate from the ripe dates and drank from the water. The Messenger of Allāh ﷺ said, 'I swear by the One in whose Hand is my soul that this is also included amongst those blessings of which one will be asked on the Day of Judgment; the cool shadow, fresh and pure dates, and

428 Sunan Abū Dawūd (5128) and Sunan Ibn Mājah (2745)

cold water.'

Abū al-Haytham ﷺ then went to prepare some food, and the Prophet ﷺ said to him, 'Do not slaughter a sheep that gives milk.' So, he slaughtered for them a sheep that had not yet reached four months. After they ate, the Prophet ﷺ asked the host, 'Do you have any servants?' He replied, 'No.' The Prophet ﷺ replied, 'When we receive captives of war, remind us.'

Thus at a later point, two slaves were brought to the Messenger ﷺ upon which Abū al-Haytham ﷺ came to the Prophet ﷺ who said to him, 'Pick from them.' He ﷺ said, 'O Messenger of Allāh! I would prefer if you chose for me.' The Prophet ﷺ said, 'The one whose advice is sought ought to be honest in his advice. I hence choose this slave for you, as I saw him praying. My advice to you is to treat him well.'

Abū al-Haytham ﷺ went to his wife, and told her what the Messenger ﷺ had advised him to do with the slave. His wife said, 'You will not be able to fulfil that which the Prophet ﷺ has commanded except by freeing him.' He said, 'Then, he is free.' The Prophet ﷺ said, 'Allāh has not sent a Prophet or a vicegerent except that He ﷻ made for them two types of close advisers. One of which ordains the good and forbids the evil. The other tries to corrupt the individual. The one that is saved from the corrupt advisor is saved from ruin and destruction."'

Ibn Hajar al-Haytamī said,

> It is evident that the Prophet ﷺ experienced periods of time when he had nothing and periods of time when he possessed riches but it was his habit to distribute the wealth he received between the needy ones and spending upon the army and delegates etc.
>
> Al-Hulaymī said in Shu'ab al-Imān that the Prophet ﷺ should be given his due respect by not describing him as a poor person. Al-Badr al-Zarkashī quoted some latter jurists who said the Prophet ﷺ was not poor; rather he was rich for Allāh sufficed him in his worldly life.

The *fiqh* of this hadith is:

1. It is permissible to express one's pain and hunger if it is intended to help oneself to endure it. This is because if the intent is to complain, it is ugly and disliked.
2. It is allowed to drink fresh water and look for it and that does not contradict *zuhd*.
3. Serving one's family is from the good manners and humbleness.
4. It is recommended to honour the guest and show happiness for hosting them.
5. It is recommended to serve fruit before serving the food and to hasten serving the food that can be eaten right away, especially if the host believes the guest is hungry. Some of the *salaf* disliked the host burdening himself with that which is beyond his capacity as that will affect one's sincerity and may result in showing worry.
6. The host should serve the best food he has even if this may take more time to cook.
7. It is allowed to eat to a full stomach and the hadīths condemning overeating relate to when it is harmful or when it becomes regular as this hardens the heart and makes one forget about the needy ones.
8. Al-Nawawī said, "The mention of the questioning on the Day of Judgement regarding the bounties that Allāh has bestowed upon us, which is mentioned in the hadīth, was to draw attention to His favours upon us and it was not intended for the purpose of condemnation or questioning."
9. The advisor should mind the best interest of the one asking for advice and must not withhold information that may benefit him.
10. It shows that those who pray are better than those who do not pray.
11. It is from evil to remain silent about evil and being good requires the person to order the good and forbid the wrong.

٣٧٣: حدثنا عمر بن إسماعيل بن مجالد بن سعيد ، حدثني أبي عن بيان حدثني قيس بن حازم ، قال : سمعت سعد بن أبي وقاص يقول : إني لأَوَّل رَجلٍ أَهْرَقَ دَمًا فِي سَبِيلِ اللهِ ا وَإِنِّي لأَوَّل رَجلٍ رَمَى بِسَهْمٍ فِى سَبِيلِ الله لَقَدْ رَأَيْتُنِي أغزوا فِي الْعِصَابَةِ مِنْ أَصْحَابِ مُحَمَّدٍ صلى الله عليه وسلم مَا نَأْكُلُ إلاَّ وَرَقَ الشَّجَرِ وَالْحُبْلَةَ حَتَّى تَقَرَّحَتْ أَشْدَاقُنَا وَإِنْ أَحَدُنَا لَيَضَعُ كَمَا تَضَعُ الشَّاةُ وَالبَعِيرِ وَأَصْبَحَتْ بَنُو أَسَدٍ يُعَزِّرُونَنِى فِي الدِّينِ ا لَقَدْ خِبْتُ إِذَنْ وَخَسِرْت وَضَلَّ عَمَلِي .[429]

373. Sa'd ibn Abī Waqqās ﷺ reported: "I was the first man to spill blood in the path of Allāh, and I was the first man to shoot an arrow in the path of Allāh. I found myself fighting besides a group of people from the companions of Muhammad ﷺ and we were in such a state where we ate nothing except the leaves of trees and shrubs. As a result, the corners of our mouths were sore and when we relieved ourselves, what came out appeared as if a camel or sheep had relieved itself. And now, the people of Banu Assad come to criticise my worship. Indeed, I am ruined and in loss if their [false] claim is true."

Alı al-Qarı said,

> The companions ﷺ used to pray in secret and it happened that some disbelievers saw Sa'd with a few other companions praying in secret. Thus, they started to abuse them and the dispute escalated so Sa'd hit one of them and made him bleed.
>
> The battle referred to in the hadīth is the battle of al-Khabat which happened in the eighth year. The number of companions was three hundred and their leader was Abū 'Ubaydah ﷺ. Before they left Madīnah, the Prophet ﷺ gave them a bag of dates and so Abū 'Ubaydah ﷺ used to divide it between the companions and reduce the share of each until it dwindled down to one date per

429 Sahīh al-Bukhārī (3728) and Sahīh Muslim (2966)

person. After they finished the dates and endured a great degree of suffering, Allāh gave them from the sea an extremely large fish that they lived on for approximately one month. It was said that the battle that Sa'd referred to was a battle that the Prophet ﷺ participated in, which is reported in Sahīh al-Bukharī and Sahīh Muslim. Regardless of which battle it was, the relevance of this hadīth in the context of this chapter is that it indicates the minimal resources that the Prophet ﷺ possessed, because if he had more he would have given his companions more.

The reason Sa'd ibn Abī Waqqās رضي الله عنه was upset with Banī Assad is because he was appointed as the ruler of Basra during the time of 'Umar رضي الله عنه and they falsely claimed that he did not know how to pray. So he expressed his objection to this, indicating to them the absurdity of their claim when he was from the first ones who embraced Islām and accompanied the Prophet ﷺ for such a long time.

٣٧٤: حدثنا محمد بن بشار حدثنا صفوان بن عيسى حدثنا محمد بن عمرو بن عيسى أبو نعامة العدوي قال : سمعت خَالِدِ بْنِ عُمَيْرٍ وشويسًا أبا الرقاد قالا : بعث عمر بن الخطاب عُتْبَةُ بْنُ غَزْوَانَ وقَالَ انطلق أنت ومن معك حتى إذا كنتم في أقصى أرض العرب وأدنى بلاد أرض العجم فأقبلوا حتى إذا كانوا بالمربد وجدوا هذا المكان فقالوا : ما هذه ؟ هذه البصرة . فساروا حتى إذا بلغوا حيال الجسر الصغير فقالوا : هاهنا أمرتم فنزلوا فذكروا الحديث بطوله .

قال : فقال عتبة بن غزوان : لَقَدْ رَأَيْتُنِي وَإِنِّي لسَابعَ سَبْعَةٍ مَعَ رَسُولِ الله صلى الله عليه وسلم مَا لنَا طَعَامٌ إلاَّ وَرَقُ الشَّجَرِ حَتَّى تقَرِحَتْ أَشْدَاقُنَا فالْتَقَطْتُ بُرْدَةً فَقسمتها بَيْنِي وَبَيْنَ سَعْدٍ بن أبي وقاص فَمَا مِنَّا من أُولَئِك السَبْعَة أَحَد إلاَّ وَهُوَ أَمِيرَ مِصْرٍ مِنَ الأَمْصَارِ وَسَتَجْرُبونَ الأُمَرَاءَ بَعْدَنَا[430]

430 Al-Mu'jam al-Awsat (4/243)

374. Khālid ibn 'Umayr and Shuwaysa narrated: "'Umar ibn al-Khattab ؓ instructed 'Utbah ibn Ghazwān and those under his command to travel to the farthest point of the lands of the Arabs and the nearest part of the lands of the non-Arabs and camp there. The army embarked on the journey and when they reached al-Mirbad, they saw some strange white stones. They asked, 'What is this?' The people replied, 'This is Basra.' Then, they proceeded until they reached a small bridge. The people said, 'This is the place that 'Umar ؓ had ordered us to set up our camp.'" [The narrator mentioned the story in its totality.]

'Utbah ibn Ghazwān ؓ said: "By Allāh, I was the seventh of the first seven with the Messenger of Allāh ﷺ, eating nothing but the leaves of trees until the corners of our mouths were sore. I picked up [from the floor] a garment and then I cut it into two halves and gave one half to Sa'd and I wore the other half. Each one from the seven became a leader of a city from amongst the cities. After us, you will find leaders that are in no way similar to us."

Abdul Razzaq al-Badr said,

> 'Umar ibn al-Khattab ؓ sent 'Utbah ibn Ghazwān with a group of people to guard the boarders from where the attacks of the disbelievers were feared. He appointed for them the location where they needed to set up their camp in.
>
> Al-Tirmidhi did not include the full story due its irrelevance to the chapter; thus he jumped to the parts that are related to the title of the chapter.
>
> The reason 'Utbah ibn Ghazwān ؓ mentioned that he and the other six companions became rulers eventually was to show them how life was difficult at that time and how it changed afterwards.
>
> The full incident is mentioned in Sahīh Muslim[431] and part of the remaining statement of 'Utbah ؓ was, "I seek refuge in Allāh from being great in this world whilst being small in His sight."

431 Sahīh Muslim (2967)

٣٧٥: حَدَّثَنَا عَبْدُ اللهِ بْنُ عَبْدِ الرَّحْمَنِ ، قَالَ : حَدَّثَنَا رَوْحُ بْنُ أَسْلَمَ أَبُو حَاتِمٍ الْبَصْرِيُّ ، قَالَ : حَدَّثَنَا حَمَّادُ بْنُ سَلَمَةَ ، قَالَ : حَدَّثَنَا ثَابِتٌ ، عَنْ أَنَسٍ ، قَالَ : قَالَ رَسُولُ اللهِ صلى الله عليه وسلم : لَقَدْ أُخِفْتُ فِي اللهِ وَمَا يُخَافُ أَحَدٌ ، وَلَقَدْ أُوذِيتُ فِي اللهِ وَمَا يُؤْذَى أَحَدٌ ، وَلَقَدْ أَتَتْ عَلَيَّ ثَلاثُونَ مِنْ بَيْنِ لَيْلَةٍ وَيَوْمٍ ، وَمَا لِي وَلِبِلالٍ طَعَامٌ يَأْكُلُهُ ذُو كَبِدٍ ، إِلا شَيْءٌ يُوَارِيهِ إِبِطُ بِلالٍ[432]

375. Anas ibn Mālik ﷺ narrated: "The Messenger of Allāh ﷺ said: 'I was made to fear [for striving] in the path of Allāh at a time when no one else was threatened. I was harmed [for striving] in the path of Allāh at a time when no one else experienced harm. Thirty consecutive nights and days passed wherein I and Bilal ﷺ had no food that even an animal would eat, except for the minute, hidden under the arm of Bilal ﷺ."'

Ibn Hajar al-Asqalānī said,

> Narrated Aisha ﷺ: "I asked the Prophet ﷺ, 'Have you encountered a day harder than the day [of the battle] of Uhud?' The Prophet ﷺ replied, 'Your tribes have troubled me a lot, and the worst trouble was the trouble on the day of 'Aqaba when I presented myself to Ibn 'Abd-Yalail ibn 'Abd-Kulal and he did not respond to my request. So I departed, overwhelmed with sorrow and proceeded on. I could not relax until I found myself at Qarnath-Thalib where I lifted my head towards the sky to see a cloud shading me unexpectedly. I looked up and saw Jibrīl in it. He called me saying, 'Allāh has heard your people's words to you, and what they have replied back to you, Allāh has sent the Angel of the Mountains to you so that you may order him to do whatever you wish to these people.' The Angel of the Mountains called and greeted me, and then said, 'O Muhammad! Order what you wish. If you like, I will let al-Akhshabain (i.e. two mountains) fall upon them.' I said, 'No but I hope that Allāh will let them beget children who will

432 Sunan Ibn Mājah (151) and Sunan al-Tirmidhī (2372)

worship Allah Alone, and will worship none besides Him.'"[433]

Ibn Hajar al-Haytamī said,

> Al-Tirmidhī said that this was during the period when the Prophet ﷺ left Makkah.

٣٧٦: حَدَّثَنَا عَبْدُ اللهِ بْنُ عَبْدِ الرَّحْمَنِ ، قَالَ : حَدَّثَنَا عَفَّانُ بْنُ مُسْلِمٍ ، قَالَ : حَدَّثَنَا أَبَانُ بْنُ يَزِيدَ الْعَطَّارُ ، قَالَ : حَدَّثَنَا قَتَادَةُ ، عَنْ أَنَسِ بْنِ مَالِكٍ : أَنَّ النَّبِيَّ صلى الله عليه وسلم ، لَمْ يَجْتَمِعْ عِنْدَهُ غَدَاءٌ وَلا عَشَاءٌ مِنْ خُبْزٍ وَلَحْمٍ ، إِلا عَلَى ضَفَفٍ[434]
قَالَ عَبْدُ اللهِ : ، قَالَ بَعْضُهُمْ : هُوَ كَثْرَةُ الأَيْدِي

376. Anas ibn Mālik ؓ narrated: "The Messenger of Allāh ﷺ would not consume bread or meat in the morning or evening twice in one day, except if he was invited as a guest."

٣٧٧: حَدَّثَنَا عَبْدُ بْنُ حُمَيْدٍ ، قَالَ : حَدَّثَنَا مُحَمَّدُ بْنُ إِسْمَاعِيلَ بْنِ أَبِي فُدَيْكٍ ، قَالَ : حَدَّثَنَا ابْنُ أَبِي ذِئْبٍ ، عَنْ مُسْلِمِ بْنِ جُنْدُبٍ ، عَنْ نَوْفَلِ بْنِ إِيَاسٍ الْهُذَلِيِّ ، قَال : كَانَ عَبْدُ الرَّحْمَنِ بْنُ عَوْفٍ لَنَا جَلِيسًا ، وَكَانَ نِعْمَ الْجَلِيسُ ، وَإِنَّهُ انْقَلَبَ بِنَا ذَاتَ يَوْمٍ ، حَتَّى إِذَا دَخَلْنَا بَيْتَهُ وَدَخَلَ فَاغْتَسَلَ ، ثُمَّ خَرَجَ وَأُتِينَا بِصَحْفَةٍ فِيهَا خُبْزٌ وَلَحْمٌ ، فَلَمَّا وُضِعَتْ بَكَى عَبْدُ الرَّحْمَنِ ، فَقُلْتُ لَهُ : يَا أَبَا مُحَمَّدٍ ، مَا يُبْكِيكَ ؟ فَقَالَ : هَلَكَ رَسُولُ اللهِ صلى الله عليه وسلم ، وَلَمْ يَشْبَعْ هُوَ وَأَهْلُ بَيْتِهِ مِنْ خُبْزِ الشَّعِيرِ فَلا أَرَانَا أُخِّرْنَا لِمَا هُوَ خَيْرٌ لَنَا[435]

377. Nawfal ibn lyās al-Hudhalī narrated: "Abdul Rahman ibn al-

---

433 Sahih al-Bukhārī (3010) and Sahīh Muslim (3358
434 Musnad Ahmad (13859)
435 Musnad 'Abd ibn Hamīd (161)

'Awf ﷺ would host gatherings for us, and verily he was a good host. Once we were returning from a place with him. On returning we went with him to his house. When we entered his home he first took a bath and then came to us. Bread and meat was served upon a large platter. Thereupon he began to cry. I asked, 'O Abu Muhammad! What causes you to cry?' He said, 'Until the demise of the Messenger of Allāh ﷺ, neither did he or his family members fill their stomachs with something as little as the bread made of barley. I never thought that we would be delayed from that which is better for us.'"

'Abdullāh ibn Sa'īd said,

> The crying of Abdul Rahman ibn al-'Awf ﷺ was due to his concern regarding the consequences of the ease which had come to engulf their lives. This is because the simple lifestyle of the best of mankind ﷺ was such that he could not eat to his full even with the barley bread. The first generation used to become worried and concerned when life became easy for them as they feared that Allāh had made their reward in this worldly life instead of the Hereafter.

CHAPTER FIFTY THREE

باب ماجاء في سن رسول اللّه صلى اللّه عليه وسلم

THE REPORTS PERTAINING TO THE AGE OF THE MESSENGER OF ALLAH ﷺ

٣٧٨: حَدَّثَنَا أَحْمَدُ بْنُ مَنِيعٍ ، قَالَ : حَدَّثَنَا رَوْحُ بْنُ عُبَادَةَ ، قَالَ : حَدَّثَنَا زَكَرِيَا بْنُ إِسْحَاقَ ، قَالَ : حَدَّثَنَا عَمْرُو بْنُ دِينَارٍ ، عَنِ ابْنِ عَبَّاسٍ ، قَالَ : مَكَثَ النَّبِيُّ صلى الله عليه وسلم بِمَكَّةَ ثَلاثَ عَشْرَةَ سَنَةً يُوحَى إِلَيْهِ ، وَبِالْمَدِينَةِ عَشْرًا ، وَتُوُفِّيَ وَهُوَ ابْنُ ثَلاثٍ وَسِتِّينَ[436]

378. 'Abdullāh ibn Abbās ﷺ narrated: "The Prophet ﷺ remained in Makkah for thirteen years during which he received revelation, and in Madīnah for ten years. He passed away at the age of sixty three."

Ibn Hajar al-Asqalānī said,

> The Prophet ﷺ was forty years old when he received the revelation on the first occasion and it was mentioned previously in the chapter of revelation that the revelation was in the month of Ramadān. The most famous and correct view is that he was born in the month of Rabī' al-Awwal.

Abdul Rahman al-Mubarakfūrī said,

> Al-Tirmidhī reported three narrations regarding the age of the Prophet ﷺ at the time of his passing. The first hadīth states that he passed away when he was sixty three years old, the next hadīth states that he was sixty years old and the last hadith states that he was sixty five years old. Al-Nawawī offered a good reconciliation between these three hadīths as he stated, "The most correct and most widely accepted view is that he ﷺ was sixty three years old when he passed and the hadīth stating his age as sixty was mentioned in respect to decades and not to give an exact number. The other hadīth was just a confusion on the part of Ibn Abbās ﷺ for 'Urwah ﷺ rejected this statement of his and said that Ibn Abbās erred as he did not accompany the Prophet ﷺ as much as other companions and did not witness the beginning of his prophethood." The scholars agreed

436 Sahīh al-Bukhārī (3903) and Sahīh Muslim (2351)

that he ﷺ was born on a Monday and died on a Monday but they differed upon which day of the month he was born, whether it was the second, eighth, tenth or twelfth of Rabī' al-Awwal.

٣٧٩: حَدَّثَنَا مُحَمَّدُ بْنُ بَشَّارٍ ، قَالَ : حَدَّثَنَا مُحَمَّدُ بْنُ جَعْفَرٍ ، عَنْ شُعْبَةَ ، عَنْ أَبِي إِسْحَاقَ ، عَنْ عَامِرِ بْنِ سَعْدٍ ، عَنْ جَرِيرٍ ، عَنْ مُعَاوِيَةَ ، أَنَّهُ سَمِعَهُ يَخْطُبُ ، قَالَ : مَاتَ رَسُولُ اللهِ صلى الله عليه وسلم وَهُوَ ابْنُ ثَلاثٍ وَسِتِّينَ وَأَبُو بَكْرٍ وَعُمَرُ ، وَأَنَا ابْنُ ثَلاثٍ وَسِتِّينَ سنة[437]

379. Jarīr narrated that he heard Mu'āwiyah ؓ saying in a speech he delivered: "The Messenger of Allāh ﷺ passed away at the age of sixty three. Likewise, Abū Bakr and 'Umar ؓ passed away at the same age. I am [currently] sixty three."

Alī al-Qārī said,

> Given the age of passing of the Prophet ﷺ and his two companions ؓ, Mu'āwiyah expected to die at the same age. In Jāmi' al-Usūl it is stated that Mu'āwiyah passed away at the age of seventy eight and it was said at eighty six years old. Mirak said, "He hoped to die at the age of sixty three just like the Prophet ﷺ and his two companions but that did not happen as he died when he was nearly eighty years old."

٣٨٠: حَدَّثَنَا حُسَيْنُ بْنُ مَهْدِيٍّ الْبَصْرِيُّ ، قَالَ : حَدَّثَنَا عَبْدُ الرَّزَّاقِ ، عَنِ ابْنِ جُرَيْجٍ ، عَنِ الزُّهْرِيِّ ، عَنْ عُرْوَةَ ، عَنْ عَائِشَةَ : أَنَّ النَّبِيَّ صلى الله عليه وسلم ، مَاتَ وَهُوَ ابْنُ ثَلاثٍ وَسِتِّينَ سَنَةً[438]

380. Aisha ؓ narrated: "The Prophet ﷺ passed away when he was

437 Sahīh Muslim (2352)
438 Sahīh al-Bukhārī (3536) and Sahīh Muslim (2349)

sixty three years of age."

٣٨١: حَدَّثَنَا أَحْمَدُ بْنُ مَنِيعٍ ، وَيَعْقُوبُ بْنُ إِبْرَاهِيمَ الدَّوْرَقِيُّ ، قَالا : حَدَّثَنَا إِسْمَاعِيلُ بْنُ عُلَيَّةَ ، عَنْ خَالِدٍ الْحَذَّاءِ ، قَالَ : أَنْبَأَنَا عَمَّارٌ مَوْلَى بَنِي هَاشِمٍ ، قَالَ : سَمِعْتُ ابْنَ عَبَّاسٍ ، يَقُولُ : تُوُفِّيَ رَسُولُ اللَّهِ صلى الله عليه وسلم ، وَهُوَ ابْنُ خَمْسٍ وَسِتِّينَ[439]

381. 'Abdullāh ibn 'Abbās ﷺ narrated: "The Messenger of Allāh ﷺ passed away when he was sixty five years old."

٣٨٢: حَدَّثَنَا مُحَمَّدُ بْنُ بَشَّارٍ ، وَمُحَمَّدُ بْنُ أَبَانَ ، قَالا : حَدَّثَنَا مُعَاذُ بْنُ هِشَامٍ ، قَالَ : حَدَّثَنِي أَبِي ، عَنْ قَتَادَةَ ، عَنِ الْحَسَنِ ، عَنْ دَغْفَلِ بْنِ حَنْظَلَةَ : أَنَّ النَّبِيَّ صلى الله عليه وسلم ، قُبِضَ وَهُوَ ابْنُ خَمْسٍ وَسِتِّينَ ، قَالَ أَبُو عِيسَى : وَدَغْفَلُ ، لا نَعْرِفُ لَهُ سَمَاعًا مِنَ النَّبِيِّ صلى الله عليه وسلم ، وَكَانَ فِي زَمَنِ النَّبِيِّ صلى الله عليه وسلم[440]

382. Daghfal ibn Handhalah narrated: "The Prophet ﷺ passed away when he was sixty five years of age."

Al-Tirmidhī said: "Daghfal did not hear any reports from the Prophet ﷺ directly, though we know that he lived during the lifetime of the Prophet ﷺ."

٣٨٣: حَدَّثَنَا إِسْحَاقُ بْنُ مُوسَى الأَنْصَارِيُّ ، قَالَ : حَدَّثَنَا مَعْنٌ ، حَدَّثَنَا مَالِكُ بْنُ أَنَسٍ ، عَنْ رَبِيعَةَ بْنِ أَبِي عَبْدِ الرَّحْمَنِ ، عَنْ أَنَسِ بْنِ مَالِكٍ ، أَنَّهُ سَمِعَهُ ، يَقُولُ : كَانَ رَسُولُ اللَّهِ صلى الله عليه وسلم ، لَيْسَ بِالطَّوِيلِ الْبَائِنِ ، وَلا بِالْقَصِيرِ ، وَلا بِالأَبْيَضِ الأَمْهَقِ ، وَلا بِالآدَمِ ، وَلا بِالْجَعْدِ الْقَطَطِ ،

439 Sahīh Muslim (2353)
440 See hadīth 381

وَلا بِالسَّبْطِ ، بَعَثَهُ اللهُ تَعَالَى عَلَى رَأْسِ أَرْبَعِينَ سَنَةً ، فَأَقَامَ بِمَكَّةَ عَشْرَ سِنِينَ ، وَبِالْمَدِينَةِ عَشْرَ سِنِينَ ، وَتَوَفَّاهُ اللهُ عَلَى رَأْسِ سِتِّينَ سَنَةً ، وَلَيْسَ فِي رَأْسِهِ وَلِحْيَتِهِ عِشْرُونَ شَعَرَةً بَيْضَاءَ[441]

383. Narrated by Rabī'a ibn Abī Abdul Rahman ﵁: "I heard Anas ibn Mālik describing the Prophet ﷺ saying, 'He was neither too tall nor short; neither absolutely white nor brown; his hair was neither very curly nor completely straight. The divine revelation was revealed to him when he was forty years old. He stayed ten years in Makkah, and stayed in Madīnah for ten more years. When he died, he was sixty years old and had [approximately] twenty grey hairs in his head and beard."

٣٨٤ : حَدَّثَنَا قُتَيْبَةُ بْنُ سَعِيدٍ ، عَنْ مَالِكِ بْنِ أَنَسٍ ، عَنْ رَبِيعَةَ بْنِ أَبِي عَبْدِ الرَّحْمَنِ ، عَنْ أَنَسِ بْنِ مَالِكٍ ، نَحْوَهُ

384. Anas ibn Mālik ﵁ reports the same through a different route.

441 See hadīth 1

CHAPTER FIFTY FOUR

باب ماجاء في وفاة رسول الله صلى الله عليه وسلم

THE REPORTS PERTAINING TO THE DEATH OF THE MESSENGER OF ALLAH ﷺ

Abdul Razzaq al-Badr said,

> The author wanted to highlight the death of the Prophet ﷺ after he finished the chapters related to his description for his death was indeed the greatest calamity that befell the Muslims.
>
> The most famous remark made upon the death of the Prophet ﷺ was said during the state of confusion that overtook the Muslims. They could not believe the news and were under the shock of it. Then Abū Bakr addressed the people, "Whoever worships Allāh, then know that Allāh is alive and does not die, and whoever worships Muhammad, then Muhammad has died."

٣٨٥: حَدَّثَنَا أَبُو عَمَّارٍ الْحُسَيْنُ بْنُ حُرَيْثٍ ، وَقُتَيْبَةُ بْنُ سَعِيدٍ ، وَغَيْرُ وَاحِدٍ ، قَالُوا : حَدَّثَنَا سُفْيَانُ بْنُ عُيَيْنَةَ ، عَنِ الزُّهْرِيِّ ، عَنْ أَنَسِ بْنِ مَالِكٍ ، قَالَ : آخِرُ نَظْرَةٍ نَظَرْتُهَا إِلَى رَسُولِ اللهِ صلى الله عليه وسلم ، كَشْفُ السِّتَارَةِ يَوْمَ الاثْنَيْنِ ، فَنَظَرْتُ إِلَى وَجْهِهِ كَأَنَّهُ وَرَقَةُ مُصْحَفٍ ، وَالنَّاسُ خَلْفَ أَبِي بَكْرٍ ، فَكَادَ النَّاسُ أَنْ يَضْطَرِبُوا ، فَأَشَارَ إِلَى النَّاسِ أَنِ اثْبُتُوا ، وَأَبُو بَكْرٍ يَؤُمُّهُمْ وَأَلْقَى السِّجْفَ ، وَتُوُفِّيَ رَسُولُ اللهِ صلى الله عليه وسلم مِنْ آخِرِ ذَلِكَ الْيَوْمِ[442]

385. Anas ibn Mālik ؓ narrated: "The last glimpse I laid upon the Messenger of Allāh ﷺ was on a Monday when the curtain of his house was lifted [the people had aligned [in rows] for the prayer]. I looked at him [and his face was bright] and it was as if it was a page of a *mus-haf* (Qur'ān). Upon seeing the Prophet ﷺ, we were about to leave the prayer [due to the overwhelming joy of seeing him]. However, he ﷺ beckoned to us to complete the prayer. Abū Bakr ؓ led the people in prayer and he let the curtain fall. Towards the end of that day the Messenger of Allāh ﷺ passed away."

Abdul Razzaq al-Badr said,

> This hadīth explains that the death of the Prophet ﷺ was on a Monday. On that day, the sickness of the Prophet ﷺ became severe and so Abū Bakr ؓ led the *Fajr* prayer. The brief moment that the Prophet ﷺ lifted the curtain and saw his companions standing in lines with humility ready for the prayer he rejoiced at witnessing that scene and smiled as stated in the hadīth in Sahīh al-Bukharī and Sahīh Muslim.
>
> The concern and worry of the Prophet ﷺ regarding the prayer did not stop there for his last words upon his death bed were to remind the people to observe the prayer and he mentioned it twice

442 Sahīh al-Bukhārī (680) and Sahīh Muslim (419)

as stated in Sunan ibn Mājah[443]. This shows the great status of the prayer in Islām.

The correct view is that the Prophet ﷺ passed away during the time of *Duha* and it seems that the meaning of Anas was that people verified the news of his death towards the end of the day. It happened when they inquired from Abū Bakr regarding the authenticity of such news. He confirmed the news, kissed the Prophet ﷺ between his eyes and delivered a speech to the people to inform them about it.

٣٨٦: حَدَّثَنَا حُمَيْدُ بْنُ مَسْعَدَةَ الْبَصْرِيُّ ، قَالَ : حَدَّثَنَا سُلَيْمُ بْنُ أَخْضَرَ ، عَنِ ابْنِ عَوْنٍ ، عَنِ إِبْرَاهِيمَ ، عَنِ الأَسْوَدِ ، عَنْ عَائِشَةَ ، قَالَتْ : كُنْتُ مُسْنِدَةً النَّبِيَّ صلى الله عليه وسلم ، إِلَى صَدْرِي أَوْ قَالَتْ : إِلَى حِجْرِي فَدَعَا بِطَسْتٍ لِيَبُولَ فِيهِ ، ثُمَّ بَالَ ، فَمَاتَ[444]

386. Aisha narrated: "The Messenger of Allāh ﷺ was resting against my chest, [or she said: in my lap]. He asked for a wash-basin to relieve himself. He relieved himself and thereafter, he passed away."

Ibn Kathīr said,

> It is reported in the two Sahīh books that in the presence of Aisha some people mentioned that the Prophet ﷺ had appointed Alī by will as his successor. Aisha said, "When did he appoint him by will? Verily when he died he was resting against my chest (or she said: in my lap), he asked for a wash-basin and then collapsed whilst in that state. I could not even perceive that he had died, so when did he appoint him by will?"
>
> Talhah ibn Musarrif related, "I asked 'Abdullāh ibn Abī Awfa,

443 Sunan ibn Mājah [585]

444 Sahīh al-Bukhārī (741) and Sahīh Muslim (1636)

'Did the Messenger of Allāh ﷺ have a will?' He replied, 'No.' I said, 'If he did not do so, why did he order us to write our own wills?' He said, 'His will was that we do not overlook the book of Allah.'"

Abdul Razzaq al-Badr said,

> The other hadīths indicate that he ﷺ was resting against her chest. The Prophet ﷺ asked the permission of his wives to be treated in the house of Aisha ﵂ and he used to lead the prayer until he could no longer do so due to his sickness. The last prayer he led was a Friday prayer and then Abū Bakr ﵁ began leading the prayer from that Friday until the *Fajr* prayer on Monday.
>
> Due to his sickness, he could not get up from his bed and this is why he asked for the container.

٣٨٧: حَدَّثَنَا قُتَيْبَةُ حَدَّثَنَا اللَّيْثُ ، عَنِ ابْنِ الْهَادِ ، عَنْ مُوسَى بْنِ سَرْجِسَ ، عَنِ الْقَاسِمِ بْنِ مُحَمَّدٍ ، عَنْ عَائِشَةَ ، أَنَّهَا قَالَتْ : رَأَيْتُ رَسُولَ اللهِ صلى الله عليه وسلم ، وَهُوَ بِالْمَوْتِ وَعِنْدَهُ قَدَحٌ فِيهِ مَاءٌ ، وَهُوَ يُدْخِلُ يَدَهُ فِي الْقَدَحِ ، ثُمَّ يَمْسَحُ وَجْهَهُ بِالْمَاءِ ، ثُمَّ يَقُولُ : اللَّهُمَّ أَعِنِّي عَلَى مُنْكَرَاتِ أَوْ قَالَ : عَلَى سَكَرَاتِ الْمَوْتِ[445]

387. Aisha ﵂ narrated: "I saw the Messenger of Allāh ﷺ just before he passed away placing his hands into a cup of water. He would wipe his face with it whilst saying, '*O Allāh help me endure the agonies of death*.'"

Abdul Razzaq al-Badr said,

> The Prophet ﷺ repeated the statement, "There is no god worthy of worship besides Allāh" and then said, "Death possesses agony." Then he stretched his hand, raised it and said, "I choose to be with

445 Sunan al-Tirmidhī (978)

the company of the higher companion" until he died and his hand fell down.

Ibn Hajar al-Asqalānī said,

> Al-Suhailī said, "The reason why these ("O Allāh, [with] the higher companion") were the last words of the Prophet ﷺ is because they refer both to *tawhīd* and to *dhikr* in the heart. It offers comfort to those who are unable to speak [when dying], because some people may not be able to speak out loud for some reason, but that does not matter if their hearts are steadfast in remembering Allāh."

٣٨٨: حَدَّثَنَا الْحَسَنُ بْنُ الصَّبَّاحِ الْبَزَّازُ ، قَالَ : حَدَّثَنَا مُبَشِّرُ بْنُ إِسْمَاعِيلَ ، عَنْ عَبْدِ الرَّحْمَنِ بْنِ الْعَلاءِ ، عَنْ أَبِيهِ ، عَنِ ابْنِ عُمَرَ ، عَنْ عَائِشَةَ ، قَالَتْ : لا أَغْبِطُ أَحَدًا بِهَوْنِ مَوْتٍ بَعْدَ الَّذِي رَأَيْتُ مِنْ شِدَّةِ مَوْتِ رَسُولِ اللهِ صلى الله عليه وسلم[446]

388. Aisha رضي الله عنها said: "I no longer rejoice at anyone experiencing an easy death after having witnessed the difficulties in death endured by the Messenger ﷺ of Allāh."

Ibn Hajar al-Asqalānī said,

> This shows that experiencing hardship and agony at the time of death does not indicate a lower status of *imān*; rather it is a means whereby the good deeds of the believers increase or the bad deeds of the believers are erased.

Al-Sindī said,

> This hadīth proves that Aisha رضي الله عنها knew that the more agony a person experiences at the time of death, the more good deeds he

446 Sunan al-Tirmidhī (979)

receives. [This is from] observing the extreme level of suffering the Prophet ﷺ endured upon his death bed.

٣٨٩: حَدَّثَنَا أَبُو كُرَيْبٍ مُحَمَّدُ بْنُ الْعَلاءِ ، قَالَ : حَدَّثنا أَبُو مُعَاوِيَةَ ، عَنْ عَبْدِ الرَّحْمَنِ بْنِ أَبِي بَكْرٍ وَهُوَ ابْنُ الْمُلَيْكِيِّ ، عَنِ ابْنِ أَبِي مُلَيْكَةَ ، عَنْ عَائِشَةَ ، قَالَتْ : لَمَّا قُبِضَ رَسُولُ اللهِ صلى الله عليه وسلم ، اخْتَلَفُوا فِي دَفْنِهِ ، فَقَالَ أَبُو بَكْرٍ : سَمِعْتُ مِنْ رَسُولِ اللهِ صلى الله عليه وسلم ، شَيْئًا مَا نَسِيتُهُ ، قَالَ : مَا قَبَضَ اللهُ نَبِيًّا إِلا فِي الْمَوْضِعِ الَّذِي يُحِبُّ أَنْ يُدْفَنَ فِيهِ ، ادْفِنُوهُ فِي مَوْضِعِ فِرَاشِهِ[447]

389. Aisha ؓ related: "After the demise of the Messenger of Allāh ﷺ, the people disagreed regarding where to bury him. Abū Bakr ؓ said, 'I heard something from the Messenger of Allāh ﷺ that I did not forget. He ﷺ said, 'Allāh does not take the life of His Prophets except in the location He [or the Prophet] wishes them buried." Thus he was buried in the place where his bed was."

Alī al-Qārī said,

> The companions differed regarding the location where they should bury the Prophet ﷺ, some suggested to bury him in his masjid, some said in al-Baqī' where his companions were buried, and some suggested in Makkah.

Al-Zarqanī said,

> Indeed, there was no darker day than the day on which he ﷺ died. Upon his death, he moved to another place that has the pleasure of receiving him, and to celebrate his coming Paradise wore its best adornment to welcome his soul.

After the death of the Prophet ﷺ, it is reported that his donkey

447 Sunan al-Tirmidhī (1018)

showed sadness until it fell in a well and died. Also, his camel refused to eat and drink anything after his death until it died.

٣٩٠: حَدَّثَنَا مُحَمَّدُ بْنُ بَشَّارٍ ، وعياش العنبرى وسوار بن عبد الله وغير واحد قالوا : أخبرنا يحيي بن سعيد عن سفيان الثورى عن موسى بن أبي عائشة عن عبيد الله عن ابن عباس وعائشة : أن أبا بكر قبل النبي صلى الله عليه وسلم بعدما مات[448]

390. 'Abdullāh ibn Abbās and Aisha ؓ both narrated: "Abū Bakr ؓ kissed the Prophet ﷺ after he passed away."

٣٩١: حدثنا نصر بن علي الجهضمي ، حدثنا مرحوم بن عبد العزيز العطار ، عن يزيد بن بابنوس ، عن عائشة أن أبا بكر دخل على النبي صلى الله عليه وسلم بعد وفاته فوضع فمه بين عينيه ، ووضع يديه على ساعديه ، وقال : وانبياه واصفياه ، واخليلاه[449]

391. Aisha ؓ narrated: "Abū Bakr ؓ entered upon the Prophet ﷺ after his death. He kissed him ﷺ between his eyes, put his hands upon his forearms and said, 'O my Prophet! O my close companion! O my best friend!'"

Ibn al-Qayyim said,

> It is permissible to express one's sadness over someone's death if the statement is simple and truthful and is not intended to wail or to show discontentment as this does not contradict the patience that one is obliged to show in such events, as can be noted in this hadīth.

448 Sahīh al-Bukhārī (4451)
449 Sunan Abū Dawūd (2137)

Ibn Hajar al-Haytamī said,

> Abū Bakr ؓ cried and kissed the forehead of the Prophet ﷺ to follow the example that he ؓ set when he kissed 'Uthmān ibn Madh'ūn ؓ after his death. It shows that it is recommended to kiss the face of the deceased pious person.

٣٩٢: حَدَّثَنَا بِشْرُ بْنُ هِلالٍ الصَّوَّافُ الْبَصْرِيُّ ، قَالَ : حَدَّثَنَا جَعْفَرُ بْنُ سُلَيْمَانَ ، عَنْ ثَابِتٍ ، عَنْ أَنَسٍ ، قَالَ : لَمَّا كَانَ الْيَوْمُ الَّذِي دَخَلَ فِيهِ رَسُولُ اللهِ صلى الله عليه وسلم الْمَدِينَةَ أَضَاءَ مِنْهَا كُلُّ شَيْءٍ ، فَلَمَّا كَانَ الْيَوْمُ الَّذِي مَاتَ فِيهِ أَظْلَمَ مِنْهَا كُلُّ شَيْءٍ ، وَمَا نَفَضْنَا أَيْدِيَنَا مِنَ التُّرَابِ ، وَإِنَا لَفِي دَفْنِهِ صلى الله عليه وسلم ، حَتَّى أَنْكَرْنَا قُلُوبَنَا[450]

392. Anas ibn Mālik ؓ narrated: "The day the Messenger of Allāh ﷺ arrived at Madīnah, everything became illuminated. The day that the Messenger of Allāh ﷺ passed away, everything darkened. We had not yet dusted off the earth of his burial from our hands, yet we felt a change in our hearts."

Ibn Hajar al-Asqalānī said,

> After the burial of the Prophet ﷺ, Fātimah ؓ chastised the companions, including Anas ibn Mālik ؓ for having the heart to place the Prophet ﷺ down in his grave [and bury him] as she knew their extreme love towards him. In response, Anas ؓ remained silent given the emotional state he was in at that time as if to indicate that they disliked doing so but they had to subdue their hearts to comply with his command.
>
> The statement where he ؓ said that they felt a change in their hearts meant that they did not find their hearts to be upon the same degree of purity, serenity and softness as before the Prophet's

450 Sunan Ibn Mājah (1631) and Sunan al-Tirmidhī (3618)

death, when revelation was still being revealed to him, and when he was still teaching them.

Ibn Abdul Barr said,

> Indeed, the death of the Prophet ﷺ made all other calamities and hardships look small and trivial. How could it not be when by his passing the divine revelation ceased descending to the earth!
>
> The Prophet ﷺ said that there is no Muslim who is afflicted with a calamity and says that which Allāh has enjoined, "*Innā lillāhi wa inna ilayhi rāji'ūn. Allāhumma ajurni fi musībati wakhluf li khayran minha*" (Verily to Allāh we belong and to Him we will return. O Allāh, reward me for my calamity and compensate me with something better than it), but Allāh will compensate him with something better than it.

٣٩٣: حَدَّثَنَا مُحَمَّدُ بْنُ حَاتِمٍ ، قَالَ : حَدَّثَنَا عَامِرُ بْنُ صَالِحٍ ، عَنْ هِشَامِ بْنِ عُرْوَةَ ، عَنْ أَبِيهِ ، عَنْ عَائِشَةَ ، قَالَتْ : تُوُفِّيَ رَسُولُ اللهِ صلى الله عليه وسلم يَوْمَ الاثْنَيْنِ[451]

393. Aisha ﵂ narrated: "The Messenger of Allāh ﷺ passed away on a Monday."

٣٩٤: حَدَّثَنَا مُحَمَّدُ بْنُ أَبِي عُمَرَ ، قَالَ : حَدَّثَنَا سُفْيَانُ بْنُ عُيَيْنَةَ ، عَنْ جَعْفَرِ بْنِ مُحَمَّدٍ ، عَنْ أَبِيهِ ، قَالَ : قُبِضَ رَسُولُ اللهِ صلى الله عليه وسلم يَوْمَ الاثْنَيْنِ فَمَكَثَ ذَلِكَ الْيَوْمَ وَلَيْلَةَ الثُّلاثَاءِ ، وَدُفِنَ مِنَ اللَّيْلِ[452]
وَقَالَ سُفْيَانُ : وَقَالَ غَيْرُهُ : يُسْمَعُ صَوْتُ الْمَسَاحِي مِنْ آخِرِ اللَّيْلِ

394. Muhammad al-Bāqir ﵁ narrated: "The Messenger of Allah

451 Sunan al-Tirmidhi (996)
452 Musannaf 'Abdul Razzaq (6209)

ﷺ passed away on a Monday. His burial waited until the day of Monday and night of Tuesday had passed, and then he was buried on the night of Wednesday. (The night between Wednesday and Thursday)." Sufyān (the narrator of this hadīth) said: "In other narrations it is stated that the sound of spades could be heard in the latter portion of the night."

Ibn al-Qayyim said,

> It is permissible to bury the deceased at night. Imām Ahmad was asked about the ruling on burying the deceased during the night and he did not object to it and said, "Abū Bakr was buried at night, and Alī ibn Abī Tālib buried Fātimah ﷺ at night."

Ibn Hajar al-Haytamī said,

> The reason why the companions ﷺ delayed his burial was either due to the fact that some of them did not believe that he had passed away, because they differed upon where to bury him or because of their busyness with the succession of the Prophet ﷺ so as to avert any possible disputes that may have arisen if there was a delay in the decision being made and the pledge being given. The burial was decided after the intervention of Abu Bakr ﷺ whose statement settled the dispute.

Ibn Battal said,

> It is narrated that Aisha ﷺ said, "We did not know of the burial of the Messenger of Allāh ﷺ until we heard the sound of spades in the latter portion of the night of Wednesday."[453]
>
> 'Uqbah ibn 'Amir ﷺ narrated, "There are three times at which the Messenger of Allāh ﷺ forbade us to pray or to bury our dead: when the sun has clearly started to rise until it is fully risen, when it is directly overhead at midday until it has passed its zenith, and

453 Sunan al-Bayhaqi (6216)

when the sun starts to set until it has fully set."

Al-Bajūrī said,

The burial preparation began on Tuesday and the burial finished during the latter part of the night of Wednesday. This can reconcile the reports stating he was buried on Tuesday and the reports stating he was buried on Wednesday.

٣٩٥: حَدَّثَنَا قُتَيْبَةُ بْنُ سَعِيدٍ ، قَالَ : حَدَّثَنَا عَبْدُ الْعَزِيزِ بْنُ مُحَمَّدٍ ، عَنْ شَرِيكِ بْنِ عَبْدِ اللهِ بْنِ أَبِي نَمِرٍ ، عَنْ أَبِي سَلَمَةَ بْنِ عَبْدِ الرَّحْمَنِ بْنِ عَوْفٍ ، قَالَ : تُوُفِّيَ رَسُولُ اللهِ صلى الله عليه وسلم يَوْمَ الاثْنَيْنِ ، وَدُفِنَ يَوْمَ الثُّلاثَاءِ[454]
قَالَ أَبُو عِيسَى : هَذَا حَدِيثٌ غَرِيبٌ

395. Abū Salamah ibn Abdul Rahman ibn 'Awf narrated: "The Messenger of Allāh ﷺ passed away on a Monday and was buried on Tuesday."

Ibn Hajar al-Haytamī said,

> To reconcile between this hadīth and the previous one, it can be said that the companions ﷺ started to prepare the body of the Prophet ﷺ at the end of Tuesday and only finished the preparation during the latter portion of the night of Wednesday.

٣٩٦: حَدَّثَنَا نَصْرُ بْنُ عَلِيٍّ الْجَهْضَمِيُّ ، قَالَ : حَدَّثَنَا عَبْدُ اللهِ بْنُ دَاوُدَ ، قَالَ : حَدَّثَنَا سَلَمَةُ بْنُ نُبَيْطٍ ، عَنْ نُعَيْمِ بْنِ أَبِي هِنْدَ ، عَنْ نُبَيْطِ بْنِ شَرِيطٍ ، عَنْ سَالِمِ بْنِ عُبَيْدٍ ، وَكَانَتْ لَهُ صُحْبَةٌ ، قَالَ : أُغْمِيَ عَلَى رَسُولِ اللهِ صلى الله عليه وسلم ، فِي مَرَضِهِ فَأَفَاقَ ، فَقَالَ : حَضَرَتِ الصَّلاةُ ؟ فَقَالُوا : نَعَمْ فَقَالَ : مُرُوا بِلالا فَلْيُؤَذِّنْ ، وَمُرُوا أَبَا بَكْرٍ أَنْ يُصَلِّيَ لِلنَّاسِ أَوْ قَالَ : بِالنَّاسِ ، قَالَ

---

454 Muwatta Mālik (539)

: ثُمَّ أُغْمِيَ عَلَيْهِ ، فَأَفَاقَ ، فَقَالَ : حَضَرَتِ الصَّلاةُ ؟ فَقَالُوا : نَعَمْ فَقَالَ : مُرُوا بِلالا فَلْيُؤَذِّنْ ، وَمُرُوا أَبَا بَكْرٍ فَلْيُصَلِّ بِالنَّاسِ ، فَقَالَتْ عَائِشَةُ : إِنَّ أَبِي رَجُلٌ أَسِيفٌ ، إِذَا قَامَ ذَلِكَ الْمُقَامَ بَكَى فَلا يَسْتَطِيعُ ، فَلَوْ أَمَرْتَ غَيْرَهُ ، قَالَ : ثُمَّ أُغْمِيَ عَلَيْهِ فَأَفَاقَ فَقَالَ : مُرُوا بِلالا فَلْيُؤَذِّنْ ، وَمُرُوا أَبَا بَكْرٍ فَلْيُصَلِّ بِالنَّاسِ ، فَإِنَّكُنَّ صَوَاحِبُ أَوْ صَوَاحِبَاتُ يُوسُفَ ، قَالَ : فَأُمِرَ بِلَالٌ فَأَذَّنَ ، وَأُمِرَ أَبُو بَكْرٍ فَصَلَّى بِالنَّاسِ ، ثُمَّ إِنَّ رَسُولَ الله صلى الله عليه وسلم ، وَجَدَ خِفَّةً ، فَقَالَ : انْظُرُوا لِي مَنْ أَتَّكِئُ عَلَيْهِ ، فَجَاءَتْ بَرِيرَةُ ، وَرَجُلٌ آخَرُ ، فَاتَّكَأَ عَلَيْهِمَا فَلَمَّا رَآهُ أَبُو بَكْرٍ ذَهَبَ لِيَنْكُصَ فَأَوْمَأَ إِلَيْهِ أَنْ يَثْبُتَ مَكَانَهُ ، حَتَّى قَضَى أَبُو بَكْرٍ صَلاتَهُ .

ثُمَّ إِنَّ رَسُولَ الله صلى الله عليه وسلم قُبِضَ ، فَقَالَ عُمَرُ : وَاللهِ لا أَسْمَعُ أَحَدًا يَذْكُرُ أَنَّ رَسُولَ الله صلى الله عليه وسلم ، قُبِضَ إِلا ضَرَبْتُهُ بِسَيْفِي هَذَا ، قَالَ : وَكَانَ النَّاسُ أُمِّيِّينَ لَمْ يَكُنْ فِيهِمْ نَبِيٌّ قَبْلَهُ ، فَأَمْسَكَ النَّاسُ ، فَقَالُوا : يَا سَالِمُ ، انْطَلِقْ إِلَى صَاحِبِ رَسُولِ الله صلى الله عليه وسلم فَادْعُهُ ، فَأَتَيْتُ أَبَا بَكْرٍ وَهُوَ فِي الْمَسْجِدِ فَأَتَيْتُهُ أَبْكِي دَهِشًا ، فَلَمَّا رَآنِي ، قَالَ : أَقُبِضَ رَسُولُ الله صلى الله عليه وسلم ؟ قُلْتُ : إِنَّ عُمَرَ ، يَقُولُ : لا أَسْمَعُ أَحَدًا يَذْكُرُ أَنَّ رَسُولَ الله صلى الله عليه وسلم قُبِضَ إِلا ضَرَبْتُهُ بِسَيْفِي هَذَا ، فَقَالَ لِي : انْطَلِقْ ، فَانْطَلَقْتُ مَعَهُ ، فَجَاءَ هُوَ وَالنَّاسُ قَدْ دَخَلُوا عَلَى رَسُولِ الله صلى الله عليه وسلم ، فَقَالَ : يَا أَيُّهَا النَّاسُ ، أَفْرِجُوا لِي ، فَأَفْرَجُوا لَهُ فَجَاءَ حَتَّى أَكَبَّ عَلَيْهِ وَمَسَّهُ ، فَقَالَ : إِنَّكَ مَيِّتٌ وَإِنَّهُمْ مَيِّتُونَ ، ثُمَّ قَالُوا : يَا صَاحِبَ رَسُولِ الله صلى الله عليه وسلم ، أَقُبِضَ رَسُولُ الله صلى الله عليه وسلم ؟ قَالَ : نَعَمْ ، فَعَلِمُوا أَنْ قَدْ صَدَقَ ، قَالُوا : يَا صَاحِبَ رَسُولِ الله صلى الله عليه وسلم ، أَيُصَلَّى عَلَى رَسُولِ الله ؟ قَالَ : نَعَمْ ، قَالُوا : وَكَيْفَ ؟ قَالَ : يَدْخُلُ قَوْمٌ فَيُكَبِّرُونَ وَيُصَلُّونَ ، وَيَدْعُونَ ، ثُمَّ يَخْرُجُونَ ، ثُمَّ يَدْخُلُ قَوْمٌ فَيُكَبِّرُونَ وَيُصَلُّونَ وَيَدْعُونَ ، ثُمَّ يَخْرُجُونَ ، حَتَّى يَدْخُلَ النَّاسُ ، قَالُوا

: يَا صَاحِبَ رَسُولِ الله صلى الله عليه وسلم ، أَيُدْفَنُ رَسُولُ الله صلى الله عليه وسلم ؟ قَالَ : نعَمْ ، قَالُوا : أَينَ ؟ قَالَ : فِي الْمَكَانِ الَّذِي قَبَضَ اللهُ فِيهِ رُوحَهُ ، فَإِنَّ اللهَ لَمْ يَقْبِضْ رُوحَهُ إلا فِي مَكَانٍ طَيِّبٍ فَعَلِمُوا أَنْ قَدْ صَدَقَ ، ثُمَّ أَمَرَهُمْ أَنْ يَغْسِلَهُ بَنُو أَبِيهِ ، وَاجْتَمَعَ الْمُهَاجِرُونَ يَتَشَاوَرُونَ ، فَقَالُوا : انْطَلِقْ بِنَا إِلَى إِخْوانِنَا مِنَ الأَنْصَارِ نُدْخِلُهُمْ مَعَنَا فِي هَذَا الأَمْرِ ، فَقَالَتِ الأَنْصَارُ : مِنَّا أَمِيرٌ وَمِنْكُمْ أَمِيرٌ ، فَقَالَ عُمَرُ بْنُ الْخَطَّابِ : مَنْ لَهُ مِثْلُ هَذِهِ الثَّلَاثِ ثَانِيَ اثْنَيْنِ إِذْ هُمَا فِي الْغَارِ إِذْ يَقُولُ لِصَاحِبِهِ لا تَحْزَنْ إِنَّ اللهَ مَعَنَا مَنْ هُمَا ؟ قَالَ : ثُمَّ بَسَطَ يَدَهُ فَبَايَعَهُ وَبَايَعَهُ النَّاسُ بَيْعَةً حَسَنَةً جَمِيلَةً[455]

396. Salim ibn 'Ubayd ﷺ narrated: "During his sickness the Prophet ﷺ fell unconscious; when he later recovered consciousness he asked, 'Has the time of the prayer commenced?' They replied, 'Yes.' Then he said, 'Order Bilāl to call to the prayer, and order Abū Bakr to lead the people in prayer.' Then again, he lost consciousness; when he was revived, he said, 'Has the time of the prayer commenced?' They said, 'Yes.' He ﷺ said, 'Order Bilāl to call to the prayer, and order Abū Bakr to lead the people in prayer.'

Aisha ﷺ said, 'My father is a man with a soft heart, prone to being moved. If he stands in that position, he will cry and he would not be able to control it. If you wish you can appoint someone else.' He again lost consciousness, and when he revived this time, he said, 'Order Bilāl to call to the prayer, and order Abū Bakr to lead the prayer, for indeed, you women are the companions of Yūsuf.' Thereupon, Bilāl ﷺ was ordered to make the call to prayer and he did so, and Abū Bakr ﷺ was ordered to lead the people in prayer, and he did so. Then the Messenger of Allāh ﷺ found some respite from his illness and so he ﷺ said, 'Find someone for me upon whom I may lean.' Barīrah and another man came and he ﷺ leaned upon them. When Abū Bakr ﷺ saw him, he began to move back so that the Prophet ﷺ could take his place, but the Prophet ﷺ indicated

455 Sunan Ibn Mājah (1234)

to him that he should remain firm in his place, until Abū Bakr completed his prayer.

Then, the Messenger of Allāh ﷺ passed away, upon which 'Umar said, 'By Allāh, if anyone mentions that the Messenger of Allāh ﷺ has died, I will strike his neck with this sword of mine.' The Arabs were illiterate and never before Muhammad ﷺ had there been a Prophet amongst them. The people desisted [from any action] and said, 'O Salīm, go to the Messenger of Allāh's companion and call him.' I came to Abū Bakr whilst he was in the masjid. I approached him whilst crying and in a state of shock. When he saw me, he said, 'Did the Messenger of Allah ﷺ die?' I replied, 'Indeed but 'Umar is saying, 'If I hear anyone mention that the Messenger of Allāh ﷺ has died, I will strike his neck with this sword of mine."

Abū Bakr then said to me, 'Come,' and so I proceeded with him until we reached the people, who had entered the room of the Messenger of Allāh ﷺ. He said, 'O people! Make way for me.' They made way for him until he bent down to the Prophet ﷺ and touched him; he then said: "{Verily, you [O Muhammad ﷺ] will die and verily, they [too] will die.}"[456]

The people asked, 'O companion of the Messenger of Allāh ﷺ, has the Messenger of Allāh ﷺ died?' He answered, 'Yes.' They knew that he had spoken the truth.

They said, 'O companion of the Messenger of Allāh! Is the Messenger of Allāh ﷺ to be prayed upon?' He said, 'Yes.' To which they replied, 'And how?' He said, 'A group shall enter, say the *takbir*, pray and then invoke Him. Then they shall leave, another group shall enter and do the same until everyone has prayed.'

The people asked, 'O companion of the Messenger of Allāh! Is the Messenger of Allah ﷺ to be buried?' He said, 'Yes.' They said, 'Where?' He answered, 'In the same place that Allāh took his soul, for indeed, Allah did not take his soul except in a good and pure place.' And they knew that he had spoken the truth. Then he ordered the offspring from the Prophet's father's side to wash him.

---

456 Qur'ān 39:30

The Muhājirūn then assembled to decide the succession to the Prophet ﷺ. They said, 'Let us go to our brothers from amongst the Ansār and include them in this matter.' The Ansār said, 'Amongst us is a leader and amongst you is a leader.' 'Umar ibn al-Khattab ؓ said, 'Who is that person from your midst who possesses these three: {The second of two; when they two were in the cave, when he said unto his comrade: 'Grieve not. Indeed! Allah is with us?'}' 'Umar ؓ then extended his hand to give the pledge of allegiance. Subsequently, all those present followed suit and wholeheartedly gave allegiance to Abū Bakr ؓ.

Ibn Hajar al-Haytamī said,

> This shows that Prophets can fall unconscious (al-Ghazalī stated that their unconsciousness can be short or long in duration and al-Subkī stated that in this state their hearts are still awake) since it is considered as a sickness that does not entail a defect or a flaw; contrary to madness and insanity which Prophets are protected from experiencing. The reason that Allāh allows His Prophets to fall sick is so that their reward can be increased and to consolidate the people (i.e. to strengthen them with the knowledge that even Prophets are subject to hardship and sickness) and to avert the possibility of any extreme glorification on the part of the people after they witness the miracles of the Prophet (i.e. to prevent people from worshipping Prophets after seeing their miracles).
>
> This hadīth shows that the person who should be asked to lead the prayer is the one with best understanding of religion, who can recite the Qur'ān in the best manner and has the most sense of piety. The fact that the Prophet ﷺ ordered Abū Bakr ؓ to lead the prayer more than once is a strong indication that he was the most deserving to be his successor.
>
> The similarity between Aisha ؓ and the woman mentioned in the story of Yūsuf ؑ is that both did not reveal the true purpose behind their requests and instead gave different justifications. Zulaykha invited the women and showed them good hospitality

whilst her real purpose was to let them see the beauty of Yūsuf so that they could relate to her for falling in love with him. Similarly, Aisha ﷺ stated that she disliked her father leading the people in the prayer because his soft heart would cause him to cry when reading the Qur'ān. In reality, she made that request because she feared that the people would dislike him for taking the place of the Prophet ﷺ, as she clearly revealed in another hadīth documented by al-Bukharī.

There are different hadīths, each of which states different people that the Prophet ﷺ leaned upon. In Sahīh al-Bukharī and Muslim it states that they were two men: al-Abbās and Alī ﷺ. In Muslim, they were al-Abbās and his son al-Fadl ﷺ, and in another hadīth, they were al-Abbās and Usāmah ibn Zayd ﷺ. In Sunan al-Daraqutnī they were Usāmah and al-Fadl, in Sahīh Ibn Hibbān they were Baryrah and Nubah, and in the book of Ibn Sa'd they were al-Fadl and Thawban ﷺ. The reconciliation between these hadīths, if all are proven authentic, is that he ﷺ went out of his house more than once and on each occasion he leaned upon different people.

The signal of the Prophet ﷺ to Abū Bakr ﷺ (to remain as the *imām* of the prayer) indicates that he prayed behind Abū Bakr. However, in Sahih al-Bukharī and Muslim it states that he ﷺ sat on the left side of Abū Bakr, thus Abū Bakr stood leading the prayer behind the Prophet ﷺ and the people followed the lead of Abū Bakr. This explains the basis of the view of al-Shafi'ī that it is allowed for a person praying in congregation to leave following the *imām* [i.e. leave the congregation by intending to pray individually] and then follow another *imām*.

The reason 'Umar ﷺ denied the death of the Prophet ﷺ and threatened anyone who dared to say that is because he thought that he was just unconscious. Regarding the meaning of the statement that Arabs were illiterate and that never before Muhammad ﷺ was there a Prophet amongst them is that the Arabs never had the knowledge of how a Prophet would die, which can be attained either through witnessing that or through scripture, and Arabs never had either (i.e. they were not from the People of the Book. Therefore they did not have a scripture and no Prophet was sent to them before the Prophet Muhammad ﷺ).

Referring to Abū Bakr as the companion of the Prophet ﷺ indicates that he was known amongst the people with that description as if they agreed that it is his description that Allāh has confirmed in the Qur'ān (i.e. the ayah wherein it says in its meaning "he ﷺ says to his companion....").

Abū Bakr addressed the people after he verified the death of the Prophet ﷺ and said, "Whoever worships Muhammad then know that Muhammad has died, and whoever worships Allāh, then Allāh is Alive and does not die." Then he recited the ayah **{"You will die and so they shall too..."}** Thereupon, the people began to cry. This shows the courage and knowledge of Abū Bakr as he quoted the ayāt to refute the claim that the Prophet did not die and stayed firm in the face of such a difficult calamity.

The response of the companions to the news differed, 'Umar could not believe the news and threatened anyone who claimed that the Prophet ﷺ had died, 'Abdullāh ibn Anīs could not get up and remained seated upon hearing the news and 'Uthmān could not speak. Abū Bakr was the firmest and he arrived whilst his eyes were full of tears.

Ibn Battal said,

> Al-Bukharī documented in his Sahīh that Aisha ﷺ narrated: "Allāh's Messenger ﷺ died whilst Abū Bakr ﷺ was at a place called al-Sunah (al-'Aliya). 'Umar stood up and said, 'By Allāh! Allāh's Messenger is not dead!' 'Umar (later on) said, 'By Allāh! Nothing occurred to my mind except that.' He said, 'Verily! Allāh will resurrect him and he will cut the hands and legs of some men.' Then Abū Bakr came and uncovered the face of Allāh's Messenger, kissed him and said, 'Let my mother and father be sacrificed for you, [O Allāh's Messenger], you are good in life and in death. By Allāh in Whose Hands my life is, Allāh will never make you taste

death twice.' Then he went out and said, 'O oath-taker! Don't be hasty.' When Abū Bakr spoke, 'Umar sat down. Abū Bakr praised and glorified Allāh and then said, 'No doubt! Whoever worshipped Muhammad, then Muhammad is dead, but whoever worshipped Allāh, then Allāh is Alive and shall never die.' Then he recited Allah's Statement: **{[O Muhammad] Verily you will die, and they also will die.}**[457] He also recited, **{Muhammad is no more than an Apostle; and indeed many Apostles have passed away, before him, If he dies or is killed, will you then turn back on your heels? And he who turns back on his heels, not the least harm will he do to Allāh And Allāh will give reward to those who are grateful.}**[458]

The statement of Abū Bakr ؓ that the Prophet ﷺ will not taste death twice was in response to the statement of 'Umar and others who said that the Prophet ﷺ died and will be resurrected again in this life. This is to state that he dies once in this life and will be resurrected on the Day of Judgment. This hadīth shows the virtue of Abū Bakr and that he was more knowledgeable than 'Umar ؓ. This event showed his sensibility, firmness and his ability to understand events in the light of the Qur'ān and it also shows his high status amongst the Muslims.

٣٩٧: حَدَّثَنَا نَصْرُ بْنُ عَلِيٍّ ، قَالَ : حَدَّثَنَا عَبْدُ الله بْنُ الزُّبَيْرِ ، شَيْخٌ بَاهِلِيٌّ قَدِيمٌ بَصْرِيٌّ قَالَ : حَدَّثَنَا ثَابِتٌ الْبُنَانِيُّ ، عَنْ أَنَسِ بْنِ مَالِكٍ ، قَالَ : لَمَّا وَجَدَ رَسُولُ الله صلى الله عليه وسلم ، مِنْ كُرَبِ الْمَوْتِ مَا وَجَدَ ، قَالَتْ فَاطِمَةُ : وَاكَرْبَاهُ ، فَقَالَ النَّبِيُّ صلى الله عليه وسلم : لا كَرْبَ عَلَى أَبِيكِ بَعْدَ الْيَوْمِ ، إِنَّهُ قَدْ حَضَرَ مِنْ أَبِيكِ مَا لَيْسَ بِتَارِكٍ مِنْهُ أَحَدًا الْمُوَافَاةُ يَوْمَ الْقِيَامَةِ[459]

397. Anas ibn Mālik ؓ narrated: "When the Messenger of Allāh ﷺ was experiencing the agonies of death, Fātimah ؓ said, 'What a

457 Qur'ān 39:30
458 Qur'ān 3:144
459 Sunan Ibn Mājah (1629)

calamity that has inflicted my father!' Thereupon, the Messenger of Allāh ﷺ said, 'No calamity will inflict your father after today. That which has befallen your father is inevitable and none will be saved from it until the Day of Reckoning.'"

Al-Sindi said,

> The meaning of the statement of the Prophet ﷺ, "No calamity will inflict your father after today" is that the agony he felt would come to a halt through his death.

٣٩٨: حَدَّثَنَا أَبُو الْخَطَّابِ زِيَادُ بْنُ يَحْيَى الْبَصْرِيُّ ، وَنَصْرُ بْنُ عَلِيٍّ ، قَالا : حَدَّثَنَا عَبْدُ رَبِّهِ بْنُ بَارِقٍ الْحَنَفِيُّ ، قَالَ : سَمِعْتُ جَدِّي أَبَا أُمِّي سِمَاكَ بْنَ الْوَلِيدِ يُحَدِّثُ ، أَنَّهُ سَمِعَ ابْنَ عَبَّاسٍ ، يُحَدِّثُ أَنَّهُ سَمِعَ رَسُولَ اللهِ صلى الله عليه وسلم ، يَقُولُ : مَنْ كَانَ لَهُ فَرَطَانِ مِنْ أُمَّتِي أَدْخَلَهُ اللهُ تَعَالَى بِهِمَا الْجَنَّةَ ، فَقَالَتْ عَائِشَةُ : فَمَنْ كَانَ لَهُ فَرَطٌ مِنْ أُمَّتِكَ ؟ قَالَ : وَمَنْ كَانَ لَهُ فَرَطٌ يَا مُوَفَّقَةُ قَالَتْ : فَمَنْ لَمْ يَكُنْ لَهُ فَرَطٌ مِنْ أُمَّتِكَ ؟ قَالَ : فَأَنَا فَرَطٌ لأُمَّتِي ، لَنْ يُصَابُوا بِمِثْلِي[460]

398. 'Abdullāh ibn Abbās ؓ narrated: "I heard the Messenger of Allāh ﷺ say, 'The person who experiences the loss of two young children [during his lifetime], Allāh shall admit him in Paradise by them!' Aisha ؓ asked, 'What about the one from your nation who experiences the death of one young child [during his lifetime]?' He replied, 'O successful! The one who loses one child shall also enter Paradise.' Aisha ؓ then inquired, 'What about those from among your nation who have not lost any children?' He replied, 'I shall be their intercession in the Hereafter for no loss equals the loss of my death.'"

---

460 Sunan al-Tirmidhi (1062)

Ibn al-Qayyim said,

> From the hadīths that encourage us to have children is this hadīth.

Al-Baydāwī said,

> The meaning of this hadīth is that the deceased children precede their parents to Paradise and prepare for their parents places therein.

Alī al-Qārī said,

> The praise of the Prophet ﷺ to Aisha ﵂ ("O successful") was due to her questioning. He mentioned this to indicate that she is guided to the good as her questions were an evidence of her concern for the Muslims.

CHAPTER FIFTY FIVE

باب ماجاء في ميراث رسول اللّه صلى اللّه عليه وسلم

THE REPORTS PERTAINING TO THE INHERITANCE OF THE MESSENGER OF ALLĀH ﷺ

Abdul Razzaq al-Badr said,

> This chapter is dedicated to mentioning that which the Prophet ﷺ left behind after his death, and to clarify that the inheritance of Prophets is knowledge and anything else is left for charity.

٣٩٩: حَدَّثَنَا أَحْمَدُ بْنُ مَنِيعٍ ، قَالَ : حَدَّثَنَا حُسَيْنُ بْنُ مُحَمَّدٍ ، قَالَ : حَدَّثَنَا إِسْرَائِيلُ ، عَنْ أَبِي إِسْحَاقَ ، عَنْ عَمْرِو بْنِ الْحَارِثِ ، أَخِي جُوَيْرِيَةَ لَهُ صُحْبَةٌ ، قَالَ : مَا تَرَكَ رَسُولُ اللهِ صلى الله عليه وسلم إِلا سِلاحَهُ ، وَبَغْلَتَهُ ، وَأَرْضًا جَعَلَهَا صَدَقَةً[461]

399. 'Amr ibn al-Hārith ﷺ, the brother of Juwairiyya ﷺ said: "The Messenger of Allāh ﷺ did not leave behind anything except his weapons, his mule and a piece of land that he allocated for charity."

Ibn Hajar al-Asqalānī said,

> The Juwairiyya referred to in this hadith is the mother of the believers, Juwairiyya bint al-Hārith.
>
> The slaves of the Prophet ﷺ who were mentioned in the hadīths were either freed or died during his lifetime [as stated in the hadith in Sahīh al-Bukharī which reads, "When Allah's Apostle died, he did not leave any *dirham* or *dinār* (i.e. money), a slave or a slave woman, neither did he leave anything else besides his white mule, his arms and a piece of land which he had given in charity."]

Ibn Barral said,

> The king of Aylah sent the Prophet ﷺ a white mule as a gift.

٤٠٠ : حَدَّثَنَا مُحَمَّدُ بْنُ الْمُثَنَّى ، قَالَ : حَدَّثَنَا أَبُو الْوَلِيدِ ، قَالَ : حَدَّثَنَا حَمَّادُ بْنُ سَلَمَةَ ، عَنْ مُحَمَّدِ بْنِ عَمْرٍو ، عَنْ أَبِي سَلَمَةَ ، عَنْ أَبِي هُرَيْرَةَ ، قَالَ : جَاءَتْ فَاطِمَةُ إِلَى أَبِي بَكْرٍ ، فَقَالَتْ : مَنْ يَرِثُكَ ؟ فَقَالَ : أَهْلِي وَوَلَدِي ، فَقَالَتْ : مَا لِي لا أَرِثُ أَبِي ؟ فَقَالَ أَبُو بَكْرٍ : سَمِعْتُ رَسُولَ اللهِ صلى الله عليه وسلم ، يَقُولُ : لا نُورَثُ ، وَلَكِنِّي أَعُولُ مَنْ كَانَ رَسُولُ اللهِ صلى الله عليه وسلم ،

461 Sahih al-Bukhārī (2739)

يَعُولُهُ ، وَأُنْفِقُ عَلَى مَنْ كَانَ رَسُولُ اللهِ صلى الله عليه وسلم يُنْفِقُ عَلَيْهِ[462]

400. Abu Hurairah ﷺ narrated: "Fātimah ﷺ came to Abū Bakr and asked him, 'Who shall inherit from you?' He replied, 'My wife and my children.' She said, 'Then why is it so, that I cannot inherit from my father?' He replied, 'I heard the Messenger of Allāh ﷺ say, 'We (i.e. the Prophets) are not inherited from.' However, I will support those whom the Messenger of Allāh ﷺ used to support and I will spend upon those whom he spent upon.'"

Abdul Razzaq al-Badr said,

> Fātimah ﷺ came to Abū Bakr ﷺ after he become the successor of the Prophet ﷺ to ask him for her share from that which her father ﷺ had left behind [as he acquired some estates from war booties]. It seems that she was not aware of his statement that no one inherits from him. This can be supported by the fact that she did not object to the statement of the Prophet ﷺ after she heard it and this is why Abū Bakr ﷺ did not distribute that which the Prophet ﷺ had between his wives and daughters ﷺ. Nonetheless, Abū Bakr ﷺ explained that he was now responsible for the affairs of the Muslims. Therefore he would make sure to keep the arrangements of the Prophet ﷺ stay as they were and thus, he would continue to give her the support that she used to receive from the Prophet ﷺ and spend upon everyone that the Prophet ﷺ spent upon during his lifetime.

Ibn Hajar al-Asqalānī said,

> The hadīths indicating that Fātimah ﷺ refused to talk with Abū Bakr after he denied her what she thought to be her right in the Prophet's ﷺ properties do not mean that she boycotted him. Rather, she refused to talk with him regarding the matter and she did not boycott him, which is forbidden to do so as stated in the

---

462 Sunan al-Tirmidhī (1608)

hadīth.

Given the high level of piety and sensibility of Fātimah ﵂, it appears that she did not boycott Abū Bakr. This can be corroborated by the hadīth documented by al-Bayhaqī who reported from the way of al-Sha'bī that Abū Bakr visited Fātimah and Alī ibn Abī Tālib said to her that Abū Bakr sought permission to visit her. She said, "Are you happy for me to allow him?" He replied, "Yes." So she allowed him to enter upon her.

Some of our scholars said that the forbidden type of boycott between Muslims is that when two people ignore each other when they meet. It is evident that what she did was avoid meeting him, as it seems to be the case that she was too busy with her sadness and sickness.

The reason she became upset though she heard the hadīth is because she understood the hadīth in a different manner to Abū Bakr. Her understanding led her to believe that she was not subject to this hadīth (meaning she was an exception to the general statement) whilst Abū Bakr understood the hadīth to be applicable to everyone, and the interpretation of both are possible.

٤٠١ : حَدَّثَنَا مُحَمَّدُ بْنُ الْمُثَنَّى ، قَالَ : حَدَّثَنَا يَحْيَى بْنُ كَثِيرٍ الْعَنْبَرِيُّ أَبُو غَسَّانَ ، قَالَ : حَدَّثَنَا شُعْبَةُ ، عَنْ عَمْرِو بْنِ مُرَّةَ ، عَنْ أَبِي الْبَخْتَرِيِّ ، أَنَّ الْعَبَّاسَ ، وَعَلِيًّا ، جَاءَا إِلَى عُمَرَ يَخْتَصِمَانِ ، يَقُولُ كُلُّ وَاحِدٍ مِنْهُمَا لِصَاحِبِهِ : أَنْتَ كَذَا ، أَنْتَ كَذَا ، فَقَالَ عُمَرُ ، لِطَلْحَةَ ، وَالزُّبَيْرِ ، وَعَبْدِ الرَّحْمَنِ بْنِ عَوْفٍ ، وَسَعْدٍ : أَنْشُدُكُمْ بِاللَّهِ أَسَمِعْتُمْ رَسُولَ اللهِ صلى الله عليه وسلم ، يَقُولُ : كُلُّ مَالِ نَبِيٍّ صَدَقَةٌ ، إِلَّا مَا أَطْعَمَهُ ، إِنَّا لَا نُورَثُ ؟ وَفِي الْحَدِيثِ قِصَّةٌ [463]

401. Abū al-Bakhtarī narrated: "Both al-Abbās and Alī ibn Abī Tālib ﷺ disputed over the inheritance of the Prophet ﷺ so they went to 'Umar ﷺ during his reign as the Caliphate whilst each of

463 Sunan Abū Dawūd (2963)

them accused the other. 'Umar ﷺ said to Talhah, al-Zubayr, 'Abdul Rahman ibn 'Awf and Sa'd ibn Abī Waqqās ﷺ, 'Do you not bear witness that you heard the Messenger of Allāh ﷺ say, 'The wealth that a Prophet [leaves behind] is for charity, except that which he used to feed and clothe his family. Indeed, we are not inherited from."This hadīth also has a story [which is being shortened here]."

Al-San'ānī said,

> The meaning of this hadīth is that all of the wealth that the Prophet ﷺ left behind was for his nation as charity. The money he used to feed his family was exempt from this ruling as Allāh allowed him to do so and it appears that even this was considered a charity for them (his family) during his lifetime.
>
> It was said that the wisdom for Prophets leaving nothing behind as inheritance was so that their heirs would not wish for their death. As for the inheritance mentioned in the ayāt: **{Sulaymān inherited Dawūd}**[464] and **{Who will inherit me and inherit from the family of Ya'qūb}**[465], both refer to knowledge.

Al-Khattabī said,

> Mālik ibn Aws said: "'Umar ibn al-Khattab ﷺ sent a messenger to call me to present myself before him. I went and found 'Umar sitting on a bare bed, with no mattress. I greeted him and sat down, and he said, 'O Mālik, some families from your people have come to us and I have ordered that some shares be allocated to them. Take them and divide among them.' I said, 'O Amir al-Muminīn! I would prefer that you appoint someone else to do this.' He said, 'Take them [and perform the task.]' Then his doorkeeper Yaria' came to him and said, 'Will you give 'Uthmān, Abdul Rahman ibn 'Awf, al-Zubayr and Sa'd ibn Abī Waqqās ﷺ permission to enter?' He responded, 'Yes.' So he let them in, they entered and sat down.

464 Qur'ān 27:16
465 Qur'ān 19:6

Then after a while, Yaria' came and said to 'Umar, 'Do you allow Alī and al-Abbās ؓ to enter?' He replied, 'Yes.' So he let them in, and they entered. Al-Abbās said, 'O Amīr al-Muminīn, judge between me and this one (Alī).'

The group, 'Uthmān and his companions, said, 'O Amīr al-Muminīn! Judge between them and give them a break from one another.' 'Umar said, 'I ask you by Allāh, by whose permission the heaven and earth exist, do you know that the Messenger of Allāh ﷺ said, 'We cannot be inherited from; what we leave behind is charity?'' The group replied, 'He did say that.' Then 'Umar ؓ turned to Alī and al-Abbās ؓ and said, 'I ask you by Allāh, do you know that the Messenger of Allāh ﷺ said that?' They said, 'He did say so.'

'Umar said, 'Allāh allocated for the Messenger something exclusive for him when He said: **{And what Allāh gave as booty (*Fai'*) to His Messenger (Muhammad ﷺ) from them, for which you made no expedition with either cavalry or camels. But Allāh gives power to His Messengers over whomsoever He wills. And Allah is Able to do all things.}**'[466] Then he said, 'And Allāh gave his Messenger the war booty of Banī al-Nadyīr but by Allāh, he did not keep it for himself and withhold it from you, rather he gave it to you and distributed it amongst you, until only this wealth was left. The Messenger of Allāh ﷺ gave his family what they needed for the whole year from this wealth, then he took what was left and put it in the Bayt al-Māl.' Then he addressed the group, 'I ask you by Allāh, do you know this?' They replied, 'Yes.' Then he said to Alī and al-Abbās ؓ, 'I ask you by Allah, do you know this?' They replied, 'Yes.'

'Umar said, 'Then Allāh took the soul of His Prophet ﷺ, and Abū Bakr ؓ said, 'I am the successor of the Messenger of Allāh ﷺ.' By Allāh, Abū Bakr took it and used it in the same manner that the Messenger of Allāh ﷺ had done. Then you and him (al-Abbās and Alī) went to Abū Bakr, you (al-'Abbās) demanding your share from the inheritance of your nephew (the Prophet ﷺ) and he (Alī)

466 Qur'ān 59:6

demanding the share of his wife from the inheritance of her father (the Prophet ﷺ) and Abū Bakr said to you that he had heard the Messenger of Allāh ﷺ say, 'We cannot be inherited from. All that which we leave behind is to be given for charity' and Allāh knows that he was honest and sincere, and sought the truth.

Then Allāh took the soul of Abū Bakr and I said, 'I am the successor of the Messenger of Allāh and the successor of Abū Bakr.' I took over and I used it as the Messenger of Allāh ﷺ and Abū Bakr ؓ had done. And you have come to me and spoken to me, when you were both in agreement. When I thought that I might give it to you, I said, 'If you wish, I will give it to you both, on condition that you make a promise to Allāh that you will use it as the Messenger of Allāh ﷺ did, as Abū Bakr ؓ did and as I have done since the beginning of my reign.' You replied, 'Give it to us on that basis.' Thus I gave it to you. I ask you by Allāh, did I not give it to them on that basis?' The group replied, 'Yes.' Then he turned to Alī and al-Abbās and said, 'I ask you by Allāh, did I not give it to you on that basis?' They replied, 'Yes.' He said, 'And now you are seeking a different judgement from me? If you are not able to manage it properly, then give it to me and I will take care of it'"

Abu Dawūd said, "Al-Abbās and Alī ؓ came the second time asking 'Umar to divide it in two halves between them so that each one could be responsible for his part but 'Umar refused to divide it." This is a very good explanation and is indicated from the context of the hadīth where it mentions that al-Abbās and Alī were in agreement regarding the matter but they differed upon a new idea that came into their mind at that time which was to divide it. Also, it cannot be that they acknowledged the statement of the Prophet ﷺ and yet still came to demand inheritance. 'Umar refused to divide it due to his fear that the people coming after al-Abbās and Alī may not possess their wisdom, insight, piety and knowledge and so they would claim its ownership.

٤٠٢ : حَدَّثَنَا مُحَمَّدُ بْنُ الْمُثَنَّى ، قَالَ : حَدَّثَنَا صَفْوَانُ بْنُ عِيسَى ، عَنِ أُسَامَةَ

بْنِ زَيْدٍ ، عَنِ الزُّهْرِيِّ ، عَنْ عُرْوَةَ ، عَنْ عَائِشَةَ ، أَنَّ رَسُولَ الله صلى الله عليه وسلم ، قَالَ : لا نُورَثُ مَا تَرَكْنَا فَهُوَ صَدَقَةٌ[467]

402. Aisha ؓ narrated: "The Messenger of Allāh ﷺ said, 'We cannot be inherited from. All of that which we leave behind is for charity.'"

٤٠٣ : حَدَّثَنَا مُحَمَّدُ بْنُ بَشَّارٍ ، قَالَ : حَدَّثَنَا عَبْدُ الرَّحْمَنِ بْنُ مَهْدِيٍّ ، قَالَ : حَدَّثَنَا سُفْيَانُ ، عَنْ أَبِي الزِّنَادِ ، عَنِ الأَعْرَجِ ، عَنْ أَبِي هُرَيْرَةَ ، عَنِ النَّبِيِّ صلى الله عليه وسلم ، قَالَ : لا يَقْسِمُ وَرَثَتِي دِينَارًا وَلا دِرْهَمًا ، مَا تَرَكْتُ بَعْدَ نَفَقَةِ نِسَائِي وَمُؤْنَةِ عَامِلِي فَهُوَ صَدَقَةٌ[468]

403. Abu Hurairah ؓ narrated: "The Prophet ﷺ said, 'My inheritance is not to be distributed by *dinārs* and *dirhams*. Whatever is remaining, after setting aside the expenditure of my wives and workers, is for charity.'"

Ibn Battal said,

> The statement of the Prophet ﷺ in this hadith does not entail an order because he did not leave behind any money to be divided as he died whilst his armour was still pawned. Thus he ﷺ meant that his heirs will not have any money from him after his death as he will not leave behind any.
>
> He ﷺ excluded the expenditure of his wives after his death because they were his dependants and leaving them without support entails what Allāh said: **{And it is not [conceivable or lawful] for you to harm the Messenger of Allāh.}**[469]
>
> The workers mentioned in this hadīth are his workers who worked in the land he possessed in Fadak, Banī al-Nadīr and

467 Sahīh al-Bukhārī (4035) and Sahīh Muslim (1758)
468 Sahih al-Bukhārī (2776) and Sahih Muslim (1760)
469 Qur'ān 33:53

Khaybar (his war booty) as he used the income generated from these lands to spend upon his family and the rest he gave in charity to benefit the Muslims. This remained until the time of 'Umar ؓ who gave the wives of the Prophet ﷺ the choice either to continue receiving their share from these lands or to allocate for them some properties. Aisha and Hafsah ؓ chose to take the properties and so he excluded them from their share in the lands and gave them what they wanted. These were then left for their heirs after they died.

Al-Tabarī said, "This is evidence that it is allowed to allocate some income for those whose time is dedicated to managing acts that are considered as good deeds such as the *muadhin* (caller to prayer), teachers, judges, rulers, scholars etc."

٤٠٤: حَدَّثَنَا الْحَسَنُ بْنُ عَلِيٍّ الْخَلالُ ، قَالَ : حَدَّثَنَا بِشْرُ بْنُ عُمَرَ ، قَالَ : سَمِعْتُ مَالِكَ بْنَ أَنَسٍ ، عَنِ الزُّهْرِيِّ ، عَنْ مَالِكِ بْنِ أَوْسِ بْنِ الْحَدَثَانِ ، قَالَ : دَخَلْتُ عَلَى عُمَرَ فَدَخَلَ عَلَيْهِ عَبْدُ الرَّحْمَنِ بْنُ عَوْفٍ ، وَطَلْحَةُ ، وَسَعْدٌ ، وَجَاءَ عَلِيٌّ ، وَالْعَبَّاسُ ، يَخْتَصِمَانِ ، فَقَالَ لَهُمْ عُمَرُ : أَنْشُدُكُمْ بِالَّذِي بِإِذْنِهِ تَقُومُ السَّمَاءُ وَالأَرْضُ ، أَتَعْلَمُونَ أَنَّ رَسُولَ الله صلى الله عليه وسلم ، قَالَ : لا نُورَثُ ، مَا تَرَكْنَاهُ صَدَقَةٌ ، فَقَالُوا : اللَّهُمَّ نَعَمْ وَفِي الْحَدِيثِ قِصَّةٌ طَوِيلَةٌ[470]

404. Mālik ibn Aws ibn al-Hadathān ؓ narrated: "I entered upon 'Umar and Abdul Rahman ibn A'wf, Talhah and Sa'd also came. At a later point, Alī and Abbās also entered whilst they were in the midst of an argument. 'Umar asked them (Abdul Rahman, Talhah and Sa'd), 'Do you bear witness by the One whose permission allows the heavens and earth to exist that the Messenger of Allāh ﷺ said, 'We are not inherited from. Whatever is left behind is charity."' They replied, 'O Allāh, yes."' There is a long story behind this hadīth.

470 See hadīth 401

٤٠٥ : حَدَّثَنَا مُحَمَّدُ بْنُ بَشَّارٍ ، قَالَ : حَدَّثَنَا عَبْدُ الرَّحْمَنِ بْنُ مَهْدِيٍّ ، قَالَ : حَدَّثَنَا سُفْيَانُ ، عَنْ عَاصِمِ ابْنِ بَهْدَلَةَ ، عَنْ زِرِّ بْنِ حُبَيْشٍ ، عَنْ عَائِشَةَ ، قَالَتْ : مَا تَرَكَ رَسُولُ اللهِ صَلى الله عليه وسلم دِينَارًا وَلا دِرْهَمًا وَلا شَاةً وَلا بَعِيرًا. [471] قَالَ : وَأَشُكُّ فِي الْعَبْدِ وَالأَمَةِ

405. Aisha ﵂ narrated: "The Messenger of Allāh ﷺ left behind no *dinārs*, *dirhams*, sheep or camels." [The narrator of this hadith] said: "I am in doubt regarding whether she also mentioned male and female slaves."

Abdul Razzaq al-Badr said,

> It is narrated that Abū Hurairah ﵁ walked in the market of Madīnah. He stood and shouted, "O people of the market! How slack you are!" The people asked, "O Abu Hurairah! Why do you say that?" He replied, "The inheritance of the Messenger of Allah ﷺ is distributed whilst you are still here and not collecting your share from it!" The people asked, "Where is it distributed?" He replied, "It is now being distributed in the masjid. Thereupon, the people rushed to the masjid and Abū Hurairah waited in the market until their return. When they returned, he asked them about what happened so they said, "We went there but we saw nothing being distributed." He said, "Have you not seen anyone in the masjid?" They said, "Yes, we did! We saw some people praying, and some people reciting the Qur'ān, and some people studying that which is lawful and that which is forbidden." He said, "Woe to you! That is the inheritance of Muhammad ﷺ."[472]

471 Musnad Ahmad (25053)
472 Al-Mu'jam al-Kabīr (402)

CHAPTER FIFTY SIX

باب ماجاء في رؤية رسول الله صلى الله عليه وسلم

THE REPORTS PERTAINING TO SEEING THE MESSENGER OF ALLAH ﷺ IN DREAMS

Abdul Razzaq al-Badr said,

> The author concluded his book with this chapter to confirm the relation between knowing the description of the Prophet ﷺ and the ability to verify seeing him in dreams. This is because a person who does not know the attributes and description of the Prophet ﷺ cannot verify if the one in his dream is the Prophet ﷺ or not.

٤٠٦ : حَدَّثَنَا مُحَمَّدُ بْنُ بَشَّارٍ ، قَالَ : حَدَّثَنَا عَبْدُ الرَّحْمَنِ بْنُ مَهْدِيٍّ ، قَالَ : حَدَّثَنَا سُفْيَانُ ، عَنْ أَبِي إِسْحَاقَ ، عَنْ أَبِي الأَحْوَصِ ، عَنْ عَبْدِ اللهِ بْنِ مَسْعُودٍ ، عَنِ النَّبِيِّ صلى الله عليه وسلم ، قَالَ : مَنْ رَآنِي فِي الْمَنَامِ فَقَدْ رَآنِي فَإِنَّ الشَّيْطَانَ لا يَتَمَثَّلُ بِي[473]

406. 'Abdullāh ibn Mas'ūd ﷺ narrated: "The Prophet ﷺ said, 'The one that has seen me in a dream has indeed seen me, for Shaytān cannot impersonate me.'"

Ibn Hajar al-Asqalānī said,

> The phrase "... for Shaytān cannot" indicates that although Allāh gave him the ability to appear in any form he wants, He does not allow him to appear in the form of the Prophet ﷺ. This was the opinion of a group who said concerning the hadīth, "What this refers to is when a person sees him as he really looked." Some of them restricted it even further and said, "He must see him as he looked when he died, so he must even take into consideration the number of his white hairs which were no more than twenty." The correct view is that he may be seen at any age or in any condition, so long as he appears as he really looked, whether as a youth, in the prime of manhood, in old age or any other time of his life.
>
> Ayyūb said, "If a man told Muhammad (meaning Ibn Sirīn) that he had seen the Prophet ﷺ [in a dream], he would say, "Describe to me the one whom you saw." If he gave a description that he did not recognise, he would say, "You did not see him."
>
> Al-Qurtubī said, "There are different opinions about the explanation of this hadīth. Some people said that it means seeing his real actual person in the literal sense, meaning that whoever sees him in a dream sees him actually, and hence seeing him in a dream is the same as seeing him whilst awake. However, the corruption of this opinion can be noticed with basic intellect

473 Sunan Ibn Mājah (3900) and Sunan al-Tirmidhī (2276)

because it necessitates that anyone who sees him [in a dream] will see him in the form he died in and also that two persons should not be able to see him at two different places if they dream at the same time. This opinion also means that he ﷺ is alive, leaves his grave, walks about in the markets, speaks to people and they speak to him. It also entails that his grave does not contain his body, and hence his grave is empty and those visiting are just going to an empty grave and greeting someone who is not there, since (according to this claim) he can really be seen at any time of the day (in a dream), in places other than his grave. Anyone who has the least grip on his senses will not hold on to such ignorance.

Another group said whoever sees him in the physical form he is known of during his lifetime [in the authentic hadīth] has truly seen him in the dream and if his physical form was different then it is a false dream. However, it is known that he ﷺ can be seen in a dream in a state that befits him but different to his state during his lifetime, such as when a person sees in his dream that the body of the Prophet ﷺ has filled the dreamer's house, which is interpreted to mean that the house is full of blessings. Let alone, if the Shaytān could impersonate his physical form or anything that is attributed to him, then that would contradict the generality of the statement of the Prophet ﷺ, 'Shaytān cannot impersonate me.' The correct understanding of this hadith is that it is possible to see him in different ways and states, so either the dream means exactly what happens in it or it needs to be interpreted for witnessing him ﷺ in a dream can occur either to warn the person against evil, give him glad tidings or to remind him."

٤٠٧: حَدَّثَنَا مُحَمَّدُ بْنُ بَشَّارٍ ، وَمُحَمَّدُ بْنُ الْمُثَنَّى ، قَالا : حَدَّثَنَا مُحَمَّدُ بْنُ جَعْفَرٍ ، قَالَ : حَدَّثَنَا شُعْبَةُ ، عَنْ أَبِي حُصَيْنٍ ، عَنْ أَبِي صَالِحٍ ، عَنْ أَبِي هُرَيْرَةَ ، قَالَ : قَالَ رَسُولُ اللهِ صلى الله عليه وسلم : مَنْ رَآنِي فِي الْمَنَامِ فَقَدْ

رَآنِي ، فَإِنَّ الشَّيْطَانَ لا يَتَصَوَّرُ أَوْ قَالَ : لا يَتَشَبَّهُ بِي[474]

407. Abū Hurairah ؓ narrated: "The Messenger of Allāh ﷺ said, 'The one that has seen me in a dream has indeed seen me, for Shaytān cannot take my form.'"

٤٠٨ : حَدَّثَنَا قُتَيْبَةُ ، قَالَ : حَدَّثَنَا خَلَفُ بْنُ خَلِيفَةَ ، عَنْ أَبِي مَالِكٍ الأَشْجَعِيِّ ، عَنْ أَبِيهِ ، قَالَ : قَالَ رَسُولُ اللهِ صلى الله عليه وسلم : مَنْ رَآنِي فِي الْمَنَامِ فَقَدْ رَآنِي[475]

قَالَ أَبُو عِيسَى : وَأَبُو مَالِكٍ هَذَا هُوَ : سَعْدُ بْنُ طَارِقِ بْنِ أَشْيَمَ ، وَطَارِقُ بْنُ أَشْيَمَ هُوَ مِنْ أَصْحَابِ النَّبِيِّ صلى الله عليه وسلم ، وَقَدْ رَوَى عَنِ النَّبِيِّ صلى الله عليه وسلم أَحَادِيثَ سَمِعْتُ عَلِيَّ بْنَ حُجْرٍ ، يَقُولُ : قَالَ خَلَفُ بْنُ خَلِيفَةَ : رَأَيْتُ عَمْرَو بْنَ حُرَيْثٍ صَاحِبَ النَّبِيِّ صلى الله عليه وسلم ، وَأَنَا غُلامٌ صَغِيرٌ

408. Tariq ibn Ashyam ؓ narrated: "The Messenger of Allāh ﷺ said, 'The one that has seen me in a dream has indeed seen me.'"

Al-Nawawī said,

> The meaning of this hadīth is that seeing the Prophet ﷺ in a dream is something true and not a false dream. However, it is not allowed to establish a ruling in religion that contradicts any of the established rulings based on a dream even in this case. This is because a dreamer does not fulfil any of the conditions of testimony. However, if a person sees the Prophet ﷺ in a dream wherein he orders the person to do something that is considered recommended in religion, or to avoid something that is considered disliked or forbidden in religion, or instructs the person to do

---

474 Sahih al-Bukhārī (110) and Sahih Muslim (6056)

475 Musnad Ahmad (15880)

something that has a benefit, then it is agreed upon that it is recommended to comply. This is because the ruling of the act that is instructed to be performed or avoided is already established in the religion before the dream.

٤٠٩ : حَدَّثَنَا قُتَيْبَةُ هُوَ ابْنُ سَعِيدٍ ، قَالَ : حَدَّثَنَا عَبْدُ الْوَاحِدِ بْنُ زِيَادٍ ، عَنْ عَاصِمِ بْنِ كُلَيْبٍ ، قَالَ : حَدَّثَنِي أَبِي ، أَنَّهُ سَمِعَ أَبَا هُرَيْرَةَ ، يَقُولُ : قَالَ رَسُولُ اللهِ صلى الله عليه وسلم : مَنْ رَآنِي فِي الْمَنَامِ فَقَدْ رَآنِي ، فَإِنَّ الشَّيْطَانَ لا يَتَمَثَّلُنِي ، قَالَ أَبِي : فَحَدَّثْتُ بِهِ ابْنَ عَبَّاسٍ ، فَقُلْتُ : قَدْ رَأَيْتُهُ ، فَذَكَرْتُ الْحَسَنَ بْنَ عَلِيٍّ ، فَقُلْتُ : شَبَّهْتُهُ بِهِ ، فَقَالَ ابْنُ عَبَّاسٍ : إِنَّهُ كَانَ يُشْبِهُهُ[476]

409. Abū Hurairah ﷺ narrated: "The Messenger of Allāh ﷺ said: 'Whoever sees me in a dream has indeed seen me, for the Shaytān cannot impersonate me.'"

Kulayb [the one narrating this report from Abū Hurairah] said: "I mentioned this hadīth to Ibn 'Abbās ﷺ and stated that I saw him ﷺ in a dream. I said to Ibn 'Abbās that I found the image in my dream very similar to that of al-Hasan ﷺ. Ibn 'Abbās said, 'Truly, al-Hasan was very similar to the Prophet ﷺ in appearance.'"

٤١٠ : حَدَّثَنَا مُحَمَّدُ بْنُ بَشَّارٍ ، قَالَ : حَدَّثَنَا ابْنُ أَبِي عَدِيٍّ ، وَمُحَمَّدُ بْنُ جَعْفَرٍ ، قَالا : حَدَّثَنَا عَوْفُ بْنُ أَبِي جَمِيلَةَ ، عَنْ يَزِيدَ الْفَارِسِيِّ وَكَانَ يَكْتُبُ الْمَصَاحِفَ ، قَالَ : رَأَيْتُ النَّبِيَّ صلى الله عليه وسلم فِي الْمَنَامِ زَمَنَ ابْنِ عَبَّاسٍ ، قَالَ : فَقُلْتُ لابْنِ عَبَّاسٍ : إِنِّي رَأَيْتُ رَسُولَ اللهِ صلى الله عليه وسلم فِي النَّوْمِ ، فَقَالَ ابْنُ عَبَّاسٍ : إِنَّ رَسُولَ اللهِ كَانَ ، يَقُولُ : إِنَّ الشَّيْطَانَ لا يَسْتَطِيعُ أَنْ يَتَشَبَّهَ بِي ، فَمَنْ رَآنِي فِي النَّوْمِ فَقَدْ رَآنِي ، هَلْ تَسْتَطِيعُ أَنْ تَنْعَتَ هَذَا الرَّجُلَ الَّذِي رَأَيْتَهُ فِي النَّوْمِ ؟ قَالَ : نَعَمْ ، أَنْعَتُ لَكَ رَجُلا بَيْنَ الرَّجُلَيْنِ ، جِسْمُهُ

476 Musnad Ahmad (7168)

وَلَحْمُهُ أَسْمَرُ إِلَى الْبَيَاضِ ، أَكْحَلُ الْعَيْنَيْنِ ، حَسَنُ الضَّحِكِ ، جَمِيلُ دَوَائِرِ الْوَجْهِ ، مَلَأَتْ لِحْيَتُهُ مَا بَيْنَ هَذِهِ إِلَى هَذِهِ ، قَدْ مَلَأَتْ نَحْرَهُ ، قَالَ عَوْفٌ : وَلا أَدْرِي مَا كَانَ مَعَ هَذَا النَّعْتِ ، فَقَالَ ابْنُ عَبَّاسٍ : لَوْ رَأَيْتَهُ فِي الْيَقَظَةِ مَا اسْتَطَعْتَ أَنْ تَنْعَتَهُ فَوْقَ هَذَا .[477]

قَالَ أَبُو عِيسَى : سقط من هنا كلام طويل من تعريف يزيد الفارسي وغيره.

410. 'Awf ibn Abī Jamīlah narrated that Yazīd al-Fārisī, who was a transcriber of the Qur'ān, said: "I saw the Prophet ﷺ in my sleep in the time of Ibn 'Abbās ﷺ. I informed Ibn 'Abbās regarding my experience and he said, 'The Messenger of Allāh ﷺ used to say, 'Verily, the Shaytān cannot imitate my form, therefore whoever sees me in his sleep has indeed seen me.' Can you describe for us the man whom you saw?' I said: 'Yes, I saw a man of a medium build; his skin was white with a hint of red. His eyes were [dark as if they had been applied] with kohl and he possessed a beautiful smile. He had a handsome, rounded face and his beard went from here to here, almost filling his upper chest."'

'Awf (one of the narrators) said: "I do not recall any other features besides these that he described."

Ibn 'Abbās said: "Had you seen him whilst awake you would not have been able to describe him better."

Ibn Hajar al-Haytami said,

> The reason 'Awf mentioned the work of Yazīd is to indicate he saw the Prophet ﷺ in his dream.

٤١١ : حدثنا أبو داود سليمان بن سلم البلخي ، حدثنا النضر بن شميل . قال : قال عوف الأعرابي : أنا أكبر من قتادة .

411. A'wf al-A'rabī narrated: "I am older than Qatādah."

477 Musnad Ahmad (2410)

٤١٢ : حَدَّثَنَا عَبْدُ اللهِ بْنُ أَبِي زِيَادٍ ، قَالَ : حَدَّثَنَا يَعْقُوبُ بْنُ إِبْرَاهِيمَ بْنِ سَعْدٍ ، قَالَ : حَدَّثَنَا ابْنُ أَخِي ابْنِ شِهَابٍ الزُّهْرِيُّ ، عَنْ عَمِّهِ ، قَالَ : قَالَ أَبُو سَلَمَةَ : قَالَ أَبُو قَتَادَةَ : قَالَ رَسُولُ اللهِ صلى الله عليه وسلم : مَنْ رَآنِي ، يَعْنِي فِي النَّوْمِ ، فَقَدْ رَأَى الْحَقَّ.[478]

412. Abu Qatādah ﷺ narrated: "The Messenger of Allāh ﷺ said, 'The one who sees me (meaning in a dream) has indeed seen a thing that is true.'"

٤١٣ : حَدَّثَنَا عَبْدُ اللهِ بْنُ عَبْدِ الرَّحْمَنِ الدَّارِمِيُّ ، قَالَ : حَدَّثَنَا مُعَلَّى بْنُ أَسَدٍ ، قَالَ : حَدَّثَنَا عَبْدُ الْعَزِيزِ بْنُ الْمُخْتَارِ ، قَالَ : حَدَّثَنَا ثَابِتٌ ، عَنْ أَنَسٍ : أَنَّ رَسُولَ اللهِ صلى الله عليه وسلم ، قَالَ : مَنْ رَآنِي فِي الْمَنَامِ فَقَدْ رَآنِي ، فَإِنَّ الشَّيْطَانَ لَا يَتَخَيَّلُ بِي وَقَالَ : وَرُؤْيَا الْمُؤْمِنِ جُزْءٌ مِنْ سِتَّةٍ وَأَرْبَعِينَ جُزْءًا مِنَ النُّبُوَّةِ[479]

413. Anas ibn Mālik ﷺ narrated: "The Messenger of Allāh ﷺ said: 'Whoever sees me in a dream has indeed seen me, for the Shaytān cannot impersonate me. The dream of a believer is one portion of the forty six portions of Prophethood.'"

Ibn 'Uthaymīn said,

> The meaning of the words of the Prophet ﷺ, "The dream of the believer is one portion of the forty six portions of Prophethood" is that the dreams of the believers come true, because they are like parables that the angels give to the one who sees them. They may tell of something that is happening or that is going to happen, so it happens in accordance with the dream. So these dreams are like the revelation of Prophethood in that they come true, yet they are

478 Sahih al-Bukhārī (6996) and Sahih Muslim (2267)
479 Sahih al-Bukhārī (6994)

different from it. Hence they are one of the forty six portions of Prophethood.

Ibn Hajar al-Haytamī said,

The reason why the dreams of the believers are likened to Prophethood is because both entail knowing some of the unseen; hence no one must interpret them without knowledge.

٤١٤ : حدثنا محمد بن علي ، قال سمعت أبي يقول : قال عبد الله ابن المبارك : إذا ابتليت بالقضاء فعليك بالأثر

414. 'Abdullāh ibn al-Mubarak said: "If you are trialled by becoming a judge, then resort to that which has been narrated [from the Prophet ﷺ and the four rightly guided caliphs.]"

Ibn Hajar al-Haytamī said,

Abdullāh ibn al-Mubarak considered taking the position of a judge a trial due to its great impact upon people.

٤١٥ : حدثنا محمد بن علي ، حدثنا النضر بن عون ، عن ابن سيرين قال : هذا الحديث دين ، فانظروا عمن تأخذون دينكم.

415. Ibn Sirīn said: "These hadīths are the religion. Therefore, pay heed to whom you take your religion from."

Ibn Hajar al-Haytamī said,

The reason why the author placed this hadīth and the one before it at the end of the book is to encourage people to learn the knowledge of the Sunnah and to refer to it, especially during the times of trials and tests. Hence, one should find pious knowledgeable people to take this knowledge from.

Ibn Abdul Barr said,

> Al-Mughīrah said, "We used to examine the conduct and prayers (piety) of the person before we would take knowledge from him."

Shams al-Din al-Safirī said,

> Al-Nawawī said, "We only learned the knowledge from those whose piety was manifested, knowledge was verified, competency was unquestionable and who were known for this.

Ibn Muflih said,

> Imam Mālik said, "Knowledge must not be taken from four types of people and can be taken from anyone besides them. It is not taken from a person whose foolishness is shown in public, a person who has lied before, a person who follows his desires and calls people to follow that which suits his desires, and an old man who is known for worship and virtue but he does not understand that which he teaches.

Al-Suyūtī said,

> Some of the scholars said, "It is recommended to start listening to (i.e. learning) the knowledge of hadīth after the age of thirty. This was the view of the people of Shām. And it was said after the age of twenty, which was the view of the people of Kufa. Sufyān al-Thawrī said, "If a man wanted to learn hadith, he would worship for twenty years beforehand." Abū Abdullāh al-Zubayrī, who was a Shafi'ī scholar, said, "It is recommended to learn hadīth in one's twenties, because it is when his mind reaches maturity. Before that, I prefer a person to occupy himself in memorising Qur'ān and studying *fiqh*.

Appendix One

Hadīth Gradings and Notes from Mukhtasar al-Shama'il al-Muhammadiyyah by the Muhaddith, Imām Nasiruddīn al-Albānī[1]

Hadīth 7: Graded as weak.

Reason: The author made a remark after narrating the hadīth saying its chain of narrators is disconnected. I say, there is no purpose to authenticate the chain [based on its narrators] since it is disconnected, let alone it has 'Umar ibn 'Abdullah, the servant of Ghufurah who is weak.

Hadīth 8: Graded as very weak.

Reason: The chain of narrators is very weak and it suffers two defects. I have explained this in al-Silsilah al-Sahihah (2053) wherein I included a supportive route for the first part of it.

---

1 Translator's note: We have sufficed with the gradings and notes that the Imām provided for the hadīths that he considered as weak. His gradings and comments regarding the hadīths he considered to be authentic have not been added herein.

Hadīth 15: Graded as very weak.

Reason: Its chain is very weak as I explained in al-Silsilah al-Da'īfah (4220).

Hadīth 33: Graded as weak.

Reason: The chain of narrators has two weak narrators and the details of this account can be found in al-Silsilah al-Da'īfah (2356). Ibn Kathīr said: "This hadīth is odd and strange."

Hadīth 36: Graded as weak.

Reason: Its chain is weak as it has Yazīd ibn Khālid who is a truthful narrator who makes a lot of mistakes. The previous hadīth narrated by 'Abdullāh ibn Mughful suffices.

Hadīth 47: Graded as weak

Reason: Its chain of narrators is weak because it has al-Nadr ibn Zurarh and Abū Janāb.

Hadīth 49: The last part of this hadīth is very weak.

Reason: The chain of narrators is very weak as I explained in Irwā' al-Ghalīl (76) but the first part of the hadīth is supported by other routes and so it is authentic.

Hadīth 57: Graded as weak

Reason: Its chain is weak because it has Shahr ibn Hawshab who is a weak narrator due to his bad memorisation. It is for this reason I included it in al-Silsilah al-Da'īfah (3457).

Hadīth 66: Graded as weak.

Reason: This hadīth I only know from the way of 'Abdullāh ibn Hassan and there are no scholars who said he is trustworthy.

Hadīth 74: The last statement of Jābir is weak.

Reason: Jābir is Ibn Yazīd al-Ja'fi who is a weak narrator.

Hadīth 86: Graded as weak.

Reason: The chain of narrators has Qais ibn Mu'awiyah who is classified as an abandoned by Abu Zar'ah and others. However, al-Tabarāni narrated this hadīth from a different route that has a weak narrator.

Hadīth 93: Graded as weak.

Reason: This is a munkar hadīth as stated by Abū Dawūd regardless of the authentication of the author and other scholars. I have explained it in Irwā' al-Ghalīl (48) and Da'īf Abu Dawūd (4).

Hadīth 107: Graded as weak.

Reason: This is a *munkar* hadīth as it was only reported from the way of Hūd and he is an unknown narrator as stated by Ibn al-Qattan and others.

Hadīth 108: Graded as weak.

Reason: The statement of the author after the hadīth, "It is a strange hadīth that we only know of it in this route. Yahya al-Qattan criticised the memory of 'Uthmān ibn Sa'īd (i.e. one of the narrators).

Hadīth 121: The chain is weak but the hadīth is authentic.

Reason: The chain has Mūsa ibn 'Ubaydah who is a weak narrator.

Hadīth 123: Graded as weak.

Reason: The chain of narrators has Ibn Lahi'ah who is a weak narrator due to his bad memorisation.

Hadīth 127: Graded as weak but it is closer to the grade of *hasan*.

Reason: Its chain is the same as that of hadīth 66.

Hadīth 136: Graded as weak.

Reason: Its chain of narrators is weak because of the existence of 'Ata ibn Muslim.

Hadīth 137: Graded as weak.

Reason: The chain is authentic but the text is odd because it opposes the hadīths narrated by the trustworthy ones in the hadīths that follow it.

Hadīth 148: Graded as weak.

Reason: The chain has Mujalid ibn Sa'īd who is a weak narrator and

I explained in 'al-Ta'līq al-Raghīb A'la al-Targhīb wal Tarhīb' that the part mentioning crying is *munkar*.

Hadīth 155: Graded as weak.

Reason: The chain of narrators has an unknown narrator.

Hadīth 170: Graded as weak.

Reason: The chain of narrators has Fulayh ibn Sulaymān who is not a strong narrator as stated by al-Dhahabi in al-Kāshif, and 'Abdul Wahhab ibn Yahya was only credited by Ibn Hibbān who listed him as from the generation following the generation of Tabi'īn. This makes the chain of narrators disconnected since he is narrating it from the grandfather of his father. The apparent meaning of the hadīth also contradicts the other authentic hadīths.

Hadīth 171: Graded as weak.

Reason: The chain has a narrator whose name is not specified.

Hadīth 178: Graded as weak

Reason: The chain of narrators has al-Fudayl ibn Sulaymān who was classified as weak as stated in al-Kāshif of al-Dhahabi.

Hadīth 183: Graded as weak.

Reason: Its chain of narrators is weak as I explained in al-Silsilah al-Sahihah (4737).

Hadīth 187: Graded as weak.

Reason: The chain has Qays ibn al-Rabī' who is a weak narrator.

Hadīth 188: Graded as weak.

Reason: It has 'Abdullah ibn La'hiya whose memorisation is bad and it has two unknown narrators.

Hadīth 191: Graded as weak.

Reason: Its chain is weak as I explained in Takhrīj al-Kalām al-Tayyib (188).

Hadīth 202: Graded as weak.

Reason: Its chain is weak and its defects I have explained in al-Silsilah al-Da'īfah (5411).

Hadīth 203: Graded as weak.

Reason: See hadīth 202.

Hadīth 211: Graded as weak.

Reason: Its chain is weak and its defects I have explained in al-Silsilah al-Da'īfah (4204).

Hadīth 221: Graded as weak.

Reason: It is a *mursal* hadīth with a weak chain.

Hadīth 222: Graded as very weak.

Reason: Its chain of narrators is very weak because of the existence of 'Umar ibn Isma'īl ibn Mujalid who is criticised by al-Dhahabi in al-Kāshif and declared as abandoned by al-Hafidh.

Hadīth 226: Graded as weak.

Reason: The chain of narrators has Hajjaj ibn Arta'ah who is a *muddalis* (i.e. one who conceals) and he narrated the hadīth without declaring clearly that he heard it from the one he is narrating it from.

Hadīth 234: Graded as weak.

Reason: It has Muhammad ibn Muhammad ibn al-Aswad who is considered in the rank of the unknown narrators and no one did credit him.

Hadīth 252: Graded as weak.

Reason: Its chain has Mujalid ibn Sa'īd. Ibn Kathīr said, "This is from the strange hadīths and it has *nakarah* (i.e. *munkar*).

Hadīth 268: Graded as weak.

Reason: The hadīth is disputed over whether it is a statement of the Prophet ﷺ or if it refers to his action. The latter is most likely the case as I stated in Da'īf Abu Dawūd (240) and this is more accurate than what I stated in al-Irwā; (453).

Hadīth 282: Graded as weak.

Reason: 'Atiyyah al-'Uwfi is weak.

Hadīth 329: Graded as very weak.

Reason: The chain has 'Abdullāh ibn Maymūn who is an abandoned narrator.

Hadīth 332: Graded as weak.

Reason: The author commented on it, "It is only reported from the way of Muslam al-A'war; he is declared as weak." Al-Hafidh also declared him weak in al-Taqrīb.

Hadīth 343: Graded as weak.

Reason: Its chain is weak because Sulaymān ibn Kharijah is unknown as indicated by al-Dhahabi in al-Mizān.

Hadīth 346: Graded as weak.

Reason: Its chain has Salim al-'Alawi who is weak as stated by al-Hafidh and al-Dhahabi.

Hadīth 355: Graded as weak.

Reason: Its chain has Musa ibn Abi 'Alqama who is unknown.

Hadīth 359: Graded as weak.

Reason: The chain has a narrator whose name is not mentioned – that is the one narrating it from Aisha ﵂.

Hadīth 371: Graded as weak.

Reason: The chain of narrators has Sayyar ibn Hatim.

Hadīth 374: Graded as weak.

Reason: The chain has Safwan ibn 'Issa Abu Na'amah who is a trustworthy narrator but a *mukhtalit* (i.e. this is one whose narration is mistaken because of senility, impaired vision, or loss of references etc.) However, part of it is reported by Muslim.

Hadīth 377: Graded as weak.

Reason: The chain of its narrators is weak due to the existence of Nawfal ibn lyās al-Hudhalī who is unknown as al-Dhahabi stated in his book al-Mizān.

Hadīth 381: Graded as odd.

Reason: The authentic hadīth from Ibn Abbās ﷺ states that the Prophet ﷺ was sixty three when he died and it is what the majority narrated and so any other opposing hadīth is either odd or reconciled with the other hadīths as al-Hafidh said.

Hadith 382: Graded as weak.

Reason: Not only is it *mursal* but also *munkar* (i.e. it contradicts the authentic hadīths stating sixty three).

Hadīth 387: Graded as weak.

Reason: The chain has an unknown narrator and I explained its defects in my book "Al-Difā' 'Aan al-Hadīth al-Nabawi wal Sīrah," on pages fifty seven and fifty nine.

Hadīth 395: Graded as weak.

Reason: It is *mursal* and it is *munkar* because it contradicts the hadīth of Aisha ﷺ.

Hadīth 398: Graded as weak.

Reason: Its chain has 'Abdul Rabbih ibn Bāriq al-Hanafi who is weak.

Appendix Two

330. 'Umar ibn al-Khattab ﵁ narrated: "The Messenger of Allāh ﷺ said, 'Do not over praise me as the Christians over praised Īsa ibn Maryam ﵇ for I am just a slave of Allāh, so call me the slave of Allāh and His Messenger.'"[2]

Abdul Karīm al-Khudair said,

> The Messenger ﷺ is the best and most perfect of creation, and the most beloved to Allāh and the most honoured by Him. But this does not mean that his human characteristics are to be denied, or that any of the duties of worship which are due only to Allāh should be directed to him. The Messenger ﷺ was a human being who suffered from sickness and real death the same as any other human being. Allāh said:
>
> إِنَّكَ مَيِّتٌ وَإِنَّهُم مَّيِّتُونَ ﴿٣٠﴾
>
> **{Verily, you (O Muhammad) will die, and verily, they (too) will die}[3]**
>
> وَمَا جَعَلْنَا لِبَشَرٍ مِّن قَبْلِكَ ٱلْخُلْدَ ۖ أَفَإِيْن مِّتَّ فَهُمُ ٱلْخَٰلِدُونَ ﴿٣٤﴾

---

2 Presented in this appendix are further notes from contemporary sources to complement the explanation from classical works provided for this hadith in the main text.

3 Qur'ān 39:30

{And We granted not to any human being immortality before you (O Muhammad); then if you die, would they live forever?}[4]

The Messenger ﷺ passed away and he was buried in his grave, hence al-Siddīq Abū Bakr ﵁ said, "Whoever used to worship Muhammad, Muhammad has died, but whoever used to worship Allāh, Allāh is alive and will never die."

The fact that the Prophet ﷺ was a witness, a bringer of glad tidings and a warner, and that he will be a witness on the Day of Resurrection, does not mean that he is present amongst all nations, or that he ﷺ will remain alive until the Day of Resurrection, or that he sees and witnesses whilst he is in his grave. Witnessing does not only mean seeing. Rather he will testify against the nations by means of what Allāh tells him, for he does not know the unseen. Allāh says:

قُل لَّآ أَمْلِكُ لِنَفْسِي نَفْعًا وَلَا ضَرًّا إِلَّا مَا شَآءَ ٱللَّهُۚ وَلَوْ كُنتُ أَعْلَمُ
ٱلْغَيْبَ لَٱسْتَكْثَرْتُ مِنَ ٱلْخَيْرِ وَمَا مَسَّنِيَ ٱلسُّوٓءُۚ إِنْ أَنَا۠ إِلَّا نَذِيرٌ
وَبَشِيرٌ لِّقَوْمٍ يُؤْمِنُونَ ﴿١٨٨﴾

{Say, "I hold not for myself [the power of] benefit or harm, except what Allāh has willed. And if I knew the unseen, I could have acquired much wealth, and no harm would have touched me. I am not except a warner and a bringer of good tidings to a people who believe!}[5]

The Prophet ﷺ does not have the ability to be present in numerous places; he is in only one place, which is his grave, and this is according to the consensus of the Muslims.

Sa'd al-Humayd said,

[In light of this evidence,] whoever wants to place the Prophet ﷺ

4 Qur'ān 21:34
5 Qur'ān 7:188

beyond the human realm and claim that the Prophet ﷺ is present in all places, he is the one who should be asked to produce evidence (*dalīl*). How does he know that the Prophet ﷺ is omnipresent at all times?

The Lajnah al-Dā'imah ruled,

The knowledge of the unseen is limited to Allāh ﷻ for He said:

۞ وَعِندَهُۥ مَفَاتِحُ ٱلْغَيْبِ لَا يَعْلَمُهَآ إِلَّا هُوَ ۚ وَيَعْلَمُ مَا فِى ٱلْبَرِّ
وَٱلْبَحْرِ ۚ وَمَا تَسْقُطُ مِن وَرَقَةٍ إِلَّا يَعْلَمُهَا وَلَا حَبَّةٍ فِى ظُلُمَٰتِ
ٱلْأَرْضِ وَلَا رَطْبٍ وَلَا يَابِسٍ إِلَّا فِى كِتَٰبٍ مُّبِينٍ ﴿٥٩﴾

{And with Him are the keys of the unseen; none knows them except Him. And He knows what is on the land and in the sea. Not a leaf falls but that He knows it. And no grain is there within the darkness of the earth and no moist or dry [thing] but that it is [written] in a clear record.}[6]

He also said:

قُل لَّا يَعْلَمُ مَن فِى ٱلسَّمَٰوَٰتِ وَٱلْأَرْضِ ٱلْغَيْبَ إِلَّا ٱللَّهُ ۚ وَمَا يَشْعُرُونَ أَيَّانَ
يُبْعَثُونَ ﴿٦٥﴾

{"Say: "None in the heavens and the earth knows the unseen except Allāh, nor can they perceive when they shall be resurrected"}[7]

However, He ﷻ informed some of his Messengers of some things from the unseen so He said:

عَٰلِمُ ٱلْغَيْبِ فَلَا يُظْهِرُ عَلَىٰ غَيْبِهِۦٓ أَحَدًا ﴿٢٦﴾

6 Qur'ān 6:59
7 Qur'ān 27:65

إِلَّا مَنِ ٱرْتَضَىٰ مِن رَّسُولٍ فَإِنَّهُۥ يَسْلُكُ مِنۢ بَيْنِ يَدَيْهِ وَمِنْ خَلْفِهِۦ
رَصَدًا ﴿٢٧﴾

{[He is] Knower of the unseen, and He does not disclose His [knowledge of the] unseen to anyone Except whom He has approved of messengers, and indeed, He sends before each messenger and behind him observers}[8]

He also said:

قُلْ مَا كُنتُ بِدْعًا مِّنَ ٱلرُّسُلِ وَمَآ أَدْرِى مَا يُفْعَلُ بِى وَلَا بِكُمْ ۖ إِنْ أَتَّبِعُ إِلَّا
مَا يُوحَىٰٓ إِلَىَّ وَمَآ أَنَا۠ إِلَّا نَذِيرٌ مُّبِينٌ ﴿٩﴾

{Say, "I am not something original among the messengers, nor do I know what will be done with me or with you. I only follow that which is revealed to me, and I am not but a clear warner."}[9]

This is also established in the long hadīth narrated by Umm al-'Ala ﷺ (an Ansārī woman who gave the pledge of allegiance to the Prophet ﷺ) that, "The Ansār drew lots concerning the dwelling of the Emigrants. It was decided that 'Uthmān ibn Madh'ūn ﷺ would dwell with them (i.e. Umm al-'Ala's family), 'Uthmān fell ill and I nursed him until he died, and we covered him with his clothes. Then the Prophet ﷺ came to us and I [addressing the dead body] said, 'O Abū al-Sā'ib, may Allāh's Mercy be upon you! I bear witness that Allāh has honoured you.' On that the Prophet ﷺ said, 'How do you know that Allāh has honoured him?' I replied, 'I do not know. May my father and my mother be sacrificed for you, O Allāh's Apostle! But who else is worthy of it [if not 'Uthmān]?' He said, 'As for him, by Allāh, death has overtaken him, and I hope the best for him. By Allāh, though I am the Apostle of Allāh, I do not know what Allāh will do to me.' By Allāh, I will never assert the piety of anyone after him. That made me sad, and when I slept

8 Qur'ān 72:26-27

9 Qur'ān 46:9

> I saw in a dream a flowing stream for 'Uthmān ibn Madh'ūn. I went to Allāh's Apostle ﷺ and told him of it. He remarked, 'That symbolises his (good) deeds.'" This is reported by al-Bukhārī and Ahmad, and it was reported in many authentic hadīths that Allāh revealed to the Prophet ﷺ the destiny of some of his companions and it was also reported by al-Bukhārī and Muslim that Jibrīl ﷺ asked the Prophet about the Hour and he replied, "The one who is asked about it does not know any more about it than the one who is asking." Then Jibrīl only mentioned the signs of the Hour, which indicate that he ﷺ knew from the unseen that which Allāh revealed to him only from the unseen and he mentioned it when there was a need to do so.[10]

Ibn al-Uthaymīn said,

> What is meant by the unseen is that which is not seen. The unseen is something relative. But that which is unseen in the absolute sense (*al-ghayb al-mutlaq*) is known only to Allāh.[11]

The Lajnah al-Dā'imah ruled,

> The Prophet ﷺ is alive in his grave in the sense of the life of *al-barzakh*, so he enjoys the blessings that Allāh has prepared for him as a reward for his great good actions that he did in this world. But the life in the grave is not like the life of this world, or the life in the Hereafter. Rather it is the life of *al-barzakh* which comes in between his life in this world and his life in the Hereafter. Hence we know that he passed away as other Prophets and other people before him passed away. Allāh says:
>
> وَمَا جَعَلْنَا لِبَشَرٍ مِّن قَبْلِكَ ٱلْخُلْدَ أَفَإِين مِّتَّ فَهُمُ ٱلْخَٰلِدُونَ ﴿٣٤﴾
>
> **{And We granted not to any human being immortality before**

10 Fatāwa al-Lajnah al-Dā'imah 2/167-169
11 Sharh al-'Aqīdah al-Wāsitiyyah (p. 158)

you (O Muhammad); then if you die, would they live forever?}[12]

كُلُّ مَنْ عَلَيْهَا فَانٍ ﴿٢٦﴾

{Whatsoever is on it (the earth) will perish.}[13]

وَيَبْقَىٰ وَجْهُ رَبِّكَ ذُو الْجَلَالِ وَالْإِكْرَامِ ﴿٢٧﴾

{And the Face of your Lord full of Majesty and Honour will remain forever.}[14]

إِنَّكَ مَيِّتٌ وَإِنَّهُم مَّيِّتُونَ ﴿٣٠﴾

{Verily, you (O Muhammad) will die, and verily, they (too) will die.}[15]

And there are other verses which also indicate that Allāh caused him to die. Moreover, the Companions washed him, shrouded him, offered the funeral prayer for him and buried him; if he had been alive in the worldly sense, they would not have done the same as is done for others who die.

Fātimah ﵂ asked Abū Bakr ﵁ for her inheritance from her father ﷺ and this indicates that she was convinced that he had died, and no one among the Companions differed with her concerning that. Rather, Abū Bakr ﵁ responded to her request by saying that nothing could be inherited from the Prophets.

The Companions agreed unanimously to choose a caliph for the Muslims to succeed the Prophet ﷺ, and that was done through the appointment of Abū Bakr ﵁. If the Prophet ﷺ had been alive in a worldly sense, they would not have done such. So this indicates that there was consensus among them that he had indeed passed away.

When the tribulations and problems increased during the time

---

12 Qur'ān 21:34
13 Qur'ān 55:26
14 Qur'ān 55:27
15 Qur'ān 39:30

of 'Uthmān and 'Alī رضي الله عنهما, and before and after that, they did not go to his ﷺ grave to consult him or ask him for a way out of those tribulations and problems, or the way to solve them. If he had been alive in a worldly sense, they would not have overlooked that when they were in such great need of someone to save them from the trials that surrounded them.

With regard to the soul of the Prophet ﷺ, it is in the highest part of 'Illiyyeen, because he is the best of creation, and because Allāh has given him *al-waseelah* which is the highest position in Paradise. The Prophets and the *shuhadah* (martyrs) are alive in *al-barzakh* as the Prophet ﷺ said: "The Prophets are alive and they pray in their graves."[16] Allāh says:

وَلَا تَقُولُوا۟ لِمَن يُقْتَلُ فِى سَبِيلِ ٱللَّهِ أَمْوَٰتٌۢ ۚ بَلْ أَحْيَآءٌ وَلَٰكِن لَّا
تَشْعُرُونَ ﴿١٥٤﴾

{And say not of those who are killed in the way of Allāh, 'They are dead.' Nay, they are living, but you perceive (it) not}[17]

This is a special life, the nature of which is known only to Allāh. It is not like the life of this world in which the soul remains with the body.

The basic principle concerning the dead is that they do not hear the words of the living sons of Adam, because Allāh says:

وَمَا يَسْتَوِى ٱلْأَحْيَآءُ وَلَا ٱلْأَمْوَٰتُ ۚ إِنَّ ٱللَّهَ يُسْمِعُ مَن يَشَآءُ ۖ وَمَآ أَنتَ بِمُسْمِعٍ
مَّن فِى ٱلْقُبُورِ ﴿٢٢﴾

{And not equal are the living and the dead. Indeed Allāh causes to hear whom He wills, but you cannot make hear those who are in graves.}[18]

---

16 Narrated by al-Mundhiri and al-Bayhaqī who classed it as sahīh because of corroborating reports in al-Sahīhayn.
17 Qur'ān 2:154
18 Qur'ān 35:22

Allāh confirmed that those whom he (the Prophet ﷺ) was calling to Islām could not hear, by likening them to the dead. There is nothing in the Qur'ān or in the authentic Sunnah to indicate that the Prophet ﷺ can hear every du'ā or call from human beings. Rather it is proven that the only thing that reaches him ﷺ is the blessings and salāms of those who send them upon him. This was narrated by Abu Dawūd (2041) with a hasan isnād from Abū Hurayrah ؓ who said that the Prophet ﷺ said, "There is no one who sends salāms upon me but Allāh will restore to me my soul so that I may return his salāms." This does not mean that he hears the words of the one who sends salāms. Rather it is possible that he comes to know of those salāms when the angels convey them to him. If we assume that he hears the words of the one who sends salāms, this is an exception from the general rule, as in the case of the dead hearing the footsteps of those who carry his bier, and as in the case of the slain disbelievers in the well at Badr who heard the call of the Messenger of Allaah ﷺ when he said to them, "Have you found your Lord's promise to be true? For we have found our Lord's promise to be true."[19]

19 See Fatāwa al-Lajnah al-Dā'imah, 1/313, 318, 321